They Spoke from God

A Survey of the Old Testament

*For prophecy never had its origin in the
will of man, but men spoke from God as they
were carried along by the Holy Spirit.*
2 Peter 1:21

Compiled and Edited by
William C. Williams, Ph.D.

Stanley M. Horton, Th.D.
General Editor

LOGION
PRESS

Gospel Publishing House
Springfield, Missouri
02-0411

Logion Press books are published by Gospel Publishing House.

A Test Bank containing suggested questions covering the entire book is available for instructors. Submit a request on your official school letterhead to the address below. Include the name of this text and your e-mail address. A PDF file will be sent to you.

Gospel Publishing House
Promotions
1445 N. Boonville Ave.
Springfield, MO 65802-1894

Photographs
William C. Williams: 167, 397, 427, 430, 441
Dwayne Braddy: 655, 680

Library of Congress Control Number: 2003113799
International Standard Book Number: 0-88243-694-5

Printed in the United States of America

Contents

Maps, Charts, and Illustrations

Maps

Charts

Illustrations

Foreword

The Old Testament is not just a "Jewish Bible" as some choose to call it. It is really a Christian book. From beginning to end it has a forward look. It gives us a chosen line that leads to Christ. Its laws, lessons, and history prepare us to understand the New Testament. Its sacrifices help us to understand the Cross. Its history helps us to understand Christian theology. When the apostle Paul describes the faith Christians must have, he goes back to Abraham. When he talks about grace, he reminds us of how God restored David. Over 350 times the New Testament quotes or refers to the Old Testament.[1] No wonder Christians need the Old Testament in order to understand the New!

During forty-six years of teaching Old Testament I enjoyed seeing the light come on in students who had probably avoided the Old Testament. It became truly God's Word to them.

I tried a number of different textbooks. Some were simple summaries of the Old Testament books. Some were in story form. Some were dull. Some were over the heads of my students. I often wished for a textbook such as this.

[1]See Gleason L. Archer and Gregory Chrichigno, *Old Testament Quotations in the New Testament* (Chicago: Moody Press, 1983).

In my teaching I found that I had to take unnecessary time explaining the 1611 language of the King James Version, so I encouraged my students to use the American Standard Version. However, its language was also difficult for them. Thus, I was glad when a new version by evangelical translators became available: the New International Version (NIV). It is a good translation, very readable, and Logion Press has chosen to use it as its basic Bible text.[2]

The writers our Logion Press team has selected to collaborate in this work are all excellent Bible scholars and teachers. Dr. William C. Williams is the editor of this work, the author of two chapters, and a contributor to footnotes and sidebars. He was one of my best students. He holds the Ph.D. in Hebrew Language and Literature from New York University with postdoctoral studies at the Hebrew University and the Institute of Holy Land Studies, both in Jerusalem. Since 1969 he has been Professor of Old Testament at Vanguard University (formerly Southern California College) and has taught Old Testament for many years on both college and graduate levels. He is an outstanding biblical scholar, writer, and Bible translator. At the same time he knows how to make the Bible relevant and alive to his students. He has pastored in Maryland and New Jersey and has taught in several overseas colleges and seminaries.

Stanley M. Horton, Th.D.
Distinguished Professor of Bible and Theology Emeritus
Assemblies of God Theological Seminary

---

[2]For a good discussion of various translations of the Bible, see James R. White, *The King James Only Controversy* (Minneapolis: Bethany House Publishers,1995).

Contributors

William Barnes is Assistant Professor of Pastoral Ministries at North Central University. He holds the Th.D. in Hebrew Bible from Harvard Divinity School. He formerly taught at Southeastern College of the Assemblies of God.

Dwaine Braddy was Professor of Pastoral Ministries and Bible at Northwest College until 2003; he is currently on staff at Renton (Washington) Assembly of God. He holds the D.Min. from Drew University.

Malcolm Brubaker is Professor of Church Ministries at Valley Forge Christian College. He holds the Th.M. from Westminster Theological Seminary.

Dale Brueggemann is Director, Eurasia Education Services, Assemblies of God World Missions. He holds the Ph.D. from Westminster Theological Seminary.

Roger Cotton is Professor of Old Testament at the Assemblies of God Theological Seminary. He holds the Th.D. from Concordia Seminary.

Andrew Davies is professor at the Assemblies of God Bible College at Mattersey, United Kingdom. He holds the Ph.D. from the University of Sheffield, England.

Steven M. Fettke is Professor of Religion at Southeastern College of the Assemblies of God. He holds the D.Min. from Columbia Theological Seminary.

Richard Israel is Vice President for Academic Affairs at Bethany College of the Assemblies of God. He holds the Ph.D. from

Claremont Graduate University.

Larry McQueen is associate pastor of the Cottonwood Church of God, Brookston, Texas. He has taught at Lee University. He holds the M.Th. in Biblical Studies, Old Testament Concentration from Columbia Theological Seminary.

Robert A. Mullins was Educational and Cultural Affairs Fellow at the W. F. Albright Institute for Archaeological Research in Jerusalem. He holds the Ph.D. in Archaeology from Hebrew University. He has been an instructor in Biblical Archaeology, history, and geography, and a research associate in the Tel Beth Shean Project, Hebrew University Institute of Archaeology. He has also taught Old Testament and Hebrew.

William Raccah, formerly Dean and President of College Biblique in Quebec, is now Director, Calgary Leadership Training Center (an extension of Northwest Bible College, Edmonton) Calgary, Alberta, Canada. He holds the Ph.D. in Old Testament Ethics from Université Laval, Quebec City, Quebec, Canada.

Robert C. Stallman is Associate Professor of Bible and Hebrew at Northwest College of the Assemblies of God. He holds the Ph.D. in Hermeneutics and Biblical Interpretation from Westminster Theological Seminary. He has taught at Central Bible College and has pastored churches in Pennsylvania and Washington.

April Westbrook is Assistant Professor of Biblical Studies at Vanguard University. She holds the M.A. from Vanguard University and is pursuing doctoral studies at Claremont Graduate University.

The late Ronald E. Wright was Professor Emeritus of Theology at Vanguard University, where he taught from 1975 to 2000. He held the M.R.E. from Central Baptist Seminary in Toronto and the B.D. from Northwest Baptist Theological College in Vancouver, Canada.

Preface

The inspiration for writing this book came from teaching students on Borneo in 1985. The only evangelical survey of the Old Testament available at that time was tedious and dry. My students were excellent, intelligent, and highly motivated, but English was their third language! They agonized over the reading level required by the material.

This book offers both student and teacher a number of innovations that will, hopefully, set it apart from other similar works. First, *it strives for simplicity.* This book addresses complex and sophisticated subject matter in simple language that does not bewilder the beginner. It defines difficult words in a glossary. It is written in a personal style, as though the teacher were addressing the student directly.

Second, this book is *not simply repetitive of the biblical text.* Rather than summarize a given portion of the Bible, the text addresses it directly. To learn the Bible, the student *must read the Bible*, not a book *about* the Bible. The text assumes the student has read the biblical material and is familiar with its general content. The textbook uses the New International Version.

Third, it provides *the basics without overwhelming* the student. It does not attempt to answer every question. Instead, it allows room for the instructor to "nuance" the course in the direction he or she desires. To this end, foot-notes and bibliography at the end of each chapter will help the student or instructor find additional material on the subject being discussed.

Fourth, it endeavors to *engage the student in creative dialogue.* Rather than technical terms, its topic headings are often phrases, couched as questions where possible. Their function is to stimulate the student's mind on the topic. It avoids jargon, except where such is defined, either in the text or in the glossary (and foreign terms are given in their popular transliterations). While it is erudite, it does not flaunt its sophistication.

Fifth, it is *designed as a textbook,* conceived from the start as a classroom instrument. As such, it attempts to be relevant to present-day concerns. For instance, the discussion of creation includes the current material for addressing the creation/evolution debate. It leaves detailed analyses of Near Eastern parallels for advanced classes. Each chapter contains study questions and suggestions for further reading. Please note the copyright page about accessing an online test bank.

Sixth, *it prioritizes the material.* It attempts to distinguish what is foundational to a holistic overview of the Old Testament and what is not. There are many great portions of Scripture. But the material of Genesis-Leviticus is foundational. Scripture in both Old and New Testaments will build on this material. It establishes our being, our primordial existence, our fallen estate and need for redemption, and the meaning and means of securing atonement.

Seventh, and most important, *it is synthetic.* As a new convert, I devoured the Bible, using every study aid I could get my hands on. But it took years of study before I had synthesized the material so I could open the Bible at will, find what I needed, and relate it to what was in another part of the Bible (e.g., to history or to a theological or ethical problem). *They Spoke From God* attempts to do this.

Finally, God, as he is revealed in the Old Testament narratives, is the object of our pursuit. After all the analysis has been done, there needs to be a synthesis that leads us to him. Accordingly, instead of following a book-by-book summary or a division by literary genre, I have used a *theology of history as the unifying theme* for this book. God reveals himself to us in history as interpreted for us through the words of Scripture. Thus, the various law codes find their places within the overarching context of the narratives within which they find themselves embedded. The prophets are treated in such a way that they are integrated into the stream of history. The poetic and wisdom materials are likewise integrated by placing them near the reigns of David and Solomon. History, therefore, is no mere incidental that can be disregarded in our quest; rather, it becomes the theological linchpin that joins everything else together to tell a story that reveals the mind of God regarding our redemption.

A word of caution: No matter how great my care, and the care of the contributing scholars, there are bound to be errors, both of omission and commission, in the first edition. I would like to encourage all readers to report to me any such omissions or errors of substance for correction in subsequent editions.

William C. Williams
Vanguard University
Costa Mesa, California

Acknowledgments

I would like to thank Logion Press for its willingness to adopt so many of my suggestions and Dr. Stanley M. Horton, the series editor, for his ever-generous spirit and help in moving the project forward. Most of what I have to contribute to scholarship I owe to others. A great Jewish sage once said, "Much have I learned from my teachers, more from my colleagues, and most of all from my students." I am grateful to people in all those categories, and to many from whom I learned through their publications. I would like to thank the contributors for their willingness to take time from work schedules that are already burdensome. It has been gratifying to have such scholarship readily available to the project. I would like to thank my dear wife, Alma, for her patience and support. I would also like to thank my research assistants, Kris Gleason Nunn, Laura Nivinskus, Rose Ottosen, and Calvin Greer for their help in gathering bibliography and in proofing the finished copy.

W. C. W.

Abbreviations

Scholarly Works

AB	The Anchor Bible
ABD	*The Anchor Bible Dictionary*
ANET	*Ancient Near Eastern Texts Relating to the Old Testament*
BA	*Biblical Archaeologist*
BAR	*Biblical Archaeology Review*
BASOR	*Bulletin of the American Schools of Oriental Research*
BZAW	*Beihefte zur Zeitschrift für die alttestamentliche Wissenschaft*
CAH	*Cambridge Ancient History*
CC	Communicator's Commentary (Word)
DSB	Daily Study Bible
ISBE	*The International Standard Bible Encyclopedia*, rev. ed., 1979–88.
NAC	New American Commentary
NBD	*New Bible Dictionary*, 3d ed.
NCB	New Century Bible
NICOT	New International Commentary on the Old Testament
OTL	Old Testament Library
TOTC	Tyndale Old Testament Commentaries

TWOT	*Theological Wordbook of the Old Testament.* Edited by R. L. Harris, G. L. Archer, Jr. 2 vols. Chicago: Moody Press, 1980.
WBC	Word Biblical Commentary
WTJ	*Westminster Theological Journal*

Bible Versions

KJV	King James Version
NASB	*New American Standard Bible*
NIV	New International Version
NKJV	New King James Version
NLT	New Living Translation
NRSV	New Revised Standard Version
RSV	Revised Standard Version

Other Abbreviations and Sigla

ANE	Ancient Near East
cf.	compare
CH	Code of Hammurabi
e.g.	for example
HL	Hittite Laws
LXX	Septuagint
MAL	Middle Assyrian Laws
MT	Masoretic Text
NT	New Testament
OT	Old Testament
//	parallel(s)

1

Ronald Wright

What Is the Old Testament?

Outline:

- In What Sense Is the Bible the Word of God?
- How Was the Word of God Given?
- What Does "Revelation" Mean?
- What Is Meant by the "Inspiration" of Scripture?
- How Should Inspiration Be Understood?
- What Value Did Jesus Place on the Old Testament?
- What Are the Characteristics of a Divinely Inspired Scripture?
- What Is Meant by Describing the Bible as "Canon"?
- What Is Hermeneutics and How Is It Used?
-

Terms:

autograph
canon
hermeneutics
inspiration
revelation
Septuagint (LXX)

The Old Testament is the first major part of a unique collection of writings called the Bible. The Bible has often been rightly acclaimed as a literary gem and prized for its contribution to the study of history. Many have pointed to its ability to elevate values within a culture. It can enrich personal and societal views of life and overall worldviews. Some have found comfort in its pages when they were pressed by the problems of everyday life. But these and a host of other claims for the importance of the Bible, even taken collectively, do not get to the heart of how valuable the Bible is. The Bible is prized *because* it is the Word of God to humanity. It reveals God and candidly describes humanity.

The English word "bible" comes from the Greek word *biblion*. This word was originally used in a general sense of any book. With the passage of time, however, "Bible" (capital "B") became a term used by believers to identify the Holy Scriptures. It still has this meaning. Yet not all who claim that the Bible is the Word of God are in agreement as to what such a claim means. Two individuals may use identical words to state a position and yet have vastly differing interpretations of that position. It is necessary, therefore, to carefully define one's claim, or confession of faith. The believer needs to ask, "What is Scripture?" Biblical understandings, personal convictions, and resulting commitments can come only after having first studied the nature of Scripture itself.

In What Sense Is the Bible the Word of God?

Every book of the Bible came through human agency; none of them was dropped from the sky. The first five books of the Bible are called the Books of Moses or the Pentateuch (Gk. *penta*, "five," plus *teuch*, "work" or "book"; Heb. *Torah*). The prophecies of Isaiah, Jeremiah, Ezekiel,

Daniel, and the twelve minor prophets are all identified by the name of their human authors. Each writer has a personal style, which includes vocabulary, sentence structure, and the tone the writer adopts toward his subject matter. Once this is recognized, two major questions must be addressed. The first is centered on human imperfections and asks, "How can fallible people write an infallible book?" The second asks, "Since humans are involved in writing the Bible, how then can it possibly be God's Word?"

Too often, unfortunately, people answer these questions without any regard to what the Bible says about itself. The Scripture is a definitive source for doctrine, including doctrine about God, humankind, salvation, and the Church. It is just as important that Scripture be consulted for the doctrine about itself. Scripture repeatedly and consistently testifies about its nature. It declares that, though written by ordinary people, its ultimate author is God.[1] This testimony of Scripture not only informs the mind but also produces in its readers a sense of wonder, about both God's person and his work.

The witness of the Bible to itself is not confined to explicit statements about inspiration, such as 2 Timothy 3:16 ("All Scripture is God-breathed"). It is also implied in how the Bible treats its various subjects: Rather than representing the perspective of a people, it consistently speaks on behalf of God. In a sense, then, all the Bible is a witness to itself.[2]

Here by Accident?

Christian philosophers use the term "open universe" to indicate God's continued activity in his creation. In such a universe, he works to bring his design to fulfillment in human redemption by his Spirit through his Word. Since he planned in creation to have a people called by his name, it follows that his plan will be executed. Because a great gulf exists between the Creator and fallen humanity, an authoritative word from him for sinful and sinning people is needed. Such a word speaks to a fundamental question of human existence: Are we here by accident or by divine design and purpose? Christians answer, "By divine design and purpose!"

[1]See, for example, Ps. 19:7–11; Isa. 40:8; 2 Tim. 3:16; and B. B. Warfield, *Inspiration and Authority of the Bible* (Phillipsburg, N.J.: Presbyterian & Reformed Publishing Co., 1948), 173.

[2]See John Frame, "Scripture Speaks for Itself," in *God's Inerrant Word,* ed. John W. Montgomery (Minneapolis: Bethany House Publishers, 1974), 180.

What Does the Bible Say About Itself?

The Old Testament teaches that God has communicated with humankind from the dawn of human history. After creating Adam and Eve, he spoke to them, both before and after the Fall (Gen. 1:28–30; 3:9–19). God chose Abram to be the father of a people that God would later commit himself to. God spoke to Abram and called him after the death of his father (Gen. 12:1–3). God later reconfirmed his covenant with Abram and encouraged, strengthened, and directed him,[3] eventually changing his name to Abraham (Gen. 17:5). God spoke to Isaac, guiding him and confirming with him the covenant promises first made to his father, Abraham (Gen. 26:1–5). God spoke to Jacob, calling upon him to build an altar (Gen. 35:1). In this way God reconfirmed to him the covenant given to Abraham and confirmed to Isaac. The voice of God was so vivid and convincing that Jacob had his son Joseph vow not to bury him in Egypt. Instead, the Israelites were to carry his body up to the land promised them (Gen. 49:29–30; Heb. 11:22).

God spoke to Moses. Almost two-thirds of the Pentateuch, or Torah, is a direct record of what God said to Moses. He first heard the voice of God from the flaming bush when God commissioned him for service (Exod. 3 through 4). As Moses obeyed, God repeatedly spoke to him. Clear statements of God's words to Moses occur throughout the story of the exodus (Exod. 6:1 through

---

Even the genealogies, often considered unimportant to the casual reader, serve an important function: They itemize the persons who played a part in God's redemption of the world. Examples are the genealogy of Shem, leading to Abraham (Gen. 11:10–32); of Judah, leading to David (1 Chron. 2:3–15); and of Adam, leading to Jesus (Luke 3:23–38).

[3]Gen. 12:7; 13:14; 15:1–21; 17:1–21.

14:18).[4] When the people wailed because there was no water, God instructed Moses to strike a particular rock (Exod. 17:5–6). Later, when the Amalekites came to war against Israel at Rephidim, God gave His people victory. Afterward He instructed Moses to write the account as a permanent record (Exod. 17:14). In preparation for Moses and the Israelites to receive the covenant at Sinai, as well as in the giving of the covenant itself, God spoke to Moses. Moses then wrote down God's revelation (Exod. 19 through 24). God gave him detailed instructions regarding the tabernacle (Exod. 25 through 31). Some of the most passionate verses in Exodus describe this intimate communion. Inside the sacred tent where Moses went for his meetings with God, God spoke to him "face to face" (Exod. 33:11; Num. 12:8). Moses also talked to the LORD (Exod. 33:12). In all these instances, it is obvious that God's communication is direct and clear. It often involves dialogue between him and human beings.

So far, only the first two books of the Pentateuch have been examined. Nevertheless, divine authorship has consistently been stated and restated. Applying the question of origins to the rest of the Old Testament produces similar results. The prophets are not identified so much by what they *fore*tell. Their distinctive is that they *forth*tell, that is, that they tell forth, or orally publish, the word of God. The Hebrew words for "prophet" in the Old Testament help the reader to understand the role the prophet played in Israel's life. *Ro'eh* and *chozeh* mean "one who sees" and

[4]The chapter divisions of this passage of Exodus convey a remarkable recurring cadence, a kind of chorus, *The LORD said . . . The LORD said . . . The LORD said.* These words compose a refrain that is striking enough when one reads the first verse of each of the chapters cited, but even more compelling when one reads the entire section with an ear tuned to this language.

nabi' means "one who calls."[5] A recurring assertion by the prophets was that they were chosen and commissioned by God to speak for him. Over and over they make statements such as "the Lord has spoken" (Isa. 1:2).[6] Henry C. Thiessen observes, "Statements like these occur more than 3,800 times in the Old Testament."[7]

How Was the Word of God Given?

The great word associated with God throughout Scripture is "holy." He is the Creator. When considering his creation, specifically human beings, one word that comes to mind is "creature."[8] And what follows is an awareness of the great distance between creature and Creator. If this were not enough, the Fall (see chap. 3) has widened the gap. Humanity is now fallen and sinful. The Bible paints a dismal picture of an abyss between the righteous God and self-centered humanity. Fallen humanity is self-deceived and deceitful. Human beings are alienated, not only from God but also from themselves (Jer. 17:9; Rom. 1:18 through 3:20). It is also very clear that God has bridged that abyss.

His Word—No Doubt

Think about it—God affirms Scripture as his Word on average almost one hundred times per book. Do you suppose he wants us to get the point?

---

[5]The derivation of nabi' remains a matter of debate among scholars. Robert Culver summarizes four views on the matter and concludes, "The essential idea in the word is that of authorized spokesman." See R. Laird Harris et al., eds., *Theological Wordbook of the Old Testament* (Chicago: Moody Press, 1980), 2:544–45. Another scholar has observed that nabi' is technically a passive participle and has suggested that it means "one called [by God]."

[6]For example, "the LORD said to me" (Isa. 8:1); "this is what the LORD says" (Isa. 43:1); "from the mouth of the LORD" (Jer. 23:16); "the word that came to Jeremiah from the LORD" (Jer. 11:1), ". . . to Ezekiel" (Ezek. 1:3), ". . . to Hosea" (Hos. 1:1), ". . . to Joel" (Joel 1:1).

[7]Henry C. Thiessen, *Lectures in Systematic Theology,* rev. Vernon D. Doerksen (Grand Rapids: Wm. B. Eerdmans, 1979), 68.

[8]See R. Otto, *The Idea of the Holy: An Inquiry Into the Non-rational Factor in the Idea of the Divine and Its Relation to the Rational,* 2d ed. (London: Oxford University Press, 1950).

He has chosen to disclose himself to the sinner in gracious acts of redeeming love.

The elements in this process, which God uses to convey his truth to us, may be diagrammed thus:

GOD
—
revelation (*unveiling* the truth)
—
inspiration (*transmission* of the truth)
—
Scripture (the *record* of the truth)
—
illumination (*understanding* the truth)
—
HUMANITY

Some elements, or categories, overlap. Revelation, for example, does not have to cease in order for inspiration to begin. Nonetheless, there is a logical and historical order to God's making himself known. Each category stands as a separate area of study.

What Does "Revelation" Mean?

The word "revelation" is often used in a popular sense to mean knowledge just acquired or insights freshly gained. *The New Webster's Dictionary* defines revelation as an "act of revealing; God's disclosure of himself to man."[9] Further, the Scriptures speak of revelation as knowledge that was formerly hidden but which is now manifest, declared by God through his Word and Spirit (Rom. 16:26; 1 Cor. 2:10–13; Eph. 3:4–5). And keep in mind that God's revealing himself took place over a long period of time in many acts of disclosure.

---

[9]*New Webster's Dictionary and Roget's Thesaurus* (New York: Book Essentials, 1991), 233.

A Demonstration of Love

The Christian has no difficulty at all in relating the love of God to the cross of Christ. Little wonder, for the cross is the supreme demonstration of divine love central to all of history. It is a dynamic and foundational love, which has always been evident in all God's dealings with his creation. Frederick Lehman (1869–1953) composed a magnificent song, "The Love of God," developing this third stanza from a portion of a poem written in 1096 by a German cantor, Rabbi Mayer:

(cont. on the next page)

A Demonstration of Love (cont.)

Could we with ink the ocean fill and were the skies of parchment made,
Were every stalk on earth a quill and every man a scribe by trade,
To write the love of God above would drain the ocean dry,
Nor could the scroll contain the whole though stretched from sky to sky.

This love, then, is itself the spring of God's gracious activity of revelation. Apart from such a revelation *by* God, the knowledge *of* God is impossible. The writer of Hebrews reminds his readers that those who come to God *must* believe not only in his being but also in his self-revelation (Heb. 11:6).

What Is General Revelation?

Theologians have long viewed God's disclosure of himself as occurring in two ways: "general" revelation and "special" revelation. General revelation recognizes that God has revealed himself generally, that is, in his creation. This may be seen in nature, in history, and in the human conscience, whether an individual's or a society's (Ps. 19:1–4; Rom. 1:20).

What Is Special Revelation?

Special revelation refers to God's disclosure of himself specifically in and through Christ and Scripture. Scripture is the means by which God, through the Holy Spirit, leads a person to Christ.[10] Theology derived from special revelation is called "revealed" theology.

How Does Revelation Work?

David refers to general revelation when he says that the heavens declare the glory of God and the earth shows his handiwork (Ps. 19:1–4; 8:1–9). He then reflects on the perfection and soul-restoring ability of Scripture, God's special revelation (Ps. 19:7–11). Paul shows that general revelation does not stop with just confronting humankind with the idea of the supernatural. Much more than that, it clearly declares something about the character of God—his everlasting power and divinity (Rom. 1:20).[11] Jesus declared the

[10]Isa. 61:1; Ezek. 36:27; John 14:21–26; 16:7b–14.

[11]Although it is beyond the scope of this introduction to deal more fully with the concept of general revelation, we cannot overemphasize its importance. It is the rejection of the general revelation of God which renders the Gentile world guilty before God (Rom. 1:18–20).

special revelation of God when he reminded the religious leaders of his day that the Scriptures pointed to him (John 5:39–47). To the questioning Philip he said that those who truly see him with discerning eyes also see the Father (John 14:9). Based on Scriptures such as these, believers may confidently say that the Bible is not merely a revelation *from* God. It is also a revelation *of* God and *by* God. It is revealed to and through the human instruments of his choosing.

What's So "Special" About Special Revelation?

The special revelation of God imparts understanding to human beings. It transcends the knowledge obtained through human reason alone. This revelation originates with God and includes both the data and its interpretation. But if revelation is spoken of as coming from God, then its nature must be defined. B. B. Warfield says, "God has intervened extraordinarily, in the course of the sinful world's development, for the salvation of men otherwise lost."[12]

It is of utmost importance to understand the difference between the terms "exhaustive" and "accurate" when dealing with the knowledge of God. The very idea of human beings possessing an exhaustive knowledge of God is sheer arrogance. What believers know about God, or of his countless acts of redeeming grace in human experience, they know because God has revealed himself. Not that anyone should claim to have an exhaustive knowledge of God! Instead, believers maintain that the revelation of God given in the Bible is accurate.

God chooses the content of what is revealed. He is infi-

Where Do Babies Come From?

What does a mother tell her child who asks where babies come from? If the child is told "The stork brings them," the response is obviously untrue, inaccurate. But suppose the mother judges her child not to be ready for a full lecture on human biology. She may say, "Babies grow in Mommy's tummy." This response, while having no degree of exhaustiveness scientifically, is true, accurate. Later questions from the child will draw out more details. Being finite, human beings will never attain exhaustive knowledge on any subject. If this is true of knowledge of everyday things, how much more is it true of knowledge of God!

---

[12]Warfield, *Inspiration and Authority*, 71.

nite. Humanity is not. There are things which belong to God alone. Yet those things that He does disclose are given so his will can be known and obeyed (Deut. 29:29).

Revelation includes both facts and their interpretation. For example, Joseph speaks to his brothers, "'You intended to harm me, but God intended it for good to accomplish what is now being done, the saving of many lives'" (Gen. 50:20).[13] So, for example, when God reveals himself, the revelation is not confined to listing attributes of his character. It also includes what those attributes mean in his relations with people.

Viewed in historical context, revelation means that God's word does more than describe an event. It also provides understanding as the event is interpreted in the context of redemption. Leon Morris writes, "The history recorded in the Old Testament is real history, but it is recorded in terms of the outworking of the divine purpose... [and], rightly interpreted, tells us about God."[14]

Revelation thus embraces both event and its interpretation: The event is made meaningful by its interpretation. I. Howard Marshall points out that "revelation for us takes place through interpreted events, and the interpretation must take place in words."[15]

What Is Meant by the "Inspiration" of Scripture?

The doctrine of the inspiration of Scripture pervades the Bible. The classic passage cited for this doctrine is 2 Timothy

[13]Cf. Gen. 45:5–8; for other examples, see 2 Kings 18:11–12; Acts 2:12,16.

[14]Leon Morris, *I Believe in Revelation* (Grand Rapids: Wm. B. Eerdmans, 1977), 43.

[15]I. Howard Marshall, *Biblical Inspiration* (Grand Rapids: Wm. B. Eerdmans, 1983), 14.

3:16. The key Greek word used by Paul in this passage, *theopneustos,* occurs in the New Testament only here. It has generally been translated "given by inspiration of God" (KJV; "inspired by God" [NASB, RSV]). This is a compound word that literally means "God-breathed" (note NIV).[16] In this verse it refers to the content of the Scripture in its entirety. It is faithfulness to the text of Scripture that leads believers to speak of the Bible as a God-breathed writing.

Even more important, inspiration is not inhaling but exhaling. That is, the word describes not so much the product of God's action as the activity itself. The words of Peter are particularly instructive here (2 Pet. 1:20–21). He shows that though Scripture came through human agency, it is nonetheless from God. Inspiration is the action of God by his Spirit through human writers. (As noted earlier, the vocabulary, syntax, and style of writing were theirs.) Yet in bringing forth the Scriptures through them, the Spirit guided.[17] I agree with L. Gaussen's definition of inspiration: "the mysterious power put forth by the Spirit of God on the authors of Holy Writ . . . to guide them even in the

[16]See Warfield, *Inspiration and Authority,* 131–33, where he says, "The Greek term . . . speaks only of a 'spiring' or 'spiration.' . . . No term could have been chosen . . . which would have more emphatically asserted the Divine production of Scripture than that which is here employed."

[17]The Bible clearly rejects a wholly naturalist interpretation of its origin. A naturalist perspective undergirds both the classic liberal and more recent postmodern interpretation of Scripture. David Dockery has shown that the antisupernaturalist philosophy of the Enlightenment period "was foundational to much of the liberal theology that dominated nineteenth-century European and early twentieth-century American thought." *Christian Scripture* (Nashville: Broadman & Holman Publishers, 1995), 51. See also Bruce Demarest, "The Bible in the Enlightenment Era," in *Challenges to Inerrancy,* ed. Gordon Lewis and Bruce Demarest (Chicago: Moody Press, 1984).

I, He, You— Biblical Writing Styles

Let's look at Luke's justification for his gospel (Luke 1:1–4), and Jude's statement about his epistle (Jude 3). Both are autobiographical and use the first person: "It seemed good also to me to write an orderly account for you" (Luke 1:3); "I was very eager to write to you" (Jude 3). On the other hand, Exodus 24:1–2 is written in the third person: "Then he said to Moses, 'Come up to the LORD, you and Aaron, Nadab and Abihu, and seventy of the elders of Israel. You are to worship at a distance, but Moses alone is to approach the LORD; the others must not come near. And the people may not come up with him.'" And the Ten Commandments (the Decalogue) are given in the second person (Exod. 20:2–17).

employment of the words they use, and thus to preserve them from all error."[18]

What Are Some Erroneous Views of Inspiration?

Not every view of inspiration meets the biblical criteria. The following are two of the most common errors in understanding this important doctrine.

THE DICTATION THEORY

Some pious believers hold to a "dictation" theory of inspiration. Not only do they agree that God spoke to the human authors, they assume that God commanded specific language to be recorded. There are places where this is true.[19] However, a basic problem arises. The dictation theory does not refer to the extent of inspiration, but to its mode. But little is known about the nature of inspiration. God spoke "at many times and in various ways" (Heb. 1:1; see sidebar on writing styles). Moreover, when what is true in particular portions of Scripture is extended as a generalization to all Scripture, we can develop doctrine that does not represent the *whole* of biblical teaching.

David Dockery observes that many faithful believers wrongly ascribe to the dictation theory. Because of this, many often associate dictation with a plenary view of inspiration (the term "plenary" will be defined later). Dockery

[18]L. Gaussen, *Theopneustia: The Plenary Inspiration of the Holy Scriptures* (London: Passmore & Alabaster, 1888), 108.

[19]For example, Exod. 20:1–17 tells us that God spoke the Ten Commandments to Moses. The tension between human and divine authorship, however, may be seen by comparing Exod. 34:1 and 34:27. In 34:1, God says he will write his words on the tablets, but in 34:27 he commands Moses to do it.

writes, "Adherents of the plenary view take great pains to disassociate themselves from the dictation theorists. It is right to judge the dictation theory as docetic and, therefore, less than orthodox."[20]

CONCEPTUAL INSPIRATION

Opposite the dictation theory of inspiration is the theory of "conceptual," or "dynamic," inspiration. In this view, God inspired the ideas. The human writer set them forth in his own words. It attempts to link the ideas to God while leaving the human writer free to express them as he chooses.

Some contemporary approaches have expanded the view to include the community of faith in the composition of Scripture. This position suggests that the Bible arose out of traditions that confess what God has done for the community. Individuals or groups of individuals within that community took up the traditions and reformulated them to address specific situations. This theory limits inspiration to God's initiating impulse; the emphasis of inspiration falls not on the product–Scripture itself–but on the purpose and process of its production.[21]

One expression of this theory considers human writers of Scripture infallible when they wrote of faith and practice but not necessarily when they wrote of the humanities or

[20]Dockery, *Christian Scripture,* 51. The term "docetic" refers to an ancient heresy that claimed that Christ only *seemed* to have a body; this heresy denied the incarnation (see the strong refutation in 2 John 7). The Bible is God's Word in human language, making it similar to the incarnation in this respect. Dockery uses "docetic" to express the danger of the dictation theory in ignoring this important human factor in its interpretation of Scripture.

[21]Ibid., 54.

the sciences. This raises a question: Why is one sentence of Scripture accepted and not another? This theory offers no answer at this point. It fails to consider that *all* Scripture is God-breathed (2 Tim. 3:16).[22]

How Should Inspiration Be Understood?

Each of the views described to this point falls far short of a biblical definition of inspiration.[23] Some, for example, blur the distinction between inspiration and one's subjective

The Dead Sea Scrolls and Your Bible

The standard printed text of the Old Testament is *Biblia Hebraica Stuttgartensia,* ed. K. Elliger and W. Rudolph, based on Leningrad Codex B19ᴬ, dating 1008 A.D. Although the autographs have long since perished, the discovery and publication of ancient biblical manuscripts over the past two centuries have confirmed that the text we now possess is remarkably accurate. Most recent of these discoveries are the Dead Sea Scrolls (DSS) found at Qumran near the Dead Sea, dating from the second century B.C. to the first century A.D.

By comparison with ancient manuscripts, we know that our text is essentially identical to the Hebrew Bible used by Jesus. Let me illustrate by using Isaiah 21:8. The traditional Hebrew text (often called the Masoretic text) literally reads "A *lion* cried, 'On the watchtower I stand.'" The Isaiah Dead Sea Scroll (1QuIsaᴬ) reads, "The *watcher* cried." In copying the text, a scribe obviously confused the letters *rw'h* ("watcher") and read them *'ryh* (lion), an easy mistake to make.

This verse marks the *most significant variant* to be gleaned from the Dead Sea Scrolls for the entire book of Isaiah (sixty-six chapters)! Even better, most scholars regard our modern text as a text that is generally *superior* to the Dead Sea Scrolls. Why? Although the DSS are chronologically much older and thus closer to the autographs, the Leningrad Codex (B19ᴬ) was copied with such care that it has preserved older forms of many words than have the Qumran texts.

[22]See Thiessen's refutation of this theory in *Lectures in Systematic Theology,* 64.

[23]Some of the finest contributors to the formulation of the doctrine of Scripture say very little—if anything—on the question of the mode of inspiration. They do this purposely because they believe that the Bible has very little to say on the subject. Peter says that the prophets spoke from God as they were borne along by the Holy Spirit (2 Pet. 1:20–21). But to say exactly what form this took, or to limit it to any one form, is certainly to go far beyond the witness of Scripture itself, especially in the light of the opening verse of the book of Hebrews (" . . . at many times and in various ways").

response to the Word of God. For example, the "encounter" theories of religious existentialism understand that the person is responding to an event in his or her own experience. Such interpretations can lead to error.

The Autographs and Verbal Plenary Inspiration

Orthodox Christianity's traditional view is that the inspiration of Scripture is both verbal and plenary. "Verbal" means that God has influenced each word of Scripture. Even though the style of each human author can be detected, God has controlled the wording. "Plenary" means that inspiration extends to the whole of Scripture. This claim is made for the words of the autographs, that is, the original biblical writings. It applies to versions and translations only insofar as these reflect the original texts.[24]

How Should Differences in Ancient Texts Be Regarded?

Undeniably there are variant readings in the ancient texts used to make translations of the Bible. But this should in no way erode the believer's confidence in Scripture. Many of the variations have no effect on interpretation. Moreover, studies in the field of textual criticism maintain the reliability of present Greek and Hebrew texts.[25] The essential accuracy of the message is not jeopardized.

Studying Scripture

Christians believe the Bible is the Word of God. This is not something to take for granted. To do so is to take God for granted. We *cannot* afford to be sloppy interpreters of Scripture. Every serious interpreter of Scripture should make an effort to recover the meaning of the Greek, Hebrew, and Aramaic texts that underlie our present translations. The various unabridged concordances and computerized search engines for the Bible are very helpful in doing word searches in multiple versions and recovering original readings.

On the other hand, we work in a culture of English language. Most of us will find ourselves using an English Bible. There are a number of fine translations available. Here are some modern English language translations I have found useful:

(cont. on the next page)

[24]See Warfield, *Inspiration and Authority*, 173.

[25]See Werner Georg Kümmel, *Introduction to the New Testament*, trans. Howard Clark Key (Nashville: Abingdon, 1973), 553–54.

Studying Scripture (cont.)

For concordant studies: The New American Standard Bible (The Lockman Foundation)

For rapid reading: The New Living Translation (Tyndale)

For study: The New International Version (The International Bible Society)

For certain environments, the dignified phrasing of the King James Version may still be useful.

What Value Did Jesus Place on the Old Testament?

Jesus' use of the Old Testament is particularly instructive. It reflects his view that the very words of the Hebrew Scriptures were given by God. They were to be valued, studied, embraced, and internalized. He saw the whole of the Old Testament as God-given. He was as saturated in its content as he was skilled in its interpretation. And he said not "the smallest letter" of the Hebrew alphabet or "the least stroke of a pen" would pass away until it all was fulfilled (Matt. 5:18). Again and again Jesus appealed to a single word as he interpreted and applied a passage to his hearers. This is particularly noteworthy when he faced opposition. Questioned by the Pharisees about his true identity, he emphasized one word from Psalm 110:1 (Matt. 22:41–45). He based His reply to the Sadducees' denial of the resurrection on the time implied by one verb in Exodus (Exod. 3:6; Matt. 22:31–32). When a crowd in Jerusalem prepared to stone him, Jesus centered his defense on a single word from Psalm 82:6 (John 10:34). He countered Satan in the wilderness by appealing to Scripture, "It is written . . ." (Matt. 4:1–11). And it is hard to imagine a scene more charged with spiritual fervor than the one in the synagogue at Nazareth after Jesus' reading from Isaiah: He closed the book and announced, "'Today this scripture is fulfilled in your hearing'" (Luke 4:21).

New Testament writers also bear witness to the verbal plenary inspiration of Scripture. For example, they often introduce their quotations from the Old Testament by saying, "He [God] says" (Heb. 1:8), or "The Holy Spirit says" (Heb. 3:7; see 10:15), or "The Holy Spirit spoke . . . through Isaiah" (Acts 28:25), or "He . . . says in Hosea" (Rom. 9:25).

In writing to the churches of Galatia, Paul used one word from Genesis 13:15 to show that Christ is the true seed of Abraham (Gal. 3:16).

What Are the Characteristics of a Divinely Inspired Scripture?

Many distinctives mark the pages of the Scripture and set it apart from other writings, even religious ones; for example, the beauty of its language, its essential unity, or the singleness of its message (redemption). These distinctives, and many more, can be gathered under three great hallmarks of the Bible: (1) its truthfulness, (2) its authority, and (3) its effectiveness.

1. How Is Scripture Truthful?

Christianity cannot be separated from its claims of truth. When Moses received the covenant, the Lord commanded him to prepare two stone tablets. He said, "'I will write on them the words that were on the first tablets, which you broke.'" After this he disclosed himself as "'The LORD, the LORD, the compassionate and gracious God, slow to anger, abounding in love and faithfulness'" (Exod. 34:1,6). Both Moses and David refer to God as the "God of truth" (Deut. 32:4, KJV; Ps. 31:5). The judges who were appointed under Moses were to be men of truth (Exod. 18:21). David prays for continual preservation in the truth (Ps. 40:11), where clearly it is Scripture that he has in mind (40:8). In Psalm 119 the psalmist extols the Word of God calling it "the word of truth" (119:43) or simply "the truth" (119:142, KJV). The truth of God was to be acknowledged. Even Nebuchadnezzar was brought to recognize God's sovereignty, calling all God's works truth (Dan. 4:37, KJV).

The "Old" Testament for a New Day

Scripture is the Word of God; it speaks truth. And the Word of God "stands forever" (Isa. 40:8). It was what we call the Old Testament that Paul described to Timothy as "God-breathed" (i.e., inspired; 2 Tim. 3:16). It was the Bible used by Jesus and the Early Church. God has not changed. These Scriptures, rightly interpreted, are as applicable to us today as they were to the Early Church. The secret, though, as emphasized in this chapter, is proper interpretation.

Mixed Signals

It is always tragic whenever a gap occurs between what believers profess and how they live.

Francis Schaeffer often spoke of the Christian before the watching world. It must be that way. The world generally will be inclined to judge us not by our philosophical positions, nor by our theological articulations, but by the way we live. Although the problem is not new (cf. Rom. 2:24; 2 Pet. 2:2), think about the mixed signals that sometimes come from the Christian community in America today. How can such possibly be justified, given (1) that Scripture is truthful, authoritative, and effective; and (2) that the Holy Spirit both motivates and enables the believer to please God in all things?

Moreover, truth in the heart was a necessity for a citizen of Zion (Ps. 15:1–2).

This close association of revealed religion and truth, so evident in the Old Testament, is carried over into the New Testament. Jesus not only professed to *speak* the truth but to *be* the Truth (John 14:6). He taught that a complete and ongoing commitment to him was the basis of one's knowledge of the truth, and he spoke of freedom as its inevitable result (John 8:31–32).

After Jesus returned to the Father, the Holy Spirit would guide his disciples into all truth (John 16:13). The early Christians were obligated to the truth (2 Cor. 13:8). They were to acknowledge it (Titus 1:1; 2 Tim. 2:25). They were to be established in it (2 Pet. 1:12) and live it out daily (3 John 3). The context of 2 Timothy 3:16 contains a charge that Paul delivers to Timothy, his "son in the faith." Paul's message is set against the somber backdrop of deception by evil men and imposters. It addresses the sharp contrast between the truth of Scripture and the error of unbelief. Paul had urged Timothy to do his best to present himself to God as one approved, a workman who treated the Word of truth honestly and fully (2 Tim. 2:15). Timothy was to continue in the Holy Writings that he had known since childhood. Those writings would strengthen his spiritual life (2 Tim. 3:15) and equip him for ministry (vv. 16–17).

The Bible's truthfulness, or inerrancy, its infallibility,[26] and its authority are all consequences of biblical inspiration.[27] "Inerrancy" means that the Bible is without error or

---

[26]By standard dictionary definition, "inerrancy" and "infallibility" are synonyms. But in the interests of accuracy in theology, they are used differently.

[27]These doctrines, while amply set forth in Holy Scripture, are results of inspiration. The Bible is not inspired because it is inerrant; it is inerrant

falsehood in all it affirms or teaches. "Infallibility" means that it is reliable, certain, absolutely trustworthy. It means that Scripture, as the standard for faith and practice, is both adequate and effective (Titus 2:11–12; 2 Peter 1:3).[28]

Theology is possible because of God's revelation and the intellectual, volitional, and emotional abilities human beings have received from him. But God's revelation is not exhaustive: On the one hand, theology is limited to what God chose to reveal. On the other hand, his creatures are limited. So theology is limited by the finiteness of human understanding. Even devout theologians are handicapped by the incompleteness of their knowledge. A further hindrance is the corruption of the human heart. It is precisely because of this human condition that the understanding and definition of inerrancy must be biblical, to keep one on track. Doctrine is taught in Scripture both explicitly and implicitly. As noted earlier, the Bible repeatedly expresses the truthfulness of its message.[29] That truthfulness is implied throughout. Paul Feinberg says that inerrancy means "when all the facts are known, the Scriptures . . . will be shown to be wholly true in everything they affirm, whether that has to do with doctrine or morality or with the social, physical, or life sciences."[30] The definition begins

because it is inspired. The One who knows all things, and who is all-powerful, so superintended the human writers of Scripture that they wrote without error or falsehood in all they said, and without any deceit in what they intended.

[28]The purpose of Scripture is not to satisfy human curiosity but to bring people to Christ, and by teaching, reproof, correction, and training, to perfect them in the way of salvation (2 Tim. 3:15–17). And God guarantees that it will achieve its intended goal (Isa. 55:11).

[29]Paul D. Feinberg, "The Meaning of Inerrancy," in *Inerrancy*, ed. Norman L. Geisler (Grand Rapids: Zondervan Publishing House, 1979), 294.

[30]Ibid., 294.

with a humble acknowledgment of human finiteness—all the data is simply not available. Moreover, the Fall has produced what Augustus Strong called "a moral and spiritual astigmatism."[31] As a result, people often misinterpret the data that they do have. This fact alone should cause the believer to shun the arrogance of judgments made without adequate bases in fact.

Technically, inerrancy, like inspiration, is limited to the autographs—the original words that were written. For this reason evangelicals have used the term to apply to copies and translations to the degree that they reflect the original writings. And there is precedent for this in Scripture itself. Greg Bahnsen cites examples of biblical writers who, fully aware of the differences between autograph and copies and translations,[32] treated those copies and translations as authoritative.[33]

Knowing the Bible means a great deal more than merely quoting it. True knowledge implies understanding. To achieve understanding of the Bible, it must be interpreted. The definition of inerrancy in this chapter promotes and

[31]Augustus H. Strong, *Systematic Theology* (Philadelphia: Judson Press, 1956), 1:34.

[32]In evaluating the New Testament use of Old Testament versions, perhaps an analogy would be useful. The New Testament was written in Greek to a Greco-Roman world. Translations always miss something of the original. That's why Christians often consult several in trying to understand a passage in the English Bible: Each one will say things a bit differently and serve to emphasize another aspect of the original. In his writings, Paul often consults the Septuagint or the Targums (early Jewish Aramaic versions), depending on which makes his point better. For a detailed examination of the problem, see E. Earle Ellis, *Paul's Use of the Old Testament* (Grand Rapids: Wm. B. Eerdmans, 1957).

[33]Greg L. Bahnsen, "The Inerrancy of the Autographa," in *Inerrancy,* ed. Norman L. Geisler (Grand Rapids: Zondervan Publishing House, 1979), 57–59.

encourages the activity of interpretation. This does not mean that the truthfulness of Scripture hangs on the human interpretation of it. It means, rather, that one receives the truth of what the Bible says only when it is properly interpreted. It means that what a person believes (or does not believe) about Scripture influences that person's interpretation of it.

Keep in mind that inerrancy has to do with all the teachings of Scripture. Those who do not accept biblical teaching as true must formulate some other objective criterion by which truthful assertions may be recognized. Such a criterion—whether philosophical, biblical, or theological—says Carl Henry, has never been laid out.[34]

2. How Is Scripture Authoritative?

Scripture makes a strong claim for its own authority. Moses gave specific instructions for the care and security of the Torah (Deut. 31:24–26). The priests were to read it to the people (Deut. 31:11). Joshua was commanded to meditate on it day and night, "'to do everything written in it'" (Josh. 1:8). It was required reading for Israel's kings (Deut. 17:18–19). David charged his son Solomon, "'Observe what the LORD your God requires: Walk in his ways, and keep his decrees and commands, his laws and his requirements, as written in the law of Moses'" (1 Kings 2:3). Some kings were praised for their obedience to Scripture,[35] but others were condemned because they disobeyed it.[36] The prophets

---

[34]Carl Henry, "The Battle for the Bible," in *Carl Henry at His Best* (Portland: Multnomah Press, 1989).

[35]See 1 Kings 15:5–11; 2 Kings 23:24–25; 2 Chron. 31:20–21; 34:2.

[36]See 1 Sam. 15:11,22–26; 1 Sam. 28:17–18.

Jesus and the Law

Again and again in segments of the gospels, such as the Sermon on the Mount, Jesus says, "You have heard . . . but I tell you" (see Matt. 5:21–22). This is frequently misinterpreted to mean that Jesus came as a new lawgiver, setting aside the law of Moses. In reality, just the opposite is true. He honored the law. What he took exception to was the religious leaders who got around the law (in effect, breaking it), by both their teachings and their lives. Jesus specifically says that he came to fulfill the law. He did this both in his teachings and in his life. In the final analysis, Jesus' endorsement of the Old Testament should settle all questions relating to its authority.

eloquently testified that their words constituted the authority of the LORD God.[37] By the time Jesus was born, the Old Testament was accepted in its entirety–Law, Prophets, and Writings–as the inspired and authoritative Word of God.[38]

Christ came proclaiming himself as the fulfillment of the promises made to Israel in a book (Matt. 5:17). The disciples, in their sermons, interpreted the Old Testament as a record of redemptive history, linking it to Jesus. In this way they associated the authority of the Old Testament with the authority of Jesus.[39]

HOW MAY AUTHORITY BE UNDERSTOOD?

Authority can be innate or derived. Only God's authority is innate. It is inherent in his being. He has the right and the capacity to do what he chooses, including the right to command belief and action. There is no one greater by whom he can swear, so he swears by himself (Gen. 22:16; Heb. 6:13–18).

Derived authority is authority that comes from a greater authority. It is clear, for example, that the centurion who asked Jesus to heal his sick servant was thinking of derived authority when he spoke, as a solider, of both being under authority himself and then having authority over others (Matt. 8:9).[40] The chief priests and the elders asked Jesus who gave him the authority to do what he did (Matt. 21:23).

---

[37]See Isa. 8:5; 31:4; Jer. 3:6; 13:1; Ezek. 21:1; 25:1; Hos. 4:6; 8:1,12; Amos 3:1; 7:1.

[38]Edward J. Young, "The Authority of the Old Testament," in *The Infallible Word* (Philadelphia: Presbyterian & Reformed Publishing House, 1946), 70–71.

[39]John 5:39–40; Acts 17:2–3,11; Rom. 1:2–4; Heb. 1:1–3.

[40]The centurion's authority had been bestowed on him by imperial Rome. He represented the full governing authority of the Roman Empire.

They too were thinking of derived authority.

Jesus was the Word of God in the flesh (John 1:14). Scripture is the Word of God in writing (John 10:34–35). Because of who Jesus is, his authority is innate. He also has authority derived from the Father by reason of his mission. So it is with the Scriptures. On the one hand, Scripture is its own genuine and valid authority because it is the Word of God. God himself addresses humanity. On the other hand, its authority is bestowed by God. Holy men spoke as they were propelled by the Spirit of God (2 Peter 1:21). H. D. McDonald uses the terms "real authority" and "conferred authority." He writes, "Because the Bible points beyond itself to God, it has a conferred authority. Yet the Bible has a real authority in itself as the authentic embodiment of God's self-disclosure."[41]

3. How Is Scripture Effective?

All Scripture is permeated by the idea that the power of God's word can produce the desired effect. God's word will not return to him fruitless but will accomplish what he wants (Isa. 55:11). Jeremiah encouraged the prophets to speak the word faithfully and boldly. He knew that nothing could successfully withstand God's word (Jer. 23:28–29). The writer of Hebrews describes the word of God as living and powerful; it discerns the thoughts and attitudes of the heart (Heb. 4:12). Paul shows that Scripture is given to make one wise unto salvation through Jesus Christ. It teaches, reproves, corrects, and instructs in righteousness (2 Tim. 3:14–16).

[41]H. D. McDonald, "Bible, Authority of," in *Evangelical Dictionary of Theology,* ed. Walter A. Elwell (Grand Rapids: Baker Book House, 1984), 139.

All authors are selective in what they write. Their intended purpose guides their choice of what to include and what to exclude. God's intention in giving Scripture determines what is given. The ultimate goal of Scripture is not simply to increase human knowledge, but to change lives. This does not mean, of course, that there is no appeal to the intellect. In fact, our experience of the Word is valid only as it is grasped by the mind and internalized in the heart (for example, see Rom. 10:9–10).[42]

God's Word is both unique and dynamic. No dull book of records, it continues to live century after century to fulfill its purpose for being written. The Psalmist tells what Scripture is and what it does (Ps. 19:7–14). Taken altogether, the synonyms the Psalmist uses reflect the idea of instruction. These are given by the righteous Judge, bearing witness to who he is. They call for obedience. They are to the soul what food is to the body. They warn God's servants, restore the soul, and make spiritually wise those who are open to them.

What Is Meant by Describing the Bible as "Canon"?

Now about which books were accepted into the Old Testament and why: The first question deals with the canon[43] of Scripture. The second one deals with canonicity.

---

[42]Acts 8:26–39 provides a classic study in the order in which the faculties of the human spirit are brought into play in the conversion experience. First comes an appeal to the intellect, "'Do you understand what you are reading?'" (8:30). This is followed by a confessed act of decision (8:36). Finally, the emotions of the Ethiopian are set before us: he goes on his way "rejoicing" (8:39).

[43]For a very useful discussion of the canon and text of the Old Testament, see R. K. Harrison, *Introduction to the Old Testament* (Grand Rapids: Wm. B. Eerdmans, 1969), 199–288.

The word "canon" comes from the Greek *kanon,* which in turn comes from the Hebrew *qaneh,* meaning "reed."[44] Reeds were used to measure things and ultimately became accepted as a standard measuring instrument, like "yardstick" (originally Old English *geard,* meaning a small stick). In time the literal term became figurative, used as a standard for human thought and action (as did the English term: "Let the general good be our yardstick on every great issue"). "Canon" was—and is—a fitting term for the books of the Bible, either the thirty-nine of the Old Testament, the twenty-seven of the New Testament, or the sixty-six combined (the sense in which Protestants use the term).[45]

Jesus recognized as canonical the same books that are in the Old Testament today. After his resurrection he appeared to a group of grieving disciples. He reminded them that the events of the previous hours had been in fulfillment of the Old Testament prophecies about him. He told them, "'This is what I told you while I was still with you: Everything must be fulfilled that is written about me in the law of Moses, the Prophets and the Psalms'" (Luke 24:44).[46] Norman L. Geisler and William E. Nix observe

[44]The word translated "rod" in contemporary versions in Ezekiel's temple vision is *qaneh,* lit. "reed" (Ezek. 40:3,5; cf. KJV). The man in Ezekiel's vision used it to measure the temple.

[45]The Roman Catholic canon of the Bible includes the Apocrypha, bringing the total number of books in that canon to eighty. Catholics also have a Canon of the Mass which involves a set form of liturgy, and Canon Law in which they present forms of discipline. For a thorough discussion of canon, see Harrison, *Introduction to the Old Testament,* 260–88.

[46]A question naturally arises about Christ's use of "the Psalms" to designate the third division of the canon. One answer is that he used the part for the whole, but this is unlikely, given its inconsistency with the earlier designations "the Law of Moses" and "the Prophets." It is much more likely that Christ referred to "the Psalms" because of their many predictions about him, best suiting them for the Christological purposes of his teaching on the occasion

that there is not enough data to form a complete history of the Old Testament canon.[47] Yet there are evidences that sketch an overall process: the gradual accumulation and collection of the books, prophetic continuity in the books themselves, and the completion of the (Old Testament) canon with the last of the prophets.[48]

Collection of the Old Testament books began with Moses, who placed the "Book of the Law" in the tabernacle (Deut. 31:24–26). Joshua added to it (Josh. 24:26). Samuel wrote concerning the kingdom and laid the book up before the LORD (1 Sam. 10:25). Hilkiah found the Law in the temple (2 Kings 22:8). Daniel shows the prophets' understanding of the character of the Law of Moses: He laments that Israel's calamities are due to its rejection of that law (Dan. 9:10–11). These passages show how the writers of Scripture characteristically used earlier canonical writings. The links of prophetic continuity extend from Moses to Joshua. They continue through the prophets, forming an unbroken chain that is completed in Nehemiah.[49] Both Josephus, a Jewish apologist writing in the first century A.D., and the Talmud, a body of Jewish writings begun before the Christian era, indicate that prophetic succession ended in Nehemiah's day with the prophecies of his contemporary Malachi. The Talmud says that after the ministries of

Luke records. The NT quotes Psalms more than any other book in the Old Testament.

[47]Norman L. Geisler and William E. Nix, *From God to Us* (Chicago: Moody Press, 1974), 76–80.

[48]Ibid., 80–85.

[49]For example, Daniel (Dan. 9:2) is reflecting on the writings of Jeremiah when he receives his revelation of "seventy 'sevens'" (9:24). It is clear that Hosea knew of a written *torah* (see Hos. 4:6; 8:1; esp. 8:12).

Haggai, Zechariah, and Malachi, the Holy Spirit left Israel.[50]

Some scholars point to the Council of Jamnia (Jabneel; see Josh. 15:11), a center of biblical study where the Sanhedrin relocated after the fall of Jerusalem in A.D. 70. These scholars argue that the Old Testament canon was decided by a Jewish synod there. This is a misconception. Jamnia was not a formal council with authority for Judaism but simply a gathering of Jewish scholarship. Any discussion of canonicity was probably raised in an academic sense. E. J. Young cites H. H. Rowley: "We . . . know of no formal or binding decisions that were made, and it is probable that the discussions were informal, though nonetheless helping to crystallize and to fix more firmly the Jewish tradition."[51]

Why Are Some Books Canonical While Others Are Not?

There is but one criterion for a book's inclusion in the Bible. It is not a book's sacredness, or its sublime contents, or the majesty of its style. Nor is it by ecclesiastical endorsement, whether by creed or by formal pronouncement.[52] The right to be in the canon of Scripture stems from the book itself: It must have canonicity to be included. Canonicity here refers to an inherent quality rather than the result of a formal action. That is, the informal recognition

[50]Geisler and Nix, *From God to Us,* 85.

[51]H. H. Rowley, *The Growth of the Old Testament* (London, 1950), 170, as cited by Edward J. Young, "The Authority of the Old Testament," in *The Infallible Word* (Philadelphia: Presbyterian & Reformed Publishing House, 1946), 73.

[52]William G. Heidt, *Old and New Testament Reading Guide* (Collegeville, Minn.: Liturgical Press, 1970), 23–24.

of the Jewish community that certain Scriptures were inspired recognizes canonicity. It is this quality that lay behind their being included in the Jewish Canon.

It is that quality which the book has because it is divinely inspired. In other words, canonicity is determined by God; it is only discovered by humans. Thus, canonicity precedes canon. Various Jewish sects claimed that many writings were canonical.[53] This led to the development of certain criteria for recognizing canonicity. Jewish scholars of the second century looked first at the book's language: Was it Hebrew or Aramaic? If not, it was discarded. Then they looked at how the book was received by the community of faith. Had it been recognized historically as coming from God? If only a sect had claimed it, the book was discarded. It had to meet both conditions to be considered for canonicity. Even so, many sharp debates followed.

Looking back over the process, a number of factors seem to have been involved in the final selection. Geisler and Nix have identified "five basic criteria": Is the book (1) authoritative? (2) prophetic? (3) authentic? (4) dynamic? (5) *"received or accepted by the people of God for whom it was originally written"*?[54]

Christians commonly believe that canonization did not come through an exclusive committee of patriarchs, or church fathers. Instead it gradually took place under the guidance of the Holy Spirit. It involved an extended process that was both natural and dynamic; the inspired writings

---

[53]Some of these writings were pseudepigraphic; that is, they claimed authorship by some great religious figure of the past or present. Examples may be seen in the Assumption (or Ascension) of Moses (first to second century A.D.) and the spurious letter sent to the believers in Thessalonica (2 Thess. 2:2).

[54]Geisler and Nix, *From God to Us,* 67.

were collected throughout the Old Testament period, for more than a thousand years. When the books of the last writing prophets–Haggai, Zechariah, and Malachi–were added, the Old Testament canon was complete.

The books as arranged in modern Jewish editions of the Old Testament reflect the following threefold division: Law (Torah), Prophets, and Writings. These divisions, found in Jewish lore, date back to the second century B.C. The Torah (Genesis through Deuteronomy) deals with creation, human rebellion against God, and God's judgments on that rebellion. It describes God's grace in forming a covenant people through whom the Savior would come and shows God's dealings with them during forty years of pilgrimage through the desert.

The section called the Prophets included the Former Prophets (Joshua through 2 Kings) and the Latter Prophets (Isaiah, Jeremiah, Ezekiel, and the twelve Minor Prophets). The Former Prophets pick up the story, telling how God brought his people into a promised land, Canaan, and describe their triumphs and defeats. God used prophets to call the nation to obedience. Some of them (like Jeremiah) left a written record of their preaching. Jewish scholars call them the Latter Prophets. Others (like Nathan, 2 Sam. 12:1–15) did not, or their writings did not survive. Despite their idolatry, God spoke to his people of the Messiah, giving precise details of his birth, life, and atoning death (Isa. 52:13 through 53:12). The prophetic writings record God's triumph over every form of evil and give marvelous glimpses into the worship and ethical expectations of Israel. They summarize its grand story in the historical books.

The Writings, or Hagiographa, contain everything else: Job, Psalms, Proverbs, and the Five Rolls (the books of

Song of Songs, Ruth, Lamentations, Ecclesiastes, and Esther, which were read on special occasions). The Writings also include the historical books (Chronicles, Ezra-Nehemiah, and Daniel).

The following chart shows how the Jewish canon is divided into Torah, Prophets, and Writings.

The Torah	The Prophets	The Writings
	The Former Prophets	**The Poetical Books**
Genesis	Joshua	Psalms
Exodus	Judges	Proverbs
Leviticus	Samuel	Job
Numbers	Kings	
Deuteronomy		
	The Latter Prophets	**The Five Rolls**
	Isaiah	Song of Songs
	Jeremiah	Ruth
	Ezekiel	Lamentations
	The Twelve	Ecclesiastes
		Esther
		The Historical Books
		Daniel
		Ezra-Nehemiah
		Chronicles

Luke records Jesus referring to this threefold division (Luke 24:24), confirming that it was used in his time.

The Septuagint is an early translation of the Hebrew Old Testament into Greek, done shortly before the time of Christ. Centuries later, Jerome produced a Latin translation, called the Vulgate. In doing this he followed the fourfold topical division of the Septuagint: Pentateuch, historical

books, poetical books, and prophetic books.[55] Bibles used
by Protestants follow this same division.[56]

Pentateuch (Torah)	Historical Books	Poetical Books	Prophetical Books
Genesis	Joshua	Job	**The Major Prophets**
Exodus	Judges	Psalms	Isaiah
Leviticus	Ruth	Proverbs	Jeremiah
Numbers	1 Samuel	Ecclesiastes	Ezekiel
Deuteronomy	2 Samuel	Song of Solomon	Daniel
	1 Kings		**The Minor Prophets**
	2 Kings		Hosea
	1 Chronicles		Joel
	2 Chronicles		Amos
	Ezra		Obadiah
	Nehemiah		Jonah
	Esther		Micah
			Nahum
			Habakkuk
			Zephaniah
			Haggai
			Zechariah
			Malachi

[55]The writers of the OT employed the Hebrew and Aramaic languages. The books were written primarily in Hebrew. Aramaic was also in use throughout the period of the Old Testament. In the sixth century B.C. it was used as an international language throughout the Near East. Sections of Ezra (4:8 through 6:18; 7:12–26) and Daniel (2:4b through 7:28) and one verse in Jeremiah (10:11) are written in Aramaic. Both Hebrew and Aramaic manuscripts were originally written without vowels. When they were translated into Greek and Latin, their increased size (due in part to vowels included in the words) necessitated the division of several of the books (Samuel, Kings, and Chronicles). This led to a rearrangement of the canon.

[56]Even though Jerome adopted the Septuagintal fourfold division of the Old Testament, for the last six centuries Roman Catholics have taught a threefold division of the Old Testament: Historical, Sapiential (i.e., wisdom), and Prophetical. The Apocryphal books are distributed among each of these divisions. See Heidt, *Reading Guide,* 39.

Bible Study: Start Now!

Although formal study is helpful, one of Martin Luther's Reformation principles was that the Bible could be understood by the common person without the help of a priest or a pope. I came to the Lord while working in the forests in Idaho. Later, in New Jersey, working in heavy industry, I would sit at noon and devour a chapter of the Bible while I ate my lunch. Later, as I began to understand what my conversion meant, I began to witness to others and then to preach a bit in rescue missions. Could I have done it better? Of course. My point is, though, that we can study from the moment we open our Bibles and can witness to God's grace as soon as we are converted.

No matter how it is arranged, the most important thing about the Bible is not its structure but its nature: It is God's Word to us. When one recognizes that, it leads into a desire to know the Bible's message and to understand its meaning.

What Is Hermeneutics and How Is It Used?

Beginning students of the Bible may feel overwhelmed by the volume of material presented at the outset of their studies. The matter of their English Bible being a translation, for example, is raised. Questions about the reliability of the various translations may come to mind. Furthermore, between today's readers and the original manuscripts are thousands of years; this raises questions about the relevance of their ancient message. The cultures and conditions of the people who lived when the Bible was being written and the cultures and conditions found in modern industrialized nations are quite different. This, too, poses unique issues for an inquiring mind. How should the Bible be considered in order to understand its message and its meaning? This should take the student to the discipline of hermeneutics.

The word "hermeneutics" is derived from the Greek verb *hermeneuo*, "interpret." Put very simply, hermeneutics is the science and art of interpretation and can refer to interpreting any kind of communication, verbal or nonverbal, secular or religious. The content of this chapter focuses on a special branch of hermeneutics. Because it deals with the interpretation of the (written) Word of God, it is sometimes called "sacred" hermeneutics. And because it examines the biblical text, it is sometimes called "biblical" hermeneutics. It tries to determine an accurate reading of what the text says. It seeks to understand and articulate clearly what the text means.

What Are the Components of Biblical Hermeneutics?

A number of things are involved in biblical hermeneutics. They include the purpose for the Scripture, prerequisites for the interpreter, precommitments in coming to the text, certain basic principles in interpreting the text, and the recognition of personal issues which may color an understanding of the text.

Why Was the Bible Written?

A focus on God's purpose in giving his Word should always be maintained. Humanity faces a problem of enormous proportions: Sin separates from God. No human effort can resolve this predicament. Yet salvation is possible. God's Word brings a message of redemption to humankind. If this is forgotten, the Bible cannot be treated fairly, nor can it be interpreted accurately. Someone has said that theology that does not become biography is simply wishful thinking. The Bible intends its message to be translated into human lives, not simply intellectualized. God is glorified in redeeming people. He frees people from sin and draws them to himself. One's thinking is changed. And when thinking is changed, a life is changed (Rom. 12:2a). Human history is filled with stories of ordinary people who were transformed by the power of God's Word, from the apostle Paul in the first century to C. S. Lewis and right up to this very day.

How Important to the Task of Interpretation Is Personal Preparation?

Before principles of interpretation can be applied to the biblical text, certain prerequisites must be met. For example,

No Ordinary Book

Mark Twain is credited with saying, "It's not the things I don't understand in the Bible that bother me, it's the things I *do* understand!" The Holy Spirit acts through the Word of God to immediately engage the reader. It is no ordinary book that causes me to face my lostness. Yet my alarm is swept away by the benediction of grace so gloriously set forth in the very Word which had earlier pointed out my pitiful condition. As John Newton observed, "'Twas grace that taught my heart to fear and grace my fears relieved." Grace frees us to be all that God wants us to be—not just through reformation, but through transformation.

the Holy Spirit guided the writers of Scripture. It follows, then, that one must be indwelt by the Spirit in order to interpret Scripture (John 16:13). Moreover, it must be recognized that the Bible is the Word of God in written form. Then the believer may have this confidence: The Spirit of God will lead him by the Word of God to know the mind of God and to have fellowship with God.

Everyone comes to the Scripture with preconceived ideas, assumptions. Believers must be careful about their assumptions. A person can read assumptions into the biblical text even though they are not supported by it, and may even run counter to it. On the other hand, certain assumptions are appropriate to study of the biblical text. For example, believers may properly expect that if they use the text reverently this will lead to understanding it. They may assume they will not meet a smorgasbord of meanings; each passage will have one meaning (though it may have many applications). They may assume that the meaning of a text can be discovered by reference to its context. They will not need to guess about its message and meaning. It is possible, even for the beginning student, to come into an ever-expanding understanding of the Bible's message and meaning.

Are There Rules of Interpretation That Can Be Used Immediately?

A process of interpretation takes place whenever one receives any communication. There are some basic principles that should govern the interpretation of Scripture. They can be put to use immediately! The heart of biblical interpretation can be stated very simply: To understand the text properly, the Bible must be interpreted in a way that respects its intentions. This means it must be interpreted literally, grammatically, historically, and according to its genre (the category of literature it falls into, for example, poetry, parable, letter). And what does this mean?

LITERALLY

To interpret a text literally is to take it at face value, asking, What is the message the author intended to convey? This applies equally to figurative and nonfigurative language. That is, to take Scripture literally does not mean to believe God actually has feathers, even though Psalm 91:4 says, "He will cover you with his feathers." The psalmist is using figurative, poetic language, likening God to a protective bird. And figurative language uses words deliberately out of their ordinary sense, employing literary devices, such as metaphor, personification, allegory, and the like, to give strength and fresh expression to their message. Literal interpretation will also involve some knowledge of the meaning of idioms used in Scripture. Idioms are modes of expression specific to a given language. That is, they usually defy word-for-word translation into another language. For example, there is no "apple" in your eye. But the pupil of the eye, besides being precious to sight, was anciently thought of as spherical. Thus developed an idiomatic phrase in English, "apple of one's eye," for greatly valuing something.

GRAMMATICALLY

The Bible is to be interpreted grammatically. The reader must pay careful attention to each word in its own context. This involves activities such as identifying the part of speech (is it a verb? a noun? an adjective? a participle?). Note its declension or its conjugation, how it fits into its context syntactically, etc. When working with a translation, you should do everything possible to recover the original words of the text and their meaning.[57]

HISTORICALLY

Third, Scripture originated in a historical context. Thus it can be understood only in the light of the history of its time. History takes place in time, with people living in a given place, with a specific manner of life. So to interpret the Bible historically is to include geographical and cultural considerations. But it means more than that. I contend that the interpreter needs a theology of history like the biblical writers had. This implies a conviction that God is at work in human affairs and that he sovereignly controls human destiny.

GENRE

Fourth, the Bible must be interpreted according to the type, or genre, of literature its text falls into. Drama cannot be interpreted in the same way as narrative; a proverb cannot be interpreted in the same way as apocalyptic writing. To ignore or misclassify genre is to distort the meaning of the text. For example, when an interpreter expects the language of scientific precision in a poem, the interpreter errs, not the author of the poem. The language of everyday speech is phenomenological—it describes things by how they are perceived. We still speak of the setting sun even though we know it is the Earth that is in motion.[58]

> ### The Indestructible Book
>
> "Keep my commands and you will live; guard my teachings as the apple of your eye" (Prov. 7:2). "Now I commit you to God and to the word of his grace, which can build you up and give you an inheritance among all those who are sanctified" (Acts 20:32). In summing up this chapter, I want to leave with you this truth: I have found that the uniqueness of Scripture is beyond doubt. My confidence in Scripture is this: It will endure simply because it *is* the Book of God. The indestructibility of the Book of God is as sure as the immutability of the God of the Book.

[57]You may wish to consult works such as Lawrence O. Richards, *New International Encyclopedia of Bible Words* (Grand Rapids: Zondervan Publishing House, 1991) or *Theological Wordbook of the Old Testament* (see n. 5), or any of the many Bible dictionaries and encyclopedias published in recent years.

[58]A person who uses the language of science at the office goes home and communicates to his family in everyday terms: "The *sun came up* as I left for

Personal Issues

Fifth, *personal issues* can color one's understanding of the text. It should be the goal of every student of Scripture to be as objective as possible. This presents a greater difficulty than might be imagined. People today are preoccupied with themselves. So they tend to isolate a single text to prove a pet doctrine and so forget that a doctrine is biblical only when it embraces *all* that Scripture has to say about it. Some people use Scripture to help them feel good. Some others attend a "Bible study" where a text of Scripture is read, followed by the opinions of each of the participants, supposedly to find its "meaning." Human opinions and experience must be judged by the light of Scripture, not the other way around.

The Old Testament is the Word of the living and true God. It speaks with the authority of God. It speaks of creation and of the Fall, with its awful legacy. But it also points to the Savior. It proclaims God's acts of redeeming grace in human history. Dwight L. Moody said, "Sin will keep you from this book. This book will keep you from sin." The prophet Isaiah declared, "'The grass withers and the flowers fall, but the word of our God stands forever'" (Isaiah 40:8).

---

work." "The sun *went down* as I pulled into the driveway." He may be angered at the suggestion that his terminology is misleading or inaccurate. In the same way, when the Bible describes the world in terms reflecting our ordinary senses such as sight, its description is true, and thus can be trusted.

Study Questions

1. Explain how the Bible is the Word of God and how that makes it valuable.
2. What is meant by revelation? What is general revelation? special revelation?
3. What is revealed theology?
4. What is inspiration?
5. Distinguish verbal plenary inspiration from dictation and conceptual inspiration.
6. What is meant by inerrancy? infallibility? authority?
7. What is meant by canon? canonicity? divisions of the canon?
8. What is genre? hermeneutics?
9. Identify the major biblical languages.

For Further Reading

THE BIBLE

Boice, James M., ed. *The Foundation of Biblical Authority.* Grand Rapids: Academie Books, 1978.

Bruce, F. F. *The Canon of Scripture.* Downers Grove, Ill.: InterVarsity Press, 1988.

Carson, D. A., and John D. Woodbridge. *Scripture and Truth.* Grand Rapids: Academie Books, 1983.

Dillard, Raymond, and Tremper Longman. *An Introduction to the Old Testament.* Grand Rapids: Zondervan Publishing House, 1994.

Geisler, Norman, ed. *Biblical Errancy: An Analysis of Its Philosophical Roots.* Grand Rapids: Zondervan Publishing House, 1981.

Harrison, R. K. *Introduction to the Old Testament.* Grand Rapids: Wm. B. Eerdmans, 1969.

Hodge, A. A., and B. B. Warfield. *Inspiration*. Grand Rapids: Baker Book House, 1979.

HERMENEUTICS

Carson, D. A., and John D. Woodbridge, eds. *Hermeneutics, Authority, and Canon*. Grand Rapids: Academie Books, 1985.

Osborne, Grant R. *The Hermeneutical Spiral*. Downers Grove, Ill.: InterVarsity Press, 1991.

Traina, Robert A. *Methodical Bible Study*. Wilmore, Ky.: Francis Asbury Press, 1952.

2

William C. Williams

In the Beginning

Outline:
- What Is the Pentateuch?
- Why Genesis?
- Where Did Genesis Come From?
- How Is Genesis Laid Out?
- What Does Genesis 1 Through 2 Teach Us?
- Interpreting the Data: Science Supports a Beginning
- How Did It Happen?
- How Should We Interpret Creation?
- Human Beings: What Are They?
- The Farmer Takes a Wife: Life in Eden and the Creation of Woman

Terms:
covenant
recombinant DNA
torah/Torah
transcendent

What Is the Pentateuch?

The Book of Genesis forms the introduction to the first five books of the Bible. In English these books are called the Pentateuch; Jews call them the Torah (Heb. *torah*, "teaching"). They are Genesis, Exodus, Leviticus, Numbers, and Deuteronomy. The theology of the entire Bible is grounded on certain key teachings found in these books.

Genesis means "beginning." The Book of Genesis tells how humans were created, sinned, and fell from fellowship with God. The spread of humanity and its sinfulness throughout the world is seen in chapters 1 through 11. But Paul tells us that where sin increased, grace did also (Rom. 5:20). The world's sinfulness implies its need for salvation (Rom. 8:19–22). Genesis hints at this in the revelation the LORD gave Abraham, calling him "a father of many nations" (Gen. 17:5). God would send a means of redemption through him to bless the entire world (Gen. 12:2–3).

Exodus means "the way out." The book sets forth God's redemptive work in freeing Israel from Egyptian bondage. It reaches its climax in the great covenant enacted at Mount Sinai (Horeb) between Israel and God. This redemptive work of God was so powerful that it later formed the core of Israel's great confession of faith (Deut. 6:21–23). In this way Exodus shows God's concern for the fallen state of humanity and his desire to redeem us from it.

Leviticus is so named for the priestly tribe of Levi. It has at its core a theology of holiness (i.e., godliness). Israel was taught that God is holy and that Israel was also expected to be holy (Lev. 19:2). In this context the sacrifices (Lev. 1 through 7) take on a redemptive meaning. The atoning sacrifices—the whole burnt offering, the sin offering, and the guilt offering—show how sin can be forgiven and the worshiper can be reconciled to God. The fellowship and grain offerings celebrate aspects of that redemption. Other laws function to define the nature of the redeemed community in terms of its ethics (e.g., care for the poor) and worship (e.g., the laws of clean and unclean).

Numbers returns to the story of Israel's wandering in the desert. It tells of the great census (Num. 1 through 4) that gives the book its English name. It also records the second Passover (Num. 9:1–14), the crisis at Kadesh Barnea (Num. 13 through 14), and the rebellion by Korah, Dathan, and Abiram (Num. 16). It describes the journey to the plains of Moab, scene of Balaam's oracles (Num. 22 through 24) and Israel's apostasy at Baal Peor (Num. 25). We learn about the bronze serpent (Num. 21:4–9), an inheritance for women (Num. 27:1–11; 36:1–12), the defeat of the Amorites in the Transjordan (Num. 21:21–30), and the settlement of Reuben, Gad, and one-half of the tribe of Manasseh in the Transjordan (Num. 32).

Deuteronomy continues the story on the plains of Moab. Its name is compounded from the Greek words *deuteros,* "second," and *nomos,* the term the translators of the Septuagint used to translate *torah.* In it Moses reviews Israel's history and reaffirms God's covenant with them. The book stresses God's love for Israel, his covenant with them, and the salvation he provided for them. It emphasizes the land Israel was about to receive and God's great works of salvation for them. At the conclusion of the book, Moses dies and is succeeded by Joshua.

Why Genesis?

Did you ever wonder where the world came from? Who God is? Why you are here? Why you have some sort

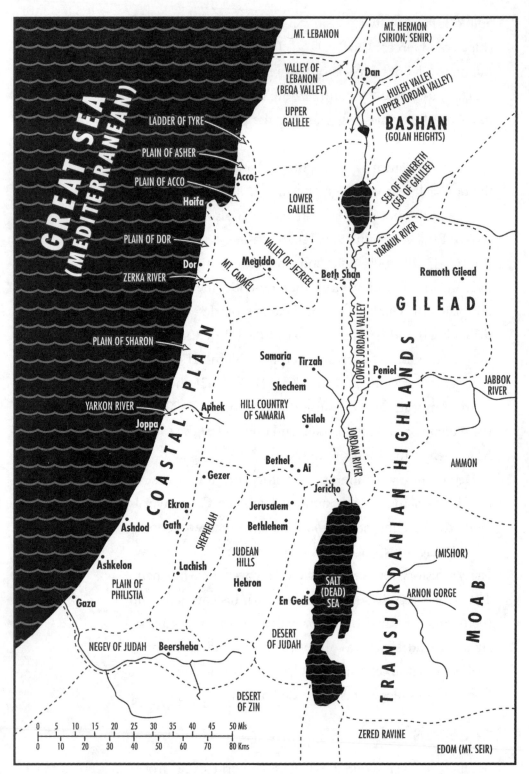

GREAT SEA
(MEDITERRANEAN)

MT. LEBANON

MT. HERMON
(SIRION; SENIR)

VALLEY OF
LEBANON
(BEQA VALLEY)

Dan

HULEH VALLEY
(UPPER JORDAN VALLEY)

UPPER
GALILEE

BASHAN
(GOLAN HEIGHTS)

LADDER OF TYRE

PLAIN OF ASHER

PLAIN OF ACCO

Acco

SEA OF KINNERETH
(SEA OF GALILEE)

Haifa

LOWER
GALILEE

YARMUK RIVER

PLAIN OF DOR

VALLEY OF JEZREEL

Megiddo

Ramoth Gilead

Dor

MT. CARMEL

Beth Shan

ZERKA RIVER

GILEAD

PLAIN OF SHARON

Samaria

Tirzah

Peniel

LOWER JORDAN VALLEY

TRANSJORDANIAN HIGHLANDS

JABBOK
RIVER

Shechem

YARKON RIVER

Aphek

HILL COUNTRY
OF SAMARIA

Shiloh

Joppa

JORDAN RIVER

Bethel

Ai

AMMON

Gezer

Jericho

Ekron

Jerusalem

Ashdod

Gath

SHEPHELAH

Bethlehem

JUDEAN
HILLS

(MISHOR)

Ashkelon

Lachish

Hebron

SALT
(DEAD)
SEA

ARNON GORGE

Gaza

En Gedi

MOAB

PLAIN OF
PHILISTIA

DESERT
OF JUDAH

COASTAL PLAIN

NEGEV OF JUDAH

Beersheba

DESERT
OF ZIN

ZERED RAVINE

EDOM (MT. SEIR)

| 0 | 5 | 10 | 15 | 20 | 25 | 30 | 35 | 40 | 45 | 50 Mls |
| 0 | 10 | 20 | 30 | 40 | 50 | 60 | 70 | 80 Kms |

Geography of Canaan

of inner voice about what's right or wrong? Why you don't always listen to that voice or act the way you should? These are some of the questions addressed in the opening chapters of Genesis. Genesis plays an important role in telling us about the creation of humanity, the fall of humanity, and God's plan to nullify the effects of that fall. To those who will hear the voice of Deuteronomy, it tells humanity of its past and God's pattern for the future, God's model for redemption.

Sometimes, though, it's important not to settle for an answer that tells you *what* without telling you *why*. For instance, did you ever ask yourself why a biblical book—Genesis, in this case—is in the Bible? Was it so we could speculate about the world's origin or the extent of the Flood or where Cain got his wife? Some people seem to think so, but this is not the reason. Instead, Genesis—and indeed all Scripture—has been placed in the Bible to reveal to us the mind and person of God and thus make us "wise for salvation" (2 Tim. 3:15). If we believers can remember that idea, our witness will be strong and united. If we forget it, our witness will be weak and divided.

Where Did Genesis Come From?

Perhaps the first question that should be asked is, How did this book called Genesis come about? The material of Genesis 1 through 11 is clearly Babylonian in its setting and origins, containing, for example, Babylonian words and Babylonian place names.[1] Such information was probably brought to Canaan from Haran by Abraham (Gen. 11:27

[1]E.g., the Heb. word for "deep" in Gen. 1:2 *(tᵉhom)* is related to the name of the Babylonian sea monster Tiamat, and the Tigris and Euphrates rivers (2:14) and the plain of Shinar (10:10; 11:2) are Babylonian place names.

What the Bible Itself Says About Mosaic Authorship

External Evidence. Material bearing on the question of authorship that comes from sources outside the material identified as being by a certain author, in this case, the Pentateuch, is called "external evidence." The first such mention is Josh. 8:31; cf. also 1:7–8; 8:32–34. Later, in David's charge to Solomon (ca. 971 B.C.), David tells his son to keep God's commands "as written in the Torah [i.e., Teaching] of Moses" (1 Kings 2:3, author's translation). Numerous other records mentioning a Torah book attributed to Moses are found in the books of Kings and Chronicles, among them 2 Kings 14:6 (also 2 Chronicles 25:4), referring to the time of Amaziah of Judah, 796–767 B.C.; 2 Chron. 35:12, to the time of Josiah, 641/40–609 B.C.; and Ezra 3:2; 6:18; 7:6 and Neh. 8:1; 10:29;

through 12:5). There it would have been preserved by the Israelites until it, together with the stories of the patriarchs, Abraham, Isaac, Jacob, could be written down.

But who wrote it down? Many people consider Moses the greatest man in the Old Testament (see Heb. 3:5). Traditionally he has been identified as the author of the Pentateuch. A large number of Bible verses record that Moses wrote, spoke, or sang something (see Exod. 15:1; Deut. 31:9,22). Others mention a "book" that has its origins with Moses (see 2 Chron. 25:4; Ezra 6:18). Mosaic authorship does not mean, however, that no portions of the Pentateuch are earlier or later than the life and times of Moses.[2] Nor should his authorship be taken to mean that he used no sources in compiling the Pentateuch. In Numbers, for example, he quotes from "the Book of the Wars of the LORD" (21:14). Like Luke would do centuries later in putting together his gospel (1:1–4), Moses examined the materials at his disposal. Guided by the Holy Spirit, he selected the information that was suitable. He then arranged and transmitted it to those who would preserve it, either orally or in writing. Mosaic authorship means, therefore, that the Pentateuch as a whole bears the stamp of Moses. It means that he set much of it down in writing. But it recognizes that much of the material already existed (for example, that of Genesis), either orally or written. And it accepts the fact that someone else wrote the material that follows Moses' death.

[2]All the events of Gen., for example, took place long before Moses' birth. And his death is recorded in Deut. 34:5–12. Verses such as Gen. 36:31 seem to presuppose the existence of Israelite kings (cf. 1 Chron. 1:43) long before the monarchy.

Some scholars in the past two centuries have denied that Moses wrote any of the Pentateuch. Instead, they identify it as being produced two to four centuries later, coming from the period of the Israelite monarchy (about 1000 B.C. or later, often called the Iron Age).[3] One strand of information in the Pentateuch was identified by its use of the divine name Yahweh (or Jehovah; "LORD" in most translations) when speaking of God, called the "Yahwistic" source (commonly dated to about 850 B.C.). A second strand was identified by its use of the Hebrew word *ᵉlohim* for God, termed the "Elohistic" source (dated about 800 B.C.). These two strands were, they say, combined with Deuteronomy (about 620 B.C.) and later with the "Priestly Code" (which supposedly addressed the priestly concerns of the Jewish community after the Babylonian exile after 550 B.C.) and in this way formed the Torah, or Pentateuch. Such a view is called the Documentary Hypothesis or the Graf-Wellhausen Theory[4] and is commonly referred to by the initials of each hypothetical source: JEDP. Some evangelicals have found this terminology useful for describing biblical texts in terms of their literary style. However, no evangelical has fully accepted the theory, recognizing that a naturalistic evolution undergirds it. Furthermore, its dates are too late for Mosaic authorship and thus call into question the truthfulness of Scripture. And lastly, archaeology has demonstrated that an overwhelming amount of the Genesis material has its origins in the Middle Bronze Age, not in the Iron Age.[5]

13:1, to the postexilic period.

Internal Evidence. Material bearing on Moses' authorship that comes from the Pentateuch itself is called "internal evidence." For example, Moses receives the command to write in the following verses: Exodus 17:14; 34:27; Deut. 31:19. The tabernacle and priesthood were revealed to Moses on Mount Sinai (Exodus 25 through 31). The laws of the worship system are also connected to Sinai (Lev. 26:46; 27:34).

There is also testimony to something actually written by Moses: the "Book of the Covenant" (Exod. 24:4,7); the book of his Torah, or teaching (Deut. 31:9, cf. vv. 24–26; 30:10); the "Song of Moses" (see Deut. 31:22); the list of campsites in Num. 33 (see 33:2).

These are only *some* of the many testimonies, direct or indirect, that attribute a Torah Book to Moses.

---

[3]Moses would be dated to the Late Bronze Age, ca. 1450–1250 B.C.

[4]The theory takes its name from Karl Heinrich Graf and Julius Wellhausen, two German scholars who popularized the view.

[5]I.e., about 2200–1550 B.C.; see Cyrus Gordon, "Biblical Customs and the Nuzu Tablets," *BA* 3 (1940): 1–12.

How Is Genesis Laid Out?

Most scholars agree that the structure of Genesis turns on the word *toledoth* or the phrase *sepher toledoth,* translated in NIV as "the account of" or "the written account of" (for example, 2:4; 5:1; 6:9). Most careful scholars agree that these words divide the book into sections.[6] Not all, however, agree as to their precise function or the sections they represent. Some, for example, hold that the words mark where each section begins. Others hold that they mark where each section ends. It is probable that some function as one or the other, and one or two as both. For the purposes of this survey, the following structural outline for the book is suggested.

The book divides into two major sections:

1. 1:1 through 11:26 — Primordial history

2. 11:27 through 50:26 — Abraham and his descendants

The *toledoth* generate the following structural pattern,[7] suggesting this: Genesis 6:9a acts as a subscript showing the end of the preceding section (5:1b through 6:8); the same verse acts as a superscript showing the beginning of the following section (6:9b through 9:29). In the same manner, 37:2 would be a subscript; it ends a section that begins with 27:46 (Jacob's preparation to depart for Mesopotamia). The histories of Esau (36:1–8; 36:9 through 36:43) would be insertions into the history of Jacob. The final section

---

[6]See P. J. Wiseman, *New Discoveries in Babylonia About Genesis* (London: Marshall, 1936), recently reprinted as *Ancient Records and the Structure of Genesis* (Nashville: Nelson, 1985); R. K. Harrison, *Introduction to the Old Testament* (Grand Rapids: Wm. B. Eerdmans, 1969), 543–47; Gordon J. Wenham, *Genesis 1–15,* WBC (Waco: Word, 1987), xxi–xxii; and Victor P. Hamilton's critique in *The Book of Genesis: Chapters 1–17,* NICOT (Grand Rapids: Wm. B. Eerdmans, 1990).

[7]I am indebted to Johnson Motilal (a graduate student at Southern California College) for the stimulus he has provided for my thinking on this matter.

(37:3 through 50:26) would be an appendix without superscript or subscript (Joseph's life in Egypt).[8]

1:1 through 2:4a	The origins of the cosmos
2:4b through 5:1a	The origins of humanity
5:1b through 6:9a	The histories of Noah, pt. 1
6:9b through 9:29	The histories of Noah, pt. 2
10:1 through 11:9	The histories of the sons of Noah
11:10–26	The histories of Shem
11:27 through 25:11	The histories of Terah
25:12–18	The histories of Ishmael
25:19 through 27:45	The histories of Isaac
27:46 through 35:29; 37:1–2	The histories of Jacob
36:1–8	The histories of Esau, pt. 1
36:9–43	The histories of Esau, pt. 2
37:3 through 50:26	Joseph

The smaller subdivisions that fall within Gen. 1:1
through 11:26 are these:[9]

1:1–2:4a	Creation of the world
2:4b through 3:24	Paradise and Fall
4:1–26	Cain and Abel
5:1–32	Genealogy: Adam's descendants
6:1 through 9:17	The Flood
9:18–29	After the Flood
10:1–32	Genealogy: the "Table of Nations"
11:1–9	The tower of Babel
11:10–26	Genealogy: from Shem to Abram

[8]In support of this perspective, it would seem that the greater story of
Scripture is carried on through Levi (Exod. through Deut.) and Judah (Josh.
through 2 Chron.). Joseph does not reappear as a major player, nor do his
sons, Ephraim and Manasseh, even though they receive large tribal allotments, testifying to their extensive populations.

[9]Adapted from G. Ch. Aalders, *Genesis: Volume I* (Grand Rapids: Zondervan
Publishing House, 1981), 43.

What Does Genesis 1 Through 2 Teach Us?

Genesis introduces a number of cardinal doctrines that will reappear throughout Scripture.

The Bible Uses Stories to Teach Theology

Have you ever pondered why God has included stories in the Bible? Each book of the Bible, including Genesis, has been put in the canon to reveal God's mind and will. We are forcefully reminded of this when Jesus speaks directly to his hearers or Paul tells what the Lord has revealed to him. We are confronted by it in the Old Testament in the prophets' words "this is what the LORD says" and in wisdom statements about God in books like Proverbs. But the mind of God is also revealed in the stories of both Old and New Testaments. Sometimes we get so absorbed in a story that we forget to look for the theology it contains. That is easy to do in the stories about Joseph in Egypt or the adventures of David, for example. Or, as in the case before us, we get so taken up by the controversies surrounding details in the creation texts that we forget to ask ourselves, "What does the story clearly tell me about God and my relationship to him?" This textbook examines the Old Testament as it tells the story of God's redeeming work as it is displayed in the lives of his people.[10]

Who Is God?

Did you ever wonder who God is? The opening chapters of Genesis do not tell us all about God. Moreover, since

---

[10]See Carl E. Armerding, "Faith and Method in Old Testament Study: Story Exegesis," in *A Pathway into the Holy Scripture,* ed. P. E. Satterthwaite and D. F. Wright (Grand Rapids: Wm. B. Eerdmans, 1994), 31–49.

God fills both heaven and earth (Jer. 23:24), it would be impossible to contain him between the covers of any book or to tell all about him in it (cf. John 20:30–31; 21:25). But these first chapters of Genesis tell us some very important things about him. These are just a few of them: (1) He is preexistent. He existed before all else. He did not come into existence at the beginning but, as the Creator, made the beginning possible (Gen. 1:1). (2) If he created space and time, it follows that he must exist independent of them. That makes him what theologians call transcendent. (3) He is a God of order. The account of God's six days of creation describes a world being transformed from a state of chaos ("formless and empty," 1:2) to a world teeming with life. (4) He is personal and has personality and personhood. He speaks the world into existence, creates human beings (persons) in his image (1:27–28), and can communicate with them (1:28–30). (5) He can reach and be reached by those he has created (2:15–18). That makes him not only transcendent but also imminent. (6) He is sovereign. He deliberates only with himself in making his decisions, asking no permission from the created world (1:26). (7) He is the life-giver. All living things owe their lives to him (1:20–27; 2:19–22).

God Has Created All That Is

How did the universe begin?[11] The first verse of the Bible tells us that in the beginning God created the heavens and earth (Gen. 1:1). The words "the heavens and the earth" might be paraphrased to say "all that is," "everything." In

---

[11]For a thorough discussion of the theological dimensions of creation, see Christoph Barth, *God With Us: A Theological Introduction to the Old Testament* (Grand Rapids: Wm. B. Eerdmans, 1991), 9–37.

this simple sentence a number of things are identified: (1) the creation and (2) the Creator. We learn who God is: He is Creator. We learn what the universe is: It is creation. We learn who we are: We are creatures. We learn when it happened: in the beginning.

The word "create" *(bara')* occurs three times in the first chapter: 1:1, 1:21, and 1:27. It describes an action as (1) performed by God, and (2) something entirely new. Genesis 1:1 shows that all there is comes from God and that existence as we know it is radically different from preexistence. The writer of the epistle to the Hebrews puts it this way: "By faith we understand that the worlds were prepared by the word of God, so that what is seen was made from things that are not visible" (Heb. 11:3, NRSV). (We will take up Gen. 1:21 and 1:27 later.)

The story of creation is simply told but has profound meaning. For one thing, it means that the universe is God's handiwork. The Bible does not tell when God created the universe; it simply declares that it was "in the beginning" and that God did it. Some scientists have attempted to argue that the universe is eternal,[12] constantly renewing itself as it decays. The Bible, however, declares that the universe had a beginning. Moreover, it did not come into existence through spontaneous generation; it had a creator.[13]

---

[12]As, for example, Carl Sagan's famous statement, "The Cosmos is all that is or was or ever will be." See Robert E. Snow, "A Critique of the Creation Science Movement," in Howard J. van Till et al., *Portraits of Creation: Biblical and Scientific Perspectives on the World's Creation* (Grand Rapids: Wm. B. Eerdmans, 1990), 188, citing Sagan's *Cosmos* (New York: Random House, 1980), 4. See also Mark G. McKim, "The Cosmos According to Carl Sagan: Review and Critique," at http://www.asa3.org/ASA/topics/Astronomy-Cosmology/PSCF3-93McKim.html.

[13]The fundamental distinctive of what J. Lindsay calls "Theistic Creation" is God's involvement in the creative work; it did not occur spontaneously.

God's Spirit Is His Active Agency

What is meant by "the Spirit of God"? Throughout the Old Testament the "Spirit of God" or the "Spirit of the LORD" appears as God's active agency. The term often describes God's immediate presence at work in the world he has created. In the Book of Judges, God's Spirit "comes upon" the judges to enable them to do the task at hand.[14] Likewise, the Spirit comes upon Saul to empower him to lead united Israel against Philistine dominance. When the time comes for David to replace Saul, the Spirit leaves Saul (1 Sam. 16:14–16) to come upon David (1 Sam. 16:13; cf. 2 Sam. 23:2). In the Old Testament the theological foundation is laid for the revelation of the Holy Spirit as the third person of the Holy Trinity (Matt. 28:19). The revelation of the Godhead in the New Testament is much fuller than in the Old Testament. In the New Testament God's Spirit manifests a distinct personality and office (e.g., John 16:13–15), whereas in the Old Testament the Spirit manifests the presence of God as living and full of power.[15]

"Creation," in *ISBE*, 1:800–802. See also Daniel Lys, *The Meaning of the Old Testament: An Essay on Hermeneutics* (Nashville and New York: Abingdon, 1967), 27–80.

[14]E.g., Othniel: Judg. 3:10; Gideon: 6:34; Jephthah: 11:29; Samson: 13:25; 14:6,19; 15:14–15.

[15]When a child is taught to read or do arithmetic, the teacher begins with simple concepts the child can understand. When God revealed himself to the biblical writers, he did so in a manner that people could understand at the time the revelation was given. Often that revelation was augmented and developed as it was addressed later in Scripture. The Godhead is just one example of this. For a discussion of the progressive nature of revelation, see B. B. Warfield, *The Inspiration and Authority of the Bible* (Phillipsburg, N.J.: Presbyterian & Reformed Publishing Co., 1948), 79–83.

Human Beings Are Jointly Created in God's Image

What are human beings? How are they set apart from the lower animals? The Bible says that humans are distinguished from lower animals by being created in the image of God (Gen. 1:27). It is what distinguishes them as theologically human, and allows them to commune with God.[16]

The Bible does not speak of the male alone as bearing God's image. Instead, it indicates that male and female—both genders—make up the human species that bears the image of God. Together, not individually, the two reflect the image of God and thus are theologically human.

As such, they are one (that is, human), yet different. And in this oneness, they reflect the unity and diversity that characterizes the Godhead itself. Christians confess that there are three persons in the Godhead, yet all are divine in essence. The harmony shown in the "let us" passages in Genesis points to a plurality acting in unison. So humanity, though diverse, was created to reflect the unity and harmony that is seen in Eden before the Fall. (See also "Human Beings: What Are They?" later in this chap.)

The Unity of the Human Species Is Shown Biblically, Genetically, and Psychologically

How are human beings related? The human species may vary in its appearance and function, but it is a single whole. The Bible clearly speaks of humans as descended from a

---

[16]See David L. Turner, "Image of God," in the *Evangelical Dictionary of Biblical Theology*, ed. Walter A. Elwell (Grand Rapids: Baker Book House, 1996), 365–67. For an exhaustive survey of current opinion on this subject, see G. C. Berkouwer, *Man: The Image of God,* trans. Dirk W. Jellema (Grand Rapids: Wm. B. Eerdmans, 1962), 67–118.

single pair of parents (see the genealogies in Gen. 4:17 through 5:32). Recent scientific evidence from recombinant DNA seems to confirm this.[17] Evidence of this relatedness may be seen in the ability of all humans to interbreed. No matter their size or color, the offspring they produce are human beings. On the other hand, horses and donkeys look very much alike, but when they interbreed, they produce mules. Mules cannot reproduce themselves; they are sterile.

Further evidence of human unity may be found in the common psychological needs shared by all normal humans. For example, most people need human companionship or they are miserable. That's one reason for Christian fellowship: We need to "encourage one another" (Heb. 10:25).

These factors point to a single human species. That means that *all* persons, whatever their race, sex, or origins, are included when we speak of mankind in God's image.

The Created Order Has a Theological Meaning

Scholars sometimes refer to a "theology of the created order" or to an "Edenic" model. But what do they mean by a "created order"? They are referring to God's own evaluation of creation recorded in Genesis 1:31: "It was very good." That means that the world as originally created by God was good and right. The Genesis account of Eden gives us a glimpse of what God's unfallen creation would have looked like. It also mirrors what God's plan of

[17]Recombinant DNA is DNA in which genes from two different sources are linked. These genetic combinations may be traced to show relationships. For an easy-to-understand discussion of the issues involved, see Karen Springes, "The Search for Adam and Eve," *Newsweek,* 11 January 1988, 45–52.

redemption labors to accomplish: to restore humanity, and with it all creation (Rom. 8:19–22), from the effects of the Fall. The Edenic narratives show how God set things up originally to help human beings make moral judgments. In proclaiming the gospel of redemption, therefore, believers work to overcome the fallen order and to restore the created order by advancing the Kingdom of God.

Human Marriage Is Not Just a Social Issue

How does God see human marriage? In Genesis 2:24 the principle is laid down that the man should leave his family to be united with his wife. The two of them would become "one flesh" (that is, inseparable). In Old Testament language, common flesh, blood, or bone indicates a relationship of the closest order. It describes one person as an extension of the other, often indicating a blood relative (as in Gen. 29:14; 37:27; Judg. 9:2; 2 Sam. 19:13). Jesus appealed to Genesis 2:24 when he spoke of divorce (Matt. 19:5). Paul used it to describe the harmony that should be a part of the Christian home (Eph. 5:31). This important verse teaches us that marriage is not just a private matter: It is of great concern to God himself.

Interpreting the Data: Science Supports a Beginning

We have already discussed God's general revelation of himself in creation, and his special revelation in Scripture.[18] You and I witness God's revelation of himself wherever we look, whether it be in the heavens (astronomy) or in the structure of the atom (atomic physics). The intricacy of the structure of

[18]See chap. 1.

creation bears witness to a great mind that designed it and a great power that executed it: God, the Creator.

General revelation functions as a complement to special revelation and to revealed, or biblical, theology. Each one speaks the truth of God's existence and his nature. They should never be represented as adversaries.[19] So when we set out to study the biblical doctrine of creation, we must also consult the natural sciences and history to see what it is we are talking about.

The obvious reason for believing in a creation is that the Bible declares it (Gen. 1:1). This works when discussing matters with believers. But what about the person who does not accept the Bible as a truthful and reliable record? Can some kind of witness be found in the created order itself? The answer is yes, an objective examination of the universe turns up compelling reasons to believe that it had a beginning.[20] Its existence is not eternal, in some sort of steady state. Moreover, it appears to have developed considerably since that beginning. Some of those reasons are given below.

The Universe Is Expanding

How big is God's creation? The universe is enormous. Our Milky Way galaxy alone is from 100,000 to 150,000 light years in diameter; it is from 25,000 to 40,000 light

[19]Although some have interpreted scientists and mathematicians such as Stephen W. Hawking as ruling out the existence of God, he calls this an oversimplification. His findings, he says, say "nothing about whether or not God exists—just that He is not arbitrary" in his act of creating. See his *Black Holes and Baby Universes and Other Essays* (New York: Bantam Books, 1993), 172; cf. 98–99.

[20]For a persuasive defense of this point, see Hugh Ross, *The Fingerprint of God,* 2d ed. (Orange, Calif.: Promise Publishing, 1991); see also Robert B. Fischer, *God Did It, But How?* (La Mirada, Calif.: CalMedia, 1981). I am deeply indebted to Dr. James Bradford, pastor of Broadway Church, Vancouver, B.C., for his help in preparing this section of the chapter.

years thick. It contains about a trillion stars or solar masses.[21] There may be as many galaxies in the visible universe as there are stars in our galaxy.

Astronomers have determined that the universe is expanding from a central location in space.[22] The speeds of the bodies increase according to the distance they are from that central point. Whole nebulae have been discovered two thousand light-years apart. They are moving away from one another at incredible speeds. The light from some of the most distant bodies has not yet reached the earth. (If all such light—coming from all over the universe—were to reach the earth simultaneously, we would have perpetual day.) This points back to a time when the universe was concentrated in a very small, dense mass. That mass exploded—an event called the big bang, leading to the theory by that name. The explosion sent the various astronomical bodies hurtling through space away from the center of the universe. If their rate of acceleration has been constant, the age of the universe can be calculated.[23] Its expansion declares it had a beginning.

The Universe Is Not Static

Can the universe keep up its speed forever? By the beginning of the twentieth century, scientists had demonstrated

[21]A solar mass represents the mass of our sun and equals 333,400 times the mass of Earth.

[22]See "Cosmology: The Study of the Universe," at the NASA MAP web site: http://map.gsfc.nasa.gov/m_uni.html.

[23]Most recent calculations yield about seven to fourteen billion years; see Robert Lee Hotz, "Universe Far Younger Than Believed, Two Studies Find," *Los Angeles Times,* 29 September 1994, and sidebar. Less recent estimates suggested about twelve to twenty billion years; see Ross, *Fingerprint of God,* 90; Hong-Yee Chiu, "Cosmology (Astronomy)," in *The New Grolier Multimedia Encyclopedia* (1993).

that there are no absolute reference frames by which absolute speeds can be measured. Yet the speed of light is always the same. These facts led Einstein to develop his special and general theories of relativity. The predictions made from these theories have since been verified experimentally to an amazing degree of accuracy.[24] Einstein's general theory of relativity showed the universe to be expanding and slowing down at the same time. Although stellar bodies near the edge of the universe are moving faster than those that lie near the center, their velocities are decreasing. In the past, therefore, those bodies that are slowing down would have been moving faster. These famous theories also had in them the making of a revolution, upsetting previously held notions about the eternal, steady state nature of the universe. They pointed to a beginning and, by inference, to a creation. Einstein was so distressed by what this discovery would imply that he arbitrarily added a "cosmological constant" to his equations. It was a kind of "antigravity" effect that could not be justified by observation or mathematics. Einstein later called it the biggest mistake of his life.[25] Although he never did admit the existence of a

[24]This treatment of the theory of relativity was written by Dr. James Bradford, and I gratefully acknowledge his assistance. It is interesting to note that, depending on what one measures, some aspects of the universe may be speeding up (see "Cosmology," NASA MAP page cited earlier). In any case, the universe is in a constant state of change.

[25]"In its simplest form, general relativity predicted that the universe must either expand or contract. Einstein thought the universe was static, so he added this new term ["cosmological constant"] to stop the expansion. Friedmann, a Russian mathematician, realized that this was an unstable fix, like balancing a pencil on its point, and proposed an expanding universe model, now called the Big Bang theory. When Hubble's study of nearby galaxies showed that the universe was in fact expanding, Einstein regretted modifying his elegant theory and viewed the cosmological constant term as his 'greatest mistake'." See "What Is a Cosmological Constant?" at the NASA MAP web site: http://map.gsfc.nasa.gov/m_uni/uni_101accel.html.

personal God, his general theory of relativity predicted a finite universe. It had a beginning and would have an end.

The Anthropic Principle

How did things happen in the early history of the universe? For many years, chaos theory dominated scientific thinking. This theory stressed the apparent randomness found in the universe. Darwin's theory of evolution, for example, was founded on the notion of random selection. Christians, on the other hand, have argued that the universe shows evidence of a great design so intricate that it could not have been the product of chance.[26] Indeed, it displays nothing less than the glory of its Creator.[27]

A recent development in the scientific community has added further weight to the design argument. A variation is called the anthropic principle. This term was coined from the Greek (*anthropikos*, "human being") by Brandon Carter, a respected astrophysicist from Cambridge University. The anthropic principle evaluates the universe from the perspective of human life, exploring the relationship between highly technical mathematical constants. These constants would have been present when the universe was formed billions of years ago. When the various and seemingly arbitrary constants of physics are examined, they are found to have one thing in common: They result

[26]For a simple explanation of this complex issue, see "A Not-So-Random Universe," in Patrick Glynn, *God: the Evidence: The Reconciliation of Faith and Reason in a Postsecular World* (Rocklin, Calif.: Forum, 1997), 21–55. For a sample list of "coincidences in values," see 29–31.

[27]Ps. 19:1. See John C. Hutchison, "Design Argument in Scientific Discourse: Historical-Theological Perspective from the Seventeenth Century," *Journal of the Evangelical Theological Society* 41, no. 1 (March 1998): 85–105. For a series of very readable articles on intelligent design, see also *Touchstone: A Journal of Mere Christianity* 12, no. 4 (July/August 1999): 18–94.

in a universe capable of producing life as we know it. These are called coincidences in values. The slightest mathematical deviation at the time of creation would have yielded a universe quite different than the one we see.[28] Without delving into theoretical mathematics, a layperson can still see some of these "coincidences." For example, (1) water violates the general laws of physics and becomes less dense as a solid than as a liquid. Therefore, ice floats, allowing water to freeze from the top down, rather than from the bottom up. (2) The particles that make up an atom are protons and electrons. Protons have positive charges; electrons have negative ones, compelling matter to hold together (opposite charges attract). (3) We have the right kind of sun to support life. Some suns give too much, too little, or the wrong kind of light. (4) The earth has just the right amount of tilt to produce changes in climate without generating devastating extremes.[29] From a consideration of these facts it would seem that the universe's support of human life is no accident—it was designed. More and more scientists are beginning to consider the anthropic principle as an option for explaining the universe.

Heat Is Distributed Unevenly Throughout the Universe

Why is the sun so hot? Why are the outer planets so cold? The law of the conservation of energy states that

---

Prepared to Answer

Even though the Bible tells us to "be prepared to give an answer to everyone who asks you to give the reason for the hope that you have" (1 Pet. 3:15), sometimes I find a student asking, "But why do I have to learn all this? Why can't I just believe the Bible?" There will be times when we will need to know more than a verse of Scripture. It may be that our faith has been shaken and we need some assurance that the Bible really is the Word of God. Or it may happen that we encounter an unbeliever. Sometimes that may be a person from our own family.

Let me tell you a story to illustrate this point. Mary (not her real name) was a student at Vanguard University where I teach. She never

(cont. on the next page)

---

[28]Most of the mathematical alignments that astronomers point to occurred in the first nanoseconds of creation and are too complex to mention here.

[29]A very readable survey of these factors may be found in David H. Levy, "Four Simple Facts behind the Miracle of Life," *Parade Magazine,* 21 June 1998, 12–14. Levy draws heavily on the work of the Nobel Prize winning scientist George Wald for his data.

Prepared to Answer
(cont.)

took a course from me so I don't know her level of understanding on these things. But one day she wrote to me, asking me to respond to a letter from her grandfather. "I'd like to see Grandpa in heaven," she wrote. It was obvious from reading her grandfather's letter that he was an intelligent, educated man. Apparently he had heard only the "literalist view" (see the section "A Young Earth") and could not accept it. His doubts were real ones and were well set forth. He could not reconcile the Bible with his knowledge of the scientific and historical record and so could not believe it.

I responded to Mary by enclosing a draft of this chapter, suggesting that the footnotes would lead her to more bibliography. But I kept wondering *why* she hadn't taken advantage of courses that would have enabled her to answer her grandfather's objections on her own.

energy cannot be created or destroyed. It can be only transformed into another form. For example, light radiated from the sun is not lost. Instead, it is captured as heat by anything it strikes (for example, the earth). Were the universe eternal, the hot spots would have cooled and the cold spots would have warmed. Heat would have evenly distributed itself throughout the universe long ago. But it has not. The universe still has some very hot spots and some very cold ones.[30] This points to a beginning when the hot spots were even hotter and the cold spots were even colder. The universe is finite! It had a beginning!

Radioactive Elements Decay Into Other Elements

If the earth is old, why are there still elements that are radioactive? Radioactive decay is the emission of atomic particles from the atom. By this process the atom is transformed into an isotope with a different atomic weight or number or both. In an unstable element, for example, uranium or radium, this goes on at a constant rate and may be calculated. These elements will continue to decay until they reach relative stability in an isotope of lead.[31] Were the universe eternal, all unstable elements would long ago have reached stability. For example, all uranium would have become lead. But it has not. This points to a time when

[30]For example, the interior of the sun, only a moderately hot star, is about 15,000,000° K (27,000,000° F). On the other hand, the temperature of Neptune is somewhere between a calculated -228° C (-378° F) and -218° C (-360° F) according to infrared measurements made by Voyager 2. Absolute zero, the theoretical point at which all molecular activity ceases, is determined at -273.15° C or -459.67° F.

[31]Lead deteriorates so slowly that it can be considered stable for our purposes.

there were even more "hot" elements and less lead than there is today. It points to a beginning.

None of these phenomena explicitly argues for creation. Yet each points to a beginning. Each argues against the idea that what we see now has always been.[32] And when we see a beginning, we must ask, "What power moved nonexistence to existence?" The Bible has an answer for this. That power was God!

How Did It Happen?

For perhaps as long as the Church has existed, scholars have diligently tried to harmonize the Bible's statements about the world with their knowledge of the world from other sources. Efforts to reconcile creation with history and science generally fall into two major classes: those who hold to an "old" earth and those who hold to a "young" one. Exchanges between scholars who have these opposite views are too often charged with harsh words and name calling.[33] As Christians, we must remember that our faith resides in a biblical doctrine of creation, not in a theory of *how* or *when* it happened. Such a doctrine is called "creationism"; those who hold it—and all evangelical Christians hold it in some form—are called "creationists." We consider creation a fact because the Bible declares it. Scientific and historical data are also facts. Believing scholars sometimes

[32]Hugh Ross, for example, estimates that the universe is "at least ten billion orders of magnitude too small or too young for life to have assembled itself by natural processes" (*Fingerprint of God,* 138).

[33]Henry M. Morris, for example, speaks of Calvin College as "notorious for its compromising position on evolution and related issues." He uses similar terms to describe Wheaton College. He thinks Davis Young is "following the same path traveled by Charles Darwin." *The Long War Against God: The History and Impact of the Creation/Evolution Conflict* (Grand Rapids: Baker Book House, 1989), 102–3, 108.

Facts and Interpretation

Let's always remember: Genuine biblical truth unites the Church and builds it up. Personal hobbyhorses divide it and tear it apart.

Let me illustrate: A teacher in a local church once asked me for help with a woman who was about to leave his church. She could not, he told me, agree with his teaching on creation. So I invited him out to lunch.

"What are you teaching on creation?" I asked, curious as to how such a basic teaching could be divisive.

It turned out that he was teaching a particular

disagree about how the facts are to be weighed and interpreted, but they generally agree about the facts themselves. The following list gives some of the more commonly held interpretations of creation.[34]

An Old Earth

Age-Day Theory (Concordism). Are the days of creation in Genesis normal twenty-four-hour days? Sometimes the Hebrew word for "day" *(yom)* represents a more or less undetermined period of time, just as it does in English. That is evident from expressions like "in the day of trouble" (Ps. 27:5) or "in the day of my distress" (Gen. 35:3).[35] The age-day theory (concordism) reckons the days of Genesis not as twenty-four-hour periods but as geological ages. It argues for a "long" Genesis day, equaling millions of years. Proponents point out that there is no end (no "evening and morning") for the seventh day as there is for each of the other six (see Gen. 1:5,8,13,19,23,31)—which, they say, argues that we are still *in* it. Thus *yom* in this context must refer to an age, not to a twenty-four-hour day. This interpretation

[34]See Stephen R. Schrader and Davis A. Young, "Was the Earth Created a Few Thousand Years Ago?" in *The Genesis Debate: Persistent Questions About Creation and the Flood,* ed. Ronald Youngblood (Grand Rapids: Baker Book House, 1990), 56–85; see Davis Young, "Genesis: Neither More nor Less," *Eternity* 33, no. 5 (May 1982): 14–21. Bernard Ramm, *The Christian View of Science and Scripture* (Grand Rapids: Wm. B. Eerdmans, 1954), 119–56, presents a good, but not unbiased, summary of the various interpretations of the creation event. Whether one agrees with Ramm's interpretation of creation or not, his book is a treasure chest of proposed solutions to knotty problems. Citations here are from the paperback edition.

[35]For this expression and similar ones, see 2 Sam. 22:19; Ps. 18:18; 27:5; 50:15; 86:7; 140:7; Prov. 11:4; Isa. 9:4; 13:13; 17:11; 30:25; 49:8; Jer. 17:17; 18:17; 51:2; Lam. 1:12; 2:1,21,22; Ezek. 7:19; 16:56; 22:24; Obad. 12,13,14; Zech. 14:3; 2 Cor. 1:14; 2 Cor. 6:2; James 5:5.

would allow time for the fossil record.[36] However, the greatest weakness in this view is that the most common usage for *yom* means a day of twelve or twenty-four hours. Analysis: This view provides enough time for the historical record but pushes the meaning of the word "day" in the creation narrative.[37]

Progressive Creationism. A variety of concordism, this view stresses the progressive nature of the creative process over a period of time.[38] Some would argue that the "days" may be of various lengths and even parallel to some other days. Analysis: same as for concordism.

Religious-Only Theory. The biblical account speaks of creation as theology: that it happened, that God did it. It's up to science to articulate *how* it happened. Analysis: This view resolves the time problem and gives the biblical text its proper theological place. The Scripture text, however, gives no hint that it is not to be considered as historical.

Pictorial-Day Theory. This perspective urges that creation was revealed in six days, rather than actually performed in that length of time. That is, creation may have taken millions of years but was revealed to the author of Genesis in six days. Analysis: similar to that of the religious-only theory.

interpretation of *how* God created the universe as though it were *fact*, rather than an *interpretation*. He did not distinguish the clear teaching of Scripture (i.e., *what* happened) from his own understanding of *how* it might have happened.

I tried to explain to him that the error was his, not the woman's. By insisting on a particular interpretation of how God created the universe, he had brought division into the church. The sad thing was that the controversy overshadowed the great doctrine of creation that the Bible clearly *did* teach.

[36]The most recent exponent of an old earth is Davis Young. See his *Christianity and the Age of the Earth* (Grand Rapids: Zondervan Publishing House, 1982); cf. Dan Wonderly, *God's Time-Records in Ancient Sediments: Evidence of Long Time Spans in Earth's History* (Flint, Mich.: Crystal Press, 1977).

[37]See Terence E. Fretheim and R. Clyde McCone, "Were the Days of Creation Twenty-Four Hours Long?" in *Genesis Debate,* ed. Youngblood, 12–35; Andrew E. Steinman, "'*Echad* as an Ordinal Number and the Meaning of Genesis 1:5," *Journal of the Evangelical Theological Society* 45, no. 4 (December 2002): 577–84.

[38]The most vigorous proponent for this view is Ramm, *Christian View.* It differs sharply with theistic evolution in that it sees any new development as a fresh creative act of God rather than as a naturalistic development.

Theistic Evolution. Rather than the selection of the species being random (Darwin), it was guided by God in an eternal plan. Analysis: This view allows the necessary time, but the use of the word "create" *(bara')* in Genesis 1:1,21,27 poses serious problems for this interpretation.[39]

A Young Earth

Flood Geology. Doesn't the Bible naturally give the impression of a recent creation? That's what flood geology argues.[40] The earth's age may be measured in thousands of years, but not billions. The present geological strata and fossils were caused by a worldwide flood in the time of Noah, not by great age. Scientific data have been misinterpreted. Analysis: This view fits well with the biblical data; but if the Flood was not global, this view is impossible. Even many who advocate a global flood do not understand the data in this way and argue for an old earth.[41]

The Literalist View. The world was created from 3000–5000 B.C. in six literal days. Analysis: This interpreta-

[39]The Heb. verb *bara'* means something slightly different from its English equivalent, "create." The Heb. word stresses a divine, rather than human, action that is entirely unprecedented. For example, the term "something totally new" (Num. 16:30) translates a noun from this same verbal root. Thus, if the creation of the cosmos in Gen. 1:1, and that of animal life in 1:21, represented something without precedent, then so did human creation in 1:27. There is no hint of development from a subhuman in the text. For further discussion, see Mark Hillmer and John N. Moore, "Was Evolution Involved in the Process of Creation?" in *Genesis Debate,* ed. Youngblood, 86–109.

[40]See Steven A. Austin and Donald C. Boardman, "Did Noah's Flood Cover the Entire World?" in *Genesis Debate,* ed. Youngblood, 210–29; see also J. C. Whitcomb and H. M. Morris, *The Genesis Flood* (Philadelphia: Presbyterian & Reformed Publishing Co., 1961); D. W. Patten, *The Biblical Flood and the Ice Epoch* (Seattle: Meridian, 1966); and A. M. Rehwinkel, *The Flood* (St. Louis: Concordia, 1951).

[41]Cf. Davis Young's *Creation and the Flood: An Alternative to Flood Geology and Theistic Evolution* (Grand Rapids: Baker Book House, 1977).

tion is virtually impossible to hold considering what we know from history. Many civilizations are much older than this.[42]

The Pro-Chronic View. Creation came into existence with age built into it: Adam had a navel, trees had rings, rocks had fossils. Analysis: The concept is logical if built-in age is assumed, but defies all modern rules for gathering evidence (induction). The view makes sense only if its basic hypothesis is assumed: built-in age. Moreover, it presupposes a "deception" built into creation—things are not what they appear. Pushed to its logical conclusion, this philosophy could lead to nihilism. Yet the Bible proclaims that creation declares "the glory of God" (Ps. 19:1) and makes known God's invisible qualities (Rom. 1:20). God is true (John 3:33). To deceive is not in him. Because of the lack of evidence for this view, it has generally been abandoned.

A Little of Both

The Gap Theory. What if there was a lapse of time between the creation of the universe and the creation of the world? Gap theorists argue that between Genesis 1:1 and 1:2 there was a great catastrophe. Prehistoric life perished and the earth became empty and lifeless. They argue that Genesis 1:2 should be translated, "The earth *became* an empty waste." Analysis: The strengths of the gap theory are that it allows plenty of time for the scientific record. It

[42]For example, the year of the Jewish calendar that corresponds to November 2001, is 5762, with the years computed after the creation event. That would mean that creation occurred in 3761 B.C. But forms of writing began in Ancient Egypt and Mesopotamia, for example, just before 3000 B.C., and archaeological remains of organized settlements date from much earlier than that. The earliest remains at Jericho, for example, date from the tenth to eighth centuries B.C.

could also account for prehistoric life forms. But the Hebrew verb *hayah* ("was") in Genesis 1:2 stands in the completed, perfect tense; it describes no movement or development. The translation "became" is thus very unlikely. This view is attractive but as with the case of the age-day theory and *yom*, it imposes too much on the biblical text.

Why should we learn these different viewpoints about creation? Isn't there just one right way to interpret Genesis? It is important to know these views because they are held among Christian scholars who believe the Bible. It is equally important to realize that each view has at least one strength and one weakness.[43] None is necessarily revealed truth. Nor do the great theological truths mentioned earlier depend on any single view. Charity toward those who differ is very much in order on this matter. The adversaries of Bible-believing Christians are not Christian scholars who differ on the interpretation of the biblical data; our adversaries are those who dismiss the data as legendary and irrelevant.

How Should We Interpret Creation? — Gen. 1:3 Through 2:4a

To interpret the biblical text accurately, we must be prepared to recognize its author's perspective. In the opening chapters of Genesis there are three authorial perspectives. In 1:1–2 the first perspective is cosmic. These verses describe creation as if the observer were watching from somewhere in space. In 1:3 the second perspective is a shift to the earth. God's creative acts are described as an observer on earth

---

[43]Conveniently summarized in John H. Walton, *Chronological and Background Charts of the Old Testament*, rev. ed. (Grand Rapids: Zondervan Publishing House, 1994), 97.

would see them. Finally, in 2:4b the third perspective, a human one, is introduced. Events are described in terms of their importance to, and perception by, human beings. This perspective remains through most (if not all) of the rest of the Pentateuch. These shifts must be taken into account when interpreting the material.

While the Bible is not trying to teach science, the creation narrative is relatively easy to reconcile to modern-day science.[44] In Genesis 1:3 through 2:4a each aspect of creation is taken up in a manner that is remarkably sophisticated when compared with the creation myths of the ancient world. The Bible differs radically from its Babylonian and Egyptian counterparts, the *Enuma Elish*[45] and the Memphite Theology of Creation,[46] in its absence of mythology (as that term is commonly understood).[47] The biblical order of events, though not the same as science would suggest, is remarkably compatible, especially for such an ancient document. In addition, it agrees with science where we would not expect it to. For example, it is natural to associate the presence of light in the world with the sun. The idea that light could reach earth before the sun was visible (cf. 1:3,14–16) is a highly sophisticated concept,

[44]One exploratory volume on science and Scripture is Vern Sheridan Poythress, *Science and Hermeneutics: Implications of Scientific Method for Biblical Interpretation* (Grand Rapids: Academie Books, 1988).

[45]See James Pritchard, *Ancient Near Eastern Texts,* 3d ed. (Princeton: Princeton University Press, 1969), 60–72. Hereafter cited as *ANET.*

[46]*ANET,* 4–6; see also "The Creation by Atum," 3–4; and "The Repulsing of the Dragon and the Creation," 6–7.

[47]Recognized even by Hermann Gunkel, *The Legends of Genesis,* 2d ed. (New York: Schocken, 1966), 11. Some scholars, however, redefine "myth" to describe any encounter with the supernatural. By using "myth" these scholars do not mean legendary or untrue. They simply want to show that such an experience cannot be measured by physical means.

suggesting that there could be light that does not come from a visible sun. That life began in the seas (1:20–23) does not appear to be something ancient shepherds would dream up on their own. Things like these show the hand of God in revealing Scripture, reinforcing Peter's statement that "prophecy never had its origin in the will of man, but men spoke from God as they were carried along by the Holy Spirit" (2 Pet. 1:21).

But we must be very careful here. To say the Bible generally agrees with science is not to say that it teaches science; the Bible is a prescientific text and to read modern science into it does it violence. The people of that time understood the world in much simpler terms than we do today; their language was often *phenomenal* (related to observation).[48] The Bible is not a scientific textbook, nor is its language the technical language of modern science.[49] It is foremost a theological document, written to declare theology. At the same time, truth is truth. And we may expect that where the Bible does treat scientific or historical data, that treatment will be in a restrained manner that allows us to understand those

---

[48]Bernard Ramm says, "The language of the Bible with reference to natural matters is popular, not scientific" (*Christian View,* 46). For phenomenology of the text, see also A. Berkeley Mickelsen, *Interpreting the Bible* (Grand Rapids: Wm. B. Eerdmans, 1963), 93–95. The elegant simplicity of the biblical narrative and its lack of any real mythology portray a world as it is seen. Observed phenomena are not myth, whether they be observed by a layman or a scientist. One can see the guidance of God's Spirit in this. There was often more in the words of the text than the writer was aware of.

[49]For example, see Bernard Ramm, "The Problem of Inerrancy and Secular Science in Relation to Hermeneutics," in *Protestant Biblical Interpretation,* rev. ed. (Boston: W. A. Wilde, 1956), 182–95. He says, concerning biblical language: "No objection can be brought against inerrancy because the language of the Bible is phenomenal. A language which is phenomenal is restricted to terms of description and observation. Its language about astronomy, botany, zoology, and geology is restricted to the vocabulary of popular observation."

data in our modern terms. There have been many efforts to reconcile the scientific and biblical data. One way of understanding the creation narrative in terms of the scientific record is given in the following chart:[50]

Reference	Day	Event	Possible Meaning in Our Terms
Gen. 1:1–2	0	Creation of heaven and earth	Formation of matter as glowing hot plasma, and the universe, the earth, and other planets from it.
Gen. 1:3–5	1	Light, day, and night	Dust, vapor, and mist envelop the earth in thick gaseous clouds. The earth is still too hot for water to condense to yield rain.
Gen. 1:6–8	2	Firmament (sky)	The gases separate from solids and liquids into an atmosphere. Water vapor condenses into clouds enveloping the earth, then later precipitates into rain to form oceans.
Gen. 1:9–13	3	Earth emerges from the sea. Plant life appears on earth.	Cooling of the earth's crust, inducing buckling, forming mountains, then continents. First primitive forms such as algae, then more developed varieties.
Gen. 1:14–19	4	Lights appear in the sky.	Volcanic activity decreases, precipitation gradually cleanses dust and ash from the atmosphere; the cloud envelope thins, permitting the sun and moon to become visible.
Gen. 1:20–23	5	The sea brings forth creeping things, flying things, sea monsters, animal life of various sorts.	The sea is the womb of animal life. It yields invertebrate life (e. g. trilobites); first flying reptiles, then birds; aquatic reptiles and amphibians; reptilian life (sea, land, and air). The creation of animal life in 1:21 marks a sharp distinction from what had existed before. The word rendered "great creatures" (Heb. *taninim*) is one of three biblical words for "monster." Here it may well represent some forms of life that are now extinct.

[50]For a similar reconstruction, see Gleason L. Archer, *A Survey of Old Testament Introduction*, rev. ed. (Chicago: Moody Press, 1994), 199–203.

Reference	Day	Event	Possible Meaning in Our Terms
Gen. 1:24–31	6	Earth brings forth life: nondomesticable animals domesticable animals (sheep, etc.) creeping things (mice, etc.) Humans created in God's image	Warm blooded animals, both large and small, domesticable and wild, appear. Human beings appear last of all.
Gen. 2:1–4a	7	The sabbath: God rests from creative activity; hallows the seventh day.	The basic life forms are already finished. No new ones are created, but those already formed are left to develop into the varieties we know today.

Does this evidence lead us to an old earth or a young one? How can we sort through all this? Scripture gives us a hint: The creation narrative offers no "evening and morning" to close the seventh day, suggesting (the age-day theory emphasizing) that the seventh day has not yet ended. Moreover, God, who does not lie or speak with two voices, declares in His Word that creation bears witness to its Creator (Ps. 19:1–5)[51] (a testimony so powerful that Paul could indict the world for having rejected it [Rom. 1:18–20],[52] and a testimony so obvious that the church identifies it as "general" revelation). Having observed the remarkable coincidence of the record in Genesis and the information from general revelation—in light of the theological evidence gathered from the special revelation of the Bible and the general revelation of creation—an old earth seems to offer the fewest number of unresolved difficulties.

[51]See also Ps. 8:1–4; 104:1–32.

[52]See chap. 1.

Human Beings: What Are They?

In 1:26–27, God resolves[53] to create human beings. The use of the word "create" (Heb. *bara'*) indicates an entirely new entity, a life form distinct from that of lower animal life which had appeared earlier. Not only are human beings created, but they are created in the image of their Creator (1:27). Various theories are held as to what the term "image of God" means. In this context at least, it seems to represent a composite of the qualities that distinguish humankind from animal life. It becomes, therefore, the definer of theological humanness.[54] Anthropological life forms that may have existed before Adam cannot be said to have been theologically human, regardless of what they may have looked like or how anthropologists have identified them. Later in the Scriptures this "image" will become the definer of what is ethical (Gen. 9:6; James 3:9; cf. Gen. 5:1): Human beings must treat one another with respect because in some way they bear the likeness of God. In the

[53]The words "let us" suggest the possibility of plurality (though not yet revealed as a trinity) within the being of God. The words are not satisfactorily explained by the interpretation that God was talking to angels or other heavenly beings, as in Job 1:6; 2:1. Job makes it clear that the heavenly beings are never the "us" of the Godhead. Instead, just as Adam is both "him" and "them" (Gen. 1:27), so there is also unity and plurality implied here for the being of God. It is worth noting the harmony in the Godhead implied in such language.

[54]For example, J. Barton Payne says, "The divine image thus implies all the various aspects of God's reflected glory and honor. . . . It may be defined, in summary, as the totality of man's higher powers that distinguish him from brute creation" (*The Theology of the Older Testament* [Grand Rapids: Zondervan Publishing House, 1962], 227). A. Bloom calls the image of God "a quality which makes a man a man" ("Human Rights in Israel's Thought: A Study of Old Testament Doctrine," *Interpretation* 8 [1954], 422–32). See also Georg Fohrer, *Studien zur alttestamentlichen Theologie und Geschichte* (1949–1966) (Berlin: Walter de Gruyter, 1969), 177–78; Berkouwer, *Man, the Image of God,* 70.

New Testament, Paul will speak of Christ as the "image of God" (2 Cor. 4:4; see Col. 1:15; cf. 1 Cor. 11:7); by our "clothing ourselves with the Lord Jesus Christ" (see Rom. 13:14), we become more like him. We also become more like the human beings we were created to be.[55]

The image of God is not the sole property of the male sex, as some have supposed. Instead, human beings corporately bear the image of God, as clearly shown by the parallelism in Genesis 1:27:

So God created man in his own image.

| In the image of God | he created | him. |
| Male and female | he created | them. |

Parallelism in Hebrew poetry points to similarities in meaning between two or more lines of poetic material. In 1:27, a line of prose (line 1) introduces the poem (lines 2 and 3). Clearly the words "he created" are the same in lines 2 and 3. It is also clear that the word "them" (line 3) defines the word "him" (line 2). The same may be said for the terms "image of God" and "male and female": the latter defines the former and makes it meaningful. That is, humanness is vested in the human species as it exists as both male and female.[56] It is not the property of the male alone, with the female as something of a divine afterthought.[57]

[55]See G. W. Bromiley, "Image of God" in *ISBE*, 2:803–5.

[56]Some scholars go so far as to suggest that since Adam's name means "human being," Gen. 1:27 means that God created any number of people. If this interpretation can be sustained it eases the problem later posed by Cain's wife, his fear of reprisal, and the city he builds (Gen. 4:14,17; see n. 59 for another possible explanation of Cain's experiences). For our purposes, Adam will be spoken of in the singular, as in the biblical narrative. Yet it should be kept in mind that the corporate interpretation seems attractive and possible.

[57]See Richard M. Davidson, "The Theology of Sexuality in the Beginning: Genesis 1–2," *Andrews University Seminary Studies* 26, no. 1 (spring 1988):

The dominion that God had given the two humans over creation was granted to the male and the female jointly.[58] As such they were to serve as God's regents, ruling his creation and maintaining it for him (Gen. 1:28–30; cf. 2:8–9,15–17).[59] Their diet was to be vegetarian (1:29–30). Killing animal life to sustain human life began only after the Fall (9:3). Biblical glimpses of the restored creation suggest that all animal life may return to a vegetable diet (cf. Isa. 11:6–9; 65:25).[60]

At the conclusion of Genesis 1, God proclaimed that everything he had created was "very good" (1:31). So God finished his six days of creative activity and "rested" on the seventh (2:2–3). The Hebrew word for "rested" does not mean that God was tired and went to sleep (as, perhaps, Baal did; 1 Kings 18:27), but as a lawyer in a modern court of law "rests" his case (ceases from further argumentation), so God ceased from further creative activity.

5–24. See also Patricia Gundry, "Why We're Here," in *Women, Authority and the Bible,* ed. Alvera Mickelsen (Downers Grove, Ill.: InterVarsity Press, 1986), 10–21. Gundry's point is, Are women human or not? If they are, she argues, they are entitled to the full rights of that humanness.

[58]The imperatives are plural in the Heb. text.

[59]It is interesting to note that when Adam appears he is already an agriculturist. The discovery of agriculture is a recent development, dating from about 10,000 B.C. It is important to note that the Bible is interested only in defining what is *theologically* human. It makes no direct mention of pre-Adamic creatures that were only *biologically* human. Yet they may be implied by Cain's fear that someone would kill him (Gen. 4:14), the famous problem of who his wife might have been (4:17), and who was to live in the city he built (4:17). For further discussion on the possibility of an ancient earth and a recent Adam, see Ronald Youngblood, *The Book of Genesis,* 2d ed. (Grand Rapids: Baker Book House, 1991), 41–49.

[60]Whether or not these passages are to be taken literally, they point to a time of peace and harmony that will be restored where none presently exists.

The Farmer Takes a Wife: Life in Eden and the Creation of Woman – Gen. 2:4b–25

We have seen a number of perspectives in the creation narrative: cosmic (Gen. 1:1–2) and that of an observer on earth (1:3 through 2:4a). From 2:4b to the end of the chapter (2:25), the third perspective occurs: The focus moves to humankind and will remain there for the rest of the Book of Genesis. What is commonly called the second account of the creation of man and woman, therefore, is told from a human perspective. In language that is dynamic for its very simplicity, we are told that God took dust and formed it into a man, just as one might sculpt a sand castle on the beach. Then he breathed into the man's nostrils the breath of life and the man became a "living being" (2:7).[61]

The earth, which had previously been covered with water (1:2), now remained without rain for an unspecified time. This seems to present a picture of the Near East at the end of the last glacial epoch. The earth was drying–and still is–yet numerous rivers water the land. The Mesopotamian setting is confirmed later in 2:11–14, where the Tigris and Euphrates rivers are mentioned by name.

Why Was Woman Created?

The only exception recorded to the pronouncement in Genesis 1:31 that everything was "very good" is found in 2:18, where God says, "'It is not good for the man to be alone. I will make a helper suitable for him.'" It was God's

---

[61]The Heb. term *nephesh* literally means a "thing that breathes." The words here translated "living being" are the same as those rendered "living creatures" in Gen. 1:20,24. As such, humans hold the act of breathing in common with other mammalian life. They are distinct, however, in that they are created in God's image.

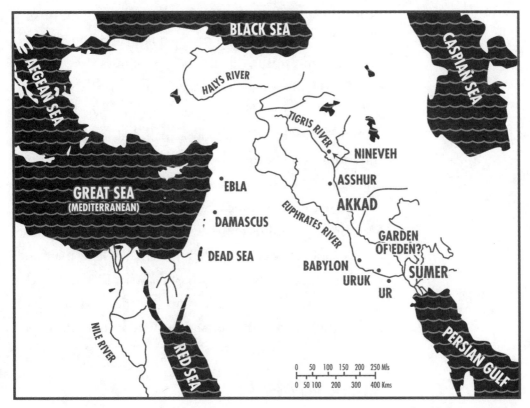

Possible Location of Eden

intention to create the human species male and female in the image of God (1:27). But without the female, the species was not complete: The man was alone. A part of humanity was lacking.

After being put in the garden, the man performed his first recorded act of dominion over creation: He named the creatures of the garden (Gen. 2:19). Yet in all his labors he could not find someone who would fill the emptiness he felt. When all the animals had been examined, it became apparent that no satisfactory relationship could be achieved with any of them (2:20). At that point God caused the man to fall into a deep sleep (2:21). Taking a rib from his side, God fashioned it into a woman and brought her to the man. There is a sense of great excitement in the man's words: "'At last! . . . part of my own flesh and bone!'" (2:23, NLT). For this reason, the narrative continues, "she shall be called 'woman,' for she was taken out of man" (NIV).[62]

The earliest recorded formulation of marriage follows in Genesis 2:24: "For this reason a man will leave his father and mother and be united to his wife, and they will become one flesh." The two that had been created by God from one flesh now would become one flesh again through marriage. Marriage would thus embody the two elements that make up the human species (male and female). The man and woman would discover in each other what they were lacking in themselves. The innocence of the relationship is recorded in 2:25: "The man and his wife were both naked, and they felt no shame."

What Do You Mean—"Helper"!

Some people think women are inferior to men in God's sight. They often appeal to the specific account of the creation of woman (2:18,20–22) because they believe it proves woman to be a secondary creation, a "helper" (NIV) for the man. This interpretation is not correct. The woman was made of the same essence and substance as the man. She could not be considered essentially inferior to him.[63]

The Hebrew text describes the woman's relationship to the man in two words: (1) she is a "help" (not a "helper," as

[62]In this case the Eng., i.e., "woman," "man," adequately reproduces the pun in the Heb. text: *ishshâ, îsh.*

[63]See William C. Williams, "Sexuality, Human," in the *Evangelical Dictionary of Biblical Theology,* ed. Walter Elwell (Grand Rapids: Baker Book House, 1996), 727–34; cf. id., "Formulating Biblical Models for a Moral Theology of Sexuality" (paper presented to the Evangelical Theological Society, Chicago, 17 November 1994).

in NIV); and (2) she is "suitable for him" (2:18).[64] The Bible's use of the word "help" ('ezer) to describe God—"he is our help and our shield" (Ps. 33:20)—demonstrates that the word has no sense of inferiority in it.[65] Instead, the term describes God as one who is strong enough to share his strength with another. The expression translated "suitable for him" (kᵉnegdo) is compounded of three elements: a preposition meaning "like" (kᵉ); a second preposition meaning "over against," "opposite" (neged); and a suffix meaning "him" (o).

It was not good for man to be alone (2:18; cf. 1:31). Some people assume that 2:18 refers to the man's loneliness. Certainly that would be part of being alone, for the man looks to every animal to see if there is a "help" for him. But there is more to being alone than feeling lonely. The word points to the creation of man as male and female (1:27). The "help" for the man would therefore designate "what was lacking, necessary for completion" that "helped" Adam become a theologically human being. Thus the woman became man's complement, not merely his supplement.[66] Together they made up what may be called theological humanity, in which both humans jointly participated.

The man and the woman seemed to exist as equals. Yet

[64]Heb. 'ezer kᵉnegdo. It is interesting that the phrase in the KJV is "a help meet for him"; this phrase evolved in popular usage to "helpmeet," then "helpmate," meaning "one serving as a companion, partner, or assistant." But the Heb. does not mean "helper." Instead it means a "help suitable (meet) to him" (cf. NRSV, "helper as his partner"). Although "helpmeet" is often used, it does not support a view that the woman was inferior.

[65]See also Deut. 33:7,29; Pss. 46:1; 54:4; 70:5; 115:9,10,11; 146:5; cf. 1 Sam. 7:12; Pss. 121:2; 124:8.

[66]See Derek Kidner, *Genesis: An Introduction and Commentary* (Downers Grove, Ill.: InterVarsity Press, 1967), 65.

equality demands neither identity nor sameness of function.[67] Sameness would be redundant. The relationship would not be complementary. The physical differences between the sexes show that God designed their roles in society to be different. A man, for example, cannot bear children. Thus, such differences are not a product of the Fall to be redeemed; they are part of the created order to be nurtured.

The biblical text makes it clear that one human being should not dominate another. Such relationships do not come from the theology of the created order but from the Fall. This is true whether a man dominates a woman or one race of people dominates another race of people. The gospel seeks to abolish biases, such as racism or sexism, that demean and dehumanize (Rom. 10:12; Gal. 3:28). By the work of God's Spirit, negating the effects of the Fall seeks to elevate people to their full humanity. The functional differences, therefore, that distinguish man from woman are in no way to be construed as superior or inferior but as complementary. Each one "helps" the other by furnishing what is lacking.

[67]Brevard Childs, *Old Testament Theology in a Canonical Context* (Philadelphia: Fortress Press, 1985), 188–92.

Study Questions

1. Why is Genesis in the canon?

2. What is the structure of the book?

3. What do the first two chapters of Genesis tell us about God? about creation? about being human? the unity of the human species? the created order? marriage?

4. Give the five major arguments for a creation, aside from the Bible, and explain each of them.

5. What is the "old earth" interpretation of creation? the "young earth"? the "gap" theory?

6. What are the varieties of "old earth" interpretation? "young earth"? What are their strengths and weaknesses?

7. How can the Bible and modern science work together in interpreting creation?

8. What is meant by the "image of God," and to whom does it belong?

9. How does the man relate to the woman? What is meant by a "helper suitable for him"?

10. How is marriage described? In what terms?

For Further Reading

See books, commentaries, and articles cited in the footnotes. You may also wish to explore commentaries such as those by C. F. Keil and John T. Willis. Victor Hamilton's commentary (NICOT) is the most helpful for English readers. Gordon Wenham's (WBC) is the most useful critical commentary for evangelicals. A good conservative introduction to critical matters may be found in Herbert Wolf, *An Introduction to the Old Testament Pentateuch* (Chicago: Moody Press, 1991).

Ross, Allen P. *Creation and Blessing: A Guide to the Study and Exposition of the Book of Genesis.* Grand Rapids: Baker Book House, 1988.

Walton, John H., Victor H. Matthews, and Mark W. Chavalas. *The IVP Bible Background Commentary: Old Testament.* Downers Grove, Ill.: InterVarsity Press, 2000.

3

William C. Williams

Paradise Lost:
The Origin and Spread of Human Evil

Outline:

- What Is the Fall?
- What Are the Consequences of the Fall?
- After the Fall: What Do These Stories Teach Us?
- How Should the Stories About Adam's Descendants Be Interpreted?
- What Happened in the Flood?
- How Was the Ark Constructed?
- The Noahic Covenant
- The "Curse on Ham" (Canaan): What Does It Mean?
- Who Were the Descendants of Noah?
- The Tower of Babel
- A Message of Hope: The Lineage of Shem

Terms:

Gilgamesh
redemption
suzerain
suzerain-vassal treaty
vassal

The Bible says that God created everything good (Gen. 1:31). He even created human beings in his own image (1:27). So why, then, do people sometimes act in such cruel ways? Why is there crime? Why are there wars? Why do people suffer from poverty and lack of food? Why do some people inflict pain on others?

The Bible provides an answer. It tells us that the original human beings sinned. They fell from fellowship with God and became strangers to him. They fell out with each other, as well, becoming strangers even to themselves. The stories of Cain's murder of Abel, the Flood, and the Tower of Babel teach us about the spread of human evil. These stories tell us that as people scattered throughout the world, so did their sin and evil. Why? Because they took it with them.

Male-female relationships before the Fall are described in Genesis 2:25: Although they were naked, the two humans felt no shame. That is, they could look at each other as God's creations without embarrassment. But sin entered the world through the episode in the Garden of Eden. The result was Adam and Eve's banishment (Gen. 3:24). Moreover, with sin came shame. It built a barrier to their naive innocence. The man and the woman found it necessary to cover their nakedness with clothing (Gen. 3:7,10–11), even though they were husband and wife. They had become ashamed of who they were.

What Is the Fall?

What Do We Mean When We Speak of the Fall?

The Christian doctrine of the Fall refers to an act of disobedience to God committed by the earliest human beings. It brought alienation, separation from God (Eph. 4:18), and death to all future generations (1 Cor. 15:22).

The foundational text for any doctrine of the Fall is Genesis 3. But how do we interpret it? A number of interpretations have been proposed. While we want to recognize that there are viewpoints other than our own, each of them must take the Bible seriously. What's more, we want to be certain to focus on the thrust of the chapter and not get lost in the details. James Orr can help us here: "I do not enter into the question of how we are to interpret the third chapter of Genesis—whether as history or allegory or myth, or most probably of all, as old tradition clothed in oriental allegorical dress—but the truth embodied in that narrative, viz. the fall of man from an original state of purity, I take to be vital to the Christian view."[1]

How do believing Christians understand the story of the Fall? Most evangelicals subscribe to one of the following interpretations:

Literal: A literal interpretation means that a physical fruit and serpent were involved. Eden had a geographic location. Many Christians believe this is the only way the story of the Fall can be interpreted. In the New Testament, Luke and Paul, they say, consider Adam a person (e.g., Luke 3:38; Rom. 5:14; 1 Cor. 15:45; compare Matt. 19:4).

Metaphoric or symbolic: A symbolic interpretation suggests that Genesis 3 teaches a truth by means of a story. Like a parable, the story need not be historical in order for its point to be true. But the truth taught by the narrative must describe something that really did happen. The story of the

---

[1]James Orr, *The Christian View of God and the World* (1897), 185, quoted in Bernard Ramm, *The Christian View of Science and Scripture* (Grand Rapids: Wm. B. Eerdmans, 1954), 223–24.

Fall, therefore, is true in the sense that it teaches truth – humans have fallen from grace – yet it need not be pressed in its details. Those who subscribe to this viewpoint point to the symbolic use of names and various other elements that would suggest a metaphoric interpretation.[2]

Evangelicals generally discard other interpretations. One such interpretation, for example, argues that the Fall really represents a psychological distance from God. The barrier of despair must be overcome by a "leap of faith." Another such view urges that the Fall is really just another myth about the civilizing of humanity. It tells about the change from an innocent rural lifestyle to a sophisticated urban one. While there is value in both of these views, evangelicals believe they are not enough. These views fail to consider mankind's separation from God because of sin. They also do not explain the alienation of human beings from one another and from themselves.

What Evidence Do We Have for the Fall?

We can find evidence for humanity's fall from innocence in both the Bible and human behavior. The Bible describes the Fall as banishment from Eden (Gen. 3:23), and as separation from life (3:22) and from God (Eph. 2:11–12). There is also a human dimension to the Fall: Human beings have become alienated from themselves and from one another. The first homicide was committed because of sibling rivalry (Gen. 4:1–16). Except for a few other creatures, human

[2]For example, Eden means "pleasure"; Adam means "humankind"; Abel means "breath"; Nod means "wandering." Those who espouse this view also point to things like the problem of Cain's wife, his city, and his fear of murder to indicate that a nonliteral meaning was intended by the author.

beings are the only ones that kill for amusement. They wage wars out of national pride. Nations have spent immense sums of money to acquire great stockpiles of weapons for destroying other human beings. These characteristics point to a "brokenness"[3] in human beings that cannot be explained simply in terms of survival needs. And because of that brokenness, creation groans (Rom. 8:22) and the land mourns (Hos. 4:3).

What Is the Nature of the Fall?

Devout Christians throughout the history of the church have believed that humans have fallen spiritually. As a result, all live under a sentence of death (Rom. 5:14). Apart from the grace of God, humankind has no hope. God's revelation of himself and of his plan of redemption in Scripture has provided a means of passing from death to life. As members of the body of Christ, the believers' covenant is with God through the blood of Jesus.[4] As such, salvation becomes a foretaste of the resurrection when everything will be made new and right again (1 Cor. 15:37–50).

Christians also believe that physical death came with the Fall. Pentecostals and many charismatic Christians believe that just as spiritual imperfections will be repaired in the resurrection, so will physical ones (1 Cor. 15:43,48,53). Our redemption in Christ, then, means a reversal of the dying process that started with banishment from Eden. It begins a life-giving process that will end with our resurrection. Because of this, Pentecostals and Charismatics often have

[3]Bruce C. Birch, *Let Justice Roll Down: The Old Testament, Ethics, and Christian Life* (Louisville: Westminster/John Knox, 1991), 92–95.

[4]1 Cor. 10:16; Eph. 2:13; Heb. 9:14; 1 Pet. 1:19.

special services where the sick are prayed for (Isa. 53:4–6; James 5:14–16; 1 Pet. 2:24). Reconciliation to God fulfills our need for spiritual redemption. Physical healing meets the need of our fallen bodies. Physical healing, therefore, is also to be seen as a foretaste of the resurrection, when our bodies will be raised imperishable (1 Cor. 15:42).

How Far Did We Fall?

Throughout the history of the church, many have held to an interpretation of the Fall set forth by Saint Augustine (A.D. 354–430). Augustine's interpretation says that all people are guilty because they descend from Adam. They are "sinners by birth." This belief is called the doctrine of original sin. It is not difficult to find biblical evidence tying spiritual death to our descent from Adam (1 Cor. 15:22). Many, however, have had great difficulty in this interpretation of the Fall because it seems unfair. Like Abraham of old, they believe God is a God of justice (Gen. 18:25). Sin is tied to a knowledge of truth (James 4:17). Newborn infants and mentally deranged people, therefore, may have no concept of sin or the need for repentance. Thus it would seem unjust to condemn one who has had no opportunity to repent.

Pelagianism, on the other hand, stresses the freedom of human will and human responsibility. Humans have not fully participated in Adam's fall and have no inclination to evil. They are capable of obeying God's law if they want to and become guilty only when they break it. From an ethical perspective, this seems fairer. We are judged by our works rather than condemned for an ancestral failure. Yet Pelagianism, too, falls short. It has little support from Scripture, which declares that no one is righteous apart from God's grace (Rom. 3:10).

Because of the deficiency in the two views outlined above, many theologians have sought a mediating view and argue that we have inherited a fallen nature. A *fallen* nature is different from a *sinful* nature. Such a view does not assume that by virtue of simply being born one has sinned, but rather that one is prone to sin. That is, humans sin because of their fallen nature, but God does not hold them guilty until they commit the act. Accordingly, we are not born with imputed sin. Instead, we are heirs to a value system that is marred by the sin of our ancestor, Adam. Such values will eventually lead us to sin and, at that point, to become guilty (Rom. 3:23). Those who espouse this view hope to comply with Scripture's general pronouncement that all are guilty, but to avoid the moral consequences that come with Augustine's interpretation.[5]

What Are the Consequences of the Fall?

We Have Been Separated From God

The wisdom and godlike nature that the woman sought in the fruit of the tree were an illusion, a deception born of a serpent's promise. By sinning, humans exchanged their fellowship with God for lives of lonely exile from his kingdom. They traded their dominion over the earth for bondage filled with sorrow (Gen. 3:22–24). This shows us something very important. The first element in the emptiness of human life involves alienation from God. Without God's help, all are strangers from his kingdom, not citizens

[5]See Bruce R. Marino, "The Origin, Nature, and Consequences of Sin" in *Systematic Theology: A Pentecostal Perspective,* ed. Stanley M. Horton (Springfield, Mo.: Logion Press, 1994), 268–69.

of it (Eph. 2:12). As a result, they stand under a sentence of spiritual death (Rom. 7:13).

We Have Become Strangers to One Another

Why do people fight? Why can't people just get along? There is no record of dissension between the two human beings before the Fall. It would appear that they lived in harmony with one another. With the Fall, however, came the dire prediction that codependency would replace mutuality. Although made in God's image, the humans, nevertheless, became separated from God, and then from one another. Now it was possible for one human to rule over another. It was after the Fall that God said to the woman, "'Your desire will be for your husband, and he will rule over you'" (Gen. 3:16). Likewise, it was after the Fall that Adam named his wife Eve, using the same naming formula (3:20) that he used in naming the animals (2:20). By using that formula he claimed the authority of a superior over an inferior.[6] It was this spirit of alienation from other humans that led to the first murder and its punishment (4:10–14).

We Have Become Strangers to Ourselves

Have you ever wondered why you did something, even though you knew it was wrong? Did you ever ask yourself afterward, "Why did I do that? That was dumb!" Do you ever think you can't understand yourself? These are signs that we are part of a fallen world. The distortion brought about by the Fall caused more than alienation from God and each other. It includes alienation from oneself (Jer. 17:9;

---

[6]The Heb. construction differs from Gen. 2:23 where Adam identifies his fellow human as "woman." The sense seems to be that the term "woman" is not a name, like "lion" or "Eve."

Rom. 7:15–24). Separated from God, in whose image they had been created, human beings could no longer understand or control themselves. They could no longer determine what was right and what was wrong; they could think only of what was good for themselves. Even then, in trying to better themselves, they made distorted choices. Even when they knew what was right, they could not always bring themselves to do it (Rom. 7:19–20).[7]

Community Has Broken Down

Why can't we work together?[8] We have seen that in God's created order, the man and woman were equals. There is no hint of disharmony found in the Edenic material. Each party, male and female, seems to have been different but equal. Sin, however, introduced a distortion; it fostered enmity and alienation where none had previously existed. Soon afterwards there is mention of one human lording it over another (Gen. 3:16). And soon after that a jealousy so intense it leads one brother to murder another (4:8). The harmony that had marked the Edenic existence had broken down and with it any sense of true community.

[7]It is easy to see the effects of the Fall in Cain. Cain's alienation from his brother and the jealousy it spawned prompted him to murder his brother (Gen. 4:8). Erich Fromm calls the alienated individual one who "experiences himself as an alien." By this he means those who no longer determine their own acts; instead their acts (and their consequences) have mastered them and they are helpless to control them ("The Sane Society," in *Alienation: The Cultural Climate of Our Time,* ed. Gerald Sykes [New York: George Braziller, 1964], 1:67). This is clearly the picture in Rom. 7:15–24 (cf. Gen. 4:7).

[8]See Christopher J. H. Wright, *An Eye for an Eye: The Place of Old Testament Ethics Today* (Downers Grove, Ill.: InterVarsity Press, 1983), 103–6; see also William C. Williams, "Family Life and Relations" in the *Evangelical Dictionary of Biblical Theology,* ed. Walter Elwell (Grand Rapids: Baker Book House, 1996), 243–45.

Human Beings Die

Why must we die? As a result of sin, humanity became cut off not only from God's presence but from life itself (Gen. 3:22). As a result, people age and die. Parts of our bodies die every day—the dandruff we brush from our clothes is telling us that we are mortal! The Bible explains that death entered the world because humankind was separated from the tree of life in the Garden. That is, although physical death did not occur immediately after Eve's disobedience, it followed. In the New Testament, Paul points out that the death that came upon humans was spiritual as well as physical (Rom. 3:23; Col. 2:13). Adam and Eve did—and so do we all—"surely die" (Gen. 2:17).

Wherever Humans Go, Their Evil Follows

Why can't we run away from evil? Perhaps if we found a cave, far from other people, we could escape their evil. No, it doesn't work that way! Why? Because we would take our own evil with us, wherever we went.

The spread of sin and evil through the world is clearly a dominant theme in Genesis 4:1 through 11:26.[9] Following the murder of Abel by his own brother, Cain (4:8–15), we meet arrogant Lamech, who boasted to his wives of killing another man (4:23–24). The story of the Flood (Gen. 6:1 through 8:12) points to a spread of evil so monstrous that God decided to blot out human life. But even with a new beginning, the human rebellion reasserted itself. The people

[9]See Gerhard von Rad, *Old Testament Theology* (New York and Evanston: Harper & Row, 1962), 1:154–60; cf. William C. Williams, "Evil" in *Evangelical Dictionary,* ed. Elwell, 221–25.

declared that they would make themselves great by their achievements, apart from God. They would build a great tower so that they would not be scattered over the earth. But the story ends with an ironic twist: God confused their languages and did precisely what their scheming had been designed to prevent–*scattered* them over the earth (11:9). Without the ability to communicate with one another, their essential alienation became apparent and they dispersed over the earth.

After the Fall: What Do These Stories Teach Us? –Gen. 4:1 Through 5:32

Human Beings Are Held Responsible

President Harry Truman had a sign on his desk: The Buck Stops Here. It was his way of saying that he understood that as president, he had the responsibility for everything done in the U.S. government. On the other hand, the story of the Fall is a masterpiece of "buck passing": Adam blamed his wife (and, indirectly, God, who had given her to him); his wife blamed the serpent (Gen. 3:12–13). And Cain, guilty as sin, shrugged his shoulders at God and tossed off a line echoed down the centuries, "'Am I my brother's keeper?'" (4:9). Much of human evil springs from human failure to accept moral responsibility for any actions. Nevertheless, what Cain meant as a rhetorical denial has been answered in the affirmative by Jesus' story of the Good Samaritan. Yes, we *are* our brother's keeper. Like it or not, people are to be responsible for one another. If our neighbor is in need, God has obligated us to do what we can to help.

Quoting and Misquoting Scripture

Paul tells his young friend Timothy, "Do your best to present yourself to God as one approved, a workman who does not need to be ashamed and who correctly handles the word of truth" (2 Tim. 2:15). Quoting the Bible does nothing good if the "quote" is really a misquote. Yet at some time or another, many have done this. I must confess that I did, especially when I was a new convert, full of zeal and little knowledge.

It's clear that Genesis includes the words of Cain, a murderer, to show just the opposite—we *are* our brother's keeper. We *are* responsible for one another.

One particularly bad misquote in my view is "an eye for an eye" to justify vindictiveness. It is clear from Jesus' use of the term in Matthew 5:38 that some Jews of his day saw it that way and needed correction. But the contexts of the phrase in the Old Testament show clearly that the intent is justice, not vengeance (Exod. 21:24; Lev. 24:20; Deut. 19:21). For example, a damaged eye is worth only an eye, not a human life.

Some have used Jesus' words, "'The poor you will always have with you'" (Matt. 26:11; Mark 14:7), to justify their own hard-hearted refusal to help the poor. But the point being made in context was that Jesus would not always be with them. The Bible's view of the poor is clearly articulated: "There will always be poor people in the land. Therefore I command you to be openhanded toward your brothers and toward the poor and needy in your land" (Deut. 15:11).

It is not money but the love of it that is "a root of all kinds of evil" (1 Tim. 6:10). It is our own lust for wealth, and for the power it can buy, that is evil.

When we misquote the Bible, we give the unsaved world tools to use against the gospel. But even worse is what such misquoting does to the one doing it: It justifies unbiblical thoughts or actions (e.g., greed) and absolves from biblical obligations (e.g., helping the poor). Finding what a verse really means before using it should be important, if it is the authoritative Word of God! Some have used Noah's curse on Canaan (Gen. 9:25) to justify the enslavement and abuse of black Africans. And although we are horrified at this abuse of the text, Jesus himself warned his disciples that when people killed them they would think they were offering "a service to God" (John 16:2). Indeed, the unconverted Paul fit this very model (Acts 9:1–2; Gal. 1:13). And unfortunately, history is replete with examples of people mishandling the word of truth.

Human Life Is Sacred

Why is the taking of human life such a major concern? Because God created human beings as bearers of his image (Gen. 1:27). Therefore, one person is not to take the life of another without cause. This doctrine is most clearly stated as a part of the Noahic Covenant (Gen. 9:5–6):

> "Whoever sheds the blood of man,
> by man shall his blood be shed;
> for in the image of God
> has God made man."

The one who needlessly takes human life has committed blasphemy against the One in whose image human life was created. The only fitting punishment for the murderer is the surrender of his or her own life.[10]

God Has Made Provision for the Redemption of Humanity

The whole world is fallen and stands to receive God's judgment (Rom. 3:23). Yet, "where sin increased, grace increased all the more" (5:20). God had created the world and pronounced it "very good" (Gen. 1:31); he saw value in his created work. This value that God saw , therefore, indirectly implies that God would desire its redemption. One could think of it this way: All humanity is God's fallen creation. God's work, however, is redemption, not condemnation (John 3:17). Since all human beings are his, his redemptive work cannot be confined to a single people. Instead, it must be extended to the entire created order

[10]See Carl F. H. Henry and Malcolm A. Reid, "Does Genesis 9 Justify Capital Punishment?" in *The Genesis Debate: Persistent Questions about Creation and the Flood,* ed. Ronald Youngblood (Grand Rapids: Baker Book House, 1990), 148–65.

Covenants in the Ancient World

"Covenant" is a word often used to define a relationship between two or more parties, including the terms for understanding and implementing that relationship. Internationally they are known as treaties. Treaties took several forms in the ancient world.[11]

Parity Treaty	A treaty between two equal parties, generally two sovereign nations of near equal power to a set of mutually agreed-upon terms. Participants called each other "brothers." A biblical example of a parity treaty is the "treaty of brotherhood"(Amos 1:9) first made informally between Hiram of Tyre and David (2 Sam. 5:11) and later renewed formally between Hiram and Solomon (1 Kings 5:1,12).
Suzerain-Vassal Treaty	The Hebrew term for suzerain literally means "king of kings," i.e., the supreme king. Under the suzerain would be subordinate, or vassal, kings and their kingdoms. A treaty between a suzerain and a vassal state was never a partnership. The treaty was set forth by the suzerain and accepted by the vassal. In it the vassal pledged allegiance, service, and support, both military and financial, to the suzerain. In return the suzerain promised protection and certain other benefits, contingent on the vassal's continued loyalty. The Sinai covenant in its various forms is an example of a suzerain-vassal treaty (see chap. 6).
Divine Charter	The divine charter is an unconditional gift, somewhat reminiscent of royal grants made by kings to loyal subjects. The grant assumed continued loyalty to the suzerain, but otherwise was unconditioned. The Noahic and Davidic covenants, as well as most of the Abrahamic covenant, are divine charters.

Covenants in the Old Testament

COVENANT	TYPE	PARTICIPANTS	CONTENT
Noahic Gen. 9:8–17	Divine Charter	Noah, his descendants, and every living thing (9:9–10)	Responsibility for all living things, especially for human life (9:6); God would never destroy the earth again with water; sign of the rainbow.

(cont. on the next page)

[11]The terminology in this chart and the next is adapted from George E. Mendenhall and Gary A Herion, "Covenant," in *ABD,* 1:1179–1202.

Covenants in the Old Testament (cont.)

COVENANT	TYPE	PARTICIPANTS	CONTENT
Abrahamic Gen. 15:9–21; 17:1–22	Mixed (Gen. 15:9–21 seem to be a charter; 12:1–3 and 17:1–22 seem to be suzerain-vassal)	Abram (Abraham) and his descendants	Promissory grant of descendants, land Certain imposed obligations: Circumcision as covenant sign; leaving his ancestral land (Gen. 12:1); "Walk before me and be blameless" (17:1).
Sinaitic Exod. 19; 20; 24	Suzerain-Vassal	Moses, Israel's leaders, and all Israel	God makes Israel his "treasured possession," a "kingdom of priests and a holy nation" (Exod. 19:5–6), granting them special privileges in terms of certain obligations (e.g., the Ten Commandments).
Davidic 2 Sam. 7:5–16	Divine Charter	David and his descendants	Establishes the Davidic kingship in perpetuity (cf. Ps. 89:19–37)
New Jer. 31:31–34	Divine Charter	Israel and Judah	A revived Davidic kingship (Jer. 33:15–16) would bring about a new covenant which, unlike the covenant broken by their ancestors, would be deeply inscribed in the hearts of the people.

The Serpent and the Seed

The immediate meaning of Genesis 3:15 is the hostility between humans and snakes, and, by extension, the animal kingdom. Yet the serpent is more than a serpent in the Genesis narrative. He is, instead, an agent of evil that leads the man and woman to disobey God, and thus be banished from Eden. The story casts him as the adversary of both humans and God. Later Scripture will reveal the identity of this adversary: He is Satan (Job 1:6–12; 2:1–4), the devil, who sinned "from the beginning" and who does indeed have offspring (John 8:44; 1 John 3:8,10; cf. Matt. 23:15). And finally the identity of Eve's "offspring" (individual, Gal. 3:16, as well as collective, Rom. 16:20) becomes clear. The One who would "crush [the serpent's] head" would also represent all mankind: Jesus Christ, the "last Adam" (1 Cor. 15:45). It is no coinci-

(Rom. 8:19–22). Genesis hints at this in the curse laid on the serpent.[12] Redemptive revelation is further developed through Abraham. Modern people often call him the "Father of the Jewish People," but the Lord called him the "father of many nations" (Gen. 17:5). It is through Abraham that the covenant for the redemption of humankind was mediated. It was to Abraham that the promise was given, "'All peoples on earth will be blessed through you'" (Gen. 12:3).[13]

How Should the Stories About Adam's Descendants Be Interpreted?

What Was Wrong With Cain's Offering?

The first homicide occurred after Cain became jealous of his brother's offering being acceptable to the Lord and his own being unacceptable. But why was Cain's offering not acceptable? Some have suggested that it was bloodless; no life was sacrificed by it. The context, however, makes it clear that the offering was to be one of firstfruits. If the harvest was to be grain, the offering would have had to be grain (Exod. 23:19). Later Mosaic revelation shows that a grain offering without blood was acceptable to God (Lev. 2).[14] It

---

[12]For the messianic implications of Gen. 3:15 and the patriarchal narratives, see T. Desmond Alexander, "Messianic Ideology in the Book of Genesis," in *The Lord's Anointed: Interpretation of Old Testament Messianic Texts,* ed. P. E. Satterthwaite et al. (Carlisle: Paternoster; and Grand Rapids: Baker Book House, 1995), 19–40.

[13]A difference must be seen between God's offer of salvation to all the world and the doctrine of universalism. The latter teaches that all humans everywhere will eventually be saved. The Bible, however, restricts salvation to those who accept God's revelation of himself and his will for their lives.

[14]See Herschel H. Hobbs and Joel D. Heck, "Was Cain's Offering Rejected by God Because It Was Not a Blood Sacrifice?" in *The Genesis Debate,* ed. Youngblood, 130–47.

is unlikely, therefore, that the bloodlessness of Cain's offering was the reason for its lack of approval.

The biblical texts show three things:

Abel offered the best he had: "some of the firstborn" (Gen. 4:4).	Cain offered a random sample, of average quality: "some of the fruits" (Gen. 4:3).
Abel made his offering "by faith" (Heb. 11:4).	It may be implied that Cain's offering was made grudgingly or without faith.
John implies that Cain's arrogance speaks of inner evil (1 John 3:12).	This seems to be confirmed by Cain's fierce anger against God.[15]

dence, therefore, that Luke traces Jesus' ancestry directly back to Adam (Luke 3:38). The first Adam brought sin into the human race; the last Adam brings redemption.

In looking over the evidence, therefore, it would seem that the thing wrong with Cain's offering was Cain himself. If we give the best we have with a willing heart in faith, God will not refuse it (Ps. 51:16–17).[16]

Where Did Cain Get His Wife?

Many people have stumbled over the question of where Cain got his wife (Gen. 4:17). Explanations range from the reasonable to the ridiculous. Some have suggested that he married his sister, while others point out the Bible does not mention the birth of a sister until later (5:4). Some have suggested that this event assumes the later mention of Adam's daughters and that the story simply jumps ahead.

[15]Compare Jon. 4:1–4,9, where Jonah's seething anger against God shows how unaligned he is with God's priorities.

[16]For a discussion of the difficulties in Genesis 4:7, see Victor P. Hamilton, *The Book of Genesis: Chapters 1–17*, New International Commentary on the New Testament (Grand Rapids: Wm. B. Eerdmans, 1990), 225–26. It is possible that the Lord was holding out a promise of redemption to Cain if he could only master the sin that threatened to consume him. That would mean repentance. Cain chose, instead, murder.

Others believe that there may have been more human beings created than only Adam and Eve (see "Human Beings: What Are They?" in chap. 2).[17] In any case, the story of Cain clearly and consistently implies that there were more human beings on earth by the time of Cain's banishment. This can be seen in his fear that someone would act as Abel's kinsman and avenge him (4:14). This also agrees with his need to build a town, not merely a house (4:17).

Where did Cain get his wife, then? We can't say for sure. But we can say that the picture of his wife, his city, and his fear of being murdered are consistent and point to more people on earth at that time than Cain and his parents.

How Do We Interpret the Genealogies of Genesis?

The genealogies of Genesis 5 and 11 have long been the subject of much discussion among scholars because of the length of life assigned some of the individuals. The most famous of these, of course, was Methuselah, who is allocated 969 years (Gen. 5:27). How do we understand these protracted life spans? What are the implications of these lists for the creation of the world?

Some Christians who see a young earth as the only interpretation possible consider the genealogies of Genesis to be chronologies. Interpreting the genealogies literally they arrive at a creation date somewhere in the vicinity of 5000–4000 B.C.[18] Most scholars, however – even many who

[17]See H. Wade Seaford and George Kufeldt, "Were There People Before Adam and Eve?" in *The Genesis Debate*, ed. Youngblood, 148–65.

[18]The Jewish calendar, for example, dates the year A.D. 2002–3 as year 5763 from the creation of the world (about 3761 B.C.); compare this with Bishop Usher's well-known date of 4004 B.C. for creation.

advocate a young earth—would recognize a world older than 6000 years. As a result, they would consider the Genesis genealogies to be abridged or to mean something more than what appears at first glance.[19]

It should be noted, however, that the age of the earth needs to be considered separately from the age of its human inhabitants. God created humanity on the sixth day, but the earth was created "in the beginning." As a result, one may argue for an old earth and yet consider human life, as the Bible defines it, as having appeared relatively recently.[20]

The genealogies of Genesis pose another problem: the long lives of the people who lived before and immediately after the Flood. Scholars have compared the Genesis account to other ancient Mesopotamian documents, such as *The Sumerian King List*.[21] By comparison to such material, the life spans assigned in Genesis are relatively short. But life spans of 969 years (Methuselah; Gen. 5:21–27) nevertheless need some comment. A few explanations of these figures follow:[22]

[19]Cf. R. K. Harrison, *Introduction to the Old Testament* (Grand Rapids: Wm. B. Eerdmans, 1969), 148–52; id., "From Adam to Noah: A Reconsideration of the Antediluvian Patriarch's Ages," *Journal of the Evangelical Theological Society* 37, no. 2 (June 1994): 161–68.

[20]One evangelical scholar who makes this argument is Ronald Youngblood in *The Book of Genesis: An Introductory Commentary,* 2d ed. (Grand Rapids: Baker Book House, 1991), 47–48. Youngblood considers Adam the first human because he was the first hominid created in the image of God. But he concedes that there were earlier life forms that were biologically human. See also Gleason L. Archer, *A Survey of Old Testament Introduction,* rev. ed. (Chicago: Moody Press, 1994), 209–12; even Stephen Hawking notes the similarity of Bishop Usher's date for the origin of human life to the end of the last ice age "when modern humans seem first to have appeared" (*Black Holes and Baby Universes and Other Essays* [New York: Bantam Books, 1993], 86).

[21]See *ANET,* 265–66.

[22]For a fuller discussion of the problem, see James A. Borland and Duane L. Christensen, "Did People Live to Be Hundreds of Years Old before the Flood?" in *The Genesis Debate,* ed. Youngblood, 166–83. Ramm, as noted,

Explanation	Evaluation
1. Sin had not yet fully devastated human life, so people did not die as early as we do.	Possible, but unlikely. If this were true, redeemed people should live longer than pagans.
2. The world was a healthier environment then.	Unlikely. The world was actually a harder place then. There was no real medical care and food was hard to come by.
3. The absence of modern vices (e.g., smoking, alcohol, caffeine) promoted longer lives.	This would certainly be a factor in long life, but would not make enough difference to account for Methuselah, for example.
4. The names are representative of clans or tribes, named after their founder (Judg. 1).	Bernard Ramm seems to favor this view: There is probably more of this type of expression (i.e., corporate) in the Bible than we moderns recognize.
5. The numbers are not calculated the same as ours (base 10).[23]	This shows great promise. It is relatively recent view and has not had time to mature yet.
6. The numbers have a symbolic, nonliteral meaning that cannot be retrieved fully.	This is possible, but unhelpful unless a symbolism can be demonstrated.

There is little doubt that the biblical numbers serve a purpose in the text. Otherwise they would not be there. Our problem, however, is that at this point we do not understand the text well enough to offer a hard-and-fast solution. We simply must wait for further light on this matter.

seems to favor the clan/family view; his discussion in *Christian View*, 236–38, is dated but still worth reading.

[23] For example, R. K. Harrison suggests a parallel to the Genesis genealogies in the numbers found in the Sumerian King List, where the reigns are reckoned on base 60 instead of on base 10 (as are our modern numbers). For a full discussion, see "From Adam to Noah," 161–68.

What Happened in the Flood?

Its Near Eastern Setting

Between 1922 and 1934, the prominent British archaeologist C. Leonard Wooley led a series of excavations to southern Mesopotamia (modern Iraq). Beneath some ancient graves he found pottery fragments that belonged to an earlier period (Ubaid), after which the workers encountered clean silt. Thinking they had reached the bottom of the delta, they dug through the layer of silt. Beneath the silt they found pottery belonging to the earliest Ubaid period. The silt layer separating the strata containing pottery was judged to have been laid down by a great flood. The layer measured between eight and eleven feet thick at Ur.[24] A similar layer, about two feet thick, was discovered at Shuruppak, with a deposit measuring a foot and a half at Kish.[25]

Parallels to the Genesis account exist in Babylonian mythology in both the Sumerian[26] and Akkadian versions. The Akkadian flood stories include the tale of Atrahasis[27] and the somewhat better known Epic of Gilgamesh.[28] In the latter version, Gilgamesh, the hero, king, and builder of Uruk (biblical Erech; Gen. 10:10), was said to have been depressed over the death of his companion, Enkidu. Realizing that, in spite of his greatness, he too would die, he roamed the world in search of immortality. Eventually

[24]See n. 19.

[25]See the fuller description in Jack Finegan, *Light From the Ancient Past*, 2d ed., rev. (Princeton: Princeton University Press, 1959), 27–28.

[26]*ANET*, 42–44.

[27]*ANET*, 104–6.

[28]*ANET*, 72–99.

he found Utnapishtim, who had built an "ark" to ride out a great flood. As a reward for his service, the gods had granted Utnapishtim immortality. He told Gilgamesh that if he could find a certain herb and eat it, he would live forever. After a long search, Gilgamesh found the plant, but while he was bathing, a serpent ate it. Thus, the serpent is made young each time it sheds its skin, while people grow old and die.[29]

Who Were the "Sons of God"?

The background for the story of the Flood lies in the pattern laid down by the biblical material. In Genesis 4:8, Cain slew his brother Abel and was cursed. Cain's descendants appear in Genesis 4:17–24. They include artists (4:21) and craftsmen (4:22). Seth, born to Eve, took Abel's place (4:25). The genealogy from Adam through Seth to Noah and his sons, Ham, Shem, and Japheth, is recorded in Genesis 5.

In Genesis 6:1 the curtain rises on a scene of ever increasing wickedness. The reason for the Flood is immediately made clear: The wickedness of the world had become intolerable to God. Although the precise nature of the wickedness is debated by theologians, Genesis 6:1–4 seems to make it turn on the identity of the "sons of God" (6:2).

Who were they? With only a few variations, scholars have generally interpreted them as either humans or as spirit beings. If the "sons of God" were fallen spirit beings in human form, then the "daughters of men" were human women. On the other hand, if the "sons of God" were men from the godly line of Seth, then the "daughters of men"

---

[29]For a detailed comparison with the biblical narrative, see Alexander Heidel, *The Gilgamesh Epic and Old Testament Parallels* (Chicago: University of Chicago Press, 1949).

would be the ungodly lineage of Cain. In either case, the problem involves sexual, and possibly marital, liaisons of an improper sort, the first view identifying the "sons of God" with fallen spirits, the second identifying the "daughters of men" with pagan women.[30]

Any discussion of identities, therefore, usually includes the following issues:

1. Were the "sons of God" (Gen. 6:2,4) angelic or human? The term "sons of God" is occasionally used in the Old Testament to denote angelic beings (Dan. 3:25; cf. in KJV Job 1:6; 2:1; 38:7). On the other hand, throughout the Old Testament (Exod. 4:22; Deut. 14:1; 32:5; Ps. 73:15; Isa. 43:6; Hos. 1:10; 11:1), Israel, God's people, is often called God's "children," "sons," "son," or "firstborn." Devout and godly persons can be called "children of God," "sons of God," or "daughters of God" (see Deut. 14:1; 32:5; Ps. 73:15; Isa. 43:6; Hos 1:10; 11:1). Therefore, "sons of God" would here represent the descendants of Seth, as opposed to those of Cain. Evidence of the New Testament is mixed: First Peter 3:19–20 and Jude 6 seem to implicate fallen angels, and Jesus seems to indicate the sin of Noah's day as a casual attitude toward human marriage, with no mention of spirit beings (Matt. 24:37–39; Luke 17:26–27).[31]

---

[30]See F. B. Huey, Jr., and John H. Walton, "Are the 'Sons of God' in Genesis 6 Angels?" in *The Genesis Debate*, ed. Youngblood, 184–209. The data are conveniently summarized by John H. Walton in his *Chronological and Background Charts of the Old Testament*, rev. ed. (Grand Rapids: Zondervan Publishing House, 1994), 98.

[31]It is noteworthy, however, that neither Jesus nor Peter and Jude offer their interpretations as dogma, but rather use them to illustrate a point. Perhaps their views simply drew on prevailing Jewish interpretations of the day to illustrate the consequences of sin.

2. Were the Nephilim produced by the union of the "sons of God" and the "daughters of men," or were they simply a people who existed when this evil was developing? Those who espouse the angelic interpretation would see the Nephilim as the gigantic offspring of alliances with supernatural beings. Those who see the "sons of God" as Seth's descendants would simply see the note as a chronological marker, denoting conditions of the time. The Anakim, later found in Canaan, were descendants of the Nephilim (Num. 13:31–33).

3. What was it about this situation that produced such evil? Surely the evil must have been monstrous for God to decide that he should utterly destroy the creatures created in his image (Gen. 6:7)! Was it intermarriage with fallen angels? or intermarriage with pagan people and thus, paganization of the godly seed?

These questions probably cannot ever be answered with certainty, but I will make these suggestions as something to think about:

1. The notion of intermarriage with spirit beings seems impossible in the Bible (Mark 12:25). The idea was common in some pagan cultures of the time. It entered Judaism much later, after the Jews had been exposed to pagan cultures in the Babylonian exile. The Bible, however, has no concept of a child born of such a union.

2. The position of the story comes immediately after the account of Cain's (Gen. 4:17–26) and Seth's offspring (5:1–32). The lineage of Cain is full of violence. Seth's is not. It would seem that the author's intent here was, by means of this story, to point to the mixing of the

lines. Intermarriage of the godly with the ungodly would be the issue (cf. 2 Cor. 6:14).

What Was the Extent of the Flood?

There are fundamentally two interpretations of the Flood:[32] Either it was a flood that covered the whole earth, or it was a flood that covered the inhabited world as it was known at that time. These views are often called the "global" and the "local" flood interpretations.

Arguments for a global flood maintain that the language of Genesis 7:18–24 is universal. The Bible describes a flood that covers "all the high mountains" and in which "every living thing" perishes. Globalists support their arguments by appealing to the universality of flood legends through-out the world. All of them, they say, demonstrate a common origin. They point to phenomena that show that the world was at one time under water. These phenomena include silt deposits, marine fossils, and similar things that could have been formed only by water or under water. They argue, for example, that the sudden death of Siberian mammoths indicates severe disturbance of the upper atmosphere at the end of the last ice age.[33]

Arguments for a local flood are based on language theory: A term means only what it meant to the people who spoke it. Thus terms that appear to us to be universal, such

[32]For a survey of interpretations of the Flood, see Davis A. Young, *The Biblical Flood: A Case Study of the Church's Response to Extrabiblical Evidence* (Grand Rapids: Wm. B. Eerdmans, 1995) and Steven A. Austin and Donald C. Boardman, "Did Noah's Flood Cover the Entire World?" in *The Genesis Debate,* ed. Youngblood, 210–29.

[33]See especially J. C. Whitcomb and H. M. Morris, *The Genesis Flood* (Philadelphia: Presbyterian & Reformed, 1961); D. W. Patten, *The Biblical Flood and the Ice Epoch* (Seattle: Meridian, 1966); and A. M. Rehwinkel, *The Flood* (St. Louis: Concordia, 1951).

as those found in Genesis 7:18–24, must be interpreted by what they meant to the people of that time. Universality of language means nothing unless a universal concept lies behind it. Since the New World had not been discovered, the term "earth" would have had a more restrictive sense. For example, in Gen. 41:57 all the world/earth/land *(kol ha'arets)* came to Joseph to buy bread. Clearly this use of "earth" means "the region," not "the world" as we now know it. NIV accordingly translates, "all the countries." Localists buttress their arguments by appealing to the amount of water available: Even if all the moisture in the atmosphere were to fall and the polar icecaps melted, to flood the globe would require eight times the amount of water obtained. Furthermore, if the entire globe were under water, there would be no place for it to drain off. Nor could it evaporate; there would be simply too much water![34] The Anakim, descendants of the Nephilim (Gen. 6:4), were still alive in Moses' time (Num. 13:31–33). This would suggest that the floodwaters did not reach Canaan or they would have perished (cf. Gen. 6:17; 7:21).[35]

Virtually all creationists who hold to a young earth believe in a global flood. Many, perhaps most, who hold to an old earth believe in a local flood. All, however, believe that the "world" of Noah's day, however defined in detail, was covered with water. All believe that human life in that "world" was extinguished by a terrible act of God's judgment and that Noah's family was spared by divine providence.

---

[34]Ramm, *Christian View,* 156–69.

[35]A useful summary of the global and local arguments may be found in Walton, *Chronological and Background Charts,* 100–101.

How Was the Ark Constructed?

Its Shape and Dimensions

Noah's ark probably bore little resemblance to the boat-like pictures in modern storybooks. The Hebrew word translated "ark" (*tebah*) indicates a box, and is apparently derived from an Egyptian word for "chest" or "sarcophagus." Rather than having a pointed bow and stern, therefore, the ark would have been a simple rectangular structure. It was designed for maximum capacity and stability rather than for speed—for floating, not cruising.

The length of the ark was to be 300 cubits, its width, 50 cubits, and its height, 30 cubits (Gen. 6:15, KJV). The Palestinian cubit was about 17.5 inches and the Babylonian cubit was 19.7 inches. The Palestinian cubit would yield about 450 feet long by about 75 feet wide by about 45 feet high, or about 1,518,750 cubic feet. The Babylonian cubit would yield about 492.5 by 82 by 49 feet, or 1,978,865 cubic feet. It was to have three decks, all of which were presumably within the hull. There was to be a door in its side and an opening about 18 inches high beneath the roof, presumably for ventilation.

Its Materials

The Hebrew indicates the ark was made of "gopher wood" (Gen. 6:14, KJV, RSV, NASB). Most scholars equate the word "gopher" with the tree we call cypress (see NIV, NEB, NRSV). The wood is relatively hard, dense, and very durable, making it an excellent material for shipbuilding. The ark was sealed with pitch, that is, raw petroleum, the principle export of modern Iraq. Sailors throughout history have used rope coated with tar as caulk, pounding it between the joints of shiplap on the hulls of wooden boats.

Its Purpose

Even children know the purpose for the ark: It was to save Noah and his family and the animals that lived on land from the waters of the flood (Gen. 6:20 through 7:3). Animals that were "unclean" (that is, unfit to eat or sacrifice) were to be taken in pairs – a male and a female, for reproductive purposes. Animals that were "clean" (that is, suitable for food or sacrifice) were taken in sevens.[36] The ark had to carry food and water for Noah's family and for the animals. This was no small problem. The Flood is commonly thought of in terms of a rain that fell forty days and nights. In reality Noah stayed in the ark much longer. By comparing Genesis 7:11–13 and 8:13–19 it can be determined that Noah, his family, and the animals were in the ark more than a year.[37] Carrying food stores and fresh water for Noah's family and the animals must have been a major concern.

The Noahic Covenant

At the conclusion of the flood narrative, Noah entered into a covenant with God (Gen 9:1–17). Most people think of that covenant in terms of God's promise to never again wipe out human life by flooding the world (9:15). But there is more to it than that. Earlier in the narrative God charged Noah to be fruitful and multiply and rule over the earth. His choice of words echoes his charge to Adam and Eve,

[36]Ibid., 23, for a helpful summary of "clean" and "unclean."

[37]About 377 days. See ibid., 14, for a convenient chronology of the Flood.

making it clear that Noah was to continue Adam's office in taking care of the earth (9:1–2; see 1:28–30). This time, however, God permitted humans to eat meat. God is the source of all life. Since blood was the symbol of animal life, meat that was to be eaten could not have blood in it (9:3–4).[38] The Bible's concern for blood showed respect for the life of the animal and for God who had given that life. Human blood, too, had to be accounted for, whether spilled by an animal or another human being (9:5). Any person or animal that shed human blood had to be put to death (9:6; cf. Exod. 21:12,29). In a larger sense, the government of human society was passed to human beings to act on God's behalf. Social ethics were to be based on the doctrine that humans were created in God's image. How we treat others reflects the value we place on God (Gen. 9:6; James 3:9).

The "Curse on Ham" (Canaan): What Does It Mean?

Genesis 9:18–29 tells the story of how Noah planted a vineyard, became drunk from its wine, and was in some way humiliated by his son Ham. There are several problems posed by the story that need to be clarified. First of all, Noah's drunkenness is in no way presented as model behavior. The Bible abhors drunkenness.[39] The story of Noah portrays him as "righteous" and "blameless among

Moral Heresy

Throughout the history of the church, great stress has been placed on confessional orthodoxy; if we don't *believe* correctly, we are seen as heretical. Further, confessional orthodoxy (correct belief) should lead to ethical behavior. If it doesn't, another type of heresy occurs, a breach in ethics or moral theology. Let me say it clearly: abusing others is wrong! Several of my former students left the Christian ministry because of how they were treated by the leadership.

Many times I've pondered the ethics of neglecting the poor in our backyards—our ghettos, barrios, and Indian reservations—to spend our money elsewhere. I come from an impoverished home in Appalachia. I remember

(cont. on the next page)

---

[38]See Lev. 17:11,14; Deut. 12:23. Animals had to be slaughtered in such a way that they were bled dry. Animals that died of natural causes or that were killed by other animals were not to be eaten because they had not been bled (Exod. 22:31; Lev. 7:24; 17:15; 22:8). Their blood was to be drained onto the ground (Deut. 12:15–16) and covered with earth out of respect for the life it represented (Lev. 17:13).

[39]E.g., Rom. 13:13; Gal. 5:21; 1 Tim. 3:3; Titus 1:7; 1 Pet. 4:3.

how grateful I was to one
of my teachers who used
to pass on her son's used
shirts to me so I didn't
have to wear rags. James
said, "But someone will
say, 'You have faith; I
have deeds.' Show me
your faith without deeds,
and I will show you my
faith by what I do"
(James 2:18).

the people of his time" (6:9), but never as flawless. Like all citizens of the fallen world, he was subject to the imperfections of that world.

The second problem presents itself as a question: What did Ham do to Noah that enraged him enough to curse his own grandson, Canaan? A number of solutions have been suggested. Perhaps Ham laughed at his father or mocked him in his drunken stupor. Some think he may have castrated or sodomized his father. Still others suggest Ham had sexual relations with his mother, Noah's wife,[40] Canaan being the incestuous offspring of that union.

All of these interpretations, tempting as they are, must assume something more than what the text says and do not fit well with what follows. The story says only that Ham "saw the nakedness of his father" and reported it to his brothers. It was the simple act of seeing, therefore, that humiliated Noah, although we may assume that the incident implies more than a casual glance. Shem and Japheth, on the other hand, carefully entered the tent and respectfully covered their father, taking care not to look at him. The offense was unabashedly gazing at Noah's nakedness; the remedy was concealing Noah's nakedness.[41]

The final problem is the question of why Noah cursed Canaan, Ham's son, and what such a curse signified. It is important to remember that the three sons of Noah were

[40]Those who urge that Ham sodomized his father or had sexual relations with his mother point to the expression "uncover the nakedness of " (see KJV, NASB, et al.) as it is used in Lev. 18 and 20 to designate sexual intercourse. In particular, they point out that having sexual relations with one's mother (or a wife of one's father) dishonors one's father (Lev. 18:6–8). A recently proposed variation of this view holds that it was Canaan, not Ham, that is mentioned in Gen. 9:24b; if this were the case, it would ease the question of why Canaan was singled out to be cursed (9:25).

[41]For a discussion of these views, see Hamilton, *Book of Genesis,* 322–23.

Slavery: Justified by the "Curse of Ham" (Canaan)?

Some interpreters of the passage containing the so-called curse of Ham have used it to justify the slavery of Africans in this country, as well as their continued treatment as inferiors even after slavery was abolished. This interpretation is built on a number of faulty premises.

The first is that slavery is somehow the will of God and not the product of a fallen world. Genesis 1:26–28 gives the world to human beings. All are descended from a common ancestor. All are created in God's image. It is in the narrative of the Fall that we first find one human being lording it over another (Gen. 3:16). The death penalty was exacted for selling an Israelite into slavery (Deut. 24:7), and even foreign slaves that had escaped from their masters were to be granted sanctuary in Israel (Deut. 23:15–16).

Second is the assumption that all descendants of Ham were black. A clear examination of the evidence shows that it is the populace of North Africa (Egyptians, Libyans, etc.) and the Near East (Canaan) that is in focus here. While there has been considerable intermarriage from earliest times, the basic substratum for these peoples is Caucasian. However one interprets this passage, its problems—and its curse—pertains to predominantly Caucasian (white) people.

So let's ask the question again: Does Genesis 9:24–25 justify slavery? The answer is no. Does it justify treating as inferiors those who are different? The answer is no.

Moreover, the Bible shows a clear sympathy for the hardships endured by slaves. It set forth laws to curb abuses aimed at them. Capital punishment was prescribed for those who kidnapped a person in order to sell him or her into slavery (Exod. 21:16; Deut. 24:7). Mosaic law even protected runaway slaves (Deut. 23:15). Paul's epistle to Philemon shows that he understood this. He urged humane treatment for Onesimus, even as he returned him to his master (10–16). The biblical doctrine of humans as created in the image of God would eventually undermine slavery in Christian society.

not just persons, but represented the peoples that would be their descendants (see the next section). In cursing Canaan, therefore, Noah addressed Ham's descendants, the Canaanites, who would later become examples of moral degradation (cf. Lev. 18:2–3,6–30).[42]

But why was Canaan singled out from all of Ham's sons? As mentioned above, the sons are ancestors of peoples. The descendants of Canaan would continue any sins committed by Canaan's father, Ham, and exceed them. When the text curses Canaan, it looks forward to a time when Canaanites would be servants to the Israelites in the Davidic empire.[43]

Who Were the Descendants of Noah? – Gen. 10:1–32

The tenth chapter of Genesis is often called the Table of Nations. Its function serves to link the descendants of Noah to Abraham, called the "father of many nations" (Gen. 17:5) through whom the earth would be blessed. The known descendants of Noah were primarily Caucasian peoples and represent the two major language groups found among Caucasian peoples: the Indo-European (Japhetic) and the Hamitic/Semitic languages of the Middle East and northern Africa.

Japheth's descendants (Gen. 10:2–5), as far as they can be identified, are largely Indo-Europeans living in southern Asia and Europe. The following can be identified with some confidence: Gomer = the Cimmerians; Madai = the Medes;

---

[42]See note on Gen. 9:25, *NIV Study Bible.*

[43]As, for example, the Gibeonites (Josh. 9) and, perhaps, the Moabites (2 Sam. 8:2).

Javan = the Greeks (Ionians); Meshech and Tubal = the Mushki and Tabali, peoples who lived in eastern Anatolia (Asia Minor); Ashkenaz = the Scythians (?); Elishah = Cyprus (Alashia) or Sicily; Kittim = Kition, a Phoenician city on southeast Cyprus; and the Rodanim = the inhabitants of Rhodes.

The descendants of Ham (Gen. 10:6–20) generally indicate people who inhabited northern Africa and southwest Asia. The following can be identified: Cush = Nubians/Ethiopians; Mizraim = Egyptians; Put = the Libyans (?); Canaan = the Canaanites. Seba and Sheba in the Hamite genealogy probably represent a Sabean colony in the horn of Africa (10:28). The Cush mentioned in connection with Babylonia is probably best explained as indicating either the Sumerians or the Kassites (10:8–12). The Philistines mentioned here in connection with the Casluhites and later with Caphtor (Crete; see Jer. 47:4; Amos 9:7) were part of a mixed group later called the Sea Peoples by the Egyptians, and probably had a heavy Aegean (Cretan) component. The classical Hittites were a fusion of Indo-European invaders and a developed culture ("Hatti") already existing in northeast Anatolia. Sidon, like Tyre, was a chief seaport of Phoenicia.

The descendants of Shem generally denote the inhabitants of southwest Asia (Gen. 10:21–31). The following can be identified: Elam = a land on the north coast of the Persian Gulf; Asshur = the Assyrians; Lud = the Lydians; Aram = the Arameans; Uz = a land east of Canaan; Eber = the Hebrews.[44] The descendants of Joktan are generally Arabian groups, with Sheba probably designating the Sabeans, an ancient culture on the site of modern Yemen (10:28).

---

[44]See Gen. 11:14–17, where Eber is an ancestor of Abraham.

The Tower of Babel — Gen. 11:1–9

The story of the tower of Babel is set in lower Mesopotamia, on a "plain in Shinar" (Gen. 11:1). The tower mentioned in this story was probably the ziggurat found at Babylon. Although the pyramids of Egypt and the ziggurats found throughout Mesopotamia look similar to the average person, they are really quite different. The pyramids were built of cut stone as royal tombs. Ziggurats were built of mud brick as worship centers to Sumerian, and later Babylonian, sky-gods. Ziggurats became part of the Sumerian, Old Babylonian, and Neo-Babylonian culture and religion. It is thought that the original builders, the early Sumerians, had come to the Tigris-Euphrates river valley from a mountainous region. The ziggurat, therefore, was built as an artificial mountain. On the top of each ziggurat the people erected a temple to one of their gods. The most famous ziggurat was at Ur, but they existed at a number of other sites, including Babylon.

In the story, the people say, "Come on! Let's build ourselves a city, and a tower with its top in heaven. Let's make ourselves famous so we'll not get scattered over the whole earth" (Gen. 11:4, author's translation). It is quite likely that the top "in heaven" imitated the Sumerian and Babylonian temples atop ziggurats. As the story develops, we are told how Babylon got its name,[45] how the ziggurat of Babylon came to be built, and how the human languages came to be so different.[46] The point of the story is to show how human

[45]The derivation of Babel from *balal* depends on a pun garnered from folk etymology and very well may reflect a Palestinian understanding of the name's meaning. Cuneiform sources, however, derive it from *bab-ilu* or *bab-ilim,* meaning "gate of god" or "gate of the gods" respectively.

[46]Stories that explain why certain things have come to exist are called "eti-

beings had become so wicked that they could not be permitted to socialize with others, lest they try to usurp the place of God. It is a sad closing to the story of Noah's children.

A Message of Hope:
The Lineage of Shem — Gen. 11:10–26

If the effrontery of Babel were the end of the Bible, what a hopeless state humanity would be in! But Babel isn't the end. The descendants of Shem are listed in these verses for one purpose: to declare the birth of Abraham. The builders of the tower of Babel had wanted to make a name for themselves. But God told Abraham that if he obeyed, God would make his name great. What's more, he promised that Abraham would "'be a blessing. . . . and all peoples on earth'" would be blessed through him (Gen. 12:2–3). We can see this first in Abraham's exemplary life, later in the covenant mediated through Moses, then in the kingship of David, and, finally, in the birth of the Messiah, the Christ. We have hope!

Evil, Orcs, and Disunity

Their evil—their pride and arrogance, as well as their construction of ungodly worship centers—brought God's judgment on the builders of the tower of Babel. He sent division among them.

J. R. R. Tolkien, author of *The Lord of the Rings,* clearly understood that divisiveness is often one of the consequences of evil and that its opposite, good, unites through love. In the second volume of the trilogy, *The Two Towers,* Aragorn, Gimli, and Legolas are pursuing a band of orcs that had abducted two young hobbits. Beside the road they discovered five orcs, murdered by other orcs. They pondered its meaning.

"I think that the enemy brought his own enemy with him," answered Aragorn. "These are Northern Orcs from far away. Among the slain

(cont. on the next page)

---

ologies." The real point of the story in its biblical setting, however, is not an etiology.

Evil, Orcs, and Disunity (cont.)

are none of the great Orcs with the strange badges. There was a quarrel, I guess: it is no uncommon thing with these foul folk. Maybe there was some dispute about the road" (Book III, Chapter 2).

The action on the builders of Babel was a judgment by God, not an arbitrary action. The arrogance of the people (their evil) brought the judgment (division). The builders of Babel, like Tolkien's orcs, had "brought their own enemy with them"—their arrogance and rebellion.

James teaches us that conflicts, even those in the church, are often caused by selfish desires (James 4:1–3), even though they may be masked by theological rhetoric. We can learn from the tower of Babel that evil will divide us if it can. A desire for God and his truth will unite us if we let it.

Study Questions

1. Reflect on sin and evil awhile. Note its divisive nature. It alienates people from God, nature, other people, and self. List the places where this occurs in the chapters of the Bible you've studied.
2. Trace God's redemptive work, from his offer of pardon to Cain to the birth of Abram (Abraham).
3. Know the arguments for global versus local world floods.
4. What is the central thrust of the Noahic Covenant?
5. What was the tower of Babel? What happened there?

For Further Reading

For commentaries, see the suggestions at the end of chap. 2. *The IVP Bible Background Commentary: Old Testament,* by John H. Walton, Victor H. Matthews, and Mark W. Chavalas (Downers Grove, Ill.: InterVarsity, 2000), is very helpful, although not exhaustive, in filling in some of the background necessary for understanding the Old Testament world.

4

Robert Mullins

What Was the Old Testament World?

Outline:

- **Why Was the Fertile Crescent Important?**
- **When Did Civilization Begin?**
  Mesopotamia
  Egypt
  Asia Minor
  Canaan: The Hub of a Wheel
  Canaan: The Land Between
- **The Contribution of Archaeology**
- **What Have We Learned?**

Terms:

cuneiform
heiroglyphics
Levant
Transjordan

The German writer J. W. Goethe once remarked, "Whoever wants to understand a poet must go to the poet's homeland." The same thing might be said about the biblical writers. After all, these were people speaking or writing to audiences well acquainted with their world. Most of us today, however, lack this acquaintance and it influences our understanding of Scripture.

Here is how you can best learn about the biblical world. First, think of yourself as an explorer and this chapter as your guide. Use it with a good Bible atlas. Second, take advantage of the study questions, which are intended to help you focus on the main points of this chapter. Third, consult the books

Geography of the Ancient Near East

listed at the end of the chapter. They will enrich your knowledge and deepen your appreciation for what some have called the "Fifth Gospel"–the land of the Bible.

We'll begin our study with the larger setting of the biblical world and then narrow it to Canaan. We start with the Fertile Crescent, a sweep of land bordered by sea and desert that stretches from the Nile Delta northward along the Mediterranean coast. It then swings southeastward just south of Anatolia and ends at the Persian Gulf.

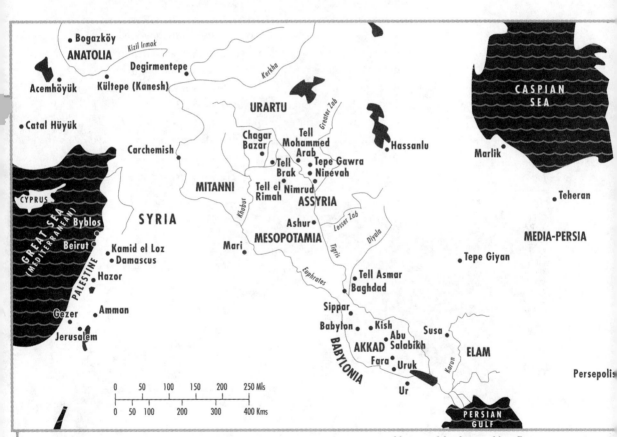

Nations of the Ancient Near East

Following Abraham

In Genesis 11:31 through 12:10, Abraham left Ur of the Chaldeans[1] and journeyed as far as Egypt. Even though the Fertile Crescent is not mentioned by name in the Bible, no doubt Abraham went along this geographic arc. Let's follow the route he took.

We first leave Ur in southern Mesopotamia and travel along the Euphrates River to Haran in northeastern Aram. Abraham could have gone by foot, but it is also possible that he traveled by boat. For a period of time, Abraham lived in Haran. In those days, Haran was a major caravan center. It linked wool-rich northern Mesopotamia with the mineral and timber regions of Anatolia. From Haran, Abraham journeyed southward to Canaan where he pitched his tent at Shechem, Bethel, and Beersheba. But a prolonged drought forced him to travel on to Egypt (Genesis 12:10). This is probably the land of Goshen, the same region in the eastern Nile Delta where the Hebrews would find themselves enslaved by the Egyptians.

The total distance Abraham traversed from southern Babylonia to Egypt by way of Haran was about 1,500 miles (2,410 km). That is about half the distance across the continental United States. Based on an estimate of 15 miles (24 km) a day for travel in antiquity, it would have taken Abraham a little over three months to go this entire distance had he traveled every day. But we know that Abraham took longer, and we can assume most other people did too.

Retracing Abraham's Journey

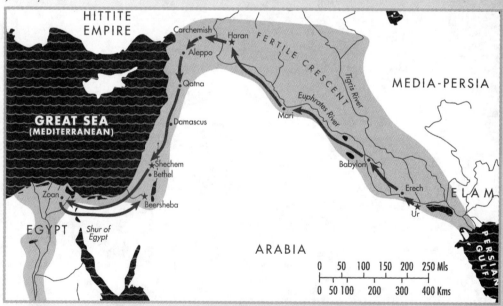

[1]The "Chaldees" (Gen. 11:31, KJV) or "Chaldean empire" is an alternative name for the Neo-Babylonian empire, which arose under King Nabopolassar around 626 B.C. Nabopolassar was the predecessor of Nebuchadnezzar who destroyed Jerusalem in 586 B.C.

Why Was the Fertile Crescent Important?

The Fertile Crescent is so named because it contained land that could be cultivated, benefiting from rainfall sufficient to grow crops or rivers that could be used for irrigation. It was the cradle and crossroads of history, a link between Europe, Asia, and Africa. Movement across this land bridge, however, was influenced by three geographic features that determined the way people traveled in antiquity.

1. *Mountains.* Along the southern side of Asia Minor, mountains form an almost continuous belt as far as Persia (Iran). Here, they turn south to border Mesopotamia on the east. Any movement across these mountains was limited to only a few passes.

2. *Deserts.* The great deserts of Syria,[2] Arabia, and Africa dominate the southern part of the area. For the most part, only nomads who knew how to survive the harsh, arid conditions would ever pass through.

3. *Seas.* Five seas frame the region. The most significant body of water on the west is the Mediterranean Sea. In biblical times, people called it the Great Sea. The Black and Caspian Seas lie to the north, while the Persian Gulf and the Red Sea are located to the south.

People avoided these natural obstacles by traveling along a narrow sickle-shaped corridor dubbed the Fertile Crescent. It is an appropriate name since this swath of land also included the best agricultural areas, the largest population groups, and the majority of powerful city-states that we read about in the Bible. From the map it is easy to see that the Fertile Crescent occupies a central part of what

---

[2]"Syria" in this context refers to the Roman province by that name (see any Bible atlas), not the modern nation, although the two overlap.

Clay or Papyrus?

The earliest known examples of writing were found on clay tablets in the ancient city of Uruk, the city of the legendary Gilgamesh. It had a population of some thirty thousand inhabitants and was one of the first (perhaps the very first) Sumerian city-state. Uruk appears in Gen. 10:10 as Erech in southern Mesopotamia. The tablets found there date to about 3300 B.C. In Egypt, the earliest evidence of writing follows not long after.

When they wrote, the people of Mesopotamia and Egypt would generally utilize material typical of their geographical locale. In the flood plains of Mesopotamia the most available writing medium was clay. In Egypt it was papyrus. This is where we get the English word "paper." Papyrus is a reedlike plant that grows along the banks of the Nile.

To do their writing on tablets made from clay,

most people today call the Middle East. When speaking in terms of its early history, though, scholars generally call this area the Ancient Near East.

When Did Civilization Begin?

At opposite ends of the Fertile Crescent lay the two great river valley cultures. At one end was Mesopotamia supported by the Tigris and Euphrates Rivers. At the other was Egypt fed by the Nile. Civilization began at both ends about five thousand years ago. Writing also first appeared at that time. When a people are able to leave behind written records, we can be more confident of our knowledge about them. Thus, the appearance of writing marks what many consider to be the beginning of history. Whatever existed of human culture prior to this is generally referred to as *pre-history*.

Let us examine these two regions in more detail. We will start with Mesopotamia, since history began there slightly earlier than in Egypt. Afterwards we will explore Asia Minor to the north and conclude by returning to the narrow land bridge of Canaan that linked those diverse areas.

Mesopotamia

The name "Mesopotamia" is a compound of two Greek words meaning "between (the) rivers," an obvious reference to the Tigris and Euphrates Rivers. Both originate in Asia Minor and pass through the entire length of Mesopotamia (present-day Iraq) and empty into the Persian Gulf. Traditionally, Mesopotamia is divided into two parts: Assyria in the north and Babylonia in the south. (Ancient Mesopotamia was about the size of the state of California.)

BEFORE **1000** B.C.

The earliest civilization was established by the Sumerians in southern Mesopotamia around 3500 B.C. (the Uruk and Jemdet Nasr periods). The Sumerians built the first cities and introduced a special form of wedge-shaped writing called "cuneiform."

Sumerian culture reached its zenith during the Early Dynastic period (ca. 2900–2350 B.C.). Although Sumerians were the predominant ethnic group, Semitic[3] people also lived in lower Mesopotamia. One of them, Sargon I, eventually seized power and established the first Semitic dynasty of Akkad around 2334 B.C. Eventually all Mesopotamia and northern Aram fell under his control. Sargon's grandson, Naram-Sin (ca. 2291–2255 B.C.), destroyed the city of Ebla with its important royal archives.[4]

Soon after, the fortunes of the Akkadian empire began to crumble. A series of transitions then took place. The region first fell under the control of an obscure group of people called the Gutians. This was followed by a short revival of

the people of Mesopotamia made use of a wedge-shaped stylus. For this reason, the writing system of Mesopotamia is called cuneiform (fr. Lat. *cuneus,* "wedge").

The Egyptians, by contrast, would use a reed pen dipped into carbon ink to write on papyrus sheets. Their writing system is different than found in Mesopotamia. It uses a series of pictorial symbols called "hieroglyphs" (lit. "sacred carvings"). It is interesting to note the "accidental" manner in which Egyptian writing has survived: Most surviving examples are not preserved on papyrus documents but on the temple walls where the signs had been carved into the stone by scribes. Hieroglyphics remained in use until the fourth century A.D.

---

[3]Like the term "Indo-European," "Semite" or "Semitic" applies solely to the speakers of a group of related languages. They cannot be distinguished racially, for example, from early Mediterranean stock who were also short, dark, and long-headed. Semitic peoples include the Assyrians, Babylonians, and Hebrews. The Sumerians, by contrast, were not Semitic; neither were the Egyptians.

[4]The Ebla texts were discovered in 1975 by an team of Italian archaeologists excavating at Tell Mardikh in northwest Syria. This discovery of some 15,000 tablets in the royal palace constitutes the largest single find of third millennium B.C. cuneiform texts. In the beginning, some thought the patriarchal period had been identified; but nearly all of these connections must be abandoned. In the end, the tablets will tell us more about the general background of Syro-Mesopotamia than about biblical characters or geography. The language of the tablets (called Eblaite) has much in common with Akkadian, the language of Assyria and Babylonia. Most of the texts are administrative. A smaller number include word lists and literary texts.

Comparative Chronology of the Ancient Near East

All Dates approx. B.C.	MESOPOTAMIA	EGYPT	ANATOLIA	PALESTINE	BIBLICAL & HISTORICAL
3100	Jemdet Nasr (3100–2900) Early Dynastic Period (ca. 2900–2350)	Late Predynastic Period (3100–2920)		Early Bronze II–III (3100–2350)	Royal Cemetery at Ur (2600–2400)
2500	Akkadian Empire (2334–3254) Post-Akkadian Period (2154–2112) Ur III (2113–2004)	Early Dynastic Period Dynasties 1–3 (2920–2575)		Early Bronze IV– Middle Bronze I (2350–2000)	Naram-Sin destroys Ebla (ca. 2250)
2000	North / South — Old Assyrian (1741–1274); Isin-Larsa (2025–1794); Old Babylonian (2004–1595); Middle Babylonian (1595–626)			Middle Bronze II A (2000–1750); Middle Bronze II B (1650–1550/1500)	Patriarchs; Mari Letters (1779–1757); Hammurabi (1792–1750); Joseph; Babylon falls (1595)
1500		New Kingdom Dynasties 18–20; Dynasty 18 (1550–1295); Ahmose I (1550–1225)	Hurrian Kingdom of Mitanni (1500–1350); Hittite Middle Kingdom (1500–1425)	Late Bronze I (1500–1400)	Expulsion of Hyksos (1550–1555); Hebrew Bondage in Egypt; Egyptians Dominate Canaan (1550–1150); Early Date Exodus: (ca. 1446); Early Date Conquest: (ca. 1406)
1400	Middle Assyrian	Dynasty 19 (1295–1186) Rameses II		Late Bronze II (1400–1200)	Amarna Age (1352–1333)

Date	Biblical / Israel	Archaeological Period	Syria / Anatolia	Egypt	Mesopotamia
1200	Joshua Hittite Empire falls (1190) Judges Philistines arrive (1180) Samuel Saul (1050–1010)	Iron Age I (1200–1000)		Dynasty 20 (1186–1069) Third Intermediate Dynasties 21–25 (1069–714)	
1000	David (1010–970) Solomon (970–930)	Iron Age II A (1000–900)	Neo-Hittite States in North Syria (1180–700) Tiglath-pileser (1115–1077)		
930	Monarchy splits (931) Shishak invades Judah and Israel (925) Omri → Ahab Battle of Qarqar (853) Mesha Stele (850) Jehu → Ahaz Samaria falls (722)	Iron Age II B (900–722)	Kingdom of Urartu (832–600)		Neo-Assyrian Empire (934–612)
720	Hezekiah Sennacherib's Campaign to Judah (701)	Iron Age II C (722–586)			
700	*Mannaseh* Ninevah falls (612) Battle of Carchemish (605)			Late or Salte-Persian Period Dynasties 26–31 (664–332)	Neo-Babylonian Empire (625–539)
600	Jerusalem falls (586)	Babylonian Period (586–539)			
539					Persian Period .... (539–332 B.C.)

Sumerian culture known as Ur III. A time of disunity then ensued with the establishment of several West Semitic Amorite dynasties (the Isin and Larsa period). Out of this emerged the Old Babylonian period (ca. 1900–1600 B.C.).

Undoubtedly, the most famous Amorite king of this time was Hammurabi (or Hammurapi), who ruled Babylon (1792–1750 B.C.). Hammurabi is best known for his law code, which dates to the time of the patriarchs. The Mari letters[5] also date from about the same time. These twenty thousand cuneiform tablets have revealed much valuable information about the daily life and customs of Abraham's time.

After Hammurabi, a period of decline followed that ended with the Hittite assault on Babylon in 1595 B.C. For about three centuries or so after this, Babylonia would be dominated by the Kassites, a people about whom we know very little.

AFTER 1000 B.C.

The great northern curve of the Fertile Crescent, passing as it did between the mountains and desert, meant that those traveling from Mesopotamia arrived in Israel from the north. In light of this, one can understand why the prophets spoke of the Assyrian and Babylonian threat coming from that direction (for example, Isa. 14:31; Jer. 1:13–16;

[5]The letters are named after the site of Mari (Tell Hariri) on the Euphrates River in Syria. The site was discovered in 1933 by a group of local Arabs who were digging a grave. While digging, they unearthed a stone statue. Eventually, archaeologists uncovered a whole palace and an archive of twenty thousand cuneiform tablets, dating mainly to the reign of Zimri-Lim of Mari (1779–1761 B.C.). Some reveal the kinds and amounts of food coming into the palace. Others are letters that tell us about the spoken languages and about everyday matters (military, civil, diplomatic, and economic) during patriarchal times.

4:6; Ezek. 26:7), even though it is obvious in looking at a map that these nations lay to the east. The armies of Assyria and Babylonia would never have gone by way of the deserts, since there was insufficient food and water for their troops.

Assyria was the first Mesopotamian empire to represent a direct threat to Israel. According to Assyrian annals, "Ahab the Israelite" and a coalition of other local rulers fought Shalmaneser III of Assyria. The battle took place in 853 B.C. at Qarqar (Karkar) in northwestern Aram.[6] Although the coalition managed to hold off the Assyrian advance for a while, further campaigns brought the Assyrians deeper into Aramean and northern Israelite territory. Then, in 722 B.C., the Assyrian army attacked and destroyed Samaria, capital of the northern Israelite kingdom.

Assyrian interests continued to dominate the region after the fall of the Northern Kingdom. Assyria, however, was weakening. With the rise of Nabopolassar to the throne of Babylon in 626 B.C., the Neo-Babylonian, or Chaldean, empire began exerting pressure on its northern neighbor. In 612 B.C., Nineveh, the Assyrian capital, fell. In 605 B.C., what little remained of a refugee Assyrian government at Carchemish was annihilated.

The shift in control from Assyria to Babylonia would spell disaster for Judah. It was only a matter of time before Nebuchadnezzar of Babylon would lay waste to Jerusalem in 586 B.C. This event finally brought four centuries of rule by descendants of King David to an end.

---

[6]See chap. 14. For an English translation of Shalmaneser's account, see *ANET*, 276–79. As important as this campaign was to the overall political history of the region, it is not mentioned in the Bible.

Egypt

The Greek historian Herodotus once called Egypt "the gift of the Nile." And indeed it is. From the air, one can view a narrow strip of green on both banks that is scarcely wider than the river itself. Beyond this spreads a desolate and sandy expanse. From the Nile's remote origins in Ethiopia (Blue Nile) and Burundi (White Nile), it threads its way northward to the Mediterranean Sea. This makes the Nile the longest river in the world. Stretching 4,142 miles (6,670 km), the Nile is twice as long as the Mississippi River. The area occupied by Egypt in biblical times is roughly equivalent to the combined states of Texas, Oklahoma, and Arkansas.

A developing civilization in the Nile Valley may be traced back to about 5000 B.C. By that time, animals had been domesticated and crops grown. Then around 3500 B.C. two distinct kingdoms emerged: Upper Egypt in the south and Lower Egypt in the north. These two halves were united around 3100/3000 B.C. by Menes (also known as Narmer), initiating the Early Dynastic, or Archaic, Period. By this time, the hieroglyphic writing system was already in use.[7] The rise and fall of two Egyptian kingdoms and eighteen dynasties of pharaohs took more than 1500 years, yet this brings us only to the time of Moses. Egypt was already ancient by his time.

OLD KINGDOM

The Old Kingdom began with the Fourth Dynasty about 2600 B.C. At this time the Egyptian capital was located at

---

"Old," "Middle," and "New" to Whom?

Egyptian history was first divided into Old, Middle, and New Kingdoms by Manetho, an Egyptian priest who lived during the third century B.C. This was the time of Greek rule in Egypt. It is he who divided up the reigns of various Egyptian rulers into "kingdoms" and "dynasties." The times of transition between the "kingdoms" are sometimes marked by "intermediate periods." Although modern research has shown that these divisions are not always accurate, western historians have nevertheless adopted Manetho's division as a helpful way to discuss Egyptian history.

---

[7]The development of this writing system seems to have been so fast that it may have been in some sense an imitation of the earliest Mesopotamian writing in its Uruk phase. Besides the development of a writing system, other indications of Mesopotamian influence on early Egypt include its art and architecture.

Memphis (south of modern Cairo). The glory of this era is well known as the Pyramid Age. Not far from Memphis is the Great Pyramid built by Khufu (Cheops) and the Sphinx built by Khafre.

MIDDLE KINGDOM

The Middle Kingdom began around 2100 B.C. This was the time of the patriarchs. It was a period of great prosperity following the social unrest of the First Intermediate Period. Art and literature flourished to such a high degree that modern historians regard it as a classic age. Toward the end of the Middle Kingdom, more and more people from Asia settled in the Delta. By 1640 B.C. they asserted political control over Lower Egypt and brought about the Second Intermediate Period. The native kings fled southward to Thebes, ancient capital of Upper Egypt. They called these Asian interlopers "rulers of foreign lands" (Egyptian *hekau khasut*). By way of Greek as preserved in the writings of Manetho, this name has come down to us in altered form as "Hyksos." In terms of biblical history, this would be the time of Joseph.

NEW KINGDOM

The end of Hyksos rule in the Delta came in 1550 B.C. with the establishment of the New Kingdom (Eighteenth Dynasty) under Ahmose. The Hyksos rulers were expelled by the native Egyptian rulers, Upper and Lower Egypt reunited, and the Hebrews were placed under bondage (Exod. 1:8–11). It was under a pharaoh of the New Kingdom that the exodus from Egypt took place.

Of the two superpowers at either end of the Fertile Crescent, Egypt was the first to exert significant economic

The Boundaries of Canaan and Israel

The boundaries of the land of Canaan as described in Deuteronomy 34:1–12 reflect the Egyptian province of Canaan as defined in the peace pact between the Egyptians led by Rameses II and the Hittites led by Muwatallis II, following the Battle of Kadesh in central Syria.

Probably the best-known biblical borders are those "from Dan to Beersheba" (Judg. 20:1; 1 Sam. 3:20; 1 Kings 4:25). This is an air distance of about 150 miles (240 km). It is also the territory most adaptable to permanent settlement. If one crosses the country by air from west to east over Jerusalem, the distance between the

and political sovereignty over the land of Canaan. Egyptian influence had begun with Narmer and continued sporadically into the patriarchal era. For much of the New Kingdom (1550–1069 B.C.), Canaan lived in the shadow of Egyptian domination. The Amarna letters date from this time (ca. 1352–1336 B.C.). These small clay tablets reflect the complex relations between various Canaanite rulers and their Egyptian overlords.[8] By about 1135 B.C., during the time of the judges, Egyptian control disappeared from Canaan. This created a political vacuum that was quickly filled by the Philistines, one of the tribes of the Sea Peoples repulsed by Rameses III in the late twelfth century. Egypt briefly reasserted itself during the reign of Solomon's son Rehoboam, when Shishak attacked the kingdoms of Judah and Israel in 926 B.C. Afterwards, Egypt was less influential in the region, although it managed to retain some political and economic ties.

Asia Minor

Asia Minor is occupied today by Turkey. When dealing with Old Testament history, scholars will often refer to Asia Minor by its Greek name, "Anatolia." Asia Minor played less of a role in shaping biblical history than did Mesopotamia and Egypt. Nevertheless, its influence was felt at certain times. One example would be the twin empires

---

[8]The Amarna letters are an archive of 380 cuneiform tablets. They were found in the ruins of Pharaoh Akhenaten's capital in Upper Egypt. The tablets span a period of about thirty years. They were written in Akkadian (the language of Mesopotamia) since this was the diplomatic language of that time. They reveal political and social conditions in the land of Canaan during a time between generally accepted dates for an Early Date or Late Date Exodus and Conquest. Included in these letters are references to the *Habiru*. Some scholars have tried to identify this group with the similar sounding "Hebrews." This, however, remains uncertain.

of the Hurrians and the Hittites. Both reached the peak of their power during the Late Bronze Age (ca. 1550–1200 B.C.). The Hurrians were the first to exert control over eastern Anatolia and northern Aram (ca. 1500–1350 B.C.). Later, the Hittites replaced the Hurrian kingdom of Mitanni as the regional superpower (1425–1180 B.C.). Rivalry for control and influence in Asia eventually culminated in a battle between the Hittites and Rameses II (whom many regard as the pharaoh of a Late Date Exodus). This battle took place at the central Aramean (Syrian) city of Kadesh around 1285 B.C.

The Hurrian empire fell first around 1350 B.C. The Hittite empire collapsed about 150 years later. In both cases, refugees may have spread southward into Canaan. Perhaps biblical Horites and Hivites were people of Hurrian extraction. The Hittites and the Jebusites may have been of Anatolian Hittite origin. Uriah, the first husband of Bathsheba, is described as a Hittite (2 Sam. 11:3).[9]

Canaan: The Hub of a Wheel

When most of us think about biblical history, we go immediately in our minds to a small stretch of land known by a variety of names, including Canaan, Israel, the Holy Land, and Palestine. And it is no small wonder. On this tiny geographic stage, no larger than the State of New Jersey, most events we read about in the Bible took place. That is an amazing amount of history to happen in such a small place! Why is that?

Mediterranean Sea and the Jordan River is about 50 miles (80 km). It is easiest to remember the traditional boundaries of Israel as being 150 x 50 miles (240 x 80 km).

At certain times the borders of Canaan extended farther. In Solomon's day, Israelite control reached south to Elath on the Red Sea and as far north as the Euphrates River in Syria. Also, Israel's boundaries fluctuated from west to east. At times the eastern boundary was located along the Jordan River (an average width of 50 miles or 80 km). At other times it included the western edge of the Transjordanian Plateau, adding another 25 miles (40 km) to the nation's width.

[9]Identifying the ethnic composition of various peoples mentioned in the Bible is difficult and controversial. For example, it is not certain that the Hivites are of Hurrian extraction or that the Hittites are the same people as the Hittites of Anatolia.

Plants and Animals of the Bible

The Jewish sages once remarked, "The land of Israel is at the center of the world, and Jerusalem is at the center of the land of Israel." One pictorial expression of this concept is the Bunting map, drawn about four hundred years ago. It depicts the world like a cloverleaf with Jerusalem at the center. In this way, the city of Jerusalem marks the meeting point between the continents of Europe, Asia, and Africa.

For many plants and animals, though, this map is not imaginary. A wide variety of flora and fauna from these three continents appear in Canaan. Furthermore, some 250 species of birds migrate between Europe and Africa by way of the Holy Land. Storks, for example, make their way south for the winter and retrace their path every spring. The significance of this was not lost on Jeremiah, who used this bird and others to warn Judah: "Even the stork in the sky knows her appointed seasons, and the dove, the swift and the thrush observe the time of their migration. But my people do not know the requirements of the Lord" (see Jer. 8:7).

Regarding plant life, the green trees and shrubs of the Mediterranean zone of southern Europe (oak, pine, carob, and olive) contrast sharply with the sparse, dry Saharo-Arabian zone found in the deserts of Asia (caper, tamarisk, juniper, and date palm). The transition between these two environments is bridged by the prairie of the Irano-Turanian zone (wormwood, lotus, jujube, and sumac). Finally, there are pockets of the African Sudanean zone (acacia, broom, and saxaul). The vegetation of this fourth zone appears mainly in the Sinai (itself a land bridge between Africa and Asia) and along the Jordan Valley as far north as Jericho. Acacia, for instance, is one of the largest trees in Sinai. It also has straight branches that make it useful for construction. The Israelites used acacia to build the ark of the covenant, as well as portions of the tabernacle and its furnishings (Exod. 25 through 26).

A variety of large and small animals also live here. In the Mediterranean zone one can find red fox, deer, gazelle, cony, and jungle cat. Unfortunately, bears and lions were hunted to extinction. In the desert zones one can find the lynx, hyena, leopard, ibex, wolf, bat, sand fox, and various rodents. There are also several varieties of scorpions and poisonous snakes, such as the viper.

Bunting Map

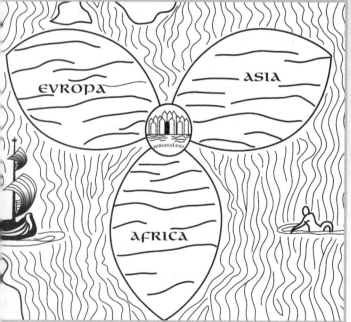

The history of any land and people is largely determined by their geographic setting. Canaan is no exception. Its importance derives mainly from its strategic location at the meeting point of three continents: Europe, Asia, and Africa. Interestingly, this is the same "world map" that appears in the Table of Nations (Gen. 10): Japheth (Europe), Shem (Asia), and Ham (Africa). Although Canaan is geographically a part of Asia, think of it as the hub of a wheel with three radiating spokes. Any movement from one spoke (continent) to another means passing by way of the hub.

As you can imagine, this unique position turned Canaan into an important land bridge in antiquity. That is why biblical geographer James Monson chose to call Palestine "The Land Between."[10] And while some people passed through, others stayed. Understanding this principle may help explain the ethnic diversity found in Canaan. For example, there were "seven nations" that the people of Israel encountered when they entered the land (Deut. 7:1).

Canaan: The Land Between

The connecting link between Egypt, Mesopotamia, and Anatolia was a middle region dominated by the land of Canaan. Some modern scholars call this region the Levant. The original French use of the word *Levant* ("rising," "raising") denoted the entire eastern Mediterranean (from where the sun "rises"). Today it has a more restricted meaning, referring to areas inhabited by the modern nations of Syria, Lebanon, Israel, and Jordan. Unlike the river valley

[10]James M. Monson, *The Land Between: A Regional Study Guide to the Land of the Bible* (Jerusalem: Biblical Backgrounds, 1983).

The Names of Canaan

1. Canaan. The land of Canaan was named after the local inhabitants known as "Canaanites." The name may derive from a word meaning "purple." Some think this relates to the production of a purple dye extracted from the murex shellfish found along the coasts of modern Lebanon and Israel.

2. The Promised Land. The Bible itself never uses the term "Promised Land." But the concept lies behind such passages as God's covenant promised to Abraham in Genesis 15:18–21 and 17:8. The territory promised to Abraham and repeated to his descendants was quite large. It stretched from the Nile River in Egypt northward to the Euphrates River. During the reigns of David and Solomon, the nation-state of Israel reached its greatest geographic extent. Throughout this time, the national boundaries included most of the territory promised to Abraham. It also comprised much of the land east of the Jordan River, even though the promise to Abraham excluded it (see Num. 34:12).

3. Israel. Following the Conquest, the territory occupied by the Israelite tribes came to be known as "Israel" or "the land of Israel" (e.g., Josh. 11:21; 1 Sam. 13:19). This was later the name given to the United Monarchy ruled by David and Solomon. Since biblical times, "the land of Israel" has been kept alive in Jewish tradition as the Hebrew name for the country. For this reason, "Israel" was the name chosen for the modern Jewish state established in 1948.

4. Israel and Judah. After the division of the United Monarchy of David and Solomon in 931 B.C., the northern state was called "Israel" (931–722 B.C.) and the southern state "Judah" (931–586 B.C.). See, for example, 1 Kings 15:25 for "Israel" and 1 Kings 14:21 for "Judah." The expression "house of David" is also used for the southern kingdom of Judah (1 Kings 12:26). The discovery of this same expression in 1993 on an Aramaic inscription from Dan (one of the two cities where King Jeroboam established worship of the golden calf, 1 Kings 12:29) is the only extrabiblical reference that we have to King David.

5. Palestine. The name derives from the Philistines. These were a people of Aegean origin who settled along the southern coast of Canaan and became enemies of the Israelites. In the fifth century B.C., the Greek historian Herodotus called this region "Philistine Syria." After the Bar Kochba Revolt in A.D. 132–135, Emperor Hadrian adopted the name for the entire country. This may have been a deliberate move, intended to humiliate the Jewish people, since their country was now named after their ancient archenemy! By the fourth century A.D. the name was abbreviated to "Palaestina" or Palestine.

6. The Holy Land. The name "Holy Land," popular among Christians, came into use during the Middle Ages. It is based on Zechariah 2:12.

civilizations that possessed continuous supplies of water, the countries of the Levant depended mainly on rainfall. This partly explains why droughts were viewed with such horror (see Deut. 11:13–14; Zech. 10:1).

Canaan occupied a key position in this Levantine land bridge, making it the coveted possession of various nations of the Near East. Such nations saw possessing the area as a way to control trade routes (both land and sea) as well as to oppose nations. Earthen mounds containing the successive remains of towns destroyed and rebuilt one on top of the other ("tells") stand as mute testimony to this strategy – destroyed by invading armies as they passed through.

CANAAN'S MAJOR REGIONS

Canaan is a land of amazing contrasts. The Bible describes it as a place with hills and valleys, springs and streams (Deut. 8:7–11). Statements like this are easy to gloss over while reading, but the geographical realities are quite dramatic. Take, for example, the reference to hills and valleys. Jerusalem sits in the Judean hills at an elevation of about 2,500 feet (760 m) above sea level. The Dead Sea lies in the Jordan Valley at about 1,300 feet (400 m) below sea level. This difference in elevation represents a drop of nearly 4,000 feet (1220 m) over a horizontal distance of only 13 miles (21 km)!

How did the landscape become so varied? Remember that Canaan sits at the meeting point of three continents. These land masses are almost always moving. They push, pull, and slide past one another – resulting in earthquakes, contorted landforms, and volcanic flows. Even to this day earthquakes are not uncommon to this part of the world.

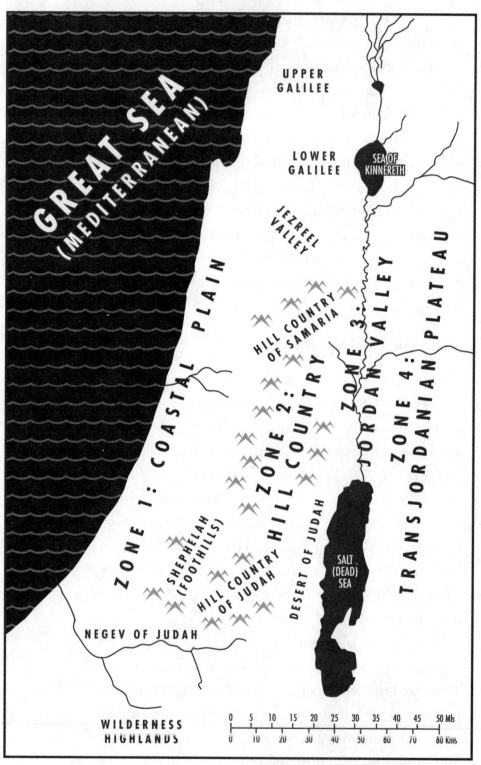

GREAT SEA
(MEDITERRANEAN)

UPPER GALILEE

LOWER GALILEE

SEA OF KINNERETH

JEZREEL VALLEY

ZONE 1: COASTAL PLAIN

HILL COUNTRY OF SAMARIA

ZONE 2: HILL COUNTRY

ZONE 3: JORDAN VALLEY

ZONE 4: TRANSJORDANIAN PLATEAU

SHEPHELAH (FOOTHILLS)

HILL COUNTRY OF JUDAH

DESERT OF JUDAH

SALT (DEAD) SEA

NEGEV OF JUDAH

WILDERNESS HIGHLANDS

| 0 | 5 | 10 | 15 | 20 | 25 | 30 | 35 | 40 | 45 | 50 Mls |
| 0 | 10 | 20 | 30 | 40 | 50 | 60 | 70 | 80 Kms |

The Four North-South Zones of Canaan

In antiquity, they could be devastating (e.g., Amos 1:1; Zech. 14:4–5).

Given its tremendous geographic variety, Canaan can be legitimately divided in several different ways. One option is four north-south zones, with zone 1 bordering the Mediterranean Sea and zone 4 at its eastern frontier.

1. Coastal Plain
2. Hill Country
3. Jordan Valley
4. Transjordanian Plateau

The Climate of Canaan

Rainfall is another example of contrast in this region. The location of Canaan between the sea and the desert means that westerly winds off the Mediterranean bring cold winter rains that generally fall between October and April (1 Kings 18:43–45). By contrast, the deserts to the east bring hot, dry summer winds (Isa. 27:8; Hos. 13:15).

The amount of rain that falls depends partly on the topography and elevation of a given area. Two additional factors are how far north and how far from the sea the area is. In the hills, Jerusalem receives 14–28 inches (350–700 mm) a year; near the Dead Sea, less than 4 inches (100 mm) a year.

This dramatic difference in climate determined where and how people lived in biblical times. Most lived in the better-watered regions to the west and north. Most Canaanites and Israelites were simple farmers who lived in small villages located in the vicinity of larger walled towns that sometimes served as administrative centers, for example, Hazor, Megiddo, Shechem, Gezer, and Beersheba. In the drier regions to the east and south there were few permanent settlements. The hostile climate there made these areas more conducive to small bands of people living in tents or caves. Such people are generally classified as nomadic. This means they moved their tents according to the need for pasture. They also depended more upon sheep and goats for a livelihood than upon farming. Based upon what we read in Genesis, this is the lifestyle that Abraham knew. Later, the Israelites were forced to adopt a similar life while wandering in the wilderness for forty years. Like the tents of the nomads, the tabernacle God dwelt in was also made of goat hair (Exod. 26:7). The Midianites, Ishmaelites, and Amalekites would be examples of a nomadic or pastoral people.

Roads of Canaan

A fragmented geography tends to promote regionalism and division. A road network, on the other hand, provides an opportunity for political and economic unity. In biblical times there were three types of roads: international highways, local roads, and local trails. All three were usually designated in the Bible by the Hebrew expression *derekh l'* . . . ("the way to . . ."). Exod. 13:17, for example, mentions "the way to the land of the Philistines" (author's translation).

There were six key routes in Canaan. The four most important north-south ones correspond with the four main north-south regions of Canaan. The two east-west valleys of the Jezreel and the Negev of Judah cut across these longitudinal regions to create natural communication lines between the coast and inland parts of the country. It should not be surprising, then, that some of the most important biblical towns were located at the strategic junctures of these arteries or along them. In general, the lines of communication tended to follow the valleys, less difficult mountain passes, and, in the case of Judah, the easier to follow mountain ridges.

1. Along the southern part of the coastal plain passed the International Trunk Road. This is the highway that linked Egypt with Syria and Mesopotamia.[11] It is also the route that followed the arc of the Fertile Crescent. This road turned inland at Mount Carmel and passed on to the Sea of Galilee by way of Megiddo. This helps explain the historical importance of Megiddo, since the town sat at the junction of the International Trunk Road and the route through the Valley of Jezreel.

2. The second north-south route was a local highway. It passed along the mountain spine or watershed line of the hill country of Samaria and Judah. This route has been popularly called the Route of the Patriarchs, because it is the only natural route linking towns associated with the patriarchs, for example, Shechem, Bethel, Jerusalem, Hebron, and Beersheba.

3. Despite its hot and dry climate, the Jordan Valley also had local highways linking towns between Elath on the Red Sea and points farther north in Syria. On the west side of the Jordan Valley these sites included En Gedi, Jericho, Beth Shan, Kinnereth, Hazor, and Abel Beth Maacah.

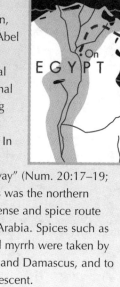

4. The fourth and final route was an international highway. It passed along the western edge of the Transjordanian Plateau. In the Bible, this route is called the "king's highway" (Num. 20:17–19; 21:22). Historically, this was the northern extension of an old incense and spice route that began in southern Arabia. Spices such as frankincense, balm, and myrrh were taken by camel caravan to Egypt and Damascus, and to the rest of the Fertile Crescent.

[11]This highway is often called *Via Maris,* a Latin expression meaning "way of the sea," based on Isa. 9:1. The prophet Isaiah, though, is probably referring to another road. Therefore, it is better to call this route the International Coastal Highway (or International Trunk Road).

ZONE 1: COASTAL PLAIN

The Coastal Plain is a narrow strip of land 140 miles (230 km) long. It is delimited in the north by the Ladder of Tyre (the present border between Israel and Lebanon at Rosh Haniqra) and in the south by Wadi el-Arish (called the "river of Egypt" in Gen. 15:18).[12] The plain begins narrow

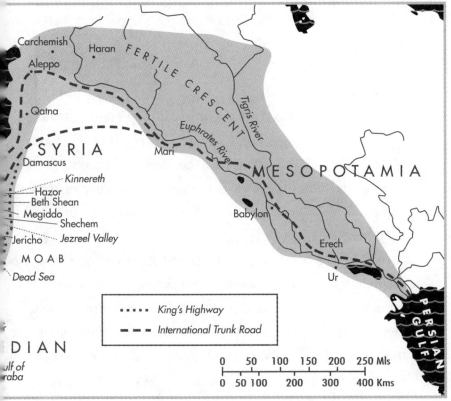

Roads of Canaan

[12]The name "Ladder of Tyre" was introduced by the Crusaders. It is an apt term since the shoreline between Tyre and Rosh Haniqra is stepped, with Tyre at the top of the geographical staircase. *"Wadi"* is Arabic for a dry riverbed that usually has water in it during the winter months when there is rainfall runoff (see Job 6:15–17). However, some wadis have perennial streams running through them as in the case of the Jabbok and Arnon gorges in the modern state of Jordan (see the section on the Transjordanian Plateau). In North America, such a ravine is sometimes called an "arroyo," though "wadi" has since been incorporated into English. Given its intermittent and varied character, one should not be surprised to find the word "wadi" (Heb. *nachal)* rendered as "brook," "stream," "ravine," "gorge," and "valley" in different verses of the same translation of an English version of the Bible.

and flat in the north (3 mi/5 km across) but grows wider and hillier towards the south (25 mi/40 km across at Gaza).

The flow of the Coastal Plain is interrupted at only one point: where the headland of Mount Carmel juts into the Mediterranean Sea. In biblical times, it served as a boundary separating Phoenicia to the north from Israel to the south. Thus, Elijah's choice of this site for the showdown between the God of Israel and Baal – the god of Phoenicia – makes good sense (1 Kings 18:20–40).

The Coastal Plain can be divided into five subregions. North of Mount Carmel are the plains of (1) Asher and (2) Acco, which belonged to Phoenicia during much of the Iron Age. South of Mount Carmel lie the plains of (3) Dor, (4) Sharon, and (5) Philistia. The border between the Sharon and Philistia plains is marked by the flow of the Yarkon River, whose waters originate in abundant springs at Aphek.

According to the Bible, the Philistines had five chief cities. Three of them (Gaza, Ashkelon, and Ashdod) were situated on or near the coast and were connected to maritime trade. Two (Gath and Ekron) were located at the eastern edge of the plain and were involved with agricultural activity. It was from Gaza that Samson carried the city gates on his shoulders 60 miles (95 km) east to a hill near Hebron (Judg. 16:1–3). And it is from Gath that Goliath came to fight the Israelites in the Valley of Elah (1 Sam. 17:2–4).

ZONE 2: HILL COUNTRY

The second north-south zone is composed of a line of hills extending from Phoenicia (Lebanon) to the Red Sea. Two east-west valleys (the Valley of Jezreel in the north and the Negev of Judah in the south) cut this range into three mountainous blocks: (1) the hills of Galilee, (2) the hills of Samaria and Judah, and (3) the Wilderness Highlands. Both east-west valleys are offshoots of the massive faulting that formed the Jordan Valley. These valleys were important because they linked the Coastal Plain in the west to trade routes in the Jordan Valley and Transjordanian Plateau in the east.

Northern Block: The Hills of Galilee. The origin of the Hebrew word for Galilee is obscure, but it may mean "district" or "region." Some think that the name originated as part of a longer phrase. For example, *galil* appears as part of the expression "all the regions [gᵉliloth] of the Philistines and Geshurites" (Josh. 13:2). In light of this understanding, one way of translating "Galilee of the Gentiles" in Isaiah 9:1 is "the region of the Gentiles."

The Galilean hills rise in two steps from the Valley of Jezreel. The first step is called Lower Galilee, where the rolling hills are generally 2,000 feet (610 m) or lower. The second step (north of the fault line of the Beth Hakkerem Valley) is Upper Galilee, where the elevations are 3,000 feet (915 m) and higher. Lower Galilee is geographically open, with east-west mountain ridges and broad valleys that connect the Plain of Acco with the Sea of Galilee. At one time roads passed through these valleys. By contrast, Upper Galilee is more closed and isolated. It was also less populated in antiquity.

Middle Block: The Hills of Samaria and Judah. The middle group of hills is bounded by the Valley of Jezreel in the north and the Negev in the south. This area is often called the Central Hill Country or the Hills of Samaria and Judah. The latter designation reflects the political circumstances following the division of David and Solomon's kingdom in 931 B.C. The Samaria hills to the north formed the heartland of the northern kingdom of Israel with its capital at Samaria. The Judean hills to the south formed the core of the southern kingdom of Judah with its capital at Jerusalem. While the hills of Galilee were under the control of Israel, much of the Wilderness Highlands were under the control of Judah.

The Samaria hills are more open, with valleys and roads approaching its strategic heart at Shechem from various directions. This may have partially motivated Jeroboam I to choose Shechem as his capital in 931 B.C. (1 Kings 12:25). Later, the capital shifted to Tirzah (1 Kings 15:33) at the head of Wadi *Farah*. Wadi *Farah* was the main route linking Israelites living west of the Jordan Valley with their brethren in the mountains of Gilead to the east (Deut. 3:13). The final capital of the Northern Kingdom was built by Omri at Samaria (1 Kings 16:24). This may have been related to his desire to locate himself nearer to the maritime coastal plain and to develop closer ties with Phoenicia.

These geographical realities made the Northern Kingdom more vulnerable to outside influence. The reign of Ahab and Jezebel, for example, brought negative influence in the form of Phoenician religion and culture. The openness of this region also made Samaria difficult territory for any centralized body to rule. This was especially true since the Northern Kingdom included Gilead east of the Jordan. Therefore, any king ruling in the north had to balance and satisfy a wide range of competing interests from both sides of the Jordan River.

In contrast to the open nature of Samaria, Judah is more uplifted, compact, and closed. Access was difficult. A single north-south road (part of the traditional Route of the Patriarchs) ran along the central spine or watershed line of the Judean hills. And fewer than a dozen east-west roads existed. These conditions did not provide Judah with much incentive to link up with the cosmopolitan coast. The dry Judean Desert and the natural barrier of the Dead Sea to the east also contributed to Judah's tendency to remain isolated and provincial.

The Hill Country of Judah can be divided into four subregions: The (1) uplifted Judean hills are in the middle. To the west lie the (2) Shephelah, or foothills. The (3) Desert of Judah lies to the east and the (4) Negev of Judah to the south.[13]

Of these four regions, the Shephelah to the west was the most vulnerable since it lay close to the heavily traveled coastal plain. Therefore, the low hills of the Shephelah functioned militarily as a buffer zone to help safeguard the heartland of Judah from invasion. One illustration of this principle is the battle of David and Goliath (1 Sam. 17). In a bid to keep the Philistines from approaching the Judean hills, the Israelites met them in the Shephelah. By stopping Goliath in the Valley of Elah, young David won a strategic victory as well as a moral victory for Israel.

Southern Block: The Wilderness Highlands. The Wilderness comprises the third and southernmost block of hills. In modern Israel, this region is considered part of the Negev. In the Bible, however, the Negev was limited to the

---

[13]The Heb. word usually rendered "wilderness" in the OT is *midbar*. Keep in mind, however, that when the OT uses this term, it is mainly referring to desert or steppe land and not the forested wilderness that one finds in North America. For this reason, some translations will render *midbar* as "desert" rather than "wilderness." The term *negev* is also potentially confusing since it has a dual meaning in Heb. The root of the word has to do with something

The Spelling of Biblical Names

English translations of the Hebrew Bible will spell words in any number of ways. The NIV has "Negev" for the Beersheba valley while the RSV renders it "Negeb." In Hebrew, if the letter "beyt" with a *b* sound does not occur at the beginning of a word or syllable, it has a *v* sound. Therefore, the RSV has spelled "Negeb"

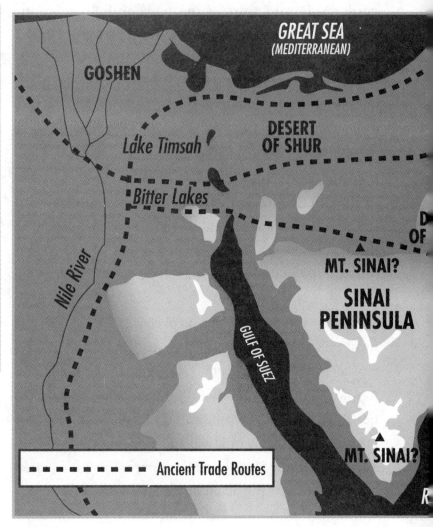

Ancient Trade Routes

east-west valley where Beersheba was located.

The Wilderness Highlands are comprised of two parts. Both were areas that the Israelites wandered in after the exodus. To the north is the Desert of Sin, where Israel expe-

that is "dry" or "parched." Since the Beersheba valley to the south of the Judean hills is dry, *negev* also took on the meaning of "south" or "southward" (see Gen. 13:1,3, KJV).

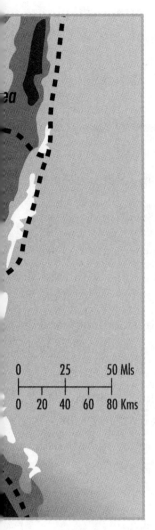

0   25   50 Mls

0   20   40   60   80 Kms

rienced the miracle of the manna and quail (Exod. 16). To the south lies the Desert of Paran (Num. 12:16). The apparent meeting point of these two regions was Kadesh Barnea (Num. 13:26; 20:1).

The Sinai Peninsula. The Sinai Peninsula is part of the same great desert expanse where the people of Israel wandered for forty years. The desolate and extreme character of the Sinai signifies a place without security or resources. Perhaps this is why it is the setting of Israel's early history, a sort of spiritual boot camp where the people of Israel were challenged to trust in God for all of their needs, spiritual as well as physical.

The Sinai Peninsula has a roughly triangular shape. It looks something like the tip of a giant dagger jabbed into the Red Sea, separating the continents of Africa and Asia. The Sinai is comprised of three main parts: In the north are low mounds of white sand dunes. In the center is the relatively flat region of the al-Tih Plateau. In the south are tall granite mountains. There, the elevations can reach well over 8,000 feet (2,440 m). This is the area of the traditional Mount Sinai.

The Bible presents us with a lot of geographic data on the wilderness wanderings, but we are unable to identify most places with any certainty. The main reason for this is a lack of continuity among those living in the desert; people do not settle down and build cities in the desert.

according to its actual transliteration value, while the NIV has rendered it according to how the letter would be pronounced when it is at the end of a word. Another example of this phenomenon is the spelling of the Sea of Galilee. In Hebrew, this word is *Kinnereth*. When the first letter appears at the beginning of a word or a syllable, it has a hard *k* sound. Otherwise, it has a *ch* sound not found in the English language, but represented in the German pronunciation of "Bach" or the Scottish "Loch." In this case, the NIV spells "Kinnereth" according to its sound value (a hard *k* since it is at the beginning of a word), while the NKJV renders it according to its transliteration value, usually regarded by scholars as *ch*. Different ideas by scholars on how to transliterate sound values not normally present in English is one of the main reasons for spelling variations between different translations of the Bible.

Without such continuity, the location of ancient place names is often forgotten. This makes it nearly impossible to identify such important landmarks as Mount Sinai with any certainty. Moreover, the virtual absence of archaeological remains from the Late Bronze Age (even those left by nomads) adds to this difficulty. It's only since the fourth century A.D. that Christian tradition has identified Mount Sinai with Jebel Musa (Mount Moses) in southern Sinai. And of course there are other possible locations as well.

The sites that can be identified tend to be those at the beginning and end of the wilderness journey, areas where populations had greater permanence. We can also understand why "God did not lead them on the road through the Philistine country," a route that passed along the sand dunes of northern Sinai (Exod. 13:17). Recent archaeology has shown that during the Ramesside era of the Nineteenth Dynasty this highway was guarded by Egyptian forts. Had the Israelites used this route, they would have encountered Egyptian opposition. Thus, they turned south and crossed the Red Sea[14] into Sinai.

ZONE 3: JORDAN VALLEY

The Jordan Valley is the northern portion of one of the largest visible tears in the earth's crust. Geologists call this kind of tear a rift. Rifts are formed when the earth's forces cause parallel cracks to develop at a certain distance apart. Afterwards, the middle part drops slowly over time, forming a deep trough-like valley. The Jordan Valley, though, is only one small segment of a more extensive system that geologists call the Syro-African Rift. Altogether it stretches

[14]The "Red Sea" in Exod. 13:18 translates the Heb. *yam suph,* "Reed Sea." See chap. 6 for a discussion of this term.

about 4,000 miles (6,400 km) from the Turkish-Syrian border to central East Africa. The deepest point of the rift is at the Dead Sea, approximately 1,300 feet (400 m) below sea level. At that point the trough is about 10 miles (16 km)

Jordan Valley

wide. From the Dead Sea, the Syro-African rift continues south into the Red Sea where it then splits into two branches: The eastern leg goes around the Saudi Arabian peninsula and up the Persian Gulf. The western branch enters Africa at Ethiopia and continues south to Mozambique.

There are five main parts to the Jordan Valley, the portion of the Syro-African Rift that passes through Israel proper: (1) the Upper Jordan, or Huleh basin, (2) the Sea of Galilee, (3) the Lower Jordan Valley, (4) the Dead Sea, and (5) the Arabah. Let us look more closely at three of these five regions.

The Sea of Kinnereth (Galilee). The body of water that the Gospels identify as the Sea of Galilee is called the Sea of Kinnereth in the Hebrew Bible (Num. 34:11; Josh. 12:3; 13:27). According to tradition, this name derives from the shape of the lake, since a *kinnereth* appears to be a kind of harp. The Sea of Galilee is known by other names as well. The Gospel of John calls it the Sea of Tiberias (6:1; 21:1) after the principal city on its western side. Luke calls it the Lake of Gennesaret (Luke 5:1) after the prominent plain on its northwestern shore.

The lake is filled at the northern end by the Upper Jordan River, which has its origin in springs and snow runoff from Mount Hermon. The lake measures 13 miles (21 km) long by 7 miles (11 km) wide at its broadest point. The surface of the lake is 690 feet (210 m) below sea level, making it the lowest fresh water lake on the earth.

The Lower Jordan Valley. Between the Sea of Galilee and the Dead Sea is the 65-mile-long (or 105 km) Lower Jordan Valley. The Jordan River leaves the southern end of the Sea of Galilee to fill the Dead Sea at its northern end. Due to its winding course, the Jordan River is about twice the length of the Lower Jordan Valley itself.[15]

The Dead Sea. At about 1,300 feet (400 m) below sea level, the Dead Sea is the lowest point on the face of the earth. Today the lake averages 50 miles (80 km) long by 10 miles (16 km) wide. The salt concentration is 25–30 percent

[15]The river's width, and especially its flow, was greater in biblical times than it is today. It has been substantially reduced by the agriculture of the modern states of Israel and Jordan. As a result, the Dead Sea is also shrinking.

compared to 4–6 percent for seawater. Since marine life cannot live in it, the Greeks called it the Dead Sea, the name commonly used today in English. However, in the Bible it is called the Salt Sea (Gen. 14:3; Deut. 3:17; Josh 15:5), the Sea of the Arabah (Deut. 3:17; Josh. 3:16; 2 Kings 14:25), and the "eastern sea" (Ezek. 47:18; Joel 2:20; Zech. 14:8). The salts found in the Dead Sea come from mineral springs that originate deep in the earth. These springs break forth along the shoreline as well as below the lake. They were opened when the Rift Valley was being formed and enrich the water with minerals such as sulfur, potassium, and magnesium. The presence of these minerals and the high level of evaporation from the hot, arid environment are responsible for the high salt concentration and putrid smell. The prophet Ezekiel, however, foresaw a time when the waters of the Dead Sea would be healed and contain life (47:6–12).

ZONE 4: TRANSJORDANIAN PLATEAU

Transjordan ("across the Jordan") is primarily a plateau. Although the western edge is well watered and fertile, the strip of arable land is no more than 25 miles (40 km) wide. As you travel further east, the rich soils and green fields give way to desert.

The plateau is cut through at several points by deep ravines. A few have streams running through them year-round. Most, however, are like the Wadi el-Arish described above – dry river beds containing water only during the winter months. Similar ravines can be found on the western side of the rift as well.

The four main wadis of Transjordan from north to south are the Yarmuk, Jabbok, Arnon, and Zered. The

Jabbok is especially notable. Jacob wrestled with an angel after crossing "the ford of the Jabbok" (Gen. 32:22–32).

Transjordan can be divided into five major regions: (1) Bashan, (2) the Hill Country of Gilead, (3) Ammon, (4) Moab, and (5) Edom. The name Bashan (Amos 4:1) comes from a Hebrew word meaning "fruitful." This is the area known today as the Golan Heights. It extends from Mount Hermon to the Yarmuk River. The second region is the Hill Country of Gilead. It begins at the Yarmuk River and extends southward to a point near the north shore of the Dead Sea. The Jabbok Ravine cuts right through the middle of these hills. The mountains of Gilead lying north of the Jabbok were given to the tribe of Manasseh, while the territory south of it belonged to Gad (Num. 32:39–42; Deut. 3:12–17).

The Ammonites inhabited the region around their capital at Rabbah (present-day Amman). All of the 50-mile (80 km) stretch of territory east of the Dead Sea was claimed by Moab. Like Gilead to the north, Moab was also bisected by a river. In this case, it was the Arnon Gorge. North of the Arnon is a flat region known as the Mishor ("tableland"). This was allotted to Reuben and Gad (Deut. 3:12) and became a point of sharp dispute between Moab and the people of Israel.[16] South of the Arnon, as far south as the Zered Ravine, was the heartland of Moab. After one crosses the Zered, the geology begins to change from limestone to a pre-

---

[16]The best evidence for hostilities between Moab and the Israelites comes from the Mesha Stele, a slab of stone with thirty-nine lines of Moabite writing on it. The stele, dated to around 850 B.C., was found by a missionary at Dhiban (biblical Dibon) Transjordan in 1868. Through it we learn that Omri, the northern Israelite king and father of Ahab, had formerly subdued Moab and exacted tribute from its king (cf. 2 Kings 1:1; 3:4–5). The stele goes on to tell us that after King Ahab died, Mesha, king of Moab, rebelled against Israel. As expected, this required Ahab's son Jehoram to confront the revolt.

dominance of red sandstone. All of this mountainous terrain from the Zered to the Red Sea belonged to Edom.[17]

The Contribution of Archaeology

Archaeology uses material culture (items that people built and produced) to study peoples of the past and how they lived. As one can imagine, this holds great potential for biblical research. As a modern pursuit, Near Eastern archaeology (the branch of archaeology that deals with the biblical world) is only about 150 years old. It began with interested individuals looking for biblical cities such as Ur and Nineveh. One landmark in the archaeology of the Holy Land came with the explorations of Edward Robinson and Eli Smith in 1838 and 1852. As a result of their scholarly expertise, they were able to identify more than one hundred biblical sites whose locations had been forgotten. They could do this because the original Hebrew names had been preserved in the modern Arabic names.

Once biblical sites were identified, archaeologists could begin excavating them. Sir Flinders Petrie was one such archaeologist. In 1890, Petrie became the first to realize that tells, which often look like cake-shaped mounds, contained the ruins of ancient towns built one on top of the other.[18]

---

[17]*Edom* in Hebrew and related languages has the connotation of "red." Indeed, this area of southern Jordan south of the Zered Ravine is rich in red sandstone. The famous rose-red city of Petra of Nabatean times (ca. 200 B.C.–A.D. 100), featured in the hit film *Indiana Jones and the Last Crusade,* is located within the territory of Edom. Another name for Edom, "Mount Seir" ("hairy one"; see Deut. 1:2 et al.), seems to allude to scrub oak forests that once covered the region.

[18]The Arabic *tell* and Hebrew *tel* have their origin in the Akkadian word *tillu,* meaning "ruin heap." One occurrence of the Heb. *tel* in the Bible comes from Josh. 8:28: "So Joshua burned Ai and made it a heap of ruins *[tel],* a desolate place to this day."

Petrie also recognized that pottery styles typical to each occupation layer of a tell changed through time and could be used for dating purposes.

Another pioneer in the field was the American biblical scholar William Foxwell Albright. At the time he began his career in 1922, several scholars questioned the historical accuracy of events recorded in the Bible. Albright tried to show how archaeology could help authenticate Israel's ancient traditions by its excavated remains and an ever-growing body of written sources. For example, the Mesha Stele (or Moabite Stone) had been found fifty-four years earlier. This black slab of stone with Moabite writing on it mentions Omri (the father of King Ahab) and Mesha (the Moabite ruler) by name (see 1 Kings 16:23–28; 2 Kings 3:4). Reference was also made earlier to the "house of David" inscription found at Tel Dan in 1993. The three broken fragments that had once made up a larger stone slab with writing on it mention the outcome of a battle that involved the Aramean ruler Ben-Hadad, Jehoram king of Israel, and Ahaziah king of the house of David (an alternate name for the southern kingdom of Judah [cf. 2 Kings 8:28]). The stele is best dated about 840 B.C.

Another similar discovery, the Merneptah Stele (or Israel Stele) in 1896, detailed the triumph of Pharaoh Merneptah, the son of Rameses II, over three Canaanite cities (Ashkelon, Gezer, and Yanoam) and a people called "Israel." Dating to around 1207 B.C., this is still the earliest reference to Israel outside the Bible. Assyrian and Babylonian monuments and annals from the era of the Divided Monarchy (931–586 B.C.) also mention Israelite and Judean kings by name. These include Jehu, Ahaz, Hezekiah, and Manasseh. Under the weight of such evidence, it became increasingly difficult for scholars to pass the Bible off as legend.

One weakness to Albright's approach, however, was that he tended to oversimplify the complexities of history by looking to archaeology as a panacea for all the historical problems of the Bible. But time is a good teacher. Since then we have learned that archaeology has limitations. Sometimes they prevent us from getting answers to our questions. These include verifying the historicity of any biblical personage or event prior to the mention of Israel in the Merneptah Stele. For example, no archaeologist has yet produced evidence for the existence of Abraham, or proved that there was an exodus from Egypt followed by forty years of wandering in the wilderness, or pointed to the fallen brick walls of Jericho. Despite the discomfort that this might engender in the heart of the faithful Christian, none of this needs to shake our faith. It does show, however, that archaeology is a long way from "proving" the Bible in the way that most people think about proof.

On the other hand, archaeology has made an important contribution that is often overlooked. Since it is a discipline that documents how people lived, archaeology provides a human dimension to the theological enterprise. Archaeology gives us a clearer understanding of the world in which the Bible was written and shaped. It helps us know how the people of that time saw the world, rather than how we *think* they saw it. In this way, we are better equipped to interpret the Bible in a responsible manner.

What Have We Learned?

This completes our tour of the Ancient Near East. Hopefully you now have a geographical context for your developing knowledge of biblical history. I also hope that you have begun to realize that biblical history is not just facts and figures. It is the record of God's conversations with historical men and women in real places and at given times. Our biblical predecessors in the faith were individuals who shared many of our hopes, dreams, and fears. Perhaps, then, in the following chapters, you can come to view yourself in perspective—beholding your image in the mirror of the biblical world.

Study Questions

1. What is it about the physical location of Canaan that made it so important historically?

2. Why did travel and trade between Asia and Africa occur mainly along the corridor of the Fertile Crescent?

3. What factors contributed to the rise of civilization in the river valleys of Mesopotamia and Egypt?

4. What were some of the key nations surrounding Canaan? What influence did they have on the development of biblical history?

5. What main factors are responsible for the climate in Canaan?

6. What are the four main north-south zones of Canaan? What is the significance of the two east-west valleys that cut across the second longitudinal zone of the hill country?

7. Why did Elijah choose Mount Carmel as the place for a showdown between Yahweh of Israel and the gods of Phoenicia?

8. What is the military or strategic significance of the

Shephelah (foothills) of Judah? Why did Israel oppose Philistia here? How did this contribute to young David's popularity?

9. Explain the phenomenon of a rift. How is the Jordan Valley a rift?

10. Does archaeology prove the Bible? What contributions can archaeology make to the study of Scripture?

For Further Reading

Aharoni, Yohanan. *The Land of the Bible: A Historical Geography.* Edited by A. F. Rainey. Rev. ed. Philadelphia: Westminster Press, 1979. This book is a must for any serious student of the Bible. It is a translation from Heb. by historical geographer Anson F. Rainey. The discipline of historical geography represents the synthesis of biblical history, extrabiblical history and documents, archaeology, and geography.

Baly, Denis. *Basic Biblical Geography.* Philadelphia: Fortress Press, 1987. Without question, Baly is the acknowledged expert on biblical geography. This book is a brief presentation of his more complete work, *The Geography of the Bible,* rev. ed. (New York: Harper & Row, 1974).

Hallo, W. W., and W. K. Simpson. *The Ancient Near East: A History.* New York: Harcourt Brace Jovanovich, 1971. A good general introduction to the Ancient Near East, especially Egypt and Mesopotamia.

Millard, Alan. *Treasures from Bible Times.* Belleville, Mich.: Lion Publishing, 1985. A popular overview of some of the more famous archaeological discoveries of the past 150 years.

Smith, George Adam. *Historical Geography of the Holy Land.* London and Glasgow: Fontana Library of Theology and Philosophy, 1966. The book is not easy to get and it is dated. But Smith was a master of the literary art, and he writes in a way that is both engaging and informative.

5

Robert Stallman

A Wandering Aramean

Terms:

covenant
election
firstborn
Habiru
hospitality
Hyksos
Pharaoh

The World of the Patriarchs: The Middle Bronze Age (ca. 2000–1500 B.C.)

It may seem difficult to imagine, but by the time of Abraham the civilized world was already about a thousand years old.[1] The glories of the Sumerian Early Dynastic Age (ca. 2900–2350 B.C.) lay in the dust, as did the remains of the Old Akkadian Empire (ca. 2371–2255 B.C.). A barbaric tribal people, the Guti,[2] had invaded from the north, but held power for only a century or so. The dark age they brought was relieved by the Sumerian renaissance known as the Ur III period (2113–2006 B.C.). In Egypt, at the other end of the Fertile Crescent, the Great Pyramids of Giza stood as monuments to the strength and sophistication of the Old Kingdom (ca. 2700–2160 B.C.). Canaan lay on the land bridge between the ends of the Fertile Crescent. For this period, little is known of Canaan. The Canaanites who lived there built the fortress-cities of Megiddo, Beth-Shan, Jericho, and Lachish. War, however, had taken its toll; all of them had been destroyed. Across Mesopotamia and spilling into Canaan, nomadic invaders known as Amorites were striking at the foundations of civilized society.[3]

Abraham's ancestors knew a world that had developed forms of literature, art, mathematics, medicine, government, agriculture, and religion. But it was also a world

---

[1] Determining the chronological location of the patriarchs in history is far from simple. In any case, the data presently available is not complete enough to fix any date with much precision. See the appendix "Where Do the Patriarchs Fit in the Past?" for a more detailed discussion of this issue.

[2] See *CAH*, vol. 1, part 2, 454–63. Dates for Egypt are taken from K. A. Kitchen, "Egypt, History of (Chronology)," in *ABD*, 2:321–31.

[3] John Bright considers the appropriateness of the term "Amorites" in *A History of Israel*, 3d ed. (Philadelphia: Westminster, 1981), 44, n. 44.

familiar with the horror of war and the upheaval of society. The Genesis account begins with Abraham at home in Mesopotamia, but he soon moved to Canaan. Eventually his descendants ended up in Egypt. Understanding these three regions will make it easier to picture the events narrated in the Bible.

Mesopotamia

Abraham was one of three sons born to Terah who lived in "Ur of the Chaldeans"[4] (Gen. 11:28). Some time after Abraham married Sarah, Terah moved the family six hundred miles north to the city of Haran (see sidebar and map "Following Abraham" in chap. 4). That city later became the staging point for Abraham's famous journey to Canaan. So for the first seventy-five years of his life, Abraham lived in the culture of Mesopotamia. He was an urban man and would have been familiar with the language and literature of the day.[5] Sumerian and Akkadian texts from this period reveal the economic and political landscape. They also describe the prevailing religious ideas. People believed in many gods that represented various aspects of nature. Supposedly the gods lived in their own "society" headed by the most powerful god of all, Enlil, who eventually was replaced by Marduk, the god of Babylon. In both Ur and Haran, however, people wor-

[4]There is some doubt among scholars regarding this location, since the LXX is more general and reads "the region of the Chaldeans." Cyrus Gordon locates Ur much farther north, closer to Haran ("Abraham and Ur," in *Hebrew and Semitic Studies,* ed. D. Winton Thomas and W. D. McHardy [Oxford: Clarendon, 1963], 77–84).

[5]For a detailed overview of the literary background of this period, see John H. Walton, *Ancient Israelite Literature in its Cultural Context* (Grand Rapids: Zondervan Publishing House, 1989).

shiped the moon god Sin.[6] Why Terah decided to leave Ur is uncertain. He may have been influenced by the instability of the times.

Western Asia: Aram and Canaan

God's call to Abraham to leave Haran pointed him to the "land of Canaan" (Gen. 12:5). In the Old Testament period the land between Mesopotamia and Canaan was called Aram. Canaan lay to the west and south of Aram. Aram and Canaan were bounded on the west by the Mediterranean Sea and on the east by the desert. North of Aram, the Fertile Crescent stretched to Mesopotamia. Southwest of Canaan was Egypt. Geographically the area is quite diverse: Along the coastline, fertile plains give way to a ridge of mountains and hills that run roughly north and south. To the east lies the Great Rift, a valley that holds the Jordan River. At the end of the Jordan is the Dead Sea, one of the driest and most barren places on earth. Further east, the landscape rises again to mountains that form the edge of the Arabian desert. Several major trade routes ran through the area, bringing the possibility of trade and cultural diversity. They also provided routes for the great armies of the superpowers to the north and south. In general, the whole region was a melting pot, rightly described as the land of the "Hittites, Girgashites, Amorites, Canaanites, Perizzites, Hivites and Jebusites" (Deut. 7:1).

There are rich data available for understanding the surrounding cultures. Except for the Ebla tablets, however, Canaan and Aram have yielded few texts outside the Bible

---

[6]This is his Akkadian name; in Sumerian he was called Nanna. Note Josh. 24:2, "'Long ago your forefathers, including Terah the father of Abraham and Nahor, lived beyond the River and worshiped other gods.'"

for this period.[7] This leaves scholars with the difficult task of reconstructing history based on artifacts unearthed by archaeologists. Results gained this way are by nature tentative and rather general. What seems fairly certain from these remains is that during the Middle Bronze Age (ca. 2000–1500 B.C.) there was a gradual influx of people from outside the region. Bible scholars label them with the broad term "Amorites."[8] The newcomers rebuilt cities and the seminomadic people of the land became more settled. Abraham and his descendants lived in the central highlands of Canaan and the areas immediately to the south. These regions were less densely populated and provided ample pasturelands.

Egypt

From the unification of Upper and Lower Egypt (ca. 3000–2700 B.C.), until the Greek invasion of Alexander the Great (332 B.C.), Egypt enjoyed a relatively stable existence. During the Middle Kingdom period (ca. 2106–1759 B.C.),

[7]About 150 miles southwest of Haran lies the ancient city of Ebla where about eight thousand clay tablets were found in 1975. Most of them are administrative texts, but some reveal more of the history, religion, and culture of the area. Preliminary studies suggested that this data would be highly relevant to biblical studies, a claim which now appears exaggerated. The finds so far date to 2400–2250 B.C., but excavations continue and may yield more information from the patriarchal period. See Robert D. Riggs, "Ebla Texts," in *ABD*, 2:263–70.

[8]The "Amorite hypothesis" maintains that there was a large migration of people southward into Canaan who came to dominate the region with a distinct culture. Evidence for the theory rests on a new style of pottery that appeared in Canaan about 2000 B.C. and the similarity of names in Canaan with those of the Amorites from Mesopotamia. This change is what separates Middle Bronze Age I (2000–1800 B.C.) from Middle Bronze Age II (1800–1650 B.C.). Though questioned by some (William Sanford LaSor, David Allan Hubbard, and Frederic Wm. Bush, *Old Testament Survey: The Message, Form and Background of the Old Testament*, 2d ed. [Grand Rapids: Wm. B. Eerdmans,

The Bristlecone Pine, Abraham, and Me

I remember a vacation in my childhood when our family spent a week in the high desert of southeastern California. The White Mountains there are home to the oldest living thing known to exist on the planet: the bristlecone pine tree. Considered by some to be the most ancient species, one tree is over 4,600 years old. Named after the oldest person in the Bible, it is called Methuselah. Standing in the presence of these "patriarchs" of the plant kingdom was (quite

Egypt experienced a high level of cultural development. It maintained loose political control over Canaan where the patriarchs lived. Egypt was wealthy and strong. Its prosperity resulted in numerous building projects. The period witnessed the expansion of knowledge in math and medicine. Works of literature flourished. When faced with famine at home, Abraham went to Egypt for help and found it (Gen. 12:10–20).

The religion of Egypt was characterized by regularity and optimism. Just as the Nile faithfully nourished the land, so the gods of nature sustained the society. The pharaoh himself was regarded as more than a representative of the gods; he was thought to have actually been a god himself. In the Old Kingdom period, only the pharaoh expected to live beyond the grave. In the Middle Kingdom this hope was extended to anybody who made the appropriate religious preparations.

The Middle Kingdom eventually weakened, however. Egypt experienced an interval of oppressive foreign rule known as the Second Intermediate period (ca. 1786–1550 B.C.). During part of this time, power was held by a dynasty of foreign chiefs called the Hyksos (ca. 1786–1550 B.C.).[9]

1996], 39), the hypothesis is widely accepted as a basis for continuing research (see William G. Dever, "Palestine in the Second Millennium B.C.E.: the Archaeological Picture," in *Israelite and Judean History,* ed. John H. Hayes and J. Maxwell Miller [Philadelphia: Trinity Press, 1977], 84–86). Eugene Merrill notes that the theory provides the best explanation for the ease of the patriarch's travel throughout Canaan but that it is not essential to those who regard the patriarchal narratives as historical (*Kingdom of Priests: A History of Old Testament Israel* [Grand Rapids: Baker Book House, 1987], 30). It is possible that Abraham's migration was not part of a broader movement of people.

[9]The Fifteenth Dynasty, the "Hyksos Dynasty" in Lower Egypt, made up of invaders from Asia, is dated at about 1674–1567 B.C. An Asian presence, however, troubled Egypt from the Middle Kingdom, increasing in the Twelfth Dynasty. Following the collapse of a unified Egypt, Hyksos local rulers doubtless established an increasing presence in the East Nile Delta (Goshen).

They gradually infiltrated from the north and were worshipers of Canaanite gods, including Baal. After seizing control, they moved the Egyptian capital from Thebes to their own city, Avaris. They were responsible for importing horses and chariots as well as other military innovations. It is likely that during their rule Joseph rose to power in Egypt and eventually brought his entire family to live there. The "new king, who did not know about Joseph," would have been Ahmose I (Exod. 1:8). He was the native Egyptian ruler who successfully expelled the Hyksos about 1550 B.C.

What Kind of People Were the Patriarchs?

God called Abraham to leave his familiar surroundings and travel to a foreign land (Gen. 12:1–3). But Abraham had to do more than trust and obey. He had to adjust. And when we start reading the stories of this great man and his family (Gen. 12 through 50), we too need to adjust: It is natural for us to wonder about a world and a lifestyle so different from ours. How did they live together as families? How did they support themselves? How did they get along with their neighbors? For all the differences we may discover, however, we must still remember that they were human – just like us.

Aside from the Bible, there are no ancient documents that mention Abraham or his descendants. And only seldom does the Book of Genesis provide background information. The biblical portrait of the patriarchs must be placed against the backdrop of what is known of ancient Canaan and Egypt. When that is done, the picture that emerges is fairly coherent.

frankly) not very exciting for me. Perhaps it was because I lacked perspective and a reference point in history. But now, I think of Abraham and know that this tree was already five hundred years old by the time he was born! Somehow this lifts Abraham and his family off of the printed page. It reminds me that they were real people like me. They walked on this earth. Sometimes they also took shelter from the scorching sun under the branches of a nearby tree.

People used to think of Abraham, Isaac, and Jacob as nomads who wandered aimlessly around the countryside; they traveled by camel, living in tents on the fringe of society. That notion needs to be revised. Actually, the population of Canaan in this era fit into two cultures that existed side by side. Those who inhabited cities and villages lived off their businesses and the produce of nearby cultivated land. Tent-dwellers raised sheep and goats. They usually lived near settlements. They moved their flocks and herds according to the seasons, looking for the best places to graze. They lived in tents not because they were poor but because it was convenient. In fact, many of them became quite wealthy and respected by their city-dwelling friends. Abraham had lived in the cities Ur and Haran; he would have been at home in both cultures.

Abraham is better described as a seminomad. He and his family managed herds of animals (Gen. 13:5–7; 15:9; 18:7). They traveled the countryside, camping near cities and towns such as Shechem, Dothan, and Hebron. They worked the land, dug wells (26:12–15), grew rich in silver and gold, and had many servants (12:16; 13:2; 24:35). Abraham could even muster a force of 318 trained men to go to war against a coalition of kings (14:1–16). Abraham was more than a tent-dwelling shepherd. Once a newcomer, he became the powerful chief of a large family business.

But more significant than his status as a tribal chief or seminomad is the fact that Abraham was a resident alien. The Hebrew word *ger* (retained in the name of Moses' firstborn, "Gershom," in Exod. 2:22) refers to one who was not native to the area he lived in and thus had no citizenship (Gen. 15:13; 23:4). Although God had promised the land of Canaan to Abraham and his descendants, the region was realistically called "the land of your sojournings" (Gen. 17:8, NASB, RSV). A resident alien needed the permission of local landowners to settle down. He did not have the rights of a citizen.

Archaeology has helped us to picture life in the Middle Bronze Age. One find in particular has received a lot of attention. From 1925 to 1931 over four thousand clay tablets were unearthed at Nuzi. An ancient city east of the Tigris River, Nuzi was about fifty miles southeast of Asshur. Although the texts date from about 1500–1300 B.C., many have used them to help fill in the cultural background of the patriarchs who lived much earlier.[10] At first, scholars were quick to find parallels that actually rested on very thin evidence. When Abraham referred to Sarah as his wife and sister (Gen. 12:12–13; apparently setting a model for his son [26:7]), one scholar thought he was reflecting a common Hurrian custom mentioned at Nuzi.[11] Further study has shown that the differences outweigh the similarities. On the other hand, valid parallels between the customs at Nuzi and the lives of the patriarchs do exist.

Abraham referred to Eliezer as his heir, even though he was only a slave and not related by blood (Gen. 15:3). The practice of adopting a slave as one's son was known to exist at Nuzi as well as at Larsa in the Old Babylonian period.[12] Sarah, Rachel, and Leah were all known as barren wives who gave a slave girl to their husbands in the hope of get-

Living in Two Kingdoms

As members and citizens of God's kingdom, Christians are "aliens and strangers in the world" (1 Pet. 2:11). Like Abraham, we are servants of God and give him our primary allegiance. Yet we must show respect to earthly authorities (Rom. 13:7). It is when such authorities call for behavior opposed to God's will that we resist them (as Naboth did, and as did Jesus' disciples [1 Kings 21:3; Acts 5:29]).

[10]For a balanced survey of scholarship regarding the relationship of the Nuzi tablets to biblical studies, see M. J. Selman, "The Social Environment of the Patriarchs," *Tyndale Bulletin* 27 (1976): 114–36.

[11]See E. A. Speiser, "The Wife-Sister Motif in the Patriarchal Narratives," in *Oriental and Biblical Studies,* ed. J. J. Finkelstein and M. Greenberg (Philadelphia: University of Pennsylvania Press, 1967), 62–82.

[12]Selman, "Social Environment," 127.

ting more children. This strikes us today as highly irregular, but the custom was practiced in ancient Nuzi. There are other parallels too, and together they help confirm the historical reality of the patriarchs as living in the Middle Bronze Age.

Another point of scholarly interest has to do with whether or not the word "Hebrew" should be equated with the West-Semitic name *Habiru*.[13] Abraham is the first person in the Bible to be called a Hebrew (Gen. 14:13). Throughout the Middle Bronze Age, the word *Habiru* was used to refer to a certain group of people. It may be tempting to think of the *Habiru* as an ethnic category. More likely, however, the word referred to a class of people who lived on the fringe of society.[14] The patriarchal "Hebrews" may have been part of the *Habiru* class, but it would be too strong to claim that they actually *were* the *Habiru* of the ancient world.

Beyond these descriptions of the lifestyle of the patriarchs, we can also say something about their character. What stands out most about Abraham is his obedient faith and belief in one God. In contrast to the polytheistic religion of his surroundings, Abraham believed that there was one God who was supreme. He created the universe and was the Judge of all (Gen. 14:22; 18:25). In obedience to his command, Abraham left Haran and moved to the land of Canaan (12:1,4). This showed his trust in God's promises. The same trust led him to lay Isaac on the altar of sacrifice, knowing that God would provide the offering (Gen. 22).

[13]The word is also spelled *Hapiru* and *'Apiru*. Much has been written on this subject. See Niels Peter Lemche, "abiru, apiru," in *ABD*, 3:6–10 for an up-to-date discussion of the issues and sources.

[14]Bright, *History of Israel*, 95.

Confident that God would meet his needs, Abraham could afford to be generous (13:9). His military rescue of his nephew Lot showed great loyalty (14:14–16). Yet for all this, Abraham had his faults. Out of fear, he deceived the pharaoh of Egypt into believing that Sarah was not his wife, but his sister (12:10–16). Later, he acted the same way with Abimelech, king of Gerar (20:2). The errors of his descendants were even more blatant, as we shall see.

Sometimes we feel compelled to defend the men and women of the Bible, even when they are clearly in the wrong. But this approach misses the point. God did not give us the stories of the Bible to show us a gallery of heroes and heroines. Instead, he wanted to point us to himself and his work of redemption. In the midst of their achievements and failures, God was active. He spoke, guided, provided, and protected. He was and is the God of promise and fulfillment; he can be trusted. As we consider the stories of the rest of Genesis, we will seek to be fair and perceptive in our treatment of Abraham and his extended family. We will keep in mind that like us, they were called to love and serve God in a very real world, complete with great opportunities and challenges.

The Election of Abraham and the Patriarchs

Genesis 1 through 11 traces the growth of humankind from an original couple of persons to a family of nations scattered over the earth. In spite of some positive events along the way, the general trend was downward and away from the knowledge of God. At this point, God's plan of redemption entered a new phase, one that focused on a single nation. So when God called Abraham to leave his homeland, God also "chose" him. He promised Abraham that he would become the father of a great nation that would, in turn, become a source of blessing to *all* nations.[15] The ideas of call and choice are what lie at the root of the theology of election.[16] In both testaments, God's people are referred to as "chosen" (Ps. 105:6; Col. 3:12) and "called" (Isa. 48:12; Jude 1). Sometimes both words appear with similar meaning in the same verse (1 Pet. 2:9; Rev. 17:14).

The theology of election is rooted in God's choice of Abraham. God promised that he would have many descendants (Gen. 12:2a), that he would personally experience God's blessing (12:2b), and that he would be a source of universal blessing (12:2c–3). He would inherit land (12:7). These promises were repeated over and over, not only to Abraham but also to Isaac, Jacob, and even the whole nation of Israel.[17] What's more, all of these benefits were promised to Abraham because God entered into a covenant with him. This divine covenant, or relationship between two parties, can be understood as a "sovereign administration of grace and promise."[18] However, a covenant meant not only benefits but obligations as well.

God's promise of descendants, however, soon met with an obstacle. Abraham and Sarah were unable to have children. So Abraham fathered Ishmael through Sarah's ser-

[15]Gen. 12:1–3; Neh. 9:7; Heb. 11:8.

[16]This is a rich doctrine in Scripture. There are several biblical words that deal with the concept of election, but the main ones are *bar* and *eklegomai* (Heb. and Gk., respectively, for "to choose").

[17]See n. 21 for a list of references of promises to the patriarchs. The promises also pertained to God's people on the national level (Deut. 7:12–15; 30:15–20). The following is a sample: descendants (Deut. 1:10–11; 6:3); blessing (Deut. 15:6); land (Deut. 1:8, 4:37–38).

[18]Willem A. VanGemeren, *The Progress of Redemption: The Story of Salvation from Creation to the New Jerusalem* (Grand Rapids: Zondervan Publishing House, 1988), 117.

vant Hagar. But he quickly found out that Ishmael was not the child of promise. God had promised he would give Abraham a son by Sarah to be his true heir (Gen. 18:10; 21:12).

Abraham's descendants eventually moved to Egypt, where they multiplied and became enslaved. This period of slavery was a dark time, yet the covenant promises were not dead. Moses prophesied that God would free his people and lead them into the Promised Land. God would be faithful to the covenant he had established. He said, "'I will bring you to the land I swore with uplifted hand to give to Abraham, to Isaac and to Jacob'" (Exod. 6:8). After God brought Israel out, they continued to look back with gratitude to God's choice of their forefathers and the promises he had made to them (Deut. 4:37; 29:12–13). Moses told them that having God's favor was not related to anything special about them. God chose their father Abraham. In love, he was remaining faithful to his promises (Deut. 7:6–9; see 1 Cor. 1:26–31). The covenant that God made with Israel on Mount Sinai was a continuation of the one he had established with Abraham (Josh. 24:2–13). Just as Israel expected to receive benefits from God, the LORD also commanded Israel to live up to certain obligations. These were spelled out in the Ten Commandments and the laws of the Pentateuch. These rules were not meant to be a heavy burden (Deut. 30:11–16). In short, Israel was to be loyal to him and keep themselves separate from the surrounding pagan world (Lev. 18:1–5). Faith and obedience were to be evidence of their commitment. Israel was to be a source of blessing, giving praise to God (Isa. 43:21; Rom. 9:5).

In the course of their history, it is clear that some

The True Children of Abraham

In the letter to the Galatians, the apostle Paul reflected on Ishmael as a natural son and Isaac as a son of promise. He concluded that not every person who was physically descended from Abraham was really one of his children. Abraham's true children are those who respond in faith and trust to God's offer of salvation in Christ (Gal. 3:7,29; 4:28–31).

This is seen in two of Abraham's grandchildren, the twins, Esau and Jacob. Esau was born first (and was thus technically the rightful heir). Yet it was Jacob whom God had chosen (Gen. 25:23). Commenting on this, Paul noted that God's choice preceded the opportunity for either of the boys to do right or wrong. God was not being unjust; he was simply showing mercy and compassion to the one he had chosen (Mal. 1:2–3; Rom. 9:10–13). Out of his own wisdom

(cont. on the next page)

The True Children of Abraham (cont.)

and mercy, God selected Jacob (Israel) to be an ancestor of the covenant people through whom the Messiah would eventually come. So, Paul rightly called the church of Jesus Christ "the Israel of God" (Gal. 6:16). In all of this, election, covenant promises, and faith remain closely tied together.

responded well to God and others did not. God allowed Israel to be captured by Babylon because most of them had abandoned him. Yet, there was always a remnant who stayed true. Through the prophets, God said that he would honor his promises with that faithful remnant (1 Kings 19:18; Isa. 1:9; 6:13). Furthermore, God would even extend those blessings *outside* the borders of Israel to the Gentile nations (Isa. 2:2–4). God had originally focused on Abraham, the man he chose to be an agent of blessing to all peoples on earth. He would again choose one individual to bring that blessing to the whole world. This "chosen servant" would be the Messiah (Isa. 42:1–4).

What Does Election Mean to Us, the Church?

As the story of redemption moves into the New Testament, the spotlight shifts to Jesus Christ. He is the embodiment of the remnant, and the only One who has perfect faith and obedience. God the Father said, "'This is my Son, whom I have chosen; listen to him'" (Luke 9:35). Peter referred to him as the foundation and called him "the living Stone – rejected by men but chosen by God and precious to him" (1 Pet. 2:4). Those who are "in Christ" are thus part of the elect community of faith. The Early Church was faced with a challenge: How were the Gentiles to be included in God's purposes? They concluded that it was by grace and faith (Acts 15:9; Rom. 3:22; Eph. 2:8). Through placing their trust in Christ, Christians became "a chosen people, a royal priesthood, a holy nation, a people belonging to God." They could declare God's praises because he had called them "out of darkness into his wonderful light" (1 Pet. 2:9).

What then should we think of the nation of Israel? Paul used the analogy of an olive tree to illustrate how God would deal with Israel and the Gentiles (Rom. 11:16–24). Just as the natural branches of a cultivated olive tree can be broken off, unbelieving Jews were cut off from the covenant blessings. They rejected God's chosen Son, Jesus the Messiah. So believing Gentiles become members of the covenant community when they respond to the offer of salvation in Christ. If God in his mercy can forgive a pagan sinner, then he can certainly forgive Jews who return to him. So in the end Paul could declare with confidence, "All Israel will be saved" (11:26).

There is something about the theology of election that is always beyond us. Though Paul knew there would be unanswered (and unanswerable) questions (Rom. 9:19–21), he ended up giving heartfelt praise to God for his mysterious wisdom (Rom. 11:33–36).

Christians today can be tempted to ignore the doctrine of election. They think it is either difficult to understand or it may seem to raise more questions than it answers. But the real question is not "Does the Bible teach election?" but "What *kind* of election does the Bible teach?" At the risk of becoming simplistic, it is fair to say that the point of debate has more to do with the *basis* of election than with the mere *fact* of it.

All agree that Israel was a chosen nation and that the covenant with Abraham was expanded through Moses and David to the new covenant in Christ (Jer. 31:31–34; Luke 22:20; Heb. 12:24). Christians are Abraham's true descendants through faith; just as Abraham believed (Gen. 15:6), so must we (Gal. 3:6–9). Those who know God have a part in spreading the good news of salvation.

Paul took the doctrine of election and used it as a spring-board to both praise God and encourage Christians. His opening words to the Ephesians brim with thanksgiving. We were chosen in Christ (Eph. 1:11) from before the foundation of the world (1:4). We were chosen by God's perfect will (1:5) to be his holy people, marked by the Holy Spirit (1:4,13). All of this is by grace (1:7) through faith in Christ (1:13) for God's praise (1:6,12,14).

The Patriarchal Narratives
–Gen. 12 Through 50

Beginning at Genesis 12, there is a clear change in focus of the text. The worldwide scope of God's blessing in Genesis 1 through 11 is now directed through one man, Abraham.[19] What would God ask him to do? How would he respond? What about his wife, Sarah? Would their children and grandchildren serve the LORD? As you read, it is good to keep such questions in mind.[20] What you find out about this family may surprise you.

Israel looked to Abraham as their founding father. God's covenant with him is the pivot of the Book of Genesis. God chose Abraham from a people that had been scattered over the whole earth (Gen. 11:9). But God was concerned for all those nations. Abraham was to be part of a grand mission to bless them (12:3). The accounts of Ishmael and Esau are

[19]God changed the name Abram, which means "exalted father," to Abraham, "father of many" (Gen. 17:5). God also changed the name of Abraham's wife, Sarai, to Sarah (17:15); the text provides no explanation for the latter change. "Sarah" means "princess," a name that is appropriate in the light of 17:6. To avoid confusion I will call them "Abraham" and "Sarah" throughout. Notice that Jacob (32:28) and Joseph (41:45) also received new names.

[20]For an outline of Genesis according to the *toledot*, see the section "How Is Genesis Laid Out?" in chap. 2.

short in comparison to those which focus on Abraham, Isaac, and Jacob (and his son, Joseph). The children of promise become the channels through which God's blessing would flow to the nations (see Rom. 9:8; Gal. 4:28). They are the ones to watch most closely.

Genesis 12 through 50 compresses centuries of events into relatively few pages. It quickly becomes clear that there is a great deal that we are not told. This can be disappointing for those who want to read these chapters as so-called normal history. A better way to approach them is to pay close attention to what we are told. God's command to Abraham is also a promise of blessing for the future. How will these promises work out? A full answer would involve a tour through the whole Bible. For now, we will simply look to Abraham and offer this thought: We want to avoid the failures that were part of Genesis 2 through 11. So those who want the blessing of God must respond to his commands with trusting obedience.

Abraham

WESTWARD HO! TO CANAAN AND BEYOND — GEN. 12

Genesis 11 begins with people traveling east and building a city. Instead of seeking God, they sought a name for themselves. Genesis 12, on the other hand, begins with a man and his small family traveling west to an unknown land. Why? Abraham had heard God's voice and did what God said. He left his home, his extended family, and his community. He put his security and future in God's hands. Some might consider that a tremendous risk. But when Abraham left Haran, he didn't show any signs of resistance or doubt, at least not yet (cf. Gen. 15:2–3). In fact, Abraham's obedience was proof of his faith and trust in God. He could set out on this lifelong "camping trip" because "he was looking forward to the city with foundations, whose architect and builder is God" (Heb. 11:8–10). His faith was more than an attitude. His faith affected his actions and made a difference in his choices (John 8:39; James 2:20–24).

But God did not just tell Abraham to go. He gave him three promises: descendants, blessing, and land.[21] What about the timing? Just because God made a promise did not mean that he would fulfill it right away. As the story of this family unfolds, we'll find there will be complications. Still, the promises are central not only to the rest of the Book of Genesis, but to the Pentateuch (and even to the whole Bible). "The theme of the Pentateuch is the partial fulfilment – which implies also the partial nonfulfilment – of the promise to or blessing of the patriarchs."[22]

God had told Adam and Eve to be "fruitful and increase in number" (Gen. 1:28). In the same way, God would make Abraham's family into a huge nation. Its population would be as the dust of the earth, the stars in the sky, and the sand on the seashore in number (Gen. 13:16; 15:5; 22:17). This seems incredible! All we know about Abraham's wife, Sarah,

[21]VanGemeren has a very helpful exposition of these promises, though he counts four. He divides the category of blessing into personal and national aspects (*Progress of Redemption,* 104–7, 122–24). These promises were repeated not only to Abraham (13:14–17; 15:1–7,18; 17; 18:9–19; 22:17–18), but to Isaac (26:2–4) and Jacob as well (28:13–14; cf. 28:3–4; 35:9–12). David J. A. Clines has assembled an impressive list of references and allusions to these promises throughout the whole Pentateuch (*The Theme of the Pentateuch,* JSOT Supplement 10 [Sheffield, JSOT Press, 1984], 32–43).

[22]Clines, *Theme of the Pentateuch,* 29.

so far is that she'd been unable to have children (11:30).

But God had promised to bless Abraham and make him a blessing to the nations. This concept is a bit hazy at first. But it comes into sharper focus when we see God make a covenant with him. Notice that in this chapter of Genesis the first people that Abraham dealt with received "serious diseases" from the Lord (12:17). That was hardly a "blessing"! Abraham's actions seem to be guided more by fear than faith (12:13). Finally, God promised to give Abraham and his offspring a land that included everything west of the Jordan River from the Euphrates down to the Negev. Such a gift! Yet Abraham himself never possessed that territory. Two generations later, his grandson Jacob was still a "wandering Aramean" (Deut. 26:5; cf. Gen. 46:5-6). Famine drove him down to Egypt. In spite of these (and other) complications, God's promises were still good. It was up to this family to trust him.

UNCLE ABRAHAM: HOW DO WE RESOLVE PERSONAL DIFFERENCES? — GEN. 13 THROUGH 14

When Abraham moved to Canaan, his nephew Lot came with him. Together they became wealthy shepherds, but beyond that their differences soon surfaced. First there was the problem of overcrowding. There was not enough pasture for both of them (Gen. 13:7).[23] To ease the friction, Abraham offered Lot the pick of the land, an offer Lot quickly took. Abraham would settle with whatever was left over. In response to this selfless act, God repeated the

---

[23]Abraham had 318 servants born in his family (Gen. 14:14). Many of these servants may have had wives and children. If Lot's group was of a comparable size, it is easy to understand how a conflict based on grazing and water rights would have arisen.

promise of land (13:14–17). Lot failed to be as generous as his uncle. To make matters worse, Lot moved in among the wicked people of Sodom. There he was made a prisoner of war by the marauding kings from Mesopotamia (14:12). Out of loyalty to his nephew, Abraham staged a brave and successful rescue (14:16).

The episode ends with Abraham meeting two kings: one from Sodom, who is unnamed, and one from Salem, Melchizedek. The two kings couldn't have been more different. Abraham's response to them shows his high character. Melchizedek brought out a meal and blessed Abraham.[24] Abraham knew his victory was a gift from God (Gen. 14:20,22). He responded by giving a gift back to God: a tenth of everything. In contrast, the king of Sodom tried to "bless" Abraham. He offered him all the spoil from the battle as a reward. But Abraham refused to take it. He wanted everybody to know that no *person* acting on his own could make Abraham rich. Only *God* could do that. Abraham must have known that the blessing of God is a gift to be received, not a payment to be earned.

"LOOK UP AND COUNT THE STARS, IF YOU CAN." — GEN. 15 AND 17

In Genesis 15 and 17 we learn that God entered into a covenant (Heb. *karath*, lit. "cut") with Abraham. A covenant is a solemn, legal agreement between two parties, though here it refers more broadly to the idea of an oath or

---

[24]The Book of Hebrews deals with the significance of Melchizedek as a priest, in distinction to the Levitical priesthood of the day, which could trace its ancestry back to Aaron. In contrast, Melchizedek's priesthood is older and doesn't depend on genealogy. Since Jesus wasn't from the tribe of Levi (he was from Judah), He couldn't be a great high priest in the normal way. His priesthood was in the line of Melchizedek (see Ps. 110; Heb. 7).

a confirmation of a promise.[25] Archaeologists have found covenant documents from the second millennium B.C. They show the words and actions that accompany the making of a covenant. One ancient text from the city of Alalakh sheds some light on the ceremony in Genesis 15.[26] In this chapter God promised to give Abraham a son and a country. To validate that promise he asked Abraham to sacrifice a few animals. He was to cut them in half and place the parts in two piles. Then when Abraham fell into a deep sleep, God spoke to him about the land again: Abraham's descendants would inherit the land. But that would happen only after they had lived in a foreign country. There they would be mistreated as slaves for four hundred years. After God told Abraham this, a smoking firepot and a blazing torch appeared to him. They moved between the pieces of the sacrificed animals (Gen. 15:17). What could it mean? In the Alalakh text, a master grants land to a servant. To do this, he takes an oath by cutting the neck of a lamb. This signified a death wish on himself if he ever went back on his word. Think of it: The fire that went between the pieces symbolized God's own presence. It is as if God had said, "Abraham, if I ever break my promise, may I die." Certainly that would be impossible, but it shows how serious God is about his word. Later generations looked back on the oath God swore to Abraham. No wonder they concluded that God would

[25]Claus Westermann, *Genesis 12–36: A Commentary*, trans. John J. Scullion, S.J. (Minneapolis: Augsburg, 1985), 229.

[26]See Richard S. Hess, "The Slaughter of the Animals in Genesis 15: Genesis 15:8–21 and Its Ancient Near Eastern Context," in *He Swore an Oath: Biblical Themes from Genesis 12–50,* ed. R. S. Hess, G. J. Wenham, and P. E. Satterthwaite, 2d ed. (Grand Rapids: Baker Book House, 1994), 67–92.

indeed give them the Promised Land (Deut. 7:8)!

The other side of the promise had to do with a son. For the very first time, Abraham questioned God (Gen. 15:2). He was concerned. Since he and Sarah could not have children, his estate would fall to one of his servants, Eliezer of Damascus.[27] But God assured Abraham that he and Sarah would have a son of their own. Eventually their descendants would be as uncountable as the stars in the sky. When God pledged to make Abraham the father of many nations he also changed his name from Abram to Abraham.[28] In chapter 17, this promise is a major part of the covenant. But unlike earlier, God now asks something of Abraham: "Walk before me and be blameless'" (17:1). The promises are still gifts that Abraham can't earn, but they come with an expectation that Abraham will remain loyal to God no matter what. In the Bible there is no such thing as "just believing" in God. True faith always leads to a life of trust in the Lord and obedience to his word.

This time, the confirmation of the covenant would be marked by something that Abraham had to do. He had to circumcise every male, whether a direct descendant or not. God declared circumcision to be a sign of his covenant with Abraham.[29]

[27] The practice of granting an inheritance to a servant who becomes an adopted son was known to exist at Nuzi (E. A. Speiser, "Notes to Recently Published Nuzi Texts," *Journal of the American Oriental Society* 55 [1935]: 435–36).

[28] The name "Abram" means "exalted father." The name "Abraham" is a longer form of Abram and essentially means the same thing. It is, however, a word play on a similar sounding Hebrew phrase meaning "father of a multitude" (Gen. 17:4–5).

[29] It would appear that Canaanites (Gen. 34) and Philistines (1 Sam. 14:6) did not circumcise. Circumcision, therefore, set Abraham's descendants apart from many of the people around them. The practice of circumcision was not totally unique to Abraham's family but the covenantal significance of it certainly was.

Trying to Do God's Work for Him: A False Start With Hagar and Ishmael — Gen. 16

Knowing that God had promised Abraham a son, Sarah became impatient and came up with a plan to give Abraham an heir. Her husband could sleep with her servant Hagar, and perhaps get a child that way. This advice seems shocking to us today, but the practice was not that unusual back then, especially in cases of infertility.[30] What really stands out in this story, however, is the way Abraham and Sarah took matters into their own hands. The whole Book of Genesis makes it clear that not only does God promise, he delivers. But God always reserves the right to do things his way and in his time. God didn't *need* Abraham's clever ideas and help any more than he needs ours today. Faith does more than believe that God *can* do what he said he would. Faith trusts that God *will* do it and then patiently endures to the end (Heb. 6:12).

The result of Abraham and Hagar's union was Ishmael. He was not the promised son. Instead, he would be a "wild donkey of a man" (Gen. 16:12). Still, as Abraham's offspring, Ishmael would be blessed of God. He would be the father of a great nation.

Abraham Among the Angels — Gen. 18 Through 19

In chapters 18 and 19 of Genesis, both Abraham and Lot "entertained angels without knowing it" (Heb. 13:2). In the

---

[30]This activity was sanctioned at Nuzi and in the Code of Hammurapi (also spelled "Hammurabi") (Selman, "Social Environment," 127–29). Abraham and Sarah were making a decision within the context of their culture, and the Bible neither commends nor condemns Abraham (nor later Jacob) for this act. Rather, the problem here is Sarah's lack of trust in God. We should not hold Abraham responsible for something he did not yet know about, namely the law against adultery (Exod. 20:14).

ancient world, showing hospitality to strangers and travelers was expected. It was a custom of common decency. Abraham, however, is to be commended for his extra generosity (Gen. 18:6–8). Lot, however, did not behave nearly so well. He almost surrendered his two daughters to the perverse Sodomites. And after God rescued Lot and destroyed the city, these two daughters got their father drunk and then slept with him. The children they conceived became the ancestors of the Moabites and Ammonites, longtime enemies of Israel. On this low note, Lot makes his exit from the stories of Genesis. In contrast, Abraham continued to serve the Lord. He even prayed for the wicked city where his nephew had chosen to live.

MY WIFE OR MY SISTER? ABRAHAM DECEIVES KINGS ABOUT SARAH—GEN. 12:10–20; 20:1–18

Abraham had lied about his wife, Sarah, calling her his sister (Gen. 12:10–20). He excused his actions by saying that he feared Pharaoh would kill him for Sarah (12:12–13). Pharaoh took her into his harem. God, however, sent plagues on Pharaoh to make him let her go (12:17–20). Later, while staying in Gerar, Abraham feared that Abimelech, the king, would kill him to get Sarah. The plan went awry again. Like Pharaoh, the king took Sarah into his harem. How could God give them a son now? God stepped in and spoke to the king in a dream. He told him to give Sarah back and have Abraham pray for him, which he did. In fact, as one who could intercede, Abraham was called a "prophet" (20:7). Normally, prophets brought God's word to people, but they also took the concerns of people to God in prayer (Num. 12:13; Jer. 32:16; 42:4).

A TIME TO LAUGH: THE BIRTH OF ISAAC—GEN. 21

In this section of Genesis (21:1–7), God's promise of a son finally comes to pass. God was still working out his promises (18:10,14,18–19). Even though Abraham was close to a hundred years old and Sarah ninety, they heard that they would have a son in about a year's time. Just as Abraham laughed when he first heard this news (17:17, so did Sarah (18:12). God told them to name the child "Isaac," which means "he laughs" (17:19). The boy's name would remind them that they had laughed in amazement when they heard the promise of Isaac's birth. But afterward, Sarah laughed with joy. In spite of Abraham's failure to trust, God still kept his word. Isaac was born and Abraham circumcised him, just as God commanded.

Abraham realized his first legal claim to part of the Promised Land, the well at Beersheba (Gen. 21:22–34). To do this, he made a covenant with Abimelech. The name *Beersheba* means "the well of the oath."

Abraham's dealings with Abimelech brought him wealth and property (20:16; 21:27–31). Abraham's quarrel with the king's men about water rights could have become quite serious. But God's favor is obvious, even on the lips of a pagan. He confessed to Abraham, "'God is with you in everything you do'" (21:22). That statement is practically the theme of Abraham's whole adventure.

THINKING THE UNTHINKABLE: THE "BINDING" OF ISAAC—GEN. 22

At this point we come to the most intense period of Abraham's entire life. Isaac the promised son had finally arrived. Surprisingly, God then asked Abraham to give

Abraham, a Pattern of Christ

One can hardly read Genesis 22 without thinking of Jesus Christ (see Heb. 11:17–19; James 2:18–24). Just as Abraham put his son on the altar, God the Father put his Son on the cross. Just as God provided the ram as a substitute, Jesus died in our place. Through him, the blessing of salvation flows to the nations. But it is also possible to read the story and see Abraham as a pattern of Christ, who is in turn a pattern for Christians. Gerhard von Rad made this connection by showing that if Abraham had carried out the sacrifice of Isaac, he not only would have lost his son; he also would have lost his faith in God

him up.[31] In Genesis 15, God confirmed His commitment to Abraham with a sacrifice. Now it was Abraham's turn to do the same. Although we read that it was only a "test" (22:1), the idea of God commanding child sacrifice is nevertheless a shock for us. Perhaps it was a *bit* less so for Abraham, who lived in a culture where people tended to think of their children more as extensions of the parents and less as individuals with their own rights.[32] Child sacrifice, particularly of the firstborn, was common.[33] Much later, God told his people that the firstborn of their animals belonged to him (Exod. 13:11–13). Although Isaac was a son, not a sheep, the Law had not yet been given. God can rightly ask for anything he wants, but the instruction to offer Isaac ought to astonish us, especially when we remember two important points: Isaac was especially dear to his parents and his birth was the result of God's own promise. God's demand for Isaac's life struck at the heart of what was important to Abraham. It involved not only his son, but also his faith. God's extraordinary command called for radical obedience from Abraham. In the bottom of his heart, Abraham must have known that both his *and* Isaac's lives belonged to God. This kind of total abandonment to God is exactly what Jesus asked of his disciples and of us as well. "Whoever wants to save his life will lose it, but whoever loses his life for me will save it'" (Luke 9:24).

[31]Gen. 22 is sometimes mistakenly called "the sacrifice of Isaac" when, in fact, it is a ram that is sacrificed. To call it "the offering of Isaac" (see NASB) may even be too strong. Jews commonly refer to the story as the *Akedah,* the "binding" of Isaac. The Heb. word *'qd* means to bind, or tie up, (an animal) in preparation for a sacrifice.

[32]R. W. L. Moberly, "Christ as the Key to Scripture: Genesis 22 Reconsidered," in *He Swore an Oath,* ed. Hess, Wenham, and Satterthwaite, 156.

[33]Cf. Lev. 18:21; Deut. 18:10; 1 Kings 16:34; Ezek. 16:21.

It is natural to wonder what Abraham must have been thinking and feeling when asked to offer his son. The text simply says that he got up and went. No resistance—no wavering. Even at the last moment, when the knife was in his hand, Abraham was determined to obey. He would let God be God. Having walked so long with God, he was confident that God would "provide" (Gen. 22: 8). He knew that God, if need be, could raise the dead (Heb. 11:19). He was right. At the last moment, God provided a ram for the sacrifice. So Abraham named the place "The LORD Will Provide" (Gen. 22:14).[34] In response to this amazing show of obedience, God confirmed his promises to Abraham. He would get descendants; he would get land; and he would get blessings both for himself and for the nations (22:15–18).

SAYING GOOD-BYE TO SARAH AND ABRAHAM — GEN. 23; 25:1–11

Abraham and Sarah spent over sixty years together. The Bible says that he mourned her death with tears (Gen. 23:2). Afterwards, Abraham took ownership of a second parcel of land, a field with a burial cave for the family, beginning with Sarah. Compared to the whole of the Promised Land, it wasn't much. Abraham still considered himself "an alien and a stranger" (23:4). If Abraham had wanted property, he could always have returned home to Haran or Ur. But he had God's promise—something far more sure and valuable. When Abraham died, Isaac and

who had both promised and given him Isaac. He would have been "Godforsaken."[35] This test, then, was designed not only to see if Abraham would obey but also to see if Abraham understood the true nature of God's promise of a son. It was (and always would be) a gift; he was never entitled to it. His life and future were in God's hands. Jesus showed that same awareness. Anticipating the cross he prayed, "'My Father, if it is possible, may this cup be taken from me. Yet not as I will, but as you will'" (Matt. 26:39). This kind of total abandonment to God is exactly what Jesus asked of his disciples (and of us as well). "'Whoever wants to save his life will lose it, but whoever loses his life for me will save it'" (Luke 9:24). This is what it means to take up your cross and follow Jesus (Luke 14:27).

---

[34]Heb. *yhwh yir'eh* (or Jehovah Jireh), which can also mean "The LORD will see" (cf. the *Living Bible,* "Jehovah provides").

[35]Gerhard von Rad, *Genesis: A Commentary,* rev. ed., trans. John H. Marks (Philadelphia: Westminster, 1972), 238–45. (See Matt. 27:46.)

A Better Country

Abraham and his family "were longing for a better country—a heavenly one. Therefore God is not ashamed to be called their God, for he has prepared a city for them" (Heb. 11:16).

Being God's Friend

What are we to make of these promises of descendants, land, and the blessing of being in a covenantal relationship with God? It is possible to trace the partial fulfillment of these promises through the Old Testament. But it is vitally important to notice that Jesus is the son of Abraham (Matt. 1:1; see Luke 1:55,72–73). And "no matter how many promises God has made, they are 'Yes' in Christ"

Ishmael buried him with Sarah. In fact, Isaac and Jacob were buried in the same family tomb.[36]

Isaac

THE MATCH-MAKER: ISAAC AND REBEKAH MARRY —GEN. 24

The story of Isaac is short in comparison to those of the other patriarchs. But it is important because the promises given Abraham are carried forward. Abraham must have been concerned about this because of the way he arranged for Isaac's marriage. If his family was to grow into a nation, Isaac had to have a son. For that, he needed a wife. Clearly, not just any wife would do. First, she could not be a Canaanite. Why not? Canaanite women had a reputation for low moral standards. The girl who would marry Isaac had to be from Abraham's own people back in Mesopotamia. However, she had to be willing to move to Canaan; under no circumstances could Isaac, the promised son, go back east (Gen. 24:5–8). Just as Abraham had trusted God, so would the girl his son would marry; she would have to trust God enough to leave her identity and security behind.

The account of how Abraham's servant found Rebekah and brought her to Isaac is unusually long, but it shows us the marvelous way that God leads. Abraham knew that God was in control and was sure that he would send an angel to guide the process (24:7). Besides that, we learn something about Rebekah, who is destined to be a key

[36]So was Isaac's wife, Rebekah. Jacob's wife Rachel was buried near Bethlehem (Gen. 35:19). Joseph died in Egypt but gave strict orders that his remains be taken to the Promised Land when the family left (Gen. 50:25; Exod. 13:19; Heb. 11:22).

player in redemption's story. Like Abraham, she was very hospitable and generous, watering the camels and offering a place to stay. Although she was pretty (24:16), her real attraction came from the quality of her character (Prov. 31:10).

LIKE FATHER, LIKE SON? — GEN. 26

Twice before, Abraham was driven from the land by a famine. In these moments he gave way to fear. The events of Abraham's sojourn are mirrored in the life of Isaac (see "Parallels" chart below). Like Sarah, beautiful Rebekah caught the sexual attention of a king. Yet, just as with Sarah, God protected her. And like the rulers who mistook Sarah for Abraham's sister, the Philistine king ends up looking more righteous than the husband (Gen. 26:10–11).

Since the story of Isaac and Rebekah having children appears in chapter 25, we may wonder why in chapter 26 the Philistines could see them as brother and sister rather than as husband and wife. The simplest solution is to treat chapter 26 as out of chronological order so as to highlight a more important theological concern.[37] The divine blessing which Isaac inherited from his father brought protection and prosperity. This is the blessing that Isaac's son Jacob stole from his brother, Esau (27:27–29).

We can understand the tendency some feel to portray Isaac as a man of faith, as his father was. But as the story of this family unfolds, Isaac clearly trusts God less and less.[38]

(2 Cor. 1:20). This means that Gentile Christians, along with believing Jews, are heirs of those blessings (Gal. 3:14,29). Together we are a vast nation (1 Pet. 2:9; Rev. 5:9). Our "land" is ultimately the new heaven and the new earth (Rev. 21:1). Our relationship with God is through the new covenant in Christ (Luke 22:20; Heb. 9:15). Who but God could have imagined the grandeur of all of this?

Who are the children of Abraham today? Those who do what Abraham did (John 8:39), walking with God in obedient trust. This is what it means to "believe" (Rom. 4:11–12; Gal. 3:7). Abraham was called the friend of God (Isa. 41:8; James 2:23). It should come as no surprise then, to hear Jesus say, "'You are my friends if you do what I command. . . . Love each other'" (John 15:14–17).

[37]Bruce K. Waltke with Cathi J. Fredricks, *Genesis: A Commentary* (Grand Rapids: Zondervan Publishing House, 2001), 367. He notes also the examples of anachronism in the Table of Nations and the Tower of Babel (Gen. 10–11) as well as the children of Keturah (Gen. 25).

[38]See the insightful analysis of Isaac by Bruce K. Waltke, "Reflections on Retirement from the Life of Isaac," *Crux*, 32, no. 4 (1996): 4–14.

In the end, he doesn't really know what is going on and gives his blessing to the "wrong" son (Gen. 27).

Parallels in the Lives of Abraham and Isaac in Genesis		
	Abraham	Isaac
Famine in the land forced a move	2:10	26:1
He moved to Gerar and stayed with Abimelech	20:1–2	26:1,6
God appeared and issued promises	12:2–3,7; 13:14–17	26:3–4,24
Out of fear, he called his wife his sister	12:12–13; 20:11–13	26:7–8
He was rebuked by the king	12:18–19; 20:9–10	26:9–10
He became wealthy	12:16; 13:2; 20:14–15	26:12–13
He quarreled over water rights	21:25–30	26:19–22
He worshiped by building an altar	13:18	26:25
Abimelech acknowledged that God was with him	21:22	26:28
He made a covenant with Abimelech	21:27	26:28–31
A well was named "Beersheba"	21:31	26:33

Jacob

FAMILY FEUD: JACOB AND ESAU—GEN. 25:19–34

Just as Abraham and Sarah could have no children at first, neither could Isaac and Rebekah. So Isaac prayed to the LORD and his wife became pregnant with twin boys. Because they were twins, there was some question as to who would be the heir. But we're told right from the start: It would be the younger son (Gen. 25:23).[39] Later on, Jacob "bought" his elder brother's birthright for no more than a hot meal. We've seen character flaws in this family before,

[39]The firstborn son usually received a larger share of the family property than the others. Evidence from Nuzi suggests that part of an inheritance could be transferred to another brother (M. J. Selman, "Comparative Customs and the Patriarchal Age," in *Essays on the Patriarchal Narratives,* ed. A. R. Millard and D. J. Wiseman [Winona Lake: Eisenbrauns, 1983]), 116, 123, 135.

but what follows is quite unexpected. For all of their differences, the only thing these twins truly shared in common was their stubborn conformity to their own natures. In the words of Thomas Mann, "Jacob has a sharp mind and no conscience, but Esau is all belly and no brain."[40]

JACOB EARNS HIS NAME: THE DECEIVER — GEN. 27:1 THROUGH 28:9

The name "Jacob" means "he grasps by the heel," which connotes the idea of deception.[41] He took advantage of his brother's hunger to steal his birthright. He also took advantage of his decrepit, blind father to steal the blessing due his brother (which echoes God's blessing on Abraham). It's hard to see how God would honor the blessing given to a cheat like Jacob. True, none of his ancestors was perfect. And it wouldn't seem right for Esau to get the blessing; his values weren't right. Before we feel too sorry for him, notice also his hatred for Jacob that produced a secret death threat (Gen. 27:41). And knowing that Isaac didn't want Jacob to marry a Canaanite, Esau went straight out and married an Ishmaelite. (Ishmaelites, like the Canaanites, stood outside the Abrahamic covenant.) On the other hand, Jacob became one who "struggled with God" (Gen. 32:28). The events of his life brought a definite change for the better. His "conversion," though, was a gradual one.[42]

[40]Thomas W. Mann, *The Book of the Torah: The Narrative Integrity of the Pentateuch* (Atlanta: John Knox, 1988), 52. This work offers a close reading of Genesis that is highly rewarding.

[41]The connection is not totally clear. There is a verb related to the Heb. word for "heel." Literally it means "to follow at someone's heel." In Gen. 27:36 and Jer. 9:4 it is used in its figurative sense of "to deceive," "to cheat." See commentaries for a fuller discussion of the issue.

[42]Mann, *Book of the Torah*, 56.

STAIRWAY TO HEAVEN — GEN. 28:10–22

Just as God spoke to Abraham before his journey, so God spoke to Jacob before his. In each case God promised descendants, blessing, and land. But there was a difference with Jacob. He headed in the wrong direction: back *east!* At Bethel he saw a vision of angels moving up and down on a stairway to heaven. Jacob realized he was at the gateway of heaven itself. He was definitely at a "gateway" of sorts (Gen. 28:17). He couldn't very well go back. The "Promised Land" was home to a spiteful brother who had plotted to kill him. We, the readers, can sense the danger that lay ahead but have to admire Jacob's vow of dedication to God (28:20–22). His pledge to tithe shows that he was beginning to realize that whatever good that came to him would arrive as a gift from God.

This is the first of four pivotal times when Jacob met with God.[43] In the twenty years that Jacob would spend outside of Canaan, God didn't seem to be very close to him. He worked more from behind the scenes, blessing Jacob from a distance.

WORKING FOR UNCLE LABAN — GEN. 29 THROUGH 31

Jacob made his way to Haran where his grandfather Abraham once lived. While there, he gained two wives, two concubines, eleven sons, plus a large herd of sheep and goats.[44] But in spite of all this success, the deceiver was now the deceived: Laban made a good first impression, but turned out to be quite the manipulator. He tricked Jacob into marrying

[43]Gen. 28:13–15; 31:10–13; 32:24–30; 35:9–12.

[44]Jacob's wives, surrogate wives, and children are named in Gen. 29:31 through 30:24; 35:18.

Leah instead of her younger sister, Rachel, whom he really loved. It was customary for an older sister to be married first,[45] but Jacob seemed unaware of the tradition. Perhaps he chose to ignore it, having fallen in love with Rachel.

When Jacob and his uncle Laban reached the place where they finally parted, Jacob made a moving speech (Gen. 31:36–42). He had worked for twenty years and suffered much because of Laban's dishonesty and injustice. It had been a struggle living with his relatives, but this was only the beginning. Not only would he have to face Esau when he got home, but before that he would have to struggle with God "face to face."

WITH GOD ON THE WRESTLING MAT —GEN. 32 THROUGH 33

The next crucial point when Jacob met God was at the ford on the Jabbok River. All Jacob could see as he approached home was the ugly prospect of meeting angry Esau. So in desperation he prayed for protection. The confession of his unworthiness is strangely uncharacteristic (Gen. 32:10). Apparently he had finally learned the same lesson that Abraham knew: The blessing of God is a gift.

After praying, he sent his servants ahead of him with a large herd of animals as a present for Esau. Then he stayed behind at the Jabbok River. All night long he wrestled with someone who came out of nowhere. Who was it he wrestled with? Genesis calls this opponent "a man" (32:24; cf. Hos.

[45]This point is generally established. Scholars have used the evidence from Nuzi to suggest parallels for several other events described in these chapters, such as Laban's "adoption" of Jacob, Jacob's marriages, and Rachel's theft of Laban's "household gods." But closer analysis has rendered these particular analogies invalid. On the other hand, Laban's legal demand that Jacob not take any additional wives (Gen. 31:50) can be illustrated from a marriage contract from Nuzi (Selman, "Social Environment," 123–25, 130).

12:4). But Jacob couldn't get a name out of him. Even though Jacob believed that he had met God face to face (Gen. 32:30), this encounter retains an air of mystery. At Bethel God had openly introduced himself to Jacob as "'the LORD, the God of your father Abraham and the God of Isaac'" (28:13). Blessings followed. But here, the "man" remained anonymous. Struggles followed. In the end, the wrestler blessed Jacob, but not before wounding him. Even though Jacob was told that he had "overcome," his limp would always remind him who was the stronger. The fact that he received a new name was further confirmation that he had met with someone far greater—someone divine.

Jacob is a complex character. On the one hand he is scheming and shrewd. On the other, he is humble. He knew how to take for himself, but in this episode he learned something better: how to *receive* from God. This change of heart immediately surfaced in the way he acted toward his brother. He bowed down seven times, called Esau his "lord" and himself his "servant" (Gen. 33:3,13–14). He pressed a lavish gift, a "blessing," on him, too. This is surely remarkable. Even though Jacob couldn't undo the past by returning Esau's birthright and original blessing, he could still give a blessing to the brother he had wronged.

Jacob was not the only one who had changed. Esau was different as well. We might want to think about that some more, but the Bible does not take us down that road. Instead, Esau was honored with a long genealogy (Gen. 36) and then left to history.

A STINKING MESS—GEN. 34

God blessed Jacob in Paddan Aram with the birth of eleven sons. They would inherit God's promises to their great-grandfather Abraham. Together with Benjamin, who wasn't born yet, they would become the heads of the twelve tribes of Israel. Their role was to be a blessing to the nations. But in Canaan they got off to such a bad start that Jacob had to say, "'You have brought trouble on me by making me a stench to . . . the people living in this land'" (Gen. 34:30).

What had they done? A Hivite prince named Shechem had seduced their sister Dinah. Afterward he asked to marry her. Her brothers retaliated by making a false promise to the man's family. They said Shechem could marry Dinah only if all the males of Shechem's city were circumcised. While the men were still sore from the operation, Simeon and Levi raided the city. They killed every man in it.

They were justly concerned for the honor of their sister, but their strategy was all wrong. Rather than uphold circumcision as a holy sign of the covenant, they used the custom in a plot of cold-blooded murder.

JACOB BECOMES ISRAEL — GEN. 35

Jacob returned to Bethel where God appeared to him the first time (see Gen. 28:10). God had safely returned him to his "father's house" (i.e., Canaan; Gen. 31:30) and Jacob worshiped at the place called "God's house" (Bethel). God changed his name and repeated the promises made earlier to Abraham and Isaac. The new name "Israel" means "he struggles with God." This seems curious, since from the start God was constantly out to bless him. Why should *this* man be honored with providing a name for the nation of God's people?

In a real sense, the history of this nation had been an ongoing struggle with God. Apparently privilege has its price. Being a guest of God's presence and generosity brings with it an obligation to behave accordingly. While we may never understand it fully, God's choice of Israel was never based on their own worth. It was simply because God loved them and promised to bless them (Deut. 7:7–8; 9:4–6). Looking back, we can wonder why God put up with these people. But we must remember that his power is made complete in our weakness. His patience ultimately means salvation (2 Cor. 12:9, 2 Pet. 3:15).

Joseph

JOSEPH'S DREAMS NEARLY COST HIM HIS LIFE — GEN. 37

The sibling rivalry that ran in this chosen family became intense in the life of Joseph, the first son of Jacob and his favorite wife, Rachel. Their two sons, Joseph and Benjamin, were both given special treatment. It is helpful to watch how their brothers reacted. In this first episode, young Joseph had dreams in which his brothers bowed down to him. He was also somewhat of a tattletale (Gen. 37:2). At the first convenient moment, his brothers planned to take his life. But they ended up selling him as a slave to a caravan bound for Egypt. Mistakenly thinking they were rid of him, they presented his special coat to Jacob, stained with goat's blood. Though no stranger to tricks, Jacob was completely fooled and mourned the death of his favorite son.

AN UGLY FAMILY SECRET — GEN. 38

Before the story follows Joseph to Egypt, there is a dark tale that concerns his brother Judah. The chapter appears as somewhat of an interruption. But as we'll discover later, it is absolutely necessary to see Judah as he really was.

Although some might credit him with sparing Joseph's life, it was Judah's idea to sell him to the Ishmaelites (Gen. 37:27). After that, Judah betrayed his family honor and earned the distinction of being the first one to intermarry with a Canaanite (38:2). The sons of this union were so bad that the LORD himself put two of them to death (38:7,10). As a father, Judah was a failure. And as if he couldn't get any worse, Judah committed fornication with his own daughter-in-law. The fact that he thought she was a prostitute hardly makes his sin any less blameworthy.

OUT OF THE FRYING PAN AND INTO THE FIRE—GEN. 39

In Egypt, Joseph became a household servant to a high-ranking Egyptian. Although he had been abandoned by his brothers, God was "with him" (Gen. 39:2,21,23).[46] It was a good thing, too. His success earned him more than a promotion. He also gained the affection of Potiphar's wife, who found him sexually irresistible and tried to seduce him. But Joseph (in contrast to his brother Judah) knew (and declared) that adultery was more than a violation of his master's rights. It was a sin against God (39:9). Yet, for all this, her accusation of attempted rape sent him to prison.

THE DREAMER KNOWS DREAMS
—GEN. 40 THROUGH 41

What happened to Joseph in prison prepared him for what was to come. In the ancient world, dreams were often considered windows on the future. Those who could interpret the details of such dreams were highly respected. Acknowledging that "'interpretations belong to God'" (Gen.

---

[46]Abraham, Isaac, and Jacob were told the same thing (Gen. 21:22; 26:3; 28:15).

40:8), Joseph correctly interpreted two dreams for his fellow inmates. That paved the way for his explanation of a double dream for Pharaoh himself. Through Joseph's interpretation of Pharaoh's dreams, God revealed the course of the next fourteen years of Egyptian agriculture. There would be seven years of abundance followed by seven years of famine. Pharaoh immediately promoted Joseph to his second-in-command and gave him the task of managing Egypt's resources.

While these astounding events put Joseph in a position to help his starving family back home, they also created a problem. Joseph was still heir to the land that God had promised to Abraham. Through no fault of his own, he had left it. Would he get back? Why should he? In Egypt, he was no longer "Joseph"; he had a new identity, "Zaphenath-Paneah," and he married into a prominent family (41:45). His new job gave him wealth, respect, and a secure future. He had it made. Some may think that these changes did not really affect Joseph "the Hebrew." Perhaps. But then why would he name his first son Manasseh, "making one forget"? At his birth he said, "'God has made me forget all my trouble and all my father's household'" (41:51). The Bible tells us nothing about what Joseph was thinking (it seldom does). From this point until he re-encountered his brothers, the only description given of Joseph is of a man successful in his work.

WHAT A STRANGE FAMILY REUNION!
—GEN. 42 THROUGH 46

What follows next is the longest narrative of the whole book. This dramatic account records a surprising development in Joseph's relationship to his brothers. It is worth reading carefully. In the end, it is no less than the story of the family's rescue from extinction.

These chapters chronicle three journeys made by Joseph's family from Canaan to Egypt. The first two times, his brothers came to Egypt for food and met with "Zaphenath-Paneah." Joseph recognized them, but kept his identity a secret in order to carry out a carefully planned trick. He was not mischievous, but shrewd. His long-range plan was to bring the whole family to Egypt. But in the process, a more immediate concern drove him. Would his brothers ever face up to their mistreatment of him? And if they were willing to get rid of Joseph, what had become of Benjamin, the only remaining son of Rachel?

To answer those questions for himself, Joseph offered to keep helping the starving family, but only on one condition: Benjamin had to leave his father and personally appear in "Zaphenath-Paneah's" court. Jacob was totally unwilling to let his son go, until his brother Judah stepped in to guarantee his safe return. Little did he know that Joseph would accuse Benjamin of stealing his cup and threaten to make him a slave, never to return home.

It is at this point that the story returns to the character of Judah, who had behaved so badly before. This man who had showed such contempt for his family was beginning to change. How could he return home to Jacob without Benjamin? His father would die from grief. The strain would be too much! So at the cost of cutting himself off forever, Judah presented a solution. In a moving speech, Judah offered *himself* for Benjamin's freedom. Though he had not taken the prized cup (and didn't know that Benjamin hadn't either), he would live the rest of his life as a slave rather than go back on his promise to his father. Think of it! Judah had once stood in front of Jacob holding

Judah's Change of Heart

I remember the first time I *really* heard the story of Judah's change of heart, and it had a profound effect on me. Here was the first person in the Bible to give up his life for another. More than that, he did it out of love for his father! Judah was more than an individual man; he was the ancestor of a whole tribe from whom Israel would receive kings, starting with David (Gen. 49:10). Judah's example must have left a powerful mark on Moses, the first leader of the nation. Rather than see God's people perish for their sin, he prayed for God to spare them but if not, to blot Moses himself out of the book he had written (Exod. 32:32). David acted much the same way when he saw punishment fall on Israel. He cried out, "'What have they done? Let your hand fall upon me and my family'" (2 Sam. 24:17). And most importantly, Jesus, the king from the tribe of

Joseph's bloody coat. Now he was offering his life for the sake of the favorite son.

The dreams of Joseph's childhood had come true. His brothers were bowing to him, including Judah! Joseph could stand it no more. The whole thing was torturing him as much as his brothers. Impressed with this show of loyalty and moved to tears, he ordered his Egyptian servants out of the room. Once in private, Joseph revealed his true identity to his brothers, who must have been shocked indeed. What irony! The man who had saved them from starvation was the brother they had tried to kill!

After an emotional reunion, Joseph sent his brothers back home to fetch Jacob and the rest of the family. Stunned when he heard the news, Jacob neverthless believed the whole story and moved the family to Egypt. Safe at last!

Egyptian wall painting found near Beni Hassan depicts Semitic nomads arriving in Egypt about 1895 B.C.

Joseph looks like the central character of the story, but he said otherwise. It was *God* who had arranged events (Gen. 45:8; 50:20). The same God who made promises to Abraham was the One still at work. God even assured Jacob that it was all right to take his family to Egypt. There he would multiply their numbers and eventually bring them back home to the Promised Land (46:4).

EGYPT: NOT EXACTLY THE PROMISED LAND —GEN. 47 THROUGH 50

The great story of the patriarchs ends with the whole family prospering in Egypt. They were safe, protected from famine. On the eve of Jacob's death, he blessed each of his sons. But each of them knew that Egypt was not their final destination. Jacob reassured Joseph that God had promised the land of Canaan to the family (Gen. 48:3–4). And it is with this controlling thought that Joseph, when he lay dying, gave one last instruction: To the brothers who once plotted his murder he said, "'Carry my bones up from this place'" (50:25). It was a statement of faith in God and hope for the future (Heb. 11:22). Loyal to the end, with great care his brothers placed him in a coffin (an Egyptian form of interment not practiced in Israel). And so Joseph remained in Egypt until God opened the next door (Exod. 13:19).

Judah, took the same attitude and willingly laid down His life (John 10:17–18). His death brought about our life.

These scenes from the Bible rush to my mind when I hear Jesus say, "'Love each other as I have loved you. Greater love has no one than this, that he lay down his life for his friends'" (John 15:12–13). Judah and the rest are more than figures from the past. They are preachers whose actions speak even today. It is as if they say, "It wasn't easy, but I learned to do the right thing—and by God's grace, so can you." As followers of Jesus, God asks us to live out our love for him by serving one another (Mark 10:42–45; Phil. 2:3–4). It is the only way to true greatness in his kingdom.

Appendix: Where Do the Patriarchs Fit in the Past?

What's the historical setting for the patriarchs? The short answer is that they fit into the Middle Bronze Age (ca. 2000–1600 B.C.).[47] But what is the evidence for this view? How reliable or specific is that evidence? The diffi-

---

[47]This statement reflects my conclusion along with that of the other authors of this textbook. Among those scholars who believe that Abraham and the

culties involved here make assigning dates to the people and events of this period quite controversial. But in spite of the obstacles, discerning where in history the patriarchs fit is an important endeavor. Because God revealed the truths of redemption in the lives of real people, we want to understand those people and their world as well as possible.

1. The Issue of Historicity

Although we do not try to prove the Bible by history, we do believe that biblical faith depends on historical reality.[48] It's not just a set of timeless ideas. For Christians, events in history are especially important. Jesus Christ really came to earth in a physical body, died for the sins of the world, and was raised to life (1 Cor. 15:3–4,14; 1 Tim. 3:16). When the Israelites confessed their faith in the LORD, they thought back to Jacob and proclaimed, "'My father was a wandering Aramean . . .'" (Deut. 26:5–10). Just as Christians believe that Jesus was a real person, ancient believers thought Abraham and his family were real persons, too. But not everybody who studies the Bible agrees on this last point.

To help clarify this discussion, let's use the word "history" to refer to human records of the past. The word "historicity," on the other hand, has to do with whether certain

---

other patriarchs really existed, very few would date Abraham's birth before 2167 B.C., or date Jacob's descent into Egypt after 1490 B.C.

[48]Those who try to prove the truth of the Bible by history fall into the trap of regarding the so-called facts of history as a standard that is somehow above the Bible. This leads to taking a stance of skepticism that says, "I will believe that the Bible is true only if I can back up what it says by logic or some archaeological discovery." In reality, it is not only the Bible that needs interpretation, so do the artifacts uncovered by archaeologists. Instead of holding the Scriptures hostage to the science of archaeology, it is better to use our ever-growing knowledge of the ancient world to illuminate and corroborate the people, places, and events of the biblical story.

events really took place or whether certain people actually lived. Before about 1900 and the recent expansion of archaeology, many biblical scholars held that all of the events described in the Book of Genesis (and the other books of the Pentateuch as well) were not written down until many centuries later.[49] Most concluded that Abraham and the other patriarchs never truly existed and that their stories amounted to little more than folklore. While archaeology has yet to discover any physical trace of the patriarchs themselves (for example, their names in inscriptions), modern finds confirm that the conditions of their stories fit the Middle Bronze Age remarkably well. Still, scholars following the lead of Albrecht Alt and Martin Noth continued to discount the historicity of the patriarchs.[50] Despite mounting evidence that countered this skepticism, the attack on historicity continued in the studies by T. L. Thompson and J. Van Seters.[51] These scholars rightly pointed out some flaws in earlier attempts to place the patriarchs in history, but their negative conclusions are too extreme.[52] For them, the Book of Genesis has no historical value. They claim it does not provide valid historical

[49]See the discussion in chap. 2 concerning the Graf-Wellhausen hypothesis. Currently, many scholars are moving away from Graf-Wellhausen in favor of a more holistic type of analysis. For a survey of the issues and available literature, see Raymond D. Dillard and Tremper Longman III, *An Introduction to the Old Testament* (Grand Rapids: Zondervan Publishing House, 1994), 38–48.

[50]But see the rebuttal of Roland de Vaux, "The Hebrew Patriarchs and History," chap. 6 in *The Bible and the Ancient Near East,* trans. Damian McHugh (Garden City: Doubleday, 1971) 111–21.

[51]T. L. Thompson, *The Historicity of the Patriarchal Narratives: The Quest for the Historical Abraham* (New York: Walter de Gruyter, 1974); J. Van Seters, *Abraham in History and Tradition* (New Haven: Yale University Press, 1975).

[52]See the critique of their position by John. T. Luke, "Abraham and the Iron Age: Reflections on the New Patriarchal Studies," *JSOT* 4 (1977): 35–47.

information about the patriarchal (Middle Bronze) period. Rather, they maintain that the narratives reflect the times in which they were written down and arranged (1000–720 B.C.). But in the end, it is hard to imagine how the faith of Israel could have even existed if people were the least bit uncertain of whether or not their founding father and his sons ever really lived.[53]

2. Locating the Patriarchs in Time

Having made that point, however, our task is far from over. Unlike political leaders of empires who would naturally leave permanent records, the patriarchs were heads of families and were quite mobile. They left no palaces or libraries behind. Furthermore, the climate of Palestine isn't as favorable to preservation as that of Mesopotamia and Egypt. In the absence of specific mention of the patriarchs outside the Bible, we must piece together information from two sources: the Bible and our general knowledge of Middle Bronze Age Palestine (i.e., Canaan).

The Scriptures contain many genealogies that provide historical information, but they aren't of much help in setting dates.[54] Genesis 14 mentions a raid on five kings, but

---

[53]A. R. Millard wrote that the historicity of Abraham "is important for all who take biblical teaching about faith seriously. Faith is informed, not blind. God called Abraham with a promise and showed his faithfulness to him and his descendants. Abraham obeyed that call and experienced that faithfulness. Without Abraham, a major block in the foundations of both Judaism and Christianity is lost; a fictional Abraham might incorporate and illustrate communal beliefs, but could supply no rational evidence for faith because any other community could invent a totally different figure" ("Abraham," in *ABD*, 1:40).

[54]Some genealogies look like they have been shortened, leaving gaps. For instance, Moses is listed as being four generations away from Jacob (1 Chron. 6:1–3), but his contemporary Bezalel (Exod. 31:1–2) is listed as being seven generations away (1 Chron. 2:1–20).

we can't identify them with anybody known at that time. Likewise, we don't know which pharaoh is the one who "did not know about Joseph" (Exod. 1:8). We do know, however, that the relatively stable history of Egypt was interrupted by a series of foreign Semitic rulers, the Hyksos, who had control from about 1786 to 1550 B.C. If Joseph rose to power under one of them, then a likely candidate for the pharaoh of Exodus 1:8 would be Ahmose I (also called Amosis, ca. 1550–1525 B.C.). He expelled the Hyksos and founded the Eighteenth Dynasty, noted for its revival of Egyptian power and culture.

Genesis 19 records the destruction of Sodom and Gomorrah, cities that were near the Dead Sea. Their remains haven't been located. We are left only with several key verses. We know that Abraham was seventy-five years old when he left Haran for Canaan (Gen. 12:4). In Genesis 15:13, the LORD told Abraham that his descendants would be enslaved in a foreign country and mistreated for four hundred years. This fits well with Exodus 12:40–41, which says the Israelites lived in Egypt for 430 years. But other evidence suggests that the 430 years stretches from Abraham's entry into Canaan to the deliverance of Israel from slavery.[55] Finally, 1 Kings 6:1 dates the beginning of Solomon's temple (probably 967 B.C.) at 480 years after the exodus. While this last point has direct bearing on the date of the exodus (see the discussion in chap. 6), it is fair to note that the Septuagint reads "440" years. The issues involved in the dating of Abraham's entry to Canaan, Jacob's descent to Egypt, the exodus, and the conquest

[55]The Septuagint and the Samaritan Pentateuch agree that the 430 years applies to the time the Israelites spent in Egypt *and Canaan*. This reading receives indirect support from Paul (Gal. 3:17).

under Joshua are all interrelated. As of yet, there is no fixed reference point to work from.[56]

When scholars examine the social conditions of the Middle Bronze age, the patriarchs seem right at home. Their names are typical of Amorites living in Canaan.[57] Many of their customs are known from elsewhere too.[58] For instance, rights of the firstborn son could be assigned to a younger brother after the manner of Jacob, who clearly preferred Joseph over Reuben, his true firstborn son, and gave a special blessing to Ephraim and not his older brother, Manasseh (Gen. 48:14). The patriarchs were known travelers as were many others during their time.[59] And alliances of kings like those described in Genesis 14 are also known to have existed.

While it is impossible to be precise, we can use the data above to assemble a tentative timeline for the lives of the patriarchs. Though open to revision, it can nevertheless serve as a convenient starting place.[60] We adopt the "Early Date" for the exodus (1447 B.C.) and hold that Israel and the

---

[56]The date of the exodus is either ca. 1450–1440 B.C., or later on, ca. 1290–1280 B.C. Likewise, the date of the conquest is either early or late. Following a thorough survey of the evidence and scholarly positions, Bruce Waltke wrote judiciously, "In sum, the verdict *non liquet* [not proven] must be accepted until more data puts the date of the conquest beyond reasonable doubt. . . . [E]ither date is an acceptable working hypothesis, and neither date should be held dogmatically." "The Date of the Conquest," *WTJ* 52 (1990): 200. For further discussion of the dates of the exodus, see chap. 6 of this textbook.

[57]Bright, *History of Israel,* 77.

[58]Selman, "Comparative Customs," 91–139.

[59]Bright, *History of Israel,* 80–83.

[60]For a fuller discussion of these issues and possible solutions, see J. N. Oswalt, "Chronology of the OT," in *ISBE,* 1:673–85; K. A. Kitchen and T. C. Mitchell, "Chronology of the Old Testament," in *NBD,* 186–93. Another study that values the biblical data, yet places the patriarchs a bit earlier is J. J. Bimson, "Archaeological Data and the Dating of the Patriarchs," in *Essays on the Patriarchal Narratives,* ed. Millard and Wiseman, 53–89.

patriarchs spent 430 years in Egypt *and Canaan* (Exod. 12:40, LXX).[61] This places the birth of Abraham close to 1952 B.C., with Isaac coming along a century later (Gen. 21:5). Jacob would then have been born about 1792 B.C. (Gen. 25:24). The birth date of Joseph is uncertain, but he would have found his way to Egypt and risen to power under a Hyksos ruler. Jacob would have joined him there, moving the family to Egypt around 1662 B.C. (Gen. 46:5–7). Egypt's change of administration in 1567 B.C. marked the earliest possible time for the beginning of the Israelites' oppression and slavery.

Time Line of the Patriarchs (approximate dates B.C.)	
1952	Abraham is born (Gen. 11:26)
1942	Isaac is born (Gen. 21:1–4)
1877	Abraham leaves Haran for Canaan (Gen. 12:4)
1866	Ishmael is born (Gen. 16:16)
1852	Isaac is born (Gen. 21:5)
1815	Sarah dies (Gen. 23:1–2)
1812	Isaac marries Rebekah (Gen. 25:20)
1792	Jacob and Esau are born (Gen. 25:25–26)
1777	Abraham dies (Gen. 25:8)
1752	Esau marries Judith and Basemath (Gen. 26:34)
1729	Ishmael dies (Gen. 25:17)
1701	Joseph is born (Gen. 30:22–24)
1672	Isaac dies (Gen. 35:28–29)
1671	Joseph enters Pharaoh's service at age 30 (Gen. 41:46)
1662	Jacob moves his family to Egypt (Gen. 41:47; 45:6; 47:9)
1645	Jacob dies in Egypt (Gen. 47:33)
1591	Joseph dies in Egypt (Gen. 50:26)
1567	A "new" (non-Hyksos) pharaoh arises (Exod. 1:8)
1447	Exodus from Egypt (Exod. 12:37)

[61]The Heb. (Masoretic) text yields 215 years as the patriarchal sojourn in Canaan, and 430 years of slavery in Egypt. The LXX allows 430 years for both Canaan *and* Egypt, a difference of 215 years.

An alternative chronology might also be held. We could take the Late Date for the exodus (ca. 1290–1280 B.C.), together with the reading of the Hebrew (Masoretic) text for Exodus 12:40.[62] This would have Abraham leaving Haran at about 1935 B.C. Jacob's descent into Egypt would be 215 years later, or 1720 B.C.[63] Both dating systems arrive at remarkably close results. Both place Joseph in Egypt under Hyksos rulers, and Abraham in the Middle Bronze Age.

1935	Abraham leaves Haran for Canaan (Gen. 12:4)
1720	Jacob moves his family to Egypt (Gen. 41:47; 45:6; 47:9)
1567	A "new" (non-Hyksos) pharaoh arises (Exod. 1:8)
1290–1280	Exodus from Egypt (Exod. 12:37)

Study Questions

1. What does archaeology tell us about the world Abraham came from?
2. Describe Abraham's lifestyle as a seminomad.
3. How does this chapter explain the doctrine of election? How might a Christian today benefit from better understanding this truth? How should we think of non-Christian Jewish people as a whole?
4. What three promises did God give Abraham? To what extent were they fulfilled in his lifetime? What is their state of fulfillment at the end of Genesis? As you move through reading the Old Testament, check the status of these promises at the end of Deuteronomy, 2 Kings, and even the Book of Malachi.

[62]430 years in Egypt (Exod. 12:40) + 215 years from Abram to Jacob's descent into Egypt = 645 years.

[63]Calculated from Gen. 12:4; 21:5; 25:26; 47:9.

5. Tell the story of Isaac's binding on the altar. Relate it to the life of Jesus.

6. How is Isaac like his father? How is he different?

7. Evaluate the life of Jacob in the light of the contemporary proverb "What goes around, comes around."

8. Why does Joseph go to such trouble to test his brothers? What does he learn from it?

9. What relevance do the Hyksos rulers have to the Joseph story?

10. What is the relationship of the *Habiru* to the Hebrews?

11. What is the difference between the words "history" and "historicity"?

12. What are the key Scriptures that help us compose a chronology of the patriarchs?

For Further Reading

In addition to the material cited in the footnotes, consider the following:

Garrett, Duane A. *Rethinking Genesis: Sources and Authorship of the First Book of the Pentateuch*. Grand Rapids: Baker Book House, 1991.

Hamilton, Victor P. *The Book of Genesis: Chapters 1–17*. Grand Rapids: Wm. B. Eerdmans, 1990.

_____. *The Book of Genesis: Chapters 18–50*. Grand Rapids: Wm. B. Eerdmans, 1995.

Janzen, J. Gerald. *Abraham and All the Families of the Earth: A Commentary on the Book of Genesis 12–50*. International Theological Commentary, ed. Fredrick Carlson Holmgren and George A. F. Knight. Grand Rapids: Wm. B. Eerdmans, 1993.

Kidner, Derek. *Genesis*. TOTC. Downers Grove, Ill.: Inter-Varsity Press, 1967.

Livingston, G. Herbert. *The Pentateuch in Its Cultural Environment*. 2d ed. Grand Rapids: Baker Book House, 1987.

Sailhamer, John H. *The Pentateuch As Narrative: A Biblical-Theological Commentary*. Grand Rapids: Zondervan Publishing House, 1992.

Waltke, Bruce K., with Cathi J. Fredricks. *Genesis: A Commentary*. Grand Rapids: Zondervan Publishing House, 2001.

Walton, John H. *Ancient Israelite Literature in its Cultural Context*. Grand Rapids: Zondervan Publishing House, 1989.

Walton, John H., and Victor H. Matthews. *The IVP Bible Background Commentary: Genesis-Deuteronomy*. Downers Grove, Ill.: InterVarsity Press, 1997.

Wenham, Gordon J. *Genesis 1–15*. WBC. Waco: Word, 1987.

_____. *Genesis 16–50*. WBC. Waco: Word, 1994.

6

Larry McQueen

With a Strong Hand and an Outstretched Arm

Outline:

- The Strong Hand of God
- From Blessing to Suffering
- The Call of Moses and the Revelation of the Name
- The Contest with Pharaoh
- Reenacting Redemption
- The Departure From Egypt
- Victory at the Sea
- A Trip Through the Desert
- Establishing the Covenant
- The Covenant Is Broken and Restored

Terms:

firstborn
Habiru
Hyksos
Passover
Pharaoh
Tetragrammaton
Yahweh

The Strong Hand of God

The story of the exodus is one of the most exciting stories in Scripture. It is filled with wicked kings, rebellious slaves, miraculous signs, and a cliff-hanging getaway. Beyond the dramatic portrayal of the beginning of the nation of Israel, the Book of Exodus reveals a God who reached a strong hand into the desperate situation of his people and delivered them in triumph.[1] He traveled with his people, made a covenant with them, and gave them a way to relive the story for generations to come. God, with his mighty hand and outstretched arm, is the main character of this amazing adventure.

Here is a brief outline of the story:

Exodus 1 through 2	From Blessing to Suffering
3 through 4	The Call of Moses and Revelation of the Name
5 through 11	The Contest with Pharaoh
12:1 through 15:21	Reenacting Redemption
15:22 through 18:27	A Trip Through the Desert
19:1 through 20:21; 24:1–18	Establishing the Covenant
32 through 34	Breaking and Renewing the Covenant

From Blessing to Suffering – Exod. 1 Through 2

Standing on the Promises

The story of Genesis 12 through 50 focuses on the relationship between God and the family of Abraham. God had promised to bless them with many descendants and with a land they could call their own. The Book of Exodus picks up where the story of the patriarchs left off—with Jacob's sons

[1]Exod. 6:6; 13:9; 15:3; Deut. 26:8.

and their families in Egypt. Exodus 1:1–7 shows how God's promise to Abraham of many descendants was being fulfilled. The Israelites are described as "fruitful" and "exceedingly numerous, so that the land was filled with them."[2]

The promise God had made to their forefathers to give them land was still in effect. It became the driving force behind God's actions to deliver the Israelites from forced labor in Egypt (Exod. 3:6–8). Consequently the exodus can be seen as part of the larger story begun in Genesis. It is an account of the promise and fulfillment of God's blessing upon Abraham's descendants.

The King Who Did Not Know – and the God Who Did

The theme of "knowing" is of major importance in the Book of Exodus. The Hebrew text of Exodus 2:25 reads simply, "And God saw the children of Israel, and God knew" (author's translation). The king who did not know Joseph (Exod. 1:8) is contrasted with the God who knew. The word "know" *(yada')* in Hebrew means much more than simply "to know about." It means "to know through relationship." To know is to experience and be affected by what is known. It is in this sense that God knew the Israelites in their sufferings (Exod. 3:7). God wanted to know and be known through relationship. The larger purpose of God in delivering the Israelites was that they would know him (Exod. 6:7). Ironically, this also applied to the Egyptians. At his first confrontation with Moses, Pharaoh claimed that he did not know the LORD (Exod. 5:2). Yet the purpose of the miraculous signs performed before

[2]These words point to the original intention of God for all of humankind (Gen. 1:28; 9:1).

Pharaoh was that he and the Egyptians would "know that [God is] the LORD."[3] In the end, Pharaoh acknowledged the LORD and even asked to be blessed by him (Exod. 12:31–32).

The identity of the new king who did not know Joseph cannot be determined with absolute certainty (Exod. 1:8). It is probably helpful to understand the arrival of this "new king" as the beginning of a new dynasty in Egypt. This is likely the dynasty that came to power after the expulsion of the Hyksos, a group of Asian invaders who had dominated Egypt for over two hundred years. It is also helpful to keep in mind that the term *pharaoh* is not a name but a title, meaning "Great House," used for all Egyptian kings. The series of Pharaohs who ruled after the Hyksos (ca. 1567–1250 B.C.) instituted oppressive policies that included slave labor for their extensive building projects. The political situation portrayed in the Book of Exodus reflects the harsh realities of this period well. (See the appendix, "Chronology of the Exodus," at the end of this chap.)

The Oppression of the Israelites and Other Hebrews

According to Egyptian documents, the kings of the Eighteenth and Nineteenth Dynasties (ca. 1550–1200 B.C.) forced the *Habiru* (or *Apiru*) to work on their extensive building projects. The *Habiru* were displaced migrants who were viewed as an inferior social class. They were found throughout the Near East and were made up of many ethnic groups, including several Semitic peoples. The "Hebrews" mentioned in Exodus 1 through 2 were likely considered by the Egyptians to be part of the *Habiru*. These

[3]Exod. 7:5,17; 8:10,22; 9:14,29.

Habiru (called "Hebrews" in Exod. 1:15–16,19, et al.) may have included groups of people who were not directly descended from Jacob (Israel). This view is supported by Exodus 12:38, which refers to "many other people" (a "mixed multitude," KJV) that went out of Egypt with the Israelites. The Israelites/Hebrews were slaves and were identified with the lower classes of Egyptian society. This is important for understanding God's concern for them and his action on their behalf. God sides with the poor. He is the "God of the Hebrews" (Exod. 3:18; 5:3).

The oppression of the Israelites represented both a political and a spiritual challenge.[4] The intensity of the oppression is shown through the repetitive use of the word "labor" in Exodus 1:11–14. It is a word that also means "service" or "worship." In this context, to "serve" Egypt meant to give one's allegiance to an empire that claimed to sustain one's life. Later the Israelites demanded to be given the freedom to "serve" the LORD in the wilderness (Exod. 7:16, KJV). When Pharaoh finally commanded them, "Go, serve the LORD" (Exod. 12:31, KJV; "worship," NIV), he understood that they would be giving their allegiance to another king. A primary question of the Book of Exodus then is this: "Whom will Israel serve, Pharaoh or God?"

The Birth and Early Adulthood of Moses

The story of Moses' birth is filled with suspense and amazement (Exod. 2:1–10). The text parallels the larger story of Genesis and Exodus. Moses was pronounced "a fine child" ("a goodly child," KJV), just like creation was

Dividing Moses' Life

Moses' life can be divided into three periods of forty years each. He was approximately 40 years old when he killed the Egyptian (Acts 7:23), 80 at the time of the exodus (Acts 7:30), and 120 at his death (Deut. 31:2).

---

[4]On the political and spiritual dimensions of the exodus story, see Walter Brueggemann, *The Prophetic Imagination* (Philadelphia: Fortress Press, 1978).

Identity and Acceptance

Christians who stand up for what is right may sometimes feel alienated. This can be very difficult when one is already struggling for acceptance and identity. Jesus said that the world would hate his followers, because it hated him (John 15:18). My identity as a Christian is more important than being accepted by everyone around me. In the end, standing up for truth will shape my character and make me a better person.

pronounced "good" (Exod. 2:2; Gen. 1:31). He was placed in an "ark" (Exod. 2:3, KJV) just as Noah and his family took refuge in an "ark" (Gen. 6 through 8). (The Heb. word is the same, *tevah,* in both instances.) Under sentence of death, the baby boy was ironically "cast" into the Nile for protection (Exod. 1:22, KJV; 2:3). Then he was drawn out of the reed-filled water (Exod. 2:10), a shadow of how Israel would later be rescued from the Sea of Reeds. The circumstances of Moses' birth foreshadowed the threatening circumstances of Jesus' birth: As a child taken to Egypt for safekeeping, Jesus also came out of Egypt (Matt. 2:13–15).

The scenes of Moses' early adulthood reveal a person who had developed a great concern for justice. The killing of the Egyptian, the peacemaking effort among his fellow Israelites, and the intervention for the women at the well— all point to a man willing to take great risks for the sake of righteousness (Exod. 2:11–22). These episodes also portray a man whose identity and character were being formed. He was reared in Pharaoh's household, yet stood against an Egyptian to defend a Hebrew slave. He attempted to mediate between his arguing kinsmen, yet was chided for acting like an Egyptian. Though he was perceived to be an Egyptian by the women at the well in Midian, he did not correct them. When naming his son, he chose a name that represented his unsettled state: Gershom, "alien." Finally, Moses himself asked the question of identity, "'Who am I?'" (Exod. 3:11). And the God who knew, answered.

The Call of Moses and the Revelation of the Name —Exod. 3:1 Through 4:17

Up to this point in the story God had been working behind the scenes through the Hebrew midwives and

Moses' rescuers,[5] as well as through Moses himself. But the groans and cries of the Israelites moved God to direct action.[6] God "heard," "remembered," "saw," and "knew" (Exod. 2:24–25, RSV). Past promises were connected to present needs. God responded by calling Moses to become his mouthpiece.

Moses: The First Prophet

Although Abraham is identified as a prophet (see "My Wife or My Sister?" in chap. 5), Moses is the first person in Scripture called to be a messenger of God. According to Deuteronomy 34:10, Moses would become the greatest of prophets, the standard by which all who followed would be measured. The call of Moses took place on Mount Horeb (Exod. 3:1), also called Mount Sinai, which may have been located in the southern part of the Sinai Peninsula.[7] The appearance of the Angel of the LORD, the burning bush that was not consumed, and the voice of God from the fiery bush (Exod. 3:2–4) all spoke of the

[5]Women play a crucial role in the opening chapters of Exod. The two Hebrew midwives took a stand against the most powerful man in the world at that time. It is amazing that they are named and the king is not! Their testimony that they feared God rather than Pharaoh is a call for everyone who reads the story to resist oppressive public policies. The mother and sister of Moses and the daughter of Pharaoh also contribute to the dramatic turn of events as they unwittingly rescued the man God later used to bring his people out of Egypt. See J. Cheryl Exum, "'You Shall Let Every Daughter Live': A Study of Exodus 1:8–2:10," *Semeia* 28 (1983): 63–82.

[6]The power of lament and grief as a form of prayer is a major theme in the Bible as well as in early and contemporary Pentecostalism. On the role of lament in Pentecostalism, see L. R. McQueen, *Joel and the Spirit: The Cry of a Prophetic Hermeneutic* (Sheffield: Sheffield Academic Press, 1995), 76–82.

[7]G. E. Wright, "Sinai, Mount," in *The Interpreter's Dictionary of the Bible*, vol. 4 (Nashville: Abingdon Press, 1963), 376–78. For other possible sites see G. I. Davies, "Sinai, Mount," in *ABD*, 6:48.

mystery and holiness of God's presence. The divine mystery is a theme that runs through the remainder of the Book of Exodus.

The conversation of Moses and God (Exod. 3:4 through 4:17) reveals much about both of them. God had come down to deliver his people. He asked for Moses' help. Moses responded with no less than five objections to God's call.

Objection	The Issue	God's Response
(1) 3:11–12	Adequacy/Identity	Assures Moses of his presence
(2) 3:13–22	Authority	Reveals his name/character to Moses
(3) 4:1–9	Assurance	Gives Moses three signs to call forth belief
(4) 4:10–12	Weakness	Assures Moses of his sovereignty to create and teach
(5) 4:13–17	Willingness	Allows for Aaron to become Moses' spokesman

Note that God took Moses' objections seriously. God remained patient with him until his final objection. At this point, the first mention of the "the LORD's anger" appears in Scripture (Exod. 4:14). God's willingness to make allowances for Moses shows how crucial Moses was to the plan of God. It is also amazing that the revelation of the divine name occurred in response to one of Moses' questions.

Does God Have a Name?

In the Ancient Near Eastern culture, a name was much more than simply a word that distinguished one person from another. A person's name revealed that person's character, or nature. To know someone's name was to know the kind of person you were dealing with. Even today, to know someone's name makes the person more accessible and vulnerable. Therefore, for God to reveal his name to Moses was an act of trust. It was a commitment on God's part to establish a relationship with Moses.[8]

Yet the name God gave to Moses is not easily understood. The phrase in Exodus 3:14, usually translated "I AM WHO I AM," speaks of God as "eternal being." Taken at face value, such an abstract way of thinking about God would be foreign to Ancient Near Eastern ears. However, the equally legitimate translation "I will be who I am" speaks of God as *being in relationship*. It turns the focus of the meaning toward God's ongoing faithfulness to fulfill the promises that he made to Moses' ancestors. In other words, the history of God's relationships defines who he is. This is apparent first with the patriarchs in the Book of Genesis and then with the Israelites in the Book of Exodus. The name "I AM" cannot be understood apart from the ongoing story of God's interaction with creation and humankind.[9] This rendering is also consistent with the context of this revelation, in which God's promise of land is repeated and the means of attaining it is laid out. Consequently, for Moses to tell the people "I AM has sent me" is to tell them that he was sent by the God who has committed himself to fulfill his promises.

God's name *Yahweh* appears throughout the Old Testament and is translated "LORD" in most English versions of the Bible. Since vowels were not written in the ancient

[8]God's vulnerability stands in tension with his eternal immutability. While he cannot be changed, yet he can be grieved (e.g., Gen. 6:6). That is what relationships entail, even for God.

[9]Thomas W. Mann, *The Book of the Torah: The Narrative Integrity of the Pentateuch* (Atlanta: John Knox Press, 1988), 83–84.

The LORD *and* the Lord

Beginning students often confuse the words LORD and Lord, as they appear in most English Bibles. They are not the same.

LORD (small caps) represents the divine name (YHWH) given to Moses in Exodus 3:15, developed from the words "I am"*('hyh)* in 3:14. The contextual proximity of the terms stresses the relationship between the "I AM" of 3:14 and the "Yahweh" (Eng. "LORD") of 3:15, both of which appear as answers to Moses' hypothetical question from the Israelites, "'What is his name?'" (3:13). I AM, therefore, must be internally related to the name Yahweh. It is. The English I AM is derived from the Hebrew root *hyh*, "to be." Yahweh is derived from the root *hwh*, which also means "to be." Thus God calls himself "I AM" (3:14), but reveals himself to Israel as the "One Who Is" (see 3:15). That is, when God speaks of

Hebrew text, the name consisted of four consonants, YHWH, appropriately called the Tetragrammaton ("four letters"). It was apparently related to the Hebrew verb "to be," and so carried with it the mystery of "being in relationship."[10]

"Go Down, Moses . . ."

The record of Moses' return to Egypt includes one of the most enigmatic passages in Scripture (Exod. 4:24–26). After all that God had gone through to call Moses on this mission, God met him on the journey from Midian[11] and would have killed him! Only the quick action of his wife, Zipporah, in circumcising her son saved Moses.[12] This account immediately follows God's instructions to Moses about the mission (Exod. 4:21–23). Zipporah's action would parallel the action of God in saving his firstborn son, Israel. It was a sign of the life-and-death struggle to come. The blood of this circumcision, shed by one to save another, anticipated the blood of Passover (Exod. 12:13,22–23) as

[10]After biblical times, the name "Yahweh" was considered too holy to be spoken aloud. Jewish rabbis substituted the word "Lord" as they read the Heb. text. Consequently, during medieval times when Jewish scribes inserted vowels into copies of the Heb. Scriptures, they assigned the vowels of the word "Adonay," meaning "my Lord," to the divine name, resulting in the word that has come down to us as "Jehovah." J. Barton Payne, *"hawa,"* in *Theological Wordbook of the Old Testament* (Chicago: Moody Press, 1980), 1:210–12.

[11]The land of Midian was probably in northwest Arabia on the eastern side of the Gulf of Aqaba. The Midianites, however, were a nomadic people who also migrated west and north of the land of Midian. Judg. 1:16 and 4:11 indicate that Jethro, Moses' father-in-law, was a Kenite, leading some scholars to believe that the Kenites were a tribe of the Midianites.

[12]Actually the text is not clear about whom God was trying to kill. Exod. 4:24 (NASB) reads, "The LORD met him and sought to put him to death." (Note the brackets for "Moses" in the NIV.) In any case, Moses was apparently at fault with respect to circumcision. See Gen. 17:14.

well as the blood sprinkled on the people to seal the covenant (Exod. 24:8).[13]

After reading this passage, one may well ask the question, "Who is this God named 'I AM'?" On the one hand, he is observant, caring, committed, and empathetic. On the other hand, he is untamed, hostile, threatening, and dangerous. This text opens up a new level of understanding for the entire episode of the exodus. God's agenda is larger than liberation. His intention is for human beings to live in his holy presence. As Moses learned here and the Israelites learned later, this means being set apart to God by blood (as in Exod. 12:7,13).[14]

The Contest with Pharaoh — Exod. 5:1 Through 11:10

The Conflict Begins

The first confrontation with Pharaoh set the pattern for the long struggle that followed (Exod. 5). It was primarily a struggle between Yahweh, "God of the Hebrews," and Pharaoh, "King of Egypt." Yahweh's command of "Let my people go" was met by Pharaoh's flat refusal of "I will not let Israel go." The request to worship Yahweh in the wilderness was met by an increase in the workload of the slave labor force (Exod. 5:6–19). In this way the conflict was defined. Obedience to Yahweh was set over against the maintenance of an oppressive social and economic system.

himself, he calls himself "I AM." When Israel is to speak of him, they are to address him as "The One Who Is" (i.e., Yahweh). The mystery of the Godhead thus pervades both these names. They express the enigma of the divine being that defies human understanding and description.

On the other hand, "Lord" or "lord" represents the Hebrew term *'adon*, with a number of meanings, ranging from a polite "sir" to "lord," "master."

When the divine name (YHWH) ceased to be pronounced, devout Jews substituted a plural form (the so-called plural of majesty) of *'adon*, suffixed with the pronoun "my," to form *'adonay*. The contrast between the two words can be seen by comparing Genesis 18:26 with 18:27. LORD (YHWH) appears in 18:26; Lord (lit. "my lord") appears in 18:27.

[13]The Heb. expression cited in n. 11 may mean "tried *[biqqesh]* to kill him" or "wanted to kill him." It is perhaps helpful here to observe that if God had really wanted or tried to kill either Moses or his son, nothing could have saved them. God is, after all, omnipotent and no one can thwart his will (Job 9:12). The expression, therefore, must be an idiom for a narrow escape from death by Moses or his son.

[14]Martin Buber, "Holy Event (Exodus 19–27)," in *Exodus*, Modern Critical Interpretations (New York: Chelsea House Publications, 1987), 52–53.

The first encounter with Pharaoh left Moses wondering why God had sent him to Egypt at all. God responded with a renewal of Moses' call, which focused on the revelation of the divine name (Exod. 6:1–12). God had not previously made himself known by his name Yahweh to the ancestors of the Israelites. Instead, he was known as *El-Shaddai*, translated "God Almighty."[15]

The restatement of the divine name to Moses assured him that God would do what he promised. And God would use Moses to accomplish his promise! As if to underscore the place of Moses and Aaron in God's plan, the text includes a genealogy that establishes them within the most respected priestly lines (Exod. 6:14–27).

Signs and Wonders

Pharaoh soon learned he was dealing with a God who was beyond his control. The "signs and wonders" occupying Exodus 7 through 11 are given an interpretive key in Exodus 7:3–5. They were acts of judgment that revealed God's sovereign rule over Egypt. Egypt was not autonomous, as Pharaoh thought. Furthermore, Pharaoh's own heart was subject to God's sovereignty. God would harden Pharoah's heart (Exod. 7:3). There is a close connection throughout the story between God's signs and wonders and the hardening of Pharaoh's heart.

[15]Because the name *Yahweh,* translated "LORD" in Eng. versions, appears throughout Gen., Exod. 6:3 has been interpreted in two major ways. Some take the verse to mean that the ancestors knew the name Yahweh but did not comprehend the full meaning of the name until the exodus. Others take the text at face value and believe that editors of the text of Gen. who lived after the exodus used the name "Yahweh" along with "El-Shaddai" to refer to the same God. The second view is more in keeping with the Heb. concept of name, which makes a strong connection between name and identity, making it unlikely that the ancestors were using the name Yahweh without knowing its full significance. On this issue, see Payne, *"hawa,"* 212; and R. W. L. Moberly, *The Old Testament of the Old Testament: Patriarchal Narratives and Mosaic Yahwism* (Minneapolis: Fortress Press, 1992), 36–78.

The term "heart" *(lev)* refers primarily to a person's will or disposition. The hardening of Pharaoh's heart can be understood as the strengthening of Pharaoh's will. In other words, God was simply causing Pharaoh to be more firmly resolved in his own will, which was already set against the LORD. The text frequently indicates that Pharaoh's heart became hard or that he hardened his own heart.[16]

The signs and wonders that are noted in the Book of Exodus have been understood in various ways. Some view the plagues strictly as a chain reaction of natural phenomena brought about by the flooding of the Nile.[17] Others view the events as supernatural acts of God with no other possible explanation. A moderate view is to acknowledge the correlation of the plagues with similar phenomena that occur naturally, with the understanding that God often uses nature to accomplish his purposes. As far as the story is concerned, the plagues are signs of God's direct intervention on behalf of his people. They all follow the same general pattern of command, threat, promise, occurrence, and response.[18]

There are several indications that Pharaoh's ability to maintain control gradually grew weaker as God exerted

[16]The Heb. text uses several terms to denote Pharaoh's stubbornness: "hard" (*qashah,* Exod. 7:3; 13:15); "strong" (*chazaq,* 4:21; 7:13,22; 8:19; 9:2,12,35; 10:20,27; 11:10; 14:4); and "heavy" (*kabed,* 8:15,32; 9:7,34; 10:1; 14:4).

[17]For example, see J. L. Mihelic and G. E. Wright, "Plagues in Exodus," in *Interpreter's Dictionary of the Bible,* vol. 3 (Nashville: Abingdon Press, 1962), 822–24.

[18]Such a stylized literary pattern has led some to believe that the narrative of the plagues has a history of use in various liturgical settings of Israel and was edited at various times for that purpose. See Bernhard W. Anderson, *Understanding the Old Testament* (Englewood Cliffs, N.J.: Prentice-Hall, 1986), 68–73.

more power. At first the court magicians were able to reproduce the signs. They could not, however, duplicate the fourth sign, the plague of gnats. They even acknowledged, "'This is the finger of God'" (Exod. 8:19). By the seventh sign, they were afflicted with boils just like the other Egyptians (9:8–12).

Second, Pharaoh's response to Moses changed as the plagues increased in intensity. Initially, he refused to acknowledge the conflict (Exod. 7:22–23). After the third plague, however, he began a pattern of making promises out of desperation, then changing his mind when relief was granted (Exod. 8:8,15). On several occasions, Pharaoh tried to bargain with Moses (Exod. 8:25,28; 10:8–11,24). Twice, he admitted his sin (Exod. 9:27; 10:16). Finally, he commanded the Israelites to leave (Exod. 12:31–32).

Third, taken in sequence, the plagues can be seen as a reversal of creation. They follow a general sequence: contamination of water and land, affliction of humans and animals, destruction of plants, and removal of light. The sign of darkness (Exod. 10:21–29) is especially telling against the cult of the sun god, Re (or Ra), head of the Egyptian pantheon. The following chart provides an overview of the plagues.

Death of Egypt's Firstborn

The death of Egypt's firstborn was a terrifying event (Exod. 12:29–30). Exodus 4:22–23 implies that the killing was punishment for the sufferings of Israel, God's firstborn. Later, Israel was told to redeem every firstborn, whether animal or human (Exod. 13:11–15). In this ritual, they were to remember the death of Egypt's firstborn. In the Ancient Near East, children, especially sons, represented the continuation of the parents' existence. Offspring

Text	Sign/Plague	Meaning	Response
7:8–13	Snake[19]	Unleashing chaos	Magicians replicate sign
7:14–25	Blood	God has power over water, the source of life[20]	Magicians replicate sign
8:1–15	Frogs	God has power over the sacred Nile River	Magicians replicate sign; Pharaoh asks for help
8:16–19	Gnats	Use of dust points to Egypt's humiliation[21]	Magicians cannot replicate sign
8:20–32	Flies	God has power over all the land	Pharaoh will allow worship within Egypt
9:1–7	Plague[22] on livestock	God has power over animal life	Pharaoh investigates
9:8–12	Boils	God has power over human well-being	Magicians are afflicted
9:13–35	Hail	God has power over plant life	Some of Pharaoh's officials fear God; Pharaoh admits sin
10:1–20	Locusts	God has power over all of creation	Pharaoh's officials plead to let the Israelites go
10:21–29	Darkness[23]	Return to chaos	Pharaoh will allow worship without livestock
11:1–10; 12:29–30	Death of the firstborn	God claims Egypt's future	Pharaoh commands Israelites to leave

[19]The Heb. term for "snake" (Exod. 7:9) most often means "sea monster." In other contexts it refers to an untamed creature that represents the forces of chaos, over which God is sovereign (Gen. 1:21; Pss. 74:13; 148:7).

[20]The significance of the blood and frogs is tied to the importance of the Nile River in Egyptian life and culture. Water is the most important commodity in an arid climate like Egypt's. Proper maintenance and control of the water supply would be high on Pharaoh's list of priorities. The Nile itself is associated with several of the Egyptian deities, including Hapi, Isis, and Khnum. Because of this, the waters of the Nile were considered life-giving.

[21]The term "dust" is used in Scripture to indicate the destiny of humankind (Gen. 3:19) and to indicate humility (Ps. 72:9).

[22]The word for "plague" is commonly used in the OT for God's judgment of his enemies (e.g., Ezek. 38:22; Hab. 3:5). Considering the next two signs, which involve the livestock of Egypt, it is best to read "all the livestock" (v. 6) as hyperbole, or as a reference to only that livestock "in the field" (v. 3).

[23]In Israel's prophetic literature, darkness is especially associated with the Day of the LORD, a future time of judgment against God's enemies and of

assured one's future. For God to claim the firstborn, whether Egyptian or Israelite, human or animal, means that God claims the future of every living creature. Indeed, all of creation belongs to God. Egypt's future, represented by its firstborn, was claimed and cut off by God. Israel's future was also claimed by God at the time of the exodus. It was redeemed and therefore secured, throughout Israel's history.[24] This understanding points to the sacrificial lamb of Passover as the means of Israel's redemption.

Reenacting Redemption – Exod. 12:1 Through 15:21

Exodus 12:1 through 15:21 is unlike the preceding eleven chapters. Various instructions and regulations are interspersed in the story of the departure (12:1–29) and the crossing of the sea (13:17 through 14:31). These include instructions about the feasts of Passover and Unleavened Bread and regulations for redeeming the firstborn. The unit concludes with songs of celebration. This literary pattern makes it clear that these activities are ways in which Israel remembered and reenacted the exodus. In this way, every generation of Israel could identify with the redemption and liberty experienced by their ancestors.

The Feast of Passover

The instructions for Passover were given before the exodus from Egypt occurred (Exod. 12:1–13).[25] Every person

purging of the people of Israel (see Isa. 8:22; Joel 2:2; Amos 5:20; Zeph. 1:15). An astounding statement appears in Isa. 45:7, where God claims to "*create* darkness."

[24]The parallel with the story of Abraham and Isaac is obvious (Gen. 22). Not so obvious is the parallel with the sacrifice of God's own son, Jesus. In the crucifixion, God cuts off his future to secure the future of all those who believe (Rom. 8:32).

[25]The primary NT parallel is the institution of the Lord's Supper (1 Cor. 11:23–26).

was to be included as families or neighbors gathered for the event. A lamb or young goat was chosen on the tenth day of the first month. It was slaughtered on the fourteenth day. Its blood, applied to the doorposts and lintel, served as a sign of God's promise to protect the participants from death (Exod. 12:13). The word "Passover" (Heb. *pesach*) is related to the verb "pass over" (*pasach;* Exod. 12:13,23,27). The feast recalls that the LORD literally passed over the Israelite houses marked with blood. In this way, the sacrifice of the Passover lamb served as the biblical model of redemption. Innocent blood was shed so that human life might be saved.

The animal was roasted and eaten in its entirety before morning. It was most important that the meal be eaten in haste, for this signified readiness for departure. According to Exodus 12:42, Passover was a night of vigil. On that night, Yahweh was especially alert and watchful over his people. The Israelites, too, watched and waited for the coming release from bondage. In the New Testament, the Lord's Supper serves a similar purpose of remembrance and anticipation (1 Cor. 11:24–26).

The Feast of Unleavened Bread

The Feast of Unleavened Bread began on Passover night. It was celebrated by eating bread made without yeast for seven days (Exod. 12:14–20). In the urgency of the exodus, there was no time for the Israelites to let their bread rise (Exod. 12:34,39). Participating in the feast reenacted the urgency of the exodus. Regulations about who could or could not partake of these feasts (Exod. 12:43–49) also point to their significance. They helped define the redeemed community. The feasts of Passover and

Reliving Redemption

Pentecostal worship functions in a similar way to the feasts of Israel. When we worship, we relive the stories of the Bible as participants of redemption. Through the Holy Spirit, we tarry with the Israelites, waiting to receive what we cannot control. As we experience spiritual victories, we are taken through the sea on dry land. Through Spirit baptism, we stand at Mount Sinai and receive the law written on our hearts (Heb 8:10).

Worth Remembering

When I visited Israel a couple of years ago, I noticed that along the roadside into Jerusalem were abandoned military trucks, apparently left in the same shell-torn positions from the time of the Six-Day War in 1967. What stood out to me, however, was that they were freshly painted. One such army truck had been converted into playground equipment for children in a neatly manicured picnic area. Then I remembered that the Jewish people had learned a long time ago how to weave their history into the fabric of their lives. Here was another occasion for a child to ask his or her parents, "What does this . . . mean to you?" (Exod. 12:26).

Unleavened Bread were also opportunities for parents to teach their children about what God had done for them. Participation by the children instilled in them the communal memory of Israel (Exod. 12:26–27; 13:8).

The Departure From Egypt — Exod. 12:31–51; 13:17 Through 14:9

The event celebrated in these two feasts was the hurried departure of the Israelites. They had asked for valuable articles from their neighbors, as commanded by Moses (Exodus 3:21–22; 11:2; 12:35–36). This action foreshadowed the requirement in the law to "supply . . . liberally" slaves who had completed their allotted time of servitude (Deut. 15:12–15). According to Exodus 12:37–38, the huge envoy consisted of 600,000 Israelite men, not counting women and children, a large number of livestock, and "many other people."[26] They were finally on their way!

There is some debate about the exact route of the exodus. It appears that "God led the people around by the desert road" (Exod. 13:17–18) because the coastal road was heavily fortified with Egyptian outposts.[27] They took instead "the desert road toward the Red Sea *[yam sûf]*." Because *sûf* means "papyrus" or "reeds," a better translation is "Reed Sea" or "Sea of Reeds" (see NIV text note). In some texts, *yam sûf* is given a wide meaning to refer to the Gulf of Suez or the Gulf of Aqaba, the two bodies of water that extend out of the Red Sea (Num. 21:4; 33:10–11; 1 Kings 9:26; Jer.

---

[26]On the controversy about the number of people who left Egypt, see chap. 8 in this volume.

[27]The reference to the Philistines in Exod. 13:17 probably reflects later usage since the Philistines did not occupy that coastal area until shortly after 1200 B.C., about one hundred years after the time of Moses.

49:21). This wider meaning was carried into the Septuagint in which every instance of the phrase is translated "Red Sea." This meaning was then passed down in the Latin translation and in our contemporary English versions.

Following the literal meaning of *yam sūf*, however, most scholars believe that the Israelites crossed what was known as the "Sea of Reeds." It was probably a marshy, fresh water lake that could support the growth of papyrus. The only fresh water lake in the area is Lake Timsah, lying to the north of the Gulf of Suez and to the south of Lake Manzala. This area also fits well with the testimony of Scripture. The texts trace the journey from Rameses to Succoth to Etham, then back to Pi Hahiroth, near Baal Zephon by the sea (Exod. 12:37; 13:20; 14:2). These sites are documented in Egyptian inscriptions. One inscription suggests that the god Baal Zephon had a temple at Taphanhes, or modern Tell Defneh, located in the area of Lake Timsah.[28]

Victory at the Sea—Exod. 14:10 Through 15:21

The story of the crossing of the sea focuses on the victory of God over Pharaoh and the Egyptian army. The primary purpose of this event was that God would "gain glory." He desired that the Egyptians would acknowledge his sovereignty, which they certainly did (Exod. 14:4,17–18,25)! The story also reveals the weakness of the Israelites' trust in Yahweh, whom they did not acknowledge until after the crossing (Exod. 14:31). Instead, they complained to Moses

[28]G. E. Wright, "Route of Exodus," in *The Interpreter's Dictionary of the Bible*, vol. 2 (Nashville: Abingdon Press, 1962), 197–99. Terence E. Fretheim, *Exodus*, Interpretation (Louisville: John Knox Press, 1991), 153, argues that the translation "Red Sea" better conveys the cosmic significance of God's victory, although the actual crossing may have been in a smaller body of water.

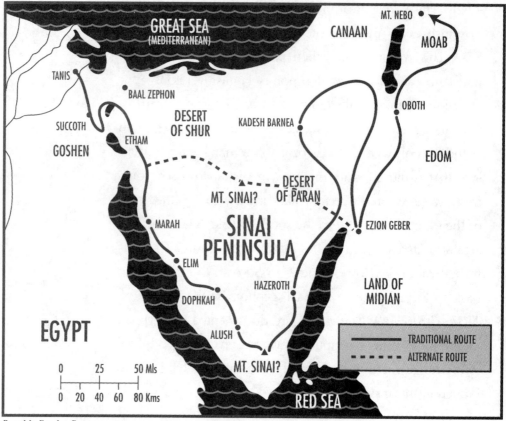

Possible Exodus Routes

about the loss of their security in Egypt. Israel's grumbling is a theme that would continue throughout their journey in the desert (Exod. 14:11–12; 16:2–3; 17:2–3). Moses responded in faith and announced the coming salvation (*yeshu'ah,* Exod. 14:13).

In both narrative and song, the story of the sea crossing is portrayed in cosmic terms. The dividing of the waters to create dry land echoes the language of creation (Gen. 1:9). This similarity in wording testifies to the creative power of God in this act of deliverance. Earlier, the use of military language was used to describe Israel's departure from Egypt (Exod. 12:51; 13:16). Here it is expanded to describe God as a divine warrior (Exod. 14:25; 15:3). The song of Moses depicts the victory in sweeping, universal terms (Exod. 15:1–18). Triumph over the Egyptians represented God's claim of sovereignty over the entire world. As a consequence, the nations would "hear and tremble" (Exod. 15:14). A notable element in the story is the wind, *ruach,* that blew back the waters (Exod. 14:21). *Ruach* can also mean "breath" or "spirit." In Moses' song, the waters parted at "the blast of [God's] nostrils" and came back together as God "blew with [his] breath" (15:8,10). Such language points to the life-giving qualities of the Spirit of God, which cannot be controlled by human will or force (John 3:8).

The long story of oppression appropriately ends with joyous celebration. Miriam and the women danced and

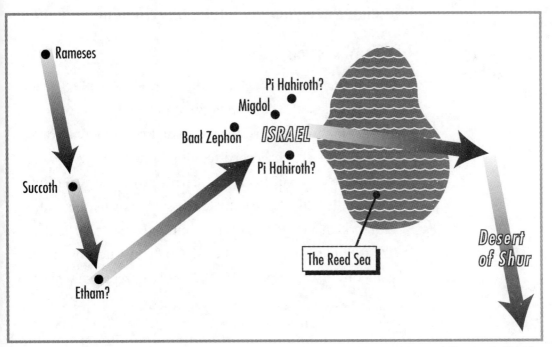

Crossing the Reed Sea

The Songs of Victory

Songs of celebration and praise are an important part of Pentecostal worship. Singing with fervor and excitement is one way of expressing the joy of the Spirit. Bodily motion such as hand clapping and "dancing in the Spirit" reflects the biblical pattern of how liberated people express praise to God. Congregational singing is also an important element of the communal life of believers who share the same testimony and destiny. Singing of victory brings deliverance!

sang (Exod. 15:20–21). Their joy was a response to Israel's long-awaited freedom of body and spirit. Joyous celebration became incorporated into Israel's worship of God. Even today Israel's songs of joy serve as a model of praise for believers during times of oppression or grief.

A Trip Through the Desert – Exod. 15:22 Through 18:27

After victory at the sea, the Israelites traveled through the desert toward Mount Sinai. The trip was marked by major crises of thirst (Exod. 15:22–27; 17:1–7), hunger (Exod. 16:1–36), war (Exod. 17:8–16), and legal administration (Exod. 18:13–26). These crises brought the issues of identity and leadership to the surface. They became opportunities for Israel and God to get to know one another. They defined Moses' role as mediator between them.

Who Was Israel?

The newly freed Israelites did not know how to relate to Moses and God. They had known nothing but the ways of oppression and slavery for the past four hundred years. Now they were challenged to adopt a new understanding of themselves apart from Egypt. This proved very difficult. They dealt with the legitimate needs of not having water and food in a childish, defiant manner (Exod. 15:24; 16:2–3; 17:3). Some blatantly disobeyed God's instructions about gathering manna (Exod. 16:20,27).[29] They repeatedly ques-

[29]Some have suggested that manna was a naturally occurring substance. Possibilities include (1) the sticky-sweet excretion of certain desert insects, (2) the product of various bushes or shrubs, (3) the secretion of aphid-infested tamarisk trees, or (4) "manna moss" found in North Africa. While it is possible that God used a naturally occurring substance, none of these suggestions fit the biblical description exactly. The point of the story is that God provided the manna.

tioned Moses' authority (Exod. 16:8; 17:2). They even tested God, as a self-centered child might test a parent (Exod. 17:2,7).

Yet, Israel quickly learned that their new master was very different from Pharaoh. They did not need to scrape and hoard to survive: God would supply their needs daily (Exod. 16:21). Neither should they accuse nor abuse one another like their former Egyptian overlords. God called them to live in righteousness and integrity (Exod. 15:26). Of course, they would come to know the full nature of this covenant relationship only at Mount Sinai. But on the way, God tested their character and their willingness to obey (Exod. 15:25; 16:4). And over and over, they failed these tests.

Who Was God?

Even before the covenant at Mount Sinai, God had begun to reveal his intention and purpose for Israel. His provision was accompanied by instructions for Israel's well-being. He gave them fresh water with the understanding that they would "keep all his decrees." In this way they would avoid the diseases of Egypt. God was their healer (Exod. 15:25–26). He gave them manna to eat with the understanding that they would "follow [his] instructions" to keep the Sabbath holy (Exod. 16:4,22–30). These events showed a close relationship between daily provision and ongoing instruction. They revealed a God whose care for Israel was grounded in his desire for them to know him and walk in his ways. He wanted to be near them (Exod. 16:9). For Israel that meant doing what was right in God's eyes.

Who Was Moses?

The water and food shortages quickly brought Moses' leadership to the fore. When the people complained to Moses, he would ask God what to do. After Moses carried out God's instructions, the crisis would be resolved. In the skirmish with the Amalekites, Moses' authority was the decisive factor for Israel's victory (Exod. 17:11). Finally, Jethro, Moses' father-in-law, helped him institute a judicial system that placed him over the highest court (Exod. 18:17–26). In these ways, Moses' role as mediator was confirmed and solidified.

The story makes it clear, however, that the real issue was not Moses' leadership, but God's authority (Exod. 16:8). On the journey toward Sinai, Israel's problems had been addressed by ad hoc regulations mediated by Moses. Yet in all this, Israel had no clear definition of their relationship with God. A covenant was needed. It would provide Israel with the identity they sought. It would also provide them a means to know who God was and what he expected of them.

Establishing the Covenant
—Exod. 19:1 Through 20:21; 24:1–18

What Is a Covenant?

Covenant is one of the most important and pervasive concepts in the Old Testament. The concept is first expressed in God's covenant with Noah (Gen. 6:18). It extends to Jeremiah's promise of a new covenant written on human hearts (Jer. 31:31–37). Although each covenant was made for a different purpose and in different circumstances, all biblical covenants share many elements.

Contracts emphasize performance of terms. They are based on the self-interests of the parties involved. A covenant, or treaty *(bᵉrith)*, emphasizes personal loyalty within a relationship. Sometimes covenants can be made between two equals (for example, Jacob and Laban, Gen. 31:44–54). At other times, they may be made between more-powerful and less-powerful parties (for example, Abraham and Abimelech, Gen. 21:27–32).

When the covenant was made between two parties of unequal power, the following characteristics were often present:

1. Covenants are person-oriented, based on a desire for relationship.
2. The stronger party usually initiates the covenant.
3. Covenant terms are not negotiated but based on the grace of the stronger party.
4. Covenant obligations are kept out of loyalty.
5. Covenants are usually in effect indefinitely.
6. Breaking a covenant involves damaging the relationship.[30]

Hittite Suzerain-Vassal Treaties

All the characteristics of covenant noted above also applied to treaties between ruling powers in the Ancient Near East. While some treaties existed between equal nations, many treaties were made between a dominant ruler, called a suzerain, and a subordinate lord, called a vassal. The discovery of treaties between suzerains and vassals in the Hittite Empire from about 1450 to 1200 B.C. has shed

---

[30]Elmer A. Martens, *God's Design: A Focus on Old Testament Theology* (Grand Rapids: Baker Book House, 1981), 73.

new light on the passages of Scripture that describe the covenant God made with Israel. In these treaties, the Hittite king (suzerain) pledged to protect a vassal from his enemies. In return, the vassal was expected to pay tribute out of gratitude to the suzerain. The form of these treaties usually consisted of the following elements:

1. Preamble (names the suzerain)
2. Historical prologue (reviews the history of the relationship between the suzerain and vassal, highlighting the gracious actions of the suzerain toward the vassal)
3. Stipulations (called the "words" of the sovereign, lists the obligations required of the vassal, including a prohibition against forming a treaty with any other king)
4. Provisions for deposit in the temple and periodic public reading
5. List of gods as witnesses
6. Curses and blessings
7. Public oath or solemn ceremony during which the vassal pledged his loyalty[31]

This same pattern, with some variation, is seen in God's covenant with Israel in Exodus, Deuteronomy, and Joshua 24.[32] (Note the comparison chart on the next page.)

[31]George E. Mendenhall, *Law and Covenant in Israel and the Ancient Near East* (Pittsburgh: Biblical Colloquium, 1955), 26–35.

[32]K. A. Kitchen, *Ancient Orient and Old Testament* (Downers Grove, Ill.: InterVarsity Press, 1966), 96–97.

Preamble	Exod. 20:1	Deut. 1:1–5	Josh. 24:2
Historical prologue	Exod. 20:2	Deut. 1:6 through 4:49	Josh. 24:2–13
Stipulations (basic)	Exod. 20:3–17	Deut. 5 through 11	Josh. 24:14–15
Stipulations (detailed)	Exod. 21 through 23	Deut. 12 through 26	
Deposit/reading	Exod. 25:16	Deut. 31:9–13,24–26	Josh. 24:26
List of witnesses[33]	Exod. 24:4	Deut. 31:16–30	Josh. 24:22,27
Blessings and cursings		Deut. 28:1–68	Josh. 24:19–20
Public oath or ceremony	Exod. 24:1–11	Deut. 27	

God had graciously delivered Israel from Egypt. The parallels show that the primary aim of the Sinai covenant was Israel's personal loyalty to God, their savior. In this context, obedience to the covenant was understood as Israel's rightful response to the God who had saved them. Grace came before law. A covenant relationship is very different from legalism. In strict legalism, if one party breaks the contract, the other party is free to leave with no strings attached. In a covenant, sin hurts and grieves the injured party. The covenant, however, continues as long as the initiator wills it. The history of Israel in the Old Testament is a story of how the repeated failure of the Israelites grieved the heart of God. Yet God remained faithful to his promises and continually called Israel back to obedience.[34] Thus the event of the exodus and the giving of the covenant may be seen as the crux of the entire Old Testament.

[33]In the place of pagan deities, the biblical texts mention memorial stones, songs, and nature as witnesses.

[34]The prophets often used a form of speech called the "controversy pattern," or covenant lawsuit *(rîb)*, to bring God's indictment against Israel for breaking the covenant. The Book of Malachi is a good example of the covenant lawsuit form.

Meeting God on the Mountain

Israel finally arrived at Mount Sinai, set up camp, and prepared to meet God. Exodus 19:3–8 records a preliminary agreement between God and Israel. It anticipates the full statement of the covenant in chapter 20. God intended for Israel to become his "treasured possession," "a kingdom of priests and a holy nation" (Exod. 19:5–6). The covenant served to form Israel as a people set apart. They were to be an example to the nations of God's intentions for the whole world. In the context of the covenant, the Law was to be a way of life. It served to reflect to the world the holy character of the God who had redeemed and called Israel to himself (19:4).

Meeting God required much preparation. For two days the people washed their garments and consecrated themselves (19:10). Moses went up and down Mount Sinai to deliver messages from God to the people. A major concern was that someone might come too close to the mountain, or try to "see the LORD," and would perish (19:12,21,24). God warned that if any crossed the boundaries, he would "break out" against them (19:24). On the third day, amid thunder, lightning, and trumpet blasts, God came down on Mount Sinai to deliver the covenant (19:16–19). The significance of this theophany is that the covenant was rooted in the awesome presence and nature of God. Biblical law is grounded in personal relationship.[35]

The Ten Words

Finally, God spoke in the hearing of the people the "words" of the covenant (Exod. 20:1; see Deut. 5:25). In the

[35]W. J. Dumbrell, *Covenant and Creation: A Theology of Old Testament Covenants* (Nashville: Thomas Nelson Publishers, 1984), 91–92.

Hebrew text of Exodus 34:28 and Deuteronomy 4:13, the
Ten Commandments are called simply the "Ten Words."
As noted above, the stipulations in Hittite suzerain-vassal
treaties were called the "words" of the king. They were
commands of a sovereign. The parallel with the Ten
Commandments is striking. Viewed as a treaty document,
the Ten Commandments served as the stipulations in the
Sinai covenant. They were the foundation upon which all
the other laws were based.

After the brief preamble and historical prologue (Exod.
20:2), Israel was commanded to give loyalty to no other
god but Yahweh (Exod. 20:3). This paralleled suzerainty
treaties in which the vassal pledged that he would not enter
into a treaty with any other king; that is, the vassal pledged
his service to the suzerain alone and to no other. By impli-
cation, Israel could not enter into political treaties with
other nations, for to do so would be to accept their gods as
witnesses and be enticed to worship them (Exod. 34:12).[36]
Because Israel's God was unique and distinct from other
gods, idol worship was forbidden. This even applied to an
image set up to represent Yahweh. God could not be contained in a visible object (Exod. 20:4–5). The prohibition
against misusing God's name meant that God's name was
not for common usage. It was only to be used carefully and
reverently. It was not to be used as a means to achieve an
end (Exod. 20:7).[37] God would remain free, both in presence and in character. By observing his Sabbath, the people
would reflect God's own practice of rest (Exod. 20:8–11).

The "words" of the covenant also included regulations
on human relationships. Honoring one's parents and for-

[36]See Mendenhall, *Law and Covenant,* 38.

[37]An example would be swearing falsely in God's name (Lev. 19:12).

bidding mistreatment of others assured a community in which every generation could live in dignity, plenty, and security (Exod. 20:12–17). Taken as a whole, the Ten Commandments summarize God's intention for Israel's life. The more detailed statements of law in Exodus 21 through 23 applied these basic stipulations to various concrete situations in the daily life of the community.

Accepting the Covenant

The immediate reaction of the Israelites to the voice and presence of God was fear. They assumed that the voice of God was life-threatening. They insisted that Moses become the mediator between them and God (Exod. 20:18–21). As mediator, Moses led in a formal ceremony to solemnize, or officially initiate, the covenant. After offering sacrifices, he recited the "words" of God to the people. They, in turn, heartily agreed to keep the terms of the covenant (24:3,7). Then blood was sprinkled upon both the altar and the people. It symbolized the unity of life between the two parties (24:8). The ceremony continued as the elders went up the mountain with Moses. There, amazingly, they saw God and shared a meal (24:9–11). In his role as mediator, Moses was called to go farther up the mountain. There he would receive the stone tablets of the covenant.[38] These were to be deposited in the ark of the covenant (Exod. 25:16).[39]

[38]The two tablets (see Exod. 34:1) probably reflected the Hittite practice of a copy of the treaty for each party in the covenant. In this instance, one copy was for God and the other for Israel. (Depictions of five commandments on one tablet and five commandments on the other misunderstand the purpose of the two tablets.) See Ronald Youngblood, *The Heart of the Old Testament* (Grand Rapids: Baker Book House, 1971), 50. Placing the tablets in the ark parallels the Hittite practice of depositing treaties in the temple of the vassal.

[39]Noah's "ark" (Gen. 6:14, NIV, KJV), Moses' "ark" (Exod. 2:3, KJV), and the "ark" of the covenant (Exod. 25:10–16, KJV) actually come from different

The Covenant Is Broken and Restored — Exod. 32 Through 34

Sin and Punishment

The Israelites' obedience to the covenant was very short-lived. While Moses was on the mountain receiving the tablets and instructions for the tabernacle, the people grew restless. In direct violation of the first and second commandments, they demanded a visible god to worship. Aaron promptly granted their request by making a calf from gold supplied by the people themselves. They held a feast and bowed before the calf as the god that delivered them from Egypt (Exod. 32:1–6). This act betrayed the heart of the covenant. So soon they had violated their relationship with God!

God's initial response was spoken to Moses in the form of a covenant lawsuit. He proposed destroying the Israelites and starting over with Moses (Exod. 32:7–10). Moses quickly and effectively interceded on Israel's behalf. He appealed to God's reputation among the Egyptians and to promises made to the patriarchs (32:11–13). However, when Moses saw for himself what the Israelites were doing, he brought judgment on the people. The covenant, along with the stone tablets it was written on, was shattered. Israel was faced once more with the question of whom they would serve. Only the sons of Levi pledged faithfulness to God. Moses authorized them to kill the violators (32:15–29). Later, in spite of Moses' intercession,

Covenant Commitment

Our Western culture emphasizes individualism and autonomy, characteristics that are detrimental to covenant keeping. The covenants of friendship, church membership, and marriage are important commitments that most of us will make sometime in our lives. Just as the unfaithfulness of Israel brought grief to God and damaged their relationship, so unfaithfulness to a friend, spouse, or faith community hurts the injured party. However, injured parties need not abandon damaged relationships altogether. Restoration is possible through repentance and forgiveness.

Heb. terms. Although Moses' "ark" changes to "basket" in a number of later translations, and the NIV begins with "chest" for the traditional "ark of the covenant" in Exod. 25:10 and Deut. 10:1–2, it reverts to "ark" in later verses because of tradition.

God also struck the people with a plague (32:30–35).[40]

Will God Go With Them?

It was not immediately evident that the covenant would be restored. Tension had developed between God and the Israelites. God was prepared to send an angel ahead of the Israelites to drive out the inhabitants of the land, but God himself had declared that he would not go with them (Exod. 33:1–6). This saddened the people, and they stripped themselves of their ornaments. This was their first sign of repentance since the shameful episode of the golden calf.

Moses, described as someone who spoke with God as a friend (33:7–11), interceded once more. At Moses' initial request, God granted his presence to go with Moses and give rest in the land (33:12–14). Insistent that the Israelites be included in God's promise, Moses gained a second assurance of God's accompaniment (33:15–17). Finally, Moses pushed God to grant a request to see his glory. In this conversation, God instructed Moses to make two more stone tablets (34:1). The covenant would be renewed!

Restoration

As in the initial covenant making (Exod. 19:16–20), God again appeared in a theophany (34:5). This time, however, only Moses was present to see and hear. In answer to Moses' request to see God's glory, God passed by Moses. He proclaimed his name, along with a list of qualities that describe his character. The list contains two very different ways in which God deals with covenant violators: He for-

---

[40]The context of Exod. 32:30–35 makes it probable that Moses' purge of the camp was an action designed to avert God's wrath. Apparently it did not succeed.

gives and he punishes (34:6–7). Moses quickly asked that God choose the first option. He requested that God forgive their sin and take them back as his inheritance. God agreed.

The renewal of the covenant included an additional promise by God to perform wonders never seen before (Exod. 34:10). This promise probably referred to exploits to be performed in the conquest of the Promised Land. The covenant required the complete obedience of the Israelites. The land they were being given would be filled with numerous temptations. They were to reserve all loyalty for God alone (34:11–17). They were to reenact their deliverance from Egypt with the annual feasts of Passover and Unleavened Bread (34:18,25). This was done through ceremonies such as the redemption of firstborn animals, Sabbath rest, and annual feasts associated with harvest. These gave Israel a reference point for their identity as the people of God in an agrarian society (34:19–26). Finally, God instructed Moses to write the words of the covenant on the new stone tablets (34:27–28). The covenant was restored.

The Shining Face of Moses

When Moses rejoined the Israelites, he discovered that his face shone from being so near to God. He began the practice of wearing a veil over his face when he was not speaking with God or the people (Exod. 34:29–35). In Moses' shining face, a portion of God's glory was revealed to the people. Later, after the tabernacle was completed, God's glory descended in the midst of Israel (40:34). The exodus from Egypt had finally reached its goal (6:7).

Appendix: Chronology of the Exodus

The discussion of the date of the exodus centers on two views, generally called the Early Date and the Late Date, each of which is supported by a verse of Scripture. The starting point for the Early Date theory is 1 Kings 6:1, which states that the departure of the Israelites from Egypt occurred 480 years before the fourth year of Solomon's reign (generally agreed to be around 967 B.C.). This would place the exodus at around 1447 B.C. during the rule of Amunhotep II (ca. 1450–1425 B.C.) and place the oppression during the preceding reign of Thutmose III (ca. 1482–1450 B.C.).

The Late Date, which places the exodus between 1300–1280 B.C., is based upon an interpretation of Exodus 1:11, which mentions Rameses and Pithom as store cities that were built by the Hebrew slaves. This theory assumes that the city of Rameses was named after the pharaoh Rameses II (ca. 1304–1237 B.C.), who had continued the work begun by his father, Seti I (ca. 1318–1304 B.C.), of rebuilding the old Hyksos capital in the Delta. In this theory Pithom probably refers to Pr-Itm, a city located west of Lake Timsah near the place where Joseph's brothers had settled.[41]

The Hebrew (Masoretic) text of Exodus 12:40 states that the Israelites were in Egypt for 430 years. The date of the arrival of Jacob and his family to Egypt may be calculated to correspond to the Early and Late Dates for the exodus at around 1877 B.C. and 1710 B.C. respectively. However, the Septuagint (Greek translation of the Hebrew) text of Exodus 12:40 includes the journey of Abram within the 430 years, allowing only 215 years for the occupation of the

[41]Anderson, *Understanding the Old Testament,* 51.

Israelites in Egypt. This places the Early and Late Dates of the arrival of Jacob at around 1662 and 1495 B.C. respectively.

The dates of the arrival of Jacob and the exodus of the Israelites are also related to the invasion, occupation, and expulsion of the Hyksos.[42] The Egyptian term *Hyksos* means "rulers of foreign countries" and is applied to a mixed group of Asian invaders who dominated Egypt from about 1786 to about 1567 B.C. during the Fifteenth through the Seventeenth Dynasties.[43] The Hyksos established their capital at Avaris in the Nile Delta, while the Egyptian princes continued to rule at Thebes in Upper (Southern) Egypt. After a long war, begun by Egyptian prince Sekenenre, the Hyksos were overthrown and finally expelled from Egypt by Ahmose (ca. 1570–1545 B.C.), the first king of the Eighteenth Dynasty.

At this time, the center of power shifted back to Thebes, and the pharaohs began the policy of drafting groups of lower class migrants called *Habiru* (or *'Apiru*) as forced labor for their extensive building projects. Although the *Habiru* cannot be directly identified with the biblical Hebrews, apparently there were groups of Semitic peoples included in their numbers. These migrants apparently were allowed to stay in Egypt when the Hyksos were driven out.

The arrival of Jacob and his family in Egypt fits best into

[42]T. O. Lambdin, "Hyksos," in *The Interpreter's Dictionary of the Bible,* vol. 2 (Nashville: Abingdon Press, 1962), 667.

[43]As I noted in chap. 5, n. 9, the Fifteenth Dynasty, the "Hyksos Dynasty" in Lower Egypt, is dated at about 1674–1567 B.C. An Asian presence, however, had troubled Egypt from the end of the Middle Kingdom. Following the collapse of a unified Egypt, Hyksos local rulers doubtless established an increasing presence in the East Nile Delta (Goshen), so the estimate of about 1786 is not an inappropriate dating.

the period of the Hyksos kings for the following reasons. First, the Hyksos' capital was in the area where they settled (Gen. 47:4–6). Second, the mention of a chariot in Genesis 41:43 fits best during or after the Hyksos occupation, since the Hyksos probably introduced the war chariot into Egypt. Third, the personal affinity shown to Joseph in Genesis 47 fits best with a Hyksos king, who was possibly Semitic like Jacob and Joseph. Fourth, the rise of a "new king" who did not know Joseph fits best with the overthrow of the Hyksos and the renewal of the native Egyptian dynasty. Furthermore, the pharaoh's suspicion of the Hebrews would have been a natural result of their association with the Hyksos.[44]

If indeed Jacob and his family came to Egypt during the Hyksos occupation, then the only two options available for the date of their arrival are the Late Date using the Hebrew text of Exodus 12:40 (ca. 1710 B.C.) or the Early Date using the Septuagint text of Exodus 12:40 (ca. 1662 B.C.).[45]

[44]There are problems with this view as noted in W. Johnston, *Exodus,* Old Testament Guides (Sheffield: Sheffield Academic Press, 1990), 15–26.

[45]For the patriarchal material that bears on the date of the exodus, see chap. 5 of this textbook. In calculating either date, we work with round numbers and estimates. Granting the nature of the material, it should be stressed that it is remarkable that the Early and Late Dates for the exodus are so close, not that they are different.

Study Questions

1. What was the purpose of God in bringing Israel out of Egypt?

2. How are the "Early Date" and "Late Date" for the exodus calculated? Know the evidence and the method of calculation for each.

3. Understand the events of Moses' "call" in Exodus 3 through 4.

4. Explain the meaning of God's name (Yahweh, I AM).

5. When and why does God "harden" Pharaoh's heart?

6. Describe the plagues that God used to punish Egypt and what they represent.

7. Summarize the important points of the first Passover. What does it represent? What are its elements?

8. Identify the main stops of the journey from Egypt to Sinai, and the events on the way.

9. Know the Ten Commandments. What do they mean? How do other documents of that time help us understand their function?

10. List the major events in the Mount Sinai and the golden calf incidents.

11. Be able to define these terms as they are used in the Book of Exodus: Pharaoh, Hyksos, Hebrew.

For Further Reading

Brueggemann, Walter. "The Book of Exodus." In *The New Interpreter's Bible*. Vol. 1. Nashville: Abingdon Press, 1994.

Gowan, Donald E. *Theology in Exodus*. Louisville: Westminster/John Knox Press, 1994.

Levenson, Jon D. *Sinai and Zion: An Entry Into the Jewish Bible*. Minneapolis: Winston Press, 1985.

Neihaus, Jeffrey J. *God at Sinai: Covenant and Theophany in the Bible and Ancient Near East.* Grand Rapids: Zondervan Publishing House, 1995.

Stiebing, William H., Jr. *Out of the Desert? Archaeology and the Exodus/Conquest Narratives.* Buffalo: Prometheus Books, 1989.

7

Roger Cotton

God Reveals Himself to His People

Outline:

- What Is the Context of the Covenant and the Ten Commandments?
- What Terms Define the Biblical Laws?
- What Is the Ancient Near Eastern Literary Context for Biblical Laws?
- What Was the LORD's Purpose in Giving the Laws?
- How Can ANE Laws Help Us Understand Biblical Laws?
- What Are the Distinctives of Israel's Laws?
- How Do Penalties in the Pentateuch Differ From Those in the ANE?
- How Do We Understand the Laws of Exodus 20:22 Through 23:19?
- Instructions for the Worship Center and Priesthood
- What Was the Tabernacle?
- How Did the Priesthood Work?
- What Did the Sacrifices Mean?
- The Theology of Holiness
- The Laws of Leviticus 17 Through 27

Terms:

atonement
case law
clean and unclean
Code of Hammurabi
command, commandment
holiness
law
lex talionis or talion
statute, statutory law
tabernacle
tithe
torah/Torah
typology
Urim and Thummim

What Is the Context of the Covenant and the Ten Commandments?

The Book of Exodus portrays Yahweh[1] speaking to Moses at the burning bush. There, on the slopes of Mount Horeb (Sinai), he commissioned Moses to deliver Israel from Egypt (Exod. 3:4 through 4:17). After he led the people of Israel out of Egypt, they met with the LORD at Mount Horeb on their way to the Promised Land. There he told them that they would be his special people (Exod. 19:4–6). They were to be his agents to bring salvation to the world. God was reaffirming the promises given to Abraham.[2] Through Israel, Yahweh would offer an eternal relationship to anyone who would be willing. To accomplish this, God would establish them as his people and give them the land of Canaan. They would be a witness to who he is and the relationship he wants with all people.

The narrative found in Exodus 19 provides the context for the laws given to Moses by the LORD. There we are told that, through the exodus from Egypt, God redeemed Israel to be his covenant people. From the beginning of the Bible the message has been clear: The true God speaks and reveals himself to people; he wants to have a relationship with all who are willing. The Bible is his Word given *to* people *through* people, so he can be known and his love experienced. The laws of the Pentateuch provide further details about the relationship God wanted to have with his people Israel. These laws illustrate the principles he wants all people to know and live by.

[1] The personal name of God for which Jews have substituted "the LORD."

[2] Exod. 3:15–17; 6:2–4; cf. Gen. 12:2–3,7; 15:18–21; 17:8; 18:18–19; 22:17–18.

Exodus 19 through 24, Leviticus 17 through 27, and all of Deuteronomy describe the covenant relationship between God and Israel in terms of a suzerain-vassal treaty.[3] The LORD would be their king and they would be his vassals. Israel, then, became God's pilot project in the world. Their covenant served as a testimony to what God wanted for humanity.

The Ten Commandments (Exod. 20:1–17; Deut. 5:1–22) are the basic stipulations, or core principles, of the covenant. The laws elaborate on and apply these principles to the everyday lives of God's people. These laws are based on God's character but are expressed in the culture of the times.

The covenant laws were to be Israel's constitution as his nation. Laws are always culturally oriented. The laws of the Pentateuch tell how the people of Israel could function effectively in their world to fulfill God's purpose. Though the details might not continue to apply as cultural situations changed, the principles behind the laws would remain stable. Obeying these laws did not save Israel or make them God's people. Instead, obedience helped them show their appreciation for their relationship to him. Without obedience to the covenant, Israel would have no basis for continuing fellowship with God.

What Terms Define the Biblical Laws?

God gives us rules for our own good (Deut. 10:13). The Hebrew word most often translated "law" is *torah*. The word, however, really means "instruction." It often refers to the whole revelation given by God to Israel (note the

[3]See George Mendenhall, "Covenant Forms in Israelite Tradition," *BA*, 17 (1954): 50–76. See also J. A. Thompson's brief but excellent *The Near Eastern Treaties and the Old Testament* (London: Tyndale Press, 1964); Kenneth A. Kitchen, *The Bible in Its World: The Bible and Archaeology Today* (Downers Grove, Ill.: InterVarsity Press, 1977).

parallelism in Ps. 119:18 and Isa. 2:3). At such times it takes on the meaning "Scripture" (see Hos. 8:1,11–12).[4]

There are three other common Hebrew words that refer to various kinds of legal pronouncements. They point to different aspects of the ancient Israelite concept of law.

The term *mitswoth*, "commands" or "commandments," focuses on the imperative nature of God's authoritative directives to his people. It is interesting that the Ten Commandments are literally called the "ten words" (cf. "decalogue"; see Exod. 34:28; Deut. 4:13; 10:4). The Hebrew term for "words" can refer to all kinds of written or spoken communication. The Ten Commandments are not true law as societies think of law. They have no circumstances or penalties listed. Rather, they are stipulations essential to God's covenant with Israel. They express statements of policy and principle for their relationship to him. This is unlike anything in the legal traditions of the Ancient Near East.[5]

The word often translated "statutes" (*choq, chuqqim*) speaks of something inscribed. Thus it refers to the specific binding and enduring nature of the laws. We call this type of law "statutory law." It presents the legal offense in its most basic sense as it comes from the lawgiver. It states only the crime and its penalty, without giving any circumstances (e.g., Exod. 21:12).

Lawgivers are not the only ones who make laws, however. Laws are also the products of court decisions. The term *mishpatim*, often translated "ordinances" or "judgments," speaks of the decisions of a judge. We call this kind of law "case law." It reflects the application of statutory law to a specific case (e.g., Exod. 21:13–14). It includes the offense,

---

[4]These occurrences are consistently translated "law" in Eng. versions but clearly denote the larger body of Scripture.

[5]"Ancient Near East" and "Ancient Near Eastern" can be signified by ANE.

penalty, and circumstances. The *torah* of Moses is made up of all these: command, statute, and case law.

What Is the Ancient Near Eastern Literary Context for Biblical Laws?

The Spirit of God inspired Moses to write the various laws, or instructions, for his people. Not all the laws in the Pentateuch, however, were totally new to the world, even though authorized by God. As can be seen by reading Ancient Near Eastern law collections like the Code of Hammurabi,[6] God had Moses include many laws already existing in the ANE cultures. God, however, modified or replaced what did not conform to his standards and values. The laws show that God did not always call for instant transformation. Often God accepted people as they were and *gradually* moved them toward his ideal. This is especially seen in his treatment of marriage. On the one hand, the worst perversions and abuses were prohibited, such as adultery, incest, homosexuality, and bestiality (Lev. 18; 20:13–21). On the other hand, polygamy (polygyny) was not directly confronted but given certain restrictions.[7] Things embedded in culture cannot be immediately overturned. People's hearts must first be transformed. God was not endorsing polygamy but dealt with it in terms of its cultural setting.[8] Frequently the Old Testament shows the

[6]James Pritchard, *Ancient Near Eastern Texts,* 3d ed. (Princeton: Princeton University Press, 1969). Also very readable is Victor H. Matthews and Don C. Benjamin, *Old Testament Parallels,* rev. ed. (New York: Paulist Press, 1997).

[7]Exod. 21:10, Deut. 17:17; 21:15–17.

[8]Much like, for example, the NT treatment of slavery. It is not abolished, but is undermined severely. It was left to the Church to work out a full return to the Edenic ideal of equal rights for all human beings.

problems and pain resulting from polygamy (1 Sam. 1:2,4–6). By degrees the LORD brought people to appreciate the way he had created marriage to function (Gen. 1:27; 2:23–24).

The literary style of the laws, especially in Exodus 21 through 23, compares to the wording of other ANE laws about half the time. Nearly all ANE laws are given as case law. They use the formula: "If . . . then." Such laws state the offense, circumstances, and penalty (e.g. Exod. 21:13–14). These laws describe an actual case or an anticipated one. Such decisions arose out of everyday life and were used as precedents for future cases. They served as illustrations of the principles God wanted to teach his people. Scholars often call such laws "casuistic," which means they are conditional. The Hebrew term for casuistic, or case, law is most often found in the plural: *mishpatim,* meaning "judgments," decisions of the court in interpreting a specific law.

The rest of the Old Testament laws are statutory law. A statute is a law that comes directly from a lawgiver or lawgiving body. Scholars call such laws "apodictic." The Hebrew word for "statute" is *choq, chuqqim.* They simply state the offense and its penalty (e.g., Exod. 21:12). Both these types of law should be distinguished from the command. The command gives neither circumstance nor penalty. It simply says "do" or "do not." Commands are not found in the ANE law collections. Some are, however, found in other documents, such as treaties and religious instructions.[9]

The literary organization of the laws of the Pentateuch is more like that of the ANE than like modern law codes. The

[9]The Heb. term for "command" is *mitswah.*

groupings are not legal categories. Instead they follow issues taken from daily life. Topics are linked by associations that naturally lead to sections of laws that follow. The Pentateuch uses literary features common in the ANE, such as various forms of repetition, to aid memorization and to emphasize certain themes.[10]

What Was the LORD's Purpose in Giving the Laws?

The flow of thought within the laws of the Pentateuch intentionally communicates theology. For example, Exodus 21 begins with the release of slaves. God is telling Israel that he values people and that their salvation from slavery in Egypt should make a difference in how they treat people. God was teaching Israel how to function together as a nation. These laws were to provide civil guidance to Israel in their cultural context.

The purpose of Old Testament laws was unique among the laws of the ANE. For example, the famous Code of Hammurabi is presented as the king's testimony of how good a ruler he was. Hammurabi's laws strive to maintain the status quo and to protect the rights of the privileged class (i.e., the *awilum*). The laws of the Pentateuch, on the other hand, were given by the LORD through Moses to the people of Israel. They revealed Israel's relationship with God (Deut. 4:6–8) and the awesomeness of his character. They expressed the specific obligations of the covenant between the LORD (Yahweh) and Israel. This was unheard of in the ANE world.

[10]For example, see Virginia Stearns, "A Study of Leviticus 18–20: Its Unity, Form and Function" (Costa Mesa, Calif.: Southern California College, 1991), wherein she shows that certain legal materials in the Pentateuch were worded and arranged for easy memorization.

The laws of Moses begin with the law collection found in Exodus 20:22 through 23:33. This collection is similar to Hammurabi's code in style and content. It deals with how Israel was to live together as God's people. The next collection is Leviticus 17 through 27, the one least like other ANE collections. It focuses on holy living. Finally, the third collection is Deuteronomy 12 through 26. The setting is Israel's preparation to enter the Promised Land. It expounds the Ten Commandments as the stipulations of God's covenant with Israel as a nation. Each of these collections picks up matters that are pertinent to the context of the particular book. Each demonstrates different emphases on the principles God was teaching his people at that time concerning who he is and how he wanted them to live.

How Can ANE Laws Help Us Understand Biblical Laws?

There are important similarities and differences in content between ANE laws and those of the Pentateuch.[11] A comparison of the subjects covered and the attitudes or principles expressed is very enlightening. Common subjects include commerce, marriage, personal offenses, and public justice.

The differences are more significant. Though absent in the Pentateuch, the following are dealt with in the ANE laws: prices, rentals, trades, adoption, physicians, and priestesses. The Pentateuch deals with commercial matters in much less detail. It usually gives only general principles.[12]

[11]See the chart of law collections in John Walton, *Chronological and Background Charts of the Old Testament*, rev. ed. (Grand Rapids: Zondervan, 1994), 87, or *NIV Study Bible* (Grand Rapids: Zondervan, 1995), xxii.

[12]For example, Israel was to have honest weights and measures, Lev. 19:36; Deut. 25:15.

On the other hand, the Pentateuch deals with all kinds of religious laws that are absent from the ANE collections. ANE laws were comparatively secular.[13] In contrast, all Israel's laws had a religious foundation. For example, there are no laws for Israel about the permanent sale of land because the land belonged to the LORD. He wanted it kept in the families he assigned it to (Lev. 25:23–24). In the ancient world, medicine was often associated with magic. Magic depends on a power other than God to accomplish its purposes. Accordingly, the LORD made it clear to Israel that He alone was to be their physician (Exod. 15:25–26).

What Are the Distinctives of Israel's Laws?

The main differences between the laws of Israel and of the ANE involve values. ANE laws served the reigning king. Israel's laws stressed the importance of an exclusive relationship to God and the worth of human life.[14] God gave Israel the laws. All crimes against the law in Israel, therefore, were ultimately crimes against God. Their moral principles were to be based on his character (Lev. 19:2). Lawbreakers were not only accountable to the community; they were, first of all, accountable to God. Therefore, their penalty could include both restitution to the victim and sacrifice to God for forgiveness (Lev. 6:1–7; 19:20–22). Another difference is that the rulers in Israel were always to be subject to the law. They were not to consider themselves better than anyone else, because God was the

---

[13]In his Prologue, Hammurabi does say that the gods commissioned him to promote the welfare of the people, although this seems more a formality to justify the document than a claim to inspiration.

[14]Human life is seen in the Bible both from quantitative (e.g., prohibition of murder) and qualitative (e.g., care of the poor, concern for the integrity of the family) perspectives.

suzerain, the great king (Deut. 17:18–20). Even their king was just another of Yahweh's subjects (Deut. 17:14–20).

Motive clauses[15] in the Pentateuch express these principles. Who the LORD is and what he has done for his people are often stated as the basis for a law. Israel had been mistreated but had been delivered by the LORD. God's people, therefore, were not to mistreat the poor or the powerless (see, for example, Deut. 24:17–18). Israel was to be holy because God was holy (Lev. 19:2). ANE laws never give such motive clauses nor relate ethical values to their gods.

Morality is a characteristic of the LORD. He expects his people to reflect his character. It goes beyond the legal requirements of law. For example, Israel was not only to love their fellow Israelite as themselves (Lev. 19:18), but they were also to love the foreigners living among them in the same way (19:34). Jesus understood this so well! In his parable of the Good Samaritan, the foreigner is the "neighbor" (Luke 10:30–37).

How Do Penalties in the Pentateuch Differ From Those in the ANE?

Capital Crimes

In terms of the covenant, Israel's rebellion against God required the death penalty. Rebellion brought death to the guilty person. What's more, it could spread to others and endanger their welfare. Therefore, rebellion had to be removed from the covenant community. It could include such things as worshiping idols and spiritual powers other

[15]A motive clause is that part of a sentence that provides the reader with the reason an action should be undertaken.

than Yahweh (Josh. 22:16–20). Such anti-idolatry legislation was unique to Israel.

God established provisions for governance in both the community and the family. Rebellion against authority, consequently, was considered to be rebellion against God. It required the death penalty. This included mistreatment of one's parents (Exod. 21:15,17; Deut. 21:18,21; 27:16). Anything that destroyed either individual lives or the family and the corporate life of the covenant people had to be dealt with decisively.

The area of sexual ethics represents another major difference between laws of the ANE and the Old Testament. The laws of the Pentateuch address the sacredness of sex, marriage, and the family. Violations hurt individuals and break down the family.[16] As a result, society begins to break down. The well-being of the family and of human society is a major value emphasized by God. Therefore, the penalty for the destruction of the family was the same as for murder. Violators had to receive the death penalty.

Marriage in Israel was seen in terms of a "one-flesh" bonding between a man and a woman (Gen. 2:23–24). In other words, sexual restrictions were based on the way God designed people to function. God's plan made possible the greatest degree of intimacy between two human beings. Sexual sins in the Bible were not just taboos but were violations of the "owner's manual."

Having illicit sexual relations is a rebellion against the way God designed us. It shows unfaithfulness in the most

Like a Cancer . . .

God's requirement of capital punishment for certain crimes can be compared to the stopping of cancer by surgical removal. If we agree with God's serious rejection of these crimes, we can see the need to "remove" the offender from the community like a cancer from the body.

[16]See, for example, William C. Williams, *An Examination of the Relationship Between Solidarity and Adultery in Ancient Israel* (Ph.D. diss., Ann Arbor, Mich.: University Microfilms, 1975), wherein the author shows that unrestrained adultery would have threatened first the family, then Israel's entire social structure.

intimate of our relationships. It was often connected to idolatry in the Old Testament. The Bible shows this by putting prohibitions against sexual sin together with those against idolatry.[17] The use of the adultery-prostitution metaphor for Israel's unfaithfulness to the LORD throughout the Old Testament illustrates this also.[18]

Only a few of the incest laws in Leviticus 18 and 20 find parallels in the ANE. The reason incest is forbidden in Scripture is because of its destructive effects on interfamily relations. Families infected with sexual sin would tend to

Social Distinctions in ANE Law

Code of Hammurabi	Exodus 21:22–25
§209–210 If an *awilum*[19] strikes the daughter of another *awilum,* causing a miscarriage, he pays ten shekels of silver. If the woman dies, the offender's daughter is put to death.	"If men who are fighting hit a pregnant woman and she gives birth prematurely but there is no serious injury, the offender must be fined whatever the woman's husband demands and the court allows. But if there is serious injury, you are to take life for life, eye for eye, tooth for tooth, hand for hand, foot for foot, burn for burn, wound for wound, bruise for bruise."
§211–212 If he [the *awilum*] has struck a commoner's daughter causing a miscarriage, he is fined five shekels of silver. If the woman dies, he must pay a half-mina of silver.	
§213–214 If he strikes a female slave and causes a miscarriage, he must pay two shekels of silver. If the slave dies, he must pay one-third mina of silver.	

[17]E.g., Lev. 18:6–20; 20:10–21; cf. 18:1–5,21–23; 20:1–6,27; Col. 3:5.

[18]E.g., Jer. 3:6–10; Hos. 1:2.

[19]The Babylonian term *awilum,* when contrasted with other classes, as in the text given in the sidebar, represents a free citizen, a member of the upper class, a person of rank. The Babylonian text is a paraphrase.

self-destruct, which would damage the larger community.

Bestiality in some forms was permitted by the Hittites (Hittite Law § 200A) and is mentioned in Canaanite epics. Homosexuality in Israel was understood as unnatural (Lev. 18:22). Both bestiality and homosexuality were forbidden because they are contrary to the way God made people (Gen. 2:18–24).

The remaining capital crimes continue to sharpen the focus on the value of human life. In Israel a murderer was to be punished by death. When a human life was taken, God even held animals accountable. Take, for example, the case of the bull that gored someone to death. It was to be stoned to death. If the owner of a bull knew it was dangerous and still let it run loose, both the owner and the bull were executed (Exod. 21:28–29).

In the rest of the ANE, however, the value of human life varied with one's social status. Criminals who committed crimes against the privileged class were punished more severely than those who did the same against lower classes. Crimes against women and slaves received lesser penalties than crimes against free men. In the laws of Israel, however, even slaves were valued as human beings and were not just property. Their masters were not allowed to do whatever they wanted with them (Exod. 21:20). Read the sidebar contrasting the famous "abortion law" in the Code of Hammurabi (CH §§ 209–214) with its parallel in Exodus 21:22–25 (see the opposite page). Note the complete lack of social stratification in the biblical law.

Property and Damages

In the ANE a thief was often punished by cutting off a hand. Sometimes thieves were killed for stealing from a

Hittite Law § 142

If you've ever had your hubcaps or wheels stolen, you'll appreciate Hittite law § 142: "[If] anyone drives [a chariot . . . and anyone steals] its wheels, he shall give 25 liters of barley [for each] wheel." Do you hear Ecclesiastes' refrain echoing in your brain? ". . . nothing new under the sun . . . nothing new under the sun."

member of the upper class. In the Bible, the penalty for theft is restitution. God does not permit mutilating the human body. Moreover, the life of the thief was protected (Exod. 22:1–4). God's law never equates the value of human life with material things. The Bible even limits the number of times a criminal can be whipped. This is to avoid demeaning the person (Deut. 25:1–3). God requires us to respect the dignity of every person, regardless of social status. Aside from the biblical text this was unheard of in the rest of the ANE.

"Lust" and "covet" are translated from the same Hebrew word. The tenth commandment forbids coveting (Exod. 20:17). Why? Because if we desire something strongly enough, we may try to take it. Furthermore, it ends up the same as idolatry (Col. 3:5). Also, rape in Israel was considered a crime against the woman (Deut. 22:25–29). This was unlike the ANE. There it was seen exclusively as a sin against the property rights of the father or husband.

Indentured servants were not to be treated harshly (Lev. 25:43). A lender was not to go into the person's house to get a thing pledged as repayment for a loan. The lender was to wait outside for the person to bring the pledge to him (Deut. 24:10–13). In this way the lender showed his respect for the borrower. Throughout the Old Testament, the LORD opposes taking advantage of others. He defends the weak and vulnerable.

The famous principle of justice called *lex talionis*—"an eye for an eye"—needs to be explained. Human nature tends to give harsher penalties to the underprivileged and more lenient penalties to the privileged classes. It also tends to escalate disputes and pay the offender back with greater hurt. God, however, told Israel to be fair and to treat everyone justly. The *lex talionis* said, "The punishment must fit the crime—no more, no less." *Lex talionis* was a principle for the administration of punishments within the public law courts. It was also intended to discourage personal retaliation in private disputes (Matt. 5:38–42). (Jesus was not saying anything negative about the application of this principle of justice in the law courts of the Old Testament.)[20]

Biblical Law and the Code of Hammurabi		
The Bible (NIV)	**The Code of Hammurabi**[21]	**Comparison**
Exod. 21:16: "'Anyone who kidnaps another and either sells him or still has him when he is caught must be put to death.'"	CH § 14: If a person of rank kidnapped the young child of another, he was to be put to death.[22]	The ANE law is the same as the OT law, except it is class-specific.
Exod. 22:7–9: A neighbor responsible for storing another's goods must be brought "before the judges" ("before God," NRSV) to determine guilt for any losses. If guilty, he must pay back double.	CH §120: In a case similar to the one cited in Exodus 22:7–9, the guilty party was to be brought before "the gods."	Penalty is the same.
Exod. 21:15: "'Anyone who attacks his father or his mother must be put to death.'"	CH §195: If a son struck his father, his hand was to be cut off.	The OT includes the mother, yet the penalty avoids bodily mutilation.

(cont. on the next page)

[20]There is no evidence that this law of retaliation was carried out literally, except for administering the death penalty in the case of murder (first commanded by God in Gen. 9:6 where he indicates the issue is a just penalty that values the image of God in the victim). In other cases a *fair* punishment, rather than bodily harm, was agreed upon (cf. Exod. 21:30 and Num. 35:31).

[21]References to the Code of Hammurabi are given by the number of the law preceded by the siglum §.

[22]Abstracted from Martha T. Roth, *Law Collections from Mesopotamia and Asia Minor* (Atlanta, Ga.: Scholars Press, 1995).

Biblical Law and the Code of Hammurabi *(cont. from the previous page)*		
The Bible (NIV)	**The Code of Hammurabi**	**Comparison**
Exod. 21:24–26: "'Eye for eye, tooth for tooth. . . . If a man hits a manservant or maidservant in the eye and destroys it, he must let the servant go free to compensate for the eye.'"	CH §§196–201: If a person of rank blinded the eye of another person of rank, his eye was to be blinded. If he blinded a commoner's eye or broke his bone, he was to pay sixty shekels of silver. If he blinded a slave's eye or broke a bone, he was to pay one-half the slave's value (in silver).	The OT and ANE both have the *lex talionis* in the context of public justice. The ANE, however, makes class distinctions that are absent from the OT.
Exod. 22:1–4: "'If a man steals an ox or a sheep and slaughters it or sells it, he must pay back five head of cattle for the ox and four sheep for the sheep. If a thief is caught breaking in and is struck so that he dies, the defender is not guilty of bloodshed; but if it happens after sunrise, he is guilty of bloodshed. A thief must certainly make restitution, but if he has nothing, he must be sold to pay for his theft. If the stolen animal is found alive in his possession . . . he must pay back double.'"	CH §§ 8, 21–22: If a person of rank stole an animal that belonged to the temple or the state, he was to pay thirtyfold. If it belonged to a commoner, he was to replace it tenfold. If the thief could not pay, he was killed. If a man broke into a house, he was to be killed and his body placed in the opening. If a man committed a robbery and was captured, he was to be executed.	Human life is of such high value in the OT that even the life of a thief is protected. Material things, on the other hand, are not as highly valued in the OT as in the ANE.
Lev. 18:6–18; 20:10–21: Incest receives the death penalty.	CH § 154: If a person of rank had sexual relations with his daughter, he had to leave the city.	The OT takes this act more seriously than the ANE.

How Do We Understand the Laws of Exodus 20:22 Through 23:19?

The first law collection in the Pentateuch has been called the Book of the Covenant because the covenant is mentioned in Exodus 24:7. These laws give the earliest instructions as to how the new nation was to function under the LORD. They begin with the laws governing the altar of the LORD (20:22–26). The LORD's priority is proper *worship* and his *people,* not material possessions. He is concerned about healthy relationships. These relationships have two dimensions: (1) those between God and the people and (2) those between individuals and/or groups.

The first social issue addressed is the treatment and release of slaves (21:1–11). The Israelites were to treat their slaves generously. They were to reflect the grace God showed them in delivering them from Egyptian slavery. From the subject of slaves, the laws move to assaults, personal injuries, and loss of property. The major principles taught here are respect for human life, responsibility for one's actions, and respect for the property of others. Along with these are accountability for agreements, restitution for violations, and penalties that fit the crimes. God also takes into consideration motive and intent. The laws of 21:12–14, for example, distinguish between murder and involuntary manslaughter.

The laws found in Exodus 21:22–25 clearly show that causing harm to an unborn child is wrong. Even within the ANE culture surrounding Israel, taking the life of an unborn child was considered a heinous act.[23] The Bible

---

[23]The penalty levied on the offender shows the act illegal in the OT. ANE law (e.g., CH §§209–214; MAL A21, §§ 50–52; cf. §53; HL §§ 17–18; Sumerian

states that God is the author and sustainer of all life. For this reason, all life is sacred, especially human life. God does not authorize private individuals to take human life. On the contrary, he works through human government, demanding a just and fair legal process (Exod. 23:6–9).

At Exodus 22:18 the Book of the Covenant divides in half. The form of the remaining material (22:18 through 23:33) shifts from casuistic to apodictic law. The content of 22:18 through 23:33 deals with improper actions toward God and with mistreatment of vulnerable people. This section contains applications of the Sabbath principle of devotion toward the LORD. It intermixes matters of Israel's vertical relationship with the LORD and horizontal relationship with people. The principles of horizontal (that is, societal) relationships given here are the consequences of a proper vertical relationship with God. A healthy relationship in either direction cannot exist without the other. Proper ethics must be based on proper theology! All of life is to be lived under the lordship of the only true God, the Creator and Savior. This is the essence of Israel's holiness (to be discussed in Leviticus). God wants a personal relationship with all who are willing. He demands devotion and loyalty. He expects love to be shown toward people. These instructions for proper relationships will become a theme for his covenant people. Here they conclude with exhortations and promises from the LORD.

Instructions for the Worship Center and Priesthood – Exod. 25 Through 40

Exodus 24, along with 32 through 34, deals with events in covenant making and covenant breaking in Israel's early

Laws §§ 1–2) records the case in almost identical language, but frequently imposes a class distinction (as in CH), absent from the biblical text.

history.[24] These chapters emphasize God's holiness, human sinfulness, and God's grace. They show that personal relationship between God and his people is the context for all the laws and instructions. Even when his people rebel, the LORD offers forgiveness and restoration to those who repent. This is grace!

Exodus 25 through 31 and 35 through 40 contain instructions for building the tabernacle and a description of its materials. The worship center was the place where God's people experienced his presence. Worship involved the priesthood described in Exodus 28. Their consecration and ordination is commanded in Exodus 29 and carried out in Leviticus 8 through 9. God established them as the only mediators between him and the people. These priests offered the people's sacrifices of worship and repentance. The sacrifices exalted the LORD and expressed faith in his Word. Leviticus 1 through 16 give instructions for those sacrifices for atonement and worship.

Finally, Leviticus 17 through 27 give instruction on living in fellowship with God through a life of holiness achieved by atonement. Leviticus 26 concludes the covenant at Sinai with blessings and cursings. Other ANE law collections and treaties also conclude this way. The literary structures of Exodus and Leviticus, as well as Numbers, alternate legal and narrative material. This style lends itself to public reading. The narrative breaks up the monotony of the legal material and illustrates its principles. It clarifies and strengthens the theological message.

What Was the Tabernacle?

God told Moses to have the people construct a sanctuary, or holy place, for him (Exod. 25:8). He empowered

[24]See chap. 6 of this textbook.

skilled workers by filling them with his Spirit (Exod. 31:1–11). Exodus 25:9 calls the sanctuary a "dwelling place" *(mishkhan)*.[25] In Deuteronomy God often says that where he puts the tabernacle, there he puts his name (Deut. 12:5,11; 16:2). Thus, God himself is associated with that place. The association includes his presence and his reputation, both in character and in deed.

From Exodus 27:21 through Leviticus and Numbers, the most common term for the tabernacle is the "Tent of Meeting." The Hebrew term translated "meeting" suggests an opportunity to get together. The word may focus on a place, like the tent, or an appointed time, like the feasts. The Tent of Meeting is the place of encounter with the king of the universe (Exod. 29:42–46).

The tabernacle became an object lesson in the biblical faith. No other religion could offer fellowship with the only true God, the Creator and Lord of the universe. In offering this to humans, God provided the only way to salvation. Through the layout of the tabernacle and its court, a clear message is dramatized: Human beings can approach the holy God and fellowship with him only on his terms. God had to be worshiped by means of one system of sacrifices, through one priesthood. Furthermore, only the high priest could enter God's very presence in the Most Holy Place, the inner sanctuary. Even this could happen only once a year, on the Day of Atonement.

Portable shrines and permanent temples with two chambers were common in many cultures in the ANE. The structure of the tabernacle bears similarities to Egyptian

---

[25]The Heb. word *mishkhan* comes from the same root as the word *sheᵏkhinah* (a postbiblical term for the presence of God experienced through human senses).

portable shrines, such as the one found in the tomb of Tutankhamen. Moving into the presence of deity by stages was a common idea. The uniqueness of the pentateuchal instructions for Israel was the *exclusiveness* of one place and one way of approaching God's presence. When Israel offered the specified sacrifices in faith, God showed himself and forgave their sins. No other religion has experienced this reality.

What Is Typology?

God's use of physical things, events, and people to demonstrate spiritual realities is called typology. It helps if we remember that Israel had no Bible. Moreover, most people could not read or write. So how could God teach them theology? Typological understanding means that God taught spiritual principles through *real* historical situations. Typology is more than mere symbolism. Its meaning is not arbitrarily attached to something. That is, typology is not an excuse to allegorize a text, ignoring its historical context.[26] Meaning is present because the principles of God's salvation are eternal. They are the same for Israel in the exodus as in the cross and resurrection of Christ. The meaning of the tabernacle was "God with us." In this its meaning was similar to the meaning of the incarnation of Jesus in the New Testament (John 1:14).[27]

Therefore, we should ask, "What was the functional significance of the tabernacle?" The tabernacle taught that

> ### The New Tabernacle
>
> The tabernacle prepared people for the message of Jesus Christ. Jesus said, "'I am the way and the truth and the life. No one comes to the Father except through me,'" John 14:6. God was present among his people in the tabernacle of Israel. He is now present through Christ in his church, the temple of the Holy Spirit (1 Cor. 3:16).

[26]The meaning of the tabernacle, for instance, must be sought in its function in ancient Israel and its significance to them at that time, not in some hidden meaning that Israel could not have known.

[27]The Gk. verb translated "made his dwelling" in John 1:14 is related to *skene,* "tent," showing that John was aware of the analogy mentioned above.

there is only one way to fellowship with the LORD. As we try to understand this, it helps to ask, "How would an Israelite of that time understand things?" For example, they would have seen no theological significance in the use of wood; it was simply the most appropriate material to accomplish God's purpose. The overlay of gold, on the other hand, would have signified to the people that the tabernacle was the place of royalty. The same for the "royal" colors of scarlet and purple. These things honored the LORD as the great king.

How Was the Tabernacle Laid Out?

The court of the tabernacle was a rectangle that measured about 75 by 150 feet (Exod. 27:9–19). It was enclosed by a series of linen screens, each 7 1/2 feet square. The entrance to the enclosure was from the east side by means of an ornate curtain embroidered with images of cherubs.

Inside the entry was the bronze altar for burnt offerings, made of acacia wood overlaid with bronze (Exod. 27:1–8). A fire was to be kept burning on it continuously. All Israel's sacrifices were to be offered there. It became the focal point of daily worship and atonement.

The next item encountered in the courtyard was the bronze basin (Exod. 30:17–21). Priests were to wash before entering the Tent of Meeting and before approaching the bronze altar to offer sacrifices (30:20–21).

At the far end of the courtyard stood the tabernacle proper, the Tent of Meeting (Exod. 26). It was constructed of frames made of acacia wood overlaid with gold. The frames were held together by a clever system of crossbars and projections. The structure was covered by two sets of curtains. One set of curtains was of linen adorned with purple and scarlet yarn and with gold. The curtains were held together with gold clasps. The second set of curtains was much plainer. They were made of goat hair and held together with bronze clasps. Exodus 26:14 also mentions two additional coverings of red ram skins and sea cow hides.[28] The entry to the tent was through an ornate curtain depicting cherubs.

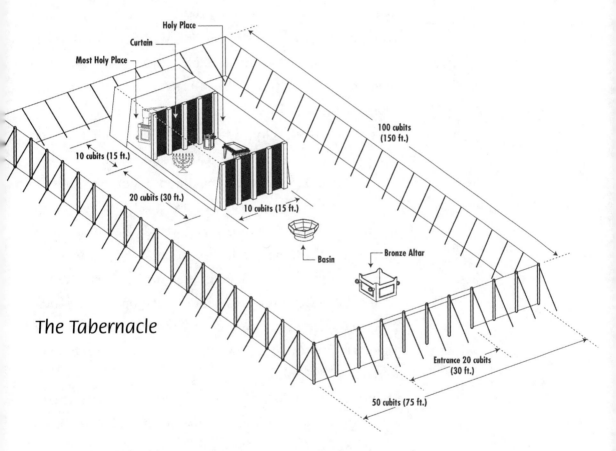

The Tabernacle

[28]Scholars are uncertain as to the nature and placement of these coverings because they are not described as being divided into sections, and if they covered the entire tent, they would have been oppressively heavy to carry. To resolve this difficulty, some rabbis thought these coverings were only partial, and some modern scholars have suggested that they were the materials for wrapping the curtains to protect them during the desert wanderings. In any case, the great detail used to describe the first two coverings stands in contrast to the single verse describing both of the leather coverings.

How Was the Tabernacle Furnished?

The outer chamber, the Holy Place, housed three pieces of furniture. On the north side, there was a table that held twelve pancake-like loaves of unleavened bread. This bread was called the "bread of the presence" (Exod. 25:23–30). The twelve loaves represented the twelve tribes of Israel before God (Lev. 24:5–9). Perhaps the bread also symbolized God as Israel's provider. It was replaced weekly, just as Israel's commitment was to be renewed every Sabbath. On the south side, across from the table, was a seven-branched gold lampstand (Exod. 25:31–40). Its light represented the presence of God. Its seven branches probably signified the days of the week. God desired fellowship with Israel on every day, not just on the Sabbath (Exod. 40:22–25).

The small altar for burning incense stood before the entrance to the Most Holy Place (Exod. 30:1–6). Its incense produced a pleasant aroma that covered all foul odors. In the minds of the people it was to be associated with the worship of God. The smoke of the burning incense represented the prayers of God's people going up to him. These prayers exalted God and were favorably received by him. Especially important among these prayers were the intercessions of the priests.

Finally, within the Most Holy Place, the inner sanctuary, was a special wooden chest overlaid with gold, traditionally called the "ark of the covenant" (Exod. 25:10–22; Num. 10:33). The chest represented the throne of the LORD. He was Israel's ultimate and eternal king. He had established his earthly headquarters in the tabernacle. The lid of the chest was called the "atonement cover" (Exod. 24:17) or the "mercy seat" (KJV). On one day each year, the high priest applied sacrificial blood to its cover. This atoned for all the sins of Israel that had not yet been forgiven. Ultimately the chest contained "the Testimony," that is, the Ten Commandments (Exod. 25:16), a jar of the manna that God provided in the wilderness (Exod. 16:33–34), and Aaron's rod after it budded (Num. 17:8–10; Heb. 9:1–5). The rod represented God's authorization of Aaron's family as the LORD's priests.

How Did the Priesthood Work?

Exodus 28:1 declares that Aaron and his sons (that is, all his male descendants) were to serve the LORD as priests. God appointed them as the mediators between him and his people: They carried the people's needs and expressions of worship to God; they communicated God's word to the people. God allowed the priests to come near his presence and offer sacrifices for the people. Through the priestly ministry, guilt was removed that would have separated the people from their holy God. He, therefore, was able to dwell among them. Israel's priests were an important part of the object lessons contained within the ceremonial laws. The ceremonies they carried out were, in a sense, acted-out prayers to God.

The priestly ministry emphasized the holiness[29] of the LORD and his requirements for fellowship. The priests blessed the people in the name of the LORD.[30] They were intercessors for God's people. They were the ones who

Eunuchs Welcome

Among other things the priesthood demonstrated that God *wanted* to have fellowship with people. Now that Christ has come and fulfilled the goal of the priesthood, no longer are eunuchs and foreigners to be excluded from the congregation (Isa. 56:3–7; cf. Acts 8:26–39); no longer are ethnicity, gender, and social status valid criteria for limiting one's participation in worship and ministry (Acts 21:9; Gal. 3:28). Every person may have direct access to God through his Son.

[29]The word "holiness" stresses the unique nature and person of God. When speaking of people, holiness speaks of a relationship between those people and God, the Holy One. See "How Was the Word of God Given?" in chap. 1.

[30]To bless, here, means to facilitate God's eternal purposes in their lives (Lev. 9:22–23; Num. 6:23–27).

taught the LORD's *torah* to the people (Lev. 10:11; Jer. 18:18). They determined what was holy and diagnosed what was clean and unclean, according to *torah* (Lev. 10:10; 13 through 14). The priests mediated answers and guidance from the LORD through the Urim and Thummim (Exod. 28:30). When they saw the LORD moving from the camp, they blew trumpets to signal Israel to get ready to move. The priests were responsible for signaling, both on occasions of battle and on occasions of rejoicing (Num. 10:8,10).

All priests were from the tribe of Levi. But not all Levites were priests. Priests were only from Aaron's descendants. The remaining Levites were support staff for the ministries of the tabernacle (Num. 8). No women were allowed to serve as priests or Levites.

The Priestly Uniforms

The overall purpose of the priestly clothing was to give the priests "dignity and honor" as mediators (Exod. 28:2). The clothing was made from fine linen. Linen garments would have indicated people held in high esteem. The colors of blue, purple, and scarlet, along with gold, would have been associated with royalty and deity.

Several items of clothing were specified for Israel's priests (Exod. 28). They were to wear "undershorts" (28:42–43, *Living Bible*) for modesty when serving at the altar.[31] The high priest was to wear a long blue robe with bells around the hem. The bells announced that the priest was acting in his official capacity, so the LORD would not kill him for entering the Most Holy Place (28:31–35). He also wore a

[31]Exod. 20:26.

kind of vest, or apron, called an "ephod." On its shoulders were two onyx stones with the names of the twelve tribes of Israel. A breastpiece hung from the ephod, on which were twelve gems engraved with the names of the tribes. In this way, the priest represented the people before the presence of God: He bore them on his shoulders and over his heart (28:12,29).

Lastly, the high priest carried the Urim and Thummim in a pocket in the breastpiece. The meaning of the words "Urim" and "Thummim" is unknown.[32] It is thought, however, that these objects were a means for determining God's will. It is likely that they were stones drawn from the pocket and cast as sacred to get a yes or no from God.

The turban of the high priest had a gold plate attached which had the words "HOLY TO THE LORD" engraved on it. This reminded everyone of the awesome responsibility that Aaron took on when he represented the LORD to the people (Exod. 28:36–38).

Commissioning the Priests

The ordination of the priests is described in Exodus 29 and carried out in Leviticus 8 through 9. It involved ceremonies that lasted a week. The new priests were dedicated to the service of the LORD and were authorized to minister in the sanctuary. Both the people and things used for ministry to the LORD had to be consecrated.[33] For a person (or thing) to be used in ministry without being sanctified

Finding God's Will

Casting lots to find God's will seems strange to us. So do things like Gideon's fleece (Judg. 6:37–39). But remember, the Israelites didn't have a complete Bible to guide them. The Scriptures and the Holy Spirit make these practices unnecessary in most cases.

[32]A possible hint may be found in the Heb. spellings: "Urim" begins with the first letter of the Heb. alphabet, while "Thummim" begins with the last letter, perhaps to encompass all possibilities.

[33]The Eng. words "sanctify," "dedicate," "consecrate" often represent the same Heb. root. In settings like this one, it means to be dedicated to the Lord in a special sense for the task at hand.

would have been blasphemous. God would destroy them.[34]

The consecration ceremony consisted of several steps. Washing, the first step, signified a new beginning, a cleansing from sin and a removal of guilt. Then, sacrifices indicated the priest's need of forgiveness of sins and communion with God. Anointing with oil signified that God had chosen the priests for leadership. It also indicated that God had delegated authority to them and had provided them with the power of his Spirit to fulfill their commission. The consecration of the priests was symbolic of the dedication of all God's people to him. The cleansing, sacrifices, and anointing ceremonies set the priests apart for ministry. They also served to teach the people about God and their relation to him.

During the week of ordination, the priests stayed in the tabernacle court until their consecration was complete. Otherwise, they would have died. The waiting period emphasized the seriousness of fulfilling one's commitments to God and the importance of letting God do his work to sanctify them. When the ordination was properly completed, the visible presence of God, his "glory," filled the tabernacle in an awesome display (Exod. 40:34–38; Lev. 9:23–24).

Leviticus 10:1–7 also shows the seriousness of obedience to the LORD's instructions and the proper way of approaching God. Nadab and Abihu, sons of Aaron, offered "unauthorized fire" to the LORD. The text may imply that they were under the influence of alcohol (note vv. 8–9); consequently, impaired in their judgment, they took lightly God's holiness. The unauthorized fire that they offered probably had a source other than the bronze altar in the tabernacle court. As a result,

---

[34]As he did Nadab and Abihu in Lev. 10:1–7. The passive verbs in Lev. 10:3 probably should be translated: "Among those who approach me I must be considered holy; in the sight of all the people I must be honored."

fire came out from God's presence and destroyed them. Because of this incident, alcohol consumption was prohibited when ministering before the LORD. The priests had to distinguish between what was holy (that is, dedicated to God) and what was common (that is, secular, not devoted to God). They were to teach the people to do so, as well.

What Did the Sacrifices Mean? —Lev. 1 Through 16

The ANE religions sought to appease angry, fickle gods with bribery. The gods represented certain forces, such as weather, love, and fertility, that the ancients wanted to con-

Old Testament Offerings				
	Name of Offering	References	What the Offering Expressed	Remarks
Worship Offerings	Vegetable: The Grain Offering	Lev. 2	Hebrew: *minchah,* gift. A tribute to the LORD, submission and dedication; often used with other sacrifices; giving to God as a worship exercise.	Provided food for the priests
	Animal: Fellowship (also called Peace) Offering	Lev. 3; 19:5-8 Three types (Lev 7:15-18; 22:18-23): thank, vow, freewill	Celebration of God's blessings in praise, thanks, and devotion	God received the fatty parts; worshiper, family, and priest ate the meat
Atonement Offerings — Note: every atoning sacrifice is a "sin" offering of some sort.	The Whole Burnt Offering	Lev. 1	Judicial substitution, general repentance for sin, worship, and total dedication to the LORD	Totally burned to the LORD
	The Sin Offering	Lev. 4:1 through 5:13	Purification from unintentional sins against God	For priest or community: totally burned; blood sprinkled in Holy Place. For lay persons: priest received the meat; blood poured out at altar.
	The Guilt Offering	Lev. 5:14 through 6:13	Paying a debt, penalty, and compensation for damages against a person or the holiness of God	Priest received the meat

trol. The powers of these gods were supposedly manipulated by means of magic. The Bible does not allow any such attitudes and rituals in the worship of the LORD. He is personal and loving. He calls on his people to trust his good purposes.

Sacrifices and Sin

The biblical sacrifices show how serious the sin problem is. Forgiveness and restored fellowship come only at a high cost. By substitution, the life of the sacrifice was given for the life of the sinner. The sacrifices proclaim that there is only one way to God—the way *he* prescribes. He has made known that way because of his great love and grace. The sacrifices, therefore, offered a message of hope. When the covenant had been violated, they provided reconciliation with God. We call this reconciliation with God "atonement."

Provision for atonement distinguished the Israelite religion from other ANE religions. It showed that the LORD, the Creator of the universe, wanted to establish a relationship with people. The sacrificial system given through Moses in the Pentateuch was intended to do this. It taught the people how to express their praise, repentance, faith, thanksgiving, submission, and devotion to their God.

Sacrifices and Worship

The sacrifices intentionally involve the whole person in acts of worship. By sacrificing an animal, the worshiper demonstrated his faith. Sacrifices provided expression for one's faith through physical activity. They effectively combined the two elements of Israelite worship: *service*[35] and *submission*.[36]

[35]The Heb. word *'abadh,* "to work," is often used to denote worship activity (e.g., Ps. 100:2).

[36]The Heb. word *hishtachᵃwah,* lit. "to prostrate oneself" (e.g., Ps. 81:9).

God specified that the animals to be offered were not to have any serious defects. The parts the people esteemed most highly were offered by fire to God. This included the animal's fat and blood. The animal used most often was a sheep. It was the most common domestic animal. For more serious sins a bull was offered.

Moreover, the animal had to fit certain criteria. It had to "chew the cud" (i.e., eat a vegetarian diet) and have split hooves (Lev. 11:3). Animals that met those criteria were deemed "clean" (i.e., acceptable for sacrifice and for food). Those that did not were considered "unclean" (i.e., unfit for sacrifice and food).[37] The terms allude to acceptability, not to hygiene. (See "The Theology of Holiness," p. 304.)

The Atoning Sacrifices

Three sacrifices atoned for sin and thus normally required blood: the whole burnt offering, sin offering, and guilt offering. They involved seeking forgiveness and atonement. Atonement lay at the heart of the Old Testament sacrificial system. The word translated "atonement" indicates removal of the sin barrier between the people of Israel and God, and reconciliation to Him. It probably meant "to cleanse" or "pay a ransom to release from a penalty."[38] This was the purpose of the burnt, sin, and guilt offerings. The

[37]Some state the principle this way: "What is acceptable for sacrifice is acceptable for food." A somewhat amusing illustration is found in Mal. 1:8. Apparently the Jews, after their return from Babylon, were offering sick animals to the LORD. Malachi says to try offering that to their governor and see if he's pleased!

[38]The Heb. word for atonement was long understood to mean "to cover from view." See Baruk Levine, *Leviticus wayyiqra'*, JPS Torah Commentary (Philadelphia: Jewish Publication Society, 1989); Jacob Milgrom, *Leviticus 1–16*, AB (New York: Doubleday, 1991); John Hartley, *Leviticus*, WBC (Dallas: Word, 1992).

sin of the worshiper was placed upon the animal; the animal's life was substituted as a ransom for the worshiper's life.

The blood of the animal represented its life (Lev. 17:11). The blood, therefore, was sacred. Blood properly used was the great purifier, but out of place, it became the great defiler.[39] The worshiper showed identification with the sacrifice by laying hands on it (Lev. 8:14). That meant that the life of the sacrifice was really given for him or her. The meat of these sacrifices was sacred and could be eaten only by the priests.

These sacrifices assumed that the sinners were repentant. The sin offering was for sins that did not represent premeditated, blatant rebellion against the LORD'S covenant (Lev. 4:2; Num. 15:27–36). For such defiant evil, the person was to be "cut off from his people" (Lev. 7:20).

Sin deeply affects one's relationship with God. The sin offering taught that sin contaminates a person. It makes people and the place where they live and worship unfit for the presence of a holy God. By the grace of the LORD, however, offerings for sin purified the people so that God's presence could continue among them.

THE WHOLE BURNT OFFERING — LEV. 1

The whole burnt offering received its name because it was totally burned to the LORD. There was no portion of it eaten. It appears from Leviticus 1:4 that it served as a general-purpose sin offering. Burnt offerings and fellowship offerings were the most frequently recorded sacrifices in 1 and 2 Samuel and 1 and 2 Kings. A whole burnt offering could be made from a bull, a sheep or goat, or a bird. This

---

[39]Any bodily discharge, including blood, could make one unclean (e.g., Lev. 15, esp. v. 25).

gradation made it appropriate for any occasion, be it simple or elaborate, and brought the offering within reach of any person, rich or poor.

THE SIN OFFERING—LEV. 4:1 THROUGH 5:13

While the whole burnt offering was made for sins in general, the sin offering removed the defilement of certain types of sin that were specifically directed against God. It purified the sinner from spiritual pollution so God's presence could continue among the people. The word "sin" means to miss an intended goal or target (Judg. 20:16). It indicates an offense against God that is unintentional (Lev. 4:2,13,22,27). It helps us see our own inability to live perfectly, even when we try. It also shows us God's willingness to forgive.

God wanted to provide atonement for *all* his people. There was even a unique allowance for poor people in the sacrificial requirements. For the burnt offering and the sin offering God allowed them to offer birds (Lev. 1:14–17; 5:7–10). The sin offering could be made even from flour (Lev. 5:11–13). No oil or frankincense was allowed on the flour. The lack of these elements expressed the seriousness of sin.

The sin offering was a powerful way of understanding the seriousness of sin in God's sight. The more serious the sin, the more serious the defilement. The requirements for leaders were greater than those for the sins of the common people.[40] The animals necessary were larger and more expensive. In the case of the anointed priest, the blood of the bull was carried into the Holy Place and the meat was

---

[40]Lev. 4:2–12,22–26; cf. vv. 27–35.

not eaten. In the case of ordinary people, however, the offi-
ciating priest received a portion of the sacrifice. This was his
to eat (Lev. 6:24–30).[41]

THE GUILT OFFERING — LEV. 5:14 THROUGH 6:7

The guilt offering dealt with sins against property.[42]
Before offering it the sinner had to pay damages of 120 percent to the person wronged. This offering dealt with making amends, reparations, and compensation. It used the
image of paying a costly debt. It atoned for accidental
offenses against holy things. It could also cover intentional
sins if they were against secular property. Making restitution through payment for the damages would help show
the sinner's repentance.

The Worship Offerings

Worship offerings were not concerned with making
atonement for sin. Instead, they represented various aspects
of worship.

THE FELLOWSHIP OFFERING — LEV. 3

The word translated "fellowship offering" *(shelem)*
comes from the same Hebrew root as the word *shalom*,
often translated "peace." *Shalom*, however, carries a wider
meaning. It means completeness, wholeness, well-being,
and harmony, especially when referring to God. The fellowship offering celebrated the blessings of God. On a few

---

[41]As part of the tribe of Levi, the priests had no inheritance in the land (Deut.
18:1; Josh. 13:14) so the LORD allowed them a portion of the sacrifices as part
of their livelihood.

[42]Recent studies have shown that the "guilt offering" was really a penalty
offering. See works cited in n. 38.

very special occasions the fellowship offering was required for certain expressions of worship. Normally, however, it was voluntary. It was the worshiper's own expression of praise, thanks, celebration, and devotion. It could be a bull or cow (3:1–5), or a sheep or goat (3:6–16). There were three specific types of fellowship offerings: thank offerings, vow offerings, and freewill offerings (Lev. 22:17–25,29–30). The first two marked certain events in the worshiper's life. The last was a spontaneous, heartfelt expression to the Lord. The fellowship offering did not involve forgiveness of sin. The meat, therefore, could be eaten. First, the blood, fat, and certain organs were offered to God. Then the meat was divided between the worshiper and his family and the priest (Lev. 7:12–18).

The Grain Offering — Lev. 6:14–23

The word translated "grain offering" (minchah) literally means "gift." It shows that we worship God through our giving. Grain offerings consisted of fine flour and were sometimes required with other offerings, especially burnt offerings and fellowship offerings. The grain offering expressed one's tribute to the divine king, and thus the worshiper's submission and dedication. It also provided food for the priests.

Salt was put on the grain offering as a reminder of its covenantal context.[43] Salt was a common element in ANE treaty ceremonies. Its use stressed the enduring nature of the promises made in a treaty.[44]

[43]Lev. 2:13.

[44]Pagan means of sacrifice were forbidden. Boiling a young goat in its mother's milk, for example, may have been prohibited to avoid associating the Lord with a worship practice performed before fertility gods. The true God is the personal, loving Source who *cannot* and *need not* be manipulated.

Firstfruits and Tithes

God's people were required to give him the firstfruits of the harvest and one tenth of all they had (a tithe). By doing this, they acknowledged that their livelihood came from him. Everything they owned belonged to him, and they were only his stewards, or managers (Lev. 25:23).

The New Moon, Sabbath, and Jubilee

Daily devotion was shown to the Lord through morning and evening sacrifices. Also on the first day of each month, the New Moon festival called for special sacrifices (Num. 10:10; 28:14). Each week, God's people were to show their devotion by resting on the seventh day. By doing this, they remembered that God rested after his work of creation (Gen. 2:1–4). The Sabbath denoted the number seven which, from all God's uses of it for special times, seems to be an important rhythm in the universe. Following the exodus from Egypt, however, the Sabbath became a covenant symbol (Exod. 31:12–17). Keeping the Sabbath testified to the relationship between the people and the LORD. The Sabbath reminded Israel that God had redeemed them from bondage. It also allowed them rest, reminding them that they were no longer slaves.

The seventh year was a Sabbath Year. The land was not to be cultivated but was to lie fallow. The fiftieth year (7 x 7 + 1) was the Year of Jubilee. In this year, debts were cancelled, slaves were released, and all land reverted to the families God originally gave it to (Lev. 25:39–43).

The Harvest Festivals

God combined commemoration of salvation events with harvest festivals in the required feasts. Israel celebrated these

Setup for the Cross

The whole sacrificial system looked forward to fulfillment in the perfect sacrifice for all sin, Jesus Christ the Son of God. His death and resurrection took away all barriers to fellowship with God. The Old Testament sacrificial system expressed this through the images of forgiveness and reconciliation, healing and purification, and payment of debt.

The Sacred Calendar of Feasts and Holy Days

Holy Day	Scripture	Frequency	Date Celebrated	Description
Sabbath	Exod. 16:23–30; 20:8–11; 31:13; Deut. 5:12–15	Weekly	Seventh day of each week	A day of no work, commemorating God's work in creation and redemption.
New Moon	Num. 28:11–15; Exod. 34:22; Num. 10:10	Monthly	New moon	Celebrates beginning of month.
Passover	Exod. 12:1 through 13:10; Lev. 23:9–14	Annual (spring)	The first month of the religious year (Nisan or Abib = March/April*)	An evening meal commemorating the exodus, God's deliverance of Israel from Egypt. Ingredients: lamb, unleavened bread (no yeast), and bitter herbs. Note that Christ was crucified on Passover.
Unleavened Bread	Exod. 12:17	Annual (spring)	The week following Passover	A week commemorating the deliverance from Egypt, with no yeast allowed.
Weeks (NT Pentecost)	Lev. 23:15–22; Num. 28:26; Deut. 16:9	Annual (spring)	50 days after Passover (May/June)	A day of worship in gratitude for the wheat harvest.
Trumpets	Num. 29:1–7	Annual (fall)	The first day of the seventh month (Sept./Oct.)	Signaling the beginning of the seventh month, culminating the sacred year and beginning the new agricultural or civil year. Similar to U.S. New Year's Day.
Day of Atonement	Lev. 16:1–34; 23:26–32; Num. 29:7–11	Annual (fall)	The 10th day of the seventh month	Not a feast! The only required fast. A day of mourning over one's sins and the high priest sacrificing to provide a fresh start for the whole nation.
Booths (Tabernacles, Ingathering)	Exod. 23:16; 34:22; Lev. 23:40–41	Annual (fall)	The 15th through the 21st of the seventh month	A week of living in shelters of branches commemorating with great joy God's provisions on the journey to the Promised Land and following. Similar to U.S. Thanksgiving.
Sabbath Year	Exod. 21:1–6; 23:10–11; Lev. 25:1–7; Deut. 15:1–18; 31:10–31	Periodic	Every seventh year	A year of rest. No sowing or reaping except for personal use. Land left fallow; produce belonged to the poor. Debts were cancelled; Hebrew slaves freed.
Jubilee	Lev. 25:8–55	Periodic	Every fiftieth year	Same as Sabbath Year, plus land restored to families from which it had been purchased or taken.

* The Jewish calendar is lunar and so the months do not match ours exactly.

events in the spring when the grain harvest began and in the autumn to mark the end of the agricultural year.

PASSOVER AND UNLEAVENED BREAD

Passover occurred in the spring. It was the beginning of the religious year because it, with the Feast of Unleavened Bread that followed, commemorated Israel's deliverance from Egypt (Exod. 12:2–28). The firstfruits of the barley harvest were offered in the Feast of Unleavened Bread. These two festivals were reminders that God had redeemed Israel from bondage to the Egyptians. He had reconciled his people to himself. They now had freedom, dignity, and a land (Lev. 23:6–8). The exodus from Egypt became a powerful illustration of God's redemption later in the Bible (Jer. 16:14–15; Heb. 3:1 through 4:16).

THE FEAST OF WEEKS

Fifty days after Passover, Israel was to offer the firstfruits of the wheat harvest. This festival was called the Feast of Weeks.[45] In it, the people thanked God for a good harvest. On this occasion, a loaf of *leavened* bread was presented to the priest at the sanctuary (Lev. 23:17,20). In later Judaism, the festival became associated with the giving of the Law at Sinai.

THE FEAST OF TABERNACLES

The last feast of the year was the Feast of Tabernacles, or Booths. This festival was named for the temporary shelters Israel was to stay in during the week of the festival. The feast was a reminder of Israel's journey through the wilderness

Different Passover Observances

Christ was crucified on Passover. However, the Jewish and Christian observances of Passover do not coincide. The Jewish calendar is composed of lunar months, the Christian (Gentile) calendar of solar months.

[45]Lev. 23:15–21; called Pentecost in Acts 2:1–4.

following their deliverance from Egypt. It was also called the Feast of Ingathering because all the harvests had now been gathered (Exod. 23:16; 34:22). This was the third and final feast of the year (Lev. 23:33–36,39–43). It began and ended with a special Sabbath. During the festival week, seventy bulls were offered. It was a time of great rejoicing for the LORD's provisions in the past year. It also looked forward to the same blessings in the year ahead and to the future fulfillment of all the LORD's promises.

The Day of Atonement – Lev. 16:1–34

The first day of the seventh month was called the Feast of Trumpets because a trumpet (ram's horn) was blown on that day (see Lev. 23:24–27). Though the ram's horn was used for a variety of signaling purposes and on other occasions, this special day was named for the blowing of the horn announcing the end of the harvest and the beginning of a new agricultural year. Later, in Judaism, it came to be called New Year's Day, the "Head" or "Beginning" of the year, *Rosh Hashanah*. The Day of Atonement came ten days later. The most solemn day of the year, it was the only required fast day. It impressed on the people their collective need of God's forgiveness. Because it represented *all* the people, only the high priest could conduct the ceremony.

On that day, the high priest entered the Most Holy Place twice: The first time he made a sacrifice to purify himself (16:11); the second time he made atonement for the people (16:15). Two goats were offered in the ceremony for the people. The priest laid his hands on each goat and confessed over it the sins of Israel. Then he slaughtered the first goat and took its blood into the Most Holy Place. There he put its blood on the cover of the ark, symbolically the

A Harvest of the World

It is appropriate that the Lord poured out his Spirit on the Church at Pentecost to usher in a spiritual harvest of the world.

"If Anyone Is Thirsty . . ."

After the Old Testament period the Feast of Tabernacles had water-pouring ceremonies, pouring out pitchers of water from the Pool of Siloam in the temple each day of the feast, except on the last day. This practice provided the setting for Jesus' words in John 7:37–38. God is the only Savior and Provider for both our physical and spiritual life. (See Leon Morris, *The Gospel According to John* [Grand Rapids: Wm. B. Eerdmans, 1971], 422.)

throne of God (16:9,15–17). The second goat was sent alive into the wilderness and never allowed to return to the camp. The word translated "scapegoat" (Heb. 'azazel) probably refers to removing the sins of the people away from the camp. Thus each year God provided a fresh start, a new beginning, for his people.

The Theology of Holiness

Holiness is a central concept of the Old Testament. It is the major theme of the Book of Leviticus. The only true God, the Creator of the universe, who revealed himself to Israel through Moses in the Pentateuch, is holy. Holiness is not just one of his attributes—it is a summation of all he is! It means he is distinct from the created world. He is the *creator;* we are his *creation* and *creatures.* Furthermore, he is totally true to his nature. His nature is the definition of what is right, both morally and spiritually. What is opposed to him is evil.

The LORD has a good purpose for all who will respond to him. Other religions of the ANE did not describe their gods as holy in any moral sense of the word. For example, the Canaanites referred to their temple prostitutes as "holy girls." Their gods were awesome, or terrorizing, and unapproachable; and often devious, acting for their own ends. They were not transcendent but simply bigger than people, invisible, and to be feared. The transcendent nature of Israel's God was unique in the ancient world.

In the absolute sense, only God is holy. Anything else can be holy only if it is granted a proper relationship with the holy God.[46] Israel became God's holy people. How? He adopted them as his son (Exod. 4:22–23; Hos. 11:1). Children take on the nature of their parents. Thus in saving

Once and for All

In Christ this fresh start through the forgiveness of sin was provided once and for all (Heb. 10:10). His sacrifice is forever sufficient to make us holy in the presence of God!

[46]Exod. 31:13; Lev. 20:8; 21:8; 22:32.

Israel from bondage to Egypt, God took them to himself and made them holy (Exod. 19:4–6). They were given a relationship with him that involved a mission of offering that same relationship to the whole world.

Holiness also meant that his people were to respond with holy living. They were to reflect his character and purposes in all they thought, said, and did (Lev. 19:2). Biblical holiness, like righteousness, is both a gift and a response, a relationship and a lifestyle, a privilege and a responsibility. Leviticus exemplifies this: Chapters 1 through 16 describe the gift by prescribing the means for continued access to the presence of God. Then, 17 through 27 instruct God's people in how to respond to the gift and live the holy life afforded through atonement. This second half of the book touches on all aspects of life because holiness is living one's life under the lordship of the covenant God, the holy king.

An important concept for Israel within the subject of holiness was the difference between what was clean and unclean. The term "clean" showed suitability for use in worship and for the presence of God. The term "unclean" meant unsuitable to function in the worship of Israel's holy God. The purpose for this distinction was not hygiene. It defined what behaviors and conditions disqualified a person or thing from participating in worship. The natural state of most things was clean but secular (not holy). Being clean allowed a person or thing to become holy through sanctification. Uncleanness, then, disqualified a person or thing from even *touching* what was holy. If that happened, serious consequences – even death – could result.

Specific areas of life covered in the clean-unclean instructions are foods, childbirth, skin conditions, and bodily discharges. The eating rules daily reminded the people of their

Object Lessons

It is important to note that God chose symbols that promoted the well-being of his people. Although health was not its *primary* focus, cleanliness *does* overlap somewhat with practices of good health. However, the Old Testament instructions were first of all object lessons given by God to train his people in spiritual principles. They were to take holiness seriously. There would be no hurtful things in the world to afflict God's people if it had not been for the Fall (Gen. 3). God did not want such things associated with him. God most holy is the Source, Sustainer, and Savior. All evil will be expelled from his presence. Yet he loves us and provides the way—the cleansing—for us to be qualified to enjoy his fellowship.

Holiness and Clean/Unclean

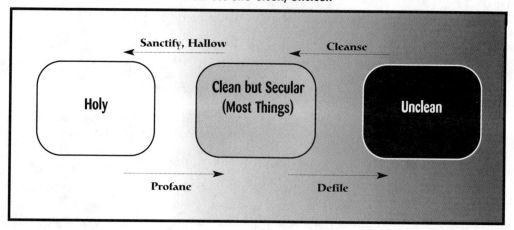

The Message of Clean and Unclean

The concepts of clean and unclean do not mean that things or people are inherently evil. Sin has distorted God's good creation. All people are separated from a holy God. There can be no fellowship between God and evil. Furthermore, his true nature and his saving purpose must be proclaimed for people to respond and be saved. This is good news. God has provided the way to fellowship with him in spite of our condition. All the instructions on clean and unclean and holiness

separation to the LORD (Lev. 7:23–27; 11:1–47). Any bodily discharge—blood, pus, menstrual fluid—made a person unclean, probably because of its association with death (Lev. 15). Finally, various skin conditions made one unclean (Lev. 14). Spiritually, they pointed to death, since they were not part of what God had pronounced "good" in creation (Gen. 1:31). The symbols reminded the people that no one in this fallen world is born in a right relationship with God. The instructions constitute a call to mourn over our fallen condition and to look to the LORD for healing.[47]

The Laws of Leviticus 17 Through 27

Appreciating the covenant relationship with God calls for all of one's life to be lived as a reflection of God's holy character. The various areas of life are summarized in Leviticus 17 through 27. Sanctification of the sacrifices and the lifeblood (Lev. 17) show an appreciation for life as the gift of God. Chapters 18 through 20 epitomize the sanctification of

[47]See the discussion in Gordon J. Wenham, *The Book of Leviticus,* NICOT (Grand Rapids: Wm. B. Eerdmans, 1979), 19–29. The chart is adapted from Wenham, 19.

the covenantal relationships – both horizontal and vertical. Chapters 18 and 20 prohibit unhealthy sexual or marital unions. The aim was to protect the integrity of the basic unit of society, the family. The structure of this section teaches an important lesson: Sexual immorality and idolatry are closely related. Chapter 20 prescribes the death penalty for both.

Leviticus 19 begins with the words, "'Be holy because I, the LORD your God, am holy,'" (Lev. 19:1b). It deals mainly with wholesome community relationships, which begin in the home (Lev. 19:18b). It ends with the treatment of foreigners (Lev. 19:33–34). It often states that proper values are dependent on the character of the LORD by concluding paragraphs with "'I am the LORD'" (e.g., Lev. 19:3,4,10). Family worship practices and everyday decisions show respect for the LORD and loyalty toward him.

The sacred calendar showed that times should be set aside for meeting with the LORD (Lev. 23). Human nature needs regular meeting and resting times to maintain healthy relationships. These relationships were to be both horizontal and vertical, toward people and toward God. Israel was particularly instructed to reach out to the poor and the alien (Lev. 23:22) on those occasions.

The presence of the LORD is portrayed in the Pentateuch as of utmost importance. It was to be honored and sought in various ways. In Leviticus 24 the priests were instructed to maintain the lights and the bread of the Holy Place in the tabernacle. These symbolized God's continued presence among his people. The account of dealing with a blasphemer (24:10–16) shows that the name of God must be respected.

Leviticus 25 presents the sanctification of the land: It is the place God chose for his people. There, he would be

teach how awesome God is. They tell us how serious is the sin condition and how wonderful is the LORD's gift of salvation. A major principle involved in the laws of clean and unclean needs to be applied by Christians today. Every choice we make, everything we say and do, sends a message to others about our values. What message does our life send about our relationship with God and his character working in us?

Responding to God's Holiness

Our holiness is our response to God's holiness. It is summed up in our love for all people. We must love God's people, as well as the foreigner or outsider.

present among them. The Sabbath Year and the Year of Jubilee showed that the land was God's. The people were only tenants (25:23). Therefore they could not permanently transfer title to it. In the Year of Jubilee, it was to come back to the family who inherited it. Whenever one was in danger of losing his property, family members were to help. They were to redeem it for him. Furthermore, people who had sold themselves as indentured servants to pay their debts were not to be mistreated in any way. No matter how much they owed, they were to serve only six years. Again, holiness to the Lord was to be shown in one's kindness to others.

Leviticus 26 serves as the climax of the covenantal instructions at Sinai that began in Exodus 20. Here, blessings and cursings are pronounced for responding to the LORD in obedience or rebellion. The judgments are given in five cycles (Lev. 26:14–39), each succeeding cycle more severe than the last. Each one is a call to repentance. This shows that God's intent was to motivate Israel to restore the relationship. Holiness takes the covenantal relationship very seriously, like the vows of a marriage. It involves commitment and accountability, with definite consequences for one's choices.

The conclusion of the Book of Leviticus in chapter 27 is a very practical appendix about taking one's commitments or vows seriously. God's people are told to follow through on their promises to him, or pay an additional twenty percent. Holiness must include self-control in one's speech, and discipline in one's obligations. A word used in this chapter that points to the essential idea of holiness is *cherem*, translated by NIV as a thing "devoted to the LORD" that could not be redeemed. If it was something that could be used, it became the property of the sanctuary (Lev. 27:14–28). If it was a person, however, the person was to be destroyed (Lev. 27:29). The term normally referred to something or someone *holy* to some *other* (i.e., pagan) *god*. It is appropriate that the laws of holiness conclude with these solemn words, expressing the danger of making rash vows and stressing the need for following through with one's promises to the LORD.

In this way, God's people were instructed in how to live with his holy presence among them. God would now lead them through the wilderness to the Promised Land. This is where the book of Numbers picks up the story.

Study Questions

1. What is the subject of Exodus 25 through 40?

2. What is the Code of Hammurabi?

3. What are the major ways the laws of the Pentateuch differ from ANE laws?

4. What is the *lex talionis*?

5. What was the purpose of the laws of the Pentateuch?

6. What are the major values of God expressed in the Pentateuchal laws?

7. What was the role of the Ten Commandments?

8. Describe the major features of the tabernacle and its overall theological message.

9. List the sacrifices and their purposes.

10. Who were the priests and what were their functions?

11. List the three special calendar events of the spring and the three of the fall and describe their purpose.

12. Locate the command "Love your neighbor as yourself" in Leviticus. What does it mean?

13. How do the references to redemption in Leviticus help you understand Christ's redemption of us?

14. Define the following terms: *torah*, suzerain-vassal treaty, theocracy, Code of Hammurabi, *lex talionis*, tabernacle, ark, (each of the) offerings, atonement, (each of the) feasts, Sabbath, Year of Jubilee, Sabbath Year, the Aaronic priests, the Levites, Urim and Thummim, ephod, glory, holiness, clean and unclean, Nadab and Abihu.

For Further Reading

Cotton, Roger D. "Leviticus." In *The Complete Biblical Library: The Old Testament.* Vol. 3, *Study Bible, Leviticus-Numbers.* Springfield, Mo.: World Library Press, 1995.

Douglas, Mary. *Purity and Danger.* London: Routledge & Kegan Paul, 1966.

Greengus, Samuel. "Law: Biblical and ANE Law." In *ABD.* Vol. 4. New York: Doubleday, 1992.

Kaiser, Walter C., Jr. "Leviticus 18:5 and Paul: 'Do This and You Shall Live' (Eternally?)." *Journal of the Evangelical Theological Society* 14 (1971): 19–28.

Kitchen, Kenneth A. *The Bible in Its World: The Bible and Archaeology Today.* Downers Grove, Ill.: InterVarsity Press, 1977.

Milgrom, Jacob. *Leviticus 1–16.* AB. New York: Doubleday, 1991.

Poythress, Vern Sheridan. *The Shadow of Christ in the Law of Moses.* Brentwood, Tenn.: Wolgemuth & Hyatt, 1991.

Roth, Martha T. *Law Collections from Mesopotamia and Asia Minor.* Atlanta, Ga.: Scholars Press, 1995.

Walton, John H. *Ancient Israelite Literature in Its Cultural Context.* Grand Rapids: Zondervan Publishing House, 1989.

_____. *Chronological and Background Charts of the Old Testament.* Rev. ed. Grand Rapids: Zondervan Publishing House, 1994.

Walton, John H., and Victor H. Matthews. *The IVP Bible Background Commentary: Genesis–Deuteronomy.* Downers Grove, Ill.: InterVarsity Press, 1997.

Wenham, Gordon J. *The Book of Leviticus.* NICOT. Grand Rapids: Wm. B. Eerdmans, 1979.

Wright, Christopher J. H. *Walking in the Ways of the LORD: The Ethical Authority of the Old Testament.* Downers Grove, Ill.: InterVarsity Press, 1995.

8

April Westbrook

Through the Vast and Dreadful Desert

Outline:

- **Numbers: Who Wants to Read a Bunch of Names, Anyway?**
  The First Census: How Many Came Out of Egypt?
  And the Moral of the Story Is…
  From Sinai to the Promised Land…Almost
  Forty Years in the Desert
  A Stubborn Soothsayer and a Talking Donkey
  The Second Census and More Laws
- **Deuteronomy: Speaking of Covenant**
  The Book of Deuteronomy: A Sepher Torah
  The Decalogue: Honoring God and Each Other

Israel From the Past to the Future
What Do We Do When We Get to the Promised Land?
Mount Ebal: The Covenant Renewed
Moses' Last Words: The End of an Era

Terms:

Asherah
bless/blessing
covenant
curse
Decalogue
'eleph
Elohim
Levites
Sabbath
seer
Yahweh

Numbers: Who Wants to Read a Bunch of Names, Anyway?

Have you ever tried to read the Bible from start to finish, only to be defeated by the Book of Numbers? After all, lists of unknown names from thousands of years ago are hardly inspiring. What does this part of the Word of God mean for our own lives? How can we apply it to our real-life situations?

Believe it or not, we can learn something about God's nature in the Book of Numbers—even in the two censuses it contains. And besides lists and numbers, this book describes several major events in the history of early Israel that address important social issues, such as gender roles and economic justice. The Book of Numbers also contains stories with definite theological challenges. For example, a man named Balaam prophesies accurately, even though he does not serve the LORD. How could this be? Overall, the Book of Numbers offers much to the modern reader.

This survey of the Book of Numbers will consider its contents in the following order:

1:1 through 2:34	The First Census: How Many Came Out of Egypt?
3:1 through 10:10	And the Moral of the Story Is . . .
10:11 through 14:45	From Sinai to the Promised Land—Almost
15:1 through 21:35	Forty Years in the Desert
22:1 through 25:18	A Stubborn Soothsayer and a Talking Donkey
26:1 through 36:13	The Second Census and More Laws

The First Census: How Many Came Out of Egypt? —Num. 1:1 Through 2:34

The Book of Numbers received its Greek (and later, English) name from its first story. Here, God instructed Moses "to number," to take a census of, the Israelites by clans and families. This census was used to estimate Israel's military forces (Num. 1:2–3). (The tribe of Levi was set apart from the other tribes: Levites were responsible for the tabernacle, rather than ordinary military service [Num. 1:47–53].) After the census, tribal divisions were assigned an official marching order.

Bible scholars are very interested in the specific numbers mentioned in this initial tribal census. One translation of the text would indicate an estimated two to three million Israelites came out of Egypt in the exodus.[1] A population of two to three million may not seem large in comparison to cities of the modern world, but in comparison to other cities and nations of the time it was enormous.[2] Some scholars believe that the true number of Israelites could not possibly have been so large. One's view concerning the inspiration of Scripture often affects one's understanding of the census in Numbers.

[1]The estimate of 2 to 3 million Israelites is based on Exod. 12:37 and Num. 1:46. The total number of Israelites was about 600 'eleph. An 'eleph has traditionally been considered to be 1,000 fighting men. Thus, the census would indicate that there were about 600,000 warriors at that time. Considering the size of the average household, the 600,000 warriors plus their families would total 2 to 3 million.

[2]In the OT era, cities covered anywhere from 50 acres (.078 square mile) to 2 square miles. Major cities such as Babylon and Nineveh were somewhat larger (Wolfram von Soden, *The Ancient Orient: An Introduction to the Study of the Ancient Near East* [Grand Rapids: Wm. B. Eerdmans, 1985], 69). The populations of ancient cities were also much smaller than we imagine. Jerusalem, for example, has been estimated at about thirty thousand (Roland de Vaux, *Ancient Israel: Its Life and Institutions* [Grand Rapids: Wm. B. Eerdmans, 1961], 67). Ai, a "city" mentioned in the conquest of the Promised Land, was actually a small village built on the site of a previously destroyed city of 27.5 acres (Victor H. Matthews and Don C. Benjamin, *Social World of Ancient Israel, 1250–587 BCE* [Peabody, Mass.: Hendrickson Publishers, 1993], 4). It had an estimated population of twelve thousand people (Donald H. Madvig, *Joshua,* Expositor's Bible Commentary, ed. Frank E. Gaebelein, vol. 3 [Grand Rapids: Zondervan Publishing House, 1992], 290).

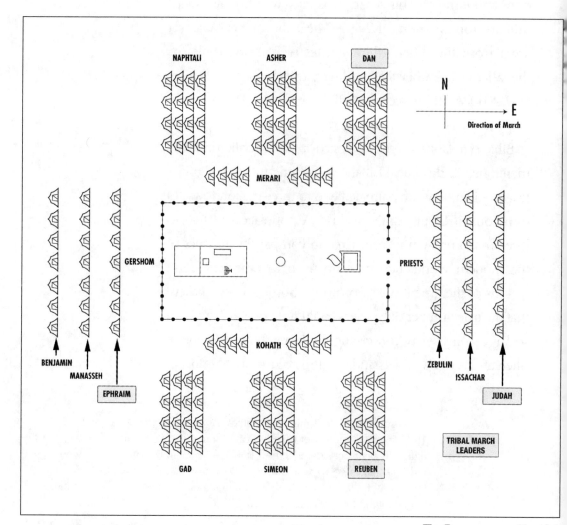

The Encampment of Israel

"THE CENSUS IS NOT HISTORICALLY TRUE," SOME SAY

Many scholars believe that the Numbers census did not occur in history as literally described in the text.[3] They point

---

[3]For example, George Buchanan Gray, *Numbers,* International Critical Commentary, ed. Samuel Driver, Alfred Plummer, and Charles Briggs, vol. 4 (Edinburgh, Scotland: T. & T. Clark, 1903), 13–15.

out several factors to support their belief. The Bible often describes the Israelite population as small. They relied on divine miracles for their victories (Exod. 23:27–29; Deut. 7:1–7). The average armies of the time have been estimated at 20,000 to 60,000 men.[4] If 600,000 Israelites defeated an army of about 40,000 Canaanites, where was the divine miracle? Further, why would such a huge army of Israelites be afraid to go into battle (Num. 13:31)?

Such scholars also consider the many difficulties of two to three million people participating in the exodus. The line of people would stretch from the Red Sea to Mount Sinai. The back of the line would always be at least two weeks behind the front![5] Food and water were miraculously provided, but what about sanitation and basic living space?[6] Also, the Numbers census seems to create impossible family units. The ratio of firstborn males to all adult males was approximately 1:27.[7] Consequently, the average Israelite family would have had twenty-eight sons. Jacob, with two wives and two concubines, had only twelve sons.

From these kinds of factors, some scholars determine that Israel could not possibly have had two to three million people at this point in their history. They often conclude that the writers of Numbers made up the census details for their own reasons. They argue that the census figures were

[4]John H. Walton and Victor H. Matthews, *The IVP Bible Background Commentary: Genesis–Deuteronomy* (Downers Grove, Ill.: InterVarsity Press, 1997), 97.

[5]Walton and Matthews, *Genesis–Deuteronomy,* 98.

[6]E. E. Carpenter, "Book of Numbers," in *ISBE,* 565–66.

[7]Gray, *Numbers,* 13–15. This figure is achieved by dividing the total number of firstborn males (22,273 according to Num. 3:43) into the total number of males counted in the census (603,550 according to Num. 1:46).

never intended as the literal record of a historical event. Some of these scholars believe the figures were symbolic. They were designed to explain the great increase of people that occurred in Egypt. Others feel that the figures were artificial and only represented the status of the tribes in relation to each other: The most important tribes were described as being larger, regardless of how many people were actually present.[8] Scholars who do not hold to a high view of inspiration may view the Numbers census as not historically true. In their opinion the story describes circumstances that are impossible if taken literally.

"HOW MANY ISRAELITES ARE IN AN 'ELEPH?": ANOTHER POINT OF VIEW

Scholars who hold a high view of inspiration believe that biblical stories must be historically true. So they explain the apparent impossibilities created by the Numbers censuses in a different way. Such scholars often point out biblical texts that describe Israel as a very large group. For example, God promised Abraham that he would be very fruitful (Gen. 12:1–3; 17:5–6). Also, the powerful Egyptians were afraid of the great number of Israelites in their land (Exod. 1:7–12).

Others simply admit that they have no solution for the practical problems of an exodus of two to three million people.[9] They maintain that unknown explanations do not affect the truthfulness of the text. Some believe that God's miraculous intervention made the impossible possible. After all, if he could miraculously provide for a few thou-

[8]de Vaux, *Ancient Israel,* 65.

[9]See Gordon J. Wenham, *Numbers: An Introduction and Commentary* (Downers Grove, Ill.: InterVarsity Press, 1981), 61ff. See also Willem Hendrik Gispen, *Exodus* (Grand Rapids: Zondervan Publishing House, 1982), 127.

sand Israelites, why not a few million?[10]

Another popular solution challenges the traditional translation of the figures found in the Numbers text. Perhaps these large numbers had a meaning to ancient Israel that the modern world cannot understand.[11] Maybe we have translated the words in the original text incorrectly. If the word *'eleph* has been mistranslated, the text may indicate a much smaller group of Israelites. If so, the practical difficulties raised by the text would be resolved without questioning its historical truthfulness.

The word *'eleph* has been traditionally translated as "1,000." Some scholars believe the word may have meant a military unit, instead.[12] For example, rather than stating that "the number from the tribe of Simeon was 59,300," the text would indicate that the number from the tribe of Simeon was 59 *units,* for a total of 300 men (see Num. 1:23). The final total of fighting men would then be 5,550 in 633 units. A problem arises, however. By using the same translation method, the text would also indicate that the final total was 3,350 in 600 units (see Num. 1:46). So the numbers do not seem to add up correctly overall. Some scholars have suggested that well-meaning scribes may have contributed to the textual problems. Perhaps they added their own totals, after assuming *'eleph* meant 1,000.[13]

[10]Ronald F. Youngblood, *Exodus* (Chicago: Moody Press, 1983), 73.

[11]R. K. Harrison, *Introduction to the Old Testament* (Grand Rapids: Wm B. Eerdmans, 1969), 633. See also Harrison's treatment of the chronology of the patriarchs of early Israel and the sojourn in Egypt, two factors that might influence the total number of Israelites at the time of the exodus (167–73).

[12]G. E. Mendenhall, "The Census Lists of Numbers 1 and 26," *Journal of Biblical Literature* 77 (1958), 52ff. See also J. Bright, *A History of Israel* (Philadelphia: Westminster Press, 1959).

[13]G. T. Manley, *The New Bible Handbook,* 2d ed. (Chicago: InterVarsity Press, 1949), 145.

Within a cultural context of tribal life, the word *'eleph* might also be translated as "clan." A clan was a social division smaller than a tribe but larger than an individual household.[14] The word *'eleph* has been translated in the NIV as "clan," rather than "1,000," in several passages (Num. 31:5; Josh. 22:14; 1 Sam. 23:23; Mic. 5:2). Such a translation would also greatly reduce the number of Israelites in question. The same concerns about the "military unit" theory would apply here, however. Also, the same language is used in Numbers 3 to describe the Levites. If *'eleph* is translated as "clan" in verse 22, then a textual problem occurs. Verse 22 would indicate a total of seven Levite clans. Verses 18–20 would indicate eight Levite clans.

The precise number of Israelites at the time of the exodus may never be known. Interpreting the text raises questions, both for those who hold to a high view of inspiration and for those who do not. Therefore, we must first decide if we are willing to accept this part of Scripture as historically true. From that point, we can consider possible explanations for the difficulties within the text. We should weigh the strengths of any view against its weaknesses. Any conclusions we draw should be tentative, not absolute.

DOES THE CENSUS TELL US ANYTHING ABOUT GOD?

While considering the challenges of this census, we must not miss the important theology it sets forth. Two factors concerning God's character are seen in his desire to include this census in the Bible. First, God finds people important, both as individuals and as related members of larger communities. The fact that there once was a Levite of the

14See G. E. Mendenhall and Christopher J. H. Wright, *Walking in the Ways of the Lord* (Downers Grove, Ill.: InterVarsity Press, 1995), 150–51.

Kohathite clan named Izhar (Num. 3:19) may not seem very important in the history of the world. If you were Izhar or one of his relatives, however, this would be important to you. As canon, however, such specific details regarding individuals tell us that people are important to God. Izhar is never described in Scripture as doing anything particularly noteworthy. But God knew Izhar by name and made sure his existence was recorded in his Word.

The second aspect of God's character seen here is his pleasure in planning and organization. He had already promised the Israelites victory over their enemies (Exod. 23:27–31). But the people also had a prominent role to play. God did not send them to take the Promised Land without forethought or planning. Rather, he instructed his people to prepare in an organized way for the challenges ahead.

And the Moral of the Story Is . . . — Num. 3:1 Through 10:10

To understand the story of Israel's journey to the Promised Land, we must remember the nature of that land. From the beginning, the Promised Land was God's idea. He chose to promise this land to Israel. He communicated that promise to the patriarchs (Gen. 15:7,18–21; 28:13). He accomplished Israel's deliverance from slavery in Egypt (Exod. 5 through 20). He led them safely across the Desert of Sinai (Exod. 40:36–38). It becomes evident that God himself is the primary character in this story. Israel's history as recorded in the Book of Numbers clearly shows God's faithfulness and holiness.

WHAT DOES HOLINESS MEAN?

The Book of Numbers devotes several chapters to the tribe of Levi (Num. 3 through 4; 8). God gave the tribe of

"Plans to Prosper You"

God's plans do not always make sense to people. Marching around Jericho seven times was not a typical method of warfare. Nevertheless, it was an organized and effective plan. In my own life, I must realize that God is a well-organized planner who is much bigger than I can fully comprehend. Just because I don't understand what God is doing doesn't mean he is untrustworthy. He is in control, he has a well-prepared plan, and he will show me what to do each step of the way, just as he did for Israel.

"'For I know the plans I have for you,' declares the LORD, 'plans to prosper you and not to harm you, plans to give you hope and a future'" (Jer. 29:11). (See sidebar "Programmatic Text" in the next chapter.)

Levi to Aaron and his sons (Num. 3:5–6). By serving the priests, the Levites also served God (see 8:16). Their new role required them to work with things that had been consecrated to God. Consequently, the Levites themselves had to be consecrated through special offerings (Num. 8:5–14). The story of the Levites can help us understand the meaning of *holiness.* They became a holy tribe because they were set apart by God to fulfill his purpose. Their holiness was a direct result of having been "given wholly" to God (8:16).[15]

Holiness is also related to godliness. Numbers 5 through 7 describes several requirements for God's people. They were to keep their promises, both to God (6:1–21) and to each other (5:11–31). They were to be generous givers (Num. 7:1–89). By doing these things, Israel would become like their faithful and generous God. This pattern of the Israelites becoming like their God is further emphasized in Numbers 9:1 through 10:10. God had faithfully delivered Israel from slavery. In response, Israel faithfully celebrated that deliverance (9:4–14). God's continual visible presence led Israel every day of their journey. In like manner, Israel continually followed God's leading (9:15–23). Such examples from Israel's history teach us that a holy people will be a godly people.

From Sinai to the Promised Land . . . Almost —Num. 10:11 Through 14:45

Numbers 10:11–36 records a very important day in Israel's history. God had miraculously freed them from

Making Israel's Experience Ours

We all have promises from God, both from Scripture and from our personal dialogue with him. Understanding Israel's relationship with God is good, but we cannot stop there. Something of God's eternal character is being revealed to us. In light of the Book of Numbers, it seems reasonable to conclude that we may experience what Israel experienced. Apparently there is a distinct relationship between the fulfillment of God's promises to us and our own faithful obedience to God's instructions.

[15]According to Walter Eichrodt, *holiness* is "the unapproachable majesty of God" that may be understood as his "divine purity and perfection." Everything and everyone else are vastly inferior to God's holiness. People and things can become holy only as they are directly associated with God, who

slavery. They had entered a covenant relationship with him and he had prepared them to take the land of Canaan.

Finally, the big moment arrived. How incredible it must have been to see the cloud of the Lord's presence move toward the Promised Land! Imagine all the tribes marching forth with their tribal standards raised high. They were God's chosen people and victory was certain. What could possibly go wrong?

A COMPLAINING PEOPLE

The victorious scene is interrupted in Numbers 11:1: "Now the people complained about their hardships in the hearing of the LORD." Only three days into the victory march the people began to grumble. This was the beginning of a cycle between God and his people in the desert. They complained, breaking their promises to him.[16] He responded with judgment, as promised (Lev. 26:14–39). The people repented. Then God ended the judgment, again as promised (Lev. 26:40–45). As a result, the people were given another chance to be faithful. The cycle is immediately repeated in Numbers 11:4–20. Here, the people craved Egyptian food and spurned God's miraculous provision of manna. God showed them their folly by sending them so many quail they became sick of them. By rejecting God's provision, they rejected him as their God. They were disloyal, but he remained faithful.

But We Had Fish . . .

The Exodus narrative describes God's provision of fresh manna each morning; God had also shown his ability to provide meat by sending quail (Exod. 16:1-36). The issue in Numbers 11, therefore, was not one of need but rather of control. The Israelites grew weary of depending on God's provision at his discretion. They preferred to control their own lives. They ignored entirely the fact that they had been slaves when they had the "luxury" of fish for dinner. How often our own experience is just like that of the Israelites. He delivers us from sin and then we look back with longing. Just like the Israelites, how quickly we forget the truth of our past!

alone is holy in his own being. See *Theology of the Old Testament,* trans. J. A. Baker (Philadelphia: Westminster Press, 1967), 2:60, 410.

[16]See Exod. 22:28; 23:20 through 24:11.

TWO MODELS OF LEADERSHIP

In the midst of the Numbers stories, two types of leadership are compared. First, Moses demonstrated the role of a humble leader (Num. 12:3). He acknowledged that the responsibility for such a difficult group was too big for him. He then selected seventy elders as leaders. God took some of his Spirit from Moses and placed that Spirit upon the other leaders.[17] Moses was thrilled with their empowerment. He was not jealous of them (11:28–29).

On the other hand, Miriam and Aaron assumed their own authority and superiority (Num. 12:1–2). Miriam and Aaron questioned God's choice of Moses and openly criticized Moses' personal life. But God made very clear the model of leadership he preferred. He upheld Moses' leadership and celebrated his strong and intimate relationship with Moses (12:5–8). At the same time, Aaron watched in horror as God struck Miriam with an ugly skin disease, making her unclean, an outcast.[18]

Some people might wonder if the story of Moses and the seventy elders was an Old Testament "Day of Pentecost." Certain similarities are present. For example, in both cases a group of people assembled in one place to wait for God's empowerment. Then the Spirit came upon them with visible signs (Num. 11:25; Acts 2:3). Also, in both cases the

[17]In context, the OT usage of the term "Spirit of God" usually refers to God's active presence. The doctrine of the Holy Spirit as the distinctive third person of the Trinity is not fully revealed until the NT (e.g., John 15:26; 16:13).

[18]Why was Miriam stricken, but not Aaron? The most likely explanation is found in Aaron's position as high priest. It was vital to the community that he remain ritually clean in order to perform his duties (Lev. 13:1–46, 21:1 through 22:16). Some hold, however, that because Miriam is mentioned first, she may have instigated the criticism (Num. 12:1,10).

Spirit enabled a group of people to prophesy (Num. 11:25–26; Acts 19:6–7).

However, several differences can be seen between the two events. Of all the Israelites only the seventy elders prophesied. Moreover, this is mentioned only one time (Num. 11:25). The Book of Acts, on the other hand, describes many believers repeatedly functioning in a variety of supernatural activities.[19] Also, the purpose for each of the events is different. The seventy elders were enabled to serve their own people as leaders (Num. 11:17). On the other hand, the New Testament believers were empowered to serve the world as witnesses of Christ (Acts 1:7–8). In spite of such differences, the empowerment of the seventy elders may be seen as an event that anticipates the New Testament happening at Pentecost. Moses' prophetic prayer in Numbers 11:29 does come to pass in Acts 2.

THE REBELLION AT KADESH BARNEA

The Israelites camped at Kadesh Barnea and sent spies into the Promised Land. In their report all the spies agreed on two facts: (1) The Promised Land was definitely good. It was a land "flowing with milk and honey" (Exod. 3:8). (2) The people who lived there were big and strong (Num. 13:31–33). Two of the spies, Joshua and Caleb, were excited about what they had found (13:30; 14:6–9). The other ten were afraid (13:31–33). The Israelites concurred with the ten. What was the difference between the two spies and the ten (to say nothing of their fellow Israelites)? Why did the two sets of spies respond in such different ways to the same information? Those who wanted to take the Promised

[19]Acts 2:43; 5:12; 6:8; 10:44–46; 21:9; cf. 1 Cor. 12 through 14.

Battles: Then and Now

There is another life lesson to be learned from the experience of the Israelite spies. When I am facing a personal battle as a believer, I need to continually ask myself, "What, and whom, am I focusing on?" Perspective makes all the difference. Any problem looks smaller when compared to the infinitely powerful God, who is on my side, as I walk in obedience to his plan for my life.

Enjoying His Relationship with You

The Israelites' interaction with God again shows us something of who he is. God is obviously a relational being. Furthermore, he seems particularly to enjoy relationships in which he can display his great faithfulness. Because this is the nature of the God we know and serve, we can expect certain things

Land focused on the size and strength of their God (14:9). Those who wanted to return to Egypt focused on the size and strength of the enemy (13:33). As a consequence, they would spend one year for each day of exploration of the Promised Land—forty (14:34)!

Ironically, God had told the Israelites about the enemy before they ever started this journey (Exod. 23:22–30). Why, then, did He send them to explore the land in the first place? He knew they would return in fear. Perhaps He intended to reveal Israel's unbelief before they faced actual warfare. In battle they would have to rely on God's faithfulness. Clearly, many Israelites were still not ready to believe. In their lack of faith, they totally rejected God. They certainly could not go to war with such a disposition. So they returned to the desert. Their futile attempt to take the Promised Land without God's blessing only proved again their unfaithfulness to God (Num. 14:39–45). In stark contrast, God's own faithfulness was clearly shown. He planned to fulfill his promises with the next generation of Israelites (14:31).

Forty Years in the Desert —Num. 15:1 Through 21:35

Numbers 15 begins almost as if the first attempt to enter the Promised Land had never happened. Israel's training process continued. The desert was still purposed as a place to learn about the holiness and faithfulness of God. Unfortunately, not everyone was willing to be taught.

A LEVITE WITH A BAD ATTITUDE

Korah and his followers rose up against Moses (Num. 16:1–2). They had come to the unreasonable conclusion that Moses was at fault for the Israelites' trouble (16:12–13). Several points in the story emphasize the intensity of this particular rebellion. Korah was a Levite. He was set apart for holy service, not rebellion. Also, the rebels questioned more than Moses' leadership. They questioned God's choice of Aaron as high priest. The people's attitude toward God had become hypocritical. They claimed to be in right relationship with him while rejecting his promises and commands (16:3,12–14). They even described Egypt – the land of their bondage – like the land God had promised: "a land flowing with milk and honey" (16:13)!

AN AMAZING RESPONSE

The Israelites' response to the terrifying scene of God's justice is almost unbelievable. Even after God destroyed Korah and his followers, they continued to grumble against Moses and Aaron (Num. 16:41). When God instructed Moses to move away from them perhaps the rebels began to realize their foolishness (16:45). Only Moses and Aaron's intervention kept them from being wiped out. The miraculous budding of Aaron's staff finally convinced the people of God's sovereign choice (17:5). However, they still refused to obey God willingly. They simply avoided the tabernacle altogether (17:12–13).

At the same time, God further confirmed the priesthood. He established a system of provision for them: The Levites were to receive the tithes of the Israelites. They, in turn, were to give a tithe to Aaron, the high priest (Num. 18:25–26). God also gave the procedure for making "water of cleansing" (19:9). The special water was to be used in purification rituals. For example, the Israelites were to cleanse anyone who had been exposed to a dead body

from him. He will give us promises and he will keep them. The response he looks for is one of trust. It would seem, then, that God wants us to trust him so that we can see who he really is. The more we trust him, the more we will know him. The more we know him, the more we will trust him. What a great cycle of relationship!

Looking Ridiculous

If you think these Israelites were being incredibly stupid, you are probably responding appropriately. Israel's actions here made them look ridiculous. Clearly, these stories are intended to show the foolishness of not trusting a loving, loyal, and faithful God. The Israelites' story shows us in a big way the tragic result of walking in willful disobedience and rebellion against God.

(19:11–22). The spoils of war were also to be purified before being brought into the Israelite camp (31:21–24). Such rituals kept diseases from spreading. The primary purpose, however, was to remind the people of God's holiness.

MOSES MAKES A MISTAKE

The Book of Numbers records an episode in which water flowed from a rock for the Israelites (Num. 20:2–13). Something similar had occurred earlier in Israel's desert experience (Exod. 17:1–7). This time, however, Moses made a mistake. In the first episode, God had told him to strike a rock, which Moses did, and water came forth. The second time, God told Moses to speak to a rock. But in Moses' frustration with the people, he struck the rock with his staff—not once but twice. Water came forth, but God told Moses and Aaron that they would not lead the people into the Promised Land; they had not trusted him. Furthermore, Moses had revealed a wrong attitude toward God. His question ("'Must we bring you water?'") and his disobedience showed that he had honored himself above the LORD (Num. 20:10–12). Even though they were great leaders, Moses and Aaron still had to answer directly to God for dishonoring him (Deut. 34:1–4).

THE EDOMITES GIVE A RUDE RESPONSE

As the Israelites continued their journey, the Edomites denied them safe passage through their land (Num. 20:18). This violated a custom of the time. Showing hospitality to travelers was expected; denying it was an expression of hostility.[20] Why did the Edomites treat the Israelites as enemies?

---

[20]Matthews and Benjamin, *Social World,* 84–86. See also de Vaux, *Ancient Israel,* 10.

First, we must remember the history recorded in Genesis. Edom came from Esau's line. Israel came from Jacob's line. The two groups were related, but their forefathers epitomized sibling rivalry. Second, we must understand the political situation when Israel arrived at Edom's border. Edom, Moab, and Ammon were negotiating their own alliances. They had united against the Amorites, who had already taken a sizeable portion of Moab's land.[21] The political situation was very touchy. Naturally, the Edomites were afraid to become vulnerable to the Israelites. So they used military force to keep Israel out. They continued to be enemies of Israel throughout the biblical period. Ultimately, they were severely punished by God for their ruthless conduct.[22]

THE BRONZE SNAKE

The Israelites continued their journey. When they came to Arad, they defeated it (Num. 21:1–3). For the first time, the Israelites believed God would give them victory and he did. Unfortunately, they disregarded God's faithfulness and spoke against him. This time, God sent a plague of snakes

Transjordan People-Groups

---

[21]For further discussion and a map, see Yohanan Aharoni and Michael Avi-Yonah, *The Macmillan Bible Atlas,* 3d ed. (New York: Simon & Schuster Macmillan Company, 1993), 52.

[22]See Obadiah; Jer. 49:7–22.

to bring the people to repentance. When they admitted their sin, God did not remove the snakes. Instead, he told Moses to make a bronze snake and lift it up on a pole. In this way the people had to rely daily upon God's faithfulness to heal (21:8–9). The Israelites took the bronze snake with them into the Promised Land. It was eventually destroyed because they began to worship it as an idol (2 Kings 18:4). Much later, Jesus would use the story of the bronze snake to symbolize the purpose of the Cross (John 3:14–15).

Israel's victory against Arad was the first of several. Like the Edomites, the Moabites and Amorites did not welcome Isarel. Rather than going around the Amorites, however, Israel attacked them. They conquered the Amorites first, then headed toward Moab (Num. 21:21–31; 22:1).

A Stubborn Soothsayer and a Talking Donkey – Num. 22:1 Through 25:18

Israel's victories caused the surrounding nations to become even more afraid of them. As Israel moved toward Moab, the Moabites panicked. Their king, Balak, acted according to normal military procedure for the time. He called in Balaam, son of Beor, who was a "seer."[23] Balak wanted Balaam to pronounce curses on Israel. In Ancient Near Eastern thought, such actions would assure victory in battle.[24]

---

[23]Archaeologists have discovered an ancient Aramaic prophetic text about "Balaam son of Beor." It describes him as a seer and a professional curse maker. R. K. Harrison, *Numbers,* Wycliffe Exegetical Commentary, ed. Kenneth L. Barker (Chicago: Moody Press, 1990), 293. While the technical term "seer" is not found in the Num. account, Balaam twice says "'I see [Israel]'" (Num. 23:9), and once, "'I see him,'" referring to the coming Davidic king (Num. 24:17).

[24]In Ancient Near Eastern thought, an opposing army was viewed "in terms of the supernatural forces which empowered it." So if a curse could be successfully made, victory was accomplished before the actual fighting even

ONE STORY OR TWO?

In Numbers 22 the story of Balaam seems to include points that contradict each other. For example, God told Balaam to go with the Moabite princes (22:20). Then God stood in anger against Balaam on his journey (22:21–31). Also, throughout the story two different names for God are used. Sometimes he is referred to as *Elohim* (translated "God"). Sometimes he is referred to as *Yahweh* (translated "the LORD"). Some scholars believe the different names show that two original stories were merged here.[25] Others look for possible solutions within the story to make sense of the details. Perhaps God's anger with Balaam on the road was not a contradiction of previous instructions. Maybe God showed his power to motivate Balaam to obey his instructions. Balaam needed the extra encouragement. Balak would offer Balaam a lot of money to be disobedient (Num. 22:17,37; 24:11).[26]

HOW DID BALAAM KNOW YAHWEH?

Scripture does not view Balaam as a positive character.[27] Divination is forbidden in God's law (Deut. 18:10,14).

began. Eryl W. Davies, *Numbers,* New Century Bible Commentary, ed. Ronald E. Clements (Grand Rapids: Wm. B. Eerdmans, 1995), 247.

[25]See Martin Noth, *Numbers* (Philadelphia: Westminster Press, 1968), 171–72. See also Gray, *Numbers,* 309–12, and Davies, *Numbers,* 236–38.

[26]Harrison, *Numbers,* 298–99. Harrison also notes that the complete story can be divided into two main sections (22:7–35; 22:36 through 24:25), each comprised of three parts (22:7–14, 15–20, 21–35, matched by 22:36 through 23:12, 23:13–26, 23:27 through 24:25). See also Walton and Matthews, *Genesis–Deuteronomy,* 201–2.

[27]Balaam is used as a negative example to believers in the NT. In 2 Pet. 2:15 he is used as an example of a false prophet who loved money more than he feared God. Jude 11 gives a very similar statement. Rev. 2:14 refers to Balaam's destructive influence against Israel. He showed Balak how to defeat them.

Prophets, True and False

The story of Balaam becomes one of several passages in the Bible that tell us something important about prophets. We cannot judge the character of a person only by his or her eloquence and ability to prophesy. The story of Balaam makes a very strong statement in this regard. Balaam was not one of God's people before *or* after this incident. Neither was he interested in having a real relationship with God. Yet, God sovereignly chose to use Balaam for his own purpose. But then again, God chose to use a donkey too. Therefore, the simple ability to prophesy may not prove much about the one prophesying. Further, it is an honor to be used by God for his own purposes, so if God should choose to speak through us prophetically, we really do not have a reason to become arrogant.

Balaam knew Yahweh, however, from the beginning of his story in Numbers. How could this be? The relationship between Balaam and Yahweh was not necessarily positive. Cursing involved a spiritual dimension. Because of his profession, Balaam was probably familiar with the gods of all the surrounding nations. It is not surprising, then, that Balaam knew of Yahweh (cf. Acts 19:13). It is more surprising that Yahweh, the one true God, chose to answer Balaam. Yet, the story quickly indicates that God had a plan here. He would use Balaam for his own purposes in blessing Israel.

A Blind Seer and a Willing Donkey

The story of Balaam and Balak is full of irony. Balaam the seer could not see into the spirit realm as well as his own donkey could. The donkey, an animal known for its stubbornness, was less obstinate than her willful master.[28] Balak, king of Moab, proved more stubborn than Balaam or his donkey. The more Balak tried to force a curse upon Israel, the more he brought a curse on his own nation. Balak refused to accept the reality that God was greater than he was. Perhaps the greatest irony, however, was seen in Israel's actions after Balaam's blessings: The Moabite men failed in military strategy against the Israelites, but the Moabite women seduced them (Num. 25:1–3).[29] A strong comparison is made in the story. Balaam, not one of God's people, had at least obeyed God out of fear. God's own people should have been obedient out of love. They did not obey, however, even out of fear.

Letting Balaam Speak to You

Balaam is a negative example in both Testaments. This tells us two things: First, the Old Testament stories provide illustrations we can learn important lessons from for our own lives. These stories may be old (they were old to the New Testament writers, too), but they are still relevant. Second, if we really want to understand the New Testament, we need to know the Old Testament first. If we don't, the full meaning of such statements as Peter's description of false teachers who "follow the way of Balaam" is lost to us (2 Peter 2:15).

[28]Davies, *Numbers*, 249.

[29]Num. 31:16 indicates that Balaam also had something to do with the actions of these women. He seems to have planned the seduction after being unable to curse Israel in battle. Perhaps he was paid for his services after all; the involvement, however, cost him his life (Num. 31:8).

The Second Census and More Laws — Num. 26:1 Through 36:13

God commanded the Israelites to take a second census. In doing so he indicated that the years of wandering in the desert were over (Num. 26:1–2,64). Like the first census, the primary purpose of counting the people was military organization. But this time God gave additional instructions: The second census would also become the basis for land distribution. Every family would receive their equal share of the Promised Land. Great care was taken to insure economic equality for Israel's future as a nation. In the midst of the process, a situation of injustice occurred.

ZELOPHEHAD'S DAUGHTERS: WOMEN ON A MISSION

Numbers 27:1–11 and 36:1–13 record the story of Zelophehad's daughters. To understand it, we must be aware of its patriarchal, cultural setting.[30] This family of only female offspring would not receive a land allotment in the Promised Land. Therefore, their family line would be forever lost from Israel. Such an event would be a tragic loss not only for the women; their deceased relatives, and yet-unborn relatives, and the entire community would suffer as well.[31] Zelophehad's daughters boldly presented the problem to their leaders. And God responded with a radical new law (27:5–7).

"Follow Justice" (Deut. 16:20)

The idea of economic justice is seen throughout Scripture—in the prophets, the proverbs, and the New Testament church. God does not seem to favor a system of haves and have-nots. For Israel, he established a system giving everyone the potential of economic success (Exod. 21:1–11, 23:2–9; Lev. 25:8–55; Num. 26:52–56). Believers cannot read the Pentateuch without asking some difficult questions about the modern American view of money and economic power. We are usually most concerned about the opportunities we do *not* have. Perhaps we should be concerned about the opportunities we *do* have—opportunities to bring economic justice to the world.

---

[30]In a traditional patriarchal system, the family's economic resources, such as land, were always passed from father to son. Daughters did not inherit or give an inheritance; rather, they received a dowry upon marriage. It is assumed in the story of Zelophehad's daughters that Israelite tradition followed this generally accepted practice (see also Deut. 21:15–17).

[31]Johs. Pedersen, *Israel: Its Life and Culture* (Copenhagen: University of Copenhagen, 1926), 1:52–56.

Bringing Injustice to Light

Some Christians believe that women, or any who believe they are experiencing injustice within the Christian community, should not question the traditional "system." They should quietly pray and endure, or humbly accept their place, as if it were not an injustice. The story of Zelophehad's daughters shows a better way. Injustice should be brought to the attention of leadership with courage and respect. Leadership should respond with genuine concern and flexibility. Over the entire process, God should be consulted, heard, and obeyed, even if he requires radical change.

God's instruction to allow daughters to inherit family land changed centuries of social custom. Even adopted adult males would have been preferred to inherit above natural daughters.[32] In this story, God made a strong statement about social traditions: When they cause injustice, they must be changed. The women in this story acted from pure motives. They took their new responsibilities seriously. They married within their own tribe, preserving its strength. As a result, justice and economic balance in Israel were maintained (Num. 36:1–13).

MISCELLANEOUS LEGAL MATTERS

Numbers 28 through 30 gives an overview of several laws concerning offerings, feasts, and vows. Many of these were previously described in Exodus. Some of them will be seen again in Deuteronomy. Why would these laws be repeated? A new generation of Israelites needed to be reminded of them.

An entirely new matter is introduced in Numbers 35: "cities of refuge" (v. 6). God assigned certain towns to the Levites. They were to provide a safe place for accused murderers. In Ancient Near Eastern culture, a person could avenge a blood relative who had been killed. In Israel, however, the law declared a difference between an intentional killing and an accidental killing (Exod. 21:12–14). Cities of refuge provided a safe place for the accused while the case was being investigated (Num. 35:6–15; Deut. 19:1–13).

[32]For a detailed description of such an occurrence see James B. Pritchard, ed., "Documents from the Practice of Law: Mesopotamian Legal Documents," in *The Ancient Near East: Volume 1, An Anthology of Texts and Pictures,* trans. Theophile J. Meek (Princeton: Princeton University Press, 1958), 168–69. See also April Westbrook, "Land, Law and Ladies: Justice and Gender Roles in the Narrative of Zelophehad's Daughters" (master's thesis, Southern California College, 1997).

TAKING THE LAND

As the Book of Numbers comes to an end, conquest of the Promised Land comes into focus. The Israelites defeated the Midianites. They received instructions concerning the spoils of war (Num. 31:1–54). The tribes of Reuben, Gad, and Manasseh began to settle on the eastern side of the Jordan River. These tribes were faithful to their promise to help the other tribes take their own lands (Num. 32:16–32; Josh. 1:16–18).

Numbers 33 records the history of Israel's journey from Egypt to Canaan, as given by Moses. Though accurate at the time, the record is difficult for the modern reader to follow with any real certainty. The names and descriptions of places have changed over extended periods of time. One fact is certain, however: God faithfully brought the Israelites out of Egypt to the land he had promised them. The Book of Numbers includes God's description of the boundaries of the Promised Land (34:1–12). Even so, Israel never fully accomplished the conquest. They were persistently disobedient and unfaithful to their covenant promises (Isa. 1 through 2; Jer. 2 through 3; Hos. 2 through 4).

Deuteronomy: Speaking of Covenant

At first glance, the Book of Deuteronomy seems to repeat the details of Israel's desert wanderings. The repetition might tempt us to give it only a quick reading. That would be a mistake. Deuteronomy helps us understand the God of covenant. The concept of covenant is very important to believers. Covenant has everything to do with relationship. We must consider the covenant relationship between God and his people in the Old Testament. Then

God Doesn't Forget Us

Sometimes it seems like God has forgotten where we are, or even that we exist. The Israelites probably thought this, too, while they were wandering around in what must have seemed like the middle of nowhere. But they learned what we can learn. God *never* forgets his people and he *always* fulfills his promises. It may look like we are going in the opposite direction (or maybe even in no direction); this doesn't mean he has decided not to do what he has said! God promised to bring Israel from Egypt to the Promised Land. Because of Israel's stubborn ways, it took them forty years; even so, God brought them to the Promised Land.

we can better understand our own covenant relationship with him according to the New Testament.

This survey of the Book of Deuteronomy will consider its contents in the following order:

1:1 through 5:33	The Decalogue: Honoring God and Each Other
6:1 through 11:31	Israel From the Past to the Future
12:1 through 26:19	What Do We Do When We Get to the Promised Land?
27:1 through 31:30	Mount Ebal: The Covenant Renewed
32:1 through 34:12	Moses' Last Words: The End of an Era

The Book of Deuteronomy: A Sepher Torah

In Deuteronomy 30:10, the book calls itself the *sepher torah,* or "Book of the Law."[33] As such, the Book of Deuteronomy records Moses' instructions to the Israelites concerning the ways of their God. In order to remain in right relationship with God from generation to generation, the Israelites would have to do four important things: remember, love, fear, and hold fast.

1. "REMEMBER THAT YOU WERE SLAVES IN EGYPT . . . "

The Book of Deuteronomy repeatedly instructs the Israelites to remember how the LORD had delivered them from slavery in Egypt.[34] They were also to remember their own failures during their journey to the Promised Land (Deut. 8:2; 9:7; 24:9). Why was it so important for Israel to remember these things? Clearly they were to learn from the results of their past mistakes. When they had rebelled against God, they were not remembering him as their deliv-

[33]See also Deut. 1:5; 4:44; 17:18–19, 28:61, 29:21,29.

[34]Deut. 5:15; 7:18; 15:15; 16:3,12; 24:18,22

ering LORD. God had miraculously set them free from slavery. He had proven his loyalty to them. He had also demonstrated his superior power. Such an awesome and faithful God was worthy of trust and obedience.

2. "LOVE THE LORD YOUR GOD . . . "

The Book of Deuteronomy describes the relationship between God and his people. Their obedience was not to be a cold and distant response; it was to be the result of their passionate love for God. Deuteronomy 6:5 explains that the Israelites were to love God with all their heart, soul, and strength.[35] In their culture, these words implied every aspect of a person's existence. No part of themselves was exempt from loving God. They were to experience a life-consuming love relationship with him. Such love would be shown through their faithfulness in keeping covenant promises (Deut. 11:1; 30:16,20). The love relationship was mutual. God showed his love for Israel by consistently fulfilling his covenant promises to them (Deut. 5:10; 7:9–13).

3. "FEAR THE LORD YOUR GOD . . . "

Frequently the Book of Deuteronomy mentions love and obedience along with the instruction to "fear" God.[36] Did God want the Israelites to be afraid of him? How can a person fear and love someone at the same time? By instructing the Israelites to fear God, Moses taught them to understand God's greatness. God had chosen them to be in relationship with him. His choice, however, did not

Rehearse Your Faith

The principle of remembering is still true. Our ability to be faithful to God flows from his own faithfulness to us. When I remember and rehearse how I responded to my call in the past, it is much easier to obey him again in the present. Human beings tend to obey only those they trust. Some people refer to "blind faith," but God did not seem to require this of Israel at all. He proved his trustworthiness many times before he asked them to walk in faithful obedience. Their deliverance from Egypt was the primary proof. Throughout the Old Testament, God often referred to this seminal event when asking for a new generation's trust and obedience (Josh. 24:5–14; Judg. 6:8; Jer. 7:21–26, 11:1–5). What has God done for you? What has this proven to you about his character? Based on that, isn't it reasonable to trust and obey him again?

---

[35]See also Deut. 10:12; 11:13; 13:3; 30:6. For further reading on the Hebrew concepts of "heart," "soul," and "strength" see Pedersen, *Israel.*

[36]Deut. 5:29; 6:2,13,24; 10:12; 31:12–13.

place them on an equal level with him. To have a real relationship with God, the Israelites had to see that he was an awesome being; he deserved their respect and honor.

The instruction to fear God came with promises. Accepting God's greatness in their own lives put the Israelites in a good place. They would be blessed and protected by him (Deut. 5:29; 6:24). From this attitude of respect, they would also be inclined to obey God's commands. His instructions were designed to give them a good life (6:2). Further, as the Israelites feared God, they would become associated with him in the eyes of others. As a result, other people would fear the Israelites. They were the people of a mighty God (28:9–11). Such respect would protect the Israelites from outside enemies.

4. "HOLD FAST TO HIM . . . "

In the Book of Deuteronomy, the Israelites were encouraged to "hold fast" to God. Usually this instruction came with the idea of loving, fearing, and obeying.[37] The Hebrew word *davaq*, translated "hold fast," literally means "to stick together." One might say that the Israelites were to "glue themselves" to God. Such a commitment would keep them from following other gods. It would also require ongoing personal choices: God faithfully committed himself to the Israelites; they would have to make their own commitment to him. Their choice would be tested. To succeed in this relationship, they would have to "stick like glue" to God. As a first step, the Israelites entered into a formal relational agreement, or covenant, with God.

In the Name of Jesus

The principle of fearing God is still true for His followers. Sometimes we think we can face spiritual enemies with great authority "in the name of Jesus," even though we are not submitted to him. "In the name of Jesus" is not a magical phrase; it is a personal understanding of who Jesus is (read Acts 19:13–16). We can have authority only where we are submitted to authority. If we don't yield ourselves to God with respect and obedience, how can we expect to command others to do so? We will be identified with God and his power only as we fear him in our own lives.

---

[37]Deut. 10:20; 11:22; 13:4; 30:20.

IS THE BOOK OF DEUTERONOMY THE RECORD OF A COVENANT ?

Some scholars believe that the Book of Deuteronomy was written in the style of a formal covenant. In the Ancient Near East, people established covenant relationships for mutual benefit. For example, someone might agree to give a percentage of his income to a landowner in return for use of that land. Such covenant relationships often required formal documentation. Written agreements included descriptions of related past events, specific requirements for the parties involved, witnesses, and blessings and cursings. The Book of Deuteronomy appears to follow such a format. Therefore, one might conclude that Deuteronomy is a record of the formal covenant agreement between God and Israel.[38] The Ten Commandments represent the heart of that agreement.

The Decalogue: Honoring God and Each Other – Deut. 1:1 Through 5:33

In the Book of Exodus, the Ten Commandments are included in the story of the Israelites at Mount Sinai (Exod. 20:1–17). Deuteronomy records the Commandments as part of the formal covenant between God and the second generation of post-Exodus Israelites (Deut. 5:6–21). The first four chapters recite God's interaction with Israel in the past.

[38]Earl S. Kalland, *Deuteronomy,* Expositor's Bible Commentary, ed. Frank E. Gaebelein, vol. 3 (Grand Rapids: Zondervan Publishing House, 1992), 4. See also M. G. Kline, *The Structure of Biblical Authority* (Grand Rapids: Wm. B. Eerdmans, 1963); G. E. Mendenhall, *Law and Covenant in Israel and the Ancient Near East* (Pittsburgh: Biblical Colloquium, 1955). The possibility of covenant format also contributes to the issue of authorship. If Deuteronomy follows a specific format, it is more likely to have been written by one author (traditionally Moses) at an early date. See the discussion of Mosaic authorship in "Where Did Genesis Come From?" in chap. 2.

Then, the Ten Commandments provide the first specific requirements for the involved parties within the agreement.

The basis for the Ten Commandments is found in Deuteronomy 5:6: "'I am the LORD your God, who brought you out of Egypt, out of the land of slavery.'" This statement summarizes God's part in his covenant relationship with Israel. He had been, and would continue to be, their God. As such, he delivered, protected, and provided for them. Because he was their God, the Israelites would be identified with him. They would share his name and add to his honor. Consequently, their responsibilities in the covenant relationship with God would reflect his own nature.

The first four commandments required Israel to honor God in their speech and worship. Their actions would acknowledge who he was. Because God alone was sovereign, the Israelites were not to seek other gods (Deut. 5:7). Just as God was passionate in his love for the people of Israel, so the people of Israel were to be passionate in their love for him (5:8–10). The Israelites would be identified as God's people. Therefore, they were not to misrepresent him in any way by their actions (5:11).[39] They also were to acknowledge their own limitations. God had initiated a Sabbath rest for his creation. The Israelites were to honor him by keeping the Sabbath holy (Gen. 2:2–3; Deut. 5:12–14). Accordingly, the fourth commandment required the Israelites to rest on the Sabbath. It was not just another work day.

The last six commandments indicate that the Israelites should honor God in their relationships with each other.

---

[39]It has also been noted that in the ANE, misusing God's name might refer to attempting to use his name "in magical ways to manipulate him" or not taking seriously oaths, vows, and treaties made in his name. Walton and Matthews, *Genesis–Deuteronomy*, 108.

Parents taught their children how to maintain the covenant relationship with God, so children were to honor their parents (Deut. 5:16). Because God created life, his people were not to commit murder (5:17). God kept his covenant promises faithfully; therefore, they were to do the same in their relationships with each other (5:18). God provided for the Israelites abundantly; they had no need to acquire wealth or personal honor by violating each other (5:19–21).[40] The Decalogue makes clear that the Israelites' interaction with each other reflected their covenant relationship with God. They were to be like him in their personal relationships.

Israel From the Past to the Future —Deut. 6:1 Through 11:31

Moses reminded the Israelites of the connection between their covenant with God and their future in the Promised Land. He repeatedly emphasized faithful obedience to God's commands within the covenant agreement. Their obedience would be challenged by pagan cultures in the new land. The Israelites would be the only people who worshiped one God.[41] Being different is never easy.

[40]The list of people and things not to be desired in the last commandment is interesting in that it represents all that made up the "house" of an Israelite. One's house represented one's personal security and honor. The forbidden desire here involved more than wanting to have something. It also involved wanting to gain personal honor by dishonoring another person. By God's choosing the people of Israel as his own, He had given them the greatest honor possible. Why should God's covenant people desire what someone else had when God would provide their every need?

[41]All of the surrounding people groups at this point in Israel's history worshiped many gods. For an overview see George Hart, *A Dictionary of Egyptian Gods and Goddesses* (London: Routledge & Kegan Paul, 1986); and William Foxwell Albright, *Yahweh and the Gods of Canaan* (Garden City, N.Y.: Doubleday & Company, 1968).

"HEAR, O ISRAEL . . . "

One of the most famous passages in the Old Testament is found in Deuteronomy 6:4–5, beginning, "Hear, O Israel." Well known to both Jews and Christians, it is sometimes referred to as the *shema'* (thus passing into the English dictionary as "Shema"), based on the Hebrew word for "hear." In this case, the word means more than just hearing words. The word includes the idea of listening with the intention of obeying what is heard. The Shema is particularly relevant to Christians because Jesus described it as the most important commandment of all.[42] By obeying this command, all the others would naturally follow. For the Israelites, the Shema would provide the ultimate test of their obedience and loyalty to God.

The Israelites would be surrounded by people who worshiped many gods. During their time in the desert they had proven themselves vulnerable to such temptation (Exod. 32:1–6; Num. 25:1–3). They also were prone to forget God's faithfulness, even while he performed miracles for them (Num. 11:1–13; 13:26 through 14:4). Would they do the same within the security of the Promised Land (Deut. 6:10–12)?

The Shema addressed each of these areas. First, it established the fact that God is *one*. The Israelites could not worship Yahweh in addition to other gods. There were, in fact, no other gods to be compared with him. Secondly, the Shema explained the meaning of total commitment to the one true God within covenant relationship. Such love and loyalty would not forget God's faithfulness or take his blessings for granted.

Mercy and Justice, a Balancing Act

Sometimes we focus so much on the great mercy of God that we forget he is also perfectly just. These two ideas are difficult to reconcile; human beings are seldom able to balance the two. But God has both qualities. Just because he does not immediately show his righteous anger over sin, we cannot assume he is unconcerned about it. The Bible indicates that God expresses his anger at the time of his choosing. The Book of Revelation gives the ultimate example of this fact. Only when I understand the depth of God's concern about my sin can I fully appreciate the grace and power of what Christ did for me at the cross.

[42]See Matt. 22:37–38; Mark 12:29–30; Luke 10:27.

I Thought He Was a Loving God

According to Deuteronomy 7, God required the Israelites to destroy seven nations. Though they were stronger than Israel, God promised to give them over to Israel. How could a loving God act in such a way? At first, this command might seem like genocide. The point has nothing to do with prejudice, however. God did not choose the Israelites because they were better than others. He chose them because of promises he made to their forefathers (Deut. 4:37,38; 7:7–9; 9:4–6). The Canaanite nations were doomed because of their own wickedness and idolatry. God had given them time to repent and they had not (Gen. 15:16). It should be noted that God promised Israel the same destiny if they practiced the same wickedness (Deut. 8:19–20).

Moreover, God removed the pagan nations so they would not tempt Israel to sin. God's instructions to destroy the wicked included a reminder of Israel's own failures. The Israelites were never to forget the golden calf incident (Deut. 9:7–21). They had to live with the consequences of their rebellion at Kadesh Barnea (Deut. 9:23–24). By remembering their failures, the Israelites had to acknowledge their weaknesses. If they forgot their vulnerability, they would be more easily tempted.

A Blessing and a Curse

Throughout Deuteronomy 10 and 11, a simple reality is repeated: The Israelites could live either in covenant relationship with God—or not. The blessings and cursings included here again reflect the content of formal covenants. In the covenant between God and Israel, their love, respect,

Some Ways to Deal with Temptation

The Israelites weren't the only ones to experience temptation. I face it in my life, and so do you. Chapters 6 through 9 of Deuteronomy teach us five things we can do to deal with temptation: (1) acknowledge that only God is worthy of our worship, remembering all of the great things he has done for us; (2) totally commit every part of our lives to him each day and love him passionately; (3) from this love relationship, faithfully trust and obey our God; (4) acknowledge our areas of weakness, instead of pretending we don't have any; (5) through God's direction and empowerment, remove from our lives all that tempts us in our areas of weakness.

and obedience would result in blessings (Deut. 10:12–13). These blessings included such things as land, abundant harvest, victory in battle, and healthy families (Deut. 11:8–9, 14–15,21–25). On the other hand, stubborn disobedience and idolatry would result in destruction (Deut. 11:16–17,28). The covenant agreement, with its blessings and cursings, would be passed on from generation to generation (Deut. 11:19–21).

What Do We Do When We Get to the Promised Land? —Deut. 12:1 Through 26:19

The Book of Deuteronomy is a record of the covenant agreement between God and Israel. As seen in the first chapters of the book, the covenant involved a love relationship. So, according to Deuteronomy, obeying God's commands maintained the covenant. Obedience also expressed one's love for God. Deuteronomy, however, is also a book of teaching *(torah)*. As such, it presents God's commands concerning life in the Promised Land. These instructions, or "laws," were part of the covenant stipulations.

ONE GOD, ONE PLACE OF WORSHIP

Within the total commitment of covenant relationship, the location of worship rituals would become significant for Israel. During their desert journey, the tabernacle moved with them (Num. 4:1–33). But soon the Israelites would be a settled people. Where would they go to worship? God emphasized that there be one place established for this purpose. The Israelites were not to worship other gods. Also they were not to worship Yahweh like the pagans worshiped their gods (Deut. 12:4). To do either would violate a full commitment to Yahweh. Having one place of worship would help the Israelites avoid both kinds of disobedience.

In keeping with this, particular attention was given to destroying the shrines of Asherah (Deut. 12:3). The Old Testament often referred to this goddess as a particular temptation to the Israelites. Some believe the Israelites tried to mix the worship of Yahweh with Asherah. Such a practice would have been simple. Asherah was probably the consort of the Canaanite chief god, El. Israel could have rationalized their idolatry by viewing Yahweh as their chief god. Then Asherah could have been worshiped as his consort.[43] In this way the Israelites could worship Yahweh and fit in with the people around them.

God addressed such thinking before Israel entered the Promised Land. He was not just the most powerful god— he was the *only* God. Deuteronomy 12 and 13 left no room for the worship of any other being, for any reason, in any way. All such practices and everything related to them were to be completely destroyed. One place of worship, for God alone, was to be established. Here, the Israelites would bring tithes and celebrate sacred feasts (Deut. 14:23; 16:2,11,15).

Rationalizing Disobedience

We are so much like the Israelites! How many times do we rationalize our disobedience by trying to mix God's way with our own sinful way. "If I go to church on Sunday, I can do whatever I want on Monday." Obviously, God has no interest in adjusting his plan to make room for sin to remain in our lives.

JUSTICE IN THE PROMISED LAND

Several laws in Deuteronomy made provision for economic and social justice. A year of canceling debts was described (15:1–11; cf. Lev. 25:8–38). Similar instructions were given concerning the release of slaves.[44] Economic

---

[43]Deut. 16:21–22 seems to support this idea by specifically commanding the people not to set up an Asherah pole beside the altar to Yahweh. See Walton and Matthews, *Genesis–Deuteronomy*, 229–34.

[44]Deut. 15:12–18; cf. Exod. 21:2–6; Lev. 25:38–55.

balance was the basis for such laws. Every seven years, all debts were canceled so that families would be spared economic disaster. Everyone would then have plenty and be able to share freely with others. Ultimately, the law was intended to discourage class distinctions.

Other factors, however, could cause poverty. A person might simply squander his wealth so that he had nothing left. Also, in the patriarchal system of early Israel, the economic status of women and children was usually linked to a relationship with an adult male.[45] As a result, the death of one's husband or father could create an economic disaster. God's commands provided for such people by instructing Israel not to take advantage of them within the community. They were not to charge interest on loans (Deut. 23:19). They were to pay hired workers fair wages each day (Deut. 24:14–15). They were to leave part of their harvest in the field for the poor (Deut. 24:19–22). In addition, every third year a family's tithe was to be given to provide for the poor (Deut. 26:12).

According to Deuteronomy, justice for everyone was also to be evident within the court system. Local judges were appointed for each tribe in every town. These judges were not to be influenced by wealth (Deut. 16:18–20). If they were unable to make a ruling on a case, the priests were to make the judgment. Priests were particularly suited for this task because they were the most familiar with the law God had given (Deut. 17:8–9).

[45]Tikva Frymer-Kensky, "Patriarchal Family Relationships and Near Eastern Law," *BA* (fall 1981): 210–11. See also R. Ivan Vasholz, "You Shall Not Covet Your Neighbor's Wife," *WTJ* 49, no. 2 (1987): 403; and related sections in Hans Jochen Boecker, *Law and the Administration of Justice in the Old Testament and Ancient East* (Minneapolis: Augsburg Publishing House, 1980).

In Deuteronomy 17:14–20 special instructions were given for the future selection of a king. This person was to be chosen by God. He was not to accumulate great personal wealth. He was not to marry many wives.[46] Most importantly, Israelite kings were to be devoted students of the *torah*. Such an emphasis would have made an Israelite king very different from other kings of the time. Kings usually created and enforced their own justice in order to secure their political positions.[47] Very few Israelite kings lived up to God's standard. Perhaps this helps to explain why God was reluctant to grant Israel a king (1 Sam. 8:1–22).

WHAT DO YOU MEAN, "DON'T LEARN"?

Learning is often spoken of in the Bible as something we *should* do (Deut. 6:7; Prov. 1:5–6; Isa. 1:17; Phil. 4:9). Deuteronomy 18:9–12, however, shows a different command for the Israelites. They were strongly told *not* to learn certain things in the Promised Land (see also Deut. 12:29–31). The Israelites were not to imitate Canaanite religious practices.[48] Particularly singled out were child sacrifice, fortune-telling, magic, and consulting the dead. These activities represented attempts to control nature and people's destinies.

The Israelites did not need additional spiritual power. God was already giving them the best possible destiny. He

[46]This requirement has much to do with politics. Kings would marry foreign wives to make treaties with other nations. Israel was to trust in their God, not in political alliances.

[47]See George E. Mendenhall, "Ancient Oriental and Biblical Law," *BA* 17, no. 3 (1954): 27; E. A. Speiser, *Oriental and Biblical Studies*, ed. J. J. Findelstein and Moshe Greenberg (Philadelphia: University of Pennsylvania Press, 1994), 313–16.

[48]For a comparison of the terms in Deut. 18:9–12 with practices in similar cultures of the time, see Walton and Matthews, *Genesis–Deuteronomy*, 244–45.

Avoiding an Old Temptation

We may live in a rational, technologically advanced society, but people still want to manipulate spiritual power, to exercise control. There is nothing new about this, and it still is not right. If this temptation is still here, then we must pay attention to God's instructions. He says to avoid *everything* that has to do with these practices. We are not even to learn how they are done (Deut. 18:9; cf. Rom. 13:14). Moreover, God did not explain whether or not these practices actually influence the spirit realm. The fascination, even among Christians, with the reality of these things isn't really the issue. His command is straightforward: *Have nothing to do with these things!*

instructed them to tear down the pagan shrines and kill all of the people who worshiped there (Deut. 7:1–5). He would raise up his own prophets from among his own people to speak his word.[49] His people would gain nothing by trying to manipulate the spirit realm. Any Israelite who engaged in these forbidden activities was to be killed (Exod. 22:18). Israel was to worship, trust, and obey God alone. He was to be their only point of connection with the spirit realm.

Rules of War

Entering a time of warfare, Israel faced two groups of enemies with two different strategies for dealing with them: Those who lived within the boundaries of the Promised Land were to be completely destroyed (Deut. 20:16–18). Those who lived nearby were to be given the opportunity to surrender (Deut. 20:10). The actions described here may seem extreme to us. Yet they were mild in comparison to warfare practices of other cultures at that time.[50]

This was particularly true in regard to the treatment of female captives. God's instructions for Israelite conquest did not sanction rape as an accepted practice in warfare. An Israelite man was required to marry a female captive before having any kind of sexual relationship with her (Deut. 21:10–14). Her legal status as a wife would then protect her socially and economically for the rest of her life. She would

[49]As seen in Deut. 18:15–19, the role of prophet in OT Israel was quite different from the NT gift of prophecy. In OT Israel, the prophet was something of a national leader, giving God's direction for all the people. The serious nature of the role came with certain risk. If a prophet spoke anything in the Lord's name that the Lord did not say, he was to be put to death (Deut. 18:20–22)!

[50]de Vaux, *Ancient Israel,* 255–57.

be fully incorporated into the Israelite community. She would not simply be used and abandoned.[51]

"UNTIL DEATH DO US PART"

The instructions given in Deuteronomy have much to say about the marriage covenant. Marriage was foundational to the community life of early Israel. God had already stated firmly that the covenant must be kept (Deut. 5:18; see also Gen. 2:24). Israelite marriage was to be highly protected. As a result, adultery was punishable by death (Deut. 22:22).[52] So what did a man do if he did not want to keep his wife?

Two possibilities are discussed in Deuteronomy. First, the husband could try to get an annulment. If a marriage contract had been negotiated concerning a virgin bride, then a virgin bride was expected at the marriage ceremony. Virgin brides were greatly prized in the Ancient Near East. Consequently, virginity became an issue in the legal marriage contract.[53] If, in reality, the bride was not a virgin, then a breach of contract occurred.

Betrothal and Marriage

In biblical times, the marriage covenant began with the legal contract between the fathers of the bride and groom. This covenant was immediately binding, even before the marriage was consummated. A betrothed woman, therefore, was considered already married, and to break the betrothal was tantamount to divorce (see Matt. 1:18–19).

The marriage laws are given from the husband's perspective. In Ancient Near Eastern culture it was definitely to a woman's advantage to be married and to have children. She did not have the social and economic options often available to the modern American woman. When this factor is understood, one can see that the laws given by God to Israel usually protected the women.

[51]This was generous treatment for a war captive; in the ANE, marriage had far more to do with legal, social, and economic status than with romance. A similar regard can be seen in the law concerning rape within the Israelite community. If a man forced an unbetrothed woman to have sexual relations with him, he was legally required to marry her. He also could never divorce her for any reason (Deut. 22:28–29); this would insure the woman's social and economic status for the rest of her life. The law would also deter rape. A man would be far better off negotiating a proper marriage contract, rather than living the rest of his life with a vengeful wife, very angry in-laws, and no way out of the marriage.

[52]This included forced adultery or the rape of a betrothed woman (Deut. 22:25–27). In such a case, however, only the man would be given the death penalty. The woman was considered an innocent victim.

[53]Matthews and Benjamin, *Social World*, 176–86.

"'I Hate Divorce,' Says the LORD God of Israel" (Mal. 2:16)

Divorce is a very common occurrence in America today. Most of us have been personally affected by it in some way. The Old Testament law concerning divorce is only the beginning of a biblical understanding of the issue. One must also consider the important New Testament texts on the subject. We can see something of God's heart in this portion of Deuteronomy, however. Clearly, his best for us is the preservation of marriage. Faithfulness in covenant relationships is precious to him. However, he is not unaware of our human tendencies to harm each other. Therefore, he also makes provision for those who have been violated.

Deuteronomy 22:13–21 addresses such a case. The marriage contract had specified a virgin bride (that is, not a widow or divorcee). The husband, however, charged that she was not a virgin; she had deceived him. The way the law was written, however, must not be misunderstood. The bride's parents held the proof of her virginity.[54] The parents' possession of the evidence gave the bride a distinct legal advantage. The groom could accuse her of not having been a virgin. Her parents, however, would undoubtedly present the evidence that would vindicate her. Then, the groom would have to pay a heavy fine and never divorce his wife for any reason. Obviously, in light of such a law, a man would think twice before making such an accusation. He did, however, have another option.

A man could end his marriage through a legal divorce. Deuteronomy 24:1–4 explains Israelite law in this matter.[55] The husband charged he had found something "indecent" about his wife. The meaning of the word "indecent" is not precise. It indicates some type of shameful exposure or activity, other than adultery; death, not divorce, would have been the penalty for adultery.

The passage also addresses remarriage after divorce. Marriage was a solemn issue. So then was divorce. A man could not simply throw out his wife. If he divorced her, he

[54]The proof is described as a "cloth," apparently showing a small bloodstain from the couple's first experience of sexual intercourse together (Deut. 22:17). The blood evidence would prove that this had been the woman's first experience of sexual intercourse with anyone. One must note, however, that it would be fairly easy to present a cloth with blood on it, even if it was not from the couple's first sexual experience. Thus, the woman was given every advantage in this type of legal dispute.

[55]Jesus refers to this passage in his discussion of the divorce issue (Matt. 5:31–32). Again, in order to understand his comments in the NT, we must first consider the original passage in its OT context.

had to grant her a divorce document. The document freed her to marry someone else. In this particular case, however, the first husband could not remarry her. He had dishonored her before the community by accusing her of something shameful. Such dishonor could not be undone.

WHAT'S THE DIFFERENCE BETWEEN "LEVITE" AND "LEVIRATE"?

Instructions concerning the custom of levirate marriage are given in Deuteronomy 25:5–10. The term "levirate" is not found in Deuteronomy and has nothing to do with the term "Levite" (even though the words sound similar). Instead, the word comes from the Latin word *levir,* meaning "husband's brother," and it describes a legal situation that happened when a married man died without a son. The relative of the dead husband was required to marry the widow. The purpose of this custom was to provide for the widow and to preserve the dead husband's lineage. If a man married and died before he had a son, his family line would end. This was considered a great tragedy. Therefore, preventive steps were taken. The first son from the levirate marriage took the name and inheritance of the deceased husband. If the male relative refused to take his responsibility here, he insulted the widow and his deceased brother.[56] Consequently, he and his own family would be disgraced before the community.[57]

[56]The story of Tamar and Onan in Gen. 38 is often misunderstood. In this case, the "wicked" thing Onan did was not that he practiced a form of birth control but that he dishonored his brother. In this story we see that greed was the motivator for Onan's actions. If he produced a son for his deceased brother, he would be disqualified from getting his brother's property. See also Ruth 4:6–10.

[57]According to Deut. 25:9, the widow responded to this insult by spitting in the man's face in the presence of the elders. From that time on, the man and

None of Us Lives to Himself Alone (Rom 14:7)

Too often we encounter a mindset that says, "That's my business and none of yours." And sometimes that's correct.

But sometimes it's not. Let's consider virtue first. We confess that Christ died for the world (Rom. 5:6–8), but don't seem to understand that his goodness becomes ours (1 Cor. 1:30). Like Jesus, we too can become vehicles of blessing to others. For example, Abraham wasn't just blessed by God; he was to *become* a blessing —through him all the world would be blessed (Gen. 12:1–3,7). His intercession for Sodom was based on the idea that the virture of the good people in it would outweigh the evil (Gen. 18). Unhappily it wasn't enough, though.

What's bad can be

ISRAEL: GOD'S SPECIAL TREASURE

Deuteronomy 26 concludes the specific instructions within God's covenant agreement with Israel. Again, God reminded the Israelites to obey his commands with all of their lives (Deut. 26:16). The relationship that they shared in covenant was one of mutual responsibility and care. The Israelites would love and honor God by obeying him. They were to show the world his wonderful character by "walk[ing] in his ways" (Deut. 26:17). God would love Israel by choosing them to be his own people. They were his "treasured possession." As such, they would be honored above all other nations (Deut. 26:18–19).

Mount Ebal: The Covenant Renewed —Deut. 27:1 Through 31:30

Mount Ebal (with Mount Gerizim) stood as a visual representation of Israel's experience in covenant relationship with God. One cannot miss the obvious comparison of this mountain event to the earlier experience at Mount Sinai (Exod. 19). This time, however, the new generation of Israelites did not face a desert. They looked toward the Promised Land itself. At Mount Ebal, the Israelites built an altar and made sacrifices to their God. They also wrote the law on stone monuments that would stand for years to come.[58] These first actions in the Promised Land showed Israel's intentions for their new life there. At this point, they

---

his entire family line would have an unfavorable reputation within the community.

[58]The fulfillment of these instructions is recorded in Josh. 8. Archaeologists may have discovered the remains of the altar on Mount Ebal described in Deut. 27:5. See Walton and Matthews, *Genesis–Deuteronomy*, 261.

wanted to be a people who worshiped and obeyed God alone.

BLESSINGS AND CURSINGS, AGAIN

Deuteronomy 27 and 28 record Moses' reminder to the Israelites of the covenant blessings and curses. The Israelites at Mount Ebal once again agreed to accept the terms of this covenant. Therefore, they understood its consequences. If they were faithful to their promises to worship and obey God, they would be incredibly blessed. If they were unfaithful and disobedient, they would be incredibly cursed.

In Israelite culture, blessing had to do with inner ability. To bless was to speak strength to a person for success. To curse someone was to do the opposite. Both cursing and blessing were considered highly effective. Either one could spread from one person to the family and even to the entire community.[59] Consequently, the renewal of the covenant was very important for this second generation of Israelites. Their parents had been given the same opportunity before and had been unfaithful. They also lived with the consequences of that decision (Num. 14:26–35; 26:63–65). At Mount Ebal, God gave the Israelites another chance to be faithful. Would they succeed where their parents had failed?

Unfortunately, future generations of Israelites would be unfaithful. But a beautiful aspect of God's character is shown in Deuteronomy 30. Here we learn that the purpose for these curses was not just punishment. The curses were intended to press Israel back to God. When they

shared also. The adulteress, for example, would bring a curse on her people (Num. 5:27). The unsolved rural murder would indict the entire population of the nearest city until resolved (Deut. 21:1–9). And we all know how Achan's sin brought defeat to an entire army (Josh. 7:12).

This understanding lies at the base for any Christian theology of ethics: We all will leave footprints in the sands of time—our deeds. We have no option that eliminates the footprints; we have only the choice of whether they speak of good or evil after we have passed.

[59]For further discussion of blessing and cursing see Pedersen, *Israel,* 182–84, 437–39.

The New Covenant Now

The New Testament also speaks of a covenant relationship with God and its consequences. "The wages of sin is death, but the gift of God is eternal life in Christ Jesus our Lord" (Rom. 6:23). Our access to this covenant relationship is based on the sacrificial work of Jesus Christ. The nature of that relationship, however, is the same as seen in Deuteronomy. In covenant relationship with God there is great blessing. Outside of that covenant relationship, there is only death and destruction. This basic truth, given throughout the Bible, is the very center of the gospel. This truth must also be the very foundation of our daily lives. Fortunately for us, God's character has not changed. He still stands ready to receive with love the unfaithful, if they will return to him. Let us "choose life."

returned to their covenant promises, he would bless them again (Deut. 30:1–10). What is the point? God is forever faithful to the covenant agreements he makes. Even when he has been rejected, mocked, and violated, his love stands ready to forgive. He will restore all who want to be in relationship with him. The future prophets of Israel would remind the people of this hope when they were an exiled and broken nation. At any time Israel could "choose life" by choosing to be God's people (Deut. 30:19–20)

Moses' Last Words: The End of an Era — Deut. 32:1 Through 34:12

The Book of Deuteronomy concludes the Pentateuch and a major era in the history of Israel. The book ends appropriately with the death of Moses, Israel's most important leader. Throughout the Pentateuch, Moses is portrayed as a real person. God had called him to lead Israel (Exod. 3:10), even though he had committed murder (2:12). He humbly led a rebellious group of people through difficult circumstances, but disobeyed God at a critical point (Num. 20:9–12). Moses' life offers great encouragement to everyone who wants to follow God. Although Moses was not perfect, God used him to do amazing things.

Moses' final words to Israel reflected their pattern of obedience and rebellion. The Song of Moses is recorded in Deuteronomy 32. In it, we see that Moses already knew about the people's future rebellion. The song was his last effort to convince the Israelites to remain faithful to God. The attempt speaks highly of his consistent leadership. Even knowing they would fail, he continued to point out the right path to the very end.

In giving his final blessings to the tribes, Moses spoke

strength to the people of Israel (Deut. 33:1–29). He blessed them before his death, as a father would bless his sons. The picture reminds us of Jacob blessing his sons, the forefathers of these tribes (Gen. 49). As Moses blessed the tribes of Israel, he spoke words of encouragement that would enable them for their future.[60]

After giving these blessings, Moses, Israel's great leader and prophet, climbed Mount Nebo. He died there and was accorded the distinction of being buried by God himself (Deut. 34:1–6). Few other details are given concerning his death. It was time for Israel to move forward into the Promised Land. Joshua would lead them from now on. But Moses' influence lives on. His life and writings have inspired generations – including ours.

Study Questions

1. Identify the purpose for, as well as the problems posed by, the censuses in the Book of Numbers.
2. Explain the various interpretations of the number of people who left Egypt in the exodus.
3. Recount the major events during Israel's wandering in the desert. Use the itinerary in Numbers 33 as an outline.

---

[60]The tribe of Simeon is not mentioned in these tribal blessings. Some believe this is because the blessings reflect a later time, after Simeon merged into the tribe of Judah. For further discussion see Harrison, *Introduction*, 660–61; S. R. Driver, *A Critical and Exegetical Commentary on Deuteronomy*, International Critical Commentary, ed. Samuel Rolles Driver, Alfred Plummer, and Charles Briggs, vol. 5 (Edinburgh, Scotland: T. & T. Clark, 1895), 386–88; Ian Cairns, *Word and Presence: A Commentary on the Book of Deuteronomy* (Grand Rapids: Wm. B. Eerdmans, 1992), 293–94.

4. Review the stories of the seventy elders, of Balaam, and of Zelophehad's daughters. What are the major details of each story? What does each story tell us about God's interaction with people?

5. Explain how Deuteronomy is a *sepher torah*.

6. Explain the centrality of the Shema to Israel's religious life.

7. Explain the laws of marriage (including the Levirate) and divorce as they occur in the Book of Deuteronomy.

8. How do blessings and cursings figure in Israel's covenant relationship with God?

For Further Reading

Brueggeman, Walter. *The Land*. Philadelphia: Fortress Press, 1977.

Grabbe, Lester L. *Priests, Prophets, Diviners, Sages*. Valley Forge, Pa: Trinity Press International, 1995.

Walton, John H. *Chronological and Background Charts of the Old Testament*. Rev. ed. Grand Rapids: Zondervan Publishing House, 1994.

Whybray, R. Norman. *Introduction to the Pentateuch*. Grand Rapids: Wm. B. Eerdmans, 1990.

Wright, Christopher J. H. *God's People in God's Land*. Grand Rapids: Wm. B. Eerdmans, 1990.

9

William Barnes

Canaan: Conquest, Covenant Renewal, and Crisis

Outline:

Terms:

ark of the covenant
chesed
Habiru
holy war
kinsman-redeemer
programmatic text
torah/Torah

357

The Book of Joshua: More Than Just About Miracles

Everyone has heard about the battle of Jericho, when "the walls came tumblin' down." And most of us have heard about the day when "the sun stood still." Joshua, the man who succeeded Moses as the Israelite leader, experienced both these miracles. And more than three thousand years later, our hearts still thrill to hear about the days "when the LORD listened to a man" (Josh. 10:14) and apparently stopped the sun dead in its tracks. As for the walls of Jericho, imagine preparing for battle by first marching around an enemy city seven times in a row (6:15). A strange way to warm up for the battle of one's life. Still, God's ways are not our ways (Isa. 55:8–9). Who would have thought that God would really make the city walls collapse so that every soldier could march straight into the city?[1]

Introduction

Even so, the Book of Joshua is not just about miracles.[2] For example, the book both begins and ends with references to

---

[1]Josh. 6:20; the Heb. reads *wattippol hachomah tachteha*, "and the wall fell in its place." (This is predicted back in v. 5, to be sure.) For a recent analysis of what archaeology indicates may have happened that fateful day, see Bryant G. Wood, "Did the Israelites Conquer Jericho?" *BAR* (March/April 1990): 44–59. Wood argues that a sudden earthquake took place just after harvest time (late spring), since large quantities of stored grain were left in the destroyed city. The toppled mud bricks of the main city walls then provided convenient ramps into the doomed city for the Israelite soldiers.

[2]The following are the main recent commentaries in English on the book of Joshua: Robert G. Boling, *Joshua: A New Translation With Notes and Commentary,* with an introduction by G. Ernest Wright, Anchor Bible (AB), vol. 6 (New York: Doubleday, 1982); Trent C. Butler, *Joshua,* Word Biblical Commentary (WBC), vol. 7 (Waco: Word Books, 1983); Richard S. Hess, *Joshua, An Introduction and Commentary,* Tyndale Old Testament Commentaries (TOTC), vol. 6 (Downers Grove, Ill.: InterVarsity Press, 1996); John Gray, *Joshua, Judges, Ruth,* New Century Bible (NCB) (Grand Rapids: Wm. B. Eerdmans, 1986); and Marten H. Woudstra, *The Book of Joshua,*

God's faithfulness, especially as described in the Torah. Almost immediately in the first chapter (Josh. 1:8), we are reminded that studying God's Torah will make us both "prosperous and successful."[3] And, likewise, in the last chapter, we are asked to "choose for [ourselves] this day" the God we will serve: the gods of our past or the LORD, the faithful God of Israel (24:15).[4] As for Joshua and his household, they chose to serve the LORD. But when the people of Israel agreed to do the very same thing, Joshua responded in a very odd way: "'You are not able to serve the LORD. He is a holy God; he is a jealous God'" (24:19). We will return to these surprising words later.

The Book of Joshua also contains a number of references to the pagan prostitute Rahab. Despite her unsavory occupation, she became a hero of the faith (Josh. 2; 6; see Heb. 11:31: James 2:25) as well as being inducted into the lineage of Jesus (Matt. 1:5).

The book also mentions the Gibeonites, a resourceful nation of seemingly doomed Canaanites. They fooled Joshua and the Israelites into fighting on their behalf, instead of against them as God had commanded (Josh. 9; 10).

Finally, the book includes some eight chapters of detailed border descriptions and lists of cities for the Israelite tribes. This is tedious material for the nonspecialist, to be sure; but it was of great concern to the parties involved. (Any real

---

New International Commentary on the Old Testament (NICOT) (Grand Rapids: W. B. Eerdmans, 1981). In the following notes, only the author's last name, and abbreviation of the commentary series will be used.

[3]This is no recipe for "claiming by faith" fancy houses, fancy cars, or any such material possession. The sense of "prosperous" here is that of fulfilling completely God's plan and calling.

[4]For further discussion of these important texts, see the sidebar "Programmatic Texts."

estate survey tends to be of little interest to us unless it's our own land.) These eight chapters also illustrate a significant theological truth: God's perfect will seems to include the principle of economic egalitarianism, that is, an equal division of wealth in God's kingdom (an idea that resurfaces in the Book of Acts [2:44–46]). Even in the earliest days of Israel, land division was to take place according to tribal size, rather than according to tribal power or prestige. The larger the tribe, the more land was given to it. Nothing was simpler than that. The Book of Joshua contains many such surprises the modern reader can benefit from.

The theme of Joshua is, of course, the conquest and settlement of the Promised Land of Israel. It may come as a surprise, therefore, that some Old Testament scholars actually wonder if there ever *was* an Israelite conquest of the land. Because the people of Israel were not native to the land, most scholars would acknowledge that at least some of the "Israelites" came from outside origins.

But some scholars doubt whether a *civilian* army of Israelites simply marched into Canaan and grabbed large portions of real estate under Joshua. Some have held that the Israelite takeover of the land was actually peaceful infiltration.[5] Others focus on the phenomenon of the *Habiru* (sometimes spelled *'Apiru*)[6] in the Late Bronze Age El-

[5]The Israeli archaeologist Yohanan Aharoni and the German OT scholars Albrecht Alt and Martin Noth were major proponents of this view, which does seem to accord with the picture of Israelite occupation of the land found in the Book of Judges (cf. the Jebusite occupation of the major city of Jerusalem until the time of David, ca. 1000 B.C.; also the clear statement in Ezek. 16:3 concerning Israel: "'Your ancestry and birth were in the land of the Canaanites; your father was an Amorite and your mother a Hittite'").

[6]Often connected with the term "Hebrew" (*'ivri*), although this identification is not universally accepted. The Bible recognizes that there were both Israelites (Exod. 1:9; 5:15,19) and "Hebrews" (1:15,16,19; 2:13) among the

Amarna tablets (fourteenth cent. B.C.). These terms appear to describe foreigners of a landless social class who represented a threat to the Egyptian governors of Canaan. They were people who had withdrawn from settled society. Joining a group of escaped slaves from Egypt, these *Habiru* transcended tribal and ethnic identities, and embraced the new religion of Yahwism.[7] As John Bright put it, "We may suppose that as Israelites of the Mosaic group entered western Canaan bringing their new faith with them, numerous towns and villages were ready to come over to their side. In some cases this was done freely and willingly, as apparently in the case of Shechem, which was not conquered, yet was a part of Israel from the first. In other cases it was done out of fear (e.g., Gibeon). In still others, the local population may simply have risen against their rulers and those who supported them, and taken control without significant fighting or general bloodshed . . . Israel conquered from within."[8]

Egyptian slaves. It is possible that here the term "Hebrew" represents the *Habiru / 'Apiru* of the Egyptian texts as a class of slaves, with the Israelites forming a subclass within it. See *ANET*, 22 n. 4. It is possible that some of these were among the "many other people" who went out of Egypt with the Israelites (Exod. 12:38).

[7] The American scholars George E. Mendenhall and Norman K. Gottwald have argued passionately and rather persuasively for this view. Certainly, the emergence of the *Habiru* must be connected somehow to the emergence of the Israelites in Canaan, as the eminent American archaeologist W. F. Albright had maintained. See Norman K. Gottwald, *The Tribes of Yahweh* (Maryknoll, N.Y.: Orbis Books, 1979); George E. Mendenhall, "The Hebrew Conquest of Palestine," *BA* 25 (1962): 66–87; and W. F. Albright, *From the Stone Age to Christianity*, 2d ed. (Garden City: Doubleday Anchor, 1957), 240, 277.

[8] John Bright, *A History of Israel,* 3d ed. (Philadelphia: Westminster, 1981), 142–43. Probably the single best resource in English on this complicated topic remains Roland de Vaux's *Early History of Israel* (Philadelphia: Westminster, 1978), 475–680. For more recent, popular discussions of this issue, with current bibliography, see n. 9.

Programmatic Text

Scholars use the term "programmatic" in reference to such editorializing texts as Joshua 1 and 24, since they introduce the major "program," or purpose, of the book. When preachers remove such texts as 1:6–9 and 24:14–15 from their original context and apply them to their audience, they are, perhaps unconsciously, doing just what the original editors of the book had in mind. Again, we are often reminded to "be strong and courageous" (1:6a,9a; see 7a), just like Joshua was. We too are to obey all the Torah that Moses gave to Joshua and to his generation (1:7b–8), so that we too might become prosperous and successful in whatever position of influence God places us

There is probably more than a little truth in each of these perspectives. Undoubtedly some people having Canaanite origins joined the Israelites. Yet the central Mosaic group must have come from Egypt, just as the Bible says. As Hershel Shanks has recently argued, "No society would invent a history of slavery for themselves and give their founding hero (Moses) an Egyptian name if they had never been there."[9] It was this group, the Israelites, whose "founding story" became the core of the unforgettable Book of Joshua.[10]

What Was Joshua's Invasion Strategy? —Josh. 1 Through 12

The Old Testament is clear that Joshua played a major role in the takeover of the land of Canaan. Indeed, the first half of the Book of Joshua (Josh. 1 through 12) seems preoccupied with bloody battles, the preparation for them, the waging of them, and their aftermath. But a closer reading shows that relatively little bloodshed occurred. This conforms to the archaeological record. In fact, Joshua's military career consists of three relatively brief campaigns. They may be called the (1) central (Josh. 1 through 8), (2) southern (Josh. 9 through 10), and (3) northern (Josh. 11 through 12) campaigns. The second half of the book, in turn, consists largely of land division (Josh. 13 through 21) and covenant

---

[9]Hershel Shanks, "The Biblical Minimalists: Expunging Ancient Israel's Past," *Bible Review* (June 1997): 38. Shanks also responds effectively to the recent attempts by Israeli archaeologist Israel Finkelstein to lower the dating of the impressive archaeological strata traditionally associated with the reigns of David and Solomon (in the tenth century B.C.): "Where Is the Tenth Century?" *BAR* (March/April 1998): 56–60; cf. also the references cited there.

[10]For indirect testimony of this see Pss. 78:51–55 and 136:10–25, which confess an exodus from Egyptian bondage as a part of Israel's faith history.

renewal (Josh. 22 through 24). We will, therefore, survey the Book of Joshua under these main headings:

1 through 12	Joshua's Takeover of the Land West of the Jordan River
1 through 8	The Central Campaign: Crossing the Jordan, the fall of Jericho, and the (eventual) victory at Ai
9 through 10	The Southern Campaign: Israel fooled by the Gibeonites but victorious over their mutual Canaanite enemies
11 through 12	The Northern Campaign: The fall of Hazor and a summary of Moses' and Joshua's victories
13 through 21	Joshua Divides the Promised Land
22 through 24	Covenant Renewal at Shechem for the Next Generation

THE CENTRAL CAMPAIGN — JOSH. 1 THROUGH 8

Introduction—Josh. 1. The Book of Joshua both begins and ends with references to God's previous covenant faithfulness to his people Israel. In both places, this leads to a moment of decision for Israel (see 1:3–5,6–9 and 24:2–13,14–15). Such symmetry is surely intentional. Clearly it represents the theology of the book. It speaks both to the original audience in the story (Joshua and the leadership in Josh. 1, and the new generation of Israelites in Josh. 24) as well as to future generations.

Two Spies and a Prostitute—Josh. 2. Chapter 2 of Joshua could be entitled "From the Sublime to the Ridiculous." It moves from the stirring and timeless advice given to military leadership in the previous chapter to the humorous and embarrassing story of two inept Israelite spies. They are nearly captured by the enemy in, of all places, a house of prostitution.[11] Good literature is honest and unpre-

(of course, our "Torah" more immediately comes from the NT, and especially the teachings of Jesus, the "greater Moses"). Similarly, we, like the aged Joshua in chapter 24, are to remind each other to "'fear the LORD and serve him with all faithfulness'" (24:14a). Indeed, we too should "choose this day" which God we will serve (see 24:15), whether the gods of our ancestors, or the gods of the pagans who surround us, or "the LORD." As for Joshua and his household, he declares once again, "'We will serve the LORD.'" The Bible speaks a clear word from God to all believers at all places and times, and this is especially true of the "programmatic texts" in both the Old and New Testaments (John 3:16 is surely the most famous of these texts—note the editorial commentary found in John 20:30–31). No wonder the Bible remains the best selling book of all time.

---

[11]Since the time of Josephus, some commentators have suggested that Rahab's establishment was an inn or tavern, a logical place to rest overnight

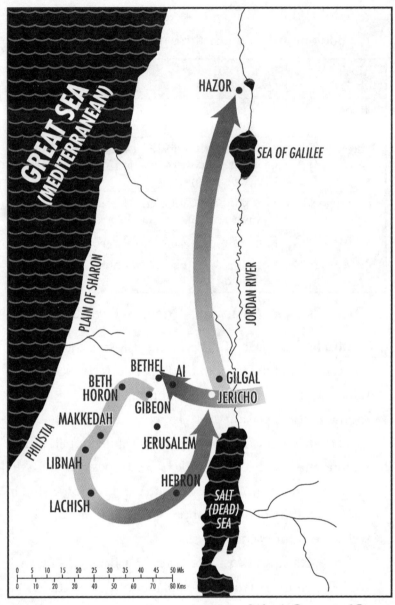

Joshua's Conquest of Canaan

and to overhear conversations by natives and travelers (see, for example, the recent comments by Hess [TOTC, 6:83–84]). But much of the verve and irony of the story are lost if this scandal-less interpretation is accepted, not to mention the force of the repeated Heb. wordplays on "bedding down" (often used in a sexual context) found in the text (see Butler, WBC, 7:31–32; cf. also the NT references to Rahab as a "prostitute" in Heb. 11:31 and James 2:25).

dictable, and the Bible certainly qualifies as good literature. We must admit its transparent honesty, even when the results can be uncomfortable.

The unnamed spies were to spy out the entire land, including Jericho (Josh. 2:1a).[12] Still, making a house of ill-repute the first stop, to say nothing of spending the night there (2:1b), appears to go beyond the assignment. Still less expected is the fact that even the king of the city knew about the visit.[13] But, as providence would have it, these spies ran into a God-fearing prostitute. After Rahab successfully hid them (2:4–7), she then proceeded to witness to them about the wonderful works of the LORD (2:8–13). Whether or not the spies were in the mood, they got a sermon. But what choice did they have, for their lives were truly in the hands of the sermonizer (2:14). So when she begged them to spare herself and her family,[14] what else could they do?

Her brave actions led to the preservation of her whole family (2:18; see also 6:22–25). With a scarlet cord, of all

[12]The NIV's emphatic reference in v. 1, "especially Jericho," is possible (cf. NLT, NRSV), but probably misleading. The spies clearly were told to scout out the *entire* land, *not* just the city of Jericho. They obviously did not do this; if they had, the Gibeonites (who lived not far from Jericho) would not have been able to fool the Israelites about where they were from (see Josh. 9:3–27).

[13]The twofold reference in Josh. 2:1–3 to the spies' task to spy out the entire land is most ironic in this context, since they have barely been able to spy out the city of Jericho.

[14]This is neither the first nor the last time in the Bible when a strong woman saved her family from disaster. Deborah, the fearless judge and military leader, comes quickly to mind (see Judg. 4 through 5), as well as Ruth and Esther, both bold heroines in the books which respectively bear their names. More obscure examples would include Zipporah, Moses' wife (see the somewhat mysterious passage in Exod. 4:24–26), and Rizpah daughter of Aiah, Saul's concubine (2 Sam. 21:1–14). Tamar, daughter-in-law of Judah, and Abigail, eventual wife of David, also deserve mention at this point (see Gen. 38; 1 Sam. 25; Matt. 1:3).

Types and Shadows

Traditional Bible inter-
preters have used the
expression "types and
shadows" when they
look for parallels
between the Old and the
New Testaments. But
more recent commenta-
tors tend to be more cau-
tious when dealing with
this issue. There is no
question that some sym-
bols and events in the
Old Testament prefigure
the New. For example,
we are told in John
3:14–15, "'Just as Moses
lifted up the snake in the
desert [see Num.
21:8–9], so the Son of
Man must be lifted up,
that everyone who
believes in him may have
eternal life.'" Just as looking at the bronze snake
in the desert brought
healing from venomous
snakebites in the days of
Moses, so focusing in
faith on the crucifixion of
Christ brings healing and
salvation from the rav-
ages of sin.

Ever since the church
fathers, commentators
have often taken the
"scarlet cord" reference
here in Josh. 2:17–21 to

things, she signaled their location when the Israelites took over the city (Josh. 2:18,21). In the New Testament, she is remembered as a woman of faith (Heb. 11:31; James 2:25). Her name is included in the genealogy of Jesus Christ (Matt. 1:5). Besides saving her entire family, her faith also preserved the lives of two wayward spies. Those spies, of course, eventually told Joshua "everything" (Josh. 2:23). They concluded, "'The LORD has surely given the whole land into our hands; all the people are melting in fear because of us'" (2:24).

Crossing the Jordan River on Dry Ground—Josh. 3 Through 4. Now from the ridiculous to the sublime: Chapters 3 and 4 describe Joshua bringing the entire Israelite nation into the Promised Land. They marched in liturgical procession, with the ark of the covenant leading the way. No initial incursion into enemy territory could have been more successful. Not even mud clung to the Israelites' sandals as they made their way across the Jordan riverbed during the flood season. The LORD had dried up the Red Sea (Sea of Reeds; see chap. 6, "With a Strong Hand and an Outstretched Arm") in the days of Moses, at the beginning of the wilderness period. And at the end of the wilderness period he rolled back the water of the Jordan, leadership having been assumed by Joshua (see Josh. 4:23–24).[15] Once again, here, as was the case back in chapter 1, Joshua is shown to be a worthy successor to the mighty Moses himself.

[15]Such literary parallels are known as "inclusios," or "bookending devices," since they indicate by repetition the limits, or boundaries, of a narrative or poem. Recent biblical scholarship has focused particularly on such literary features as inclusios and "palistrophes" (sets of interlocking inclusios), which the modern Western reader might otherwise easily miss (for a particularly dramatic inclusio, see the first and last verses of Ps. 8).

The Commander of the Army of the LORD—Josh. 5:13–15. Although space limits discussing every section of the Book of Joshua, the last three verses of chapter five should not be excluded. Joshua encountered a mysterious man standing with drawn sword. So Joshua asked him, "'Are you for us or for our enemies?'" (Josh. 5:13). The reader is hardly prepared for the odd response, "'Neither'" (5:14).[16] Many commentators note the parallels between Moses' encounter with God (Exod. 3 through 4) and Joshua's encounter here,[17] but fewer focus on the differences. Moses repeatedly had to be encouraged to lead God's people out of Egypt. But here Joshua apparently had to be cautioned against overconfidence.

Jericho's Walls Collapse—Josh. 6 Through 8. The fall of Jericho is one of the most famous stories in the Bible. But the casual reader may not notice the liturgical emphasis found throughout the chapter. We see this in the careful description of the various movements of the priests and of the ark (hardly a typical battle description). Also the "military" procedure is far from orthodox. The priestly procession marched around the city once each day for six days (Josh. 6:8–14). They made seven circuits on the seventh day.[18] As is the case in Joshua 3 through 4, "liturgical pro-

mean the shed blood of Christ. In this case, however, there is no biblical support. No one could dispute that it is indeed the blood of Christ that alone brings salvation. But this is hardly prefigured by a red-colored cord that Rahab hung in her window to signal the Israelites that her family should be spared. Red can mean many things other than salvation. For instance, it can indicate the bloodshed of judgment (see Isa. 63:3) or war (Rev. 6:4; 9:17). We must be most careful, even if we mean only to bring honor to God and God's Word, whenever we look for "types and shadows." This is especially true when Scripture itself gives us no clear support for our conclusions.

[16]The text literally reads the single word "no" (Heb. *lo'*). Most modern translations agree with NIV's "neither" (cf. "on neither side" in the New Jerusalem Bible). "The visitor does not fit Joshua's categories exactly" (Woudstra, NICOT, 105).

[17]One of the closest parallels is the command, "'Take off your sandals, for the place where you are standing is holy ground'" (Exod. 3:5; see. Josh. 5:15). This command to proceed barefoot finds no other exact parallel in Scripture, although such a procedure does seem to be implied in Exod. 29:20 (Gray, NCB, 79–80).

[18]The city of Jericho is one of the oldest towns on earth (established by 8000 B.C. and fortified by 7000 B.C.). But it was not large. Boling (AB, 6:205) describes the site as covering only some eight and a half acres, but domi-

Taking Sides

We can never just assume that God is on our side. When one of Abraham Lincoln's supporters exclaimed, "We trust, Sir, that God is on our side," he is said to have responded, "It is more important to know that we are on God's side." That is good advice for any leader in any era.

cession" dominates the account. The ark represented the very presence of the LORD, the earthly throne of Israel's deity (see 2 Sam. 6:2). With such a holy God among the people, strictest obedience to the stipulations of "holy war"[19] was essential. After the city had fallen, Achan, one of the tribe of Judah, chose to disregard the rules. His disobedience brought dire effects on the entire Israelite community (see Josh. 7:1–26). It was only after Achan had been punished that Israel was able to take Ai and thus seize the center of the land. With the LORD'S help, the Israelites set an ambush against the king of Ai that resulted in their taking the town (Josh. 8:1–29).[20]

THE SOUTHERN CAMPAIGN — JOSH. 9 THROUGH 10

The Gibeonite chapters in the Book of Joshua illustrate well the observation that actual warfare often diverges considerably from war-theory.[21] Four Canaanite towns (Josh.

---

nating an extensive oasis. Still, this sevenfold circuit of the city must have proved tiresome indeed.

[19]The concept of "holy war," though often used by biblical scholars, remains controversial. Also, the technical term used here, and throughout the OT (Heb. *cherem*), is notoriously hard to translate (suggested translations include "put under the ban," "set apart to destruction," "devote [to the deity]"; cf. NIV footnote to Josh. 6:17). The root idea of *cherem* is that everything the warriors and their weapons come in contact with would be infected by "holiness," thus unsafe for common use (Gray, NCB, 63). This practice is attested elsewhere in the ANE world as well (e.g., in ninth century Moab, where the same word appears in the Mesha Stele; as well as in Assyria and Egypt [Hess, TOTC, 6:42–43]). Indeed, the familiar Modern English term "harem" (women "set apart" for one particular man) is also related to this root.

[20]This in turn introduces the covenant renewal ceremony in front of Mounts Ebal and Gerizim (Josh. 8:30–35). These mountains flank the central town of Shechem and provide a natural amphitheater for such a ceremony (cf. Deut. 27, as well as Josh. 24).

[21]Carl von Clausewitz, as cited by Peter C. Craigie (*The Book of Deuteronomy*, NICOT [Grand Rapids: Wm. B. Eerdmans, 1976], 56–58; cf. also his monograph entitled *The Problem of War in the Old Testament* [Grand Rapids: Wm. B. Eerdmans, 1978], 45–48). At least in theory, war

9:17) were able to turn the tables on the invading Israelites. Representatives pretended to come from a far country (9:9–13). They really came from the territory just west of Jericho and Ai.[22] Their ruse worked: The Israelite leaders made a treaty with them, one which could not be revoked.[23] But this treaty soon worked to Israelite advantage. For Gibeon itself was soon threatened by a southern Amorite coalition (10:1–5). Because of their treaty with them, the Israelites were expected to march to Gibeon's defense. The ensuing battle was the setting for the famous "sun standing still" incident.[24] Joshua desperately sought divine assistance

---

must end in clear victory for the aggressor; otherwise there is no reason to initiate war in the first place. But if complete victory is to be obtained, no effort can be spared and, above all, no principle of moderation can ever be introduced. In actual warfare, however, unforeseen factors, such as chance or the psychological state of the enemy, may modify this theoretical perspective. In the present case, of course, the cleverness of the Gibeonites, plus the spiritual carelessness of the Israelite leadership (Josh. 9:14b), led to a very different result.

[22]The classic text on "holy war" (Deut. 20) distinguishes clearly between total annihilation of the peoples who live in the Promised Land itself (vv. 16–18), and relative leniency toward those living on the periphery, the nations which are not directly allied with the enemy (vv. 10–15). The Gibeonites obviously were in the former category, but they pretended to be in the latter. They, like Rahab back in Josh. 2, seem to have known their Bible well.

[23]Here is one of the few times in the OT that the people seem to be entirely justified in having "grumbled" against their leaders (Josh. 9:18b). Although the Bible emphasizes time and again that we should show proper respect to our spiritual and political leaders, it never whitewashes their failings.

[24]How this actually happened is a matter of much study. The classical discussion is found in Bernard Ramm, *The Christian View of Science and Scripture* (Grand Rapids: Wm. B. Eerdmans, 1954), 107–10. It is important to note that the Bible often speaks in phenomenological language (52–53). That is, it recorded what people perceived when describing events such as this—just as we do today, people then spoke of the sun (and the moon as well) as moving across the sky (Ps. 19:5–6; Eccles. 1:5). The Heb. term for "stand still" in Josh. 10:12 is *dom* (root, *d-m-m*), which literally means "be silent or dumb." So some modern scholars take Joshua's request as asking for the sun to "be silent," or cease shining. Thus we should envision a long

as he counterattacked the Amorite coalition on Gibeon's behalf (10:12–14), for their combined strength was frightening. But with the LORD fighting for Israel, their enemies were of course doomed. And such a coalition then only made the enemies' defeat take place more quickly. This section of the Book of Joshua concludes with accounts of devastation against the Amorite leaders as well as their territories (10:10–11). The result was that Joshua and the Israelites gained political domination over the central and southern regions of Canaan. "Surely the LORD was fighting for Israel!" (10:14b).[25]

---

night, not a long day. This would correspond quite nicely to the providentially timed hailstorm mentioned in 10:11. But these scholars fail to reckon adequately with the statements found in the rest of the passage, such as the parallelism found in the poetic citation from the "Book of Jashar"(Josh. 10:13): "The sun stood still [again, the verb *d-m-m*], and the moon stopped, till the nation avenged itself on its enemies." Here, the unambiguous verb *'amadh*, "to stand," is found. Also, the prose commentary in 10:13b clearly states, "The sun stopped *['amadh]* in the middle of the sky and delayed going down about a full day." The word translated "delayed" by NIV is *'a-w-ts*, "to hasten, hurry," here used with the negative word *lo'*, "not." Despite the astronomical difficulties we moderns must acknowledge (i.e., did God actually stop the rotation of the planet earth for a full day?) it would seem best to follow the natural meaning of the Heb. text. Indeed, "there has never been a day like it before or since, a day when the LORD listened to a man" (10:14a). Ramm records three attempts by evangelicals to solve the problem: (1) The language was poetic and refers to added strength given Joshua's soldiers; (2) there was a supernatural refraction of the light of sun and moon, miraculously extending the daylight; or (3) there was a supernaturally induced thunderstorm, giving Joshua's troops relief from the heat. For more recent discussions of the possible alternative explanations for these verses, see Hess, TOTC, 6:196–99; Boling, AB, 6:282–85; Woudstra, NICOT, 173–76; also William Barnes, *The Complete Biblical Library: The Old Testament,* vol. 5, *Joshua, Judges, Ruth* (Springfield, Mo.: World Library Press, 1996), 113–17.

[25]Boling (AB, 6:303) makes the apt observation that only at Jericho and at Ai do the Israelites take the initiative in warfare. God's great victories often result from successful defense of our previous position. This explains the famous reference to the "full armor of God" in Eph. 6:10–18, where after the fierce battle is over, Paul hopes his audience will still be standing their ground: "Use every piece of God's armor to resist the enemy in the time of evil, so that after the battle you will still be standing firm" (6:13, NLT).

THE NORTHERN CAMPAIGN—JOSH. 11 THROUGH 12

In the north another coalition of kings, led by Jabin king of Hazor, arose to threaten Israel (11:1–5). Once again, Joshua launched a single, fast-moving campaign. The city of Hazor was easily the most significant city in Canaan, large[26] as well as strategic.[27] Once again, however, it must have been nothing less than the grace of the LORD that led to Joshua's stunning victory at the Waters of Merom (11:6–9). For the first time in the Book of Joshua the use of war chariots appears. Normally they would have posed an insurmountable obstacle to Israel's victory, but Yahweh's power proved more potent than the most modern war equipment. Details are lacking, but the Israelite victory must have been overwhelming. The Israelites chased the retreating enemy westward all the way to the Mediterranean Sea ("Greater Sidon," probably what is called "Misrephoth Maim," 11:8). They also drove them to the east ("Valley of Mizpah"). However, only the city of Hazor was burned (11:11b,13).[28]

[26]Even back in the eighteenth century B.C., Hazor consisted of a citadel located on a mound of some 30 acres overlooking the lower city of some 175 acres (ten times the area of Jerusalem, Megiddo, or any other biblical site yet excavated). The population numbered easily in the tens of thousands. No wonder Hazor is described in Josh. 11:10b as "the head of all these kingdoms."

[27]Located eight miles directly north of the Sea of Galilee, Hazor sat at the crossroads of two important trade routes: (1) The Great Trunk Road stretched from the Egyptian delta to the city of Damascus, and eventually to upper and lower Mesopotamia. This route is often termed the Way of the Sea, but inaccurately so, according to Barry J. Beitzel (*The Moody Atlas of Bible Lands* [Chicago: Moody Press, 1985], 65–69). And (2) the Beqa' Valley Road stretched north from the Jordan River Valley and the Sea of Galilee into the Beqa' Valley of central Lebanon.

[28]Depending on when one dates the exodus and the conquest, the massive "burn layer" of Stratum XIII, which Yigael Yadin dated to ca. 1250–1230 B.C., may or may not be that of Joshua, as described in Josh. 11:11 (Yadin thought

The first half of the Book of Joshua (Josh. 1 through 12) ends with a summary of both Moses' and Joshua's victories, concluding with a list of some thirty-one deposed kings (12:9–24). The overwhelming effect is one of complete and total victory over the enemy. Thus the reader is not prepared for the bold statement at the very beginning of the next chapter: "There are still very large areas of land to be taken over'" (13:1). Such statements as this, as well as similar ones in Judges 1, must be kept in mind when reading the account in Josh. 11:14–23. This passage records that Joshua "left nothing undone of all that the LORD commanded Moses" (11:15b). It adds that he "took the entire land, just as the LORD had directed Moses" (11:23a). Likewise, we read that the Israelites put all the enemies "to the sword until they completely destroyed them, not sparing anyone that breathed" (11:14b). And, "It was the LORD himself who hardened their hearts to wage war against Israel, so that he might destroy them totally, exterminating them without mercy" (11:20). When these accounts are weighed against those in Judges 1, we recognize that this is only one side of the picture. Decisive, stunning victory for the Israelites, yes, yet still much land to be conquered. This is the balanced perspective that the Book of Joshua presents to us. The second half of the book deals with the division of the land (Josh. 13 through 21). In it, this picture will be developed

---

it was, but other scholars connect it to the arrival of the Sea Peoples, such as the Philistines). As Boling (AB, 6:309) notes, the issue is far from settled, and the fact that the next stratum also attests a pagan temple makes the alleged Israelite occupation of the site problematic. But the most recent excavators of Hazor do conclude that it was indeed the Israelites who were responsible for the city's destruction (see Amnon Ben-Tor and Maria Teresa Rubiato, "Did the Israelites Destroy the Canaanite City?" *BAR* [May/June 1999]: 22–39).

further. We must recognize the references to complete destruction found repeated in these earlier chapters[29] are offset by the disclaimers found in the later land-division chapters.[30] The text usually describes the defeat of enemy kings, not their cities.[31] Maybe, as some biblical scholars have maintained, the Israelites were indeed joined by some of the land's inhabitants. Thus the "takeover" of the Promised Land probably came from both within and without: *coup d'état* as well as invasion.[32]

How Did Joshua Divide the Promised Land? —Josh. 13 Through 21

The next major section of the Book of Joshua deals with land allocation. These nine chapters are filled with detailed border descriptions and lists of cities. As already noted, there is a very pertinent theological teaching contained here. It may be called economic egalitarianism for the people of God. Can it actually be God's perfect will that God's people share all things in common, giving to each according to need?

[29]For example, in Josh. 10:28,30,32,33,35,37,39,40b; also in 11:11,12, 14,20.

[30]Besides the passages already mentioned, note the parenthetical notes at the end of several of the tribal allotment passages (Josh. 15:63; 16:10; 17:12–13).

[31]It is instructive here to note that only Hazor was burned. See the plain statement found in Josh. 11:13. It would make little sense to burn the cities the Israelites planned to live in. (Note the caution found in Deut. 6:10–12 concerning the time when the Israelites would gain control over the Promised Land, with "large, flourishing cities you did not build, houses filled with all kinds of good things you did not provide . . . then when you eat and are satisfied, be careful that you do not forget the LORD, who brought you out of Egypt, out of the land of slavery." Such a warning loses its force if the Israelites had largely destroyed the cities and their houses in the conquered territories).

[32]See my discussion in the introductory part of this chapter; also nn. 5–9, above.

Sharing the Wealth

This dividing of the land sounds fair enough. But is all this too utopian, akin to the brief period in the Early Church when God's people had all things in common, as described in Acts 2:44–46? Certainly we cannot argue that the Bible insists that God's people must accept one particular political or economic system of government, be it feudalism, democracy, capitalism, socialism, or the like. Still less can we say that biblical Christians are expected to force fellow believers to share their material wealth with the less fortunate (or with us). But here, as in so many other instances, God's perfect plan seems to be in evidence: Those who care most about the

In chapter 13 we learn that Joshua honored Moses' previous decisions concerning the Transjordanian tribes. Reuben, Gad, and East Manasseh were tribes that had asked to settle east of the Jordan River (Num. 32; Josh. 1:12–18). Chapters 14 through 17 discuss the land divisions of the Judah and the Joseph tribes (Ephraim and West Manasseh). Chapters 18 through 19 tell how the other seven "lay" tribes (Benjamin, Simeon, Zebulun, Issachar, Asher, Naphtali, and Dan) received their inheritance at Shiloh. Finally, chapters 20 through 21 designate the "cities of refuge" (see Num. 35), and the "towns of the Levites."[33] Joshua and Eleazar the priest are given special mention. The basic method of land division was by casting lots. Personal initiative was also taken into account (both male and female).[34] Because of their numbers, the Joseph tribes successfully asked for more property (Josh. 17:14–18). Indeed, the land division procedure in 18:1–10 is the model of fairness. Joshua told the Israelites to appoint three men from each tribe to survey the remaining land. They were to divide it into seven parts, with a written description of each portion. Joshua himself would then cast lots "in the presence of the LORD" (18:8,10) and thus distribute the land.[35]

The implied theology of these chapters is that God's perfect political and economic plan for his people Israel was set forth. Various methods are used: honoring decisions of

[33]The Levites were the "clerical" tribe that assisted the priests.

[34]For example, the "men of Judah," especially Caleb, approached Joshua at Gilgal (Josh. 14:6–15); Caleb's daughter Acsah (wife of Othniel the judge) approached Caleb (15:13–19); the "people of Joseph" approach Joshua (17:14–18); and the "family heads of the Levites" approach Eleazar, Joshua, and the other tribal chieftains (21:1–3). Finally, Joshua himself respectfully asked the tribal leadership for an inheritance in Ephraim (19:49–50).

[35]I am reminded of the time-honored procedure of dividing a piece of pie or cake between two young siblings: One cuts; the other chooses.

past leadership (Josh. 13; 14; 21), recognizing legitimate requests of petitioners (15:13–19; 17:14–18; 19:49–50), making provision for the future (20:1–9). This could be carried out by leadership fiat (13:8; 14:13; 15:13; 17:17–18), or by the casting of lots (14:2; 18:1–10). The section concludes: "So the LORD gave Israel all the land he had sworn to give their forefathers, and they took possession of it and settled there. . . . The LORD handed all their enemies over to them. Not one of all the LORD'S good promises to the house of Israel failed; every one was fulfilled" (21:43–45).

kingdom of God and for God's glorious presence in their lives will care little for economic advantage. They will be most pleased when all of God's children are adequately blessed, and they will gladly give away some of their own economic excess so that others' needs may be met.

Tribal Territories

How Was the Covenant Renewed at Shechem?
—Josh. 22 Through 24

Both the first and final chapters of Joshua emphasize the importance of exclusive loyalty to God. They call for obedience to God's Torah. Before the final chapter, however, chapters 22 and 23 set the stage for Joshua's farewell.

Chapter 22 discusses at length the return of the Transjordanian tribes to their homeland east of the Jordan. There they built an altar near the river. The tribes west of the Jordan feared that this altar marked an apostasy (22:16–20). Civil war threatened to break out. The tribes west of the Jordan sent a delegation of tribal leaders led by Phinehas the priest. The tribes east of the Jordan assured the delegation that they had intended only to honor God (22:21–29). They named the altar "A Witness Between Us that the LORD is God" (22:34).[36]

The narrative resumes in chapter 23 with Joshua's "last words" to the tribal leadership. He addressed the Israelites concerning both the past (23:2b–11) and the future (23:12–16). In both sections of his address Joshua warned his audience of the ever-present dangers of idolatry.[37] He stressed the need for caution as Israel lived among the surrounding nations and their idolatrous practices. His words grew more ominous as his short speech drew to a close. His final words were gloomy indeed: "'If you violate the

---

[36]Heb. *ki 'edh hu' beynotheynu ki YHWH ha'elohim*. This is probably best understood as "There is a witness between us, / Yahweh is truly God" (Boling, AB, 6:504, 516).

[37]"Idolatry" in both senses of the word: worship of pagan gods and bowing down to their physical idols or images. The first sense is a violation of the first commandment (Exod. 20:2–3, Deut. 5:6–7); the second is probably a violation of both the second and third commandments (Exod. 20:4–7; Deut. 5:8–11).

covenant of the LORD your God, which he commanded you, and go and serve other gods and bow down to them, the LORD's anger will burn against you, and you will quickly perish from the good land he has given you'" (23:16). This solemn warning would sadly come true for later generations exiled to Assyria (2 Kings 17:22–23) and Babylon (2 Kings 24:14–16).

This sets the stage for Josh. 24. Most of this chapter (vv. 1–27) takes the shape of a suzerain-vassal treaty.[38] Here we find evidence of nearly all of the typical subsections of such a treaty: preamble (24:2), historical prologue (24:2b–13), general stipulations (24:14,16,18b,21,23–24), specific stipulations (no clear parallels), divine witnesses (24:22,27), and blessings and cursings (24:19–20).[39] But the actual literary setting is again the last words of the aged leader Joshua.[40] And his words once again are tied geographically to the covenant town of Shechem (cf. 8:30–35; see also n. 20). The present chapter is also tied thematically to chapter 1 of the book: In both places leadership transitions lead to renewed allegiance to the Torah and to Yahweh

[38]The Book of Deuteronomy has often been analyzed in the same fashion, for it also seems to take the shape of a second millennium B.C. Hittite suzerain-vassal covenant or treaty (see Craigie, *Book of Deuteronomy,* 20–24, and the references cited there). The term "suzerain" refers to the overlord of great power and the term "vassal" to an underling, or king of a smaller subservient nation. These formal treaties would include a rehearsal of the previous history leading up to the making of the treaty, as well as the "stipulations" (legal obligations) placed upon the vassal to indicate his future obedience and loyalty to the suzerain. See chap. 6 in this textbook for a more complete discussion.

[39]This delineation comes from Butler (WBC, 7:268), who notes that we do not have here an actual treaty between Yahweh and his people but rather "a report of the making of an agreement" based on such a political model.

[40]In contrast to the explicit words of Josh. 23:1, Joshua's advanced age must be surmised by the editorial placement of chap. 24 after chap. 23, plus the death notice (24:29–31) which immediately follows the present passage.

Joshua, Pointing Back and Forward

If there is any hope we can ever serve the LORD, clearly it must be found in this Book of Torah. Therefore, the Book of Joshua of necessity points beyond itself, both back to the "classic" Torah (i.e., the Pentateuch) and forward to the New Torah (i.e., the New Testament). Let us reaffirm our commitment to the LORD, just as Joshua did in 24:15c of the book that now bears his name: "'As for me and my household, we will serve the LORD.'"

the God of Israel. While the first chapter ends on a positive note, the present passage is more ambiguous. Joshua repeatedly challenged the people to "serve the LORD" (24:14–15,22; see also 19a,23). The people answered, "'We will serve the LORD'" (24:21,24; cf. 24:16,22b). But then Joshua responded, "'You are not able to serve the LORD. He is a holy God; he is a jealous God'" (24:19).[41] Both the words "holy" and "jealous" deserve further comment. "Holy" (Heb. root *q-d-sh*) means "separated" from creation and the mundane.[42] But this is not to be understood as an impersonal theological principle. Trent Butler observes, "[T]he holiness of God impresses the worshiper to imitate the purity of God, acting in accordance with the demands of God."[43] They (and we) cannot serve such a God.

Secondly, Yahweh is a "jealous" God (Heb. root *q-n-'*). "Yahweh . . . loves [his worshipers] so much that he wants their undivided love in return. He will not share them with any other god."[44] Yahweh, as a jealous husband, will tolerate no rivals. No wonder Joshua told his audience (and, indirectly, us), "'You are *not able* to serve the LORD'" (24:19a).

But the people persevered. They declared they *would* serve the LORD. And so must we. They (and we) are witnesses (24:22,27). The Book of the Torah is also a witness:

---

[41]Butler (WBC, 7:274) aptly comments, "Joshua's answer [in vv. 19–20] is perhaps the most shocking statement in the OT. He denies that the people can do that which he has spent the entire chapter trying to get them to do. Having won their statement of faith and allegiance, he rejects it."

[42]J. Muilenburg ("Holiness," in *The Interpreter's Dictionary of the Bible* [Nashville: Abingdon, 1962], 2:617) categorizes the "elemental meaning" of the Heb. root *q-d-sh* as "separation."

[43]Butler (WBC, 7:275).

[44]Ibid. The Heb. root *q-n-'* connotes "zeal," "envy," and especially "jealousy" in the marriage relationship (Leonard J. Coppes, *TWOT*, 2:802–3). In Exod. 34:14, Yahweh's very "name" is said to be "Jealous."

The Book of Joshua both begins and ends with references to the "Book of the Law" (1:8; 24:26a).

The Book of Judges: Times of Agony and Ecstasy

Introduction

The Book of Judges[45] is probably not as well known as the Book of Joshua. But most of us have heard of Samson and Delilah and that infamous haircut.[46] And many have heard of Gideon and the time he put a fleece before the LORD (Judg. 6:36–40).[47] Women leaders are not lacking in this book either. Deborah, for example, served both as prophet and judge. This remarkable woman led Israel to a great military victory over the Canaanites. What's more, the honor of the victory went to another woman, Jael.[48]

[45]Important recent commentaries in English on the Book of Judges include Robert G. Boling, *Judges: Introduction, Translation and Commentary,* Anchor Bible (AB), vol. 6a (New York: Doubleday, 1975); Arthur E. Cundall, *Judges, An Introduction and Commentary,* Tyndale Old Testament Commentaries (TOTC), vol. 7 (Downers Grove, Ill.: InterVarsity Press, 1968); and John Gray, *Joshua, Judges, Ruth,* New Century Bible Commentary (NCB) (Grand Rapids: Wm. B. Eerdmans, 1986). Only the author's last name and abbreviation of the commentary series will be cited in the following notes.

[46]See Judg. 16:16–19; as explained later in the main text, Samson had taken a solemn vow not to have his hair cut.

[47]Actually, he did it twice: once the fleece was to be wet from the dew and the surrounding ground dry, the second time the other way around. Commentators note that God likewise soon tested Gideon's faith twice: once when more than two-thirds of Gideon's volunteer army (some 22,000) chose the home front over the battlefront (Judg. 7:2–3); and then again when the remaining 10,000 were reduced to only 300 (vv. 4–8), depending on how they drank water from a spring. I imagine that the moral of the story is that when we put a "fleece" before God to determine his will and to encourage our faith, we may expect God to do the same for us.

[48]See the prose account in Judg. 4:4–22, also the poetic version in 5:24–30, a passage usually entitled "The Song of Deborah." Note that credit for the victory over the enemy general Sisera *did* go to a woman! That honor was given to Jael the Kenite, a member of a tent-dwelling tribe who had previ-

There is, however, much more to the Book of Judges than a few familiar stories. Judges is in many ways a dreary book. It begins with a rather lengthy summary of the conquest of the land of Canaan, tribe by tribe. Unlike the account in the Book of Joshua, the account in Judges emphasizes how much of the land was not conquered. It tells how most of the tribes failed to take over their territories. And, likewise, Judges ends on a correspondingly dismal note. Two sections, often termed "appendixes" (17 through 18; 19 through 21), illustrate most effectively how terrible things were in the land of Israel before there was a king.

But Judges should not be dismissed simply because it contains much heartache and tragedy. It is compelling reading. In it are Samson's foibles and juvenile escapades, Gideon's all-too-human timidity, and Deborah's bold and sarcastic leadership. For the height of poignancy and irony there is the story of Jephthah, son of a prostitute, who inadvertently assigned his own daughter as a sacrifice. But there is also Ehud, the warrior whose left-handedness enabled him to dispatch the enemy king Eglon in his own house. Desperate victories, ignominious defeats. The Book of Judges is like life itself, with its twists and turns and inevitable surprises. And behind and beneath it all is the one and the same God who always listens to desperate prayer. When wayward Israel had once again fallen from God's grace, the LORD said to them: "When the Egyptians, the Amorites, the Ammonites, the Philistines, the Sidonians, the Amalekites and the Maonites oppressed you

---

ously been friendly with Sisera's nation. But Jael, after granting the fleeing enemy general Sisera both food and sanctuary (4:17–20), later killed the sleeping general by pounding a tent peg into the temple of his head (4:21–22).

and you cried to me for help, did I not save you from their hands? But you have forsaken me and served other gods, so I will no longer save you. Go and cry out to the gods you have chosen. Let them save you when you are in trouble'" (Judg. 10:11–14). In response to these doleful words, the Israelites once again acknowledged their sin, put aside their foreign gods, and renewed their worship of the LORD. And sure enough, "he could bear Israel's misery no longer" (10:16b); once again he set out to rescue his people.

God is most of all a God of love, a God of second chances. Whether it be the prodigal son (Luke 15:11–32) or the rebellious nation of Israel, God is there, waiting and watching eagerly for their return. This is the underlying message of the Book of Judges.

What Is a Judge?

This brief summary indicates that the Book of Judges is about something quite different from strictly legal controversies. Much of the book is about military matters. Yet, the title of the book in both the Hebrew (shophᵉṭim) and the Greek (kritai) traditions is generally translated "Judges." What, then, was the role of these "judges" as leaders of God's chosen people? And are there any present-day applications to make concerning the nature of their leadership?

The word shophet, "judge," comes from the root sh-ph-ṭ, which carries the idea of governmental administration.[49] Thus a ruler can be a "judge" (Exod. 2:14). So can a king, because court decisions go along with kingship (1 Kings 3:27–28). But when Absalom desired to be "judge in the

[49]See J. P. M. Walsh, *The Mighty From Their Thrones: Power in the Biblical Tradition* (Philadelphia: Fortress Press, 1987).

land" (2 Sam. 15:4), he was seeking the throne, not a court appointment.

These judges were not kings or queens, however. None of the judges was succeeded in office by a family member. The usurper Abimelech, born to Gideon by a concubine, was the only exception (Judg. 8:30–31). The people had offered a perpetual judgeship to Gideon, but he had wisely refused (8:22). Later the people would ask Samuel to give them a king (1 Sam. 8:4–5), complaining that his children were unworthy to succeed him (1 Sam. 7:15 through 8:5). Later on, however, nearly all of Israel's kings would inherit the throne. By way of contrast, each of the judges was chosen by God's Spirit,[50] not by birth. The divine appointment of the judges was recognized by tribal leadership.[51] (On the issue of kingship vs. judgeship in Israel, see also the appendix, "Judges or Kings for Israel?").

But the judges did take on the trappings of kingship in other respects. For example, they tended to be strong military leaders. Indeed, the nature of the Book of Judges is that of cyclical patterns of apostasy leading to severe military

[50]See Judg. 3:10 (for Othniel); 6:34 (for Gideon); 11:29 (for Jephthah); and 13:24–25 (for Samson); also 9:23 for the counterexample of Abimelech's leadership being rejected by God's Spirit. The Samson cycle contains three additional references to God's Spirit "rushing with great power" (Heb. *tsalach*) upon him (see 14:6,19; 15:14—note that similar language is used of Saul in 1 Sam. 10:6,10; 11:6 [cf. also the negative reference in 18:10]; and of David in 16:13).

[51]There was much tribal disunity at the time. Most of the judges were local figures. So in most instances only some tribes, or clans within the tribes, recognized God's choice of judge. See, for example, Judg. 6:28–32 where the "men of the town" first opposed, then supported Gideon. In 7:23 through 8:21 some tribes and clans supported Gideon, but others opposed him. In the story of Jephthah (10:17 through 11:11), the elders of Gilead sought him out. See also the indirect references to tribal leadership in the Song of Deborah (5:9–18, where, again, some tribes supported Deborah, others did not).

oppression by Israel's enemies. These situations called for heroic military actions by the judges.[52] So the verb "judge" (Heb. *shaphat*) came to signify both judicial activity and unique acts of military deliverance.[53] For example, Deborah "had become a judge in Israel" and would "hold court under the Palm of Deborah" in the hill country of Ephraim. There the Israelites would come to her "to settle their disputes" (Judg. 4:4–5, NLT). Still the term "judge" is not simply a synonym for "king," even though the two offices clearly overlapped. In the concluding formulas for certain judges, the length of their service is listed: Jephthah, six years (Judg. 12:7); Ibzan, seven years (12:9); Abdon, eight years (12:13–14); Samson, twenty years (15:20; 16:31). Obviously this included much more than sporadic military activity. (I must admit, though, that picturing Samson as a distinguished magistrate takes some imagination.)[54] Probably the single greatest distinction between judgeship and kingship is mode of initial selection: Most kings were

[52]Examples of such actions by the major judges are found in Judg. 3:10–11 (Othniel), 3:15–30 (Ehud), 4 through 5 (Deborah), 6:33 through 7:21 (Gideon), 11:4–33 (Jephthah), and 14 through 16 (Samson, most of where the Philistines are the enemy).

[53]See Boling, AB, 6a:5–6, who argues that the larger Semitic context of the verb means "to rule," or "[designates] a series of acts of government." The verb can also refer to mobilization for war (Judg. 3:10; see Boling, AB, 6a:81).

[54]Other trappings of kingship may also be noted: multiplication of wives, concubines, and/or children (Gideon, Judg. 8:30–31; Jair, 10:3–4; Ibzan, 12:8–9; Abdon, 12:13–14, and in a sense Samson, Judg. 14 through 16). Sometimes they were wealthy (Gideon, Judg. 8:24–27; Jair with his thirty towns, 10:4, as well as his sons' thirty donkeys; see also the seventy donkeys of Abdon, 12:13; and the wealth Samson acquired in his various escapades). Many scholars think that Abimelech's attempt to succeed his father Gideon as king (9:1–6) may be related to Gideon's not entirely convincing protestations in 8:23—"Abimelech" literally means "my father is king." Thus the later mixture of judgeship and kingship characteristics in the Saul and David accounts is not without precedent.

born into the royal family (the "dynastic principle"), but judges were chosen, or at least recognized, by their innate ability (the "charismatic principle").[55]

In fact, in one place (Jephthah's speech to the enemy Ammonite king), we are told that Yahweh himself should be recognized as "Judge." Here, the context is military, but the judicial role remains paramount: "'Let the LORD, the Judge, decide the dispute this day between the Israelites and the Ammonites'" (Judg. 11:27). Yahweh is thus more than Israel's national God. He is, to use Robert Boling's terminology, "Suzerain [Overlord] of the Universe."[56] So he will decide (by peaceful means or otherwise) the justice of Jephthah's cause. Therefore, in a sense, the judicial and military roles correspond, as long as different (enemy) nations are in view: "to judge" meant to put things in their proper order. In the international sphere, this seemed inevitably to involve military action.

Several times the judges are also termed "saviors" or "deliverers" (Judg. 3:9,15; Heb. *moshia'*), and the analogous verb "to save" (Heb. *yasha'*) is used of their activity (2:16; 3:9,31; 6:14–15; 8:22; 10:1; 13:5). In conclusion: Once again, these judges were the chosen instruments of Yahweh, who is the One who truly saved or delivered his people time and again from their enemies (2:18; 6:36–37; 10:11–12).

[55]These men and women were "charismatic" in the sense that they possessed unmistakable ability and unique endowment of the Spirit of the LORD (this meaning of the term "charismatic" was first used by the prominent German sociologist Max Weber; see Cundall, TOTC, 7:15–16; Boling, AB, 6a:26).

[56]Boling, AB, 6a:204; in this context he cites Laban's comments to Jacob in Gen. 31:53 for the God (or gods) of the two different national groups to "judge" *(shaphaṭ)* between the two disputants.

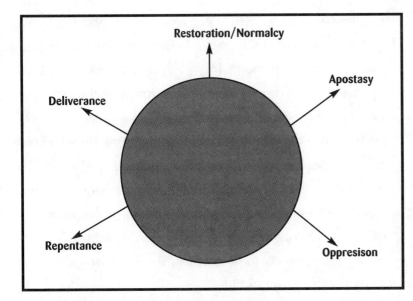

The Judges Cycle

The Cyclical Pattern of Rebellion and Deliverance in the Book of Judges

The Book of Judges presents a gloomy, circular scheme (even downward spiral) of rebellion, defeat, repentance, and deliverance. This stands in sharp contrast to the optimistic flavor of the Book of Joshua. The cyclical pattern of events is well-defined in the passages found in Judges 2:6 through 3:6; and 10:6–16.[57] A similar pattern recurs throughout the book in connection with most of the major judges (biblical scholars typically characterize the judges as "major" or "minor" depending on how much space is given them in the narrative). This cyclical pattern introduces Othniel (3:7–11), Ehud (3:12–15), Deborah (4:1–3), and Gideon (6:1–12). Echoes of this pattern also introduce Jephthah and Samson (10:6–10; 13:1). Unfortunately, the deliverance phase always seemed to lead to a new cycle of

---

[57]Note the following sequence: apostasy or rebellion in Judg. 2:10–13; 10:6; judgment or defeat in 2:14–15; 10:7–9; supplication or repentance in 10:10–16; and restoration or deliverance in 2:16–18.

rebellion and defeat, which got worse and worse (see 2:19). When the two appendixes that conclude the book are considered (Judg. 17 through 18; 19 through 21), the effect is all the stronger. What a sadly realistic portrayal of the people of God is found here! They had a glorious beginning and occasions for revival and reformation. Yet the book shows a general downward slide to apostasy and depravity. It is only by the grace of God that his people could draw closer to him. So it is for us today. Secular culture still gives us little evidence of lasting religious reform or moral improvement.

Let us, therefore, look briefly at the Book of Judges utilizing the following outline:

1:1 through 2:5	The Incomplete Conquest of Canaan
2:6 through 16:31	The Period of the Judges Proper
2:6 through 3:6	The Generations after Joshua
3:7 through 16:31	From Othniel to Samson
17 through 21	Two Appendixes to the Book, Illustrating What Life Was Like "When Israel Had No King"
17 through 18	Micah and the Danite migration
19 through 21	Tribal warfare against Benjamin

The Incomplete Conquest of Canaan —Judg. 1:1 Through 2:5

I've already pointed out that the Book of Judges starts off and ends with remarkably pessimistic perspectives. And its atmosphere is quite different from the victorious one of the Book of Joshua. (There are hints already in the Book of Joshua that the takeover of Canaan was incomplete.)[58] There are some stark vignettes of conquest (including cutting off the

[58]See "The Northern Campaign" earlier in this chap., and the references cited there; also Cundall, TOTC, 7:19–21.

thumbs and big toes of the tyrant Adoni-Bezek [Judg. 1:5–7]). The reader is nonetheless surprised to read time after time of how the Israelites did not take over much of the land, being unable to "drive out" the inhabitants (see 1:19b,21,27,29, 30,31,33). In fact, the text focuses on listing compelling reasons as to why the Israelites failed to conquer the land.[59] The section ends with a particularly dismal etiology[60] explaining the origin of the place name *Bokim* (Heb. for "weepers"). It was there that the Israelites wept aloud before the LORD when he declared that due to their disobedience, the native inhabitants would not be driven out (2:1–5). They would remain as "thorns" in the Israelites' sides, and their gods a "snare." Regrettably, the rest of the Book of Judges gives ample attestation to the truth of this divine prophecy.

The Generations After Joshua
–Judg. 2:6 Through 3:6

The Lord chose to test his people by refusing to drive out their enemies completely.[61] The primary reason for this was

[59]These reasons include the Canaanites' iron chariots (Judg. 1:19b) and their determination to remain in the land (1:27,35a). The Canaanites had successfully confined the Danites to the hill country (1:34). Various Israelite tribes were content to reduce their opponents to forced labor (1:28,30,33,35). There is an apparent contradiction between 1:8 and 1:21. The Judahites seemingly conquered the city of Jerusalem in 1:8, but in 1:21 the Benjamites were unable to dislodge the Jebusites who were living in Jerusalem (see Josh. 15:63). Boling (AB, 6a:55–56) suggests that probably only the unfortified southwest hill of Jerusalem was conquered at this time.

[60]Biblical scholars use this term to indicate the assigned cause or origin of a name or practice. Etiologies are found throughout the Old Testament. The Book of Genesis is especially filled with them (there are no less than three of them in the brief passage about Jacob wrestling with the angel, Gen. 32:22–32: the patriarch's change of name, the naming of the location of the encounter, and the Israelite avoidance of consuming a certain tendon).

[61]See Cundall, TOTC, 7:23–24; the following comments are greatly indebted to his observations.

the Israelite tendency to sin against God. This is most clearly stated in Judges 2:22–23 (also 3:4). Analogous to this is the bald charge that Israel failed to keep her part of the covenant. Therefore the LORD had every right to be angry and not keep his part (2:20–21). But yet another, more positive reason is given in 3:1–3, where the enemy nations remain to "teach warfare" to future Israel.[62] Consequently, scholars usually conclude the Israelites had actual control only of the hill country during the period of the judges.

From Othniel to Samson —Judg. 3:7 Through 16:31

The section from Othniel to Samson composes the bulk of the book. Space permits only a brief look at the six major judges. There are, however, brief notices of six minor judges as well.[63] The following is a list of all twelve[64] judges,

[62]Other reasons given in the OT for the failure of Israel to fully occupy the land include their disposition to make foreign alliances (see Judg. 2:1–5) and their small numbers (see Exod. 23:29–30; Deut. 7:22). The mixture of practical and theological reasons found in these texts again indicate the Bible's realistic portrayal of life. Similarly we usually cannot give simplistic, one-sided reasons for why God does or does not do something in our lives.

[63]The term "major" may not mean a judge who is more important. It simply denotes one that the Bible tells us more about. This is similar to the use of the terms "major prophets" and "minor prophets." As is often pointed out, most of the so-called minor prophets are "minor" only in length. They may well be "major" in historical or theological significance. But unfortunately we have no way to ascertain whether this is the case of these six "minor" judges. They are mentioned only briefly in the Book of Judges. One of these, Shamgar, currently merits only one verse (3:31), but his work may well have been quite significant (cf. his exclusion from the list of "minor" judges in Boling, AB, 6a:7, 89–90).

[64]This biblical number, corresponding to the "twelve tribes of Israel," has often led scholars to try to link each judge to a different tribe. The results of these attempts, while suggestive, remain problematic (concerning the numbering of the twelve tribes of Israel, see the sidebar "The Tribal League of Israel" later in this chap.).

with their corresponding sections from the Book of Judges.

Major judges are in boldface:

Judge	Enemy	Period of Peace*	Reference
Othniel	Cushan-Rishathaim, king of Aram Naharaim	40 years	3:7–11
Ehud	Eglon, king of Moab	80 years	3:12–30
Shamgar	600 Philistines		3:31
Deborah	Jabin, king of Hazor, and Sisera, his commander	40 years	4:1 through 5:31
Gideon	Midianites	40 years	6:1 through 8:35
Abimelech (not reckoned as a judge)			9:1–57
Tola		23 years?	10:1–2
Jair		22 years?	10:3–5
Jephthah	Ammonites	6 years?	10:6 through 12:7
Ibzan		7 years?	12:8–10
Elon		10 years?	12:11–12
Abdon		8 years?	12:13–15
Samson	Philistines	20 years?	13:1 through 16:31

*Note that the "periods of peace" listed for Othniel through Gideon are actually described as when "the land had peace." This is not the case for the later judges. Also, some of these periods probably overlapped chronologically. The question marks refer to the period the judge ruled, which may not be the same as the figures introduced by the phrase "the land had peace."

OTHNIEL — JUDG. 3:7–11

Othniel is the first judge. Yet the text devoted to him is the briefest of any of the major judges. In these few verses is the clearest example of the cycle of rebellion, defeat, repentance, and deliverance. At the same time, many scholars see Othniel as the prototypical judge,[65] the first example of what the proper nature of judgeship should be. If this is the case, then perhaps Samson, the last of the examples found in this lengthy section of the book, shows us most everything a judge should *not* be. Othniel was Caleb's younger brother. Due to his bravery in capturing the town of Debir, he became Caleb's son-in-law, being given his daughter, Acsah, in marriage. At this time Cushan-Rishathaim, a king from Mesopotamia, invaded Israel and colonized much of it. The Spirit of the Lord came upon him, and he mustered the people and defeated the enemy.

EHUD—JUDG. 3:12–30

Ironies pervade this humorous narrative about a left-handed judge, Ehud, from the "right-handed" tribe of Benjamin.[66] He defeated Eglon, king of Moab, a man of immense size. Pretending to pay tribute to him, he delivered a very pointed message instead, plunging his dagger into the corpulent belly of the king. Being left-handed, Ehud carried his dagger on his right thigh (Judg. 3:16), opposite where most members of his tribe would have been expected to

[65]E.g., Boling, AB, 6a:82–83. Also, in contrast to all the other judges, major and minor, whose narratives are found in this section, we have already been introduced to Othniel twice in the closely parallel passages found in Josh. 15:13–19 and Judg. 1:9–15; see Cundall, TOTC, 7:55; Boling, AB, 6a:56. Ironically, in these passages, emphasis is placed more on Acsah than Othniel, as she successfully obtained springs of water from her father, Caleb, for her semiarid land in the Negev (the southern desert). This is not the only place where (in both the books of Joshua and Judges) women successfully take the initiative in that male-dominated culture.

[66]"Benjamin" (Heb. *ben-yamin*) literally means "son of (my) right hand," usually understood as "son of the south." The ancients would orient themselves by facing east, with the south on their right, and the north on their left. Later on, the incongruity of the famous left-handed warriors from the tribe of Benjamin ("each of whom could sling a stone at a hair and not miss" [Judg. 20:16]) also plays on the double meaning of this name.

carry theirs. Managing to appear unarmed, he gained audience with the king alone. Most scholars take the "upper room of [the king's] summer palace" (3:20) to mean an indoor toilet. This is one reason the king's servants delayed checking on him. Apparently they thought the offensive odor they smelled was natural (3:24–25). In any case, Ehud succeeded in escaping past "the idols" near Gilgal (3:19,26).[67] He then mustered the Israelite militia and succeeded in breaking the Moabite yoke. A stirring and most diverting tale this is. It is one that must have entertained generations of Israelites as it was told and retold at the waterholes and around the campfires.[68]

DEBORAH — JUDG. 4:1 THROUGH 5:31

There is irony also in the story of Deborah, a judge and a prophetess (Judg. 4:4). Israel's military leader, Barak, would play only a supporting role, while a peasant woman would receive the honor of victory over the Canaanite enemy.[69] Unique in the Book of Judges are the prose and poetic accounts of Israel's struggle.[70] The battle itself is summed up in only two verses of prose (4:15–16). Four

[67]The verses thus form an inclusio (concerning this term, see n. 15), bracketing the major actions of the story.

[68]Cf. the references in the Song of Deborah to the storytellers who "recite the righteous acts of the LORD" at the watering places, and presumably around the campfires (Judg. 5:10–11,16). Boling, AB, 6a:86 in particular notes the oral style of the Ehud story.

[69]The Song of Deborah (Judg. 5:2–31a) plays on this incongruity. In it there is also the bitter irony of the Canaanite general's mother pictured waiting with her court ladies for the triumphal homecoming of her son. She assumes that his delay must have been due to the magnificence of his victory (5:28–30). How wrong she and her court attendants were!

[70]The closest parallel is the account of victory over the Egyptians at the Red Sea (prose account, Exod.14; poetic account, the "Song of the Sea" in Exod. 15:1b–18). It is probably not coincidental that here too the poetic account

verses of the Song of Deborah give us additional information (5:19–22). Apparently a cloudburst sent from heaven caused the Kishon River to flood (5:20–21). The water rendered the Canaanite chariots useless, bogged down in the mud. Both heavenly and earthly forces are joined in the Deborah narrative. The poetic account singles out a number of Israelite tribes for their participation. Others are noted as conspicuously absent. As Michael Coogan points out, "The activity of the Divine Warrior [Yahweh] is expressed primarily in the activity of those who fight for him. His enemies are the enemies of his people, his friends are those who destroy those enemies, for whatever reasons."[71] Note that "friends" of the LORD here include both fighting men and women. They may be of prominent or subservient status, native Israelite or foreign. What's more, the highest honor of all goes to a woman. She is not Deborah, the exalted prophet and judge. Rather, she is Jael, the humble hammer-wielding wife of a tent-dwelling chieftain.

GIDEON AND ABIMELECH
—JUDG. 6:1 THROUGH 9:57

The narrative of Gideon and his (slave) son Abimelech is the longest yet, encompassing four complete chapters, the fourth dealing with Abimelech. There are ironies to be

---

Humble Heroes

God can and does raise up a person of humble position to do mighty things for God's people, but God never expects us to plot and connive to obtain high position. Maybe this is why the story of Gideon and Abimelech is told in such detail; we dare not misunderstand or misapply either God's unusual choices or his amazing blessings!

---

was probably first composed by a woman (Miriam, in this case—see 15:20–21). There have always been influential women in the history of God's people, in both the Old and New Testaments, as well as up to the present day.

[71]Michael David Coogan, "A Structural and Literary Analysis of the Song of Deborah," *Catholic Biblical Quarterly* 40 (1978): 165–66; the full article (143–66) is a fine analysis of the song's literary structure.

found here as well.[72] A huge number of invading Midianites and their allies (Judg. 6:3–5) were stopped by Gideon's tiny force (three hundred men, 7:7–8). Gideon, by his own account, was the least in his family, from the weakest clan in the tribe of Manasseh (6:15).[73] Finally, Gideon, the "Baal-hacker,"[74] demolished the Baal altar and the Asherah pole in his hometown. As a result, he had to contend with his own neighbors, who wanted to kill him (6:27–32). Yes, the story of Gideon is filled with irony.[75] Gideon had already refused an offer of dynastic rule (8:22–23) when after his death Abimelech attempted to renew and accept it. Pursuing his treacherous ambition, he managed to murder all but one of his seventy brothers (Judg. 9).[76]

[72]An irony can be defined as an unexpected outcome to a course of events, sometimes with a humorous twist (e.g., Abimelech, the would-be king, killed by a millstone dropped by a woman; Samson, the he-man of his day, also undone by a woman; Gideon's victory over the Midianites, using the most unlikely weapons and tactics).

[73]Manasseh itself was weaker than Ephraim, the other Joseph tribe, yet it contended with the vast enemy host of the Midianites. They also dealt with the contentious Ephraimites (Judg. 8:1–3) as well as with a number of other uncooperative Israelite enclaves (8:4–17)

[74]This is the meaning of the other name given to Gideon: "Jerub-Baal" (see Judg. 6:32). As is often the case in biblical narrative, there is wordplay here; the name Jerub-Baal probably originally meant "May Baal give increase" or the like, but here it is reinterpreted to mean "May Baal contend (with him, the bearer of the name)" (see Gray, NCB, 207; Cundall, TOTC, 7:106–7).

[75]"Irony" in the sense of reversals of normal expectation. Many biblical accounts take delight in the humble overtaking the mighty, and the weak the strong (cf. 1 Cor. 1:25). One of the best discussions of biblical irony remains Edwin M. Good, *Irony in the Old Testament* (Philadelphia: Westminster, 1965).

[76]The only survivor was Jotham, the youngest (Judg. 9:5). After hearing about Abimelech being crowned king by the citizens of Shechem, Jotham bravely climbed up Mount Gerizim to address the people (Mount Gerizim is one of the two well-known mountains flanking the town of Shechem—Mount Ebal being the other—and this terrain provides a natural amphitheater for the city

Like the Canaanite king Sisera before him, Abimelech met his match in a woman, who received the honor of killing an enemy of God (see Judg. 9:53). The weapon this time was an upper millstone. One of the final verses in the Gideon traditions somberly reminds us, "Thus God repaid the wickedness that Abimelech had done to his father [Gideon] by murdering his seventy brothers" (9:56). Paul reminds us, "Do not be deceived: God cannot be mocked. A man reaps what he sows" (Gal. 6:7).

JEPHTHAH — JUDG. 10:6 THROUGH 12:7

The story of Jephthah contains what is perhaps the most tragic event — the bitterest irony of all — in the Book of Judges (11:30–40). Jephthah was the son of a Canaanite prostitute (11:1). Driven out by his people, the Gileadites, Jephthah formed a band of raiders (11:3). But when the Ammonites began to oppress the Gileadites, they called him back to lead them (11:6–10). In his speech to the Ammonite king, Jephthah memorably acknowledged that it is Yahweh who is the true Judge (11:27). The justice of Jephthah's cause would most certainly prevail. Unfortunately, Jephthah's pagan background becomes visible at this point. Before leaving for battle, he vowed to sacrifice "to the LORD" (11:30) whatever would come out of his house to meet him when he returned victorious. Tragically, it was his only child, his daughter, who came dancing to greet him (11:34). The text tersely records that

[cf. Deut. 27:12–26; Josh. 8:30–35]). What is often called "Jotham's Fable" (Judg. 9:8–15) remains a classic parable of the relatively unimportant role political leaders have (or should have) in society; for of all the trees who were candidates to be crowned king (olive tree, fig tree, grapevine, thornbush), only the thornbush had nothing better to do. Unfortunately, then (and many times since), the people paid no attention to Jotham's wise words.

"he did to her as he had vowed" (11:39).[77]

Jephthah is not as well-known to the average reader as some other judges. Yet his story teaches much about Israelite religious thought and practice. Being a prostitute's son meant his origins were not only humble, they were pagan. He was a loner and the leader of an outlaw gang (11:2–3). He was edgy and combative when contending with the Gileadite elders (11:4–11) and with the self-important Ephraimites (12:1–6). He seemed proud and inflexible (11:30–31).[78] But he accomplished mighty things for the LORD. The narrator recounts his many personal failings more in a spirit of sympathy and sorrow than in the spirit of censure. God loves us all, no matter what our background, and he may well use us mightily for his kingdom.

Near the end of Jephthah's speech to the Ammonite king, there is a curious reference to "three hundred years" (Judg. 11:26). Apparently this refers to the period between the time of Moses and the time of Jephthah. We have not discussed the chronological problems attending the period

A Dangerous Zeal

Some scholars flinch at interpreting that Jephthah sacrificed his daughter, but most scholars recognize what the text seems plainly to say: Jephthah, a judge in Israel, committed human sacrifice in the name of Yahweh, and the victim was his only daughter, whom he loved dearly. Religious impulse can be a most dangerous thing in a person's life, especially when zeal overtakes reason.

[77]Cundall, TOTC, 7:146–49, has a particularly perceptive discussion of this event. It must be faced that human (especially child) sacrifice was not uncommon among Israel's neighbors (e.g., 2 Kings 3:27, in reference to Mesha, king of Moab), and it was even practiced by some of the later kings of Judah (2 Kings 16:3; 21:6).

[78]This is my interpretation concerning Jephthah's fulfillment of his hasty vow to sacrifice whatever first meets him when he returns home in victory. Almost certainly Jephthah expected to have to sacrifice some farm animal, not a human being. Boling (AB, 6a:208, ill. 8) points out that Israelite Iron Age houses generally included a courtyard in which livestock would be kept. Most scholars emphasize that Jephthah felt he had no choice but was indeed compelled to keep his most unfortunate vow. Probably Jephthah's parentage and childhood upbringing greatly contributed to this tragic inflexibility. In any case, vows were (and are) very serious matters (but see 1 Sam. 14 where Saul's similar vow is correctly condemned and nullified by the people). It is therefore no wonder that Jesus told us not to make any vows at all (Matt. 5:33–37)!

of time of the judges. If taken literally, the combined terms of all the judges exceeds three hundred years.[79] A possible solution is that some of the judges overlapped chronologically, but not enough is known about these "Dark Ages" in Israel for dogmatic conclusions.

Finally, the well-known term "Shibboleth" is found in 12:4–6. The Ephraimites protested that Jephthah had not included them in his victorious struggle against the Ammonites. Civil war ensued. To distinguish the enemy, the Ephraimites, the Gileadites came up with a password: "Shibboleth." The Ephraimites pronounced it "Sibboleth." Those who mispronounced the term[80] were killed by the Gileadites—a total of forty-two thousand Ephraimites. It was indeed a bloody age in the land of Israel. Jephthah's story includes several stern lessons for life from a grim era in Israelite history.

SAMSON—JUDG. 13:1 THROUGH 16:31

Samson's enemies were the powerful Philistines.[81] Israelites must have rejoiced in Samson's clever victories

---

[79]Those who support an early date for the exodus (ca. 1450 B.C.) often cite this number, as well as the later reference to 480 years between the time of Moses and the founding of Solomon's Temple (1 Kings 6:1).

[80]The term "Shibboleth" meant either "ear of corn" and/or "flood, torrent"; but the meaning of the word was not at issue, rather its precise pronunciation. Boling cites E. A. Speiser as suggesting that the difference in pronunciation probably was between *th* and *sh,* with the Gileadites preserving the traditional distinction, and the more linguistically "advanced" Ephraimites merging the sounds (as is the case in the standard Heb. alphabet still in use today). Boling, AB, 6a:212–13, citing E. A. Speiser, "The Shibboleth Incident (Judges 12:6," *BASOR* 85 (1942): 10–13. In popular English usage, the term "Shibboleth" has come to denote any phrase, practice, or custom that is distinctive for any particular group of people. It goes without saying that we Christians have rather many "Shibboleths" which can be off-putting for nonbelievers.

[81]The Philistines were the foremost adversaries of Israel during the reigns of Saul and David and proved troublesome even up to the time of King

over the Philistines. Yet their delight must have been tempered with embarrassment over his adolescent appetites, especially his weakness for Philistine women.

Multichambered City Gate

We have already taken note, of course, of the most infamous haircut in Old Testament history (Judg. 16:4–22). But Delilah's success over Samson is only the last of a lengthy series of dalliances. Samson consorted with a number of Philistine women, some of quite questionable background. To be sure, the Samson story ends in tragedy. The Philistine temple in Gaza came crashing down on the blinded judge and on the wildly celebrating crowd (16:23–30).[82] But most of the Samson story contains much

---

Hezekiah in the late eighth century B.C. They appear to have been one of the tribes of the Sea Peoples defeated by Rameses III at Pelusium about 1200 B.C. The Sea Peoples were responsible for the Hittite Empire and a number of powerful city-states on the eastern seaboard of the Mediterranean.

[82]Samson was able to topple the two central supporting pillars of the temple to avenge the gouging out of his two eyes (Judg. 16:29–30). Boling notes that a recently excavated Philistine temple at Tell Qasile consisted of a long room that supported its roof by two wooden pillars, set on stone bases along the center axis. AB, 6a:252.

Going It Alone?

Samson seems to break the mold of a proper Israelite judge in yet another way: He consistently acted as a loner, a "free-lancer," a kind of "Rambo." This is even more striking in such a community-minded society as Old Testament Israel. Samson sought no advice from elders. He mustered no troops. What a reminder to our more individualistically minded culture of the dangers of "going it alone"! God used Samson despite his flaws, not because of them!

that is ironic. On one occasion he had come to Gaza to spend the night with a prostitute. Imagine Samson grabbing the bar, doors, and doorposts of the closed Gaza gate at midnight and carrying them nearly thirty-eight miles uphill toward Hebron (16:1–3). Talk about "power ministry." Also imagine him catching three hundred foxes, tying them tail-to-tail in pairs, and fastening a torch to each pair. He used them to burn down the standing grain of the Philistines, thus avenging the loss of his Philistine bride (15:1–5). Samson was never boring, but far from a role model for the believer.

We do read that God's Spirit "began to stir him" as Samson grew up (Judg. 13:25). Three times God's Spirit "came upon him in power" (14:6,19; 15:14). Still, Samson, who was called to be a Nazirite from birth (13:5),[83] seems systematically to break all his vows, one by one.[84] What a frustrating "hero" he must have been![85] Still, God chose to effect much good, despite the very serious failings of this most injudicious judge (14:4).

[83]Nazirites were to abstain from alcohol and grape products, contact with the dead, and, of course, haircuts (Num. 6:1–21). The term "Nazirite" comes from the Heb. verb *nazar*, "to dedicate or consecrate, to separate," and both men and women could become Nazirites for fixed periods of time, not necessarily all their lives.

[84]Besides Delilah's notorious haircut, Samson seemed repeatedly to enjoy "the fruit of the vine" (cf. the seven-day wedding feast Samson hosted in Judg. 14:10–18; also presumably his "night on the town" in 16:1–3; not to mention his dalliances with Delilah later in the same chap.), and he certainly came in contact with the dead (the carcass of a lion where he found the honey [14:8–9]; the corpses of the thirty Philistines whom he killed to get thirty sets of clothing [14:19]; and that famous "fresh jawbone of a donkey" which he used to strike down a thousand men [15:15–17]).

[85]All of Samson's physical strength, as well as the "rush" of God's Spirit, still prove inadequate without a will to withstand the tears or nagging of an unhappy woman (see Judg. 14:16–18; also Delilah in 16:15–17). A significant test of true strength, after all, is to know your weaknesses.

Two Appendixes to the Book —Judg. 17 Through 21

The Book of Judges seems to save its most extreme stories for the end. In these two appendixes are horrific atrocities that took place among God's people Israel.

The first of these stories is of Micah and the Danite migration (Judg. 17 through 18). It opens with the account of an Ephraimite who robbed his very own mother (17:1–2) and concludes with the Danites' brutal and thorough ethnic cleansing of a peaceful, unsuspecting nation (18:27).

The second story tells of the tribal war against Benjamin (Judg. 19 through 21). It begins with the repeated rape and abuse of an Israelite concubine, not to mention the later methodical dismembering of her corpse (19:25–30). It ends with the intertribal warfare against Benjamin (Judg. 20), with the later forcible seizure of unsuspecting women to become wives for the Benjamite survivors (21:20–23).

The repeated theme of this section is how horrible things were in Israel before there were kings in the land (Judg. 17:6; 18:1; 19:1; 21:25; cf. the sidebar "The Tribal League of Israel"). The Book of Judges is a most pessimistic book. It suggests that without the transforming power of God's Spirit, things will only get worse and worse.[86] These two appendixes were not written to entertain but to teach and admonish. Our modern cultures are *still* permeated with grotesque examples of godlessness. Whenever people do "whatever seems right in their own eyes" (see 17:6;

---

[86]Indeed, in its own way the Samson story has already confirmed this. For Samson, the "Spirit of the LORD" gave him power, amazing power, but no personal transformation. Mighty power without personal holiness can lead only to disaster.

The Tribal League of Israel

Most readers of the Bible have heard of the twelve tribes of Israel. These tribes trace their origin back to the twelve sons of Jacob (also known as "Israel"), and they mostly take their names directly from these sons (see Gen. 35:22b–26; cf. 29:31 through 30:24; 35:16–18). Strictly speaking, there were thirteen tribes, the Levites being reckoned as the liturgical tribe, and Ephraim and Manasseh, the two sons of Joseph, both becoming important northern tribes. Most biblical references to the nation of Israel, however, envision "twelve" as the tribal number.

Most scholars today would agree that at least some of the elements of premonarchial Israel stemmed from different ethnic origins. Note, for example, the "many other people" who went out of Egypt with Israel (Exod. 12:38), and the Egyptian father in Leviticus 24:10. What united them in the early

(continued on next page)

21:25), let us remember the Book of Judges. Any society that purports to believe in God but does not follow his ways will only deteriorate until God's true people finally call out desperately to him once more for relief.

The Book of Ruth: A Woman of Valor, A Narrative of Grace

Introduction

The short Book of Ruth has long been recognized as a literary masterpiece.[87] The German poet Goethe once called it the most beautiful "little whole" in the Old Testament.[88] Its setting is "in the days when the judges ruled" (Ruth 1:1a). In the first chapter we immediately read of famine, untimely death, and the heartache of family separation (1:1–15). But this narrative is different from those in the Book of Judges. What makes it different is Ruth herself (1:16–18). A woman, a widow, a foreigner, Ruth, through the providence of the LORD, would prove to be an instrument of remarkable blessing. This was to benefit not only the widow Naomi, but in a larger sense, the entire nation of Israel.[89]

[87]The following are important recent commentaries in Eng. on the Book of Ruth: Frederic W. Bush, *Ruth, Esther,* Word Biblical Commentary (WBC), vol. 9 (Dallas: Word, 1996); Edward F. Campbell, Jr., *Ruth: A New Translation, With Introduction, Notes, and Commentary,* Anchor Bible (AB), vol. 7 (New York: Doubleday, 1975); John Gray, *Joshua, Judges, Ruth,* New Century Bible Commentary (NCB) (Grand Rapids: Wm. B. Eerdmans, 1986); Robert L. Hubbard, Jr., *The Book of Ruth,* New International Commentary on the Old Testament (NICOT) (Grand Rapids: Wm. B. Eerdmans, 1988); and Leon Morris, *Ruth, An Introduction and Commentary,* Tyndale Old Testament Commentaries (TOTC), vol. 7 (Downers Grove, Ill.: InterVarsity Press, 1968).

[88]As cited by Campbell, AB, 7:3. Much of what follows is heavily indebted to this fine commentary.

[89]Bush, WBC, 9:51–55, sees the overall theme as that of *chesed,* a word most important in OT theology, and a word most difficult to translate. It is

---

The Tribal League of Israel (cont.)

period was their common religious faith. The tribal splintering of Israel during the period of the Judges was quite clearly evident. Also evident, however, was their distinct sense of intertribal solidarity. Ironically, the second appendix of Judges (Judg. 19 through 21), where the tribes form an alliance against their fellow Benjamites to wage bitter war against them, proves the point. The allied Israelites later "grieved for Benjamin, because the LORD had made a gap in the tribes of Israel" (21:15). The clans and tribes of the ancient nation of Israel had at least one major thing in common: It was their radical faith in the radical God of Moses and Joshua, the God of the covenant, whose name was Yahweh. He was the One who comforted the afflicted, and who afflicted the comfortable (Deut. 32:39–43; 1 Sam. 2:1–10). That was the unifying factor in biblical Israel, as well as in the new Israel, the Church, the people of God.

Structure of the Story

As is often pointed out, this brief book is quite carefully constructed. The following structural analysis[90] shows the way the first part of the book mirrors the second:

1:1–5		**A** Brief introduction, spanning more than a decade of time	
1:6–22		**B** Ruth and Orpah, focusing on the *complaint* of Naomi, her "emptiness"	
	2:1–23	**1** Ruth gleaning in Boaz's field	
		2:1–3	**a** Ruth and Naomi, brief introductory scene
		2:4–17	**b** Ruth and Boaz, encounter, blessing, act of *chesed*
		2:18–23	**a'** Ruth and Naomi, brief concluding scene; Naomi "full"
	3:1–18	**2** Ruth meeting Boaz at the threshing floor	
		3:1–6	**a** Ruth and Naomi, brief introductory scene
		3:7–15	**b** Ruth and Boaz, encounter, act of *chesed*, blessing
		3:16–18	**a'** Ruth and Naomi, brief concluding scene; Naomi again "full"
4:1–12		**B'** Boaz and so-and-so, focusing on the *resolution* of Naomi's complaint	
4:13–17		**A'** Brief conclusion, spanning three generations of time	
		[4:18–22]	[Appendix: genealogy of David]

CONVENTIONAL AND UNCONVENTIONAL MEANS OF BLESSING

Stephen Bertman has made the important observation that in the Book of Ruth we find only "conventional" people. There are no actual villains, in contrast to the Book of

---

traditionally rendered "loving-kindness," but perhaps it is better understood as "covenantal loyalty" or the like. Both God and God's people are to give evidence of this "going beyond the call of duty" (Bush, WBC, 9:53; see also Campbell, AB, 7:29–30). As Bush notes, the outcome of this *chesed* in the Book of Ruth is nothing less than the preservation of the family line from Perez, son of Judah the patriarch, through Boaz and Obed, to David the king.

[90]Adapted from Campbell, AB, 7:15–16.

Ruth
Date: Uncertain
Story: Timeless

The Book of Ruth is hard to date. Its emphasis on a Moabite hero—a woman—contrasts sharply with the Bible's usual condemnation of Moabites (e.g., Deut. 23:3-6). The tradition about the inclusion of Ruth in David's genealogy must be early. But the composition of many Old Testament books can be considerably later than the events that they describe. The author is anonymous, and the book's date of composition remains uncertain.[92] Its message, though, remains timeless: God's ways are not our ways (see Isa. 55:8–9). He may well use the most unlikely candidates to further his purposes. Tragedy may come our way, but the end of the story remains to be told. Dare to expect the unexpected. Our God is faithful. Act heroically when the opportunity presents itself is the encouragement from this little book for all believers of all times.

Judges.[91] As is the case today, most people of faith try to meet their expected obligations, but little more. Yet, a few individuals (most notably Boaz and Ruth) exceed these obligations. And it is by such heroic actions that they and their friends and relatives get blessed.

NAOMI'S COMPLAINT AGAINST HER UNJUST SUFFERING — RUTH 1

Naomi was hit by a series of hardships. First there was the famine. Hoping for happiness in a new land (Moab), she faced the unexpected deaths of her husband and sons. She was left with the seeming impossibility of finding new husbands for her two foreign daughters-in-law, now young widows. No wonder she complained, "'Call me Mara [Bitter], because the Almighty has made my life very bitter. I went away full, but the LORD has brought me back empty. Why call me Naomi [Pleasant]? The LORD has afflicted me; the Almighty has brought misfortune upon me'" (Ruth 1:20–21). The rest of the book will show how Naomi's bitter, but quite understandable, complaint would be answered.[93] Indeed, Ruth's own extraordinary announcement of loyalty to her new clan and family was to pave the way (1:16–17).

---

[91] See ibid., 7:16, and passim.

[92] Campbell (AB, 7:23–28) sees the book possibly written as early as the ninth century B.C.; Bush, however, prefers the late preexilic, or (more likely) the early postexilic period (WBC, 9:18–30). Hubbard prefers a preexilic date (NICOT, 23–46), possibly as early as the time of Solomon (or even earlier).

[93] Ibid., 31–32; also 83–84, where he notes that not only in such circumstances is complaint tolerated by God, but it can even be the *proper* response of a person who takes God seriously (the Book of Job comes immediately to mind).

RUTH'S BOLDNESS, BORN OF DESPERATION —RUTH 2

The opportunity for poor people to glean a freshly harvested field was mandated in the Torah (Deut. 24:19–22). Boaz clearly went far beyond the obligations of the Law. He truly was "a man of standing" (Ruth 2:1). But Ruth was to be the one who took the initiative (2:2). Already Naomi was less "empty" and more "full" due to Ruth's brave (cf. 2:9b) and industrious (2:7b,17) actions. Even Naomi herself began to recognize this (2:20,22).

RUTH'S BOLD ACTION WITHOUT COMPROMISE —RUTH 3

In chapter 3 the narrative gets delicate. Naomi recognized Boaz's potential to be Ruth's husband (see Ruth 2:20b). She instructed Ruth how to help bring this about, using questionable means (3:1–4). We must remember that harvest time was an occasion for revelry (3:7–8). Ruth did as Naomi suggested, but not entirely. She was supposed to allow Boaz to take the initiative (3:4b). Once she was discovered, however, she herself told Boaz what to do (3:9). Boaz was her "kinsman-redeemer" (Heb. *go'el*), a near relative to her husband's family. He could redeem property that was no longer in the family, as well as a relative in dire straits. Ruth's bold adherence to the Torah, rather than the questionable instructions of her mother-in-law, show her heroic stature in a new light. She truly was a woman of noble character (3:11b),[94] worth more to Naomi than "seven sons" (see 4:15b).

[94]Heb. *'esheth chayil,* the feminine equivalent of the narrator's highly respectful description of Boaz back in Ruth 2:1b. This is also the very same Heb. term for the "wife of noble character" described in Prov. 31:10–31.

BOAZ'S HEROIC ACTIONS: THE BIBLICAL RESPONSE TO JUSTIFIED COMPLAINT — RUTH 4

Now it is Boaz's turn to be the hero. He courteously gave the unnamed closer relative a chance to "redeem" Naomi and her property (Ruth 4:1–8). But when the fellow realized he would have to support Ruth as well as Naomi, he declined. (The man acted prudently, but timidly, so as not to endanger his own financial status.) So Boaz boldly took the initiative. He formally announced his intentions to the town elders: He would marry Ruth (4:9–10). Thus he would preserve the lineage of Naomi and her family. The elders responded with a memorable blessing (4:11–12), as did Naomi's friends later on when Ruth bore Boaz a son (4:14–15). The book ends with the genealogy of none other than King David. Indeed, Matthew's royal genealogy for Jesus, son of David, also includes Ruth's name, along with Boaz's (Matt. 1:5).

As we come to the end of this chapter on the books of Joshua, Judges, and Ruth, we should once again recall three most unlikely heroes of the faith. There is one in each book: three women, three foreigners, three bold and resourceful champions of the faith. One is Rahab the Canaanite prostitute, who saved the two Israelite spies and thereby her own family from certain destruction. The second is Jael the Kenite, whose killing of Israel's enemy Sisera will be forever celebrated in the Song of Deborah. The third is Ruth the Moabitess, who preserved the family line of Judah, thus becoming the great-grandmother of King David and ancestor of Jesus.

Appendix: Judges or Kings for Israel?

Concerning the basic principles of the faith there are no contradictions in the Bible. Scripture uniformly teaches that there is only one God, that Jesus Christ was truly the Son of God, and that he was indeed resurrected on the third day, etc. But concerning other less crucial issues, the Bible shows various viewpoints, often taken from the cultures that formed them. This can cause some younger believers distress when they expect everything to be the same. Perhaps the issue of kingship is the best example. We worry little about the "divine right of kings" any more (although for centuries this used to be a major issue in the political arena). We soon discover that the Bible says a lot about kings, both positively and negatively. Kings seemingly were not in God's ideal plan for his chosen people (1 Sam. 8:6–9). The Bible clearly indicates many drawbacks to a monarchial government (see, for example, Deut. 17:14–20, the so-called Law of the King; see also Samuel's stern words in 1 Sam. 12:12–17). The greatest kings Israel ever had were David and his son Solomon. The biblical text, however, spells out in remarkable detail the sins and weaknesses of both these leaders (2 Samuel 12 through 20; 1 Kings 11:1–13). Still, God was pleased to raise up King Saul as the "LORD'S anointed" (1 Sam. 24:6; 26:9,11; see also 10:24; 12:3). After Saul forsook his God, Yahweh raised up David and his posterity as an "eternal dynasty" (see 2 Sam. 7:4–16). Indeed, the Messiah comes from the "house of David" (see Isa. 9:6–7; 11:1). It is probably in light of these positive portrayals of kingship that the words "In those days Israel had no king; everyone did as he saw fit" (Judg. 21:25) should be read. Monarchy in Israel had its definite drawbacks, but it has been said that anarchy is the cruelest form of government. (Going back to the time when Yahweh was truly "king" seems to be out of the question.) In the days before the monarchy, living conditions deteriorated and the political situation was often quite unstable. Winston Churchill noted, "It has been said that democracy is the *worst* form of government, except all others"–perhaps that is what the Bible is saying about monarchy in Old Testament times.

Study Questions

1. What is a "programmatic text"?
2. Identify the people and events that led to the capture of Jericho.
3. How many military campaigns did Joshua make in taking the land? What were they?
4. Know the names and locations of all important cities in the conquest.
5. What were some of the criteria underlying the dynamics of the land allocation in Joshua 13 through 21?
6. What happened at Shechem in Joshua 24?
7. Who were the judges of Israel? What is the pattern of Israel's life described in the Book of Judges?
8. Know the names of the major judges, their adversaries, and what they did to defeat them.
9. Know the main characters and the story told in the Book of Ruth.

For Further Reading

The commentaries cited in the footnotes at the beginning of the discussion of each book remain the best sources for further study. These authors have immersed themselves in the latest archaeological discoveries as well as the best in literary approaches to the material. More popular articles, often handsomely illustrated, may be found in *Biblical Archaeology Review* and *Bible Review,* usually written by experts in the field.

10

William Raccah

From Tribal League to Kingdom

Outline:

- Who Wrote These Books?
- The Gathering Storm
- Who Was Samuel?
- The Philistines Capture the Ark
- The End of the Judges
- Was Saul Really Anointed King?
- Major Events in Saul's Reign
- Saul and David
- Saul's Tragic Death

Terms:

amphictyony
holy war
prophets/prophetism
ruach
seer

The period of Samuel's leadership and the institution of the monarchy are of particular importance to biblical history. There's much more to it, however, than the story of how David brought down Goliath with a well-aimed stone (1 Sam. 17). Both 1 and 2 Samuel chronicle a structural change within Israelite society. This development had profound political and religious consequences for the people of Israel.

Who Wrote These Books?

Like 1 and 2 Kings, 1 and 2 Samuel were originally one volume in the Hebrew text.[1] They were divided when the Septuagint was translated. The books of Samuel were named after the prophet because he appears as the principal character of the earlier narratives. He also played a part in anointing the two other prominent characters, Saul and David.[2] The Babylonian Talmud says that Samuel was the author of the books that bear his name.[3] The prophet dies, however, and his death is mentioned twice before the end of the books (1 Sam. 25:1; 28:3). It would appear that

[1]The Masoretes, Jewish scribes of the seventh and eighth centuries A.D., treated 1 and 2 Samuel as a unit, designating it the "Book of Samuel." It was divided in two in the Septuagint because the Greek language was written with vowels and required more space than the Hebrew, which was written using only consonants. The Latin Vulgate in the course of time dropped the term "Book of Kingdoms" (libri regnorum) and, shifting to the Hebrew division between Samuel and Kings, came out with the titles that the Western Church has used ever since. The Eastern Church, however, still refers to 1 and 2 Samuel as "1 and 2 Kingdoms" and 1 and 2 Kings as "3 and 4 Kingdoms." See Gleason L. Archer, Jr., *A Survey of Old Testament Introduction* (Chicago: Moody Press, 1974), 288; and J. Albert Soggins, *Introduction to the Old Testament,* rev. ed. (Philadelphia: Westminster Press, 1980), 185.

[2]R. K. Harrison, *Introduction to the Old Testament* (Grand Rapids: Wm. B. Eerdmans, 1969), 695.

[3]Baba Bathra 14b.

Samuel's prominence in the first book was considered sufficient explanation for the title of both books.[4]

The two books of Samuel describe the transition from the chaos of the judges' era to the more settled conditions under the monarchy. They show Samuel's part in establishing the social and political foundations of David's kingdom.[5] Samuel was the dominant religious figure of his time. He introduced the prophetic office to counter the priestly domination of Israel's worship. Only one other place in these two books do we find reference to the priestly line of Eli after his death (1 Sam. 14:3).[6] Furthermore, despite the monarchy's potential, many Israelites did not accept it as either politically expedient or theologically legitimate. The fundamental question underlying these books is "Who really was king—Yahweh or David?"[7] The tragic climax of 2 Kings with the exile to Babylon points to Israel's failure to come up with the proper answer.

[4]Soggins, *Old Testament,* 185. Various independent sources are evident for the books. Harrison, 697, lists the following parallel accounts: the announcement concerning the end of Eli and his house on two occasions (1 Sam. 2:31–33; 3:11–14); the secret anointing of Saul (9:26 through 10:1), followed later by two public ceremonies (10:21; 11:15); two occasions on which Samuel rejected Saul as king (13:14; 15:23); two introductions of David to Saul (16:21; 17:58); two escapes of David from the court of Saul (19:12; 20:42); two occasions on which David spared the life of Saul (24:3; 26:5); three different covenants between David and Jonathan (18:3; 20:16; 23:18); two flights by David to Gath (21:10; 27:1); and the tradition concerning the killing of Goliath (1 Sam. 17:51; 2 Sam. 21:19).

[5]By the time of Solomon, Israel's empire was without equal in the ANE. See Harrison, *Old Testament,* 709.

[6]Interestingly, the tabernacle and the ark are also notably absent from the text after the Philistines ravaged Shiloh. See Harrison, *Old Testament,* 710.

[7]J. Kenneth Kuntz, *The People of Ancient Israel: An Introduction to Old Testament Literature, History, and Thought* (New York: Harper & Row Publishers, 1974), 171.

The Gathering Storm

Samuel ministered from about 1050–1000 B.C. His ministry was the culmination of the 200- to 300-year period of government by the judges. During that time the fortunes of the people of Israel had alternated between prosperity and God's judgment. This lack of stability was due to these important factors: (1) Egypt's impressive period of empire had come to an end;[8] (2) Israel was experiencing increased Philistine pressure; (3) the judges were unable to rally Israel against the Philistines; and (4) the priesthood had fallen into decay. Israel's transition to monarchy must be viewed in light of these factors.

How Was Israel Organized Before the Monarchy?

Some biblical scholars considered Israel's tribal league to have been an amphictyony. In ancient Greece and Italy, an amphictyony was a league of states that took part in the cult of a common deity.[9] In ancient Israel, an amphictyony would refer to the league of Israelite tribes organized around sanctuaries such as Shiloh. The shrine was sanctified by the presence of the ark.[10] There, it was thought, the tribes gathered regularly to hear the Torah and to offer sacrifices.

More recent scholarship, however, suggests that the

---

[8]The Egyptian tale "The Journey of Wen-Amon to Phoenicia" (ca. 1060 B.C.) gives a vivid, humorous, and ironic account of Egypt's rapidly waning influence in western Asia. The conversations in this short story present a situation that contrasts sharply with an earlier era when Egypt's influence in Asia was strong. See *ANET*, 25–29; Kuntz, *Ancient Israel*, 174.

[9]An example of an amphictyony may be found in the well-known Delphic league, founded around the oracle of Apollo at Delphi, Greece.

[10]Kuntz, *Ancient Israel*, 167.

tribes cooperated to cope with a common enemy.[11] Such cooperation would have been influenced by political and geographical conditions. It may be better, therefore, to refer to Israel's organization as a tribal league. The tribes did sometimes unite in a concerted attempt to overthrow their common enemy. Shiloh's prominence was due to its custody of the ark of the covenant. We can see this in the annual trip that Samuel's parents made to Shiloh where Yahweh's ark was located (1 Sam. 1:3). The same trip may have been undertaken by many devout Israelites. In this centralization of the tribal league we may detect the foundations of Israel's monarchial government.[12]

Who Was Samuel? — 1 Sam. 1 Through 4:1a

The move from tribal organization to kingship, the development of the priesthood, and the appearance of the prophet are all associated with Samuel. Israel stood in need of effective leadership. The portrait of Samuel presented in 1 Samuel is multifaceted. In one instance, Samuel is described as judge over all Israel (1 Sam. 7:3–14). The office of judge describes him as one able to deliver Israel from impending enemy threat. His circuit as judge was the area between Ramah, Bethel, Gilgal, and Mizpah (1 Sam. 7:15–17). In 1 Samuel 9:9 he is depicted as a "seer," an earlier title for the prophetic office. He was a man of God, consulted to find the lost donkeys owned by Saul's father, Kish (9:3,6). Moreover, Samuel is the one who anointed

[11]Harry M. Orlinsky, "The Tribal System of Israel and Related Groups in the Period of the Judges," in *Studies and Essays in Honor of Abraham A. Neuman,* ed. Meir Ben-Horin et al. (Leiden, Netherlands: E. J. Brill, 1962). Other scholars have criticized the amphictyonic hypothesis as imposing an Indo-European model on an Asian culture.

[12]Kuntz, *Ancient Israel,* 169.

Israel's first king (1 Sam. 9 through 11). On two occasions, Samuel is linked with what might be called "ecstatic prophetism" (1 Sam. 10:5–7; 19:18–24).[13]

Hannah's Vow – 1 Sam. 1:1–19

Elkanah, a man from the hill country of Ephraim, had two wives, Hannah and Peninnah. Hannah was barren. Ancient Israelis thought a childless wife had suffered divine displeasure. Many biblical stories, like this one, mention how a woman is blessed by the birth of a son.[14]

The story of Samuel begins with one of Elkanah's annual journeys to the sanctuary at Shiloh. He took with him his wives, Hannah and Peninnah–and Peninnah's children. Hannah took this occasion to make a request and a vow to God (1 Sam. 1:11). Her request was not simply for a child, but for a "man child" (KJV). Her vow reminds us of the Samson story: He would be devoted to the LORD; no razor would ever touch his head.[15] After an awkward incident with Eli, the presiding priest, Hannah returned home and in due course gave birth to a son.

What's in a Name? – 1 Sam. 1:20–28

The name "Samuel" and its explanation present a puzzle. Samuel (sh⁀emu'el) means "[His] name is El [God]." It is a

---

[13]Ibid., 176.

[14]Peter R. Ackroyd, *The First Book of Samuel* (Cambridge, England: Cambridge University Press, 1971), 21–22. See the stories of Abraham and Sarah, Jacob and his wives, Samson's parents, and in the NT, Elizabeth and Mary.

[15]Although the vow appears similar to a Nazirite vow, the prospective mother is the one making it for a child not yet conceived. A parallel can be seen in Judg. 13:2–7; however, on this occasion, it is the angel of the LORD who tells the woman to dedicate her as-yet unconceived son as a Nazirite. See Ackroyd, *Samuel*, 24–25.

Comparing the Prayers of Hannah and Mary[16]	
Hannah's Prayer **(1 Sam. 2:1–10)**	**Mary's Prayer** **(Luke 1:46–55)**
[1]Then Hannah prayed and said: "My heart rejoices in the LORD; in the LORD my horn is lifted high. My mouth boasts over my enemies, for I delight in your deliverance. [2]"There is no one holy like the LORD; there is no one besides you; there is no Rock like our God. [3]"Do not keep talking so proudly or let your mouth speak such arrogance, for the LORD is a God who knows, and by him deeds are weighed. [4]"The bows of the warriors are broken, but those who stumbled are armed with strength. [5]Those who were full hire themselves out for food, but those who were hungry hunger no more. She who was barren has borne seven children, but she who has had many sons pines away. [6]"The LORD brings death and makes alive; he brings down to the grave and raises up. [7]The LORD sends poverty and wealth; he humbles and he exalts. [8]He raises the poor from the dust and lifts the needy from the ash heap; he seats them with princes and has them inherit a throne of honor. "For the foundations of the earth are the LORD's; upon them he has set the world. [9]He will guard the feet of his saints, but the wicked will be silenced in darkness. "It is not by strength that one prevails; [10]those who oppose the LORD will be shattered. He will thunder against them from heaven; the LORD will judge the ends of the earth. "He will give strength to his king and exalt the horn of his anointed."	[46]And Mary said: "My soul glorifies the Lord [47]and my spirit rejoices in God my Savior, [48]for he has been mindful of the humble state of his servant. From now on all generations will call me blessed, [49]for the Mighty One has done great things for me– holy is his name. [51]He has performed mighty deeds with his arm; he has scattered those who are proud in their inmost thoughts. [52]He has brought down rulers from their thrones but has lifted up the humble. [53]He has filled the hungry with good things but has sent the rich away empty. [54]He has helped his servant Israel, remembering to be merciful [55]to Abraham and his descendants forever, even as he said to our fathers."

[16]Text is from the NIV.

name that glorifies God. The explanation given in 1 Sam. 1:20 does not fit this exactly. Instead, it corresponds to the name Saul *(sha'ul)*, "that which has been asked for." The explanation of Samuel's name from the Hebrew verb *sha'al,* "to ask," can thus be seen as punning. Perhaps it draws on the story of Saul, showing that Samuel, not Saul, was the one approved by God.

Hannah's Psalm – 1 Sam. 2:1–11

The prayer of Hannah is really a psalm (1 Sam. 2:1–10). Perhaps it was one already known to Hannah. It was common for a psalm to be used as a prayer by an individual worshiper. Furthermore, placing the psalm at the beginning of Samuel's story also stresses what this meant for Israel. A new age was about to dawn in which God's will would be expressed in the monarchy (2:10).

The Priesthood of Shiloh – 1 Sam. 2:12–25

The outrageous conditions at the shrine at Shiloh contrast with the piety and devotion of Elkanah and Hannah. Eli's sons were not satisfied with the portions they were entitled to as priests. They abused their privileged position and stole, both from the people and from God (1 Sam. 2:12–17). Their failure to burn the fat, the part specifically belonging to God, was seen as an even worse crime. They even dared to take what should have been given to God. Their moral standards had slumped to the level of the Canaanites, treating the women serving at the Tent of Meeting as prostitutes (1 Sam. 2:22).

We can easily understand the reasons why God rejected Eli's priestly lineage. The text makes clear that Eli's line was corrupt and immoral. This was completely alien to the tradition of the Sinai covenant.[17]

How Did God Call Samuel to Ministry?
—1 Sam. 3:2–21

The narrative of Samuel's call is in the form of an "audition," or interview, with Yahweh (1 Sam. 3:1–14). Samuel was sleeping in the sanctuary, an appropriate place to receive a divine call. It was during this dialogue with God that Samuel learned that God would destroy Eli's priestly house. The story anticipates the coming transfer of authority from the house of Eli to Samuel. There were two factors involved in Samuel's calling. One was the corruption of Eli's sons. The second was the strength of Samuel's own personality. Later in Israel's history it would not have been possible for an individual to combine the offices of prophet, priest, and judge-administrator. These ministry functions would become more specialized.[18]

In 1 Samuel 2 through 3 the main lines of Samuel's career are established. He is depicted as heir to the functions and authority exercised by the priesthood of the house of Eli. Chapter 3 starts with the declaration that during those days visions were infrequent in Israel. This is probably to emphasize the events that follow in the chapter. Samuel was one through whom God spoke (3:19–20). He was called to be a messenger of God, the mediator of God's word.[19] As prophet he anointed and deposed kings and interceded for his people. Samuel was also associated

[17]Harrison, *Old Testament,* 710.

[18]R. P. Gordon, *1 and 2 Samuel* (Sheffield, England: JSOT Press, 1984), 27.

[19]Ackroyd, *Samuel,* 42, 190.

with the prophetic movement of his time.[20] Perhaps he founded the "school" called "the prophets" that later became the "sons of the prophets."

Samuel was also a priest, the successor to Eli, although this role appears to have been secondary. Besides Samuel, other priests, such as Abiathar, were prominent during the reign of David. We do not know for certain whether Samuel came from the priestly tribe of Levi. He is described initially as an Ephraimite of the Zuphite clan (1 Sam. 1:1). Elsewhere, though, he is referred to as one of a family of Levite singers (1 Chron. 6:16–30). Perhaps he was later adopted into that tribe.

Along with his priestly duties, Samuel was also a judge.[21] He led all Israel as judge and unsuccessfully tried to pass on the office of judge to his sons upon his retirement (1 Sam. 8:1–3).

Finally, Samuel is presented as the first great religious reformer after Moses. He set out to reverse the political and spiritual losses that mark the concluding chapters of the Book of Judges. He founded a prophetic school and established local sanctuaries after Shiloh was destroyed.[22]

The Philistines Capture the Ark
−1 Sam. 4:1b Through 7:2

What Happened at Aphek? − 1 Sam. 4:1b–11

A detailed report of a national disaster immediately follows the enthusiastic appraisal of Samuel as "a prophet of

[20]Kuntz, *Ancient Israel,* 176.

[21]Ackroyd describes Samuel as "one who adjudicates in the affairs of Israel, traveling on a circuit (7:15–16), and one who delivers Israel from her enemies" (1 Sam. 7:2–14; Ackroyd, *Samuel,* 190).

[22]Harrison, *Old Testament,* 710.

the LORD" (1 Sam. 3:19 through 4:1a). If Israel was to remain in Canaan, the Philistine threat needed to be addressed. The situation finally reached a climax at the battle of Aphek in the territory of Ephraim, not long after 1050 B.C. (1 Sam. 4). There the Philistines defeated the Israelite army and killed Eli's sons, Hophni and Phinehas. The Philistines then carried away the ark of the covenant. Probably the sanctuary at Shiloh was destroyed at that time.

Samuel himself, however, is conspicuously absent from the account. The text ascribes him no role in the preliminaries to the battle with the Philistines at Aphek/Ebenezer (4:1). Neither is he included in the arrangements for leaving the ark at Kiriath Jearim (7:1).

What Happened to the Ark?
—1 Sam. 4:12 Through 6:21

The circumstances surrounding the captured ark are reported in two short chapters. The gods of the Philistines met Yahweh in representative combat. This confrontation, interestingly, took place in Philistia, in the temple of Dagon at Ashdod.[23] It was customary for victorious armies in the Near East to place the gods of defeated nations in their temples. But, as the Philistines discovered, the God of Israel was not captured with the ark. The ark soon engendered considerable curiosity and was placed on public display (1 Sam. 5:4,6,9–10). The scene was now set for the contest to begin. The story that follows uses Dagon[24] as the repre-

[23]See Gordon, *1 and 2 Samuel*, 35.

[24]The older view that Dagon was represented partly as a fish is erroneous. The Ras Shamra texts give us insight into some of the forms of Canaanite religion and mythology. In them, Dagon, a vegetation and fertility god, especially connected with grain, appears as the father of Baal in ancient Ugarit. The Philistines probably combined the worship of the local people with

sentative god of Philistia. The ark was placed as a trophy in Dagon's temple. To the Philistines' consternation, Dagon was found prostrated before the ark on the following morning. From this point in the story, there is no further mention of the gods of the Philistines. In fact, Philistine priests begin to sound like Hebrew prophets (6:6).

What Afflicted the Philistines? —1 Sam. 5:9–12

The nature of the disease that afflicted the Philistines is uncertain. The Hebrew text itself is not clear. Was it "tumors" or "hemorrhoids"? Perhaps the word denotes swellings of the lymph glands, symptoms of bubonic plague. Rats could have spread such a plague.[25]

The Philistine priests and diviners decided on an appropriate "payment" to ease God's wrath; this payment took the form of their affliction (1 Sam. 6:1–6). The five tumors modeled in gold represented payment for each of the five rulers; the gold rats were payment for each of their towns.[26]

When the Philistines realized its connection to the plague, they decided to get rid of the ark. So, with magic and ceremony, they sent it to Beth Shemesh (1 Sam. 6:9,12). While it was there, seventy men carelessly looked inside it. They were slain immediately (6:19). After the disastrous reception at Beth Shemesh, the ark was deposited in Kiriath Jearim, where it remained throughout the entire reign of Saul.

Before *Raiders of the Lost Ark*

The abrupt nature of the narrative in 1 Samuel 6:19 warns about keeping a respectful distance from whatever is asssociated with the holy God. And certainly God himself is not to be taken casually!

---

their own. A shrine to Dagon was also found at Gaza (Judg. 16:23). See Ackroyd, *Samuel*, 54–55.

[25]Ibid., 55. A similar suggestion has been made for the disaster of the Assyrians in the time of Isaiah in 2 Kings 19:35//Isa. 37:36.

[26]An ancient principle of "Like cures like" is preserved for us here.

The End of the Judges
—1 Sam. 7 Through 8

The purpose of 1 Samuel 7 becomes clear when viewed in relationship to what follows. Already during the time of the Judges, proponents of monarchial rule were making themselves heard. Gideon, hero of the famous Midianite encounter, rejected the suggestion that he should assume royal power (Judg. 8:22–23). A short-lived royalist experiment even took place at Shechem (Judg. 9). Behind both these events was the Israelites' desire for immunity from attack by hostile neighbors. It was the Philistine crisis that reawakened these feelings in Israel. The rise of the monarchy marks Israel's transformation from a group of tribes to a nation. The importance of the development is reflected in the space given to it in 1 Samuel.

The Mizpah Crisis—1 Sam. 7:3–17

Samuel convened the people at Mizpah. There he challenged them to renounce their pagan ways and serve the God of their forefathers. He reminded them that only by trusting in God could they be delivered from the Philistines. Ironically, this very convocation attracted the attention of the enemy. The Philistines promptly attacked them. But God intervened, sending a great storm that unnerved the enemy. The Israelites were victorious and expelled the Philistines from their territory. In the victory celebration that followed, Samuel named the place "Ebenezer," meaning "Helpstone."[27]

[27]"Ebenezer" is a compound of 'eben, "stone," and 'ezer, "help"; see Gordon, *1 and 2 Samuel*, 41–42.

Israel Asks for a King — 1 Sam. 8:1–22

When Samuel grew old, the elders of Israel asked him for a king. They pointed out the failure of Samuel's sons to follow in his ways and asked for a king like other nations. Kingship was not something totally foreign to Israel. City-states in Canaan had kings, like Adoni-Bezek of Jerusalem (Judg. 1:5). Some of these kings were city kings, rulers of cities and the areas surrounding them. Others ruled people groups not unlike Israel.[28]

The monarchy was a controversial issue, and the pros and cons of the new institution are argued through 1 Samuel 7 through 12. Here, we are made aware of the differences between Israel's tribal governments and monarchial government at the end of the eleventh century B.C. In these chapters potential abuses of kingly power are outlined (8:11–18). (See Appendix 1: "Theology of Kingship.")

Was Saul Really Anointed King? — 1 Sam. 9 Through 11

This was no easy time to be chosen king. Although Saul had no standing army (1 Sam. 14:52), he found it necessary to constantly wage war. Tribal factions, however, made it difficult to unify the people. Saul, as king, was "a transitional figure standing somewhere between the Israelite judge and the Israelite king to follow."[29] And while he tried to present himself as a religious person, he did not really gain the support of the religious elements in Israel. Consequently, in his role as king, Saul inevitably competed with previously established religious offices and functions.

Confessing the King-Savior

The word translated "anointed" is the word *mashiᵃch*. It frequently designates Judah's or Israel's kings. This Hebrew word was rendered *christos* in Greek. From this we have the English "Christ" (and corresponding words in other modern languages). This title was given to Jesus in the New Testament. The term is itself a confession that he was the expected King-Savior. The Jews thought he would restore Israel's political independence and ultimately lead it to a position of world dominance. The record of Jesus' descent from David shows that early Christians considered him the Davidic Messiah.

[28]Ackroyd, *Samuel,* 71–72. See Gen. 36:31–39 for a list of kings of Edom.

[29]Kuntz, *Ancient Israel,* 180.

The question to ask, therefore, is whether Saul was really anointed king to rule over the people of Israel. Or was he to be a freedom fighter in the tradition of the judges of old, thus chosen for a specific purpose and a limited time?

Any answer to these questions must start with the warning note sounded by Samuel in 1 Samuel 8. Samuel condemned Israel's rejection of the theocratic ideal and also condemned their demand for an earthly king—*melekh*. God empowered Samuel to appoint a leader—*nagidh*—for the people (1 Sam. 9:16).[30] Some scholars see Samuel at Mizpah yielding with angry protest to popular pressure (10:17–27). What Samuel actually did was to remind the people of the covenant provisions. Samuel's attitude was essentially in harmony with his feelings expressed in chapter 8.

Following Saul's brilliant defeat of the Ammonites at Jabesh Gilead (1 Sam. 11:1–11), he was confirmed by the people as king at Gilgal (11:14–15). Following this, Samuel warned the people of the nature of the obligations they were about to assume (12:6–25). In one sense, the ceremony was similar to other enthronement ceremonies of monarchies in the Ancient Near East.[31] In these cultures, titles were important. Accordingly, Samuel's preference for *nagidh* rather than *melekh* in Saul's anointing would have been deliberate (1 Sam. 10:1). It is then possible that Saul's installation as king was a concession to the demands

[30]It is interesting to note that in 1 Sam. 9:16, when the prophet Samuel received his instructions from God to anoint Saul, the narrative uses the word *nagidh* (leader, "one who stands in front") and not the word *melekh* (king). The same word is used of David in 13:14; 25:30; and elsewhere. For a definition of *nagidh,* see Harrison, *Old Testament,* 707–8; see also Ackroyd, *Samuel,* 79.

[31]See John L. McKenzie, *A Theology of the Old Testament* (Garden City, N.Y.: Doubleday & Co., 1974), 247.

of the people (1 Sam. 11:14–15; cf. 8:4–9).[32]

Saul, Warrior and "Administrator"

Saul established the base for his rustic government at Gibeah, his hometown. There he began to assemble a militia. Saul was an effective military leader, yet he made no attempt to override tribal loyalties. He did not try to establish an elaborate government bureaucracy. Neither did he expend impressive sums and human effort to build a splendid capital.[33] Furthermore, in contrast to 1 Samuel 8:5, Saul does not appear as a king "such as all the other nations" had. Ancient kings exhibited two functions: They led in war and administered the law. While much is said about Saul's war activity, nothing is said of his role in law. Perhaps at this time Israel's king was not expected to function in this capacity. Throughout Saul's reign, tribal elders and tribal assemblies maintained their own laws.

Saul and the Prophets – 1 Sam. 10:9–12

Scholars have discussed at great length the nature of the ecstatic prophetism that suddenly appeared in the days of Samuel. Much of the debate centers on the meaning of the expression *han^evi'im,* "the prophets," later called the "sons of the prophets."[34] These were members of a prophetic

---

[32]See Harrison, *Old Testament,* 708.

[33]Excavations at Tell el-Ful (biblical Gibeah) have uncovered the ruins of a large, well-fortified building (169 by 114 ft.), thought to have been Saul's palace. Its interior lacked the gold, silver, and ivory found in the courts of later Israelite kings. Storage jars, grinding stones, arrowheads, and stones for slings found in the debris testify to Saul's "rustic simplicity" (Kuntz, *Ancient Israel,* 181).

[34]1 Kings 20:35; NIV translates the expression *b^eney han^evi'im* as "company of the prophets" in 2 Kings 2:3,5,15; 4:1,38; 5:22; 6:1; 9:1.

guild, or "school," possibly founded by Samuel. In the Old Testament the word *nabi'* designated a charismatic religious figure, someone who was authorized to speak or act on God's behalf. It could refer to someone not put in office by hereditary right or political appointment. This situation was in general accord with Ancient Near Eastern religious traditions. Nothing seems to indicate, however, that the prophetic guilds directed by Samuel had their origins in pagan religions. "Like other manifestations of the divine spirit they appeared spontaneously, and the ecstatic functions for which they were notable constituted but one aspect of their basic spirituality."[35]

Saul's encounter with the prophets appears strange. No previous indication is given that he was inclined to ecstatic spiritual expression. Prophetic rapture engendered by the divine Spirit, however, was manifest in both individuals and groups within the prophets' guild. It seems to have been one of its most powerful external elements. It appears as something contagious and overpowering, overtaking even bystanders (1 Sam. 19:18–24).

Saul's encounter with the divine Spirit was similar to the experiences of many of the judges. For example, the Spirit of the LORD "came upon" Gideon, and he was empowered to act (Judg. 6:34; see Appendix 1). When the divine Spirit ("wind" or "breath") rested upon a man, that man became something new. The words used in 1 Samuel 10:6 suggest a dynamic experience to describe the sense of power that overtakes such a person.[36]

The people who knew Saul recognized that something

[35]Harrison, *Old Testament,* 711.

[36]Ackroyd, *Samuel,* 84.

special had taken place. They expressed surprise at what they saw and asked whether Saul was also among the prophets.[37]

The Length of Saul's Reign – 1 Sam. 13:1

Throughout 1 and 2 Kings the reign of each king is introduced by means of a formula. For example, 2 Kings 22:1 says, "Josiah was eight years old when he became king, and he reigned in Jerusalem thirty-one years." In 1 Samuel 13:1, however, the Hebrew text omits Saul's age.[38] Only a few late manuscripts of the Septuagint have "thirty years old." However, this immediately calls into question Jonathan's age in relation to his responsible position in verse 2. Some scholars have offered the phrase "fifty years old."[39]

The length of Saul's reign is also uncertain. The Hebrew text does not have the word "forty." Acts 13:21 and Josephus[40] give Saul a forty-year reign. This assertion of both Acts and Josephus is very similar to the pattern found in the Book of Judges and to the length of Eli's rule over Israel (1 Sam. 4:18).[41]

---

[37]For an analysis of the expression "Is Saul also among the prophets?" see Ackroyd, *Samuel*, 85.

[38]See the NIV text notes on 13:1. Both "thirty" and "forty" are indicated as conjectures in NIV by the use of brackets. Translated literally, the Heb. text would read, "Saul was a year old when he became king, and he reigned over Israel two years." This is clearly an unacceptable meaning, hence the attempts to make sense of the text by emendation.

[39]This suggestion is based on two considerations: Saul had a grandson before his death (2 Sam. 4:4), and 1 Sam. 13:1 may contain a misunderstood abbreviation for the numeral. See Ackroyd, *Samuel*, 104.

[40]Josephus *Antiquities* 6.14.9 has eighteen years before Samuel's death and twenty-two after, though 10.8.40 has only twenty years altogether.

[41]Ackroyd, *Samuel*, 104.

Major Events in Saul's Reign — 1 Sam. 11 Through 15

Lifting the Ammonite Siege of Jabesh Gilead — 1 Sam. 11:1–15

In those days, a treaty accompanied the surrender of a town to its enemy. The terms were negotiable. The terms offered the inhabitants of Jabesh by the Ammonites were especially harsh. They were intended to humiliate Jabesh and "so bring disgrace on all Israel" (1 Sam. 11:2).[42]

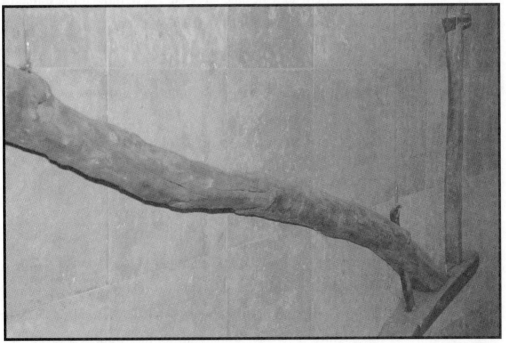

Arab Plow

Messengers brought Saul news of the town's impending surrender. They found him behind his oxen, returning from the fields. Saul was filled with anger at the Ammonite

[42]The Assyrians and the Babylonians gouged out the eyes of their captives (see 2 Kings 25:7). A similar provocation is found in the story of Ammon in 2 Samuel 10.

barbarity. The Spirit of God suddenly seized him.[43] Saul performed a gory and graphic act: He cut his oxen into pieces and sent a piece to each tribe as a summons to battle.[44] A great victory for Israel ensued. Saul's heroic exploit established his kingship and persuaded those who doubted him. Like Gideon and Jephthah, he had delivered his people from the enemy.

Samuel's Farewell – 1 Sam. 12:1-25

Having granted the people's request for a king, Samuel bade them a passionate farewell. He reminded them that he had been honest in his dealings with them. Then he summarized the history of the people. He emphasized God's deliverance through his chosen leaders. In verse 13 we find, side by side, two ironic reminders of their pleas for kingship: "'the king you have *chosen,* the one you *asked for.'"* He uses these words to remind them of the king asked for in lack of faith but granted by God.[45]

Where Did Saul Go Wrong? The Gilgal Incident – 1 Sam. 13:3-15

Quick to be proclaimed king by the people, Saul was as quickly rejected. From a group of 330,000 volunteers, Saul chose only 3,000 as a standing army (1 Sam. 11:8; 13:2). In a lightning strike, Jonathan, Saul's son, captured the Philistine outpost at Geba. The Philistines advanced and encamped at Micmash (13:5). Apparently Samuel had com-

---

[43]The same expression is used in 1 Sam. 10:6,10, where the Spirit empowered Saul for assuming leadership and transforming him in the process.

[44]The shock value of this action is similar to that of the Levite's with his concubine in Judg. 19.

[45]Ackroyd, *Samuel,* 99.

manded Saul to meet him at Gilgal so he could offer a sacrifice before the coming battle. As Saul waited for Samuel,
his men began to desert him. Since Samuel did not come at
the appointed time, Saul decided to offer the sacrifices himself. Saul's actions revealed his lack of faith; Samuel declared
him unfit to be king.[46] This was a "holy war." Prophets or
priests, not warrior-kings, were to offer sacrifices to God.[47]

Saul offered only pious excuses when confronted by
Samuel.[48] How could he face the enemy if the proper
offering had not been made and the favor of God sought?
Samuel reprimanded Saul for his disobedience. Obedience
could have saved Saul's dynasty, but now his line would
not endure. His heir, Jonathan, hero of the coming battle
at Micmash, would not succeed him.[49]

Jonathan and the Battle of Micmash
—1 Sam. 13:16 Through 14:45

At the opening of the story, Saul has stayed in Gibeah,
apparently uncertain of what to do. Israel, however, was
armed only with farm implements, because the Philistines
held a monopoly on the technology for smelting and forg-
ing iron. Ahijah,[50] the great-grandson of Eli, was serving as
priest in Saul's camp at Gibeah.

[46]This incident may be compared to Ahaz's lack of faith in a political emer-
gency and Isaiah's judgment of him (Isa. 7:1–17). Ackroyd, *Samuel,* 105, can
thus declare that the true king "must be one who is not deceived by external events into distrust of the God whose anointed he is."

[47]A similar judgment for usurping the priests' duties may be seen in
Azariah's (Uzziah's) leprosy (2 Chron. 26:16–21). Was Saul now trying to
add religious power to his office as king? See Kuntz, *Ancient Israel,* 182.

[48]See the similar excuse in 1 Sam. 15:15.

[49]See David's lament at his death in 2 Sam. 1:23.

[50]Ahijah can possibly be identified with Ahimelech (1 Sam. 21:1,8), since

Battle of Micmash

OPRAH

BETHEL

Lower
Beth Horon

GILGAL

Upper Beth Horon

MICMASH

AIJALON

GEBA

GIBEON

Kiriath Jearim

GIBEAH

JERUSALEM

BETH SHEMESH

BETHLEHEM

Wilderness of Judah

SALT
(DEAD)
SEA

0	2.5	5	7.5	10	12.5 Mls
0	5	10	15	20 Kms	

Wadi Suweinit
Where the battle against the
Philistines began

In a daring venture, Jonathan and his armor-bearer made their way down the steep side of the ravine that divided Geba from Micmash. Predicating his plan on God's favor—in contrast to his father's action—Jonathan and his aide climbed the far side of the crag and surprised a Philistine outpost. The Philistines had expected Saul to attack from the west, not from the rugged ravine to the south. They panicked! Saul, roused to action, inventoried his troops and discovered that his son Jonathan was missing. He quickly attacked and routed the Philistines while they focused on Jonathan and his armor-bearer. The result was the first military victory of Israel over the Philistines.

To impose an oath on an army was common in those days. Saul, however, required his soldiers to go without eating. Consequently, they were faint from hunger and exertion. Jonathan, because of his temporary absence, did not know about the oath (1 Sam. 14:27), so, innocently, he ate honey he found in the woods. Saul was ready to execute his own son for violating the oath, but the army came to Jonathan's defense. They pointed out that his victory clearly indicated divine favor. The focus of this story, however, is not that Jonathan was spared. It was, rather, that Saul had broken off his pursuit of the Philistines to concentrate on a petty matter—the oath. The enemy had escaped! Saul's failure clearly forecast his downfall.

When Do We Run Out of Second Chances? The Amalekite War—1 Sam. 15

The mounting tension between Saul and Samuel reaches a climax in this story. Through Samuel, God commanded

---

the divine title *melekh* (king) could be an alternative to the divine name *jah* (Yahweh): Ahijah = "Yahweh is my brother" and Ahimelech = "Melech [God as king] is my brother."

Saul to destroy the Amalekites.[51] After warning away the Kenites,[52] Saul attacked the Amalekites and defeated them. But he deliberately ignored the command to completely destroy the Amalekites. He spared Agag, the Amalekite king, and the best of the Amalekite livestock. Saul retained them as spoils of war to symbolize his victory. When Samuel confronted him, Saul tried to argue that he had saved the animals for sacrifice. Samuel responded in a classic example of prophetic speech: "'To obey is better than sacrifice, and to heed is better than the fat of rams'" (1 Sam. 15:22). Rejected by Samuel *and* by God, Saul's undoing was inevitable.[53]

Saul and David – 1 Sam. 16 Through 31

David Anointed King – 1 Sam. 16:1-13

We are introduced to David just after Samuel rebukes Saul for his conduct in the Amalekite war. God has sent Samuel to Bethlehem to anoint the youngest of Jesse's sons as Saul's replacement.[54]

---

[51]The Heb. text of 1 Sam. 15:3 tells Saul to make the Amalekites *cherem,* that is, to destroy them as a religious act (see Lev. 27:29; Exod. 22:20). This custom, sometimes rendered by "ban" or "devotion to destruction," required the slaughter of a captured people and their flocks. The language reflects the language of the conquest (for example, Josh. 2:10; 6:21). This practice was not confined to Israel (Harrison, *Old Testament,* 714; Ackroyd, *Samuel,* 122). The Moabite Stone, an inscribed pillar recording victories by Mesha, king of Moab in the ninth century B.C., describes his taking Nebo from Israel in identical terms: "taking it and slaying all, seven thousand men, boys, women, girls and maid-servants, for I had devoted them to destruction for (the god) Ashtar-Chemosh" (*ANET,* 320).

[52]The Kenites had very ancient ties with Israel. According to Judg. 1:16, Moses' father-in-law (Jethro) was a Kenite.

[53]Kuntz, *Ancient Israel,* 183.

[54]The Chronicler does not mention this anointing; see Kuntz, *Ancient Israel,* 183; Ackroyd, *Samuel,* 132.

Contrary to the selection criteria applied to Saul, David's tall and handsome brothers did not qualify.[55] The LORD told Samuel to pick David, the youngest. David's anointing, like Saul's, is associated with the power of the Spirit of the LORD coming upon him. For David, the manifestation of the power of the Spirit would be in his heroism and military prowess.

David Becomes Saul's Armor-Bearer and Musician —1 Sam. 16:14–23

The divine power and divine favor that had enabled Saul to win victories were withdrawn and transferred to David. In their stead "an evil spirit from the LORD" took possession of him (1 Sam. 16:14). That is, God gave Saul a destructive spirit, or disposition, that would eventually remove him from the throne.[56] As a result, Saul suffered bouts of paranoia and extreme depression. Apparently, music was the only thing that could bring him relief.[57]

After some time had passed, Saul sent for David to play the harp in his time of affliction. David is described not as a shepherd boy but as a warrior of experience, a "fine-looking" man skilled in the use of words (1 Sam. 16:18).

Saul made David one of his armor-bearers. As armor-bearer David was a close associate of the king and stood by his side in battle. His major function, however, was to soothe Saul with music "whenever the [evil] spirit from

[55]A good comparison can be made between the picture of Saul in 1 Sam. 9:2; 10:23 and that of David in 1 Sam. 16:12.

[56]See Judg. 9:23; and the discussion in William C. Williams, "Evil," in *Evangelical Dictionary of Biblical Theology,* ed. Walter Elwell (Grand Rapids: Baker Book House, 1996), 221–25.

[57]See also 2 Kings 3:15, where Elisha called for a musician to play, and the hand of God came upon him so that he prophesied.

God came upon" him (1 Sam. 16:23). There is irony here: Saul unwittingly took into his closest service the one who would replace him.

David Defeats Goliath – 1 Sam. 17

In this chapter we are introduced to an important aspect of warfare as practiced in ancient times. Instead of armies fighting each other, often a "champion" from one army would challenge a champion from the opposing one. The winner of this one-on-one combat would, in effect, win the battle for the whole army.[58] The uttering of curses and threats was part of the contest preceding the actual engagement. This strategy helped to muster courage before combat and to fluster the enemy and therefore gain a slim advantage. So the champion from the ranks of the Philistines was Goliath of Gath, a man of imposing stature,[59] wearing armor and brandishing a bronze spear, the point of which weighed about fifteen pounds or around seven kilograms.

At this point, David arrived on the scene. First Samuel 17:15 suggests that David – already in Saul's service according to 16:21–23 – spent part of his time at court and part at home. On this particular occasion he had come to bring

---

[58]A similar practice appears in 2 Sam. 2:12–16, where twelve young men from each side are to decide the outcome of the battle. The story of Sinuhe, dating from the second millennium B.C., tells how Sinuhe was forced into such combat. Single combat is also found in Greek stories, as between Achilles and Hector in bk. 4 of the Iliad, and much later in the sad Persian tale of Rostam and Sohrab.

[59]Harrison observes that some inhabitants of Canaan were "remarkable for their gigantic stature" (see the exploits of David's warriors in 2 Sam. 21:16–22). He believes these giants were "the remnant of a prehistoric group that inhabited areas of the Promised Land (Num. 13:33), and may have been connected with the Nephilim of Genesis 6:4" (*Old Testament,* 716).

some food to his brothers, since Israel's militia, not unlike those of other countries, was dependent on provisions from home to sustain itself. David was then made aware of Goliath's challenge and of the rewards to be given the one who would defeat him.

Declining Saul's armor, David resorted to his staff, his sling, and five smooth stones as his weapons.[60] More insults were exchanged. As the fight started, David won by throwing a well-aimed stone that struck the giant in the forehead. Standing over the dead Goliath, David then cut off his head.

The Philistine army was routed by fear, having lost confidence when their hero died. The Israelites were quick to give chase and plunder their camp.[61] David's exploit prompted Saul to inquire about David's parentage.[62] Satisfied, Saul let him remain at court.

A Loss of Courage?

David's conviction was that God is the deliverer; no human power could withstand, or bring victory against, him. Under the terms of the Philistines' challenge, if Goliath won, Saul and his army would surrender to them. One has to ask why Saul did not answer the challenge himself. Why did he send someone else? Is it possible that when the Spirit of God departed from him, so too did his courage?

[60]Slingers were a regular part of ANE armies, as can be seen on some Assyrian monuments. The accurate throwing of stones in this manner was a prized skill (see Judg. 20:16; 1 Chron. 12:2).

[61]The reference to Jerusalem in 1 Sam. 17:54 seems to be an anachronism. It was still a Jebusite city and did not come into David's possession until later (2 Sam. 5). It could also be that David was using Goliath's head to engage in a little psychological warfare with the residents of Jerusalem. Also, there is some ambiguity as to whether Goliath's weapons were taken to "his [David's] tent," or to "his (Yahweh's) tent-sanctuary," because in 1 Sam. 21:9 the "sword of Goliath" is in the sanctuary at Nob.

[62]There is no real contradiction here. Archer points out that in 1 Samuel 16:14–23 David is introduced as "a harpist employed to soothe Saul's troubled spirit" (*Old Testament Introduction*, 292). The "second introduction" of David to Saul (1 Sam. 17:55–58) is simply an inquiry about David's family (his father's name). Saul wanted only the best warriors as his personal bodyguard (1 Sam. 14:52). Archer adds, "It was quite appropriate for him to look into the possibilities of appointing Jesse or some of his other sons to his elite corps, after being treated to an example of the prowess of his youngest son in slaying the giant Goliath. First Samuel 18:1 suggests that a lengthy conversation ensued after Saul put his question to Abner concerning David, and we may reasonably infer that much more than mere names would have been discussed at that time."

Saul Becomes Jealous of David – 1 Sam. 18

David had many things going for him: He was physically attractive (1 Sam. 16:12), he was a skilled musician (16:16), he spoke well (16:18), he could be a man of combat when necessary (16:18; 17:1–54), and he enjoyed the support of Yahweh's presence (16:18). He also had developed a close and lasting friendship with Jonathan, Saul's eldest son (18:1). The bond between them took the form of a solemn covenant (18:3), being the same word (berith) used for the covenant between God and His people.[63]

The women from the surrounding towns came out to greet Saul with singing and dancing when he returned home. The words of the brief refrain given in 1 Sam. 18:7 are repeated in 21:11 and 29:5.[64] David's emergence into prominence paralleled Saul's own declining influence. Saul became jealous, realizing that David's popularity would have a negative effect on his own rule.

Back in his palace and under the influence of the evil spirit, Saul prophesied.[65] While in this state of confusion he tried to kill David with his spear, missing him twice. Driven by fear, Saul removed David from the court. He made him a military commander and sent him to fight the

[63]The fullest expression of the covenant with Jonathan may be found in David's lament at the death of Saul and his sons (2 Sam. 1:19–27, esp. vv. 25–26). See Ackroyd, *Samuel,* 147.

[64]In Exod. 15:21 a similar refrain is quoted, while in Exod. 15:1–18 there is a long psalm based on the same theme. In view of the tragic story in Judg. 11:31,34–40, it appears to have been customary for women to greet returning heroes with music and dancing.

[65]Ackroyd, *Samuel,* 150, comments: "We may note that the external effect of possession is the same whether the spirit is thought to be good or evil." The term used is that appropriate to prophetic ecstasy and speech. Saul, influenced by an evil spirit, may have been simply raving (see also 1 Sam. 19:18–24).

Philistines.[66] David was still victorious, however. Saul then offered David his eldest daughter, Merab, in marriage.[67] But Saul gave Merab to another. To pacify David, Saul offered him his second daughter, Michal.[68] Saul's evil intention of a hazardous assignment is now exposed. With Michal as the bait, Saul names the bride-price—one hundred foreskins of the Philistines![69]

The text does not say whether David suspected Saul's intentions. Marriage with Saul's daughter, however, would strengthen his eventual claim to be Saul's legitimate successor. Not satisfied to simply meet Saul's terms, David and his men brought back two hundred foreskins of the Philistines. This granted him the right to have Michal, but earned him greater animosity from Saul (1 Sam. 18:29).

David Pursued by Saul
—1 Sam. 19:1 Through 28:2; 29 Through 30

Through these chapters the relentless pursuit of David by Saul takes on dramatic proportions. Saul schemed to murder David. Jonathan, however, warned David and interceded with Saul for him. So David came back to Saul's court, playing his harp for the king. When "an evil spirit from the LORD came upon Saul," however, he tried a sec-

[66]David will use this same ploy to rid himself of Uriah after David's affair with Bathsheba.

[67]By all rights she was already David's, for Saul had promised his daughter to the champion besting Goliath (1 Sam. 17:25).

[68]This story is a reminder of the switch pulled on Jacob (Gen. 29:15–30); see also the incidents in the stories of Samson (Judg.14:1 through 15:2).

[69]Again, David's disclaimer that he was "only a poor man" (1 Sam. 18:23) seems to indicate that Saul has not met the terms set for the victor against Goliath (17:25). Furthermore, David was not "little known," since he is constantly, and favorably, compared to Saul by the people. Could it be that David was trying to diffuse some of the tension he sensed from Saul?

ond time to kill David with his spear (1 Sam. 19:9–10). David had no choice but to flee; nevertheless, instead of taking to the hills, he went back home to his wife. Saul dispatched his men to watch for him and kill him. David's house was apparently on the city wall, so he was able to escape from a window. Michal then took an idol, disguised it, and put it on David's bed.[70] She told Saul's men that David was too sick to be disturbed.

Saul and his men ardently pursued David.[71] David fled and went with Samuel to Naioth, near Ramah, where a group of prophets was prophesying. As Saul's men approached them, the Spirit of God came upon them and they prophesied. This situation forced Saul himself to go after David. On the way God's Spirit came upon Saul[72] and he, too, prophesied, apparently in an ecstatic state.

David, however, fled from Naioth and joined Jonathan. They renewed the covenant between them. It was called a "covenant of the LORD,"[73] suggesting that it may have been ratified before God, perhaps in a shrine.[74] The renewal of their mutual obligation now included a pledge that David would deal kindly with Jonathan's descendants when David became king (1 Sam. 20:15).

David and Jonathan devised a plan to discover Saul's true intentions. This plan, though, required Jonathan to tell Saul

[70]For a discussion of Michal's actions, see Ackroyd, *Samuel,* 158.

[71]This story is similar to the relentless attempts at arresting Elijah in 2 Kings 1:9–17.

[72]Ackroyd compares the incident to Num. 11:25–26, where "prophetic ecstasy" spreads from one group to another (Ackroyd, *Samuel,* 160).

[73]The Heb. text of 1 Sam. 20:8 calls it a *berith Yhwh,* "covenant of the LORD."

[74]Their bond (faithful love, *chesed*) corresponds to the bond which exists between God and Israel.

that David had gone to Bethlehem to make a sacrifice.[75] Upon hearing Jonathan's plea for David, the king, in a rage, called Jonathan an offensive name, implying that Jonathan's mother was a prostitute and that he was not a legitimate son. Saul worked himself into such a fury that he even tried to kill his own son. Having no other recourse, Jonathan put into action the previously devised plan. Once again, David had to flee for his life.

This time David went to Nob to get food and weapons from the priest Ahimelech (1 Sam. 21:1–9). The priest protested that he had only "the bread of the Presence" (v. 6).[76] Receiving the holy bread and Goliath's sword, David fled from Nob to Philistine Gath, hoping there to be safe from Saul. He received less than a warm welcome, however, from the Philistines. Some of them recognized him as Israel's champion. Fearing for his life, David pretended to be insane.[77] The Philistines allowed him to leave Gath and he fled to the cave of Adullam.

[75]This is not the first time that a lie is used in the story of David. Michal did the same thing (1 Sam. 19:11–17). While in its very essence a lie is something said with intent to deceive (i.e., Jer. 23:14), the Bible seems to permit such behavior only when a "greater good" is in view. Here that greater good is human life. Thus we can accept the action of Corrie ten Boom and her family who lied to the Germans in order to save Jews they were hiding.

[76]The "bread of the Presence," or "holy bread" (NKJV), was twelve loaves that were placed in the sanctuary on each Sabbath (Lev. 24:5,8). Only priests were allowed to eat it (see Mark 2:23–28), and ritual cleanliness was a requirement. The priest, apparently feeling that he was under duress, allowed the men to eat it. Ackroyd suggests that Jesus may have used this passage to identify himself as the new Davidic king. See *Samuel,* 171.

[77]The insane were regarded by the ancients as being possessed by a god and therefore untouchable. A humorous note is seen in this passage, however, where King Achish says: "'Look at the man! He is insane! Why bring him to me? Am I short of madmen that you have to bring this fellow here to carry on like this in front of me?'" (1 Sam. 21:14b–15a).

David's brothers and other relatives joined him in the cave of Adullam because they feared for their lives as well.[78] David was also joined by a band of malcontents.[79] To protect his mother and father, David left them in the care of the king of Moab.[80]

The prophet Gad, however, told David he must return to Judah.[81] Hearing of his return, Saul once again became intent on killing David. Saul's madness had driven him to extremes. He turned against the whole priestly house at Nob because they had helped David. He sent Doeg the Edomite to kill Ahimelech, eighty-five other priests, their families, and all their livestock.[82] Only Abiathar, one of Ahimelech's sons, escaped.[83]

David's quarrel, though, was with the Philistines, not with Saul. Upon hearing that the Philistines were pillaging the walled city of Keilah, David and his men delivered it from them. Hearing that David was in Keilah, Saul went there to lay siege to it. But David fled with his men before

[78]The risk to those who are connected with David becomes plain very quickly; see 1 Sam. 22:9–23.

[79]Compare Jephthah, Judg. 11:3.

[80]One can certainly see here the old maxim "The enemy of my enemy is my friend" in action.

[81]This same Gad appears as prophetic adviser in 2 Sam. 24. Later tradition (1 Chron. 29:29–30) ascribes to Samuel, and to Gad and Nathan, the other prophets closely associated with David, the recording of the events of the period of David.

[82]Josephus (*Antiquities* 6.12.7; 14.9) attributes Saul's downfall to this atrocity and to the failure described in 1 Sam. 15. Ackroyd comments, "It is as if the city had been put to the ban, a terrible reversal of that holy war which is waged against the opponents of God." *Samuel,* 179.

[83]Abiathar, strangely, would later support Adonijah's bid for the throne (1 Kings 1:7; also see chap. 11, "Israel Acquires Empire").

the citizens could betray him to Saul.[84] They took refuge in the Desert of Ziph, and while they were there, Jonathan came to encourage David. Once again they renewed the covenant they had made. Jonathan, who saw himself as occupying second place, made the most explicit statement yet of David's coming kingship (1 Sam. 23:17); even Saul was aware of it.

The Ziphites were only too happy to betray David to Saul. The picture we are given is that of the relentless Saul, going from cave to cave, looking for David (1 Sam. 23:19–26). It was only increased Philistine aggression that forced Saul to give up the chase–for the moment!

Waterfall at En Gedi
Where David found rest

[84]By handing him over, the villagers could hope for clemency, most certainly fearing that what had happened to Nob might also happen to them. This story may be compared with that of Sheba at Abel Beth Maacah in 2 Sam. 20:14–22; such might have been David's fate had he not been divinely warned to escape.

David went to En Gedi to find some rest. There he had the opportunity to kill Saul when he came into the cave where David and his men were hiding.[85] Killing Saul would have been easy, and it would have ended David's life as a hunted man. David, however, would not harm the LORD's anointed (1 Sam. 24:6,10).[86] He cut off a piece of Saul's robe to show him that he had been in his power.[87] After Saul left the area, David revealed himself and showed Saul the piece of his robe. He affirmed his loyalty to Saul, who reacted positively. He recognized David's coming kingship and asked a solemn oath from David that he would not harm his family.[88]

At Samuel's death, he was buried in Ramah, his home-town (1 Sam. 25:1). In the same chapter we learn how David, still in the desert,[89] came to marry the beautiful Abigail, former wife of the miser Nabal. Apparently David offered the wealthy men in the area the services of him and his men to protect them from desert raiders.[90] Those who

[85]This story (1 Sam. 24) is the first of two narratives that relate how David, having Saul in his power, refuses to take advantage of the situation. The second can be found in 1 Sam. 26.

[86]In 2 Sam. 1:1–16 David executes the Amalekite who claims to have "killed the LORD's anointed." It is David's respect for the divine will expressed in Saul's position that is the motivating factor.

[87]R. A. Brauner, "Old Aramaic and Comparative Semitic Lexicography," *Gratz College Annual Jewish Studies* 6 (1977), 26–27, argues that on the basis of ANE parallels, one could understand David's action as not only removing Saul's sovereignty over him, but also eliminating that by which David could ally himself with Saul. See also Ackroyd, *Samuel*, 188.

[88]The outcome of this can be seen in David's lament in 2 Sam. 1:19–27, and especially in his protection of Mephibosheth, the surviving son of Jonathan (2 Sam. 9). However, another, darker, side of David's conduct toward the house of Saul is shown in the grim tale in 2 Sam. 21.

[89]The place-names Carmel and Jezreel in this story are generally considered to be southern locations, not to be confused with their northern counterparts.

[90]Ackroyd, *Samuel*, 195; 1 Sam. 25:15–16,21; see also 1 Sam. 27; 30.

responded to his demand for "gifts" were protected; those who did not were not. Nabal defaulted on what David perceived as a debt, insulting him in the process. In the events that ensued, Abigail was able to head off bloodshed, winning David's admiration. When Nabal died after a drunken party (25:36–39), David saw it as an act of God. Nabal was a Calebite, a member of a powerful tribe in the south, closely associated with Judah. An alliance by marriage with that group would prove advantageous for David.[91] Nabal's death offered David the opportunity to marry into that tribe. David's marriage to Ahinoam of Jezreel also represents the purposeful establishing of links with the southern clans.[92]

But what had become of Michal, daughter of Saul, earlier given to David as his wife? In David's absence, she had been given to another husband, probably because she played a part in saving David (1 Sam. 19:11–17).[93]

The story found in 1 Sam. 26 is similar to that of chapter 24. Accompanied by his nephew Abishai,[94] David sneaked into Saul's camp during the night and took Saul's spear and water jar. David again had the opportunity to kill Saul but did not raise a hand against him. Taunting Abner, Saul's general, for being unable to adequately protect his king, David demonstrated once again that he could have taken Saul's life. Upon hearing David, Saul again repented,

[91]David was made king at Hebron, the main town of the Calebites (see Judg. 1:20).

[92]Some further details of David's marriages are given in 2 Sam. 3:2–5.

[93]She would later be restored to David as part of a political bargain (2 Sam. 3:13–16) and would again be involved in David's affairs (2 Sam. 6).

[94]Abishai, along with Joab, plays an important role in the story of David; there is also a third brother, Asahel. According to 1 Chron. 2:16 their mother was Zeruiah, David's sister.

but his change of heart did not last. David went back to his life as an outlaw, while Saul returned to Gibeah.

David and his wives, along with his men and their families, took refuge with Achish, king of Gath. By this time, Achish had heard that Saul was David's enemy. So when David asked Achish for a town, Achish gave him the town of Ziklag. From there David raided the desert tribes that had troubled Judah's southern frontier. To the Philistines, however, he pretended he was attacking Judah and its allies. David's position was very delicate and liable to be misunderstood. The story is full of irony, however. While Achish thought David had become a Philistine vassal, David was steadily preparing the way for his own rule.

The eerie story of Saul's consultation with the "witch" of Endor follows (1 Sam. 28). It interrupts the narrative of the Philistine war. At one time Saul had taken action against necromancy and other religious practices that were contrary to Yahweh's claim to exclusive worship.[95] But as chapter 28 opens, we find Saul in the hills of Gilboa on the eve of battle with the Philistines. Naturally, Saul wanted a word from the LORD, but he could not get one. He received no guidance from Urim,[96] dreams, or prophets. Accordingly, he turned to necromancy. Without apparent difficulty, Saul's servants found a woman who could answer Saul's inquiries. The device she would use, an 'ov, was probably a pit used for summoning the gods of the underworld, the

Predicting the Future

Divination was a common way of predicting the future in the ancient world. Types of divination included belomancy (lots or arrows), rhabdomancy (rods), physiognomy (human behavior and facial expression), cheiromancy (palms), oneiromancy (dreams), teratology (unusual or monstrous births), hepatoscopy (animal livers), ornithomancy (birds), ophimancy (reptiles), dendromancy (trees), empyromancy (flames), kapnomancy (smoke), lecanomancy (oil in water), astrology (heavenly bodies and meteorology; see Matt. 2:1–7).[97]

[95]Deut. 18:10–11 provides a list of forbidden practices. "But witchcraft and astrology and necromancy and the like always hold a certain fascination for those who have no secure faith" (Ackroyd, *Samuel*, 211). See also Isa. 8:19.

[96]The Urim and Thummim were probably lots carried by the priest for making decisions at times when the *torah* provided no guidance.

[97]See McKenzie, *Old Testament*, 68.

abode of the dead (cf. Isa. 8:19; 19:3).[98] When Saul asked the woman to bring up Samuel, the result was not what the woman had expected.[99] And Samuel did not intercede for Saul nor did he reveal to him the purposes of God. Instead, Samuel pronounced a chilling judgment on Saul, his family, and his soldiers.

Meanwhile, David had joined Achish, who was on his way to fight Israel. But the commanders of the Philistine army were not so eager to have him. A man who has once deserted can hardly be trusted not to do so again. A judicious change of sides in the middle of the battle could certainly affect its outcome. It would possibly decide the battle, restoring David to favor with Saul. David was spared the decision of whether to fight against Israel or the Philistines, however. Achish sent him back to Ziklag and the Philistines went against Saul without him.

Upon returning home, David and his men discovered that the Amalekites had raided the town. They had taken captive all its inhabitants and burned the city. In great distress, David and his men pursued the Amalekites. Overtaking the raiders, they rescued their wives, sons and daughters, and all their possessions. They also seized a great quantity of livestock. The booty was shared equally among David's men, both those who had gone to battle and those who had stayed behind (1 Sam. 30:24).[100] The plunder was

[98]Harry A. Hoffner, "Second Millennium Antecedents to the Hebrew '*ob* ['ov]," *Journal of Biblical Literature* 86 (1967): 385–401. The '*ov* was apparently opened on certain occasions, offerings poured into it (including honey, forbidden in biblical offerings), and the infernal deities of the netherworld summoned. The Heb. text of 1 Sam. 28:13b literally says "I see gods ascending out of the earth" (see NIV footnote). This was, after all, what she had expected to see.

[99]See Ackroyd, *Samuel*, 213–14.

[100]The same principle is enunciated in Num. 31:27 and Josh. 22:8.

so plentiful that David sent some of it to numerous places in the area where he and his men were active.[101]

Saul's Tragic Death
—1 Sam. 31; 2 Sam. 1; 1 Chron. 10

Israel's army suffered defeat in the battle in the Gilboa hills. Many were slain, three of Saul's sons among them.[102] Saul was critically wounded and rather than fall into Philistine hands,[103] asked his armor-bearer to kill him. When the armor-bearer refused, Saul fell on his own sword, committing suicide.[104]

When they saw the defeat of Israel's army and the death of Saul and his sons, the Israelites who inhabited the region fled. The Philistines acquired the whole fertile area to the north and east of the central hill country.

Not satisfied with their victory, the Philistines cut off Saul's head and stripped off his armor. They put the armor in the temple of the Ashtoreths.[105] Saul's body was nailed to the walls of Beth Shan, together with the bodies of his

---

[101]Ackroyd, *Samuel,* 225; see 2 Sam. 2:4.

[102]It appears that Saul had four sons. The three mentioned here, Jonathan, Malki-Shua (see 1 Sam. 14:49), and Abinadab, appear to have been the older ones. The fourth son, Ish-Bosheth, challenged David's claim to be Saul's heir and successor. It appears from 2 Sam. 2:8 that the challenge succeeded only because of Abner's backing.

[103]The story of Samson (Judg. 16) is a good example of what could happen to Saul if captured.

[104]See William Raccah, "Kill Me, Kill Me Not: The Bible's Moral and Ethical Dimensions to Suicide," *Eastern Journal of Practical Theology* 4, no. 2 (fall 1990): 18–25.

[105]A temple dedicated to a goddess and belonging to this period has been discovered at Beth Shan; this is probably the temple of the Ashtoreths mentioned here.

three sons.[106] The men of Jabesh, however, remembered that Saul had saved them from the Ammonites (1 Sam. 11:1–11). At the risk of their lives, they went by night to Beth Shan and took down the bodies. So the Philistines could mutilate them no further, they brought the bodies back to Jabesh, burned them, and buried the ashes.

An Amalekite brought David news of Saul's and Jonathan's deaths. Hoping to curry favor with David, he claimed to have killed Saul. David, however, saw him for the villain he was and ordered him to be executed. David sang a lament over these dead heroes and the defeat of Israel's army (2 Sam. 1:17–27).

Appendix 1: Theology of Kingship

The peoples of the Ancient Near East justified their political systems by appealing to their gods. For example, in Egypt, the pharaoh was the incarnation of one of the gods, often Horus, son of Re.[107] Ideas like this furnished the context for Israel's interpretation of kingship. Small wonder that some Israelites saw kingship as an act of rebellion against God! Others, however, considered it a necessity. The old tribal organization had provided a degree of stability for the community. Yet this did not seem to be enough. Divine election, or approval, of the monarch was a very important element of Ancient Near Eastern thought. Neither the king nor his subjects felt at ease without explicit declarations that the king was the god's man.

Ancient Near Eastern kingship was no mere political

[106]The exposure of enemy bodies was a common Assyrian practice. First Chronicles 10:8–10 records that Saul's head was deposited in the temple of Dagon.

[107]McKenzie, *Old Testament,* 178.

convenience. Rather, it was an essential element in the divinely ordered structure of the universe. In both Egypt and Mesopotamia, the king-god had an important part to play in the religious ritual of the community. In fact, he was an indispensable link in the chain that bound the community to its gods.[108] The Israelite king, however, was not to be thought of as divine. Hebraic thought was too conscious of the gulf between God and even the greatest of men.[109]

Why did kingship appear at this moment? Why not before, when Israel was establishing itself in Canaan? Answers to these questions are varied. The Philistine pressure necessitated a more central and uniform control. Surrounding nations had kings. Earlier heroes (e.g., Gideon and Jephthah) had already been kings in everything but name.

Conflicting attitudes about kingship are found in 1 Samuel 8 through 9. Chapter 8 criticizes the people's lack of faith in desiring a king. Chapter 9 (especially 9:16) promises a blessing to the leader whom Samuel was to anoint. The old tribal organization—local heroes, priests, and prophets—was highly valued by the community. But a change was in the winds! The promonarchic view may be seen in God's choices, made known by revelation to Samuel (1 Sam. 9:16; cf. 16:1). The antimonarchic perspective emphasizes the candidate as chosen by lot (1 Sam. 10:17–27).

From the biblical evidence, we can see that God gives kingship. Yet he criticizes it as an institution prone to failure. On the one hand, the monarchy was known to be a source

---

[108]Robert Davidson, *The Old Testament* (New York: J. B. Lippincott Co., 1964), 216–17.

[109]Ibid., 218; Deut. 17:14–20.

of blessing. The king was God's chosen, the mediator of God's blessing, He was called God's anointed, the "lamp of Israel" (2 Sam. 21:17). On the other hand, it was a failure. Israel's kings led their people to disaster.[110] Therefore, kingship, as a human institution, came under divine judgment.

Yahweh was experienced through the institutions of the tribal confederation. Based on Deut. 17:14–20, some within ancient Israel, therefore, concluded that Yahweh could not be experienced through monarchic institutions.[111] When human kingship was given absolute power, it was seen as an infringement on the kingship of Yahweh.[112] Limitations on the monarchy can be found as early as the Book of Deuteronomy.[113] In the beginning, it seems that Israel's kingship was considered an extension of Israel's judgeships.[114] In David's later years, however, political and economic abuses began to appear. They became progressively more severe with Solomon and his successors in the divided kingdoms.

Kings as Charismatic Leaders

A feature that set Israel's kings apart from other Near Eastern kings was their charismatic endowment. The term "charismatic leader," coined by Max Weber, has become a

[110]Ackroyd, *Samuel,* 93.

[111]McKenzie, *Old Testament,* 246.

[112]See Judg. 8:23; 1 Sam. 8:7; 12:12.

[113]See Deut. 17:14–20 for the criteria for kingship: He must be chosen by God, one from among the people of Israel; he must not acquire many horses for himself, nor have many wives, nor accumulate much gold or silver; he is to have a copy of the law and read it daily, and should not consider himself better than his fellow Israelites.

[114]Ackroyd, *Samuel,* 73.

commonplace term in Old Testament theology.[115] It has been applied to Moses, Joshua, and all the ancient prophets. More precisely, it pertains to men who received the Spirit of Yahweh, for this is what the Israelites believed the charisma was.[116] Charismatic figures first appear in the Book of Judges. They were heroes, most of them military leaders, who delivered Israel from its enemies.[117] The Spirit's coming upon Saul was altogether in character with the Spirit's action in the Book of Judges (1 Sam. 11:6).[118] The Spirit that fell upon these heroes was unpredictable and came from no visible source. It was like the wind, the same Hebrew word (ruᵃch) rendered "spirit." The "breath of Yahweh" moved ordinary people to do heroic deeds.[119] For the judges, the Spirit's anointing was for a very specific time and purpose. But the king's anointing would be relatively permanent.

In ancient monarchies the king was both the source of law, and its enforcer. The period of Israel's monarchy seems to have been a setback for covenant law. Yet Israel's kingship came into existence in a community with an extensive and well-defined tradition of common law. The Old Testament says very little about royal law, but presents the king as

[115]See Gerhard Von Rad, *Old Testament Theology* (New York: Harper & Row, 1962), 1:93–102.

[116]McKenzie, *Old Testament,* 248.

[117]Accordingly the Spirit is said to come upon Othniel (Judg. 3:10), Gideon (6:34), Jephthah (11:29), and with strange frequency upon the most unlikely of the judges, Samson (13:25; 14:6,19; 15:14).

[118]The Spirit's falling upon Saul in 1 Sam. 19:23 (and upon his messengers in 19:20), however, was quite another matter. Its effect was ecstatic worship, not charismatic leadership, which had earlier been taken from Saul (1 Sam. 16:14).

[119]McKenzie, *Old Testament,* 249.

judge and shows the institution of royal judges.[120]

For Israel, kingship was an institution rich in theological meaning. Its model was the kingship of God over Israel and over all nations.[121] The way the human king established his rule and his justice parallels God's activity. Thus the true king was to uphold justice and righteousness. In doing this, he would become a source of blessing to his people.[122] The creation of an Israelite kingdom and empire, however, resulted in state bureaucracy and taxation. These components contributed greatly to the schism of the late tenth century.

The Rise of the Monarchy —1 Sam. 9 Through 15

The story of Saul's emergence as Israel's first king proceeds through a number of stages. First, the tribal elders of Israel request a king (1 Sam. 8:1–22). Saul's private anointing follows (9:1 through 10:16). Then, there is a divine nomination and a public presentation (10:17–27). Military success ensues, leading to a public acclamation (11:1–15). Samuel then makes a final speech (12:1–25).[123]

Saul's physical strength and handsome appearance were considered divine gifts. He seemed a man of limitless valor and was regarded as a hero in the tradition of the judges. From the tribe of Benjamin, Saul was a man of wealth; the list of ancestors given in 1 Samuel 9:1 indicates a family of

[120]Ibid., 82.

[121]See 1 Sam. 8:7 and such Psalms as 47; 96 through 98.

[122]Ackroyd, *Samuel,* 94. See Isa. 11:1–9 and Ps. 72 for pictures of the ideal king.

[123]Gordon, *1 and 2 Samuel,* 40.

standing. In anointing Saul, Samuel conferred upon him a further status. (For a discussion of anointing, see Appendix 2.)

Appendix 2: Theology of Anointing

Throughout the Ancient Near East, anointing was used in many different settings and for different purposes. Oil was used in private life for cosmetic as well as hygienic purposes. It was also believed that anointing had healing powers. In the legal sphere, "it was used in the manumission of slaves, to confirm betrothals and purchases, to install vassals, substitutionary kings and probably also real kings."[124] It is very likely that the Hittites practiced anointing and that it was a part of their enthronement ceremony. It was also practiced in Egypt. Canaanite vassal kings were anointed to install them in office.

The practice of anointing priests is an ancient one, dating from Sumerian times. In the Old Testament we find mention of the practice of anointing and a short description of the act itself.[125] Among the Israelites, priests were anointed with oil and blood to install them in office (Lev. 8).[126] In due time, anointing was extended to kings as well. The oil signified the anointed one as designated for a certain purpose.

Contrary to the neighboring nations, in which the king's anointing bore legal functions, Saul's (1 Sam. 10:1) reflected a theological purpose. It emphasized the divine election of the king. The same is true of David's anointing (1 Sam. 16:13) in which divine election was the principal function of

---

[124]Ake Viberg, "The Concept of Anointing in the Old Testament," *Journal of the European Pentecostal Theological Association* 16 (1996): 19.

[125]Ibid., 19.

[126]Daniel Fleming, "The Biblical Tradition of Anointing Priests," *Journal of Biblical Literature* 117, no. 3 (fall 1998): 414.

Samuel's action. God, and no one else, chose Saul's successor.

An important distinction must be noted regarding Saul's
and David's anointing. Persons and objects—for example,
priests, the Tent of Meeting and its furniture, the ark of the
covenant, and kings—were anointed to show their sacral
character. The sacredness of kingship is clearly seen in
David's reverence for Saul (1 Sam. 24:6–7,11; 26:9,11,23;
2 Sam. 1:14). The king was the anointed of Yahweh. The
sacredness of the office of king is the one element that
characterized the reigns of both Saul and David. Only in
the stories of Saul[127] and David[128] are we told that the Spirit
came upon them during their anointing.[129]

[127]Viberg notes that with the anointing of Saul (1 Sam. 10:5–6,9–10; cf.
11:6; 16:14), "the Spirit of God comes upon Saul afterwards, and the two
seem to relate like cause and effect." Saul's anointing has led to his transformation (1 Sam. 10:9), "which is precisely what the coming of the Spirit is
said to accomplish, as well (1 Sam. 10:6, 11)." Saul's prophesying is "the initial indication that he has changed, but the fundamental change is what
comes afterwards, i.e., his dynamic actions (compare Jdgs 14:6,19; 15:14)"
(*Concept of Anointing*, 27).

[128]Viberg notes the similarities of David's and Saul's anointing and reception
of the Spirit. It is only after receiving the Spirit that David does his mighty
deeds (e.g., slaying Goliath) (Ibid., 27).

[129]McKenzie observes that Solomon does not receive the Spirit, but wisdom,
which he terms "another charism" (1 Kings 3; McKenzie, *Old Testament*,
252).

Study Questions

1. What factors led to the emergence of the Israelite monarchy?

2. Compare the story of Samuel's birth to its parallels elsewhere in the Bible. Hint: See note 15.

3. Compare Samuel's "call" (1 Sam. 3:1–14) with Jacob's at Bethel (Gen. 28:11–18) and Isaiah's upon the death of the king (Isa. 6).

4. How does Deuteronomy 18:22 apply to Samuel?

5. Describe Canaanite religion, with its deities and temple worship.

6. Compare the rise of the monarchy in 1 Samuel to similar situations in the Book of Judges.

7. Compare the idealized Israelite concept of monarchy (Deut. 17:14–20) and that held by its neighbors. What are the differences between a "leader" and a "king"?

8. Compare the anointings of Saul, David, and Jesus.

9. Explore ancient prophetism and how it manifested itself in ancient Israel.

10. In which instance is "holy anger" acceptable? Compare Saul's actions in 1 Samuel 11 with Jesus' cleansing of the temple.

11. Why did Samuel regard Saul's sacrifices in 1 Samuel 13:7–15 as sacrilegious? How did they lead to Saul's downfall?

12. Define the concept of "holy war" in Israel.

13. Discuss 1 Sam. 14:24–45 in terms of a conflict between the principles of divine favor and divine displeasure.

14. Using 1 Samuel 17; 2 Samuel 21:19; and 1 Chronicles 20:5, take a closer look at the story of David and Goliath.

15. Analyze the covenant between David and Jonathan. What are its main points?
16. Summarize David's attitude toward Saul. What principles can we draw from this?

For Further Reading

Campbell, Antony F. *The Ark Narrative (1 Sam. 4–6; 2 Sam. 6): A Form-Critical and Traditio-Historical Study.* Missoula, Mont.: Society of Biblical Literature and Scholars Press, 1975.

Dunn, D. M. *The Fate of King Saul.* JSOT Supplement 14. Sheffield, England: JSOT Press, 1980.

Foresti, Fabrizio. *The Rejection of Saul in the Perspective of the Deuteronomistic School.* Rome: Edizioni del Teresianum, 1984.

Garsiel, Moshe. *The First Book of Samuel: A Literary Study of Comparative Structures, Analogies and Parallels.* Ramat Gan, Israel: Revivim Publishing House, 1985.

Horn Prouser, Ora. "Suited to the Throne: The Symbolic Use of Clothing in the David and Saul Narratives." *Journal for the Study of the Old Testament* 71 (1996): 27–37.

McCarter, P. K., Jr. *1 Samuel.* Garden City, N.Y.: Doubleday & Co., 1980.

Miscall, Peter D. *1 Samuel: A Literary Reading.* Bloomington, Ind.: Indiana University Press, 1986.

Noth, Martin. *The History of Israel.* New York: Harper & Row, 1960.

Philips Long, V. *The Reign and Rejection of King Saul: A Case for Literary and Theological Coherence.* Atlanta, Ga.: Scholars Press, 1989.

Yadin, Y. *The Art of Warfare in Biblical Lands.* New York: MacGraw-Hill Book Co., 1963.

11

Dale Brueggeman

Israel Acquires Empire

Outline:

- What Are the Sources for This Story?
- Shouldn't Israel Have Expected a Monarchy?
- David and the Empire
- Solomon and the Temple
- Theological Aspects of David's Dynasty

Terms:

cherem
chesed
Chronicler
covenant
Davidic covenant
dynasty
myth/mythology
Transjordan

What Are the Sources for This Story? —2 Sam. 1 Through 1 Kings 11; 1 Chron. 10 Through 2 Chron. 9

Parallel accounts provide contrasting perspectives on the rise of the monarchy (2 Sam. 1 through 1 Kings 11; 1 Chron. 10 through 2 Chron. 9).[1] Having parallel accounts of the monarchy's history is like having four gospel sources for Jesus' life. Samuel was responsible for some of the material (1 Chron. 29:29–30), but he dies early in the books (1 Sam. 25:1; 28:3), and 2 Kings concludes with the exile (586 B.C.). So the final editing of Samuel-Kings should be dated sometime between 561 and 539 B.C.[2]

Shouldn't Israel Have Expected a Monarchy? — Gen. 17:6; 35:11; 49:10; Num 24:7; Deut. 17:14–20

Before Saul, Israel had nothing resembling a king. God ruled, announcing his decisions through his anointed

---

[1]Robert L. Cate lists the following parallel accounts: the sudden end of Eli's house (1 Sam. 2:21–26; 3:11–14), Saul anointed as king (1 Sam. 9:26 through 10:1; 10:17–24; 11:15), Saul deposed from throne but still ruling until his death (1 Sam. 13:14; 15:26–29), David introduced to Saul (1 Sam. 16:14–23; 17:55–58), David offered a daughter of Saul in marriage (1 Sam. 18:17–19,20–21a,22b–29a), David escapes from Saul's court never to return (1 Sam. 19:12; 20:42b), Saul aware of David's first flight but later wonders why David was not at dinner (1 Sam. 19:17; 20:26–29), David has Saul in his power and spares his life (1 Sam. 24:3–7; 26:5–12), David makes a covenant with Jonathan (1 Sam. 18:3; 20:26–42; 23:18), David seeks refuge from Achish king of Gath (1 Sam. 21:10–15; 27:1–4), Goliath slain by David or by Elhanan (1 Sam. 17; 19:5; 21:9; 22:10b,13; 2 Sam. 21:19; 1 Chron. 20:5), proverb about David's and Saul's military prowess (1 Sam. 10:11; 19:24), the Ziphite treason (1 Sam. 23:19; 26:1), Saul's death (1 Sam. 31:4; 2 Sam. 1:6–10). See Robert L. Cate, *An Introduction to the Old Testament and Its Study* (Nashville: Broadman, 1987), 238–39.

[2]Samuel-Kings shows an acquaintance with the beginning of Evil-Merodach's reign in Babylon (2 Kings 25:27), which is dated at 561 B.C., but shows nothing of the return from exile that began in 539 B.C.

leaders.[3] But God had spoken of legitimate kingship to come.[4] Deuteronomy even included regulations for the future king, "The Law of the Kings" (17:14–20).[5]

Samuel-Kings begins with the sorrow of a barren woman, Hannah, a humble mother with royal expectations that manifest themselves in song: She foresees that the coming anointed king will enjoy the LORD'S protection. This will be one of the unifying themes in Samuel.[6] Further, her song is echoed by David's royal song toward the end of his reign (and the Book of Samuel: 2 Sam. 22:1 through 23:7).

Comparing the Songs of . . .	Hannah	David[7]
Rejoicing over deliverance from enemies	1 Sam. 2:1	2 Sam. 22:3–4
Celebrating God as a rock	1 Sam. 2:2	2 Sam. 22:32; 23:3
Sh^eol (i.e., the grave)	1 Sam. 2:6	2 Sam. 22:6
God thundering in the darkness	1 Sam. 2:10	2 Sam. 22:14,29
Rejoicing in protection of the faithful	1 Sam. 2:9	2 Sam. 22:26
Rejoicing in God's *chesed* for the anointed one	1 Sam. 2:10	2 Sam. 22:51; 23:1
Twin motifs of exalting and debasing	1 Sam. 2:6	2 Sam. 22:28
Killing and making alive	1 Sam. 2:6	2 Sam. 22:17–20

Saul had made a mediocre start on the concerns of Deuteronomy 17. He left the tribal organization intact and didn't impose a heavy bureaucracy. Instead, he ran things from a practical, fortified headquarters rather than from an

[3]For example, Moses or the priests using the Urim and Thummim (Exod. 28:30; Num. 27:18–21).

[4]Gen. 17:6; 35:11; 49:10; Num. 24:7; Judg. 8:22,23; 9:1–6; 17:6; 18:1; 19:1; 21:25.

[5]See chap. 9, "Canaan: Conquest, Covenant Renewal, and Crisis."

[6]1 Sam. 16:3,6,12–13; 24:6; 26:9,11,16,23; 2 Sam. 1:14,16; 3:39; 19:21.

[7]R. Polzin, *Samuel and the Deuteronomist* (San Francisco: Harper & Row, 1989), 24–25; Brevard S. Childs, *Introduction to the Old Testament as Scripture* (Philadelphia: Fortress, 1979), 272.

ostentatious palace with a harem and retinue.[8] But there is no report of Saul copying the Torah—or showing any special piety. On the contrary, Saul was destroyed because he consulted a medium in disobedience to the Torah.[9] Not until David does Israel get a king for whom God expresses substantial approval.

David and the Empire

The Selection and Rise of David
—1 Sam. 16 Through 2 Sam. 2

David was born into a Judean family of moderate means, with perhaps some influence.[10] His family also had Moabite connections.[11] Samuel went to the insignificant town of Bethlehem (Mic. 5:2, cf. Matt. 2:6) and chose the youngest rather than the eldest son in the family. This choice follows a countercultural pattern of passing the promise to the younger rather than the oldest son.[12]

David began his courtly life serving Saul, but he replaced him when Saul's reign ended in psychological disorder and

[8]John Bright speaks of a "fortress rather than a palace," and Norman K. Gottwald of a "headquarters rather than a capital" (Bright, *A History of Israel,* 3d ed. [Philadelphia: Westminster, 1972], 186; Gottwald, *The Hebrew Bible: A Socio-Literary Introduction* [Philadelphia: Fortress, 1985], 320).

[9]1 Sam. 28:5–19; Deut. 18:9–20; and see chap. 10, this textbook.

[10]The family had its own flocks, rather than working for others (1 Sam. 17:15,34), and may have hired shepherds in addition to David and his brothers (17:20). David's ancestor was Nahshon, the leader of the tribe of Judah (Num. 1:7; 2:3; 1 Chron. 2:10).

[11]Ruth was the mother of Obed, David's grandfather. The connections may have continued, because David placed his parents under the care of the Moabite king while he was fleeing from Saul (1 Sam. 22:3–4).

[12]The favored one was Abel rather than Cain; Isaac rather than Ishmael; Jacob rather than Esau; Judah and Joseph rather than Reuben; Ephraim rather than Manasseh.

spiritual apostasy. The people always assumed that they had some voice in who would be the next king in Israel. So, in an almost democratic fashion, they acclaimed David as king (2 Sam. 2:4; 5:1–3). But remember, Samuel had already designated David as "anointed" king (1 Sam. 16:1–23).

The biblical narrative is frank about how cunning David was in gaining the throne. But then, the biblical record is *history* rather than *mythology*. It's the story of real people rather than the stuff of legend. The biblical account neither hides nor lays blame for the darker events featuring people you might have thought were pure, religious characters. The Davidic dynasty originated in history; it didn't claim to descend from heaven. So the biblical record "sets before us with very matter-of-fact realism the tortuous path trodden by this erstwhile warrior in the service of Saul and then of the Philistines, until he attained to the dignity of king over all Israel."[13] And the biblical writers make no later efforts to sanitize this bloody picture in Samuel–Kings. In Samuel–Kings this is all a part of the dismal story explaining why exile became unavoidable. But the postexilic Chronicler, resurrecting monarchial hopes, produces a parallel account that points to the more helpful signs in the monarchy's history (1 through 2 Chronicles). At the same time, the narrative resists any idea that David's cunning aimed to advance himself at Saul's expense.

How Did David Develop Into Israel's Great Warrior-King? — 1 Sam. 16 Through 30

We first meet David when Samuel anoints him as Saul's announced *replacement*—not merely his successor (1 Sam.

---

[13]Gerhard Von Rad, *Old Testament Theology*, trans. D. M. G. Stalker (New York: Harper & Row, 1962), 1:308.

16:1–13). We're told, "From that day on the Spirit of the LORD came upon David in power" (16:13). The very next verse tells us more: "Now the Spirit of the LORD had departed from Saul, and an evil spirit from the LORD tormented him" (16:14). But David's earliest role in the monarchy is as Saul's choice court musician and armor bearer—not as heir apparent (1 Sam. 16:14–23).

Soon we learn that David gained a reputation as a consummate warrior by killing Goliath (1 Sam. 17). There must have been other victories as well, because the women kept singing, "'Saul has slain his thousands, and David his tens of thousands'" (1 Sam. 18:7; 21:11; 29:5).[14]

David's growing popularity—even with Saul's own son Jonathan—provoked Saul into a murderous rage. He tried

[14]It's not clear when Saul first became acquainted with David. When Saul asked for a court musician, his attendants told him of David's military prowess (1 Sam. 16:18); however, after David killed Goliath, Saul didn't know who he was (17:5–58). There are various possible explanations: (a) First Sam. 16:14–23 may be out of chronological order so that the Spirit's anointing on David and lack of it on Saul can be contrasted. (b) David may have been one of many people assigned to Saul and just a face without a name at that point. Joab himself had eighteen armor bearers. (c) Saul's failure to recognize David may have been the result of his mental breakdown. In fact, there is some confusion about who killed Goliath. We read that David killed Goliath during Saul's reign (1 Sam. 17:50,57; 18:6); however, we also read that Elhanan killed a "Goliath" during David's reign (2 Sam. 21:19). There are four different approaches to explaining this apparent contradiction: *First,* say it is indeed a contradiction in the original manuscript. *Second,* say the error was introduced by a copyist sometime in the pre-Christian era, which the chronicler attempted to resolve by saying Elhanan killed the *brother* of Goliath (Robert D. Bergen, *1, 2 Samuel,* NAC, vol. 7 [Nashville: Broadman, 1996], 449). *Third,* say "Goliath" was a typical name given to giants, and that the one in 2 Sam. 21:19 was a different Goliath from the one David killed (suggested but not defended by A. A. Anderson, *2 Samuel,* WBC, vol. 11 [Dallas: Word, 1989], 255). *Fourth,* say both accounts are about the same giant and same giant killer, that David was his regnal (royal) name, and Elhanan was his earlier family name (Joyce Baldwin, *1 and 2 Samuel: An Introduction and Commentary* [Downers Grove, Ill.: InterVarsity Press, 1988], 286). Of those choices, I think the *second* or *fourth* most likely.

various methods to get rid of David, all futile. He tried to spear him (1 Sam. 18:10–11; 19:9–10).[15] He made David a military commander, hoping he would die in battle (18:12–17).[16] Saul even demanded a suicidal bride-price of one hundred Philistine foreskins for his daughter's hand in marriage (1 Sam. 18:25). But David doubled the ante and survived to deliver–and to become Saul's son-in-law. When Saul began lying in wait for David and hunting him down (1 Sam. 19:9–17), Saul's own children Michal and Jonathan sided with David (1 Sam. 19:11–17; 20:1–42).

David had to flee Saul's court. He first fled to Gath, then to Adullam, and then to Moab (21:10–15; 22:1–4). The priests at Nob helped David make his flight. So Saul slaughtered them, driving the survivors into David's camp (1 Sam. 21:1–9; 22:9–23). Saul tried again to kill David with his own hands (23:7–29). Then, in David's absence, he gave David's wife, Michal, to another man (25:44).

David has been described as an outlaw leading "malcontents, fugitives . . . flotsam, ruffians and desperadoes" and running a protection racket that intimidated the wealthy of the region[17] (see 1 Sam. 25:7–8,15–16). That was certainly how Nabal saw him when he rejected David's request for supplies (1 Sam. 25:10–11). Apparently Saul had been neglecting his kingdom to chase David (1 Sam. 24; 26). The bandit problem in the Judean foothills was such that only a soldier of fortune like David could provide any relief. The

Saul's Rage, David's Advantage

Since Saul was the weaker character and David the better politician, it would be Saul rather than David who suffered ruin from David's flight. David was not only fleeing the palace, he was preparing for the palace.

[15]Saul's rage even led him to try spearing his own son Jonathan (1 Sam. 20:33).

[16]David later did something like this to Uriah (2 Sam. 11:15).

[17]Bright, *History of Israel,* 189. Note that the chronicler's account idealizes David. It omits the stories of David's conflict with Saul and his intimidation of Nabal and marriage to Abigail.

Lord himself had directed David to oppose the Philistines who were looting Judah's people at Keilah (23:1–6). Even Nabal's own wife, Abigail, said that David "fights the LORD's battles" (25:28). But she was also concerned about protecting him from "the staggering burden of needless bloodshed or of having avenged himself" (25:31). David himself acknowledged that he had been pushing the limits of bloodguilt (25:33–34).

David had been rescuing people from Philistine plundering (1 Sam. 23). He had kept Nabal's own shepherds and belongings safe (25:7). He had even shared his plunder with the people in the region where he operated (30:26–31). Consequently, Abigail's positive sentiments must have been common in the region. Her prediction of a "lasting dynasty" (25:28) is one that 2 Samuel 7 develops at length.

While running from Saul, David offered his military services to the Philistines (1 Sam. 27:1–12; 29:1–11). He hoped to use this Philistine alliance to ensure his safety (27:1–2). The Philistines, however, probably wanted to use him to exercise indirect control over the region. David's ploy may have been a bit of tactical genius, but it was fraught with political danger. He could easily be perceived as – or even forced to become – a traitor to his own people. Nevertheless, David skillfully walked the tightrope. He made some raids into Judah but mostly plagued Israel's neighbors (27:8–12). The record shows that he never fought with the Philistines against Israel, even in the north, from which Saul's main support came (28:1–2; 29:1–11).

Saul had failed to appreciate the religious aspects of kingship. He had alienated the priests. He turned Samuel against him by ignoring the religious requirements of *cherem* warfare during his battles with the Amalekites.[18] Saul also usurped the priestly role by sacrificing before battle. And he slaughtered the priests who gave aid to an escaping David. So the surviving priest Abiathar joined David and brought the ephod with him (1 Sam. 22:20; 23:6). The prophet Gad also joined David. Of course, David had already built himself a powerful personal army, which would support his regime for the rest of his life (2 Sam. 23:8–9; 1 Chron. 11:10–47; 1 Chron. 12:1–37). With such a court in exile, it's little wonder that the people in the south began to see him as royal material.

David was ready to deal with the priests and prophets, rather than alienating them.[19] He even backed off plans to build the temple when the prophet Nathan forbade it because David had shed so much blood (1 Chron. 22:8; 28:3). As a result, David united the charismatic and institutional conceptions of religion and linked them both to the monarchy.[20] This made his throne less vulnerable than Saul's.

Even as David was building a military and religious power base, he maintained a high regard for the reigning king. He passed over two chances to eliminate Saul (1 Sam. 24; 26). He took pains to avoid looking like an opportunist capitalizing on Saul's troubles. An Amalekite came to him with Saul's crown and armband, falsely claiming to have finished off the wounded warrior-king

[18]For *cherem,* see chap. 9, "Canaan: Conquest, Covenant Renewal, and Crisis," and "holy war" in the glossary.

[19]He himself could sometimes speak with prophetic authority. For example, his last words were a prophetic oracle (2 Sam. 23:1–7, esp. vv. 1–3a). It's important to see Israel's kingship "as *predominantly a religious institution,*" though not in the cultic sense of divinized kingship.

[20]Walther Eichrodt, *Theology of the Old Testament* (Philadelphia: Westminster Press, 1961), 1:446.

(2 Sam. 1:15–16). Rather than receive this news with satisfaction, David executed the messenger. Two factors explain this response: First, David was genuinely grieved at this shameful death for Saul. His moving elegy for Saul and Jonathan shows that (2 Sam. 1:17–27). Second, this politically savvy execution distanced David from Saul's death. It thus helped to keep open the door for the north to join his unified kingdom, although they tended to support the claims of Saul and his descendants.

How Did David Come to Rule Over Both North and South? – 2 Sam. 1:1 Through 5:5; 1 Chron. 11:1 Through 12:40

Nevertheless, critics sometimes say David usurped the throne through brute military force. David had grown stronger while Saul's military and political support weakened. We cannot dismiss his role as a warrior. By it, he exercised the charismatic function of a deliverer. On the other hand, the LORD had designated David as king some time before he actually took the throne (1 Sam. 16:13; 1 Chron. 11:1–3).

DAVID FIRST RULED THE SOUTH FROM HEBRON — 2 SAM. 2–4; 1 CHRON. 12:23–40

Upon Saul's death, David moved to Hebron and rallied his supporters. Those who were influential in the south "anointed David king over the house of Judah" (2 Sam. 2:4). For seven years he ruled the south from Hebron (2 Sam. 5:5; 1 Chron. 3:4).

In the northern Transjordan, Saul's surviving son, Ish-Bosheth, began ruling.[21] Saul's cousin Abner, serving as

---

[21] The Heb. text in Samuel gives his name as *Ish-Bosheth,* "man of shame"; however, 1 Chron. 8:33; 9:39 gives us the name *Esh-Baal,* "man of Baal." The

general, exercised actual control (2 Sam. 2:8–9). For two years Ish-Bosheth tried to assert the right of dynastic succession in Saul's line. A representative battle at Gibeon proved indecisive (2:14–17).[22] So on the one hand, "the war between the house of Saul and the house of David lasted a long time. David grew stronger and stronger, while the house of Saul grew weaker and weaker" (3:1).

Joab, David's commander, never won a clear victory over Saul's forces. But when Ish-Bosheth accused Abner of political intrigue with Saul's former concubine (2 Sam. 3:6–11), an enraged Abner offered his allegiance to David (3:12–21). David responded, "'I will make an agreement with you. But I demand one thing of you: Do not come into my presence unless you bring Michal daughter of Saul when you come to see me'" (3:13).[23] Perhaps David was hoping for a son from his marriage into the house of Saul, which would cement relations with the north. Whatever the case, the picture that results is pitiful: "Ish-Bosheth gave orders and had her taken away from her husband Paltiel son of Laish. Her husband, however, went with her, weeping behind her all the way to Bahurim. Then Abner said to him, 'Go back home!' So he went back" (3:15–16).[24]

---

change in Samuel both eliminates the pagan divine name "Baal" and disparages this "shameful" pretender to the messianic throne.

[22]Here twelve of Abner's troops fight twelve of David's, with the implied promise that the victorious twelve would win victory for their whole army (cf. David fighting Goliath, 1 Sam. 17; see "David Defeats Goliath," in chap. 10, and n. 58).

[23]Some suggest that this violates the spirit of the Law (Deut. 24:1–4; Jer. 3:1). But the law dealt with divorce, rather than the wrongful alienation of a wife. Saul had given her away to Paltiel when David fled. On the other hand, the biblical narrative does call Paltiel, rather than David, "her husband."

[24]It seems strange that Ish-Bosheth went along with this request, which undermined his own claim to the throne. Not only was it a response to

An element of the north had already been considering a move to support David (2 Sam. 3:17). So Abner's switch unraveled Saulide hopes. Then a jealous and vengeful Joab murdered Abner (3:22–36).[25] This could have caused serious problems for the newly formed union. But as had been the case with the death of Saul, David went to great lengths to disassociate himself from this murder (3:30–37).

Abner's murder rang the death knell over attempts in the north to maintain a dynasty descended from Saul: "When Ish-Bosheth son of Saul heard that Abner had died in Hebron, he lost courage, and all Israel became alarmed" (2 Sam. 4:1). Recab and his brother Baanah assassinated Ish-Bosheth and brought his head to David (4:2–8).[26] Instead of rewarding the brothers, David reminded them of what he had done to the man who had brought evidence of Saul's death (4:9–11). He executed them and mutilated their corpses before hanging them on public display for this foul deed (4:12). Then he gave Ish-Bosheth's head an honorable burial in Abner's tomb (4:12b).

DAVID RULED "ALL ISRAEL" AND "THE NATIONS" FROM JERUSALEM — 2 SAM. 5; 1 CHRON. 11:1 THROUGH 16:45

The north finally abandoned the royal pretenders among Saul's descendants and came over to David (2 Sam. 5:1–3;

David's peremptory demands, but it also involved returning to David a princess with connections to the royal house of Saul.

[25]Perhaps Joab was jealous of Abner's rising star in David's camp and vengeful because Abner had killed his brother Asahel (2 Sam. 2:18–28).

[26]They appear to have been foreigners living in the Northern Kingdom (2 Sam. 4:2–4). They were living in the Benjamite town of Gittaim, but they were originally from Beeroth, one of the Canaanite cities that succeeded in deceiving Israel into making a covenant with them (Josh. 9). Apparently, they were Hivites (Josh. 9:7).

1 Chron. 11:1–3). Accordingly, David's kingdom united Israel and Judah into "all Israel."[27]

David's Own Person Was a Unifying Factor—1 Chron. 11:1–3. David was a seasoned military leader who owed much of his reputation to his large personal guard. First, Judah came under his rule. And when the north joined his kingdom, they forged a link to more than just the southern tribes. They said, "We are your own flesh and blood. In the past, even while Saul was king, you were the one who led Israel on their military campaigns. And the LORD your God said to you, "You will shepherd my people Israel, and you will become their ruler"'" (1 Chron. 11:1–2).

This created a new state based on a "personal union" with David.[28] But it seemed prone to separation over rivalry between the northern tribes and Judah. David's authority in the south included not only Judah but also various other tribal elements: Simeonites, Calebites, Othnielites, Jerahmeelites, and Kenites (1 Sam. 27:10; 30:14; see also Judg. 1:1–21). So a southern state of Judah emerged as a separate entity alongside the Israel that Ish-Bosheth had

[27]The postexilic chronicler's idealized account begins here, skipping all the intrigue and dark dealings that led up to David's rule over the United Kingdom. With only a brief note about rule from Hebron (1 Chron. 3:4), the chronicler's account begins the story with David's rule over all Israel (1 Chron. 11; cf. 12:23–40). Samuel–Kings had the task of explaining why exile was unavoidable, given the nation's long-term disobedience of the laws in Deuteronomy. Chronicles is resurrecting monarchial hopes by focusing on the more positive signs in the history of the nation, and especially of the monarchy.

[28]J. Alberto Soggin, *A History of Ancient Israel* (Philadelphia: Westminster, 1985), 41; citing A. Alt, "The Formation of the Israelite State in Palestine," in *Essays on Old Testament History and Religion* (German original, 1930; Oxford: Basil Blackwell & Mott, 1966), 171–237. Soggin defines "personal union" as "the form of government by which two or more nations, politically independent of one another, have the same sovereign; otherwise each has its own political and administrative organization" (62).

tried to rule in the north. Both "Israel" and "Judah" gained connotations beyond mere tribal names.

David's Own City, Jerusalem, Was a Key Unifying Factor— 2 Sam. 5:6 Through 6:23; 1 Chron. 11:4–47; 13:1 Through 16:43. David had conquered Jebusite Jerusalem with his own personal guard. He therefore claimed it as the "City of David" (2 Sam 5:6–10; 1 Chron. 11:4–9). Jerusalem proved acceptable to both Judah in the south and Israel in the north because it had been a part of neither territory until David seized it.[29] This enabled him to move his headquarters up

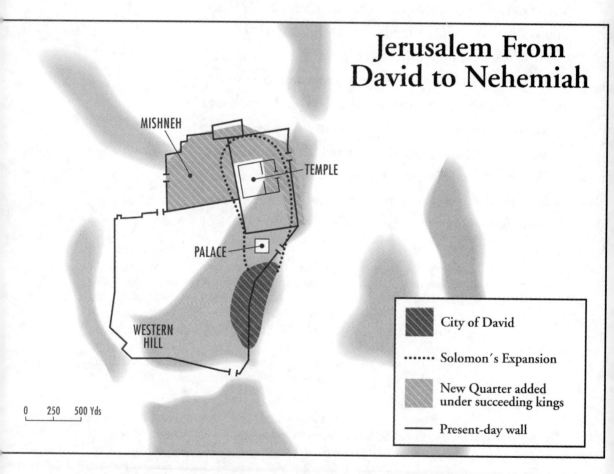

Jerusalem From David to Nehemiah

MISHNEH

TEMPLE

PALACE

WESTERN HILL

0   250   500 Yds

▨	City of David
⋯⋯⋯	Solomon's Expansion
▨	New Quarter added under succeeding kings
——	Present-day wall

[29]In fact, it probably still had somewhat of a Jebusite character. David conquered Jerusalem without displacing or slaughtering its Jebusite population (2 Sam. 24:18–25), so it wasn't even a *Judean* city after he conquered it.

from its southern location in Hebron to a central capital.

He then transferred the sacred ark from Kiriath Jearim. It had lain neglected there for more than a generation (2 Sam. 6:1–23; 1 Chron. 13:1–14; 15:25 through 16:3). With ecstatic ceremony, David brought it to Jerusalem, where Michal despised his exhibitionism (2 Sam. 6:20; 1 Chron. 15:29). But he reminded her that God "'chose me rather than your father'" (2 Sam. 6:21), a remark that cut deep and alienated his wife. "David never showed the same genius in dealing with his family that he exhibited in ruling his people."[30]

To oversee the ark, David appointed Abiathar of the priestly line at Shiloh (1 Sam. 22:20; 14:3) and Zadok of the Levitical line.[31] He also appointed a group of Levites to minister around the ark (1 Chron. 16:4–6,37–38). This merged the various populations of the empire on the religious level. But at an ethnic or political level unity proved impossible. This attempt to exercise sovereignty in the religious sphere was one of the key causes of Saul's downfall. It certainly would have been tempting to use religion "as just one more horse harnessed to the chariot of dynastic and nationalistic designs."[32]

But the biblical record shows that David proved to be wiser than Saul. Saul had neglected the ark and driven its priesthood away from him. David, on the other hand, set himself up as the patron of Israel's religion.[33] As royal

---

[30]Cate, *Introduction to the Old Testament,* 253.

[31]2 Sam. 8:17; 1 Chron. 6:4–8; 16:39–42; 18:16; 24:1–3.

[32]Eichrodt, *Theology of the Old Testament,* 1:442.

[33]It is interesting to note that Chronicles expounds at length on David's role as temple patron, noting his extensive preparations for building the temple, which effectively makes David the real founder and sponsor of the Jerusalem temple (1 Chron. 23 through 28). Kings pretty much ignores David's role and focuses on Solomon's initiatives in building the temple.

upholder of the covenant, he validated the monarchy for the independent-minded tribes. The unifying effect of this upon the tribes cannot be overestimated.

The Philistines watched the all-Israel acclamation of David's rule and saw him establish a unified capital in Jerusalem. They knew this constituted a declaration of independence. So they fought two campaigns to resubjugate David—both unsuccessful (2 Sam. 5:17–25). The failure of these offensives reversed the relationship between them and David, making them *his* vassals (2 Sam 8:1–14; 1 Chron. 18:1–13). Now they provided him with mercenaries, such as the Kerethites and Pelethites (2 Sam. 8:18; 15:18), and perhaps Hittites like Uriah (11:3).

How Great Did David's Empire Become?
—2 Sam. 8; 10; 1 Chron. 18:1 Through 20:8

David liberated Israel from Philistine oppression and incorporated their territories and peoples under his rule (2 Sam. 5:17–25; 2 Chron. 18:1–2; 20:4–8). Then he started building an extended empire. Israel became the dominant power in western Asia. In fact, Israel was for a while as strong as any power in the world.

David Conquered the Transjordan and Much of Aram—2 Sam. 8; 1 Chron. 18

David gained considerable influence in the region by making alliances. For example, he married the daughter of the king of Geshur, an Aramean kingdom in Syria (2 Sam. 3:3).[34]

---

[34]This marriage gave him Absalom as son and temporary successor by rebellion (1 Chron. 3:2).

David Overran the Southern Transjordan Territories of Moab and Edom—2 Sam. 8:1–4; 1 Chron. 18:12–13. David crippled the Moabite fighting force with cold-blooded mass executions: "He made them lie down on the ground and measured them off with a length of cord. Every two lengths of them were put to death, and the third length was allowed to live" (2 Sam. 8:2; cf. 1 Chron. 18:2).[35] And in Edom, David's men slaughtered 18,000 Edomites—"all the men" (1 Kings 11:15–16; 1 Chron. 18:12). He wiped out Edom's royal house, except for the child-prince Hadad, whom retainers whisked away to sanctuary in Egypt. David then ruled Edom and Moab as vassal states. Although he may have left a Moabite vassal king on the throne (2 Sam. 8:2), Israelite governors ruled in Edom, which David garrisoned with his own troops (1 Chron. 18:13).

David Subdued Aram—2 Sam. 8:5–12; 1 Chron. 18:3–11. David attacked King Hadadezer of Zobah and captured most of the Aramean infantry and chariot forces (2 Sam. 8:3–8). Israel had never used chariots and fought mainly on foot. So David hamstrung "all but a hundred of the chariot horses" (8:4). He also defeated the Arameans of Damascus who had come to Hadadezer's aid (8:5). The campaign paid well in loot, especially copper from Hadadezer's realm. The king of Hamath also paid lavish tribute (8:6–10). He was probably glad to be rid of Zobah and wanted good relations with the newly powerful Israel (8:9–10; 1 Chron. 18:9–11).

David Established Profitable Relations With the Phoenicians of Tyre—2 Sam. 5:11; 1 Kings 5:1–16;

[35]Note David's own Moabite connections and note that David had left his parents with the Moabite king for protection while he was on the run from Saul (1 Sam. 22:3–4). Did something go wrong at that incident with his parents to provoke David's brutal conquest?

2 Chron. 2:1–18. David's relations with King Hiram of Tyre initiated an enduring and profitable alliance. It lasted until Jehu overthrew the Omrides and assassinated the brutal queen mother Jezebel, a princess of Tyre (2 Kings 9:30–37).

David's empire was a complex geopolitical entity. It would prove difficult to hold together. There were long-standing north-south tensions and occupied territories that had majority alien populations. Communication between regions of a large empire proved difficult. These all threatened imperial unity. At the death of Solomon, the union forged by David would break, and the empire would disintegrate.

How Did Sin in David's Family Affect His Ability to Rule? —2 Sam. 11 Through 1 Kings 2

Second Samuel 11 through 20 gives us such an unvarnished account of the violence and intrigue in David's family that you would almost think an enemy of the Davidic line wrote the narrative.

DAVID SINNED AGAINST BATHSHEBA AND URIAH —2 SAM. 11 THROUGH 12

David slept with Bathsheba, the wife of his loyal Hittite soldier Uriah who was away at battle.[36] When David found

---

[36]This points out how even Israel's greatest king was a sinner, contributing to the accumulating guilt that results unavoidably in exile. The chronicler's postexilic idealized account of David omits mention of his sin with Bathsheba and Uriah's refusal to sleep with his wife during battle season; in fact, it makes nothing of the recurring sexual motif found in Samuel-Kings: sleeping with Bathsheba, a son's rape of his half sister, Absalom's seizure of David's concubines, competition for the aged David's bedmate Abishag, and the childlessness of Saul's daughter Michal (Raymond B. Dillard and Tremper Longman, *An Introduction to the Old Testament* [Grand Rapids: Zondervan Publishing House, 1995], 142). Including these issues after the exile would only cloud the shining hopes for a renewed monarchy ruling over a repentant people. God had threatened exile (Deut. 28:63–68), but he had also promised that a repentant people would return and again experience God's blessing on their nation (Deut. 30:1–5). In fact, Deut. 30:1–5 informed the basic thesis of the chronicler (2 Chron. 7:14).

that he had gotten her pregnant, he gave Uriah a leave, with implied conjugal visitation rights, to conceal the origin of the pregnancy. But Uriah, the soldier's soldier, would not sleep with his own wife during battle season—even if the adulterous king would! (2 Sam. 11:1–13). So David essentially murdered Uriah by telling Joab to abandon him at the battlefront (11:14–18). After Bathsheba's period of mourning passed, she became another of David's wives (11:27). "No doubt all Israel admired their sovereign for marrying Israel's newest widow, and one with child at that."[37] However, "the thing David had done displeased the LORD" (11:27b).

NATHAN ANNOUNCED DAVID'S JUDGMENT — 2 SAM. 12:10–12

Nathan's judgment oracle provides the theological explanation for the sad storyline that follows.[38] Nathan's parable provoked David into pronouncing a fourfold judgment on the rich man who had stolen the poor man's beloved lamb: "'He must pay for that lamb four times over'" (2 Sam. 12:1–6). In effect, David pronounced judgment on himself: (1) His first child by Bathsheba died immediately (2 Sam. 12:14–23); (2) his son Amnon was killed by another son, Absalom (2 Sam. 13:28–29); (3) his son Absalom was killed by Joab during the rebellion (2 Sam. 18:15); and (4) his son Adonijah was murdered by another son, Solomon (1 Kings 2:23–25). The sword would "never depart from [David's] house" (2 Sam. 12:10).

[37]Barry L. Bandstra, *Reading the Old Testament: An Introduction to the Hebrew Bible* (Belmont, Calif.: Wadsworth, 1995), 265.

[38]Ibid., 266.

BITTER RIVALRIES AMONG THE CHILDREN OF
DAVID'S POLYGAMOUS MARRIAGES
—2 SAM. 13 THROUGH 20

David's polygamous household proved to be treacherous.[39] The story of how David's promised son (2 Sam. 7:11–16; 1 Chron. 17:10–14; 22:6–13) ascended to the throne is filled with treachery and rebellion against God's chosen heir to the throne. Absalom's understandable fury over the rape of his sister by their half brother Amnon prompted his cold-blooded retaliation (2 Sam. 13:1–39).[40] This necessitated Absalom's exile to Geshur, his mother's hometown in Aramea (13:37–38). The removal of two potential heirs to the throne, Amnon and Absalom, probably reopened the possibility that a descendant of Saul might succeed David on the throne.

With Joab's conniving and prompting, David eventually permitted Absalom's return from exile (2 Sam. 14:1–23). At first, Absalom was barred from the court (14:24), and members of the court wouldn't acknowledge his summons (14:29). After two years in Jerusalem "without seeing the king's face" (14:28), Absalom grew frustrated. Again, with Joab's help, he got himself readmitted to the court (14:33).

But he then began plotting against the throne. David himself had been the consummate politician, always attentive to public opinion while he was accumulating power.

---

[39]The Bible never presents polygamy in a positive light, and sometimes it presents a combative picture: Abraham with Sarah and Hagar (Gen. 21), Jacob with Rachel and Leah (Gen. 29 through 30), and Samuel's father Elkanah with his mother Hannah and her rival Peninnah (1 Sam. 1).

[40]Amnon would have been David's oldest son (2 Sam. 3:2), and therefore most likely heir to the throne.

Finally, David had to flee Jerusalem (2 Sam. 15:13 through 16:14). "The whole countryside wept aloud as all the people passed by" (15:23). One man even gave supplies to the fleeing royal party (16:1–4). But a man named Shimei pelted David with dirt and rocks and cursed him as a murderer and "scoundrel" who had stolen Saul's throne (16:5–6). He taunted David, crowing that he was tasting some of his own medicine now that Absalom had taken the throne (16:7–8). One of David's followers said, "'Why should this dead dog curse my lord the king? Let me go over and cut off his head'" (16:9). David's response is a telling study in David's character: "'If he is cursing because the LORD said to him, "Curse David," who can ask, "Why do you do this?" . . . Leave him alone; let him curse, for the LORD has told him to. It may be that the LORD will see my distress and repay me with good for the cursing I am receiving today'" (16:10,11–12).

Absalom even took David's harem to the palace roof and slept with them, a public claim that he had triumphed and taken the throne (2 Sam. 16:21–23).

The royal pretenders among Saul's descendants and their supporters also welcomed the rebellion as a time for vengeance (2 Sam. 16:1–8). So Absalom's coup gained scattered support throughout the land. Some even came from David's own household, for example, David's chief Ahithophel (2 Sam. 15:12; cf. Josh. 15:51; 2 Sam. 23:34)[41] and Amasa who was kin to Joab and David (2 Sam. 17:25; 1 Chron. 2:15–17). Even Judah proved reluctant to approach

---

[41]Perhaps he joined the plot to get revenge for David's seduction of Bathsheba: Ahithophel was the father of an Eliam (2 Sam. 23:34) and Bathsheba was the daughter of an Eliam (2 Sam. 11:3)—she may have been Ahithophel's granddaughter (see Cate, *Introduction to the Old Testament*, 256)!

David after the rebellion was quashed (2 Sam. 19:11–15). Nonetheless, most of the court and priestly personnel, and David's all-important personal bodyguard, stuck with him as he fled Jerusalem.

When David heard that his counselor Ahithophel was with Absalom, he prayed, "'O LORD, turn Ahithophel's counsel into foolishness'" (2 Sam 15:31). It happened— Ahithophel proposed rapid pursuit of David. But Hushai, David's loyal plant in Absalom's court (15:32–37), played on Absalom's fears and on his ego. He called to mind David's cunning as a warrior. And he called for a huge troop buildup before pursuing David so they could use overwhelming force (2 Sam. 17:7–16). Because pursuit of him began too slowly, the coup fizzled for lack of a royal *corpus delicti,* David having made his escape.

An extended narrative records Absalom's death (2 Sam. 18), after which David returned to the throne (19:9–10). As for his shamed rooftop harem, "He provided for them, but did not lie with them. They were kept in confinement till the day of their death, living as widows" (20:3).

David's generous settlement with Absalom's followers from Judah in the south angered the northern tribes (2 Sam. 19:11–30). They saw it as favoritism and rebelled (19:41–43). Sheba son of Bicri, a "troublemaker" from Benjamin,[42] led an attempt to withdraw Israel from union with Judah. Ephraim and Manasseh led the northern rebel cry, "We have no share in David, no part in Jesse's son! Every man to his tent, O Israel!'" (20:1). The north probably felt they could leave the union by their own choice, since they had entered it by their own choice. So they fol-

[42]Perhaps the same as Becorath, Saul's kinsman (1 Sam. 9:1).

lowed Sheba (20:2). But not claiming a share in David was tantamount to rejecting their share in the kingdom of God. They were gathering "against the LORD and against his Anointed One" (Ps. 2:2, cf. 2 Sam. 12:7; 22:51; 23:1; Pss. 18:50; 89:20).

During the rebellion, Absalom had appointed Amasa over the army in place of Joab (2 Sam. 17:25). Oddly, David sustained that appointment after he regained the throne (19:13), perhaps tired of Joab's schemes, which eventually allowed Absalom to take the throne. So David commanded Amasa to bring him the army of Judah. But Amasa's regular army call-up went too slowly to meet David's three-day deadline (20:4–5). Instead, David's foreign mercenaries—led by Abishai and his demoted brother Joab—pursued Sheba to put down the rebellion (20:7). In the midst of this pursuit, Joab found the opportunity to murder Amasa, his replacement (20:8–10).

Sheba fled to the far north, deep into territory from which Saul and his main support had come, where he probably considered himself safe. But he was assassinated by the people of Abel Beth Maacah, where he was hiding, when Joab threatened it. They decapitated Sheba and threw his head down from the wall to Joab (2 Sam. 20:15–22), who then turned and left.

More Philistine Opposition
– 2 Sam. 21:15–22; 1 Chron. 20:4–8

Such internal conflict encouraged the Philistines to renew their opposition. David's troops had to defeat them in battle at places like Gob, Gezer, and Gath. But the fire of war in David had dimmed. At one point, he grew so faint in battle that he had to be protected, and his men said,

"'Never again will you go out with us to battle, so that the lamp of Israel will not be extinguished'" (2 Sam. 21:17).[43]

Why Did David Turn Over Saul's Sons to the Gibeonites? – 2 Sam. 21:1–14

When a three-year famine hit, David asked why. The LORD said the cause was Saul's guilt for murdering the Gibeonites, which now rested on his descendants (2 Sam. 21:1).[44] When David asked the Gibeonites what they wanted to make things right, they complained that they had no recourse in Israel's judicial system to ask for money or for blood.[45] But they asked David, "'Let seven of his male descendants be given to us to be killed and exposed before the LORD at Gibeah'" (21:6). David agreed, and all seven were killed and exposed "on a hill before the LORD" (21:9). We might be tempted to reject this as unjust and contemptible. But in heaven, the bloodguilt of Saul, which now extended to his descendants, had been purged from the corporate account of the United Kingdom.[46] God was still sanctioning a covenant made before him, even though a Gibeonite ruse had occasioned it (Josh. 9). After this act

[43]The chronicler omits this story, which detracts from David's military glory toward the end of his reign.

[44]The biblical narrative of Saul's reign is silent about this incident. Saul was a Benjamite, and the Gibeonites lived on land in Benjamite territory. Some nationalistic strife between the Benjamites and Gibeonites must have precipitated this covenant-breaking genocide (Josh. 9:15–20).

[45]They were subject aliens, and the monarchy must have forbade them the right to legal recourse, for the law permitted it (Exod. 22:21; Lev. 19:34; 24:22; Deut. 1:16–17; 24:17; 27:19).

[46]The Law and the Prophets repeatedly state this principle behind this punishment falling on a later generation (Exod. 20:5; 34:7; Num. 14:18; Deut. 5:9); however, the Law and the Prophets also qualify that principle by noting the presence of personal guilt as well as the corporate guilt inherited from the fathers (Deut. 24:16; 2 Kings 14:6; 2 Chron. 25:4).

of expiation cleared the records, "God answered prayer in behalf of the land" (21:14).[47]

Why Did David Conduct His Misguided Military Census?–2 Sam. 24; 1 Chron. 21

> ### Habits of the Heart
>
> It's important to note that in relying on his military forces, David was only doing what he had done all his life—and with God's repeated blessing. It was what brought him to power, restored him to power after Absalom's rebellion, and ensured his ability to transfer power to Solomon. The story should remind us that we must develop habits of the heart, so that an obedient heart can withstand lifelong habits in times when they cut across God's daily will for our lives.

The parallel descriptions of David's military census display a provocative contrast. The Book of 2 Samuel depicts this overreliance upon military forces as something *the Lord* incited David to do because he was angry with the people (2 Sam. 24:1). David took this militaristic census because God incited it. But David had his own dangerous reasons for doing it. Even Joab opposed the move because it would bring guilt on Israel (2 Sam. 24:3–4; 1 Chron. 21:3–4). But the postexilic Chronicles says *Satan* incited David to provoke God into angry judgment (1 Chron. 21:1). This shows a postexilic tendency not to allow God to be the instigator of anything bad. This should not be understood as a contradiction of the earlier account. It's a matter of God exercising dominion over all powers and authorities (Eph. 1:20–21). And it's important to remember that the ancient Hebrews did not use the modern theological concepts of God's permissive will and his active or causative will. To them, whatever happened came directly from its agent, from God—or by exilic times, perhaps from Satan. Taken together, the parallel accounts show that Satan can operate only by God's permission.[48]

God allowed David multiple choices when it came to his punishment (2 Sam. 24:11–13). But what was David doing when he chose pestilence coming directly from the LORD

---

[47]This is the same wording describing the relief from God's plague that came in judgment for David's ill-advised census (2 Sam. 24:25).

[48]See also the Book of Job.

rather than a calamity brought about by men? (24:14). Dillard and Longman decry the choice: When David was a young boy he risked his life to kill a lion for the sake of the sheep (1 Sam. 17:34–35). When David was a man, he was willing to let the sheep die for him, though this time the sheep were people (2 Sam. 24:14,17). "David will not be the good shepherd that will give his life for the sheep—we must keep reading to find another (John 10:11)."[49] Perhaps the story could be read that way. There's certainly some truth to their conclusion about waiting for "the good shepherd." But Gerhard von Rad sees something redeeming about David's choice: "In so doing he flung himself through the dark curtain of anger directly on God's heart."[50] David reasoned, "'Let us fall into the hands of the LORD, for his mercy is great; but do not let me fall into the hands of men'" (2 Sam. 24:14).

As a result, the LORD sent a plague that killed seventy thousand people all over the land. But God relented as his destroying angel was preparing to hit Jerusalem itself (2 Sam. 24:15–16). As David watched the destruction, he interceded: "'I am the one who has sinned and done wrong. These are but sheep. What have they done? Let your hand fall upon me and my family'" (24:17). The prophet Gad commanded David to build an altar on "the threshing floor of Araunah the Jebusite" (24:18). Chronicles tells us that David decided, "'The house of the LORD God is to be here, and also the altar of burnt offering for Israel'" (1 Chron. 22:1). Here on the site of the future temple, David offered his sacrifices. "Then the LORD

---

[49]Dillard and Longman, *Introduction to the Old Testament,* 146.

[50]Von Rad, *Old Testament Theology,* 1:318.

answered prayer in behalf of the land, and the plague on Israel was stopped" (2 Sam. 24:25; cf. 2 Sam. 21:14).

David Prepares for the Temple – 1 Chron. 22:2 Through 26:32; 28:1 Through 29:9

The Chronicler records David's extensive preparations for building the temple and organizing its ministry. David united royal and priestly offices. He, rather than Solomon, initiated the building of the temple (1 Chron. 22 through 26).[51] Like a second Moses, he had the pattern ready and handed it over to Solomon, who was not only a second Joshua but even a second Bezalel (Exod. 31:1–11).[52]

Why Didn't God Remove David From Office After All His Sins?

Don't David's sins seem just as serious as Saul's—or even worse? What about David's adulterous and murderous outrage with Bathsheba and Uriah? What about his "inspired" census toward the end of his reign? These things make us wonder why David was left on the throne. Because of Saul's sins, the LORD had removed his favor, denying

[51] The account found in Samuel-Kings gives little attention to David's preparations for building the temple. The writer attributes this pretty much to Solomon (1 Kings 5:1–16; 2 Chron. 2:1–18). But the chronicler depicts David as the one who really prepared for building, decorating, and staffing the temple (1 Chron. 22:1 through 26:32).

[52] 1 Chron. 28:11–12,18–19; cf. Exod. 25:9,30. This makes for an interesting convergence of the pictures of Moses and David at this late date in Israel's history (von Rad, *Old Testament Theology,* 1:351). To the Chronicler, David was a second Moses, and the records of Solomon's preparations are anticlimactic (2 Chron. 2:1–18). Moses was Israel's first tribal leader, and David was their first acceptable king. Other typological comparisons are used. We see Solomon as a second Bezalel (Bandstra, *Reading the Old Testament,* 491) and Moses passing leadership to Joshua as a pattern of David passing it to Solomon (Dillard and Longman, *Introduction to the Old Testament,* 351–61).

kingship to Saul's descendants. But he left David on the throne forty years and promised him an *eternal* dynasty.[53] Why didn't the Lord react the same way with David as he had with Saul?

God allowed David to remain on the throne for two reasons: *First* and foremost, God faithfully kept his covenant promises and blessed David. *Second,* in spite of his serious faults, David displayed a degree of faithfulness and willingness to be corrected. This allowed him to be seen as the ideal king. David could be depicted as a righteous person who was blameless (2 Sam. 22:21,24; 1 Kings 9:4); as one who obeyed God's law (2 Sam. 22:23; 1 Kings 11:33,38) and followed his ways (1 Sam. 22:22; 1 Kings 11:33); and as a typological forerunner of the "LORD'S anointed," the *Mashiach* who was to rule over God's people. Consequently, God steadfastly upheld his eternal covenant with him.[54]

What Do We Make of David's Final Words to Solomon? – 1 Kings 2:1–9

Barry L. Bandstra describes David's charge to Solomon in a positive way (1 Kings 2:1–9, esp. 2:2–4, something the chronicler omits). He says it was "reminiscent of Yahweh's charge to Joshua in Joshua 1, and recollecting the promises of the Davidic covenant."[55] Robert L. Cate is more on target when he says, "David's final words do not show the great king in his best light. His command to Solomon to

---

[53]For seven years ruling the south from Hebron and for thirty-three years ruling "all Israel" from Jerusalem (2 Sam. 5:5; 1 Chron. 3:4).

[54]1 Sam. 16:3,6,12–13; 24:6; 26:9,16,23; 2 Sam. 1:14,16; 3:39; 19:21; 23:5; 1 Kings 8:23; Ps. 89:1,3,28.

[55]Bandstra, *Reading the Old Testament,* 274.

execute both Joab and Shimei reveal the dying king to be an embittered old man." This doesn't sound very positive. But then, it's difficult to maintain a uniformly positive view of David's rule. Perhaps it's best to adopt Cate's final word: "It was not David's greatness which made him great but God's."[56]

David died after a forty-year reign (1 Kings 2:10–12; 1 Chron. 29:26–28).

Solomon and the Temple

Just as was the case with David, it is possible to interpret Solomon in a mottled light, portraying him in ways that detract from the splendor of his rule – even more so than with David. For example, we could compare Solomon's efforts to stabilize his throne to those of a typical despot of his times. On the other hand, the biblical record depicts his actions as fulfilling holy prophecy. Yes, Solomon did immediately eliminate anyone who might threaten his kingdom. But in this he was following his father's deathbed counsel, which the Scriptures allow to stand without condemnation.

At best, royal succession could be ill-defined. As for Israel, it had never yet had a dynastic succession, making the situation even more open ended. How do you get to be the king's successor when others want it so badly? David had apparently promised Bathsheba that her son Solomon would succeed him on the throne (1 Kings 1:13,17), but he had done nothing about it. Outside the palace, there was no consensus that the next king should even be one of David's sons. Rivalries were inevitable (2 Sam. 15:1–6; 1 Kings 1:5). The claims of the house of Saul were still in the air. Amnon,

[56]Cate, *Introduction to the Old Testament*, 266.

David's eldest son and presumed heir to the throne, had been destroyed by his own incestuous lust. Absalom, another prince, had died a victim of his own coup. Of course, David had minimized options for those who still wanted to see a king from Saul's line. He delivered Saul's surviving male offspring to be executed by the Gibeonites, sparing only Jonathan's lame son Mephibosheth (2 Sam. 21:1–10).

J. Alberto Soggin calls Solomon's enthronement a takeover accomplished under the transparent cover of a senile father's appointment. It became possible only after Bathsheba badgered David into making the appointment public. But the narrative's focus on David's debility at the close of his reign adds something more: It places Solomon in relation to the declining David as David had been in relation to the declining Saul. This is "perhaps a didactic aim of the 'succession narrative.'"[57] David was doing what he had sworn to do (1 Kings 1:13,17) and what God had foreordained.

In the Samuel–Kings narrative describing the move from David to Solomon, only three texts mention God's intervention in royal affairs: He was displeased and sent Nathan to rebuke David (2 Sam. 11:27 through 12:12). He "loved Solomon" and sent Nathan to announce that election (12:24–25). He frustrated Ahithophel's advice (17:14). Earlier biblical narratives of key moves in redemptive history *frequently* display God's activity in powerful signs and wonders.[58] But here God doesn't isolate his actions to a few key miraculous events. Instead, he controls everything,

---

[57]Soggin, *History of Ancient Israel*, 66.

[58]For example, the miracles performed in the exodus from Egypt. Other such moves are signaled by manifestations of God's presence at the shrine, such as the glory of the LORD that filled the tabernacle in the wilderness (Exod. 40:34–35), which God repeated later when Solomon was dedicating the temple (1 Kings 8:11; 2 Chron. 7:2).

public and private, religious and secular. God does this to fulfill the Nathan prophecy in spite of many threats to it, both during David's lifetime and at the succession of Solomon.

How Did Adonijah Make a Try for the Throne? —1 Kings 1:5–27; cf. 1 Chron. 29:21–25

Upon becoming the oldest living son (he was originally number four [2 Sam. 3:4]), Adonijah made a try for the throne before it could be given to Solomon. As Absalom had, he attempted to usurp power. In fact, he was sort of a second Absalom: (1) He worked, as Absalom had, to impress the populace (1 Kings 1:5b, cf. 2 Sam. 15:1–6), (2) he too was very handsome (1 Kings 1:6b, cf. 2 Sam. 14:25), and (3) he was born next after Absalom (1 Kings 1:6b). So he began negotiations with Joab, who was now unwelcome in David's court, and with Abiathar, a disgruntled priest (1 Kings 1:7).[59] Then he called his brothers and some dignitaries together and had himself declared king at a feast at the spring En Rogel (1:9,25).

The military, clergy, and palace personnel chose up sides, backing one or another of the claimants to the throne.

Text	Rival Claimant	Location of Spring	Supporting Military	Supporting Clergy
1 Kings 1:5–9	Adonijah	En Rogel	Joab	Abiathar
1 Kings 1:32–40	Solomon	Gihon	Benaiah	Priest Zadok, prophet Nathan

Solomon's supporters informed David of developments and pled for a quick announcement of David's choice

---

[59]Bright, *History of Israel,* 206.

(1 Kings 1:11–27). David finally made clear his choice of Solomon (1 Kings 1:28–53; 1 Chron. 29:21–25). In the end, the throne went to the team with the crack troops. David's own troops accompanied Solomon to the sacred spring at Gihon. There, Zadok anointed Solomon as king, and the crowd acclaimed him as such (1 Kings 1:32–40). Adonijah and his panicked followers knew the game was up. His followers scattered and Adonijah took refuge in the tabernacle (1:41–50). When Adonijah pled for his life, Solomon sent him home with the guarantee of safety if he would remain loyal (1:51–53). Of course, he didn't (2:13–17).

How Did Solomon Build on the Base That His Father, David, Had Fought to Establish? — 2 Kings 2:13–46

Solomon consolidated his political power base and solidified the national defenses. He pursued an ambitious foreign policy based upon alliances rather than on conquest. He essentially maintained the Davidic empire but did not continue its expansion.

Solomon Consolidated His Political Power Base at Home

Solomon was no conquering king. All he had to do was consolidate and maintain the realm his father had handed him. Solomon disbanded his father's foreign legion composed of Kerethites and Pelethites, who had been his father's loyal bodyguard and shock troops. He fortified his frontier towns, but this was a purely defensive measure. He also strengthened the army, especially the cavalry (1 Kings 4:26; 10:26). Solomon apparently never made any use of this new cavalry. It's likely that it was as much for show as his collection of gold armor (1 Kings 10:16–17,25), ornamental but useless.

Once David died, Solomon ruthlessly purged any challenge to his authority (1 Kings 2:10–46). He surrounded himself with mediocre officers. They would be less likely to force his hand, as Joab had done with his father, David (2 Sam. 3:39).

When Bathsheba came to Solomon with Adonijah's request to marry David's companion Abishag, Solomon exclaimed, "'You might as well request the kingdom for him—after all, he is my older brother—yes, for him and for Abiathar the priest and Joab son of Zeruiah!'" (1 Kings 2:22).[60] He executed Adonijah for this apparent continuing claim to the throne (1 Kings 2:21–25; cf. 2 Sam. 16:21–22). Solomon also deposed Abiathar from priestly office and banished him to Anathoth.[61]

When fellow-rebel Joab heard that Solomon was mopping up after Adonijah's rebellion, he fled to the sanctuary altar. Solomon ordered Benaiah to go in after him and kill him (1 Kings 2:28–34). Shimei, the Saul sympathizer who had cursed David as he fled from Absalom (2 Sam. 16:5–8), was confined to the city. He was executed the first time he was caught going out of town, even though he had a legitimate reason (1 Kings 2:36–46). The removal of these last two was to fulfill David's deathbed orders (1 Kings 2:1–9). As John Bright notes, "Solomon obeyed with what can only be called alacrity."[62]

To be fair, the following mitigating circumstances should

---

[60]Adonijah was now attempting something like what Absalom had done to signal his takeover by sleeping with David's harem on the palace roof (2 Sam. 16:21–23).

[61]This fulfilled the prophecy against the house of Eli (1 Kings 2:27; cf. 1 Sam. 2 through 3) and brought the Zadokites to priestly preeminence.

[62]Bright, *History of Israel*, 207.

be noted: (1) David knew that he himself could barely control Joab (2 Sam. 3:39), so he feared for his son's safety. (2) Adonijah got better treatment than he would have given Solomon and Bathsheba (1 Kings 1:21), considering the ANE custom of slaughtering all pretenders to the throne. (3) As for Shimei, he was due (2 Sam. 16:5–13; Exod. 22:28).

SOLOMON SOLIDIFIED HIS NATIONAL DEFENSES

Solomon was no warrior, but he fortified defenses on his borders and in key cities. They included Jerusalem; Hazor in Galilee facing the Arameans to the east; Megiddo at the main pass to Carmel; and Gezer, Beth Horon, and Baalath guarding the western approaches from the coastal plains (1 Kings 9:15–19). This nonwarrior even developed a chariot corps. Chariots would have been of no use to David's campaigns in rugged hill country (2 Sam. 8:4). But they may have proved useful in the extended imperial flatlands. More likely, the 4,000 horse stalls, 1,400 chariots, and 12,000 men were on decorative display in his "chariot cities" (1 Kings 10:26) like his gold shields.[63]

SOLOMON PURSUED AN AMBITIOUS FOREIGN POLICY

Rather than conduct military operations on his frontier, Solomon formed alliances. Many of them he sealed with marriages to foreign noblewomen, such as the daughter of Egypt's Pharaoh (1 Kings 3:1; 11:1–3).[64] Law would have

[63]First Kings 10:16–17,25–26; 2 Chron. 9:25, cf. Deut. 17:16.

[64]Bright points out that this marriage "illustrates both the relative importance of Israel and the low estate to which Egypt had sunk: Pharaohs of the Empire did not give their daughters even to kings of Babylon or Mitanni!" (*History of Israel*, 208). And 1 Kings records, "Pharaoh king of Egypt had attacked and captured Gezer. He had set it on fire. He killed its Canaanite inhabitants

forbidden most of these marriages.[65] It's interesting to note the absence of any mention of an Israelite wife in Solomon's palace. Especially important was Solomon's renewal of his father's alliance with Tyre (1 Kings 5:1–12).

SOLOMON MAINTAINED A VAST EMPIRE, BUT NOT WITHOUT OPPOSITION

Opposition arose in Edom after the death of David and Joab. Hadad returned to Edom from Egypt, where he had fled from David's troops, and began making trouble for Solomon (1 Kings 11:14–22). But Solomon never actually lost Edom. If he had, his activities in Ezion Geber and the Arabian caravan trade would have been impossible. Solomon's troubles in Aram, however, were more serious. He still controlled the caravan routes leading northeastward toward the Euphrates (cf. 2 Chron. 9:26; 1 Kings 4:24). But Rezon seized Damascus and made himself king there (1 Kings 11:23–25). It isn't known what action Solomon was able to take or the extent of his losses in Aram. He probably maintained some control, but his influence in the area weakened.

Did Solomon Eliminate and Neutralize All of His Potential Threats? – 1 Kings 11

Solomon did much to stabilize his kingdom by eliminating internal threats and neutralizing external ones. But other threats would crop up, often as God's judgment on Solomon (see below).

and then gave it as a wedding gift to his daughter, Solomon's wife" (9:16). This effectively gave it to Solomon.

[65]Deut. 7:1,3, cf. Ezra 10:2; Neh. 13:26–27; Mal. 2:11.

SOLOMON EVENTUALLY FACED EXTERNAL ENEMIES
—1 KINGS 11:14–25

In spite of all Solomon's alliance-building marriages, he retained old, or developed new, international foes. Hadad of Edom had fled from David's brutal conquest (1 Kings 11:14–22; cf. 2 Sam. 8:14). Like Solomon, he had allied himself to Egypt through marriage to one of Pharaoh's daughters (1 Kings 11:19). Now he came back to haunt the Israelite kingdom (11:22).

We also read that "God raised up against Solomon another adversary," Rezon (1 Kings 11:23). He had fled from the kingdom of Zobah, which David had also conquered. Using Damascus as a base, he plagued Solomon with border raids.[66]

JEROBOAM REBELLED AGAINST SOLOMON
—1 KINGS 11:26–40

In addition to external threats, Solomon eventually experienced internal threats. This came to a head with the palace revolt headed by one of his construction supervisors (1 Kings 11:27–28). Ahijah, a prophet from the old sanctuary town of Shiloh, had prophesied to Jeroboam, "'The LORD, the God of Israel, says: "See, I am going to tear the kingdom out of Solomon's hand and give you ten tribes. . . . But I will not take the whole kingdom out of Solomon's hand; I have made him ruler all the days of his life for the sake of David my servant, whom I chose"'" (11:31–34). We are not told what Jeroboam did to rebel at this time, but whatever it was, Solomon learned of it and tried to kill him. But Jeroboam escaped to sanctuary in

[66]First Kings 11:23–25; cf. 2 Sam. 8:3; 10:8,18–19.

Egypt, where he stayed until Solomon died (11:40). Of course, he came back to fulfill Ahijah's prophecy (1 Kings 12) and to earn himself decidedly different prophetic announcements from the same Ahijah (14:1–18).

How Did Solomon Get So Wealthy?
—1 Kings 10; 2 Chron. 1:14-17; 9:13-28

Solomon's true genius was industry and trade; he was essentially a merchant-prince. In this capacity, he displayed his ability to do two things: (1) benefit from his position astride the trade routes between Egypt and Arabia in the south and Aram in the north and (2) capitalize on the huge commercial possibilities of his alliance with Tyre. Because foreign trade was a royal monopoly, it brought huge wealth into Solomon's personal coffers.

SOLOMON PURSUED EXTENSIVE MARITIME TRADE
—1 KINGS 5:1–12; 9:26–28; 10:11–12,22

Red Sea trade became important under Solomon. Using Phoenician shipbuilders and sailors, he built a merchant fleet at Ezion Geber and ran far-flung trading routes. His ships brought back gold, silver, rare woods, jewels, ivory, and perhaps baboons from the south (1 Kings 10:22; 2 Chron. 9:21).

Even more important was Solomon's trade with the Phoenician maritime city-state Tyre (1 Kings 5:1–12). His alliance with Tyre, established by his father, David, allowed mutually beneficial trade with Israel. Commodities such as wheat and olive oil were shipped out, and cedar and pine came in from Lebanon. Tyre also held copper-producing colonies on the Mediterranean islands of Cyprus and Sardinia, and possibly also in Spain and North Africa. These provided ore to Solomon's own smelting furnaces in the Jordan valley that supplied copper for temple vessels (1 Kings 7:45–46). His furnaces probably also produced a surplus for foreign trade.

SOLOMON PURSUED CARAVAN TRADE WITH ARABIA — 1 KINGS 10:1–13; 2 CHRON. 9:1–12

The Queen of Sheba's visit should be understood in the light of Solomon's interest in overland trade with the south (1 Kings 10:1–13). The Sabeans, inhabitants of Sheba, had been only nomadic raiders in Job's day (Job 1:15).[67] Now, however, they were settled at the starting points for incense trade routes running north out of southern Arabia. Solomon controlled the crossroads from which caravans departed to Egypt, Babylonia, and the lands of the eastern Mediterranean. His maritime routes constituted competition for Sheba's overland routes. As a consequence, the Sabean queen sought and probably got a trade agreement. At any rate, the Arabian trade brought huge wealth to Solomon's treasury (1 Kings 10:15).

SOLOMON TRADED IN HORSES AND CHARIOTS — 1 KINGS 10:28–29; CF. DEUT. 17:16

Solomon imported horses and sold them to the kings of the Hittites and of Aram. Deuteronomy 17:16 had forbidden this practice, especially if he bought from Egypt's horse markets.[68] Solomon may have begun dealing in horses to supply

---

[67]Sheba = Saba, located in southern Arabia around modern Yemen.

[68]The exodus was never to be reversed by sending men back to Egypt, not even to buy horses at its market. This warning would have been all the more important if they were trading men for horses, as Gerhard Von Rad and Craigie suspect (Von Rad, *Deuteronomy: A Commentary*, OTL [Philadelphia: Westminster, 1966], 119; Peter C. Craigie, *The Book of Deuteronomy*, NICOT [Grand Rapids: Wm. B. Eerdmans, 1976], 255–56).

his own military. But he also made himself the indispensable middleman in this lucrative international trade.

Were Solomon's Days Israel's Golden Age?

This was a time of unique prosperity, security, and flowering culture in Israel. Trade brought huge wealth to Solomon himself.[69] The whole land's living standards must also have climbed rapidly with the employment required for all his building and trade projects. The population may have doubled over that of Saul's time, to reach as high as 800,000.[70] On the other hand, by the time Solomon's rule ended, schism threatened because of his harsh socio-economic policies.

SOLOMON FOSTERED MASSIVE BUILDING PROJECTS — 1 KINGS 5 THROUGH 7

Solomon started numerous civil and military building projects, but the temple was his most notable construction. For this, he employed a Tyrian architect (1 Kings 7:13–14). The pattern for this magnificent temple was like other temples found in Palestine and Aram (1 Kings 6:37–38). It served as a royal chapel, but it was just as much a national shrine. The temple took seven years to complete.

When it was finished, Solomon moved the ark to the temple (1 Kings 8:1–21; 2 Chron. 5:2 through 6:11). Then he led a massive ceremony of temple dedication, with prayers and sacrifices (1 Kings 8:22–66; 2 Chron. 6:12 through 7:10; Ps. 132:8–10).

It took thirteen more years to erect his own palace com-

---

[69]First Kings 10:14–29; 2 Chron. 1:14–17; 9:13–28.

[70]Bright, *History of Israel*, 217.

plex called the "Palace of the Forest of Lebanon" (1 Kings 7:1–7). It had an armory (1 Kings 10:16–17; Isa. 22:8), a judgment hall with its throne (1 Kings 10:18–20), and a treasury (1 Kings 10:21). He also built a similar palace for the Pharaoh's daughter (1 Kings 3:1; 7:8; 9:16,24). It's interesting to note that even Solomon knew that the presence of a Pharaoh's daughter in the royal palace was bad. "Solomon brought Pharaoh's daughter up from the City of David to the palace he had built for her, for he said, 'My wife must not live in the palace of David king of Israel, because the places the ark of the LORD has entered are holy'" (2 Chron. 8:11; cf. 1 Kings 8:24a).[71]

SOLOMON CONTRIBUTED TO THE FLOWERING OF HEBREW CULTURE—1 KINGS 10

This period also saw the beginning of well-organized records. Bright calls one such collection "The Court History of David."[72] The Bible calls another "the book of the annals of Solomon" (1 Kings 11:41). Music and literature flourished. Solomon was the quintessential sage.[73]

Was Solomon the Finest Manifestation of Kingship or a Burden on the People?

We know of Solomon's proverbial wisdom, divinely granted. We also know of his excesses. His oppressive taxation led to the rapid dissolution of the united monarchy

[71]By this note, Chronicles provides a positive interpretation of Solomon's palace for Pharaoh's daughter built outside the city of David.

[72]Bright, *History of Israel,* 215; see 2 Sam. 9 through 20; 1 Kings 1 through 2.

[73]See 1 Kings 3:4–28; 4:29–34; 10:7,23–24, and authorship notes in Prov. and Eccles.

after his death. As for the biblical record, its assessment of Solomon is ambivalent (1 Kings 3:2–3; 11:9).

SOLOMON ASKED FOR WISDOM TO RULE WELL —1 KINGS 3:4–15; 2 CHRON 1:2–13

An evaluation of Solomon should begin by noting that God answered Solomon's request to rule well. He had not asked for wealth, longevity, or military security. God gave him all these things as well (1 Kings 3:1–14). Solomon's wisdom was celebrated both inside the kingdom and abroad. Men as diverse as the fuzzy-cheeked simpleton in Proverbs[74] and the grizzled sages of the ANE benefited from his wisdom. Women as diverse as the Queen of Sheba (1 Kings 10:1–13; 2 Chron. 9:1–12) and the two prostitutes claiming one child (1 Kings 3:16–28) marveled at his wisdom. He composed 3,000 proverbs and 1,005 songs.[75] He became noted for his kingly botanical analysis, after the tradition of Adam, who called all animals by name as earth's first ruler (1 Kings 4:29–34; see Gen. 2:20).

SOLOMON FAILED TO RULE ALL THAT WISELY

However, even this initial analysis of Solomon's rule is ambivalent: It begins, "Solomon showed his love for the LORD by walking according to the statutes of his father David" (1 Kings 3:3a; also 2 Chron. 8:12–16). But in Samuel-Kings the analysis continues, "except that he offered sacrifices and burned incense on the high places" (1 Kings 3:3b).

---

[74]Prov. 1:4,22,32; 7:7; 8:5; 9:4,6,16; 14:15,18; 19:25; 21:11; 22:3; 27:12; also 2 Kings 20:10; Job 5:2; Pss. 19:7; 119:130.

[75]1 Kings 4:32. It's interesting to note that the Psalter contains none of them, unless the note "of Solomon" refers to his authorship rather than to him as the subject or object of dedication (Pss. 72; 127).

SOLOMON ESTABLISHED TWELVE ADMINISTRATIVE DISTRICTS—1 KINGS 4:7–19

Lavish building projects, governmental expansion, and support of temple projects generated huge expenses. The twelve tribes had been unequal in size, economic output, and political clout. Now Solomon redistricted his kingdom for taxation and temple supplies. He formed twelve administrative districts to equalize the economic clout of each district. This neutralized "the dangerously powerful northern tribes."[76] Each district had a governor accountable only to the king. It was responsible for providing one month of the court's provisions each year (1 Kings 4:7–19). This weakened tribal loyalties and apparently put a real financial strain on the districts.[77]

Economic pressure even drove Solomon to cede some of Israel's frontier towns to Hiram, king of Tyre (1 Kings 9:10–14). This was a land-for-money rather than land-for-peace trade. It was not even payment for goods purchased. Rather, it was security for a loan, which Solomon never redeemed.

SOLOMON IMPOSED EXTREME SOCIO-ECONOMIC MEASURES

Massive building projects eventually meant that taxes, already high, were not enough. Solomon then imposed forced labor.[78] At first, this involved only captive or conquered peoples, but it eventually included Israelites

[76]Gottwald, *Hebrew Bible,* 322.

[77]Bright, *History of Israel,* 221.

[78]1 Kings 4:6; 9:15–23, esp. vv. 22–23; cf. 2 Sam. 20:24; 2 Chron. 2:17–18; 8:7–10.

(1 Kings 5:13–15). This may have existed in isolated cases even from the earliest times in Israel's history (Josh. 9:21). Solomon, however, had made it permanent and national. This constituted both an assault on Israel's freedom and a drain on private manpower. It led to contradictory demands: "Stay on the land and produce more crops for export! Leave the land and serve in the army and build cities."[79] This forced labor and the heavy taxation, especially on the northern districts, caused a lot of tension in the kingdom.

SOLOMON LED A GLORIOUS KINGDOM TO THE PRECIPICE OF DESTRUCTION — 1 KINGS 9 THROUGH 11

Even more than the forced labor and land swaps, the blame for Solomon's downfall originated in his own harem (1 Kings 11:1–3).[80] It is on these terms that 1 Kings blames Solomon for the schism that occurred after his death.[81] Of course, Solomon's one thousand women were not an indication of his sexual appetite. Instead, they indicated the vast political contacts he had established and maintained through diplomatic marriages. But diplomatic ties brought religious ties. Although he may have built the Pharaoh's daughter a palace outside Jerusalem, ultimately he succumbed to his wives—allowing them to worship their

[79]Gottwald, *Hebrew Bible,* 322.

[80]Harems were an indication not necessarily of an overactive sex drive but rather of foreign alliances made through marriage. But alliances sealed with marriages could cost more than they were worth. The wife of a foreign prince was either an ever-present ambassador in her husband's court—or a spy. These pagan wives also tended to encourage apostasy (e.g., the Tyrian princess Jezebel who sponsored the worship of Baal and Asherah after marrying Ahab [1 Kings 16:31; 18:19]).

[81]Chronicles idealizes Solomon, even commending Rehoboam for "walking in the ways of David and Solomon" (2 Chron. 11:17).

own gods and goddesses right in Jerusalem.

SOLOMON LED BECAUSE HE WAS DAVID'S PROMISED "SON" — 1 KINGS 11:9–13

The idea that David's line would rule forever was used to legitimize Solomon's rise to the throne. The Royal Psalms reflect this language:

1. The LORD's choice of Zion and David's house is eternal (Pss. 89:3–4; 132:11–14).
2. Kings might be chastened, but the dynasty itself would remain (2 Sam 7:14–16; Ps. 89:19–37).
3. The king ruled as the LORD's "son" (Ps. 2:7; see 2 Sam. 7:14), his "firstborn" (Ps. 89:27), and his "anointed" (Pss. 2:2; 18:50; 20:6).
4. No foe would prevail against Zion or its king (Pss. 2:1–6; 18:31–45; 21:7–12; 132:17–18; 144:10–11).
5. Even foreign nations must submit to his rule (Pss. 2:7–12; 18:44–45; 72:8–11).

And God's covenant with David was what sustained a flawed Solomon on his faulty throne. Although the Chronicler's record does not reveal it, Kings says, "The LORD became angry with Solomon because his heart had turned away from the LORD, the God of Israel, who had appeared to him twice. Although he had forbidden Solomon to follow other gods, Solomon did not keep the LORD's command" (1 Kings 11:9–10).

WHY DIDN'T GOD REMOVE SUCH A FAULTY KING FROM HIS THRONE?

Eventually, God served notice on Solomon: "'Since this is your attitude and you have not kept my covenant and my decrees, which I commanded you, I will most certainly tear the kingdom away from you and give it to one of your subordinates'" (1 Kings 11:11). But the Davidic covenant was still Solomon's bulwark. Even in his anger at Solomon, God said, "'Nevertheless, for the sake of David your father, I will not do it during your lifetime. I will tear it out of the hand of your son. Yet I will not tear the whole kingdom from him, but will give him one tribe for the sake of David my servant and for the sake of Jerusalem, which I have chosen" (11:12–13). In other words, Solomon continued to lead because he was David's covenant son.

Solomon Died After a Forty-Year Rule —1 Kings 11:41–43; 2 Chron. 9:29–31

God sustained Solomon on the throne in spite of his wickedness. His rule spanned an impressive forty years, the same length as his father's.

Theological Aspects of David's Dynasty

Covenant: How Is the Monarchy Defined by the Davidic Covenant? —2 Sam. 7; 1 Chron. 17

What was the nature of the Davidic covenant (2 Sam. 7; 1 Chron. 17)? David had found himself comfortably settled in a house of cedar while his God was housed in a mere tent. He wanted to build God his own palace, that is, a temple. At first, the prophet Nathan liked David's plan, but after hearing from God, Nathan forbade it. Using play on words, Nathan told David that before he could establish a "house" (that is, a temple) for the LORD, the LORD would need to establish a "house" (that is, a dynasty) for him (2 Sam. 7:5–16).

God had promised David a great nation and a great name. This both echoed and fulfilled provisions of the Abrahamic covenant.[82] Under David, Israel finally possessed the land promised to Abraham (Gen. 12:16–17). God's election of David's house as an eternal dynasty gave David a tremendous sense of security (2 Sam. 7:18–29). This dynasty lasted until the exile and then appeared to end for good. But the promise continued as a hope among the exilic prophets. The return from exile brought with it an eschatological emphasis on messianism. This raised Israel's hopes for the Davidic dynasty to even greater heights.

KEY WORDS IN THE DAVIDIC COVENANT

Nathan's promise doesn't use the word "covenant."[83] However, it includes several terms that evoke the covenant. Some of them speak of a royal dynasty that God establishes, for example, "house," "offspring," "throne," and "kingdom." Others speak of a divinely instituted and assured special relationship between the Davidic king and God: "father" and "son," "lovingkindness" (NASB), "promise" and "good."

To promise the dynasty, Nathan used a play on the word *bayith*, which can mean "house," "family," or "dynasty" (2 Sam. 23:5; 1 Kings 2:24; 11:38). When David asked to build a "temple" *(bayith)* for the Lord, the Lord said he would build up David's "dynasty" *(bayith)*. To the latter end, he promised David a royal "offspring" (2 Sam. 7:12). This referred initially to Solomon, then to all of David's

[82]See 2 Sam. 5:12; 7:23,26; 1 Chron 14:2; 17:21; 1 Kings 5:7, cf. Gen. 12:1–3.

[83]Nathan's promise clearly entails the concept of a covenant. Accordingly, the other texts reflect this in their own use of *berith* (covenant) and *sheva'* (oath) to describe the Lord's promise to David (2 Chron. 13:5; 21:7; Pss. 89:3,28,34,39; 132:2,11–12; Isa. 55:3; Jer. 33:21).

dynastic descendants (Pss. 89:4; 132:11; Jer. 33:22). To this line, God promised a throne (that is, a kingdom) that would last forever.

To define the special relationship between God and the dynastic offspring, Nathan used father-son language. A basic element of Hebrew kingship was the king's status as son of Yahweh. This relationship already applied to the nation as a whole, which God called "my son" (Exod. 4:23; Deut. 32:19; Hosea 11:1). But the term would now apply particularly to the Davidic king. God would adopt him as his son to sit on his throne in Zion (2 Sam. 7:14; Ps. 2:7). And God made an eternal promise (2 Sam. 7:15,25–28): He would maintain *chesed* with David's dynasty. This term denotes God's loyal love and unfailing mercy.[84] Similarly, God promised eternal good for David's dynasty. God would assure that things remained eternally beneficial to Davidic rule.

Conditional vs. Unconditional Covenant

In some places, the covenant appears to be eternal and unconditional; in others, it appears to be conditional.[85] The biblical record shows that the promise was indeed an eternal covenant with David's descendants. However, its blessings would be withheld from those who ignored its provisions. Disciplining the recipient of a covenant promise—or his successors—was consistent with an irrevocable

---

[84]Eng. Bibles translate *chesed* with terms such as "kindness," "lovingkindness," or "love" (KJV, NASB); "steadfast love" or "loyalty" (RSV); or even "mercy" (KJV).

[85]The covenant appears *unconditional* in texts such as Ps. 89:28–29,36 and the Chronicles record, which omits the idea of punishment for David's successors. It seems *conditional* in 2 Sam. 23:5; 1 Kings 2:4; 8:25; Pss. 89:30–37; 132:11–12.

covenant.[86] So the covenant stood even when hopes for a restoration of the dynasty appeared to have failed because of the exile.[87] That durable expectation is what the New Testament writers found fulfilled in Jesus Christ the faithful son of David.[88]

Priest and Temple: How Did the Monarchy Relate to the Worship of God?

Saul's key problem had been a failure to appreciate the religious aspects of kingship. This led him to marginalize Samuel.[89] Furthermore, he slaughtered the priests who had harbored David during his flight from Saul's court (1 Sam. 22:18–19). But David saw the priesthood as indispensable to the monarchy. He made every effort to build a close association between the royal and religious functions. He strengthened those ties by his patronage of the ark and its attendants. He got personally involved with the temple in sacrifice, hymn composition, and temple plans. In the end, he is even depicted as a prophet (2 Sam. 23:1–7).

[86]Gottwald, *Hebrew Bible,* 335, citing Moshe Weinfeld, "Covenant, Davidic," in *Interpreter's Dictionary of the Bible, Supplementary Volume,* ed. George Arthur Buttrick (Nashville: Abingdon, 1962), 190.

[87]Ezek. 34:23–24; 37:24–25, cf. Hosea 3:5.

[88]E.g., Matt. 1:1,20; 9:27; 12:23; 20:30–31; 21:9,15; 22:42–45; Mark 10:47–48; 12:35–37; Luke 1:32; 3:31; 18:38–39; 20:41–44; Acts 2:30–36; Rom. 1:3; Heb. 1:5 = Ps. 2:7. For more on the Davidic covenant see Walter C. Kaiser, Jr., "King and the Promise: Davidic Era" in *Toward an Old Testament Theology* (Grand Rapids: Zondervan Publishing House, 1981), 143–64; William Dumbrell, "The Davidic Covenant," *Reformed Theological Review* 39 (1980): 40–47; J. E. Runions, "Exodus Motifs in First Samuel 7 and 8," Evangelical *Quarterly* 52: 130–31.

[89]Samuel was obviously in mortal fear of Saul when he went to Bethlehem to anoint David (1 Sam. 16:2).

Theocracy: How Did the Monarchy Relate to the Rule of God?

David also kept the prophets on his side, even as he set about establishing all the elements of constitutional kingship. He acquiesced to them, even when refused his dearest wish (to build the temple). Samuel had worried because the people were turning away from him and asking for a king. But God told him, "'It is not you they have rejected, but they have rejected me as their king'" (1 Sam. 8:7).

The Davidic covenant turned the Davidic kingship into a messianic type of God's rule. It would find its fullest realization in Jesus Christ, the Son of David.[90] The Old Testament uses *mashiach* ("messiah," or "anointed one") to refer to Old Testament kings and even to priests (Lev. 4:3,5,16; 6:22). Its main use is for Israel's kings.[91] The Old Testament rarely applies it to the unique eschatological king.[92] But certainly the eschatological king was expected to be an extraordinary manifestation of the principles of kingship exhibited in David and promised in the Davidic covenant. Isaiah foretold of this extraordinary eschatological king who would be "God with us" (Isa. 7:14). Ezekiel alluded to the LORD'S "servant David" who would forever be a "prince" or "king" over a reunited people (Ezek. 34:23–24; 37:24). Zechariah spoke of a royal figure called "the Branch" (Zech. 3:8–9). Amos talked of a restoration and reunion under David's line (Amos 9:11). Jeremiah spoke of "a righteous Branch" raised to David (Jer. 23:5–6; 30:9).

[90]See Matt. 1:1; Luke 2:11; 2 Tim. 2:8.

[91]E.g., Saul (1 Sam. 24:6,10), David (2 Sam. 19:21), Zedekiah (Lam. 4:20), and kings in general (2 Sam. 23:1; Ps. 2:2; Hab. 3:13).

[92]Dan. 9:25–26 is the only clear reference.

New Testament: What Can the Monarchy Teach Us About the Kingdom of God?

The Davidic covenant is crucial to the evangelical faith; it's the key source for biblical messianism. The messianic import of this account is something that the Psalms and the prophets develop. The prophets describe eschatological kingship in messianic terms.[93] The Royal Psalms describe the ideal king in nearly deified terms—but still from the Davidic line (Pss. 45; 72; 110). They write "prophetic exegesis of the Nathan prophecy."[94] David's rule became a type of God's reign that spoke largely of Israel's hopes for God's rule. "David and Solomon in Chronicles are not just the David and Solomon who were, but the David and Solomon of the Chronicler's eschatological hope."[95] They were great prefigurations of Israel's royal hopes, used to define Israelite kingship in spite of their faults.

Their lives warn us that we should not take our besetting sins lightly, as though they will never have consequences. Their sins bore horrible consequences in their lives and for the kingdom they led. But their stories also encourage us to believe that if our hearts turn toward God, his face will turn toward us with blessing and honor. And this can bless everything we touch, perhaps for generations after us.

[93]Isa. 9:6–7; Jer. 23:5–6; Ezek. 34:23.

[94]Von Rad, *Old Testament Theology,* 1, 321.

[95]Dillard and Longman, *Introduction to the Old Testament,* 174–75.

Study Questions

1. Compare and contrast David and Solomon, noting their respective relation to the following institutions: military, empire, tabernacle/temple and priestly office, and civil government.

2. Detail the progression and extent of family sin's effect on David's throne.

3. How did David and Solomon measure up to the "Law of the King" (see Deut. 17:14–20)?

4. How does the Davidic covenant and the promise to David's "son" relate to New Testament expressions of the kingdom of God?

5. Recognize the north-south tensions, and how they influenced the ability of Saul, David, and Solomon to rule regionally and/or over "all Israel."

6. What evidence shows that both David and Solomon could be ruthless kings when they felt the need?

7. What was the basis for Solomon's wealth? List both the benefits and the dangers of this wealth.

For Further Reading

Allen, Leslie C. *1 and 2 Chronicles*. CC. Dallas: Word, 1987.

Baldwin, Joyce G. *1 and 2 Samuel: An Introduction and Commentary*. TOTC. Downers Grove, Ill.: InterVarsity Press, 1988.

Braun, Roddy. *1 Chronicles*. WBC. Dallas: Word, 1986.

Dilday, Russell. *1 and 2 Kings*. CC. Dallas: Word, 1987.

Dillard, Raymond B. *2 Chronicles*. WBC. Dallas: Word, 1987.

Dumbrell, William. "The Davidic Covenant." *Reformed Theological Review* 39 (1980): 40–47.

McConville, J. G. *1 and 2 Chronicles*. DSB. Philadelphia: Westminster, 1984.

Selman, Martin J. *1 Chronicles*. TOTC. Downers Grove, Ill.: InterVarsity Press, 1994.

_____. *2 Chronicles*. TOTC. Downers Grove, Ill.: Inter-Varsity Press, 1994.

Thompson, J. A. *1 and 2 Chronicles*. NAC. Nashville: Broadman, 1994.

Williamson, H. G. M. *1 and 2 Chronicles*. NCB. Grand Rapids: Wm. B. Eerdmans, 1982.

Wiseman, Donald J. *1 and 2 Kings*. TOTC. Downers Grove, Ill.: InterVarsity Press, 1993.

12

Dale Brueggeman

Sweet Singers and Sages: Israel's Poetry and Wisdom

Outline:

- What Is Old Testament Poetry and Wisdom Literature?
- Job: Israel's Debate About Suffering
- Psalms: Israel's Prayer Book and Hymnal
- Proverbs: Israel's Accumulated Wisdom
- Ecclesiastes: Israel's Hard Questions
- Song of Songs: Israel's Love Poetry

Terms:

acrostic
chiasm
imprecation
lament
ma'at
mashal
metaphor
parallelism
Psalter
Sitz im Leben
typology

Some of the most beloved material in Scripture is found in Israel's songs and wisdom. We read of Israel's sweet singers[1] and wise men—and women.[2] The Psalms' prayer and praise heal our spirits, whether we're rejoicing or weeping as we turn the pages. The poetic and wisdom books together give us devotional guidance, messianic hope, and even philosophical reflection.

What Is Old Testament Poetry and Wisdom Literature?

We call Job, Psalms, Proverbs, Ecclesiastes, and Song of Songs poetic because (1) poetry predominates in them and (2) they do not fall into the divisions called Pentateuch, Prophets, or History. And we classify Job, Proverbs, and Ecclesiastes as wisdom. But you'll find poetry and wisdom throughout the Old Testament.[3]

Why Is It Called Poetry?

In English poetry we notice rhyme and meter. But Hebrew poetry uses a different set of artistic devices. These include parallelism, repetition, verse and chorus, chiasm, and figurative language.

HOW DOES PARALLELISM WORK?

The Old Testament's most significant poetic device is parallelism. Two or three short lines in a verse of poetry may

---

[1]Second Sam. 23:1, KJV, NLT; 1 Chron. 16:4.

[2]Prov. 1:8; 6:20; 23:22; 30:17; 31:1.

[3]Jer., Ezek., Hos., and Amos have sections of poetic material. Lam., Joel, Obad., Mic., Nah., Hab., and Zeph. are entirely poetry. Only Lev., Ruth, Ezra, Neh., Esther, Hag., and Mal. have no poetry.

be parallel to one another in meaning or form. In the mid-
eighteenth century, Bishop Robert Lowth introduced a system of classification that held the field for a long time:[4] He
classified poetic parallelism as synonymous, antithetical, or
synthetic. Synonymous verses pair lines, saying the same
thing in different words (for example, Prov. 14:19).
Antithetical parallelism uses contrast to make a single point
(for example, Prov. 10:1). Synthetic verses build from one
idea to the next (for example, Prov. 21:16). Lowth's
approach was decidedly an improvement over earlier
approaches.[5] At least it recognized that there was poetic
parallelism. But Lowth tended to eliminate the worth of
the second half of each parallel unit—since it was just some
form of repetition anyway. James L. Kugel, Robert Alter,
and Tremper Longman have developed a more insightful
approach to parallelism.[6] Most importantly, they note that
the second half of the parallel is where the emphasis falls,
by virtue of repetition, elaboration, contrast, and so forth.
One simplified adaptation of this newer approach is the
following sixfold classification scheme: subordination,

[4]Robert Lowth, *Lectures on the Sacred Poetry of the Hebrews* (1753; a new edition with notes, Andover: Crocker & Brewster, 1829). Lowth's approach is reflected in works like the following: G. B. Gray, *The Forms of Hebrew Poetry* (1915; reprinted with prolegomenon by David Noel Freedman, New York: KTAV, 1972); Karl Budde, "Poetry (Hebrew)," in *A Dictionary of the Bible*, ed. James Hastings (New York: Scribner's, 1905–11), 4:2–13.

[5]For the history of approaches to parallelism, see James L. Kugel, *The Idea of Biblical Poetry: Parallelism and Its History* (New Haven, Conn.: Yale University Press, 1981), 96–286; Adele Berlin, "Parallelism," in *ABD*, 5:155–62.

[6]Kugel, *Biblical Poetry*; Robert Alter, *The Art of Biblical Poetry* (New York: Basic Books, 1985); Tremper Longman III, *Literary Approaches to Biblical Interpretation*, Foundations of Contemporary Interpretation 3 (Grand Rapids: Zondervan Publishing House, Academie Books, 1987), esp. "The Analysis of Poetic Passages," 119–34; "Examples of Poetic Analysis," 135–50.

contrast, continuation, comparison, specification, and intensification.[7]

Type	Description	Example
Subordination	One parallel element is subordinate to the other, supplying the means, reason, purpose, or time of its parallel	Prov. 20:4
Contrast	Arranged to contrast, but not necessarily antithetical	Prov. 10:1
Continuation	A progression of thought building on earlier phraseology	Ps. 93:3
Comparison	Parallels form a simile or metaphor	Ps. 125:2
Specification	Makes specific what was stated in the opening of the parallel	Ps. 145:10
Intensification	Restates in a more forceful way, often with elaborate vocabulary	Ps. 88:1–12

DOESN'T HEBREW POETRY USE OTHER ARTISTIC DEVICES TOO?

A poem might use *repetition*. It can repeat the initial words from line to line (for example, Ps. 29, repeating "ascribe to the LORD" and "the voice of the LORD;" Pss. 146 and 148 repeating "Praise the LORD;" and Ps. 136 repeating "His love endures forever"). It may repeat the last words of a line at the beginning of the next line; it might even reuse words from the opening of the section at its close (Ps. 98:4–6).

> <u>Shout for joy</u> to the LORD, all the earth,
>> burst into jubilant song [and <u>make</u>] <u>music</u>;
>> <u>make music</u> to the LORD <u>with the harp</u>,
>> <u>with the harp</u> and the sound of singing,
>> with trumpets and the blast of the ram's horn –
> <u>shout for joy</u> before the LORD, the King.

[7]Proposed by William W. Klein, Craig L. Blomberg, and Robert L. Hubbard, *Introduction to Biblical Interpretation* (Dallas: Word, 1993), 230–36.

A poem might use verse and chorus. Psalms 42 through 43 follow this arrangement, with the chorus repeated in 42:5–6,11, and 43:5. This shows us that this is really a single psalm rather than two.[8] A poem might use an acrostic, which is an alphabetizing poem. For example, Psalm 119 is a complex acrostic that begins each of the first eight verses with *aleph,* the first letter of the Hebrew alphabet. It works through the whole Hebrew alphabet, from *aleph* to *taw,* as you see in the NIV headings for each eight-verse section. Psalms 25; 34; 37; 111; 112; 119; and 145; Proverbs 31:10–31; and Lamentations 1; 2; 3; and 4 are also acrostics. Psalms 9 and 10 taken together compose a single acrostic, rather than two psalms as the numbering has it. A poem might use a chiasm. This term comes from the x-shaped Greek letter *chi.* A chiasm takes an x-shaped form. In the following example from Proverbs 2:4, notice that the parallel elements are in a reversed order diagramed with an "x":

and if you look for it as for silver

X

and as for hidden treasure search for it

A poem will almost certainly use lots of figurative language, like similes and metaphors. All of these artistic devices appear throughout the Old Testament. But they occur more often in Hebrew poetry.

WHY IS IT CALLED WISDOM LITERATURE?

You might think of wisdom as the search for where you fit in God's creation. This is no merely secular routine for getting along in the world—it's *very* religious. It's linked with "the fear of the LORD" (Ps. 111:10; Prov. 1:7; 9:10) and tied

[8]See also Pss. 39:5,11; 42:5–6,11, and 43:5; 46:7,11; 59:9,17; 67:3,5; 80:4,7,19; 107:6,13,28.

closely to the law and sacrifice (Deut. 4:6; 1 Kings 3:4–15).

HOW MANY WAYS CAN WISDOM BE EXPRESSED?

Proverbs, Job, and Ecclesiastes reflect common vocabulary, words like "wisdom," "proverb," "insight," "counsel," "guidance," "instruction," "discernment," "discipline," "knowledge," and "understanding." These books also share a concern for defining, defending, implementing, or questioning the following orderly connection: known character → predictable action → general consequences.

The wisdom material throughout the Bible employs a wide range of expressions. Among them are Jotham's fable (Judg. 9:7–15), Samson's riddle (Judg. 14:10–18), popular sayings about Saul and David (1 Sam. 10:12; 18:7), the "proverb of the ancients" (1 Sam. 24:13, NASB), and the parables of Nathan and of the wise woman of Tekoa (2 Sam. 12:1–14; 14:5–14).

Proverbs, Job, and Ecclesiastes express the mandate of wisdom in a variety of forms. Sometimes wisdom is expressed with an *explicit* imperative (for example, Prov. 25:16–17, 21). Often descriptions of normal consequences in life carry an *implied* imperative. For example, you could make a straightforward assertion of truth, without metaphor. But if it could be applied to many situations, it could be proverbial (for example, Ezek. 16:34). One might state a practical truth through metaphor (for example, Prov. 25:4–5). In other words, metaphor has a representative capacity that can be intuited by future interpreters and thus has the ability to carry the message to a broader audience.

IS WISDOM LITERATURE UNIQUE TO ISRAEL'S RELIGION?

The Old Testament had no respect for pagan priests and prophets, but it did not insist that foreign wisdom was false.

Scripture shows considerable regard for the Gentile sage. Moses went to the head of the class among Egypt's sages (Acts 7:22). Daniel excelled as "chief of the magicians, enchanters, astrologers and diviners" of Babylon (Dan. 5:11–12).

Solomon is the key figure in Israel's wisdom tradition. Critical scholarship says he brought about a humanistic enlightenment, emphasizing the potential and responsibility of leaders. But Solomon's wisdom was not just royal and secular. First, God granted it in the context of sacrifices and offerings (1 Kings 3:3–5; 2 Chron. 1:4–6). Second, God tied it to covenantal obligations and blessings. He promised, "'If you walk in my ways and obey my statutes and commands as David your father did, I will give you a long life'" (1 Kings 3:14). Because wisdom finds its source in God, Proverbs' personification of Wisdom as a lady speaks to us with prophetic authority (Prov. 1:20–33).

How Is "Wisdom" Related to "Knowledge"?

Biblical wisdom isn't *theoretical* knowledge, it's *applied* knowledge. We could even translate the Hebrew term *chokhmah*, often translated "wisdom," as "skill." We see that term used for the skill in crafts needed to build the tabernacle (Exod. 31:1–6; 35:10). It's used to describe a seaman's skills (Ezek. 27:8). It's even used for a drunken man's lack of motor skills (Ps. 107:27). In Proverbs it is social, verbal, administrative, or diplomatic skill.

Job: Israel's Debate About Suffering

Job records an ancient debate about suffering. In it, Israel's wisdom tradition defined suffering as past human

---

Wisdom in the New Testament

The New Testament calls Jesus Christ the source and model of wisdom. In fact, Christ *is* the wisdom of God (1 Cor. 1:24,30). Wisdom was with God before the creation (Prov. 8:24–31). So too Christ, the *Logos,* "was with God in the beginning" (John 1:2). Moreover, we see Jesus depicted as a wise youth. He astounded teachers and grew in favor with God and man (Luke 2:21–52). He was a wise teacher who amazed listeners (Mark 6:2–3; 7:28–29). A key feature of his teaching ministry was the parable, a wisdom form.[9] His parables at times parallel the content of the Old Testament proverbs (for example, Matt. 23:12 and Prov. 29:23). In the end, Jesus will appear as a wise judge and king. He will fulfill the Old Testament messianic hopes connected with wise kingship (Isa. 42:1–4; Matt. 12:18–21).

---

[9]In the Gk. the term is *parabolé,* used in the LXX to translate *mashal,* the Heb. term for "proverb."

understanding but under God's sovereign control. The structure of Job may be briefly outlined in this way:

1 through 2	Prologue
3 through 27	Dialogue: Eliphaz, Bildad, and Zophar
28	Essay on Wisdom
29 through 31	Job's Apology and Conclusion
32 through 37	Elihu
38:1 through 42:6	Theophany: Yahweh speaks from the storm; Job repents
42:7–17	Epilogue

Job's Cultural and Literary Setting

HOW IS JOB TO BE DATED?

Early Jewish traditions and some conservative Christians teach that Moses wrote the Book of Job. Other equally conservative scholars date the book in the period of the monarchy or later. Certain features of the book indicate a more developed stage of Israel's theology than existed in Moses' time,[10] so it's best to leave the date of composition an open question.

The story's setting is like that of the patriarchal narratives. Job's wealth, like Abraham's, consisted of livestock and slaves.[11] He acted as a family priest, as did Abraham.[12] The Sabeans and Chaldeans were nomadic raiders, showing no hint of their later international and economic importance (Job 1:15,17). Most importantly, the story's religious hero is not even an Israelite. He lived in Uz, to the east of Canaan.

[10]Among these are the relationships between the sons of God, Satan, and God (Job 1 through 2).

[11]Job 1:3; 42:12; cf. Gen. 12:16; 32:5.

[12]Job 1:5; 42:8; cf. Gen. 13:4,18; 17:7–8; 22:1–13.

WHAT IS JOB'S LITERARY CONTEXT?

Some have suggested that Job is historical fiction. But key indicators point toward historicity. The opening verses of Job adopt a historical note (compare Judg. 17; 1 Sam. 1). And the Bible elsewhere mentions Job alongside Noah and Daniel, historical figures from the Old Testament (Ezek. 14:14,20). The author adapts the story of a historical personage to illustrate the age-old problem of suffering and God's sovereignty. Unexplained suffering has provoked writers since the earliest times.[13]

HOW MAY JOB BE SUMMARIZED?

Job has a prose introduction and conclusion (Job 1 through 2; 42:7–17), which describe the heavenly perspective on Job's condition. Sandwiched between them is a lengthy poetic dialogue between Job and his friends—the earthly perspective on Job's predicament (3:1 through 42:6).

Prologue: Key to Understanding the Book—Job 1 Through 2. The prologue reveals what none of the story's human characters know: Job's suffering is a test of his faithfulness to God. This is our key to understanding the

---

[13]For numerous ANE parallels see Frances I. Anderson, *Job,* TOTC (Downers Grove, Ill.: InterVarsity Press, 1976), 23–32. The "First Job" of ancient Mesopotamia complained that his gods were being unfair to him (*ANET,* 589–91). The "Babylonian Job" protested that no one can understand the ways of the gods (cf. Job 11:7–9). He worries that everyone has abandoned him. In the end, Marduk restores his fortunes (*ANET,* 596–600). Subsimesre-Sakkan complained that he had met the fate of someone else—obviously a wrongdoer. Eventually an exorcist priest appeased his god's wrath, and each demon was sent packing in florid style—his disease moving out with him (W. G. Lambert, *Babylonian Wisdom Literature* [Oxford: Clarendon, 1960], 21–26). The Egyptian "Dispute Over Suicide" (2500–2000 B.C.) says, "My wretchedness is heavy. . . . Pleasant would be the defense of a god for the secrets of my body" (see Job 9:33; 16:19–21; 19:25–27; *ANET,* 405–7).

story on God's terms rather than on the confused terms of Job and his friends.

Job Interacting with Human Wisdom—Job 3 Through 31. The dialogue portion of the book is not a verbatim transcript of the tedious arguments. Rather, the author couches it in a poetic dialogue comprising three cycles of speech and response (Job 4 through 14; 15 through 21; and 22 through 31). Job's three friends keep pressing on Job their threefold mechanistic application of retribution theology. They believed that God rewarded good and punished evil in this life so predictably that they could analyze the pattern in Job's life.

Table 1: The Logic of Job's Friends

Point	Their Argument	True/False
One	God justly blesses the righteous and curses the wicked.	*True*
Two	Job is suffering.	*True*
Three	Job must be a sinner deserving his just punishment, and he should repent so God can lift his curse.	*False*

Against point three of their argument, Job says, "'I am blameless'" (Job 9:21). Job's friends falter at this because they lack the heavenly insight from Job 1 through 2. And to their consternation, Job objects even to point one, "'It is all the same; that is why I say, "He destroys both the blameless and the wicked"'" (9:22). Toward the end, Job's three friends run out of steam. Their speeches get shorter and shorter.

Job 28 is a poem on divine wisdom. Job doesn't know about the conditions set out in Job 1 through 2 any more than his friends do. But if this poem is part of a third response, it reflects a proper knowledge that all wisdom comes from God; "'God understands the way to it and he alone knows where it dwells'" (28:23). Job concludes, "''The fear of the Lord—that is wisdom, and to shun evil is understanding"'" (28:28). Another way of seeing chapter 28 is as the work of the author, not of Job. It provides a contrast to the futile arguments that had gone before.

Even after this flash of insight about divine wisdom, Job argues that he does not deserve this suffering (Job 29:1–25). He complains that God himself does not consider his plight (30:20–30). But he keeps on appealing to God, seeking vindication (31:1–40).

Elihu Summarizes Human Wisdom—Job 32 Through 37. By this point in the dialogue, Job's three friends have given up on Job as one who is "righteous in his own eyes" (32:1). Along comes another debater. At best, he gives a slightly better but still inadequate answer to Job's situation. It looks like he just rehashes the weary words we have already heard: Job suffers because he's a sinner (34:11,25–27,37).

Job wants a revelation from God, but God reveals himself to Job by imposing suffering on him (Job 33:19–22). Job is saying that God is unjust, but Job should be "'tested to the utmost for answering like a wicked man'" (34:36). Job wants restoration—well then, he ought to repent (35:1–8). Elihu runs on and on. "'Job, listen to my words; pay attention to everything I say'" (33:1). "'Hear my words, you wise men'" (34:2). "'I would like to reply to you and to your friends'" (35:4). "'Bear with me a little longer and I will show you that there is more to be said in God's behalf'" (36:2). By the time he's done, we're ready to hear God speak for himself.

Job Interacting With Divine Wisdom—Job 38:1 Through 42:6. Job has pleaded for a session with God. Sometimes he displayed confidence that he would be justified (Job 9:14 through 10:17; 13:3,22–23; 19:7–8; 23:2–7; 24:1). But sometimes he worries that such a confrontation would only display God's might (9:14,17). Sure enough, God overwhelms him by appearing in the form of a threatening storm (38:1; 40:6; c.f. Pss. 18; 19; Nahum 1). Rather than allowing Job to cross-examine him, God insists, "'I will question *you,* and you shall answer *me*'" (Job 38:3). "Will the one who contends with the Almighty correct him?'" (40:2). "'Would you discredit my justice? Would you condemn me to justify yourself?'" (40:8). A speechless Job humbly repents of his overreaching claim to wisdom (42:1–6).

Epilogue—Job 42:7–17. You might be tempted to do a bit of pious head-nodding at Job's three friends and their stodgy defense of God's justice. You might also be tempted to do some self-righteous head-shaking at Job's doubts,

Another View on Elihu

Some have suggested that Elihu is the mediator Job had sought (Job 9:32–35). This is the older interpretation. Proponents of this view note that Elihu has the only Hebraic name among the five. This is no accident. Job had hoped for a mediator to argue *his* cause (see 9:19; 16:18–22). To Job's chagrin, Elihu proved to be a *true* mediator. He not only rebuked the friends (32:10–14) but also Job (33:12; 35:2–16). He spoke only for God, who "gives songs in the night" (35:10). Elihu pointed out that Job did not suffer *because* he sinned, as the friends had alleged. Instead, he sinned in his suffering by accusing God of injustice (9:22–24,29–31; 34:5–9,36; 36:17; see also 6:29; 10:7, cf. Job 9).

In a direct challenge to Eliphaz's claims to a unique revelation through a vision (4:12–21), Elihu pointed out that God speaks with us in many ways (33:14). Sometimes he does speak in visions (33:15–18). But he also speaks to us through our pain (33:19–28). He thus demonstrated that suffering can be not only punitive but also redemptive (33:17–19,24–25,29–30).

As a true mediator, Elihu prepared the way for the theophany (38 through 41), for Yahweh's rebuke that followed, and for Job's ultimate repentance (42:1–6). God showed that he *does* govern the world justly and that it is beyond Job's understanding (38:4 through 39:30). He also showed how he has the power to govern and Job does not (40:7 through 41:34). These factors led Job to realize he had spoken rashly. His reaction was to repent (40:4–5; 42:2–6). Once he had realized and confessed his bad judgment, his restoration followed.

It can be a great encouragement when we suffer if we realize that God may be doing something redemptive in our lives and not just punishing us. We can also see in Job's restoration God's willingness to forgive.

accusations, and anger. But in the end God tells Eliphaz, "'You have not spoken of me what is right, as my servant Job has'" (42:7). Indeed, Job had spoken rightly when he noted that wisdom is from God (chap. 28) and later disavowed his own claims to wisdom (42:1–6). This is something Job's three friends should also have done early in the debate. So God appoints Job as an intercessor for these friends who had demeaned God's sovereignty by discrediting what he was doing through Job (42:7–9).

WHAT DOES JOB TEACH ABOUT LIFE?

If you approach Job seeking an answer to help you explain the meaning of suffering, you'll be conducting the same futile search that Job and his friends belabored. God often has hidden holy purposes in suffering. If you come searching for wisdom *as God reveals it on his own terms,* you will gain considerable insight. This book shows that you can refuse pat answers in the face of life's complexities—even when answers come from an essentially sound theological base like that of Job's three friends. It teaches that you need not move from God's just sentence, "If you sin, then you will suffer," to Satan's condemnation, "If you suffer, then you have sinned."

When "the sufferings of Christ flow over into our lives" (2 Cor. 1:5), we must learn to confess that "this happened that we might not rely on ourselves but on God, who raises the dead" (v. 9).

Psalms: Israel's Prayer Book and Hymnal

We rejoice with the singing psalmist, and we weep when he weeps. We are stunned at his cries for vengeance (for example, Ps. 137:8–9). Nevertheless, we *read* the Psalms more than any other portion of the Old Testament.

The Structure of the Book

WHAT ABOUT THE MATERIAL IN THE PSALM HEADINGS?

The Hebrew title for the whole collection of psalms is *Tᵉhillim*, which means "praises." The LXX uses *Psalmos* to translate the Hebrew word *mizmor*, a term for music sung with stringed instruments. We get the English title "Psalms" from that.

Titles ascribe 73 out of 150 psalms to David. And all fourteen of the historical notes link their psalms to events in David's life. But other authors receive mention too, such as Solomon, the Sons of Korah, Asaph, Heman and Ethan the Ezrahites, and Moses. Fifty-five times we see "for the director of music." We get various tune names (Pss. 9; 22; 45:1; 56 through 60; 75). Sometimes the title classifies the musical form, such as a "song," "psalm," "prayer," or "praise." The meanings of many terms are uncertain. Some of them are *shiggaion, miktam,* and *maskil.* Another Hebrew term, used in the body of some psalms, is *selah.*

Critical scholarship generally sees little value in the notes about authorship and history. But evangelical scholarship sees more authenticity in them. Derek Kidner even treats them as inspired canonical Scripture. Although E. J. Young doubts that they are inspired scripture, he says, "Unless the testimony of the title is actually contrary to the contents of the psalm, the title may be regarded as trustworthy."[14]

[14]Derek Kidner argues that the NT treats the psalm titles as "holy writ." He even builds some of his arguments on the authorship notes (e.g., Mark 12:35–37 and Acts 2:29–36; cf. Ps. 110:1; Acts 13:35–37; cf. Ps. 16:10). *Psalms 1–72,* TOTC (Downers Grove, Ill.: InterVarsity Press, 1973), 32–46, esp. 32; E. J. Young, *An Introduction to the Old Testament* (Grand Rapids: Wm. B. Eerdmans, 1940), 301.

How Did We Get Five "Books" of Psalms?

The process of writing and collecting the 150 psalms found in the Psalter spanned the millennium from Moses' time (for example, Exod. 15; Deut. 31:30 through 32:47; Ps. 90) to the postexilic period. But most of the individual poems come from the period of the monarchy. As time passed, small collections of what was known and valued were gathered. The books may have been used independently for some time before being linked.[15] Eventually these collections were gathered into the five books that make up the Psalter. To each book of the five-book collection was added a doxology, e.g., "Praise be . . ."

Table 2: Books and Doxologies

Book	Doxology
I–Pss. 1 through 41	Ps. 41:13
II–Pss. 42 through 72	Ps. 72:19
III–Pss. 73 through 89	Ps. 89:52
IV–Pss. 90 through 106	Ps. 106:48
V–Pss. 107 through 150	Ps. 150:6

How Can I Use the Different Psalm Types for Prayer and Worship?

Various Approaches to Interpreting the Psalms

The traditional historical approach relates as many psalms as possible to events in David's life. It applies the non-Davidic psalms to events in Israel's history. This kind

[15]Pss. 42 through 49 relate to "the Sons of Korah," but Book III adds four more of their psalms (Pss. 84; 85; 87; and 88). The divine name *Yahweh* predominates in Book I, but Book II generally uses *Elohim,* even in psalms duplicated from Book I (e.g., Ps. 53 = Ps. 14; 70 = 40:13–17; 108 = 57:8–11 and 60:7–12).

of historical awareness is useful. But the critical approach tried to discover the original sources and reconstruct historical settings. Brevard S. Childs says, "This move was basically unsuccessful. As if one could write the history of England on the basis of the Methodist hymn book!"[16] Pressing an invented historical background upon a psalm and then forcing the psalm to explain that history involves circular reasoning that leads to useless—if not perverse— conclusions.

Eventually, scholarship moved away from this attempt to situate each psalm in a historical event; instead, it has sought a *Sitz im Leben* (life-setting) for each psalm genre. A solid consensus has developed around the main features of this approach. It has not been all gain; it is useful, however, when employed with care.

THE PSALM GENRES AS GUIDES TO INTERPRETATION

One advance in the foregoing approach to the study of Psalms was to classify them. Several adaptations of that approach exist. For our study we can classify the psalms as hymns, laments, thanksgiving psalms, psalms of confidence, psalms of remembrance, wisdom psalms, and kingship psalms.[17]

Hymns. The Psalter's hymns can elevate the content and style of our own worship. They open with a "call to worship." Often this is the familiar *Hallelujah*, or "Praise the

---

[16]Brevard S. Childs, *Introduction to the Old Testament as Scripture* (Philadelphia: Fortress, 1979), 509.

[17]I follow Tremper Longman, *How to Read the Psalms* (Downers Grove, Ill.: InterVarsity Press, 1988), 19–36; also Raymond B. Dillard and Tremper Longman, *An Introduction to the Old Testament* (Grand Rapids: Zondervan Publishing House, 1993), 219–24.

LORD!"[18] The "reason for worship" forms the body of the hymn, often introduced with a "for" or "because." The psalmist may call upon his listeners to declare the glory of the LORD as Creator,[19] as ruling and conquering King,[20] or as Protector.[21]

Laments (Petition Psalms). Laments may seem a little harder for a believer to use—until we find our faith being tested. The psalmist's laments open with an "invocation," a cry to God (for example, "My God, my God," Ps. 22). Then he raises a "plea for help." He asks God to hear, deliver, or vindicate him. Sometimes he even asks that God would punish those who wrong him.[22] Generally, the cry for help includes a "motive for confidence." The strongest motive is God's own merciful character (for example, Ps. 25:6). The psalmist might also rely on repentance or innocence (for example, Pss. 17:3–5; 69:5). Finally, the lament psalms end with either a "hymn of praise" or a "vow to praise" God upon deliverance (for example, 26:12). This move from desperate petition to confident praise can form a healthy part of any believer's worship.

Thanksgiving Psalms. Thanksgiving psalms open with a declaration of the psalmist's intent to give praise, probably fulfilling the vow of praise that often ends the laments. The psalmist says, "I am under vows to you, O God; I will present my thank offerings to you" (Ps. 56:12). A narrative

[18]*Hallel* is a command to "praise" and *Jah* is a short form of *Jahweh,* generally spelled *Yahweh.* See the NIV Preface for an explanation of how *YHWH* came to be translated "LORD."

[19]Pss. 8; 19; 65; 104; 148.

[20]Pss. 47; 93; 95 through 99.

[21]Pss. 46; 48; 76; 84; 87; 122.

[22]See appendix, "Imprecation."

How the Psalter Teaches Life in Christ

Just as the Father is the LORD *God of the Psalter, so too Jesus Christ the Son is* LORD *God:* (a) He receives the worship given to the LORD (Ps. 97:7; Heb. 1:6). (b) He is the founder of the cosmos, whom Psalms calls the LORD (Ps. 102:25–28; Heb. 1:10). (c) He is the divine warrior who saves his people (Ps. 98, cf. Rev.). (d) He is the ascended gift-giver (Ps. 68:18; Eph. 4:8).

David or his offspring was the anointed king (messiah) *in the Psalter, but Jesus is all the more "the Christ":* (a) The Old Testament title *messiah* ("anointed one") referred to Israel's leaders, especially to its Davidic kings. The LXX translated the Hebrew term *messiah* with the Greek term *christos.* (b) David and his descendants were the anointed ones in the Psalms. (c) The New Testament applied this "messianic" term to Jesus, the Son of David,

follows, telling the story of a crisis, plea for help, vow of praise, and deliverance. This encourages the readers to remember that God will deliver them when they're in trouble. The conclusion renews the vow of praise or testimony. Psalm 30 is a good example of this pattern. The introductory praise (vv. 1–5) is followed by a narrative. This tells the story of the crisis (vv. 6–7), the psalmist's plea for help (vv. 8–10), and his deliverance (v. 11). A concluding praise rounds out the psalm (v. 12).

Psalms of Confidence. In psalms of confidence, the psalmist asserts his trust in God's goodness and power (Pss. 11; 16; 23; 27; 62; 91; 121; 125; 131). Enemies may be present (11:2; 23:5), but he can be at peace and sing with joy. He knows God as his refuge (11:1; 16:1) or rock (62:2), shepherd (23:1), light (27:1), and help (121:1). These psalms teach us that even when we mourn, we can trust God (3:3–6; 52:8).

Psalms of Remembrance. Two key events in Israel's history prompted their thankful remembrance: (1) the exodus, which was the key Old Testament model of salvation (Ps. 77:16), and (2) the Davidic covenant, which founded the messianic dynasty (Pss. 89; 132; 2 Sam. 7; 1 Chron. 17). Psalm 105 recounts God's faithfulness to the Abrahamic covenant, which he showed at the exodus. Psalm 106 tells of God's faithfulness even in spite of Israel's wilderness rebellion. And Psalm 78 speaks about "things from of old . . . what our fathers have told us" (vv. 2–3). The psalmist alternates between times when Israel enjoyed God's blessing and when they suffered God's judgment. He recounts their history from the exodus to the founding of the dynasty of David, who "shepherded them with integrity of heart" (v. 72). Psalm 136 praises God with the recurring reason for thoughtful remembrance: "His love endures forever."

Wisdom Psalms. The psalmist often adopts wisdom language similiar to that of the Book of Proverbs.[23] Like the wisdom writers, the psalmist sees God's wisdom displayed in his orderly universe (Ps. 19). He pays close attention to the contrast between the prosperous way of the righteous and the way of the wicked. The way of the righteous is informed by God's life-sustaining law (Pss. 1:1–3; 112; 119; 128) but the way of the wicked is cursed (Ps. 1:4–6).

Kingship Psalms (Royal Psalms). The kingship psalms extol God's rule. Sometimes they proclaim that God himself is Israel's eternal warrior (Pss. 110; 144), their king in Jerusalem (46 through 48). Actually, he's king over all the earth (47:7). A common way to extol God's rule is by focusing on Jerusalem's Davidic king.[24] He enjoys a special relationship with the LORD as his "son" and "anointed one" (Pss. 2; 20; 72) as well as his war chief (2; 18; 20; 21). As God's "son" (2:7), he can rule over all Israel and over all the earth (Ps. 72); the dynasty itself will be eternal, even if it suffers the harsh consequences of sin.[25] Ultimately, of course, exalted language like this can be fulfilled only in Christ. So these psalms are often called messianic psalms.

who fulfills the messianic promise (Rom. 1:1–4, cf. 2 Sam. 7; Pss. 16; 110). This is the rationale for most of the New Testament's use of the psalms.

Jesus Christ is himself a psalm-singing high priest: (a) Jesus is our brother in suffering and our brother in rejoicing; therefore, he is the congregation's priest, who leads the brethren in singing the Psalter (Heb. 2:12 = Ps. 22:22). (b) It is appropriate for him to sing the hymns and give victory shouts because of his exaltation at his resurrection. (c) It is also appropriate for him to sing the laments because of his humiliation (Pss. 69; 22:1 = Matt. 27:46).

What Does the Book of Psalms Teach About Life?

The Psalter has much to teach us about prayer and worship. Genre identification should not straitjacket your understanding of the Psalms. Rather, it should provide

[23]E.g., Pss. 1; 19; 73; 113; 119; 127; 128; and 133.

[24]Pss. 2; 18; 20; 21; 45; 47 through 48; 72; 89; 101; 110; 132; 144.

[25]Ps. 89; 132; see also 2 Sam. 7:8–16; 1 Chron. 17:1–13.

guidelines that point your inquiries in the most fruitful direction. Christ sang these psalms, and we can sing them to him, including the laments.

Proverbs: Israel's Accumulated Wisdom

What Is the Date and Authorship of Proverbs?

It has been popular among scholars to late-date the Book of Proverbs. Some even dated it to postexilic times because of supposed signs of Aramaic, Persian, and Greek influence. But discoveries of early Sumerian, Egyptian, and Babylonian wisdom texts have shown that the materials found in Proverbs were around well before Solomon.

The Book of Proverbs is an anthology of materials collected between 1000 and 400 B.C. On the early end of that time span, we have three links to Solomon during whose time much of the material originated (ca. 950 B.C., Prov. 1:1; 10:1; 25:1). On the late end, the work was still being edited at least as late as Hezekiah's time (ca. 700 B.C., Prov. 25:1).

What Is the Setting of Proverbs?

The Book of Proverbs shows many connections to its Ancient Near Eastern setting. Sumerian proverbs from 1700–1200 B.C. insist, "Wealth is distant, poverty is always at hand" (cf. Prov. 28:22).[26] Akkadian proverbs from the same period warn, "As long as a man does not exert himself, he will gain nothing" (cf. Prov. 10:4; 12:11; 13:4). Or, "Let your mouth be restrained, guarded your speech; like a man's

---

The Psalms as a Christian Hymnal

You can know that Christ, our great high priest, intones the laments with us because of his humiliation (Matt. 27:46 = Ps. 22:1). You can sing to a Lord who is able to sympathize with your weaknesses.

You can know that Christ sings the Psalter's *hymns* with you in the congregation (Heb. 2:12 = Ps. 22:22). He not only weeps with you but also rejoices with you in his exaltation.

Thanksgiving psalms should be examples for your thanksgiving to God, especially for his indescribable gift Christ Jesus (2 Cor. 9:15).

Israel sang the *historical psalms,* looking back to the exodus and the Red Sea crossing as Israel's decisive redemptive events. How much more can we look back on Calvary as the decisive moment, singing

---

[26]E. I. Gordon, *Sumerian Proverbs* (Philadelphia: University of Pennsylvania Press, 1959), 49.

wealth, let your lips be precious" (cf. Prov. 13:3).[27] Aramaic proverbs from the eighth century B.C. warn, "Withhold not thy son from the rod" (cf. Prov. 23:13), and "From thee is the arrow, but from God is the [guidance]" (cf. Prov. 16:1,33).[28] But Egyptian wisdom materials provide us with the most striking parallels. Amen-em-Opet, writing sometime between the time of Moses and Solomon, produced a list of "thirty sayings" much like Prov. 22:17 (note v. 20) through 24:14. And the prefect Ptah-hotep (2450 B.C.) taught his "son" to behave at royal dinner parties (cf. Prov. 23:1–3), to keep from getting into woman troubles (cf. Prov. 6:24; 7:5,27), to be a reliable messenger (cf. Prov. 25:13), and to order his life according to *ma'at* (justice).[29]

Most of this Ancient Near Eastern material has a royal setting. This fits the picture of King Solomon as the father of Israel's wisdom movement. Derek Kidner notes that the expression "my son" may be "a teacher's fatherly way of speaking to a pupil, as in the old Egyptian instruction manuals." But Kidner concludes that in Israel this instruction went on in the family. He notes the role of both parents in teaching (Prov. 1:8; 6:20), and even of the grandparents (Prov. 4:3).[30]

these songs to Jesus who saved us. And we can recount our personal history of God's involvement in our lives with the same prayerful historical reflection.

As we sing the *wisdom psalms,* which praise wisdom and exhort us to follow its ways, we are reminded that Christ is the wisdom of God, so we sing them to him.

As we sing the *royal psalms,* we sing them to and about *the* Christ, who is the eternal Son of David.

---

[27]James Pritchard, *Ancient Near Eastern Texts Relating to the Old Testament: New Material,* 2d ed. *(ANET)* (Princeton, N.J.: Princeton University Press, 1955), 425.

[28]"Words of Ahiqar," in *ANET,* 427–30.

[29]*Ma'at* plays something of the role in Egyptian literature that *chokhmah* (wisdom) plays in Proverbs.

[30]Derek Kidner, *The Wisdom of Proverbs, Job, and Ecclesiastes: An Introduction to Wisdom Literature* (Downers Grove, Ill.: InterVarsity Press, 1985), 19–20.

How Is Proverbs Organized?

Introduction—Prov. 1:1–7

The first seven verses of Proverbs provide the book's title (v. 1), purpose (vv. 2–6), and motto (v. 7). Proverbs 1:1 may be a general statement of authorship for the entire book. It probably applies especially to Proverbs 1 through 9, since Proverbs 10:1 gives us a new section title.[31] Verses 2–6 of chapter 1 tell us the book aims to foster intellectual "understanding," which grasps "words of insight" (v. 2), such as "proverbs and parables, the sayings and riddles of the wise" (v. 6). The book also fosters moral excellence: "wisdom and discipline" and the "prudent life" that knows and does "what is right and just and fair" (vv. 2–3).

A Father's Exhortation of the Young —Prov. 1:8 Through 9:18

After the introduction, a series of longer poems exhort the "simple" one, introducing this naive student to a pair of key women. The first, Dame Folly (Prov. 7), is a street corner prostitute. This seductress, either literal or figurative, appears in Proverbs 2:16–19; 5:3–20; 6:23–35; 7:6–27; 9:13–18. She glitters with flattery and seductive charm but drags her young victim down into dark death (9:13–18). The second, Dame Wisdom, the street preacher with a prophetic message,[32] is "the soul's true bride, true counselor, true

---

[31]E. J. Young takes Prov. 1:1 to be the title for Prov. 1 through 9, rather than the whole book; otherwise, this would be the only section in the book that had no title; cf. Prov. 10:1; 25:1; 30:1; 31:1 (*Introduction to the Old Testament,* 311). Derek Kidner argues that it is the title for the whole book, because otherwise the title for Prov. 10:1 would read, "These *also* are Proverbs of Solomon," after the analogy of Prov. 24:23; 25:1 (*Proverbs,* TOTC [Downers Grove, Ill.: InterVarsity Press, 1964], 22).

[32]Bruce K. Waltke believes Dame Wisdom is pictured as a prophetess in

hostess, and . . . the very offspring of the Creator" (1:20–33; 8:1 through 9:6, cf. 31:10–31).[33]

This section describes folly in terms of sexual immorality. But it also speaks of other temptations young men are prone to, such as gang violence (Prov. 1:10–19; 3:27–32; 4:14–19), mockery (1:22; 3:34; 9:7–8), or even laziness (6:6–11).

MORE PROVERBS OF SOLOMON—PROV. 10:1 THROUGH 22:16; 25:1 THROUGH 29:27

This material contains two collections: the Proverbs of Solomon (Prov. 10:1 through 22:16) and the Proverbs of Solomon Collected by Hezekiah's Sages (Prov. 25:1 through 29:27). They are made up of mostly short two-line proverbs. Contrasting parallelism displays the "two ways." You see *wisdom* contrasted with stupidity, mockery, shame, disgrace, recklessness, and chattering fools. *Right* is contrasted with wickedness, folly, perversity, sin, disgrace, and death. *Life* is contrasted with violence, punishment, crushed spirits, rotten bones, and death.

WORDS OF WISE MEN —PROV. 22:17 THROUGH 24:22

The "sayings of the wise" (Prov. 22:17) begin a new section, which is ended by a new heading at 24:23. This section

---

Prov. 1:20–33 (*The Book of Proverbs,* a course of 24 lectures on 12 sound cassettes [Grand Rapids: Institute of Theological Studies, 1986]). He points to features of her address that are typically prophetic: (a) Her accusing question, "'How long?'" (v. 22; cf. Jer. 4:14; 31:22; Hos. 8:5), (b) her call to repentance (vv. 24–25; cf. Jer. 15:19; 18:11), (c) her sentence to destruction in the prophetic first person (vv. 26–30, cf. Isa. 1:15; Jer. 11:11,14; Hos. 5 through 6; Mic. 3:4), and (d) her condemnation of the faithless (v. 32; cf. Jer. 2:19; 3:6,11–12; 8:12; 14:7).

[33]Kidner, *Introduction to Wisdom Literature,* 22.

displays striking links with the Egyptian *Teaching of Amen-em-Opet*. Only a few verses lack an Egyptian parallel.[34] This raises the question of which text used the other. Most scholars suggest that Proverbs either borrowed from Amen-em-Opet or that they both drew on a common source, though some doubt any direct dependency either way.[35]

This section develops such themes as quiet trust (Prov. 23:17–18; 24:19–22). It speaks of generous compassion for strangers and even enemies (24:1–12,17). It introduces dangerous characters like the banqueting social climber (23:1–8), the prostitute (23:26–28), and the drunkard (23:29–35).

FURTHER WORDS OF WISE MEN — PROV. 24:23–34

Proverbs' "further sayings of the wise" is set off by the titles in Proverbs 24:23 and 25:1 and by the ending of the list of thirty sayings at 24:22. It comprises two- and four-line proverbs on accurate testimony (vv. 23–26,28–29) and proper priorities (v. 27), plus a longer poem on the fate of the sluggard (vv. 30–34).

WORDS OF AGUR — PROV. 30:1–33

Agur confesses an inability to know or obey God (vv. 1–4) except by his grace and revelation (vv. 5–9); then he

---

[34]Kidner says, "Almost the whole of Proverbs 22:17–23:14 . . . is closely paralleled in widely-scattered sayings in *Amenemope*. (The exceptions are 22:23,26,27; 23:13,14)" (*Proverbs,* 23); see *ANET,* 421–25, for a list of connections.

[35]R. O. Kevin suggested that *Amen-em-Opet* borrowed from Job, because he thought he saw signs of Hebraisms in *Amen-em-Opet* ("The Wisdom of Amen-em-apt and Its Possible Dependence Upon the Hebrew Book of Proverbs" [Ph.D. diss., University of Pennsylvania, 1931]). Many commentaries say Proverbs shows some kind of dependence either upon *Amen-em-Opet* itself or upon a literary background that both works share. See Roland E. Murphy, *Proverbs,* WBC (Nashville: Nelson, 1998), 22:290–94. Some reject any kind of direct dependence, see R. N. Whybray, *Proverbs,* NCB (Grand Rapids: Wm. B. Eerdmans, 1994), 323–25.

moves through a series of mostly numerical two- and three-line proverbs on assorted topics.[36]

WORDS OF KING LEMUEL—PROV. 31:1–9

King Lemuel's two- and three-line proverbs come from the queen mother, who taught the king about royal behavior, such as avoiding wine and women (Prov. 31:3–7) and speaking up for the weak and helpless (vv. 8–9).

AN ACROSTIC ON THE WISE WIFE —PROV. 31:10–31

The last two-thirds of Proverbs 31 is an A to Z description of an ideal wife (cf. Prov. 18:22). She cares for the husband, family, and home (31:11–15,21–23). She strengthens the family economy through real estate purchases and sales of handicrafts (vv. 16–18,24). She guides her household well (vv. 25–27). She cares for the poor (v. 20). She is certainly praiseworthy (vv. 28–31). These remarkable standards are not an exhortation demanding that a young woman become a super-wife. Rather, they encourage a young man to choose a wife carefully, seeking qualities reflected in Dame Wisdom rather than in Dame Folly (Prov. 9).

How Is Proverbs To Be Interpreted?

Proverbs can be taken for oversimplification. But even a genius should be able to recognize the value of simple statements. We just don't take a single proverb as the last word on a subject. For example, the attentive reader will balance the insights of Proverbs 15:22 and 19:21 (compare 16:1,9; 20:24; 21:30–31) and catch the nuance implied in the bold

[36]On numerical proverbs, see Job 5:19–27; Prov. 6:16–19; Amos 1:3 through 2:8; and the lists of duties in Exod. 20 and 34.

contradictions of Proverbs 26:4–5.

Even what seems obvious has its value for the untutored, inexperienced one. Such a person can learn from generally applicable "compressed experience" that has been tested by time. Derek Kidner says, "They may be self-evident to us by now, only because at some stage they were dinned into our reluctant ears with small regard for novelty."[37]

A key feature of this book is the *mashal,* a short, simplistic, and often ironic saying that communicates wisdom pictorially and even playfully. R. B. Y. Scott has identified the following patterns:[38]

Identity or equivalence	"Whoever flatters his neighbor is spreading a net for his feet" (Prov. 29:5).
Nonidentity, or contrast	"He who is full loathes honey, but to the hungry even what is bitter tastes sweet" (Prov. 27:7).
Similarity	"Like cold water to a weary soul is good news from a distant land" (Prov. 25:25).
Contrariety to proper order, indicative of absurdity	"Of what use is money in the hand of a fool, since he has no desire to get wisdom?" (Prov. 17:16).
Classification of persons, actions, or situations	"A simple man believes anything, but a prudent man gives thought to his steps" (Prov. 14:15).
Valuation, or priority of one thing relative to another	"A good name is more desirable than great riches; to be esteemed is better than silver and gold" (Prov. 22:1).[39]
Consequences of human character or behavior	"Humility and the fear of the LORD bring wealth and honor and life" (Prov. 22:4).

These proverbs encourage the reader to live in harmony with the general God-given order. They describe a world where behavior results in generally predictable consequences, which only a fool would ignore.

[37]Kidner, *Introduction to Wisdom Literature,* 27.

[38]R. B. Y. Scott, *Proverbs, Ecclesiastes,* AB (Garden City, N.Y.: Doubleday, 1965), 5–8.

[39]Often this form challenges easy assumptions that might lead the reader to settle for the good rather than the best.

What Does Proverbs Teach Us About Life?

Proverbs displays less God-talk than expected in a book of the Bible. But it carries a call to decide between God's way and the world's way. This was the choice Joshua offered the people of Israel at Shechem (Josh. 24:15) and Elijah offered Israel on Carmel (1 Kings 18:21). The same choice is required of a Christian believer. Peter described the lifestyle of the pagans as consisting of "immorality and lust, . . . feasting and drunkenness and wild parties, and . . . terrible worship of idols" (1 Pet. 4:3, NLT). This is the same imagery that Proverbs used to describe the way of folly. However, believers, called followers of "the Way" in Acts (Acts 24:14, also 9:2), walk in the Spirit. This is their way of life.

Ecclesiastes: Israel's Hard Questions

What Does Solomon Have to Do With Ecclesiastes?

Ecclesiastes perplexes its readers. Despair about finding meaning extends to nearly everything that anyone would find worthwhile. Even wisdom comes out with bruises: It is a "heavy burden" that can bring "much sorrow" and sometimes produces few results (Eccles. 1:13,18). Not only that, it's nearly impossible to obtain (7:23–24). Whatever wisdom does accomplish is so fleeting as to be "meaningless and a great misfortune" (2:21). Reading this book for edification (2 Tim. 3:16) will take some doing.

Derek Kidner says, "While the author wears at times the mantle of Solomon to explore the ultimate rewards of wealth and wisdom, the only name he uses is 'the

Qohelet.'"[40] The term *qoheleth* carries the idea of a lecturer speaking to an assembly of people (see Eccles. 1:1–2 and 12:8–10). Solomon was known for his wisdom, wealth, and enjoyment of pleasures. Often the "I" in these sections sounds like a king (1:12,16; 2:1–24; 4:15?). But many of these reflections seem out of character for a king (4:1–4; 5:13,18; 6:1,3; 8:2,9–17; 10:5–7).

Traditional Jewish and Christian interpreters see an apostate Solomon as the author. But others find it difficult to see an apostate writing Scripture. Since the language fits neither Solomon's writings nor Solomon's times, the book was probably written sometime after the return from exile.[41]

How Is Ecclesiastes To Be Read?

Ecclesiastes' ambiguities have provoked various approaches to it. The German Kaiser Wilhelm thought it was the greatest book in the canon. However, he was applauding what he took to be denial of a righteous moral order.

More serious readers have tried various interpretive approaches. *Is this a contradictory editorial patchwork?* Critical scholars say later editors tried to rescue the book for the canon by inserting enough orthodoxy in it to mitigate the "dangerous" material and give the whole some redeeming value. *Is this the nihilistic debate of a doubter?* On this view, the brooding twists and turns represented by strongly worded contradictions define a debate. At one point the

[40]Kidner, *Introduction to Wisdom Literature,* 105.

[41]The conservative commentator Gleason Archer argues for a Solomonic date ("The Linguistic Evidence for the Date of Ecclesiastes," *Journal of the Evangelical Theological Society* 12 [1969]: 167–82). An equally conservative Franz Delitzsch says, "If the Book of Koheleth [Ecclesiastes] were of old Solomonic origin, then there is no history of the Hebrew language" (*Canticles and Ecclesiastes* [Edinburgh: T. & T. Clark, 1891], 190).

book praises God for excellent things; at another point it gives up hope of finding significance in anything. *Is this a sarcastic challenge to the believer?* Some see this book as a series of pious quotations meant only for bitter rebuttal. One commentator even considered the book to be amoral.[42] This view does not take seriously the summarizing language about God's eternal judgment at the book's end. *Is this a godly challenge to the secularist?* Some suggest that Ecclesiastes is a digest of the best a secular mind can offer. They say that the author repeatedly subjects these ideas to the searching light of eternal judgment (Eccles. 3:17; 8:12–13; 11:8; 12:11–14).[43]

To understand Ecclesiastes, consider the conclusion (12:9–14). Then watch the unifying refrains throughout the work's main body, which is bracketed by the identical opening and closing verses (1:2; 12:8). If you do this, you'll hear a strong statement: Life lived with a view *only* of this world is meaningless. But with an eternal perspective, you can find meaning and joy in creation.

This book has a "narrator," who provides us with the key to understanding the book. He speaks in the third person. He analyzes the judgments of the spokesman who talks about what "I saw" from the limited perspective

[42]Duncan B. MacDonald, *The Hebrew Philosophical Genius: A Vindication* (Princeton, N.J.: Princeton University Press, 1936), chap. 5.

[43]Since Nicolas de Lyra (ca. 1270–1349 A.D.) this has been a widely held view among Christian commentators. Martin Luther, Cocceius, Matthew Poole, Matthew Henry, John Wesley, and C. I. Scofield have held this view. Luther even thought some savant had made a research trip to Alexandria's library to gather up the best of cynical aphorisms to shoot down. And Scofield considered these sayings an inspired survey of human wisdom, but not revealed and therefore not authoritative for life—inspired but not revelatory (cf. the serpent's words in Gen. 3:4, Satan's words in Job 1 through 2, or Herod's words in Matt. 2:8).

"under the sun."[44] This third-person analysis is both sympathetic and critical (for example, Eccles. 1:2; 7:27; 12:9–14). Using the third person, he points to the speaker's thesis: "'Meaningless! Meaningless!' says the Teacher. 'Utterly meaningless! Everything is meaningless'" (1:2). But he subjects that cynical idea to a critique. In the end, the narrator provides his key to the interpretation of this book (12:9–14). He issues neither absolute denial nor approval of the teacher. We are to respect the teaching of the first-person spokesman. At the same time we must be cautious and critical of his conclusions.

What Does Ecclesiastes Teach About Life?

The Teacher can discover meaning in nothing when he examines life only from the human perspective (i.e., "under the sun"). This includes toil (Eccles. 1:14; 2:11,17; 4:4,7–8), wisdom (2:15), righteousness (8:14), wealth (2:26; 5:10; 6:2), prestige (4:16), pleasure (2:1–2), youth and vigor (11:10), life (6:12; 7:15; 9:9), and even the future after death (11:8). Even a wise lifestyle may end up proving to be meaningless (1:16–18; 2:12–17), because you may never get to enjoy labor's fruits (2:18–26; 5:1 through 6:9). And the wisest labor cannot alter God's immutable, inscrutable providence (3:1 through 4:3; 6:10–12; 7 through 8; 9:11 through 10:11).

Song of Songs: Israel's Love Poetry

The provocative sexual imagery in the Song of Solomon is straightforward love poetry. But Jewish and Christian authors have labored to find a more "spiritual" message in the book. Perhaps young lovers are better equipped to read

[44]E.g., Eccl. 1:3–14; 2:1–24; 3:16–22; 4:1–15; 5:13–18; 6:1–3; 8:9–17; 9:11–16; 10:5–7.

Ecclesiastes and the New Testament

The New Testament never quotes Ecclesiastes. But the concept of foolish vanity is certainly there. The rich, self-satisfied farmer plans to "build bigger" without so much as a tip of the hat to God's sovereignty (Luke 12:16–21). He would have done well to read Ecclesiastes. And the businessman who says he will "carry on business and make money" without considering the Lord's will should read it too (James 4:13–16; cf. 1 Cor. 4:18).

Ecclesiastes drives home the reality of the curse of sin. The Teacher notes that everything he tries is frustrated and potentially "meaningless." So too, Paul points out that "creation was subjected to frustration" (Rom. 8:20). In Ecclesiastes, Solomon was the wisest human—but he still came to no good end (cf. 1 Kings 11:1–6). Apart from Christ, our wisdom, our plans, our end, will be just as frustrated.

To free us from this, Jesus Christ took on humanity (John 1:14). He left his rightful glory with the Father. From the humble manger to the humiliating cross he often found no place in the hearts of those he was sent to (John 1:10). He was betrayed by his disciples during his trial and felt abandoned on the cross by his Father.

Paul recognized any message limited to hope "under the sun" as futile: "If only for this life we have hope in Christ, we are to be pitied more than all men" (1 Cor. 15:19). Thank God he continued, "But Christ has indeed been raised from the dead, the firstfruits of those who have fallen asleep" (v. 20). We are no longer limited to life under the sun; indeed, "God raised us up with Christ and seated us with him in the heavenly realms in Christ Jesus" (Eph. 2:6). For Jesus Christ is the wisdom of God who was with God at creation. He is the one in whom every promise God ever made finds its unfrustrated "yes" (2 Cor. 1:20; Col. 2:3).

So we ought to heed the counsel of Ecclesiastes' narrator: Balance enjoyment of good gifts with a sense of eternal responsibility before God (Eccl. 11:9–10). Recognize that God "rewards those who earnestly seek him" (Heb. 11:6). John looked forward to the time when "each person [would be] judged according to what he had done" (Rev. 20:12–13). The narrator in Ecclesiastes concluded this too: "Now all has been heard; here is the conclusion of the matter: Fear God and keep his commandments, for this is the whole duty of man. For God will bring every deed into judgment, including every hidden thing, whether it is good or evil" (Eccl. 12:13–14).

this book than old theologians. To choose a *natural* approach to the book does not mean we must adopt a *nontheological* perspective. Ecclesiastes shows us "vanity of vanities" (KJV), that is, futility. The Song of Solomon shows us a "song of songs"–that is, the greatest of songs. And it's about a young couple's love!

What Does Solomon Have to Do With Song of Songs?

The opening verse calls this "Solomon's Song of Songs" (Song 1:1), but the connection with Solomon is a bit troubling. It's difficult to harmonize the wholesome sexuality of this book with the historical books' picture of a man with too many wives and concubines. In fact, 1 Kings 11:6–11 blames Solomon's apostasy on his many wives. Wherever this book mentions Solomon by name, it's pretty impersonal (3:6–11; 8:10–12). Perhaps it's best to say that Solomon wrote some of its poems just as he wrote or collected much of the Book of Proverbs.

How Is Song of Songs To Be Read?

Do we read the Song of Songs as an allegory? Traditionally, Jewish and Christian interpreters have allegorized the book. One Jewish writer said that the expression "We will praise your love more than wine" (Song 1:4) meant that the oral exposition of the rabbis was more valuable than the mere written Law.[45] Christians from Hippolytus to modern preachers have proposed their own

---

[45]Marvin Pope provides an abundance of examples of the various interpretive approaches to the book (*Song of Songs,* AB [Garden City, N.Y.: Doubleday, 1977], 7C:299).

allegories.[46] Hippolytus said that "Let the king bring me into his chambers" (1:4) referred to converts being brought into the church.[47] He said the "two breasts" of 4:5 were the old and new covenants. Origen said, "If you have despised all bodily things . . . then you can acquire spiritual love."[48] So you might imagine how he would interpret the breasts and legs mentioned in the Song of Songs. Watchman Nee says the beams of cedar and fir at 1:17 point to the new humanity in Christ. Or at 7:5–7, talk of hair "speaks of the strength of her dedication, as with the Nazarite." The praise of her teeth (4:2; 6:6) "points to her capacity to digest the spiritual truth."[49]

Do we read Song of Songs as typology? Martin Luther wanted to get at "the simplest sense."[50] Instead of allegorizing all the details, he said the overall book typified the relationship of the bridal church to Christ the groom. But the book itself shows no typological indicators, for example official, institutional, cultic, and overtly theological elements. In addition, the maiden pursues her lover. This would depict the church pursuing Christ, whereas the pursuit of divine love runs the other direction.[51] Most impor-

[46]Various influential figures in church history have proposed an allegorizing interpretation of the book: Hippolytus (A.D. 230), a Roman presbyter; Origen (254), an Alexandrian theologian; Jerome (419), the translator of the Latin Vulgate Bible. Even Watchman Nee (1972), leader of an indigenous local church movement in China, wrote a commentary on it following this mode of interpretation (*Song of Songs*, trans. Elizabeth K. Mei and Daniel Smith, rev. ed. [Fort Washington, Pa: Christian Literature Crusade, 1966]).

[47]This and the following examples are from Pope, *Song of Songs*, 114ff.

[48]Origen on Song 1:4, cited by Pope, *Song of Songs*, 115.

[49]Nee, *Song of Songs*.

[50]Martin Luther, *Luther's Works*, ed. Jaroslav Pelikan, American ed. (St. Louis, Mo.: Concordia, 1955–86), 15:191.

[51]G. Lloyd Carr, *The Song of Solomon: An Introduction and Commentary,*

tantly, the eroticism of these poems might well typify the mythology of pagan fertility rituals. In any case, it just doesn't serve well as a picture of Christ's relationship to his church.

Do we read Song of Songs as love poetry? The natural view has not been very popular in church history. Theodore, bishop of Mopsuestia in Cilicia (A.D. 427), defended the literal interpretation. But the Council of Constantinople (550) outlawed this approach. Others followed with a similar lack of success at defending literal interpretation. For example, a ragged, barefoot, celibate monk named Jovinian attacked the ascetic teachings of his times (ca. 342–420). He said there was no moral difference between virginity, marriage, or widowhood. He said sexual expression could be just as holy as repression. People who had formerly chosen virginity began deciding to marry. This upset the hierarchy in Rome. Augustine of Hippo (345–430) responded with two books.[52] Synods in Rome under Siricius (392) and in Milan under Ambrose (393) condemned Jovinian and his followers.

Nevertheless, sexuality is a wholesome part of God's created order. Before the fall into sin the command went forth, "'Be fruitful and increase in number'" (Gen. 1:28). Scripture sustains this delight in sexuality. For example, the father in Proverbs teaches his son, "May you rejoice in the wife of your youth. A loving doe, a graceful deer—may her breasts satisfy you always, may you ever be captivated by her love" (Prov. 5:18–19; cf. Song 1:13; 4:5; 7:3; 8:10).

TOTC (Downers Grove: Ill., InterVarsity Press, 1984), 24–31 (a solid evangelical commentary on this book, with sensible, balanced treatment).

[52]Augustine, *De Bono Conjugali* [On the Good of Marriage], in *A Select Library of Nicene and Post-Nicene Fathers of the Christian Church (NPNF)*, ed. Philip Schaff and Henry Wace (Grand Rapids: Wm. B. Eerdmans, 1890), 1:3(13), 732ff; idem, *De Virginitate* [Of Holy Virginity], *NPNF*, 1:3(13), 753ff.

What Does the Song of Songs Teach About Life?

History shows us three approaches to sexuality: profane, prudish, and pure. The modern secular world has been seduced by the *profane* approach. This is displayed in the increase of pornography, prostitution, and loose arrangements between sexual partners. The medieval church of Rome lapsed into a *prudish* approach. This was evidenced by the dismissal of Jovinian's interpretation in favor of sexual asceticism as a spiritual virtue. But the Song of Songs offers believers a *pure* approach to sexuality. The book models mutually submissive sexual behavior between a loving couple. It affirms a wholesome delight in the marriage bed. The intimacy that Adam and Eve lost, so that their nakedness made them ashamed, can be restored in a return to Eden's boudoir. As Paul said, "The husband should not deprive his wife of sexual intimacy, which is her right as a married woman, nor should the wife deprive her husband. The wife gives authority over her body to her husband, and the husband also gives authority over his body to his wife. So do not deprive each other of sexual relations" (1 Cor. 7:3–4, NLT).

Appendix: Imprecation

You might be troubled by the incessant lamentation in the Psalms. The really distressing aspect of lament psalms is their periodic call for a judgment, calamity, or curse upon enemies.[53] You cannot automatically dismiss these texts

[53]Imprecatory Psalms are 7; 35; 58; 59; 69; 83; 109; 137; and 139. Imprecatory language occurs in other Psalms as well, e.g., Pss. 5:10; 6:10; 9:19; 10:2,15; 17:13; 28:4; 31:17–18; 40:14–15; 55:9,15; 68:1–2; 70:2–3; 71:13; 79:6,10,12; 94:1; 97:7; 104:35; 109:9–11; 141:10; 143:12. We see

without ignoring 2 Timothy 3:16–17 and Matthew 5:17–19. But neither can you automatically adopt these sentiments without defying Matthew 5:39–45 and Luke 6:29–35.

Christian interpreters have attempted to diminish the offense of these imprecations by various explanations.

- Some say they do not express the psalmist's own wish but are announcements of what God plans to do. But this is grammatically unlikely in most places and impossible in Psalms 3:7 and 69:2–36. And clearly Psalm 137:8–9 is expressing the psalmist's own attitude of personal satisfaction when judgment overtakes wrongdoers.

- Some deny that this is David cursing his enemies. They think David may be quoting his enemies' curses against him, much like Hezekiah put the threatening Assyrian letter before the LORD (2 Kings 19:14; Isa. 37:14). This might work with the addition of implied words in some psalms,[54] but it will clearly not work in most of them, where the imprecation is against a plurality of David's enemies rather than the singular language that enemies would employ when cursing him.

- Many insist that this vindictive language shows David at a low spiritual level. But this paints David in more spiteful colors than he ever showed (1 Sam 24:1–7; 26:5–11). It also ignores indicators that David spoke both from

---

much imprecation elsewhere in the OT, e.g., Num. 10:35; 31:2–4; Judg. 5:31; Jer. 11:20; 15:15; 17:18; 18:21–23; 20:12. And we see it in the NT too: 1 Cor. 16:22; Gal. 1:8–9; 5:12; Rev. 6:9–10.

[54]E.g., one might read Ps. 109:5–6 with the addition of the bracketed words I include: "They repay me evil for good, and hatred for my friendship. [They say,] Appoint an evil man to oppose him; let an accuser stand at his right hand." This would be the same pattern understood to be necessary in Ps. 2:2–3: "The kings of the earth take their stand and the rulers gather together against the LORD and against his Anointed One. 'Let us break their chains,' *they say,* 'and throw off their fetters.'"

his own emotions and by the Spirit, even the imprecatory language (Acts 4:25–26; Ps. 2:1–2).

- Others tell us that this is David's imprecation against spiritual rather than human foes. But several of these psalms were written in response to oppression by human enemies. The inclusion of the families of the enemies requires that the enemies be understood as human (Ps. 109:9–14).

It's better just to recognize that these are human enemies and acknowledge the following factors:

- The fundamental basis for these imprecations is the Abrahamic covenant, which promised, "'I will bless those who bless you, and whoever curses you I will curse'" (Gen. 12:3a).
- The rhetoric is full of hyperbole, which should not be taken too literally (compare Jer. 20:14–17; Matt. 5:29; 18:9; Mark 9:47).
- The one doing the cursing was not just anybody. It is God's theocratic king, his anointed one *(messiah)* who was meant to rule on an earthly throne serving heavenly purposes (Ps. 2).
- These imprecations served just and moral purposes. They displayed a concern for the establishment of justice (Ps. 7:6–10). They cared about God's own righteous reputation (Pss. 7:17; 35:18,28; 58:10; 59:13; 83:17–18).

The imprecatory prayers of the psalmist were appropriate for the old covenant. But that doesn't mean the New Testament believer can readily adopt them into the language he uses in prayer. The New Testament saint knows more than the Old Testament saint (John 15:15):

- More about the spiritual nature of the enemy (Eph. 6:11–18)

- More about the method that God is using to establish his kingdom, the word rather than the sword
- More about the time of judgment (Matt. 13:30; Luke 4:18–19; 2 Cor. 6:2)
- More about the eternal rather than temporal nature of judgment (Matt. 25:46; 2 Thess. 1:5–9)

If imprecatory prayers are proper for Christians at all, they must be prayed with an awareness of God's sovereignty. This was the case even with Old Testament believers who prayed them (Exod. 33:19). Remember, vengeance comes in God's timing (Isa. 61:1–2; Jer. 46:10). God says, "'It is mine to avenge; I will repay'" (Deut. 32:35; Rom. 12:19).

Study Questions

1. List the five poetic books and explain why we label just these five as "poetic books."
2. Explain how Lowth categorized poetic parallelism, and recognize examples of parallelism of the following types: subordination, contrast, continuation, comparison, specification, and intensification.
3. Label the verse and chorus structure in Psalms 39; 42 through 43; 59; and 107.
4. Highlight poetic repetition in Psalms 29; 83; 98; 146; and 148.
5. Define the general use of the Hebrew term *chokhmah*, which the Old Testament often translates "wisdom."
6. List and give references for five common terms found in wisdom literature.
7. List and give references for at least five wisdom passages outside the wisdom books themselves.

8. Define Solomon's role in the development of Israel's wisdom tradition, giving references.

9. What does the New Testament add to our understanding of wisdom?

10. Describe the significance of distinguishing between the date of Job's narrative setting and the date of its being written.

11. List evidence that places the narrative setting of Job in the patriarchal age.

12. Describe why Job 1 through 2 and 42:7–17 are essential for our interpretation of the meaning of Job.

13. Describe the role that the Book of Job plays in explaining why bad things happen to good people.

14. Critique the following statement: "If you suffer, then you have sinned."

15. Define the limits of the five books that constitute our present Psalter.

16. List the kinds of information that the psalm titles provide.

17. List the elements of a hymn, showing examples from verses in Psalm 46; 47; or 48.

18. List the elements of a lament, showing examples from verses in Psalm 17 or 22.

19. Analyze and critique the various suggestions in the appendix of how we should interpret the imprecatory psalms.

20. Label the following psalms as wisdom, remembrance, or kingship: Psalms 1; 2; 17; 110; 119; 144.

21. Describe the implications of confessing Jesus as the LORD, Messiah, and Priestly Singer of the Psalms.

22. Describe how we sing each of the psalm genres in the light of Jesus' work.

23. What is the time span for the collection of most of the Book of Proverbs?

24. List the various collections that Proverbs comprises, giving references.

25. List ten positive traits that wisdom encourages and ten negative traits that folly produces, giving three references for each trait.

26. List three dangerous kinds of people that Proverbs warns about, giving references for each kind.

27. List the evidence that wisdom's counsel is authoritative rather than just good advice.

28. Describe the key to understanding the Book of Ecclesiastes.

29. List and critique the various mistaken ways of interpreting Ecclesiastes.

30. Show references that define how the Teacher values wisdom in Ecclesiastes.

31. Explain how the New Testament enlightens our reading of Ecclesiastes.

32. Explaining the Song of Songs as the story of Israel's history is an example of what interpretive approach?

33. Label the following interpreters as proponents of allegorical, typological, or natural interpretation: Origen, Watchman Nee, Lloyd Carr, Martin Luther, Hippolytus, Augustine, Ambrose, Jovinian.

34. Explain what the text means when it talks of a return to Eden's sexual intimacy as a work of grace.

For Further Reading

Besides the following, see the books, commentaries, and articles cited in the footnotes.

HEBREW POETRY

Alter, Robert. *The Art of Biblical Poetry.* New York: Basic Books, 1985.

Berlin, Adele. "Parallelism." In *ABD,* 5:155–62.

Harrison, R. K. "Hebrew Poetry." In *Zondervan Pictorial Encyclopedia of the Bible,* ed. Merrill C. Tenney, 3:76–87. Grand Rapids: Zondervan Publishing House, 1975.

Longman, Tremper III. *Literary Approaches to Biblical Interpretation.* Foundations of Contemporary Interpretation 3. Grand Rapids: Zondervan Publishing House, Academie Books, 1987. Esp. "The Analysis of Poetic Passages," 119–34; "Examples of Poetic Analysis," 135–50.

WISDOM

Bullock, Hassel. "Introduction" and "Theology in the Wisdom Books." In *An Introduction to the Old Testament Poetic Books,* 17–62. Chicago: Moody Press, 1979.

Kidner, Derek. *The Wisdom of Proverbs, Job, and Ecclesiastes: An Introduction to Wisdom Literature.* Downers Grove, Ill: InterVarsity Press, 1985. Esp. "A Meeting of Minds," 11–17; "Voices in Counterpoint: The Three Books Compared, Contrasted and Integrated," 116–24; and "Some International Reflections on Life," 125–41.

Mouser, William E. *Walking in Wisdom.* Downers Grove, Ill.: InterVarsity Press, 1983. Pp. 80–123 are helpful concerning figures of speech.

JOB

Anderson, Francis I. *Job*. TOTC. Downers Grove, Ill.: InterVarsity Press, 1976.

Bullock, Hassel. "Job." In *An Introduction to the Old Testament Poetic Books*, 63–112. Chicago: Moody Press, 1979.

Kidner, Derek. "The Book of Job: A World Well Managed?" In *The Wisdom of Proverbs, Job, and Ecclesiastes: An Introduction to Wisdom Literature*, 56–74. Downers Grove, Ill.: InterVarsity Press, 1985.

Kline, Meredith G. "Job." In *Wycliff Bible Commentary*, ed. C. F. Pfeiffer and E. F. Harrison, 459–90. Chicago: Moody Press, 1962.

Smick, Elmer B. "Job." In *Zondervan Pictorial Encyclopedia of the Bible*, ed. Merrill C. Tenney, 3:615. Grand Rapids: Zondervan Publishing House, 1975.

PSALMS

Bullock, Hassel. "Psalms." In *An Introduction to the Old Testament Poetic Books*, 113–54. Chicago: Moody Press, 1979.

Kidner, Derek. *Psalms 1–72*. TOTC. Downers Grove, Ill.: InterVarsity Press, 1973.

_____ . *Psalms 73–150*. TOTC. Downers Grove, Ill.: InterVarsity Press, 1975.

Lewis, C. S. *Reflections on the Psalms*. New York: Harcourt, Brace, & World, 1958.

VanGemeren, Willem. "Psalms." In *The Expositor's Bible Commentary*. Vol. 3, *Psalms – Song of Songs*, ed. F. E. Gaebelein, 1–880. Grand Rapids: Zondervan Publishing House, 1991.

PROVERBS

Bullock, Hassel. "Proverbs." In *An Introduction to the Old Testament Poetic Books,* 155–88. Chicago: Moody Press, 1979.

Hubbard, David A. *Proverbs.* CC. Dallas: Word, 1989.

Kidner, Derek. "The Book of Proverbs: A Life Well Managed," and "Proverbs and Modern Study." In *The Wisdom of Proverbs, Job, and Ecclesiastes: An Introduction to Wisdom Literature,* 18–55. Downers Grove, Ill.: InterVarsity Press, 1985.

————. *Proverbs.* TOTC. Downers Grove, Ill.: InterVarsity Press, 1964.

Ross, Allen P. "Proverbs." In *The Expositor's Bible Commentary.* Vol. 5, *Psalms – Song of Songs,* ed. F. E. Gaebelein, 883–1134. Grand Rapids: Zondervan Publishing House, 1991.

ECCLESIASTES

Bullock, Hassel. "Ecclesiastes." In *An Introduction to the Old Testament Poetic Books,* 189–222. Chicago: Moody Press, 1979.

Hendry, G. S. "Ecclesiastes." In *The New Bible Dictionary.* Wheaton, Ill.: Tyndale House, 1962.

Kidner, Derek. "Ecclesiastes: A Life Worth Living?" and "Ecclesiastes—A Sample of Opinions." In *The Wisdom of Proverbs, Job, and Ecclesiastes: An Introduction to Wisdom Literature,* 90–115. Downers Grove, Ill.: InterVarsity Press, 1985.

Kidner, Derek. *A Time to Mourn and a Time to Dance: The Message of Ecclesiastes.* Downers Grove, Ill.: InterVarsity Press, 1976.

SONG OF SONGS

Bullock, Hassel. "The Song of Songs." In *An Introduction to the Old Testament Poetic Books*, 223–55. Chicago: Moody Press, 1979. A solid evangelical introduction to the Old Testament poets and wisdom literature.

Carr, G. Lloyd. *The Song of Songs: An Introduction and Commentary.* TOTC. Downers Grove, Ill.: InterVarsity Press, 1983.

Hubbard, David A. *Ecclesiastes, Song of Solomon.* CC. Dallas: Word, 1989.

13

Andrew Davies

The Great Divorce

Outline:

- History and Destiny
- The Earliest Kings of Israel
- History: Why Do We Need It and What Can We Do With It?
- Kings and Chronicles: Why Do We Need So Much History?
- The Monarchy and the Kingdom of God: Who Would Be King?
- What Provoked the Great Divorce?
- Decree Absolute: The Conference at Shechem
- The Rejection of Rehoboam
- Israel's Hope? The Northern Kingdom Under Jeroboam
- Southern Discomfort: Judah Under Rehoboam
- From Bad to Worse: Abijah of Judah

Terms:

Chronicler
syncretism

History and Destiny

All of us can look back upon certain defining moments in our lives. Plenty of actions, events, or occasions have had a significant effect on the course of our lives and the development of our characters. Many of them have been times of great joy and happiness, like a childhood vacation or a first romance. A fair portion of them, though, may well have been times of despair and trauma. In fact, the difficult times actually make the most difference to our lives. These low points in our lives often become significant stages in our Christian walk. If we allow them, they can lead us to a new understanding of God's character and his plans for our future.

If that is true of our lives, it is also true of a nation's history. After all, nations gain their identity mainly from the collective memories of their people (e.g., Deut. 26:5–11). In this chapter, we will consider one of the defining moments of Israel's history. We will see how, after the death of King Solomon, the kingdom of Israel split into two nations: Israel in the north and Judah in the south. This "Great Divorce" left a bitterness between the two nations that would last for many years.

It is dealt with at length in the OT historical books. Let's begin by considering an outline of the biblical material we will be covering in this chapter.

The Earliest Kings of Israel

Information about the lives and events we are looking at can be taken from the Bible's two main historical sources: the Joshua-Kings narrative and the books of Chronicles.[1] Here's where to look for the various parts of the story:

[1]For a more detailed discussion of these two historical traditions and the differences between them, see the section "Kings and Chronicles: Why Do We Need So Much History?" later in this chapter.

Historical Era	King	Date B.C.	Events	Bible Reference
The United Monarchy	Saul	ca. 1040–1010		1 Sam. 8:1 through 31:13; 1 Chron. 9:35 through 10:14
	David	ca. 1010–970		1 Sam. 16:1 through 1 Kings 2:12; 1 Chron. 11:1 through 29:30
	Solomon	ca. 970–931/30		1 Kings 2:1 through 11:43; 1 Chron. 28:1 through 2 Chron. 9:31
			Early revolts under Solomon	1 Kings 11:14–25
			Jeroboam's revolt and Ahijah's prophecy	1 Kings 11:26–40
			Solomon's death	1 Kings 11:41–43; 2 Chron. 9:29–31
The Revolt of the Northern Kingdom		ca. 931	Division of the united monarchy into two kingdoms	1 Kings 12:1–19; 2 Chron. 10
Early Kings of Judah (South)				1 Kings 12:1 through 15:24; 2 Chron. 11:1 through 16:14
	Rehoboam	931/30–913		1 Kings 12:1–19, 14:21–31; 2 Chron. 10:1 through 12:16
			Rejection by north	1 Kings 12:1–19; 2 Chron. 10
			Idolatry	1 Kings 14:21–24
			Shishak's attack on Jerusalem	1 Kings 14:25–28; 2 Chron. 12:1–12
			Wars with the north	1 Kings 14:30; 2 Chron. 11:1–12
	Abijah	913–911/10		1 Kings 15:1–8; 2 Chron. 13:1–22
			Wars with Jeroboam	2 Chron. 13:2–19
	Asa	911/10–870/69		1 Kings 15:9–15
			Religious revival	1 Kings 15:11–15; 2 Chron. 14:1–6; 15:1–18
			Ethiopian invasion repelled	2 Chron. 14:9–15
			Alliance with Aram against Israel	1 Kings 15:16–22; 2 Chron 16:1–10

(cont. on the next page)

(cont. from the previous page)

Historical Era	King	Date B.C.	Events	Bible Reference
Early Kings of Israel (North)				1 Kings 12:20 through 16:8
	Jeroboam I	931/30–910/09		1 Kings 12:20 through 14:20
			Religious alterations	1 Kings 12:25–33
			The man of God from Judah	1 Kings 13
			Prophecy of judgment on Jeroboam's dynasty	1 Kings 14:1–18
	Nadab	910/09–909/08		1 Kings 15:25–31
	Baasha	909/08–886/85		1 Kings 15:32 through 16:7

The division of the monarchy and its immediate aftermath were among the most difficult times the Israelites ever went through. Even some two hundred years after these events, the prophet Isaiah used them to illustrate the terrible threat that Assyria was posing for the people of his day. He warned of a time "'unlike any since Ephraim broke away from Judah'" (Isa. 7:17).[2] We might wonder, along with Isaiah, if Israel and Judah ever really learned the lessons of their history. But first we need to be absolutely clear that there is plenty that *we* can learn from history.

History: Why Do We Need It and What Can We Do With It?

Perhaps we need to think about what history really is and what good it is to us. All the contributors to this textbook

---

[2] Isaiah regularly uses the name "Ephraim" when he wants his readers to be clear he means the ten northern tribes as distinct from greater Israel as a whole.

believe that the Old Testament is an accurate historical record of God's dealings with humankind. But that doesn't mean that the record answers all the questions we might want to ask. Nor does it mean that the Bible gives us a detailed explanation of all the events it describes. For example, consider Omri, one of the more interesting kings of the northern kingdom of Israel. Though he reigned for barely more than a decade, he had a significant influence upon Israel's destiny. It was Omri who made Samaria Israel's capital city (the Southern Kingdom having Jerusalem). Archaeological evidence shows that he presided over some tremendous military, architectural, and economic achievements. Yet, despite Omri's importance, he is mentioned in only a handful of verses (1 Kings 16:15–28). His weaker and politically less successful son Ahab is given six whole chapters (1 Kings 16:29 through 22:40).

The editors of Kings focus attention on those aspects of Israelite history that are most directly relevant to their particular presentation of the relationship of God to his people. This means they have omitted plenty of information that biblical scholars would dearly love to know. Although such omissions may be frustrating, they do not represent an oversight. We must remember that the historical books of the Old Testament have a clear agenda. They don't just provide us with history for history's sake. Instead, biblical history serves to reveal theology. It tells of the intervention of God in human affairs. It sees the divine hand where otherwise we might have missed it. This way of thinking sees all biblical history as "salvation history."[3]

[3]You will sometimes find the original German term *Heilsgeschichte* used instead. See the section "The Bible Uses Stories to Teach Theology" in chap. 2.

So What Is Salvation History?

To view the Bible as a book of salvation history acknowledges that "God actually has in concrete historical fact saved his people from destruction; and it proclaims that the historical salvation thus attested is but the foreshadowing or 'type' of the salvation that is to come."[4] Israel remembered the great moments of Yahweh's saving intervention in its past, particularly the exodus from Egypt. They found faith for the future in those traditions. This way of thinking came naturally to the people, since they understood every event in their lives as being the work of God.[5]

I do not mean to imply that Israel saw no role for human responsibility, however. In the broader picture, every human skill or ability came from God, the first cause of any and every event. So even though developments in the course of history had external political causes, they were still ultimately attributable to God. First Kings 12:15 makes this explicit. The editors first describe how the free actions of Solomon's son Rehoboam directly caused the division of the kingdom. Then they add the comment: "This turn of events was from the LORD, to fulfill the word the LORD had spoken." Even Scripture itself finds it difficult to disentangle the divine and human origins of a particular action! This shows how closely the two are related.

[4] A. T. Richardson, "Salvation," in *The Interpreter's Bible Dictionary,* ed. G. A. Buttrick et al. (Nashville: Abingdon Press, 1962), 168.

[5] See W. S. LaSor, D. A. Hubbard, and F. W. Bush, *Old Testament Survey: The Message, Form and Background of the Old Testament* (Grand Rapids: Wm. B. Eerdmans, 1982), 259.

How Helpful Is the Concept of Salvation History?

The salvation-history approach to the Bible is not without its problems.[6] For example, clearly the concept of God's saving intervention in history is not the only theme of the Old Testament;[7] the idea is almost entirely absent from the wisdom books. Furthermore, God steps into history not only to save his people, but also sometimes to judge them.[8] Perhaps we should think in terms of "intervention history" as much as "salvation history" if we are to do justice to the biblical understanding.

On the other hand, the salvation-historical approach is very helpful when we try to relate biblical studies to the real world of contemporary living. History isn't "more or less bunk" (as Henry Ford thought) if we can gain from it. We all continually learn from our experiences. If you hit a punching bag, it may swing back and knock you over. But if you know enough to duck the next time, you've learned a lesson that will stop you from making another painful blunder. Similarly, if God has helped us in the past, we can be absolutely confident that he will help us again in the future. Hopefully, the experience we go through will teach us to rely on him more—and help us avoid making the same mistakes again! That was certainly the way the

---

[6]To assess these problems is really beyond the bounds of this discussion; refer to J. Goldingay, *Approaches to Old Testament Interpretation* (Leicester, England: Inter-Varsity Press, 1981), chap. 3, for a more detailed survey, and see also the articles on "Salvation" in the *Anchor Bible Dictionary* and *Interpreters' Bible Dictionary*.

[7]Goldingay, *Old Testament Interpretation*, 67.

[8]Although judgment almost always functions as a part of salvation, in the bigger picture.

inspired writers of the Old Testament viewed their faith, their writing, and their God.

But Why Do We Need History?

Let's consider the importance of history a little more carefully. When written from a perspective of faith, history is actually one of the best ways of teaching theological truth. This is the case for a number of reasons. First, storytelling is so graphic and memorable. Have you ever realized how much of what you know about life you learned from stories? Did you ever wonder why all kinds of cultures throughout history have used stories to explain why things are the way they are?[9] It's because stories communicate so well, so vividly. They inspire our creative thinking and imagination. Stories invite us to participate in their retelling within each new generation. It's easy to put ourselves into them— to imagine ourselves being there at the time. We can almost see the sights and feel the emotions. It's difficult to think of a more direct means of communicating than storytelling.

A second advantage of presenting theology through narrative is that this helps us keep our feet firmly on the ground. The Christian life is not just a philosophy, or an ideology. It isn't just something for discussion in church and seminary. Believers must live out their relationship with God in the real world every day. It often helps to be reminded that the great heroes of faith had to do this too. They had the same blessings, opportunities, weaknesses, failures, and feelings as we do. Recalling that fact as we read history stops our discussion from becoming abstract and otherworldly.

---

[9]This is such a common phenomenon, it even has a technical term to denote it—"etiology."

History also shows the consistency of God in dealing with us. We ought to be amazed at his patience in enduring the same mistakes and failures of generation after generation of his people, within the Bible and outside of it. We can also see that God has an eternal purpose, a plan for the world, which he is still working out today. Now of course we can learn from our own lives, our own "stories." But history is so helpful to us because it means we can learn from the successes and failures of *others.* That is one reason the Bible records God's dealings with Israel so openly and honestly. We can find out more about God, his expectations of us and his intentions for us. How? Simply by considering his actions on behalf of his people in biblical times. We can use their past to affect our futures (see 1 Cor. 10:11). Those are just a few of the many good reasons for paying attention to the large amount of historical information in the Old Testament.

Kings and Chronicles: Why Do We Need So Much History?

We have seen that biblical history has an agenda different from that of modern history. Nevertheless, we can still uphold it as a wholly reliable and trustworthy account of events. It is a double standard to presume the accuracy of other historical records from the ancient world and at the same time approach the Bible with suspicion. The events that we are considering in this chapter were obviously important to the development of the Israelite states. They are covered therefore in some detail in the biblical texts. For the whole period of the monarchy, we have two separate accounts of the history of Israel and Judah. The account that began with Joshua and Judges continues through

Samuel and Kings.[10] Then Kings is also paralleled by the rather later account of 1 and 2 Chronicles.[11]

The Value of Chronicles

The book of Chronicles (1 and 2) is not often given the attention it really deserves. Admittedly, it borrows heavily from Kings, and it deals only with the destiny of the southern kingdom, Judah. But Chronicles also adds a substantial amount of data that is not present elsewhere. Much of this is of great historical and theological interest. Yet the Chronicler would not have rewritten Israel's story just to include a few supplementary details. Beyond that, he clearly had a strong theological reason for writing. Kings and Chronicles were written in different historical contexts,[12] and with different intentions.

What were these different motives for writing? In simple terms, Kings provides an explanation for the terrible punishment of the exile, and it attempts to show the righteousness of God's judgment. Chronicles, though, has an eye on the future of God's people, and looks instead to the restoration and rebuilding of the community. It provides a more wide-ranging and comprehensive theological

---

[10]This account is known as the Deuteronomistic History, because of its close relationship to the teaching and theology of the Book of Deuteronomy.

[11]In the Heb. text, none of these books is divided into parts one and two, as they are in our modern English Bibles. There is one book each of Samuel, Kings, and Chronicles. The books were first divided in the early Gk. translation of the OT, the Septuagint (LXX), which confuses the matter slightly by calling 1 and 2 Samuel by the name 1 and 2 Kings (or Kingdoms) and our present books of Kings by the name of 3 and 4 Kings.

[12]Kings seems to have been written early on during the exilic period, say 580 B.C. or thereabouts. Chronicles is some two hundred years later, dating probably from the fourth century.

assessment of the situation after the exile.[13]

History in Chronicles

Even more so than Kings, Chronicles is a work of salvation history. For the Chronicler, the history of Israel is merely the arena in which God's righteousness is demonstrated publicly. Chronicles concentrates on the twin topics of the God of Israel and the people of Israel. These themes and the relationship between them are worked out fully in the course of the book. Many of the other important topics in Chronicles are really the result of the interaction of these two central characters. These topics include an understanding of the election of Israel and of God's sovereign plan for Israel's destiny. The book's theological stress, naturally, is on those areas where the author has his own special contribution to make. Accordingly, some of the basic concepts of the Old Testament faith are presumed rather than expounded in Chronicles. They are referred to only in passing, if at all. However, Chronicles does make a significant contribution to our understanding of kingship in Israel.

Can We Trust Chronicles?

As I mentioned, Chronicles has often been neglected in the past. This is largely because its historical accuracy was questioned. Old Testament scholars have long felt that the two books of Kings seem to be reliable and based on accurate ancient sources. Some say, on the other hand, that the additional data contained in Chronicles has the character of

[13]This is the view of Sara Japhet, which is stated more fully and effectively in the very helpful introduction to her remarkable commentary, *1 and 2 Chronicles*, OTL (London: SCM Press, 1993).

"alterations, additions and falsifications."[14] Fortunately, scholarship today sees the folly of that opinion. The two most important recent commentaries on Chronicles acknowledge that the book does make use of ancient traditions and reliable historical sources.[15] Chronicles is certainly different from Kings and has its own interests, but scholars can still take seriously its contribution to understanding Israel's history.

The Monarchy and the Kingdom of God: Who Would Be King?

For the Chronicler the kingship of Judah and of all Israel belongs to Yahweh. The practical administration of the kingdom, however, is given to David and his descendants. The human king sits on the throne of the Lord (1 Chron. 29:23) and governs as his regent. Yet the kings are kept firmly in their places: They are portrayed as very human and fallible in all areas of their lives, particularly in their relationships with the people and with God himself.

In this respect, Chronicles makes a distinction between Israel's "glory days" under David and his son Solomon and the rest of the Judean kings. David and Solomon are portrayed in a more positive light in Chronicles than in Kings, in both political and religious realms. Yet it is not true to say that they are considered perfect or infallible. David is rejected from completing the temple because he had "shed much blood" (1 Chron. 22:7–8; see 28:3). Twice he is said to have

[14]W. M. L. de Wette, writing in 1806, and quoted by G. H. Jones, *1 and 2 Chronicles,* Old Testament Guides (Sheffield, England: Sheffield Academic Press, 1993), 12.

[15]I.e., Japhet, *1 and 2 Chronicles;* and Hugh Williamson, *1 and 2 Chronicles,* NCB (London: Marshall, Morgan & Scott, 1982).

sinned (1 Chron. 15:13; 21:1,3,8). Several of Solomon's positive qualities are stressed by Kings but downplayed in Chronicles. For example, Chronicles deliberately understates his wisdom in comparison with the Kings account. Also, the changes that Kings attributes to Solomon were almost always preempted by David. So, for Chronicles, neither David nor Solomon was perfect, but they were both appointed by Yahweh. Their combined reign was the most glorious period in Israel's history.

The Chronicler handles the kings who followed David and Solomon quite differently. Those later kings of Judah are certainly not presented as role models. Their sins and faults are not played down and are sometimes highlighted. This is true for the accounts of both the "good" as well as the "bad" kings.[16] So we might conclude that Chronicles brings us a more realistic, if less systematic, account of the later kings. It provides us with useful additional details of their military, economic, political, and religious activities. At the same time it subtly portrays their inconsistent religious conduct.

What Provoked the Great Divorce?

As I pointed out earlier, the historical books of the Old Testament see just about everything that happens as being the direct will of God for his people. Yet human beings are still responsible for their own actions. So, while there were some "spiritual" reasons for the division of the kingdom, there were also a number of political and relational factors

[16]For example, look at the treatment of the end of Josiah's life in 2 Chron. 35:20–24 (esp. v. 22) and contrast it with the parallel in 2 Kings 23:29, which removes any blame from Josiah himself. Also, you might consider the apostasy of Joash (2 Chron. 24:17–22), which is not present in Kings.

that came into play. Many of these causes of the division go back to the time of David and even earlier. From a human perspective three factors are of particular importance.

1. Was There Ever a Wedding?

Some critical scholars have suggested that Israel and Judah really were always distinct nations. They were united only in that they had the same king at the time of David and Solomon. Some radical critics, such as the German scholar Martin Noth,[17] have proposed that the twelve tribes were originally independent of each other. Noth felt he could not rely on the historicity of the patriarchal narratives, especially the account of the twelve sons of Jacob. He pointed out what he believed to be important differences between some of the lists of tribes throughout the Old Testament. For him, the names of the tribes all came from the geographical areas where they originally lived in prehistoric times. Thus Israel and Judah did not share the same ancestry. We must reject this suggestion on the basis of the biblical evidence. There is no need to think that we cannot take the patriarchal narratives quite literally, and no clue that we should not. Furthermore, the concept of the twelve united tribes existing and working together for many generations is central to the Old Testament. It cannot have been mere invention.

2. Unreasonable Behavior?

On the other hand, it is not impossible that there were tensions and even quite bitter disagreements among the different tribes. Genesis shows us quite plainly the jealousy

[17]Martin Noth's ideas are summarized conveniently for the English reader in *The History of Israel,* 2d ed. (New York: Harper & Row, 1960).

that existed among the original twelve brothers, and even their ancestors. Over the early years of the Israelite monarchy, a deep resentment for the south does seem to have built up among the northern tribes. There was growing unrest even before the death of David. In his struggle for the throne, David first became king of Judah (2 Sam. 2:4). He had to contend with Ish-Bosheth (also called Esh-Baal in 1 Chron. 8:33; 9:39) for control of Israel (that is, the northern tribes; 2 Sam. 3 through 5). Moreover, he had to cope with a revolt led by his son Absalom (2 Sam. 15) and another led by Sheba son of Bicri (from Saul's tribe, Benjamin; see 2 Sam. 20).

Solomon made things much worse, however. In the eyes of the northerners, he frequently showed favoritism to the southern tribes, especially to Jerusalem, a comparative newcomer to the nation of Israel. Worse still, the northern tribes felt he had little regard for some of Israel's most ancient and precious traditions. Solomon's vast expenditure on building programs soon stretched beyond what the country could reasonably afford.[18] Furthermore, the forced labor program he introduced to provide workers for the building projects really amounted to slavery for some groups of society (1 Kings 9:20–23).

Without consulting tribal elders, he appointed a new "civil service" to administer these schemes. He divided Israel into twelve taxation districts that had little regard for tribal boundaries (1 Kings 4:1–19). In Jerusalem too, Kings records a dramatic increase in the number of officials and advisors Solomon employed (at the nation's expense). You might like to compare his list of officials in 1 Kings 4 with

[18]See 1 Kings 9:10–14, which implies he was unable to pay his debts.

those of David (2 Sam. 8:15–18) and of Saul (1 Sam. 14:50), which are hardly worth mentioning. Also, consider the daily provisions demanded by his bloated court (listed in 1 Kings 4:20–28). This provides a rather extravagant picture of Solomon's excesses at the expense of his people.

This regional animosity grew into a bitter resentment of Solomon himself. In fact, we know that at least three substantial revolts took place late in Solomon's reign. The first two were colonial rebellions led by foreigners: Hadad the Edomite (1 Kings 11:14–18) and Rezon of Damascus (1 Kings 11:23–25). The third uprising was the significant one for our purposes. Its leader was Jeroboam son of Nebat, one of Solomon's high officials, later to become the first king of the Northern Kingdom (1 Kings 11:26–27).

3. Early Signs of Dissent

Although 1 Kings 11:26 states that Jeroboam "rebelled" against the king, there is no suggestion in the text that he formally organized a revolt or incited resistance to the king. What did happen is recorded at length in 1 Kings 11:29–40. Jeroboam was met on his way out of the city of Jerusalem by the prophet Ahijah the Shilonite. Ahijah took hold of the new cloak he was wearing, tore it into twelve parts, and gave ten of them to Jeroboam. This was a symbolic enactment of the word of Yahweh to him: "'See, I am going to tear the kingdom out of Solomon's hand and give you ten tribes. But for the sake of my servant David and the city of Jerusalem, which I have chosen out of all of the tribes of Israel, he will have one tribe'" (vv. 31–32).[19]

---

[19]Ten and one clearly don't add up to twelve, though. See n. 36 for one possible explanation. Another possibility is that the twelfth segment signified the tribe of Levi, which the Lord was retaining for himself.

This judgment was prescribed because "they" (v. 33), the people of Israel, had forsaken God and gone after the gods of the heathen nations. Yahweh had decreed, however, that because of his promise to David, the kingdom would not actually be taken away in Solomon's time. That tragedy would take place in the days of his son instead. Even then, one of the tribes would always remain under the rule of the Davidic line. God promised Jeroboam that his dynasty would be as enduring as David's if he would only follow him faithfully and keep his commands. We do not know exactly how Jeroboam responded to this oracle. The proclamation of this prophetic message posed a threat to Solomon. It is probable that the oracle was reported back to him. He then sought to do away with his rival out of jealousy, just as Saul had tried to do away with David. Either way, Jeroboam sought sanctuary at the Egyptian court. He remained there, out of Solomon's reach, until after Solomon's death.[20] On his return, however, he was welcomed back by his fellow Israelites as something of a liberating hero.

[20]The story of Jeroboam's life is made slightly more complicated by the fact that the Septuagint (LXX) account of his life (which appears between vv. 24 and 25 of 1 Kings 12) differs from the Heb. text in a number of small details. The LXX account duplicates and restates much of the Heb. account, altering the order of events slightly, and adds that Jeroboam was a harlot's (Sarira) son who "made good" and built the city of Sarira (=Zeredah?) for Solomon. He himself owned some three hundred chariots; and it was he, rather than Solomon, who built the Millo (see 2 Sam. 5:9 et al; NASB, KJV) and fortified the old City of David. In this account, it was because of his aspirations to the kingship that Solomon tried to kill him, but Jeroboam fled to Shishak in Egypt and in fact married the pharaoh's sister-in-law, Ano. Also in the Septuagint, it is Jeroboam who actually summons the congregation of the people to Shechem and invites Rehoboam to attend. Immediately before the conference begins, the prophet Shemaiah (not Ahijah as in the MT) tears a new garment into twelve pieces. He gives ten of them to Jeroboam, as a sign of what God would do with the nation of Israel. The negotiations proceed as in the Heb. text, and Jeroboam is appointed king of Israel in Rehoboam's

Divine Judgment

The human factors mentioned above are significant but must be interpreted as to their theological meaning. The Bible also presents the division of the kingdom as God's punishment upon Israel, and in particular upon the royal house. Nathan's rebuke of David after his affair with Bathsheba includes the prophecy of judgment upon his house: "'Now, therefore, the sword will never depart from your house, because you despised me and took the wife of Uriah the Hittite to be your own'" (2 Sam. 12:10). Also, 1 Kings 11:9-13 reminds us that Yahweh was angry with the apostate Solomon later in his life. He had made alliances and trading agreements with other nations (notably Egypt, 1 Kings 3:1; cf. Isa. 31:1, 30:1-5). These treaties were often sealed by his marriage to foreign princesses. The alliances and marriages gave rise to much of Solomon's idolatrous behavior in later life. But God also recognized that the people as a whole were also to blame for the increasing theological and moral breakdown. The division was in a very real sense a judgment upon all Israel. Perhaps it was a way of preserving a "righteous remnant" at the same time.

These three factors were important underlying reasons for the schism, which after Solomon's death came to a head over how a new king was to be appointed. This time the problem of royal succession was not just a matter of court intrigue. It became more serious than that.

---

place. These are interesting variations, but they are not particularly significant and are not to be preferred to the Heb. account. The MT surely records the earlier tradition and is probably more reliable. It seems to me that the LXX is kinder to Jeroboam. For example, he hears of his divine designation only after he has called the tribes together to negotiate with Rehoboam over his appointment as king. The Gk. account may simply be a rewritten and slightly more sympathetic version of his life story.

From the United Monarchy to the Fall of Samaria

Dates[21] written with a diagonal slash (e.g., 931/30) indicate a year that begins in one year and ends in another on the Gregorian calendar we use today. Overlapping dates (e.g., 872/71–870/69–848) indicate coregencies. All dates are B.C.

United Monarchy		Egypt	Assyria	Significant Events
Saul	ca.1040–1010			
David	ca.1010–970		Ashur-rabi II 1010–970	
Solomon	ca.970–931	*21st Dynasty* Siamun 978–959		Hiram king of Phoenicia 968–935
		22nd Dynasty Sheshonq I (Shishak) 945–924	Tiglath-Pileser II 966–935	Rezon king of Damascus (Aram) ca. 950 onwards
Divided Kingdom				
Judah	Israel			
Rehoboam 931/30–913	Jeroboam I 931/30–910/09	Osorkon I 924–889	Ashur-dan II 934–912	Sheshonq I's attack on Israel, 926
Abijah/Abijam 913–911/10 Asa 911/10–870/69	Nadab 910/09–909/08		Adad-nirari II 911–891	
	Baasha 909/08–886/85			

(cont. on the next page)

[21]Dates for Assyria are taken from H. W. F. Saggs, *The Greatness That Was Babylon,* 2d ed. (London: Sidgwick & Jackson, 1988); and A. Kirk Grayson, "History and Culture of Assyria," in *ABD,* 4:732–55. Dates for Egypt are from K. A. Kitchen, "Egypt, History of (Chronology)," in *ABD,* 2:321–31. Israel and Judah are taken from J. N. Oswalt, "Chronology of the OT," in *ISBE,* 1:673–85; and Edwin R. Thiele, *The Mysterious Numbers of the Hebrew Kings,* rev. ed. (Grand Rapids: Zondervan Publishing House, Academie Books, 1983). For the sake of simplicity and clarity, only the more important and better-known rulers of Egypt are listed here. This period of Egyptian history (1069–714 B.C.) is known as the Third Intermediate Period. Egypt was

Divided Kingdom		Egypt	Assyria	Significant Events
Judah	Israel			
	Elah[22] 886/85–885/84		Tukulti-Ninurta II 890–884	
	Omri 885/84–880–873	Osorkon II ca. 874–850	Ashurnasirpal II 883–859	
Jehoshaphat 872/71–870/ 69–848	Ahab 874/73–853			Battle of Qarqar, 853
	Ahaziah 853–852		Shalmaneser III 858–824	
Jehoram 853–848–841	Joram/Jehoram 852–841			
Ahaziah 841	Jehu 841–814/13			Assyria at war with Babylon, 818–811
Athaliah 841–835				
Joash/Jehoash 835–796			Shamshi-Adad V 823–811	
	Jehoahaz 814/13–798		Adad-nirari III 810–783	
Amaziah 796–767	Jehoash/Joash 798–782/81			

(cont. on the next page)

fragmented politically during this time, and a number of different dynasties overlapped, having their seats of government in different parts of the land. The pharaohs of the Twenty-Fifth Dynasty were Ethiopian invaders who took over Lower Egypt under the leadership of Piankhi and his father, Kashta. They were able to reunify the two kingdoms of Egypt by about 712 B.C., during the reign of Shabaka. For biblical evidence of the link between Egypt and Ethiopia at this time, see, for example, Isa. 20.

[22]Elah was actually succeeded briefly by Zimri, who ruled for only a week (1 Kings 16:9–20). After Zimri's death, Tibni contested the kingship with Omri before the latter was acclaimed king (1 Kings 16:21–22).

(cont. from the previous page)

Divided Kingdom		Egypt	Assyria Events	Significant
Judah	Israel			
Azariah/Uzziah 792/91–767–740/39	Jeroboam II 793/92–782/81–753		Shalmaneser IV 782–772	
			Ashur-dan III 771–754	
	Zechariah 753–752		Ashur-nirari V 753–746	
	Shallum 752			
Jotham 750–740/39–732/31	Menahem 752–742/41			
Ahaz 735–732/31–716/15	Pekahiah 742/41–740/39	*25th Dynasty* Piankhi 747–ca. 716	Tiglath-Pileser III/ Pulu 744–727	Ministry of Isaiah, ca. 740–690
	Pekah 752–740/39–732/31			
	Hoshea 732/31–723/22			Merodach-Baladan begins Babylonian revolt against Assyria, ca. 721
Hezekiah 716/15–687/86			Shalmaneser V 726–722	
	Fall of Samaria 722	Shabako 716–702	Sargon II 721–705	
			Sennacherib 704–681	Assyrian attack on Jerusalem, 701

Decree Absolute: The Conference at Shechem –1 Kings 12:1–19

After the death of Ish-Bosheth, elders from the northern part of the kingdom had come down to David at Hebron to anoint him as their king. This act ushered in the period of the united monarchy. When we note the significance of that event, it is interesting that there is no record of a similar thing happening to Solomon. He had come to power as David's chosen successor in Jerusalem. Therefore, his authority over the north seems to have been presumed and accepted. As far as we can tell, the citizens of Jerusalem had no problem in welcoming Solomon's eldest son Rehoboam as his successor. But it does appear that the northern tribes were hesitant about renewing their agreement with the Davidic house. They felt they had been slighted and mistreated over the last few years. Before they would sanction his coronation as king of all Israel, the elders of the northern tribes wanted to have a clearer idea of Rehoboam's plans for their future.

It is noteworthy here that Rehoboam himself traveled to Shechem to meet with the northern tribes after Solomon's death. This is somewhat unexpected. The more normal procedure would have been for them to come to him at Jerusalem.[23] First Kings 12:1 states that he had gone there so that "all the Israelites . . . [might] make him king." Yet the fact that the heir apparent himself made the journey suggests that all was not well. It seems Rehoboam was hoping to secure his position by appearing to take the northerners' difficulties seriously. This was undoubtedly a clever diplomatic move. Unfortunately for him, that wisdom did not extend to his handling of the negotiations.

What Was the Main Issue at the Shechem Conference?

Jeroboam son of Nebat, who had attempted to overthrow Solomon a few years earlier, had by this time returned from Egypt. He was among the Israelite tribal heads who brought to Rehoboam their very real complaints about their treatment under Solomon. They asked

[23]See J. M. Miller and J. H. Hayes, *A History of Ancient Israel and Judah* (London: SCM Press, 1986), 229.

Rehoboam to reject his father's oppressive system of forced labor gangs and heavy taxes. They promised, "'Lighten the harsh labor and the heavy yoke he put upon us, and we will serve you'" (1 Kings 12:4). The threat behind their plea was clear, though: They would serve him, but only if he would promise to improve their lot. Rehoboam asked for three days to make his decision and went off to consult his advisers. First he sought the advice of the elders who had been his father's most trusted officials. They saw the very real threat to the unity of the kingdom brought on by Solomon's harshness. They urged Rehoboam to "'give them a favorable answer'" (v. 7). He was to consider himself as much the servant of the people as their master. Rehoboam, perhaps because of his pagan heritage (1 Kings 11:3,14–21), did not favor a servant style of leadership.[24] Instead, he wanted to follow in Solomon's despotic footsteps. Accordingly, he did not find the elders to his liking. So he went to discuss the matter with the friends who had grown up with him in the royal court. Their advice was quite different: "'Tell these people . . . "My little finger is thicker than my father's waist. My father laid on you a heavy yoke; I will make it even heavier. My father scourged you with whips; I will scourge you with scorpions"'" (1 Kings 12:10–11).

The Rejection of Rehoboam

Although this manifesto would never be popular with the people, its swagger found favor with Rehoboam.[25]

[24]As described, e.g., in Deut. 17:15,20.

[25]Rehoboam's mother, Naamah, was actually an Ammonite princess—perhaps that was another factor which contributed to his lack of sympathy for the common people of Israel, shown so clearly by his response here.

After three days, he returned to the council at Shechem. There he informed the northern tribal heads that he would not agree to their request. And they reacted to his words exactly as we might expect them to, answering Rehoboam:

"What share do we have in David?

What part in Jesse's son?

To your tents, O Israel!

Look after your own house, O David!" (1 Kings 12:16)[26]

In other words, "You don't care about us—you're concerned only about yourself and your friends in Jerusalem. So we don't want anything to do with either of you!" The breakup of northern Israel and southern Judah had begun: The north had rejected the south's chosen leader. Rehoboam quickly realized his mistake and chose one of his officials to negotiate with the tribal leaders. But hoping to intimidate them, he sent out Adoniram, the man who had been Solomon's official in charge of forced labor. Of all the Jerusalem administrators, he was among the most hated and feared. The people's priority had always been to end the forced labor system. Consequently Rehoboam's power play backfired. Adoniram as a negotiator was taken as a personal insult. He met with the full fury of the crowd and was stoned to death. Rehoboam had to flee for his life. The editors of Kings add the footnote, "Israel has been in rebellion against the house of David to this day" (1 Kings 12:19).

Israel's Hope? The Northern Kingdom Under Jeroboam—1 Kings 12:20 Through 14:20

Israel was not left without a king for long, however. They had in Jeroboam an obvious candidate. He had high-level

---

[26]Compare these words with the war cry of Sheba, who led a revolt of the northern tribes in David's time (2 Sam. 20:1).

government experience but was not tainted with the corruption and excesses of the court. He had contacts abroad, especially in Egypt. He had actively resisted the hated Solomon and had also been involved in the negotiations with Rehoboam. When it became clear that the Davidic dynasty was not going to comply with their wishes, the assembly summoned Jereboam to Shechem, where they crowned him king "over all Israel" (1 Kings 12:20). Only Judah remained loyal to Rehoboam.

The Concept of Kingship

Note that there does not seem to have been any discussion about whether Israel should retain the monarchical system. This is probably significant, since it has been suggested that the rejection of Rehoboam was essentially a rejection of the whole concept of dynastic kingship.[27] According to this view, many of the people wanted a return to the charismatic leadership that was characteristic of the judges. In particular, they were outraged at the "royal theology" advocated by the throne. It presented Jerusalem and the Davidic dynasty as God's untouchable representatives on earth. Certainly both had been chosen by Yahweh, and Yahweh had promised to protect them. But some court insiders seem to have thought that made the king and the priesthood untouchable. It is easy to see how this concept could cause resentment in the north. It is possible that some such sentiments lay behind the frequent assassinations that plagued the Northern Kingdom. I suggest, however, that throwing off the oppressive yoke of royal theology was not the *major* reason behind the Israelite

[27]The view of Murray Newman, cited approvingly by B. W. Anderson, *The Living World of the Old Testament,* 4th ed. (Harlow, England: Longman, 1988), 256.

Kingship or No Kingship?

In recent years, due to the apparent moral failings of the present Royal Family, the future of the British monarchy has been a popular topic in Great Britain. A number of alternatives for the future have been discussed, both in the media and on the streets. Do we need a monarch at all? Do we skip a generation and then give the kingship to the young and innocent Prince William? Do we instruct the Royal Family to economize and keep out of trouble? Do we introduce new privacy laws, so no one knows what they are doing? These discussions have dominated the British media for some time now. Whether the debate will result in any changes, we have yet to see. But that's not the point. It would be impossible to write a history of the United Kingdom in the 1990s without dealing at length with the rise of the republican movement. So, I wonder if the contemporary British situation can help us understand the circumstances in ancient Israel? Certainly it is dangerous to argue from silence! Yet I find it puzzling that there is no record of any such discussion of alternatives in Israel. If the theological basis of kingship was really the major issue for the northern tribes, one would certainly expect it to appear somewhere.[28]

revolt. If it were, the very existence of kingship would have been threatened.

Instead, only one particular manifestation of kingship was rejected: the Davidic dynasty. The frequent changes of dynasty in Israel over the next fifty years or so, therefore, are to be seen as principally caused by something else. That is, they were the result of Israel's moral depravity and the all-consuming human lust for power. There were undoubtedly some people in the north who questioned the need for a king. However, there was not a pronounced search for charismatic leadership in the old style of the judges. It's also worth remembering that Israel's own assessment of the rule of the judges was in fact a negative one (see Judg. 21:25).

Jeroboam's Early Years as King

Although the events at the Shechem conference were obviously a surprise to most of the people, they were only

[28]See Miller and Hayes, *History of Ancient Israel,* 232.

what Jeroboam had expected. Remember, at the time of his earlier revolt he had received a prophetic designation as king over ten of the tribes (1 Kings 11:29–40). He seems to have settled in quickly as the new ruler of the northern tribes. He established his capital at Shechem, one of the great historic cities of Israel. It was at Shechem that Joshua had conducted his great covenant renewal ceremony after Canaan had been taken by the Israelites (Josh. 24). Jeroboam settled there and strengthened the city's defenses. He also fortified Peniel, another town with important historical ties (1 Kings 12:25). Later still, he also established a palace or fort in Tirzah, about ten miles away from his principal base at Shechem.

Where he lived, however, was not the most pressing issue that Jeroboam faced. He also had to deal with the religious significance of Jerusalem. Since the time of David, the Judean capital had become the center of religious life in all Israel. The people acknowledged Jerusalem as his seat. The king had an important role to play in the national religious system. Much more than this, everyone understood the city temple in Jerusalem to be the residence of Yahweh on earth. It was the place he had chosen to dwell. This was a comparatively new concept in Israelite religion, less than a century old. Yet the association of particular gods with particular sanctuaries was an ancient pagan practice; ironically the idea probably met with little resistance. And since Solomon's temple had been completed, the many small local Yahwistic shrines throughout the whole land had declined in importance. Instead there was a tendency to centralize the major religious festivals in the capital. Even at its largest, Israel was never a huge kingdom. Jerusalem was situated quite centrally, so it was always easy for pilgrims from all corners of the nation to head to the temple for the ceremonies conducted there. Jeroboam was quick enough to realize that his subjects would still make that journey south for the festivals. He had to find some alternative within his own borders. Apart from any risk to their personal safety, these travelers would be exposed to Judean propaganda about the corruption of the Northern Kingdom. They might easily be tempted to stay in the south. Worse still, they might come back home as spies and rebels to work for a reunited kingdom under Rehoboam. Jeroboam feared for his life and his nation.

How Did Jeroboam Influence Israelite Religion?

Jeroboam's basic approach to the problem of Jerusalem's religious importance was quite a clever one. He proposed to establish new national shrines for his people in two of the ancient tribal sanctuaries, Dan and Bethel. These sites would seek to continue the worship of Yahweh in the north. At the same time, they would reject the royal and Jerusalem ideologies that had become a part of the national religion. (These traditions may not have found much acceptance in the more traditional north, anyhow.)[29] Of course, Jeroboam's motives were certainly not good—he was not attempting to restore the true worship of Yahweh. Rather, he sought to deny the Davidic house its religious authority in the eyes of the people. He wanted to gain some public acclaim for himself in the process. The real problem, though, was with his execution of the plan. In trying to find

[29]While it is clear there is a genuine royal theology in the Bible (e.g., 2 Sam. 7), it is also clear from the historical books that it was later taken to excess, sometimes, for example, wrongly understood as meaning that Jerusalem could never be destroyed.

an earlier religious tradition that would be acceptable to the people, Jeroboam turned back to the Exodus period. He remembered that Aaron had made a golden statue of a calf centuries before while Moses was receiving the Law on Mount Sinai. Drawing on this precedent, he made a calf statue as a central feature of the sanctuaries.

There are a couple of striking parallels between Aaron and Jeroboam. Two of Aaron's sons were called Nadab and Abihu (Lev. 10:1); Jeroboam also had sons called Nadab (1 Kings 15:25) and Abijah (1 Kings 14:1).[30] Both Aaron and Jeroboam built their statues in response to a particular need: Their people were uncertain about the destiny of the religious system that was in operation. Both of them introduced their statues to the people with the words "'These are your gods, O Israel, who brought you up out of Egypt'" (Exod. 32:4; see also 1 Kings 12:28). There is enough evidence here to suggest that the writer of Kings believed that Jeroboam was consciously copying the work of Aaron.[31]

In addition, both Jeroboam and Aaron chose to build statues of a calf, a young bull. At this time, bulls were revered animals in many parts of the ancient world because of their strength and power. In Egypt, for example, the sacred Apis bulls were worshiped as divine incarnations. Their tombs were constructed as finely as those of the greatest pharaohs. As far as we can tell, however, bulls were not worshiped in this way in Canaan. They were seen instead as symbols of various deities, particularly of El, the chief god of the Canaanite pantheon.[32] Actually, many of

[30]"Abijah" is only a small variation from "Abihu" in Heb.

[31]For more discussion of these parallels, see Miller and Hayes, *History of Ancient Israel*, 242.

[32]See J. A. Soggin, *An Introduction to the History of Israel and Judah*

the more powerful and warlike gods of Ancient Near Eastern religion were at times pictured astride or standing on the backs of bulls. Presumably this was to represent the superiority these gods claimed over natural powers. For example, an eighth-century relief of the Aramean storm god Hadad has been found in Arslan-Tash in northern Syria, where the deity is pictured standing on the back of a bull with arrows of lightning in his hand.[33] Aaron and Jeroboam both had Egyptian connections, of course. It is much more likely, however, that their use of the bull images was, like that of the Canaanites, symbolic. Neither apparently intended to establish the bulls as idols. They were probably not representations of Yahweh or of any other gods. Most scholars admit that the bulls functioned as a symbol of the presence of Israel's God, similar to the ark of the covenant.

Jeroboam's Alterations to the Cult

At the same time, Jeroboam made a number of other practical changes to the religious system. He upgraded the status of some of the small local sanctuaries and approved them for regular use. This made it even easier for the people to worship without journeying to Jerusalem. He also needed to find additional priests and officials to staff the new sanctuaries. Most of the Levitical priests were probably still attached to the Jerusalem system and unavailable to Jeroboam. So he did away with the traditional requirement that all clergy should be members of the tribe of Levi and appointed "all sorts of people" to priestly office (1 Kings

---

(London: SCM Press, 1993), 205–6; and Anderson, *Living World,* 261.

[33] Anderson, *Living World of the Old Testament,* 261.

12:31). He also made at least one significant alteration to the religious calendar. He instituted a festival on the fifteenth day of the eighth month, "a month of his own choosing" (v. 33). This was intended to replace the great Feast of Tabernacles held a month earlier in Jerusalem. These technical cultic details were designed by God and established in Mosaic law. Yet on the surface, these adaptations appear to be relatively minor. Perhaps the writer of Kings condemned these events so forcefully because he saw how these minor alterations eventually eroded Yahwistic worship in Israel. The small local shrines quickly became centers of syncretistic worship. The new priests lacked the firm grounding in traditional belief and practice held by the Levites. Thus they were unable to resist paganizing influences. Some of them may even have been the original Canaanite sanctuary officials who merely switched allegiances to retain their jobs. This was certainly what happened centuries later when Roman emperors accepted Christianity. Large numbers of officials at the pagan temples "converted" overnight.

The Downward Spiral

The bull statues may not have been intended as idols, but they quickly took on that status in the eyes of ordinary people. This is surely what the editors of Kings meant when they wrote, "this thing *became* a sin" (1 Kings 12:30). It would always be difficult for the people to remember that they were offering sacrifices to Yahweh at the bull shrines. They were not supposed to be bringing offerings to the bulls themselves. In a little while, however, the people were doing exactly that. Even Jeroboam himself began to offer sacrifices to them (v. 32). Moreover, for years some of the Canaanite people within Israelite territory had associated bulls with their gods El and Baal. So it was only natural that these pagan gods would come to be linked to and confused with Yahweh. As a result, Dan and Bethel quickly became places of pilgrimage for the worshiping of idols, as well as the worship of Yahweh.[34]

Those in Israel who remained faithful to Yahweh were likely indignant. The establishment of the two shrines was neither initiated nor sanctioned by Yahweh. They were founded on questionable motives and opened the door for paganism. On two recorded occasions, prophetic warnings were brought to Jeroboam. They declared that he was embarking on a course of action that would lead to destruction for him and for Israel.[35] Yet only from the vantage point

Mixing True and False

Even today we need to remember the contrast that often exists between popular religious conceptions and the true biblical doctrines that they imitate. When I was a Bible college student, we took a survey on religious belief as part of our evangelism course. We would poll people in the town centers and around housing estates. The results were really interesting. I was astonished to see how many churchgoers believed there was more than one way to salvation. Many weren't convinced about the deity of Christ or even of the existence of God! (Why on earth go to church if there's no one there to worship?) Only a few days ago I recall hearing a high-profile British Christian on the BBC. He said that he believed in reincarnation—which the Bible clearly rejects! Solid scriptural teaching in our churches will equip us to deal with such misunderstandings. But we should also be aware that a similar situation certainly existed in Israel. There may have been people who had been equally influenced by both the Canaanite religious thinking and the true Israelite faith, making them syncretists. Furthermore, there was probably a substantial minority of the nation who were not fully orthodox in their belief.

[34]See J. Bright, *A History of Israel* (London: SCM Press, 1980), 238.

[35]See 1 Kings 13:1–34; 14:1–16. The fascinating story of the man of God from Judah who comes to prophesy against the altar at Bethel is well worth examining in some depth.

of later Israelite history can we really see how disastrous the consequences were. By the time of the early writing prophets, just over a century later, Bethel was a degenerate pagan shrine. Hosea urged the Northern Kingdom to recognize that the bull idol was not God and to throw it out (Hos. 8:5–6). Amos associated Bethel ironically with sin rather than with sanctification (Amos 4:4). Seek Yahweh, he pleaded, but not Bethel (Amos 5:4–5). How could a holy God be found in such an evil place? Dan and Bethel had been established as shrines to Yahweh. Yet in just a few years, they had become monuments to human arrogance and apostasy.

Jeroboam's Legacy

Despite Jeroboam's genuine achievements, the Bible treats him with scorn, resentment, and even hatred. His dynasty didn't last long. His son and successor Nadab was assassinated in the second year of his reign and replaced by Baasha. Furthermore, Jeroboam's legacy troubled the Northern Kingdom for the rest of its two-hundred-year existence. It dragged each successive Israelite king further and further down into the mire of idolatry, syncretism, and apostasy. Time after time we read that later kings "walked in all the ways of Jeroboam son of Nebat and in his sin, which he had caused Israel to commit" (1 Kings 16:26; cf. 22:53; 2 Kings 13:6,11). In 2 Kings 17, the editor explains in moving language why Yahweh had to give Israel over to destruction. Even there, Jeroboam is condemned as one of the prime causes of Israel's fall. He is described as the one who "enticed Israel away from following the LORD and caused them to commit a great sin. . . . until the LORD removed them from his presence" (vv. 21–23). His story is a solemn reminder of our responsibilities before God. It tells us the consequences of apostasy.

Southern Discomfort: Judah Under Rehoboam —1 Kings 14:21–29

Meanwhile, back in the south, Rehoboam's place as king of the southern tribe of Judah seemed assured (1 Kings 12:17). He was in no danger of losing his authority in Jerusalem. He immediately took steps to ensure the loyalty of the Benjaminite territory. The Benjaminites, the tribe of King Saul, bore no allegiance to David's house.[36] Rehoboam reinforced the border and fortified some of the major cities of the region.[37] He installed his sons in those cities to keep him informed of any threat to his position (2 Chron. 11:5–10,18–23). He also designated Abijah, son of his favorite wife Maacah, as his heir apparent.

Attempts at Forced Reconciliation

Rehoboam did not intend to give up his northern territories without a fight, either. On his return to Jerusalem, he summoned all the fighting men of Judah and Benjamin. Some 180,000 soldiers were sent to do battle with the Israelites and retake the Northern Kingdom for the Davidic

[36]The Bible drops hints that the Benjamites were quite resentful of Rehoboam. When Ahijah redistributed the twelve pieces of his garment, he gave ten to Jeroboam, but only one to Solomon. This left the twelfth, which presumably signified Benjamin, unaccounted for. Some writers see here a suggestion that Benjamin was kept within the new Judean kingdom only by force. Yet since Jerusalem was actually just in Benjaminite territory, there was no way this region could have been conceded to Jeroboam. See R. Rendtorff, *The Old Testament: An Introduction* (London: SCM Press, 1985), 39; Bright, *History of Israel*, 233.

[37]Archaeological evidence of these fortifications has been discovered, according to H. Jagersma, *A History of Israel in the Old Testament Period* (London: SCM Press, 1982), 131.

line. He was stopped at the last minute by an oracle delivered by Shemaiah, "the man of God" (1 Kings 12:21–24). He instructed Rehoboam not to fight against his sister nation but to send his men home. Nevertheless, this was not the end of the conflict between Judah and the larger state of Israel. Even during the reign of Rehoboam's grandson Asa, we read that the conflict continued. For a while the Israelite king at the time, Baasha, even overran the town of Ramah, just five miles north of Jerusalem (1 Kings 15:16–17). This caused Judah to request help from the Aramean king Ben-Hadad.[38]

Early attempts by Israel to force a reconciliation were finally brought to an end by an outside force, the assault of Pharaoh Shishak on both Israel and Judah (1 Kings 14:25–28; 2 Chron. 12:1–11). The biblical pharaoh is usually identified as Sheshonq I. Sheshonq ruled from about 947–925 B.C. and was the first pharaoh of the Twenty-Second Dynasty.[39] Regrettably, the real motive for the Egyptian invasion has been lost in the mists of time.[40] But

---

[38]This was, however, only the final results of the bitterness and resentment that had built up over the split, rather than a serious attempt at the reestablishment of a united Israelite state. By the time of Ahab of Israel and Jehoshaphat of Judah, relations between the two nations were quite cordial (1 Kings 22).

[39]See appendix, "Problems of Egyptian Chronology."

[40]There was no obvious reason for Shishak to want to attack Israel or Judah at all. Egypt was in disarray and decay and had lost her former territories. Perhaps it was a final attempt to halt the decline and to reassert Egyptian authority over Palestine. Even so, Egypt would have been unable to retain any control in the area, so many scholars have found themselves unconvinced by this explanation. Clearly Shishak was a contemporary of Solomon, since he gave asylum to Jeroboam when he fled Solomon's court. Perhaps then we should think of the attack on Judah as an intervention on behalf of Jeroboam, during the later years of Solomon's reign. This suggestion has two principal advantages. First, such an attack would easily fit the picture we have built up of the general decline of the Israelite empire at the time.

it is worth remembering that the Bible does provide us with a far broader and more fundamental reason: Second Chronicles 12:1–4 reminds us that what happened was all part of God's will. Ultimately, this attack upon Israel, like many others, was designed as a punishment for the unfaithfulness of the people to the covenant.

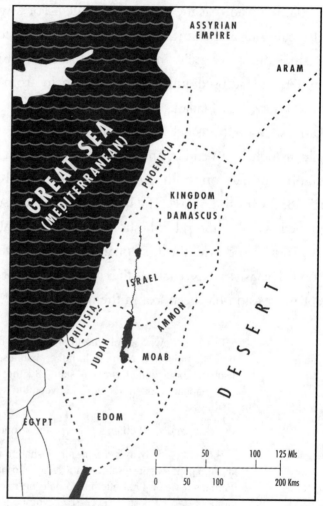

Israel and Judah Among the Nations

(Remember that Edom and Damascus both reasserted their independence shortly before Solomon's death—see 1 Kings 11:14–25.) And second, it would explain why Jeroboam is said to have revolted against Solomon (cf. 1 Kings 11:26). As we noticed earlier, this statement is something of a puzzle, since nothing of a specific revolt is recorded in either Kings or Chronicles, making this is all very hypothetical.

One factor in ending the conflict between Israel and Judah was that their national securities were in serious danger. While they were preoccupied, their vassal states took the opportunity to reassert their independence. After Damascus had been lost, the rest of Aram was quick to regain its independence. The Philistine city-states on what is now the Gaza Strip threw off their chains. Moab broke free from Israel in the middle of the ninth century (2 Kings 3:5), and Edom and Libnah rebelled against Judah slightly later, during the reign of Jehoram (2 Kings 8:20–22). Many of these nations immediately became threats to the two new smaller nations. Israel in particular, without its protective outer territories, became a target for the larger world empires, such as Assyria. Assyria wanted control of the major trading route to Egypt. Part of this route ran along the Mediterranean coast and turned inland through Israelite territory.

Although the threat to Judah was real too, it was less pressing. Judah retained only a small portion of the original Solomonic empire. It held only about a sixth of the population. The region was isolated in the mountains and of much less strategic importance. It is easy to get the impression from reading Kings and Chronicles that Judah, rather than Israel, was the larger and more significant state. In terms of the global balance of power, however, this was certainly not the case.

Rehoboam: The Verdict

For all these reasons, Rehoboam's reign was certainly no success. But as far as the editors of Kings are concerned, his biggest failing was religious, not political. He continued the syncretistic policies of his father, Solomon. Furthermore, he displeased Yahweh by permitting pagan worship in Judah. Even cultic prostitution existed in the land (1 Kings 14:22–24). His beloved queen, Maacah, was a worshiper of the goddess Asherah (1 Kings 15:13). Religious ceremonies were soon as corrupt and pagan under Rehoboam as they had been under Canaanite rule!

From Bad to Worse: Abijah of Judah
—1 Kings 15:1–25; 2 Chron. 13

Rehoboam was succeeded by his son Abijah, whose brief reign was even less distinguished. His only obvious success came when he sought God's help for a successful assault upon the Israelites (2 Chron. 13). This episode shows us that Abijah still saw himself as the legitimate ruler over all Israel. He considered Jeroboam to be nothing better than a rebel and usurper (vv. 4–7). He proudly boasted that Judah still retained its Levitical priesthood and still kept its temple service (vv. 10–12). Israel had corrupted the worship of Yahweh. Yet it is significant to read, "his heart *was not fully devoted* to the LORD his God" (1 Kings 15:3). Abijah had followed the example set by of both of his parents, Maacah as well as Rehoboam. He encouraged, rather than opposed, the introduction of pagan religion. Remember, the problem throughout the history of Israel and Judah was not their rejection of Yahweh in favor of other gods. It was rather their rejection of his claim to absolute allegiance. They sought to worship him as one deity among many. Yahweh, however, never treated Israel as one among many. In this particular instance, as always, he remembered his special commitment to David. He ensured, for David's sake, that Abijah's son Asa would succeed him. He would become a "lamp in Jerusalem" (1 Kings 15:4) to stand for righteousness. This guaranteed the survival of the Southern Kingdom for a while longer. Although the future was bleak, in Asa there was a glimmer of hope for Judah.

Appendix: Problems of Egyptian Chronology

In the nineteenth century, much of the interest in the newly developing disciplines of Ancient Near Eastern studies and Egyptology came because of their connections with the Bible. Archaeological finds became important focal points in the efforts to develop a chronology of the ancient world. You can imagine the excitement, then, when a hieroglyphic inscription, found on the south wall of the Temple of Amun at Karnak in Egypt, the site of the ancient Thebes, first seemed to provide an account of the assault on Israel and Judah from the Egyptian point of view. Champollion, the 19th century French Egyptologist who first managed to decipher hieroglyphs, translated the inscription in 1828 and found it made reference to some 150 cities of Palestine destroyed during an incursion into the area. The name of the pharaoh who claimed to have led the attack was Sheshonq I. Better still, the inscription placed the attack in the twenty-first year of his reign, and from 1 Kings 14:25, Champollion already knew that the events in Judah took place in the fifth year of Rehoboam's reign, usually dated to about 926 B.C. This was, therefore, a firm date for the start of the Twenty-Second Dynasty in Egypt. Chronology aside, the temple inscription unfortunately poses as many questions as it solves. For instance, of the 150 cities Sheshonq lists, not one of them is a Judean city. Yet, according to the biblical account, the Egyptians not only attacked the capital Jerusalem, they even took some of the temple and royal treasures away (1 Kings 14:25–28). It would be most strange for such an achievement not to have been included in the official write-up–especially since Egyptologists now think the inscription presents us with a highly exaggerated account of Sheshonq's expedition.[41] If we are to believe the Karnak inscription, it is curious that Jeroboam's Israel should have suffered the brunt of the attack, since, according to 1 Kings 11:40, it was with Shishak that he took refuge in Egypt during the later years of Solomon's reign. It is possible that Jeroboam made certain agreements with Shishak during his time in Egypt that he failed to keep when he became king of Israel. The Egyptian assault may well have been intended as punishment upon him in particular, rather than upon the two states of Israel and Judah. But this fails to explain the concentration in the biblical account of the attacks on Judah.

Study Questions

1. Why is history so helpful as a means of communicating theology?
2. How do the books of Chronicles and Kings differ?
3. What were the reasons for the division of the kingdom?
4. Describe the events and significance of the Shechem conference.
5. How did the division of the kingdom affect the later history of the two nations?
6. What were the central features of Jeroboam's religious alterations?
7. Why is Jeroboam given such bad press by the biblical historians?

[41]Though it should be noted that scholarly opinion on matters such as these does (and should) change from time to time as new discoveries are made.

8. Why is the division presented (especially by Chronicles) as a revolt of the Northern Kingdom?

9. Are the parallels between Jeroboam and Aaron coincidental, or is there a significant message being made by the biblical author here?

10. What lessons for today's church can be taken from this story?

For Further Reading

Anderson, B. W. *The Living World of the Old Testament.* 4th ed. Harlow, England: Longman, 1988; published in the U.S. as *Understanding the Old Testament* (Englewood Cliffs, N.J.: Prentice-Hall, 1988).

Bright, J. *A History of Israel.* 3d ed. Philadelphia: Westminster Press, 1980.

DeVries, S. J. *1 Kings.* WBC. Waco, Tex.: Word Books, 1985.

Japhet, Sara. *1 and 2 Chronicles.* OTL. London: SCM Press, 1993.

Jones, G. H. *1 and 2 Chronicles.* Old Testament Guides. Sheffield, England: Sheffield Academic Press, 1993.

Miller, J. M., and J. H. Hayes, eds. *Israelite and Judean History.* Philadelphia: Trinity Press, 1977.

_____. *A History of Ancient Israel and Judah.* London: SCM Press, 1986.

Rogerson, J. W., and P. R. Davies. *The Old Testament World.* New York: Cambridge University Press, 1989.

Soggin, J. A. *An Introduction to the History of Israel and Judah.* London: SCM Press, 1993.

Thiele, Edwin R. *The Mysterious Numbers of the Hebrew Kings.* Rev. ed. Grand Rapids: Zondervan Publishing House, Academie Books, 1983.

14

Robert Stallman

Long Day's Journey Into Night:
Israel, the Northern Kingdom

Outline:

- Unhappily Ever After
- Seeing the Big Picture
- Jeroboam's Dynasty: Shechem in the West and Peniel in the East
- Baasha's Dynasty at Tirzah
- Civil War Follows Destruction of Baasha's Dynasty
- Omri's Dynasty at Samaria
  The International Situation
  Omri
  Ahab and Jezebel
  The Remaining Omride Kings
- The Careers of Elijah and Elisha
  The Career of Elijah
  The Career of Elisha
- Jehu's Dynasty at Samaria
  Jehu's Revolt and Its Consequences
  Jeroboam II and His Reign
- Disintegration and Anarchy
- A "Deuteronomistic" Conclusion

Terms:

Baalism
syncretism
Yahwism

You can tell a lot about a story by looking at how it ends. For instance, the concluding phrase "and they all lived happily ever after" signals that you've got a fairy tale. Real life stories usually don't end like that. The story of the decline of the northern kingdom of Israel is certainly no fairy tale. In fact, it is the most consistently negative narrative of the entire Old Testament.

Unhappily Ever After

At the very beginning, however, we get the sense there might be some hope. Jeroboam was a very capable administrator under King Solomon. Ahijah the prophet met him and declared that God would make him king over ten of Israel's tribes! Appointed by God and on the rising tide of public opinion, Jeroboam looked like the man of the hour. But it was not to be. When he became king, he turned from the LORD. He was so wicked that he became a yardstick of evil: The worst thing that could be said about any ungodly king that came after him was that he "did not turn away from the sins of Jeroboam son of Nebat" (e.g., 2 Kings 10:29). Sadly, this story starts on a poor note and ends on an even worse one: the loss of the entire kingdom to the Assyrians. Here is the final verdict: "All this took place because the Israelites had sinned against the LORD their God, who had brought them up out of Egypt from under the power of Pharaoh king of Egypt" (2 Kings 17:7).

So why would anyone want to read this story? Good role models don't show up very often. In fact, readers get a much clearer idea of what *not* to do. But like most books of the Bible, this one is not really *about* people. The story is *for* people, but it is ultimately *about* God.

From a human point of view historians tend to ask social,

political, and economic questions. What type of class structure did Israel have? How did this country relate to its
international neighbors? What were its foreign and
domestic policies? Seen this way, the story of the Northern
Kingdom reveals plenty of ancient facts. It also leaves out
some important information and events, such as the
famous Battle of Qarqar (or Karkar). But the questions that
flow from a theological point of view are quite different.
For example, what does this account tell us about who
God is and what he has done? What can we learn about
the kind of relationship he wants to have with us?

These are the significant issues. Probing their answers is
both spiritually challenging and enriching. But getting a
clear view of the Northern Kingdom is difficult for several
reasons. Most obviously, the story is not told in a continuous narrative. Instead, it is chopped up and integrated into
the larger story of the Southern Kingdom, Judah. It is
sometimes difficult to correlate the kings and events of the
Northern Kingdom with what we know of the international situation. Moreover, the names of the kings can be
hard to sort out. Sometimes kings had multiple names.
Some had both a long and short version of the same
name.[1] Some of the names occur in both the Israelite and
Judean lists of kings.

---

[1]For example, "Joram" and "Jehoram" are variants of the same name. Both
Israel and Judah had kings by these names. Israel and Judah also had kings
by the name of "Shallum." "Elah" was the name of Israel's fourth king and
also the name of the father of Hoshea, the last king of Israel. Zechariah was
the fifth king of Jehu's dynasty in the north, but most people associate the
name with a different man, the famous prophet and book of the Bible he
wrote.

The Confusing Names of the Israelite Kings

Israelite King	Identifier	Don't Confuse With . . .	Identifier
Jeroboam I (931/30–910/09)	•Son of Nebat •1st king of Israel	Jeroboam II (782/81-753)	•Son of Jehoash •4th king of Jehu's dynasty
Nadab (910/09–909/08)	•Son of Jeroboam I •2nd king of Israel	Aaron's eldest son, also a priest	
		A member of the tribe of Judah	•Son of Shammai (1 Chron. 2:28)
		A Benjaminite	•Son of Gibeon (1 Chron. 8:30)
Elah (886/85–885/84)	•Son of Baasha •2nd king of Baasha's dynasty	Tribal prince of Edom (Gen. 36:41)	
		2nd son of Caleb (1 Chron. 4:15)	
		Father of Hoshea, last king of Israel	
		Postexilic Benjaminite (1 Chron. 9:8)	
Zimri (885/84)	•Son of Elah •3rd king of Baasha's dynasty	Simeonite prince executed by Phinehas in the wilderness (Num. 25:6–15)	
Ahab (874/73–853)	•Son of Omri •2nd king of Omri's dynasty	A false prophet denounced by Jeremiah (Jer. 29:21)	

(cont. on the next page)

(cont. from the previous page)

Israelite King	Identifier	Don't Confuse With . . .	Identifier
Ahaziah (853–52)	•Son of Ahab •3rd king of Omri's dynasty	Ahaziah king of Judah (841)	•Youngest son of Jehoram, king of Judah (not the Jehoram who was king of Israel, and also known as "Joram")
Joram (852–41)	•4th king of Omri's dynasty •Son of Ahaziah •Full name is "Jehoram"	Jehoram, king of Judah (848–41)	•Son of Jehoshaphat •His reign over-lapped with the Israelite kings Ahaziah and Joram
		A Levite in David's lifetime (1 Chron. 26:25)	
		A prince of Hamath (2 Sam. 8:9–12)	
		A priest in Judah during Jehoshaphat's lifetime (2 Chron. 17:8)	
Jehu (841–814/13)	•Son of Jehosha-phat son of Nimshi (not to be confused with King Jehoshaphat [son of Asa] who reigned in Judah) •Dynastic head of Israel	A Benjaminite warrior who helped David (1 Chron. 12:3)	

(cont. on the next page)

Israelite King	Identifier	Don't Confuse With . . .	Identifier
		A seer who prophesied against King Baasha of Israel and also to King Jehoshaphat of Judah	
Jehoahaz (814/13–798)	•Son of Jehu •2nd king of Jehu's dynasty	Jehoahaz (732/31–716/15)	•12th king of Judah •Most commonly called Ahaz
		Jehoahaz (609)	•17th king of Judah
Jehoash (also known as Joash)	•Son of Jehoahaz •3rd king of Jehu's dynasty	Joash (835–796)	•8th king of Judah
		Father of Gideon (Judg. 6:11–32)	
		A Benjaminite warrior who helped David (1 Chron. 12:3)	
		An official in Ahab's court, called the king's "son"	
Zechariah (753–52)	•Son of Jeroboam II •5th king of Jehu's dynasty	28 people in the Bible are called "Zechariah" In the Old Testament, the most famous man named Zechariah was a prophet who was a contemporary of Haggai and lived after the exile	

(cont. on the next page)

(cont. from the previous page)

Israelite King	Identifier	Don't Confuse With . . .	Identifier
Shallum (752)	•Son of Jabesh •16th king of Israel	15 people in the Bible are called "Shallum"	
Pekahiah (742/41– 740/39)	•Son of Menahem •18th king of Israel	Pekah 740/39–732/31)	•Son of Remaliah •19th king of Israel
Hoshea (732/31– 723/22)	•Son of Elah •20th (and last) king of Israel	Hoshea was the original name of Joshua, changed by Moses (Num. 13:16)	
		An official in David's lifetime (1 Chron. 27:20)	
		A member of the postexilic Jewish community (Neh. 10:23)	
		Hosea the prophet	

There is one more point that must not be overlooked. The writer drew heavily on material from the Northern Kingdom.[2] Yet he supported not only the dynasty of David (that is, Judah) but also the worship of Yahweh at Jerusalem. He believed that God had made an eternal covenant with David (2 Sam. 7:5–16). To him, the political and economic problems of the Israelites were not nearly as

[2]Most scholars believe that the books of 1 and 2 Kings were not written by a single person, but it is often more convenient to speak in terms an "author" who is sometimes called "the Deuteronomist." The same situation is true with respect to the books of Chronicles. The Bible does not name the "author" of that material either. Scholars routinely refer to this person as "the Chronicler," though of course in reality the composition of the books may have been a group effort consisting of researchers, writers, and editors.

significant as the spiritual ones. Geographically cut off from Jerusalem, Israel worshiped Yahweh at Bethel and Dan instead. But much worse than that, those "unauthorized" shrines held images of golden calves. The writer repeatedly said that through the worship of these images King Jeroboam led Israel into a depth of sin that would plague the rest of the nation's history.

Seeing the Big Picture

It is helpful to start with a brief overview of the Northern Kingdom, hereinafter referred to as Israel (in distinction to Judah, the Southern Kingdom). It began with the split of Solomon's kingdom in 931/30 B.C. and lasted 208 years, until 722 B.C.[3] (For an index of ANE sources used in developing the international relationships that follow, see Appendix 1 at the end of this chapter.)

To the southwest, Egypt was not much of a military threat. To the distant east the Assyrians controlled major territory. Eventually they would make their presence well known in Israel. During the reigns of Omri and Ahab, the Assyrian king Ashurnasirpal II (883–859 B.C.) moved westward as far as Lebanon and Philistia. Assyria's pressure on the west continued with his son Shalmaneser III (858–824). At Qarqar around 853 he confronted a coalition of ten kings, including Ahab. But the pressure really increased when Tiglath-Pileser III (744–727, also known as "Pul" and

---

[3]Thiele dates the division of the kingdom at 931/30 B.C. That is, the biblical year began in 931 according to our modern (Gregorian) calendars and ended in 930. Accordingly, there may be a year of difference in the calculations made for the reigns of the kings, depending on whether the schism is reckoned as occurring in the year 931 or 930. See Edwin R. Thiele, *The Mysterious Numbers of the Hebrew Kings,* rev. ed. (Grand Rapids: Zondervan Publishing House, Academie Books, 1983), 217.

"Pulu") moved into Palestine. He dominated the last four kings of Israel. It was he who placed Israel's final king, Hoshea, on the throne. It was Tiglath-Pileser's son Shalmaneser V (726–722) who captured Israel's capital city of Samaria in 722 B.C. Under his successor Sargon II (721–705) the Assyrians deported a large part of the population. This put an end to Israel's status as an independent nation. Never again would Israel have its own king, currency, or national army.

On Israel's northeast border, both Omri and Ahab had to deal with Ben-Hadad, from the land known in the Bible as Aram. It lay between Israel and Assyria, thus acting as a buffer. Israel's relationship with the Arameans was complex and will be treated later in this chapter.

Within Israel there was a succession of several dynasties. In contrast to the single Davidic family that ruled in Judah, the royal history of Israel was marked by internal violence and political disarray. Jeroboam's dynasty of only two kings ended with the assassination of Nadab at the hand of Baasha, the next king. Baasha brought some measure of stability throughout his twenty-four-year reign. But at his death, Israel plunged into a period of civil war and a quick succession of kings. Zimri, for example, lasted only one pathetic week!

The next dynasty was headed by Omri. His infamous son Ahab occupies center stage in the books of Kings more than any other Israelite ruler. The last king of the Omride dynasty, Joram (Jehoram), died in battle at the hand of Jehu, the next dynastic leader. Jehu reigned for twenty-eight years, longer than any Israelite king before him. His dynasty is also the longest, lasting for eighty-eight years. For nearly half of that period, Jeroboam II, son of Jehoash, was in charge. Over the course of his forty-one-year reign, Jeroboam's military conquests expanded Israel's borders to their greatest extent in nearly a century. But in typical fashion, the king who followed him had a short reign. The last member of his dynasty was Zechariah, who reigned only six months. Like many before him, Zechariah persisted in the sins of Jeroboam. He died in a public assassination by Shallum, who became Israel's next king. The Bible teaches that "a man reaps what he sows": Shallum wore his crown for only one month, murdered by the next king, Menahem.

By this point the kingdom was in sharp decline. The government was virtually disintegrating right before the people's eyes. The times were worse than during the period of the judges; anarchy prevailed for an entire generation. Eventually the Assyrians besieged Israel's capital, Samaria, for nearly three years. In 722 B.C. the city walls were finally breached. The Assyrians invaded and marched tens of thousands of Israelites about five hundred miles away to resettle them and dash any hope of further revolt. In turn, immigrants entered Israel and intermingled with the native population.[4] As a nation the northern kindom of Israel had come to a bitter and permanent end.

It would have been possible for an ancient observer to conclude that Israel's god, Yahweh, either had lost interest in his people or was simply overpowered by the gods of the Assyrians. Either way, people could have thought that Yahweh was not worthy to be trusted. The writer of 2 Kings was therefore quick to clarify the perspective that had guided

---

[4]Josephus identified the people of mixed ancestry that resulted as the Samaritans (*Antiquities* 9.277–91); 2 Kings 17:29, Heb. *shomᵉronim*. Most modern scholars agree. The Samaritan people themselves, however, trace their lineage directly to the northern tribes of Ephraim and Manasseh, claiming to be pure Israelites.

the story so far. The great empire of Assyria was no more than a stick in God's hand. Yahweh was a gracious God who redeemed his people from Egypt. But Israel betrayed him and worshiped pagan gods. They adopted the sinful lifestyles of their neighbors. In short, they violated the covenant and reaped the harvest foretold by Moses (Deut. 28).[5] God had been more than patient. He sent prophet after prophet to point Israel's kings in the right direction. God's persistent mercy was met with Israel's persistent rebellion. Given this scenario the inevitable outcome had to be judgment.

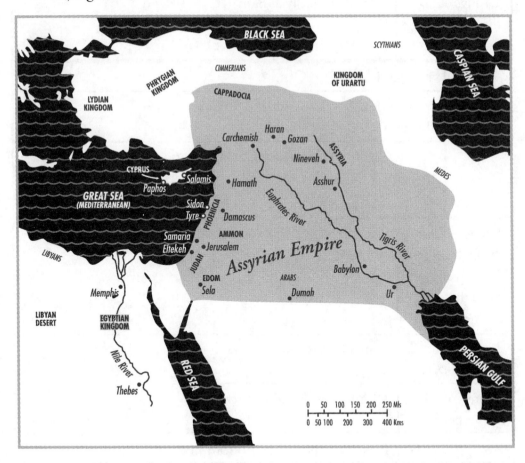

[5]This is what is known as "retribution theology." That is, they experienced the consequences of their actions.

The biblical account of the Northern Kingdom thus stretches from the coronation of Jeroboam I to the Assyrian capture of Samaria with Shalmaneser's deportation of the Israelites. This is how it unfolds:

1 Kings 12:20 through 15:32	Jeroboam's Dynasty: Shechem in the West and Peniel in the East
1 Kings 15:33 through 16:20	Baasha's Dynasty at Tirzah
1 Kings 16:21–22	Civil War Follows Destruction of Baasha's Dynasty
1 Kings 16:23 through 2 Kings 8:29	Omri's Dynasty at Samaria

	1 Kings 16:23–28	Omri
	1 Kings 16:29 through 22:40	Ahab and Jezebel
	1 Kings 22:51 through 2 Kings 9:26	The Remaining Omride Kings

1 Kings 17:1 through 2 Kings 2:11; 1 Kings 19:16 through 2 Kings 13:20	The Careers of Elijah and Elisha
2 Kings 9:1 through 15:12	Jehu's Dynasty at Samaria
2 Kings 15:13 through 17:6	Disintegration and Anarchy
2 Kings 17:7–41	Final Comment: The Bottom Line

Jeroboam's Dynasty: Shechem in the West and Peniel in the East – 1 Kings 12:20 Through 15:32

Israel's first king, Jeroboam (931/30–910/09), was a strong and capable individual who had proven himself under Solomon.[6] He supervised Solomon's program of forced labor. But Solomon's harsh policies – heavy taxation and forced labor conscriptions – stirred Jeroboam to resist. Solomon then sought Jeroboam's life, so he fled to Egypt. Following Solomon's death, Jeroboam returned. He led the delegation of northern tribes that met with Solomon's son Rehoboam at Shechem. They asked for relief from Solomon's harsh policies. When Rehoboam refused, his kingdom fragmented. The northern ten tribes formed a coalition and named Jeroboam king, in fulfillment of the prophecy of Ahijah the prophet from Shiloh (1 Kings 11:29–39).

Jeroboam reigned for twenty-two years and accomplished several significant things. He established the capital at Shechem, an important religious site. To the east, in the Transjordan, he fortified the ancient site of Peniel, thus establishing the reach of his influence. He launched a new expression of religion by choosing Dan and Bethel as worship centers and erecting the images of golden calves there. Although this did turn Israel away from the LORD, Jeroboam thought of himself as much nobler than that. He didn't want to remove the worship of Yahweh. He merely sold Israel a "new and improved" version.[7] These two locations, near the northern and southern borders of his

---

[6]See chap. 13 for a closer look at the life and policies of Jeroboam.

[7]It seems likely that the "new" version of Yahwism drew on the earlier model furnished by Aaron in the wilderness, where a golden calf represented Yahweh (Exod. 32; 1 Kings 12:28). This gave his religious innovation the appearance of something old and therefore authentic. The use of pagan

The Kings of Israel Correlated With the Kings of Judah

Dynastic heads are shown in bold. Overlapping dates denote coregencies. Dates shown with a slash (e.g., 931/30) note that the Israelite/Judean year spanned portions of two years on the Gregorian calendar.

ISRAEL	Reign	Dates*	Kings	Chronicles	JUDAH	Dates
Jeroboam I son of Nebat	22 years	931/30–910/09	1 Kings 12:20 through 14:20		Rehoboam	931/30–913
					Abijah	913–911/10
					Asa	911/10–870/69
Nadab	2 years	910/09–909/08	1 Kings 15:25–31			
Baasha	24 years	909/08–886/85	1 Kings 15:32 through 16:7			
Elah	2 years	886/85–885/84	1 Kings 16:8–14			
Zimri	7 days	885/84	1 Kings 16:15–20			
(Tibni)	5 years	885/84–880	1 Kings 16:21–22			
Omri	11 years	885–874/73	1 Kings 16:23–28			
Ahab	22 years	874/73–853	1 Kings 16:29 through 22:40	2 Chron. 18:2–34	Jehoshaphat	872/71–848
					Jehoram	853–841
Ahaziah	2 years	853–852	1 Kings 22:51 through 2 Kings 1:18			
Joram (Jehoram)	12 years	852–841	2 Kings 3:1 through 9:26		Ahaziah	841

(cont. from the preceding page)

Ruler (Israel)	Reign	Dates	Scripture
Jehu son of Jehoshaphat	28 years	841–814/13	2 Kings 9:1 through 10:36
Jehoahaz	17 years	814/13–798	2 Kings 13:1–9
Jehoash (Joash)	16 years	798–782/81	2 Kings 13:10 through 14:16
Jeroboam II	41 years	793/92–753	2 Kings 14:23–29
Zechariah	6 months	753–752	2 Kings 15:8–12
Shallum son of Jabesh	1 month	752	2 Kings 15:13–15
Menahem son of Gadi	10 years	752–742/41	2 Kings 15:16–22
Pekahiah	2 years	742/41–740/39	2 Kings 15:23–26
Pekah son of Remaliah	20 years	752–732/31	2 Kings 15:27–31
Hoshea son of Elah	9 years	732/31–723/22	2 Kings 15:30; 17:1–6

Scripture	Ruler (Judah)	Dates
2 Chron. 22:6–8	Athaliah	841–835
	Joash	835–796
2 Chron. 25:17–24	Amaziah	796–767
	Azariah (Uzziah)	792/91–740/39
	Jotham	750–732/31
	Ahaz	735–716/15
	Hezekiah	716/15–687/86
	Manasseh	697/96–643/42
	Amon	643/42–641/40
	Josiah	641/40–609
	Jehoahaz	609
	Jehoiakim	609–598
	Jehoiachin	598–597
	Zedekiah	597–586

* Dates according to Edwin R. Thiele, *The Mysterious Numbers of the Hebrew Kings*, rev. ed. (Grand Rapids: Zondervan Publishing House, Academie Books, 1983), 10.

kingdom, provided a realistic alternative to Jerusalem as a worship center. The reason for this is plain. If Jeroboam's people had to travel south to Jerusalem to worship Yahweh, they might have encountered anti-Israel propaganda and either defected, or worse, sparked a revolution. Thus it was that Jeroboam started what turned into a false religion. Consequently, he did not respond well to prophetic criticism (1 Kings 13:1–32). In spite of Jeroboam's strengths as a leader, Israel would always remember him for these faults.

After Jeroboam's death (from natural causes), his son Nadab (910/09–909/08) came to power. He lasted only two years (1 Kings 15:25–31). Nothing much is known about him except that he continued in the wicked ways of his father and was assassinated by Baasha, Israel's next king (908–886). Baasha did not stop with killing the king. He went after every member of Jeroboam's family. Obviously, Jeroboam knew how to lead a rebellion, but Baasha made sure that no descendant of Jeroboam's would live to do the same. This fulfilled the prophecy of Ahijah given directly to Jeroboam himself: "'"I will burn up the house of Jeroboam as one burns dung, until it is all gone"'" (1 Kings 14:10).

Baasha's Dynasty at Tirzah
—1 Kings 15:33 Through 16:20

Sometime following Baasha's accession to the throne, he moved the capital about seven miles northeast, from Shechem to Tirzah. The Bible doesn't even record the event,

---

elements in this expression of Yahwism clearly marks it as syncretistic. As such, it violated the second commandment (Exod. 20:4). Eventually the symbol became the essence. That is, instead of *representing* Yahweh to the people, it became the object of worship itself. By the time of the fall of Samaria in 722 B.C. the calves were probably seen as idols, just as the various Baal images were.

much less does it tell why. It was probably designed to make a clean break with the previous dynasty of Jeroboam.[8]

In any case, the defining characteristic of Baasha's reign was war. Yet the relatively brief formal account of his reign bypasses his military activity (1 Kings 15:33 through 16:20). It focuses instead on the role of Jehu the prophet in the king's life. Jehu had said that God himself made Baasha king. But Baasha never turned from the sins of Jeroboam. His dynasty would suffer the same fate as Jeroboam's— complete annihilation!

It is notable that the same prophet spoke of both God's blessing and judgment on Baasha. The relationship of the prophetic and royal traditions was complex, often marked by serious conflict. From a theological point of view, kings needed to hear the prophet's voice because they naturally tended toward two ungodly traits: They developed a strong appetite for absolute power and a great aversion toward either correction or criticism.[9]

Politically, Baasha found himself in a border dispute with Asa, the king of Judah. Baasha marched his troops south to Ramah, only five miles from Jerusalem.[10] He thus

[8]Later, Omri would move the capital to Samaria when he established his dynasty.

[9]Bruce C. Birch et al., *A Theological Introduction to the Old Testament* (Nashville: Abingdon, 1999), 265.

[10]There is a chronological conflict at this point. The parallel account beginning in 2 Chron. 16:1 dates this event in the thirty-sixth year of Asa. First Kings 16:8 locates the death of Baasha in Asa's twenty-sixth year. Every harmonistic explanation places a strain on credulity; appeal to theological and literary license strains the doctrine of inerrancy. See the discussion in William F. Albright, "A Votive Stele Erected by Ben-Hadad I of Damascus to the God Melcarth," *BASOR* 87 (October 1942): 23–29; id., "The Chronology of the Divided Monarchy," *BASOR* 100 (December 1945): 16–22; Thiele, *Mysterious Numbers*; and Raymond B. Dillard, "The Reign of Asa

established a checkpoint to control his border. Asa was justifiably threatened and bribed Ben-Hadad, king of Aram, to break his treaty with Baasha and invade Israel from the northeast. Baasha had to redirect his forces to deal with Ben-Hadad. Asa then took advantage of the situation and recaptured Ramah. He reused Baasha's building materials to reinforce the towns of Geba and Mizpah, which lay slightly to the north. From an international perspective this war did not amount to much more than family bickering. Nevertheless, it was costly for both Israel and Judah. In the final analysis all it did was weaken each side.

Unlike many kings of Israel, Baasha died of natural causes. His son's reign was short, but not sweet: Elah reigned in Tirzah for only two years (886/85–885/84), assassinated while drunk at a party. Elah's assassin was one of his own officials, Zimri (885/84). Zimri quickly took the throne and proceeded to wipe out the members of Baasha's family, just as Baasha had done to Jeroboam's family. This so enraged his countrymen that they promptly appointed Omri, commander of Israel's army, as king (1 Kings 16:16). He soon gathered his forces to besiege Tirzah, pinning Zimri inside. Realizing that there was no way out, Zimri committed suicide by burning the palace down around himself. He thus earned the distinction of having the shortest reign of any king in Israel—just seven days.

(2 Chronicles 14–16): An Example of the Chronicler's Theological Method," *JETS* 23, no. 3 (1980): 213–18. My provisional conclusion is that the Chronicler adjusted the chronology of Asa to better illustrate the doctrine of immediate retribution. In this instance, the Chronicler demonstrated that blessing followed Asa's fidelity and punishment followed his failure to trust God, choosing instead to bargain with a pagan king.

Civil War Follows Destruction of Baasha's Dynasty—1 Kings 16:21–22

Omri's succession to the throne was rushed, designed to quickly stop Zimri's murderous actions. There is no record of prophetic support for his kingship, and politically he did not have a decisive majority. Unlike most dynastic heads, Omri did not seize the throne for himself. He was given the title of king by Zimri's opponents. Actual control of the government, however, had to be earned over time. Accordingly, Israel was plunged into a period of civil war. Part of the population supported Omri's rival, Tibni son of Ginath. The conflict likely lasted for four to five years. Finally, Omri prevailed and became the undisputed king of Israel.

Omri (885/84–874/73)[11] came to power during the forty-one-year reign of King Asa in Judah. The stability of the Davidic dynasty was never more in contrast with the changing administrations of Israel. During the single reign of Asa in Judah, Israel had *seven* kings, not counting Tibni. Its stronger economy, larger population, and greater land mass (three times that of Judah) did not bring Israel an increased measure of stability. To this point, the kings of Israel who lived by the sword usually died by the sword.

Omri's Dynasty at Samaria—1 Kings 16:23 Through 2 Kings 8:29

The Omride dynasty lasted for forty-four years, nearly twice as long as the dynasties of Baasha and Jeroboam before it. On the positive side, it brought material prosperity,

[11]Omri reigned from 885/84 to 880 as rival to Tibni and thereafter to 874/73 as sole regent (Thiele, *Mysterious Numbers,* 62).

stability, and international recognition. On the negative side, the gap between rich and poor led to widespread oppression and abuse of power. Spiritually, it was horrible. Baalism and the worship of Asherah spread like cancer. Few considered exclusive loyalty to Yahweh as very important. Kings and true prophets usually found themselves at odds.

The story of Israel's kingdom is dominated by the consecutive dynasties of Omri and of Jehu. Omri reestablished Samaria as Israel's capital, which it would remain until the end of the kingdom in 722 B.C. But most of the Omride dynasty as described in Kings has to do with Omri's son Ahab. He was known for his marriage to the idolatrous Jezebel, his military activity, and his extreme resistance to prophetic correction. The books of Kings have a decidedly theological interest; nevertheless, a sketch of the international situation, a historical backdrop, can be helpful.

The International Situation

At the beginning of his rule, Omri had his hands full with the would-be king, Tibni. But far away to the east, Ashurnasirpal II, arguably the cruelest Assyrian king, assumed control of his country (883 B.C.). Near the end of Omri's relatively short reign, Ashurnasirpal II had made a series of military drives westward all the way to the Mediterranean Sea. He did not seriously threaten the kingdom of Israel, not right away. But his son Shalmaneser III would make his fearsome presence felt by four Israelite kings, from Ahab all the way to Jehu.

The more immediate threat to Israel was the Aramean kingdom with its capital, Damascus. While Israel was fighting internal battles, the Arameans were gaining strength. Ben-Hadad, son of Tabrimmon, had already caused trouble for Baasha. Afterward, his successor Ben-Hadad II invaded Israel, even attacking its capital city of Samaria, where Ahab lived.[12] The relationship between these two kingdoms proved to be quite complicated. Most often they were hostile to each other. But on at least one occasion Ahab and Ben-Hadad had to form a coalition army to stop the advance of Shalmaneser III at Qarqar in 853.

To the northwest of Israel lay the small but economically significant Phoenician city of Tyre, ruled by Ethbaal. Like David and Solomon before him, Omri entered into a formal alliance with Tyre. The deal was sealed by the marriage of Omri's son Ahab to Ethbaal's daughter Jezebel (1 Kings 16:31). The arrangement was economically good for each side. But the Bible focuses on its religious impact. Tyre had long been the site of a temple to its main god, Baal Melkart. Through Jezebel the worship of Baal, as well as Asherah, spread throughout Israel.

To the south Israel sought peace with Judah. The marriage of Athaliah (Omri's granddaughter) to the Judean king Jehoram is evidence of a positive relationship. The two kingdoms fought alongside each other in the famous battle to recapture Ramoth Gilead from the Arameans.

Omri—1 Kings 16:23–28

The Book of 1 Kings devotes only six verses to Omri's reign. Yet he proved to be an extremely capable and well-known ruler. Like his predecessors, he did not deviate from

[12]The real identity of Ben-Hadad is not immediately clear. W. F. Albright had originally suggested that the men named Ben-Hadad in the Bible were all the same person. On this account, his reign would have to have been very long indeed (about 880 to 842 B.C.; see Albright, "Votive Stele," 23–29). More likely, there was a Ben-Hadad I who attacked Israel during Baasha's reign (1 Kings 15:18,20). The Ben-Hadad mentioned in the Bible from

the pattern of the calf cult. He "walked in the ways of Jeroboam son of Nebat and in his sin, which he had caused Israel to commit" (1 Kings 16:26). But internationally Omri's legacy was outstanding. He took Israel from weakness to unprecedented vitality and respect. Long after his death, the Assyrians still referred to the kingdom of Israel as *Bit-Humri*, "the House of Omri."[13]

Omri was a military commander and so was skilled at warfare. He knew how to organize and earn the respect of people. About six years into his reign, Omri moved the capital to make a clean break from preceding dynasties. He was a man with big dreams and the skills to make them happen. Omri purchased a small town named Samaria (Heb. *shomron*) and then heavily fortified it. He added a lavish royal palace and some buildings to house the government and, *voilà*, a new capital! Not only was the city strategically located on a major trade route, it stood atop a high hill that was easy to defend. Samaria successfully withstood attack until it finally fell to the massive Assyrian army in 722 B.C.

Omri's talent for building was carried on by his son Ahab. Archaeologists once thought the stablelike structures at Megiddo were built under Solomon. Now they are more correctly dated to Omri's century.[14] Along with

---

1 Kings 20 to 2 Kings 8:14 would thus have been Ben-Hadad II (about 870–842). After that, the Ben-Hadad of the Bible would have been Ben-Hadad III (about 796–770) who ruled during the time of the Israelite king Jehoash (2 Kings 13:24–25).

[13]For example, Sargon II. See James Pritchard, *Ancient Near Eastern Texts Relating to the Old Testament*, 3d ed. (Princeton: Princeton University Press, 1969), 285. This source is elsewhere cited as *ANET*.

[14]John Bright, *History of Israel*, 4th ed., with an introduction and appendix by William P. Brown (Louisville: Westminster John Knox, 2000), 213 n. 67. I am indebted to Bright for much of the archaeological and historical data in this chapter.

Hazor, Megiddo features water tunnels built to help the inhabitants survive during long military sieges. A new kind of protective wall guarded the cities. Artifacts from Omri's palace that were recently unearthed include pieces of carved ivory from Phoenicia. He also imported the finest materials for it.

In spite of these accomplishments, Omri came up short when measured by God's standards of righteousness. The verdict of 1 Kings 16:25 is blunt: "Omri did evil in the eyes of the LORD and sinned more than all those before him." The harm he caused Israel can be measured along two lines. The first standard is theological: "He walked in all the ways of Jeroboam son of Nebat and in his sin, which he had caused Israel to commit, so that they provoked the LORD, the God of Israel, to anger by their worthless idols" (1 Kings 16:26). This "sin" was without a doubt the "new" syncretistic worship that Jeroboam promoted at Bethel and Dan (1 Kings 13:34). By outfitting his two main sanctuaries with golden calves and a new priesthood, Jeroboam had opened the gate to a flood of paganism. The Bible does not record any specific religious activities of Omri, but his decision to ally with Tyre and Sidon was pivotal. Omri arranged a marriage between his son Ahab and Jezebel the daughter of Ethbaal, the pagan priest-king of Sidon. True, most of the blame for the swelling of outright paganism in Israel should be placed on Jezebel's shoulders, but Omri certainly did his part to pave the way for it.

The second standard of measurement is economic. Here the testimony of the Bible is not as direct, but it is still relevant. About a century after Omri's time, the prophet Amos condemned the wealth of Israel: "'On the day I punish Israel for her sins, . . . I will tear down the winter house

The Worship of Baal Melkart

Ever since Israel entered the Promised Land under Joshua there was the danger of Canaanite influence. The second commandment is clear: "'You shall have no other gods before me'" (Exod. 20:3). The country was teeming with pagan shrines, and Israel never got rid of them all. And Solomon didn't help matters when he built additional shrines for his foreign wives. But in the Northern Kingdom proper it was Jeroboam who used the image of a bull to worship Yahweh. This really opened the door to idolatry for it blurred the distinction between true and false worship.

Another step down was taken by the Omride kings. When Jezebel married Ahab she moved into Israel with quite a show. She had no interest in serving her gods in private. She brought with her 450 prophets of Baal and 400 prophets of Asherah (1 Kings 18:19).

Baalism was widespread throughout the world of the Old Testament and was usually adapted to fit various regions. Since Jezebel came from Phoenicia it is likely that she promoted the worship of Baal Melkart along with that of the feminine deity Astarte. According to Josephus,[15] Ethbaal the king of Sidon was also a priest of Astarte. One of Solomon's wives worshiped her (1 Kings 11:5), but under the influence of Jezebel paganism spread swiftly.

In Tyre stood a well-known temple to Baal Melkart. The name "Melkart" means "king of the city" and may be a reference to the underworld.[16] Baal was also worshiped in the ancient city of Ugarit, north of Tyre. Religious texts from Ugarit reveal that people regarded Baal as a storm god who controlled the weather.

Since weather had a direct bearing on the success or failure of crops, Baal became associated with life, death, and healing. It is therefore easy to see how the ancient Israelites faced a real temptation. On the one hand, their traditional religion from Moses taught them that Yahweh was their life (Deut. 30:20). On the other hand, their new Canaanite neighbors prayed to Baal for rain, food, and life. Thus Israel was faced with two clear options: either worship Yahweh or defect and worship Baal. But it didn't take a genius to come up with a third option. Perhaps one could have the best of both worlds. Why risk stirring up the anger of either Yahweh or Baal by serving one and ignoring the other? This tendency to merge religions, to mix and match, is known as "syncretism." Certainly many social and political reasons can be sought for the fall of Israel as a kingdom, but for the writers of Scripture, only one basic fact was sufficient: "They worshiped other gods and followed the practices of the nations the LORD had driven out before them, as well as the practices that the kings of Israel had introduced" (2 Kings 17:7–8).

For those who think that religion ought to be constructed by and for people, syncretism is a powerful and creative tool. Of course, the problem for biblical faith is that Israel did not construct or choose Yahweh. Rather, Yahweh chose and created Israel (Ezek. 20:5). He chose Abraham, Moses, Aaron, Canaan, David, Jerusalem, and so on. In the same vein, Jesus said to his disciples, "'You did not choose me, but I chose you'" (John 15:16).

[15]Josephus *Contra Apion* 1.18.

[16]D. Winton Thomas, *Documents from Old Testament Times* (New York: Thomas Nelson, 1958), 240.

along with the summer house; the houses adorned with ivory will be destroyed and the mansions will be demolished'" (Amos 3:14–15). Such wealth was gained at the expense of the poor, who were subjected to horrible mistreatment. During the Omride dynasty the Bible indicates that sometimes creditors even took the children of those who couldn't pay (2 Kings 4:1). This is a far cry from the just society that Moses had commanded Israel to seek (Deut. 15:7–11).

Ahab and Jezebel
—1 Kings 16:29 Through 22:40

Ahab (874/73–853) and his wife Jezebel were quite a pair. During his long twenty-two-year reign, "Ahab son of Omri did more evil in the eyes of the Lord than any of those before him" (1 Kings 16:30). The list of his sins numbered only five, but they were huge. First, the sins of Jeroboam son of Nebat were trivial next to those of Ahab. In other words, on the scale of evil he picked up where Jeroboam left off. Second, he married Jezebel. Although this was certainly an arranged marriage, Ahab did little to restrain her cruelty and idolatry. She was a wicked political operator who cared nothing for justice. She killed many of the LORD'S prophets, virtually putting out a contract on Elijah (1 Kings 19:2).[17] Third, Ahab engaged in Baal worship. This was not a mere "Sunday-only" type of activity. Ahab's moral standards were set by the religion of Baal Melkart and not by Yahweh. He even built a temple for

[17]The very name "Jezebel" became equivalent to disgusting paganism. Nearly a thousand years after her death, God said to the church at Thyatira, "'I have this against you: You tolerate that woman Jezebel, who calls herself a prophetess. By her teaching she misleads my servants into sexual immorality and the eating of food sacrificed to idols'" (Rev. 2:20).

Baal in Samaria and set up an altar in it. Fourth, he also made an Asherah pole, another object of pagan worship. Fifth, Ahab refused to turn to the LORD even when the LORD addressed him directly through the prophets. For example, even after seeing Elijah triumph over the 450 prophets of Baal, Ahab still didn't understand. He made no effort to turn Jezebel aside from her crusade to slaughter Israel's prophets (1 Kings 18). In general, Ahab would do what God said only as long as he thought there was something in it for him. As we'll see in this section, he failed to show the obedience that comes from a willing heart.

No Israelite king receives as much attention as Ahab in 1 and 2 Kings. Indeed, no king in Israel was as bad as he was. Later he was compared to the evil king of Judah, Manasseh (2 Kings 21:3). Three episodes from Ahab's life illustrate his twisted priorities.

EPISODE 1: PROLOGUE TO QARQAR: AHAB AND BEN-HADAD — 1 KINGS 20

Together with thirty-two kings, Ben-Hadad of Aram marched against Samaria, Ahab's capital city. After the failure of tense negotiations for Ahab's surrender, Ben-Hadad prepared to attack. Then a prophet came to Ahab and announced that God would give victory to Israel. The overriding purpose was clear: "Then you will know that I am the LORD'" (1 Kings 20:13). Ahab fought that battle and won. The very next spring he fought Ben-Hadad a second time, and won. At this, Ben-Hadad humbled himself and met with Ahab. He promised to give back the cities that the Arameans had earlier taken from Israel. On top of that, Ben-Hadad promised to open the markets of Damascus to Ahab. This last suggestion proved to be what Ahab liked best, for at that point Ahab made a treaty with Ben-Hadad and let him go back home. When money talked, Ahab listened.

But an unnamed prophet pronounced judgment on Ahab for this. He rebuked Ahab for making a deal with Ben-Hadad his enemy when he should have finished him.[18] This had been the understanding from the start, but Ahab hadn't followed through. Why? Because he served God only when it was convenient for him. The prophet announced that Ahab would pay for that disobedience with his life. But rather than repent and obey God by hunting down Ben-Hadad, Ahab went home "sullen and angry" (1 Kings 20:43).

EPISODE 2: AHAB AND NABOTH'S VINEYARD — 1 KINGS 21

Ahab had a palace in Jezreel.[19] Near that palace lay a vineyard owned by Naboth. Like all the land in Israel, it was family land; that is, the vineyard had been in Naboth's family for generations. But the king wanted to buy it from Naboth and was willing to trade for a better piece of land or pay fair price. On the surface it seemed like a good deal for Naboth. With the king living next door, real estate had certainly appreciated in value. Naboth stood in a position to reap a profit. On top of that, he had an opportunity to

[18]First Kings 20:42 uses the Heb. word *cherem,* which indicates that in the context of holy war, certain things (including people) ought to be utterly destroyed (Lev. 27:28–29). Earlier, King Saul had violated this standard by failing to execute King Agag of the Amalekites (1 Sam. 15:9). Ahab follows in the same footsteps by sparing Ben-Hadad. In each instance, the king received a stiff prophetic rebuke for his disregard of the LORD.

[19]Jezreel is lower and warmer than Samaria. The Jezreel palace was probably a winter palace, one of the "winter houses" mentioned by Amos as possessions held by the wealthy oppressors in Israel (Amos 3:15).

King Ahab and Naboth

It is possible to read the story of Ahab and Naboth as a lesson against greed. Certainly Ahab wanted something that wasn't his, violating the commandment against coveting (Exod. 20:17). Further, it is important to note that Ahab was not a private citizen; he was a king. Ahab had little concern about living according to God's standards and behaved more like the pagans who lived around him. In those other kingdoms the land was the property of the king. Not so in Israel, and both Naboth and Ahab knew it. The land really belonged to God. Naboth respected that but Ahab didn't. Even though Naboth wanted to obey God and keep his land, Ahab still decided to seize it because he believed he had the right. As a leader, Ahab overstepped his authority under God and took to himself what ultimately belonged to God.

The Church today has

win the favor of the king. But Naboth refused. Why? The reason can be found in Israel's history as recorded in the books of Moses. God had promised to lead Abraham and his descendants into a land that would be their inheritance (Exod. 32:13). Because of that, individual property had to remain within the family. It could never be permanently sold (Lev. 25:13-17,25-28). Naboth's answer to Ahab showed his high respect for God's word and his intent to obey it: "'The LORD forbid that I should give you the inheritance of my fathers'" (1 Kings 21:3).

Again Ahab went home "sullen and angry" (v. 4). (Are we seeing a pattern?) When Jezebel saw that "he lay on his bed sulking and refused to eat," she came up with a plan: By bribing witnesses to perjure themselves, she would frame Naboth for blasphemy and treason, both capital offenses. Under the control of Jezebel, the elders of Jezreel not only executed Naboth, but killed his male heirs as well (2 Kings 9:26). With the dirty work out of the way, Ahab wasted no time in taking over the coveted vineyard. But on the way he encountered Elijah the prophet. Elijah accused Ahab of murder. In the name of the LORD, Elijah said, ""In the place where dogs licked up Naboth's blood, dogs will lick up your blood – yes, yours!""" (1 Kings 21:19). Even worse than that, God said that he would put an end to Ahab's dynasty. Surprisingly, when Ahab heard this pronouncement, he repented! God honored his response and delayed the inevitable until after Ahab's death.

The story of Naboth's vineyard illustrates the extent of injustice in Israel. It also shows us the king at his worst, murdering his own citizens. But it also reveals another side of Ahab: He had not totally lost his ability to repent. At first he seems to have listened to the prophet Elijah. Remember, at Mount Carmel this man had just triumphed over Jezebel's prophets of Baal and Asherah, 850 strong. Following that demonstration Elijah had overseen their slaughter.[20] He was hardly a friend of the royal family! How sincere then was Ahab's repentance? How ready was he to obey the prophetic word and change his life? The next episode answers these questions.

QARQAR—853 B.C.

A world-changing event forms the background to Ahab's death in the battle for Ramoth Gilead. In 853 B.C. the Assyrian king Shalmaneser III (858–824 B.C.) moved west. A powerful west Asian alliance met him in his sixth year at Qarqar. Shalmaneser's "Monolith Inscription" from the Black Obelisk describes the battle.[21]

These are the principal allies who opposed him:

King	Nation/City-State	Chariots	Infantry
Irhuleni	Hamath	700	10,000
Hadadezer (Ben-Hadad)	Damascus	1200	20,000
Ahab	Israel	2,000	10,000

Shalmaneser lists a total of twelve kings who contributed varying amounts of aid. Although Shalmaneser boasted shamelessly that he won a great victory, it is quite likely that the battle was a draw, at best. In any case Shalmaneser

many leaders, but we all belong to God. No matter how much authority a person may have, every believer is part of the Church—which belongs to God. We are his bride and the body of Christ (Rev. 19:7; 1 Cor. 12:27). No part of the Church (such as a local assembly) ever really "belongs" to anybody except Christ. It is important for everyone to remember that truth, especially leaders.

[20]The Bible speaks of "four hundred and fifty prophets of Baal and the four hundred prophets of Asherah" (1 Kings 18:19). Whether this totaled 850 depends on whether some of the Baal prophets were also prophets of Asherah. Since the religions were related, this seems likely.

[21]See *ANET,* 278–79.

withdrew from western Asia, presumably to regroup and lick his wounds.

EPISODE 3: EPILOGUE TO QARQAR: AHAB'S DEATH AT RAMOTH GILEAD — 1 KINGS 22:1–40; 2 CHRON. 18:2–34

Some time in the past the Arameans had occupied a substantial part of the Transjordan, and Ben-Hadad had failed to return it (1 Kings 20:34; 22:3). After Qarqar, Ahab decided that it was time to recapture a border town of the disputed Transjordan, Ramoth Gilead. Ben-Hadad's Damascus had been weakened by the battle at Qarqar but was nevertheless a powerful foe. Accordingly, Ahab secured the help of the king of Judah, Jehoshaphat. The story that unfolds in 1 Kings 22 is a showcase of the strained relationship between kings and prophets of the LORD. In typical Ancient Near Eastern fashion, Ahab sought the blessing of the prophets. They said, "The Lord will give it into the king's hand'" (22:6).[22] There was one exception: Micaiah son of Imlah, a prophet of the LORD. But when Jehoshaphat suggested that they both seek his counsel, Ahab, in his typically immature fashion, said, "'I hate him because he never prophesies anything good about me, but always bad'" (1 Kings 22:8). In spite of the tremendous pressure from his peers, Micaiah told the truth: Ahab would die in the battle for Ramoth Gilead.

[22]The two different spellings, "Lord" and "LORD," should not be overlooked. The Bible is trying to tell us that these were illegitimate prophets, speaking either in the name of the calf cult or of the Baals. Micaiah, by contrast, speaks in the name of the LORD (i.e., Yahweh). (See, for example, ASV: "Then the king of Israel gathered the prophets together, about four hundred men, and said unto them, Shall I go against Ramoth-gilead to battle, or shall I forbear? And they said, Go up; for the Lord will deliver it into the hand of the king. But Jehoshaphat said, Is there not here a prophet of Jehovah . . . ?")

The king was so enraged that he ordered that Micaiah be locked up in prison until he returned from the fighting. Micaiah knew that the test of a true prophet was whether his word came true. So he said, "'If you ever return safely, the LORD has not spoken through me'" (1 Kings 22:28). Ahab headed off to battle – disguising himself for safety. But a "random" arrow wounded him, and he bled to death, propped up in his chariot, just as Micaiah and Elijah before him had said (1 Kings 21:19; 22:35–38).

Again it is clear that Ahab was willing to listen to the LORD only when it suited him. Ahab's previous battles against Aram had been successful. With Jehoshaphat's help, he thought victory in this case would be certain. But it was not to be. The way Ahab both lived and died earned him the legacy of being a man who trusted in his own strength and cared little for the word of God.

The Remaining Omride Kings
–1 Kings 22:51 Through 2 Kings 9:26

After Ahab's death, his son Ahaziah (853–852 B.C.) assumed control of Israel. He was a true son of Ahab and Jezebel, at heart a worshiper of Baal. Near the end of his short two-year reign, Ahaziah was injured. To see if he would recover, he sent messengers to Ekron, a Philistine city, to consult Baal-Zebub.[23] Why not seek the LORD

23 The original name of this god was probably Baal-Zebul ("Lord Zebul"). The change to Baal-Zebub in the Old Testament may have been an intentional inside joke by Israelite scribes who were unwilling to write the name of a pagan god. It made his name sound like "Lord Fly." It is noteworthy that the Gk. NT refers to the devil as "Beelzebub" (Matt. 10:25; 12:24,27; Mark 3:22; Luke 11:15,18–19). See Raymond B. Dillard, *Faith in the Face of Apostasy: The Gospel According to Elijah and Elisha,* The Gospel According to the Old Testament (Phillipsburg, N.J.: Puritan & Reformed, 1999), 76–77.

instead? Long ago when the Philistines captured the ark of the covenant, they took it to Ekron. There they broke out with tumors (1 Sam. 5:6–12)! Like his father Ahab, Ahaziah also had a fateful meeting with Elijah, who prophesied Ahaziah's imminent death.

Since Ahaziah did not have a son to take the throne, his brother Joram (also known as Jehoram) became king (852–841). Although Joram did remove a sacred stone of Baal (2 Kings 3:2), he nevertheless continued in the ways of Jeroboam. He met his end at the hands of Jehu, the next king.

The Careers of Elijah and Elisha – 1 Kings 17:1 Through 2 Kings 2:11; 1 Kings 19:16 Through 2 Kings 13:20

A large portion of the narrative in 1 and 2 Kings revolves around the lives of two powerful men of God, Elijah and Elisha. These two books cover a time span of four hundred years, but about a third of that material is devoted to the eighty-year period of these two lives.[24] Aside from the miracles they performed why are they so important to the story? Remember that the books of Kings were completed during the Babylonian exile. Second Kings records the fall of Jerusalem but not its return from captivity. The writers must have thought that the lives of Elijah and Elisha contained important lessons for this exilic community. Let's consider a few.[25]

The Books of Kings flesh out the theology of Deuteronomy. Moses had warned Israel about the dangers of Canaanite religion and idolatry (Deut. 29:16–18). Both Elijah and Elisha lived during a period of thorough syn-

---

[24]Dillard, *Faith in the Face of Apostasy*, 7.

[25]Summarized from ibid., 7–9.

cretism of Yahwism and Baalism. They both remained absolutely committed to Yahweh and were extremely brave in the face of considerable opposition from kings, false prophets, and priests. In the exile God's people faced similar pressures. The example of these two prophets would have both encouraged and challenged them.

Moses had also instructed Israel about true and false prophets (Deut. 13:1–11; 18:9–22). Either could perform signs and wonders. But true prophets pointed only toward serving the LORD. Furthermore, if a prophetic word did not come true, then that prophet's message did not come from the LORD.

Deuteronomy also spelled out the qualifications and role of kings in Israel (17:14–20). A long reign was to be a sign of God's approval. It is therefore important for us to realize that the destruction of wicked Ahab's dynasty was foretold by Elijah (1 Kings 21:20–24). Jehu, the man responsible for carrying out this judgment, was chosen by God and anointed by none other than Elisha (2 Kings 9:1–10). Should God's people ever hope to get out of the exile, they would have to follow the leader whom God had chosen and hold him to a high standard of righteousness.

The Career of Elijah

The stories of Elijah's life are known as the "Elijah cycle." There are six main parts:

1 Kings 17:1 through 18:15	Elijah predicted a drought and hid across the Jordan River
1 Kings 18:16–46	On Mount Carmel, Elijah confronted the false prophets
1 Kings 19	Elijah fled to Horeb, encountered God, and commissioned Elisha
1 Kings 21	Elijah prophesied against Ahab for the murder of Naboth
2 Kings 1	Elijah rebuked Ahaziah for trusting in Baal
2 Kings 2:1–18	Elijah was taken up into heaven

The Two Elijahs

The name "Elijah" out-
lived even the man him-
self. Malachi predicted
his reappearance before
the Day of the LORD
(Mal. 4:5). And Jesus
plainly said that John the
Baptist was "the Elijah
who was to come" (Matt.
11:14; cf. Luke 1:17).
Both had clothes of hair
and a leather belt
(2 Kings 1:7–8; Matt.
3:4). Both faced power-
ful, evil women. Elijah
tangled with Jezebel and
John with Herodias
(1 Kings 19:2,10,14;
Matt. 14:3–12). Each
went to the Jordan River
to appoint his successor
(2 Kings 2:6–8; Matt.
3:13). Furthermore, it is
interesting that just as
Elisha saw Elijah go up to
heaven (2 Kings
2:10–12), Jesus also saw
Elijah in heavenly glory
(Matt. 17:2–3).[26]

Elijah's personal background is unclear; he seems to appear out of nowhere. Gilead was a large, rather unde-fined territory that lay along the outskirts of Israel. From there, God called Elijah to the halls of power, where he boldly spoke out for righteousness and covenant loyalty. He was a man of action and extreme commitment. He was a man of the Spirit (1 Kings 18:12). Never since Moses and Samuel had a person been so powerfully used by God. The parallels between the lives of Moses and Elijah are indeed striking. Both met God at Horeb and saw his glory (Exod. 3:1–4; 1 Kings 19:8–13). Both experienced the fire of God (Exod. 19:16–19; 1 Kings 18:38; 19:12). Both had the help of prophets (Num. 11:16–17; 1 Kings 19:16–17). Each was given an assistant who would succeed him and experience God's special help (Joshua, Elisha). And the death of each one was somewhat mysterious and strongly marked by God's pres-ence (Deut. 34:1–6; 2 Kings 2:11–12).

The Career of Elisha

The ministry of Elisha spanned approximately fifty years. He lived through the reigns of six kings, from Ahab to Jehoash, including one violent dynastic change in the purge by Jehu. Both he and Elijah confronted heads of state. But their most passionate joint concern was to demonstrate the superiority of Yahweh over Baal.[27]

Jehu's Dynasty at Samaria—2 Kings 9:1 Through 15:12

The dynasty of Jehu was the longest in Israel's history, about eighty-eight years. It is dominated by its founding

---

[26]Dillard, *Faith in the Face of Apostasy,* 10–12.

[27]See the parallels in Leah Bronner, *The Stories of Elijah and Elisha* (Leiden, Netherlands: Brill, 1968), 50–122.

king Jehu, who reigned for twenty-eight years, and Jeroboam II, who reigned for forty-one. It began in an exceedingly bloody way and ended with a pair of royal assassinations. Internally Israel was self-destructing. Externally it faced the growing threat of the Assyrians, who would eventually put an end to it all.

Jehu's Revolt and Its Consequences — 2 Kings 9:1 Through 10:36

Near the end of Joram's life the prophet Elisha sent a disciple to anoint Jehu. The army hailed him as the next king of Israel. The son of Jehoshaphat (not the Judean king), Jehu (841–814/13) was a military commander who knew how to take lethal action. His first task was to put an end to the Omride dynasty. Joram had just returned wounded from battle and was recuperating in the royal palace at Jezreel. When he saw Jehu ride toward the palace, he rode out to meet him at the site of Naboth's vineyard. He soon learned that Jehu was out for blood. He retreated, only to be fatally hit in the back by Jehu's arrow. Jehu continued on to Jezreel where he ordered Jezebel put to death too. Before he was finished, Jehu also slew Ahaziah the king of Judah (2 Kings 9:27–29). Moreover, he slaughtered all the remaining males in Jezreel who were associated with Ahab (2 Kings 10:1–11), forty-two relatives of Ahaziah king of Judah (2 Kings 10:12–14), the remaining descendants of Ahab in Samaria (2 Kings 10:17), plus all the ministers of Baal in Samaria (2 Kings 10:18–27). He is credited with destroying the worship of Baal, turning his temple in

Elijah and Elisha in the New Testament

We've seen that the New Testament compares the ministries of Elijah and John the Baptist. The same is true for their successors, Elisha and Jesus. When John the Baptist was in prison he wondered about the real identity of Jesus. He sent messengers to ask Jesus about it. Jesus sent them back with this word, "'Go back and report to John what you hear and see: The blind receive sight, the lame walk, those who have leprosy are cured, the deaf hear, the dead are raised, and the good news is preached to the poor'" (Matt 11:4–5). The similarity to the ministry of Elisha is unmistakable. He gave sight to the blind (2 Kings 6:18–20), cured leprosy (2 Kings 5), and raised the dead on more than one occasion (2 Kings 4:32–37; 8:4–5; 13:21). He also brought good news to the poor (2 Kings 4:1–7; 7:1–2; 8:6).[28] Elisha had a

(cont. on the next page)

[28]These parallels are drawn by Dillard, *Faith in the Face of Apostasy,* 12. Dillard also notes that this list of miracles is merged with the works of the promised Servant of the LORD (Isa. 61:1–3; Luke 4:17–19).

Elijah and Elisha in the New Testament (cont.)

double portion of Elijah's spirit. Clearly Jesus' ministry shone more brightly than that of John the Baptist. In these ways the narratives of the Old Testament pointed forward to the Messiah God would send to redeem his people, Jesus the Christ.

Samaria into a public outhouse!

From the start, Jehu knew that his mission was to bring an end to the house of Ahab. Elijah had prophesied it and anointed his disciple, Elisha, for that very purpose. But Jehu's zeal was extreme. His brutality weakened Israel, both inside and out. On the political side, Jehu's purging of Ahab's officials left the nation without experienced leadership. This must have led to disorganization and incompetence. Moreover, many in Israel were justifiably disgusted at his cruelty (Hos. 1:4).

On the religious side, Jehu received credit for removing the worship of the Phoenician god, Baal Melkart. But he continued to worship the golden calves at Dan and Bethel and did not truly serve the LORD. So, as it does with many others, the Bible charges him with repeating the sins of Jeroboam.

Politically, Jehu's violent start immediately smashed Israel's treaty with Phoenicia. With that relationship gone, Israel lost a major trading partner. The prosperity of the Omride dynasty began to evaporate. Jehu's action against the king of Judah deprived Israel of a military partner. Without a strong coalition force, Jehu could not successfully resist the growing power of the Arameans. Under Jehu, Israel lost its holdings east of the Jordan River all the way to Moab (2 Kings 10:32–33). Within fifty years of Jehu's ascendance, Israel would become dependent on Damascus for its survival.[29]

Under Shalmaneser III, Assyria began to flex its muscle, boding worse things to come. In 841 Shalmaneser marched westward and attacked Damascus. He then continued on to

[29]Bright, *History of Israel*, 255.

Sidon, Tyre, and eventually Israel. Rather than face utter defeat, Jehu paid tribute to Shalmaneser. Although there is no biblical record of it, the famous Black Obelisk shows a picture of Shalmaneser receiving this tribute from Jehu.[30] With an official holding a type of whip behind him, Jehu bows on all fours in front of Shalmaneser who stands upright looking very authoritative. It appears as though the great king Jehu is almost kissing the ground!

After Jehu's death Israel had two kings, Jehoahaz and Jehoash, before the rise of the strong king Jeroboam II. Both of them followed in the sins of Jeroboam I. Under Jehoahaz (814/13–798) Israel was dominated by the Arameans. The situation improved under Jehoash (798–782/81). From the Arameans he recovered the cities taken during the reign of his father. To the south, Jehoash fought with the Judean king Amaziah, who had boasted of a recent victory over Edom. In the ensuing battle, Jehoash captured Amaziah. He broke through the city wall of Jerusalem. Along with hostages, he took all the gold and silver from the temple and the royal bank.

JEROBOAM II AND HIS REIGN — 2 KINGS 14:23–29

The biblical account of Jeroboam II (793/92–753)[31] is relatively short. Yet his reign lasted forty-one years – the longest of any Israelite king. Although he too committed the sins of Jeroboam son of Nebat, his military success expanded Israel to its largest extent since Solomon. This

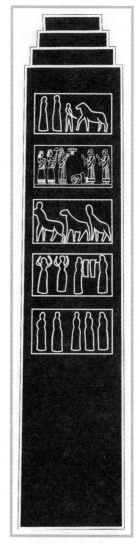

Facsimile of the Black Obelisk, in the British Museum

[30]It is possible that the Israelite in the panel is merely one of Jehu's representatives.

[31]Jeroboam reigned from 793/92 to 782/81 as coregent with Jehoash and thereafter to 753 as sole regent (Thiele, *Mysterious Numbers,* 62–63).

can be explained in two ways. From a theological point of view, the LORD responded to the suffering of the Israelite population, empowering Jeroboam to recover the territory Israel had lost to Aram. Moreover, he subjugated Damascus. From a political point of view, there was a power vacuum in the Near East. Egypt was in a state of decline. In about 802 B.C., Adad-nirari III took Damascus but was forced to withdraw because of pressure on his northern border.[32] About twenty years into Jeroboam's reign, Ben-Hadad of Damascus was defeated by Zakkur of Hamath. It is unclear whether or not Ben-Hadad died in that battle.[33] In any event, it was not until Jeroboam's death that Damascus again raised its hand against Israel. To the south, Judah, under the leadership of Uzziah (Azariah), was rapidly expanding and rebuilding. Israel and Judah made peace and together enjoyed a strong measure of prosperity.

For Israel, life under Jeroboam was good – if you were born into the right family. Archaeologists testify to the existence of exquisite buildings and elaborate furnishings. These could have been constructed only in a time of peace and prosperity. Trade was up and a river of money flowed through the country. But the prophetic ministries of Amos and Hosea paint quite a different picture.[34] The familial ties of the old tribal structure of society had given way to a sharply segregated upper and lower class. To those in control of the legal system, the LORD said, "I know how many are your offenses and how great your sins. You oppress the

---

[32]Bright, *History of Israel,* 256.

[33]Eugene H. Merrill, *Kingdom of Priests: A History of Old Testament Israel* (Grand Rapids: Baker Book House, 1987), 374–75.

[34]The bulk of Hosea's prophecy details a long list of Israel's social and religious sins.

righteous and take bribes and you deprive the poor of justice in the courts" (Amos 5:12).

Spiritually, the worship of Yahweh had become so mixed with Baalism that it had little positive effect on the people. The priests were employed by the government and so would hardly be critical of state policies. Few prophets spoke out, because their ministries were totally compromised. Through Micah the LORD said, "'As for the prophets who lead my people astray, if one feeds them, they proclaim "peace"; if he does not, they prepare to wage war against him'" (Mic. 3:5). With injustice, idolatry, and abuse so rampant, the future was indeed grim.

Disintegration and Anarchy —2 Kings 15:13 Through 17:6

The prosperity and stability of Israel under Jeroboam II began to unravel soon after his death. Within a generation, Israel would cease to exist as a nation. Certainly the ultimate cause of Israel's fall was God himself, in whose hand Assyria was merely an instrument (Isa. 10:5). But the immediate cause was the fierce rise of the Assyrian Empire. Israel's religious and social problems were hardly of much concern to Tiglath-Pileser III (744–727 B.C.).[35] He wanted nothing less than world domination. He dealt with the great powers of Babylonia and Urartu. The smaller states of the west—Hamath, Tyre, Byblos, Damascus, and Israel— had all fallen to him by 738.[36] So from the outside, Israel faced increasing pressure. But from the inside, the government was rapidly falling apart on its own.

---

[35]Also known by his Babylonian name, Pul (2 Kings 15:19; 1 Chron. 5:26).

[36]Bright, *History of Israel,* 271.

Zechariah the son of Jeroboam II became king in 753, the year his father died. Zechariah would last only six months. The great dynasty of Jehu was finally over (2 Kings 15:12). Zechariah was publicly assassinated by Shallum, who was king for a month. After him Menahem (752–742/41) managed to hold on for ten years.

During Menahem's reign, Tiglath-Pileser came to Samaria and demanded a large sum of money to spare the king. Menahem quickly imposed a tax on the wealthy—fifty shekels of silver (over a pound). From this collection, Menahem was able to pay Tiglath-Pileser one thousand talents of silver (about thirty-seven tons!). This was clearly an exorbitant sum of money. Tiglath-Pileser intended to cripple Israel's economy and thus reduce Menahem's ability to fund a rebellion. For a time, Assyria withdrew – but not for long.

When Menahem died, his son Pekahiah took over (742/41–740/39). This was the last time that the son of an Israelite king followed his father to the throne. Pekahiah was assassinated in Samaria by Pekah, who ruled for the next twenty years (752–732/31).[37]

Pekah son of Remaliah was firmly opposed to Assyrian control and broke the treaty made by Menahem. Pekah found a like-minded king in Rezin of Damascus. Together they joined forces with the hope of repelling Assyria. But they needed more help and sought it from Judah. Righteous Jotham (750–732/31)[38] would have no part of it;

[37]Pekah began his rule in 752 as a rival of Menahem. Their reigns overlapped for ten years. For two more years Pekah's reign overlapped with that of Pekahiah. From 740 to 732/31 Pekah was the only king of Israel (Thiele, *Mysterious Numbers*, 63).

[38]From 750 to 740/39 Jotham's reign overlapped Azariah's (Thiele, *Mysterious Numbers*, 64).

so when his son Ahaz came to power in 735, Pekah and Rezin invaded Judah and marched on Jerusalem (about 735/34). Out of desperation, Ahaz called out to Tiglath-Pileser for help. He would become Assyria's vassal and would pay a hefty tribute for Assyrian aid. Tiglath-Pileser happily complied. Not only did he kill Rezin of Damascus, but he also destroyed numerous cities in Israel. Earlier Tiglath-Pileser had been content to drain Israel of its wealth. Now he would be satisfied only with absolute rule. Pekah's aggression against Judah had sealed his fate by giving Tiglath-Pileser a reason to invade. His suffering ended when he died at the hands of the man who would become Israel's last king, Hoshea son of Elah.

Hoshea (732/31–723/22) recognized that surrender to Assyria was the only realistic option but that Pekah would never do that. Therefore, upon taking the throne, Hoshea paid tribute to Tiglath-Pileser and was allowed to rule as a puppet-king over what was left of Israel. When Shalmaneser V (726–722) took over from Tiglath-Pileser, Hoshea decided it was time to reassert his sovereignty. He stopped the vassal tribute payments to Assyria. At the same time, he appealed to Egypt for help, which would never come. Shalmaneser took Hoshea prisoner and went about claiming the rest of Israel. Only the capital city of Samaria was able to hold out. The siege lasted nearly three years.

Siege warfare of the eighth century B.C. was extremely cruel. People trapped inside the city were cut off from the outside world and died deaths of unimaginable horror. In the case of the citizens of Samaria, it was for nothing. Israel had no chance of survival. Their valiant hold on life was nothing more than a final gasp for air. In 722 the city fell. The kingdom of Israel would never rise again.

Tiglath-Pileser and the kings who followed him did not seek merely to control the nations they captured; they sought to obliterate them. This they accomplished by shifting populations. They deported the officials and leaders of one land and settled peoples of other lands in their place. This made it extremely difficult for the indigenous to conspire in hopes of sparking a rebellion. In the long run it resulted in the mixing of people groups. In time it would thus be impossible for Israel to reorganize and revolt. "Pure" Israelites had been virtually bred out of existence. Another name for this policy might have indeed been "you can't go home again."

A "Deuteronomistic" Conclusion—2 Kings 17:7-41

The story of the Northern Kingdom, Israel, presents a rich theological lesson. The social, religious, and political developments provide only a chronological backdrop; they are not the heart of the story. Historians of the Ancient Near East have integrated biblical texts and records from other countries to supply an account of what happened, enabling us to better appreciate the lives of the biblical characters. They were indeed real people with ideals and needs not much different from our own. But the books of Kings do not seem to be designed simply as a historical record. Instead, they make a profound theological statement. After telling of Israel's demise, the writer of 2 Kings devotes considerable space to a theological explanation. This account is often called "Deuteronomistic" because it lines up with the theology of the Book of Deuteronomy.

This theology has several main features. First, Yahweh and Israel stood in a covenantal relationship: Yahweh was the Great King who graciously delivered Israel from

Egyptian bondage. As vassal, Israel was to gratefully serve Yahweh and experience the blessings of his provision and protection. Second, Yahweh was not a distant or unconcerned God; as the God of history he intervened in Israel's life again and again. He had a goal for his people. This truth means far more than "God helps those who help themselves." Third, God's Word had authority for Israel. The Book of Deuteronomy not only told Israel who they were; it also contained laws and instructions concerning how they were to worship and work together. Fourth, worship was to be centralized in the place that Yahweh would choose (Deut. 12:5). This turned out to be the city of Jerusalem, located in the kingdom of Judah, not Israel. Perhaps more important than the identity of that place, Deuteronomy envisioned a *single* place, in contrast to many smaller shrines scattered throughout the land. Fifth, Yahweh would provide a land for his people. It was a gift, an inheritance. But in order to stay in this land God's people would have to live in obedience to God's commands. This is the theology of retribution. As Raymond Dillard and Tremper Longman explained, "Obedience to the righteous commands of God not only will result in possessing and keeping the land, but also will bring prosperity and well-being, whereas disobedience issues in disaster, disease, death, and the loss of the land."[39]

Seen from this perspective, the history of Israel is essentially the story of a long disobedience in the same direction. Sadly, the story does not end with the death of Israel only. By the end of the book Judah also meets its end. This should not surprise the first-time reader, because 2 Kings

[39]Raymond B. Dillard and Tremper Longman III, *An Introduction to the Old Testament* (Grand Rapids: Zondervan Publishing House, 1994), 105.

17:19 tells us that neither did Judah keep the LORD'S commands. They did the same kinds of things that Israel did.

There are many obvious spiritual lessons that flow from this story that can be framed as simple moral commands: Don't worship other gods. Don't disobey the LORD. Don't oppress one another. Do follow the commandments. Do listen to the word of the prophets.

But another type of lesson takes shape when one thinks of God. What is he like? What does he want? What is his intent? Reading the story of the Northern Kingdom in the light of Deuteronomy is quite revealing and helpful. God is both just and merciful. God is patient and involved. God expects not only to be obeyed but also to be loved; after all, he first reached out to Israel in love. God wants his word to be taken seriously because he means what he says. In spite of despicable people who abuse their power, God is guiding the course of history. He directs the courses of whole nations, not just Israel and Judah.

One other lesson ought not be ignored. This has to do with the value of theological reflection. How can one reconcile the dependability of God and his ways with the rapidly changing situations of his people?[40] It is not enough for us to know *what* happened, *to whom* it happened, and *when* it happened. We must also ask *why* it happened. Like the writer of 1 and 2 Kings, we are to weigh the theological significance of events. Learning is the result of experience *plus* reflection. In the end, we ought to better know who God is, who we are, where we are headed, and what he expects each of us to do.

---

[40]T. R. Hobbs, *2 Kings,* WBC (Waco: Word, 1985), 13:241.

Appendix 1: Ancient Near Eastern Sources and the History of the Northern Kingdom

The following chart shows sources for extrabiblical material relative to the Northern Kingdom:[41]

Mari Prophecies	Examples of Prophecy From 1800–1750 B.C.	Scripture Reference
Mesha Stele	Mention of Omri and Ahab	1 Kings 16:23–24
Annals of Shalmaneser II	Victory at Qarqar	1 Kings 16:29 through 22:40
Mesha Stele	Moab rebels against Israel	2 Kings 3:5
Black Obelisk of Shalmaneser III	Treaty with Jehu around 841	2 Kings 9:1 through 10:33
Annals of Tiglath-Pileser III	Israel (Menahem) becomes a satellite of Assyria	2 Kings 15:17–22
Annals of Sargon II	Israel moves from Assyrian ally (738) to colony (732) and finally to province (721)	2 Kings 17:3–6

[41]See Victor H. Matthews and Don C. Benjamin, *Old Testament Parallels: Laws and Stories From the Ancient Near East* (New York: Paulist, 1991).

Appendix 2: Parallels Between 1 Kings 14 Through 2 Kings 16 and Chronicles

Bold applies to Northern Kingdom

Kings	Event	Chronicles
1 Kings 14:21 1 Kings 14:29–31	Rehoboam's accession and death notices	2 Chron. 12:13 2 Chron. 12:15–16
1 Kings 15:1–2 1 Kings 15:7–8	Abijah's accession and death notices	2 Chron. 13:1–2 2 Chron. 13:22 through 14:1
1 Kings 15:11–15 1 Kings 15:16–22 1 Kings 15:23–24	Asa's righteous acts War between Asa and **Baasha** Asa's death notice	2 Chron. 14:2–3; 15:16–18 2 Chron. 15:19 through 16:6 2 Chron. 16:11 through 17:1
1 Kings 22:1–35	**Micaiah's prophecy against Ahab**	2 Chron. 18:2–34
1 Kings 22:41–50	Jehoshaphat's reign	2 Chron. 20:31 through 21:1
2 Kings 8:17–22 2 Kings 8:23–24	Jehoram's reign and death notice	2 Chron. 21:5–10 2 Chron. 21:20
2 Kings 8:26–27 2 Kings 8:28–29 2 Kings 9:15–16 2 Kings 9:27–28	Summary of Ahaziah's reign (the great-grandson of **Omri** by Athaliah) Ahaziah's alliance with **Joram** against Hazael **Joram's** attempted recuperation The death of Ahaziah	2 Chron. 22:2–4 2 Chron. 22:5–6 2 Chron. 22:6 2 Chron. 22:9
2 Kings 11:1–21 2 Kings 12:1–13 2 Kings 12:17 2 Kings 12:20–21	Athaliah and Joash Joash's repair of the temple Hazael's attack on Gath and Jerusalem Death of Joash by conspiracy	2 Chron. 22:10 through 23:21 2 Chron. 24:1–14 2 Chron. 24:23 2 Chron. 24:25–27
2 Kings 14:2–6 2 Kings 14:7 2 Kings 14:8–14 2 Kings 14:17–22	The beginning of Amaziah's reign Amaziah's defeat of Edomites Amaziah's goading of **Jehoash** into war Amaziah's death notice	2 Chron. 25:1–4 2 Chron. 25:11 2 Chron. 25:17–24 2 Chron. 25:25 through 26:2

(cont. on the next page)

(cont. from the previous page)

Kings	Event	Chronicles
2 Kings 15:2–4	The beginning of Azariah's (Uzziah's) reign	2 Chron. 26:3–4
2 Kings 15:5–7	Azariah's leprosy and death	2 Chron. 26:21–23
2 Kings 15:33–35	The beginning of Jotham's reign	2 Chron. 27:1–3
2 Kings 15:36–38	Jotham's death notice	2 Chron. 27:7–9
2 Kings 16:1–4	The beginning of Ahaz's reign	2 Chron. 28:1–4
2 Kings 16:7	Ahaz's submission to Tiglath-Pileser	2 Chron. 28:16
2 Kings 16:17	Ahaz's damage to the temple	2 Chron. 28:24
2 Kings 16:19–20	Ahaz's death notice	2 Chron. 28:26–27

Study Questions

1. Describe the theological perspective of 1 and 2 Kings. What was most significant in them? What was not as significant?
2. From the reign of Omri to the ultimate destruction of the Northern Kingdom, how did the rise in Assyrian power influence Israel?
3. Describe the differences between how an ancient witness might view the fall of Israel and how the biblical writers viewed it.
4. Discuss Jeroboam's rise to power. What were Jeroboam's accomplishments, and how did he lead Israel to worship other gods?
5. How did the prophets function during the reign of Baasha? Discuss the political aspects of Baasha's reign.
6. What difficulties did Omri face early in his reign?
7. What was the international situation like during Omri's reign? Who were his neighbors? What contributed to the tension in their relationship with Israel? How did he attempt to solve his problems with his neighbors?

8. Explain how Omri was a capable and well-known ruler. In what two general areas did Omri fall short of God's standard of righteousness?

9. What were the five sins of Ahab during his twenty-two-year reign?

10. Why was Naboth unwilling to sell his vineyard? What did Ahab and Jezebel do to take it from him?

11. How did Ahab respond to the various prophets who spoke to him?

12. How does the theology of Deuteronomy relate to the Books of Kings?

13. Discuss the parallels that can be drawn between the careers of Elijah and Moses.

14. What changes did Jehu bring to Israel? Consider this question with reference to religion and to politics.

15. What was Israel's relationship with Aram and Judah like during the reigns of Jehoahaz and Jehoash?

16. What was Israelite life like under the leadership of Jeroboam II?

17. Know the significance of the following names: Ahab, Ahijah, Amos, Ashurnasirpal II, Baasha, Ben-Hadad, Elijah, Elisha, Jehu, Jeroboam I, Jeroboam II, Jezebel, Mesha, Omri, Sargon II, Shalmaneser III, Shalmaneser V, Tiglath-Pileser III (Pul), Zimri.

18. Know the significance of the following places: Aram, Assyria, Damascus, Jerusalem, Judah, Qarqar, Samaria, Shechem, Tirzah.

For Further Reading

DeVries, Simon J. *1 Kings.* WBC. Waco, Tex.: Word, 1985.

Dillard, Raymond B. *2 Chronicles.* WBC. Waco, Tex.: Word, 1987.

Evans, Craig A. "Luke's Use of the Elijah/Elisha Narratives and the Ethic of Election." *JBL* 106 (1987): 75–83.

LaSor, William Sanford, David Allan Hubbard, and Frederic Wm. Bush. *Old Testament Survey: The Message, Form, and Background of the Old Testament.* 2d ed. Grand Rapids: Wm. B. Eerdmans, 1996.

Long, V. Philips. *The Art of Biblical History.* Foundations of Contemporary Interpretation 5. Grand Rapids: Zondervan Publishing House, 1994.

Matthews, Victor H., and James C. Moyer. *The Old Testament: Text and Context.* Peabody, Mass.: Hendrickson Publishers, 1997.

Merrill, Eugene H. *Kingdom of Priests: A History of Old Testament Israel.* Grand Rapids: Baker Book House, 1987.

Nelson, Richard D. *First and Second Kings.* Interpretation. Louisville, Ky.: John Knox, 1987.

Thomas, D. Winton. *Documents from Old Testament Times.* New York: Thomas Nelson, 1958.

Wallace, Ronald S. *Elijah and Elisha: Expositions from the Book of Kings.* Grand Rapids: Wm. B. Eerdmans, 1957.

Walton, John H. "Historical Literature." In *Ancient Israelite Literature in Its Cultural Context.* Grand Rapids: Zondervan Publishing House, 1989.

Wiseman, Donald J. *1 and 2 Kings: An Introduction and Commentary.* TOTC. Downers Grove, Ill.: InterVarsity Press, 1993.

15

Dwaine Braddy

Just Stayin' Alive: Judah From Rehoboam to Hezekiah

Outline:

- Introduction
- How Do We Read the Books of Kings and Chronicles Today?
- What Are the Historical and Theological Perspectives of Kings and Chronicles?
- Who Was the Audience for 1 and 2 Kings?
- A Pattern Is Established
- The Parade of Judean Kings: From Abijah to Hezekiah
  The Pre-Assyrian Era
  Jehoshaphat
  Jehoram to Amaziah
- Assyrian Domination
  Assyrian Aggression and Expansion
  Isaiah and the Kings of Judah
- Conclusion

Terms:

historiography
reform, reformation

Introduction

In one of the "Peanuts" comic strips, Snoopy is sitting on his doghouse typing a novel. He begins with the words, "It was a dark and stormy night." Snoopy always begins his stories that way. Lucy comes by and puts in her two cents' worth. In her usual abrasive manner, she scolds him: "You stupid dog! That is the dumbest thing I've ever read. Whoever heard of such a silly way to begin a story? Don't you know that all good stories begin, 'Once upon a time'?" After Lucy berates him some more she leaves. The last frame of the comic strip shows Snoopy starting over. This time he types, "Once upon a time, it was a dark and stormy night."

Some stories seem to begin with something like Snoopy's description of things. One such story is found in the books of Kings and Chronicles. It's the story of the Southern Kingdom, the nation of Judah.[1]

How Do We Read the Books of Kings and Chronicles Today?

There are two basic ways to read the books of Kings and Chronicles: from the perspective of history or from the perspective of theological narrative. Before examining these perspectives, a brief overview of the books would be helpful.

These books deal with the past – history. To many people, history means something dry and uninteresting, with no direct impact on our lives today. It deals with places, names, events, and dates of a bygone era. Richard Nelson recalls the words of poet and Lincoln biographer Carl Sandburg,

---

[1]"Story" is not meant to imply "fiction," but rather the account of the southern kingdom of Judah after the division of Israel in 930 B.C. as told by the writers of Kings and Chronicles. See chap. 14 for the story of Israel, the Northern Kingdom.

"History is a bucket of ashes"; many people encountering Kings or Chronicles today might be tempted to agree. At first glance, many modern readers of these books may see them as "nothing but record[s] of rulers long dead and battles long forgotten."[2] However, the critical eye of the historian reads these books carefully and examines the historiography. This includes the chronological framework, significant events, people, and places. The historian also considers the structure of the books and whether they are reliable sources of historical evidence.

These books *do* deal with history. Yet we still must ask the question: Is this their major purpose? I don't believe so. It is more profitable for us to read these books as theology. They are "theological literature which happens to be in the form of writing, that is, 'preached history.'"[3] The intent was transformational. But how? As we will see, the author of Kings addressed the concerns of a community in exile. The Chronicler addressed the concerns of a community newly returned from exile. What were the concerns of each of these communities? In Kings the community in Babylon would have been asking, "Why are we here in humiliation if we are God's special people [see Exod. 19:5,6]? What's the reason for our present disastrous condition?" In Chronicles the restored community was asking, "Is God still interested in us? Are his covenants still in force? Do his promises to David still have meaning for us? What is our relationship to Israel of old?"[4]

[2]Richard D. Nelson, *First and Second Kings* (Louisville, Ky.: John Knox Press, 1987), 1.

[3]Ibid., 2.

[4]Adapted from "1 Chronicles," Introduction, in *The NIV Study Bible,* ed. Kenneth Barker et al. (Grand Rapids: Zondervan Publishing House, 1985), 578.

I believe these books were written primarily to answer these kinds of questions. They make up a powerful theological narrative. They present a living message filled with hope for God's people. The author of Kings writes, "Nevertheless, for the sake of his servant David, the LORD was not willing to destroy Judah. He had promised to maintain a lamp for David and his descendants forever" (2 Kings 8:19).

When they are read from a theological perspective these books become relevant. Nelson observes that they offer insight into the nature of God and that, when read from a human perspective, they are filled with human interest. Readers find themselves "moved by the art of fine story-telling."[5] My concern with Judah's "dark and stormy night" is its struggle to keep alive faith and hope. Through the events of its history, I will focus on the relevance that the text has for its modern readers.[6]

What Are the Historical and Theological Perspectives of Kings and Chronicles?

Although the author[7] of Kings is unknown, it is clear that he was familiar with Deuteronomy. He wrote to explain why Judah found itself in the Babylonian exile, pinpointing its persistent, stubborn violation of the covenants with God. Thus he writes from a prophetic and covenantal perspective.

The author of Chronicles compiled his material to produce a narrative sermon.[8] Judah was back in its land, strug-

---

[5]Nelson, *First and Second Kings,* 2.

[6]Ibid., 3.

[7]Since it appears that these books were compiled from a number of ancient sources, it may be more accurate to use the term "editor" rather than "author."

[8]The author, or editor, of Chronicles is often called "the Chronicler."

gling to reorient itself to God, his covenants, and his promises. Judah was God's restored people. The author's views
seem to mirror those of a priest-scribe. They reflect the
period of Ezra, the scribe of the restoration.

The next question is this: "When and to whom were
these books written?" King Jehoiachin's release from a
Babylonian prison is the last event referred to in 2 Kings
25:27–30 (ca. 561 B.C.). So the final form of Kings must
reflect a date somewhat after that time.[9] It is obvious, however, from statements in Kings that the author used earlier
sources, such as the "annals of the kings of Israel" (1 Kings
14:19), "annals of the kings of Judah" (14:29), and "annals of
Solomon" (11:41). It is likely that Kings was compiled
sometime during the exile, with the author using
Deuteronomy and the source materials mentioned above.

What about Chronicles? Chronicles also mentions
sources that the author used, such as: "the records of
Samuel the seer, the records of Nathan the prophet and
the records of Gad the seer" (1 Chron. 29:29); "the records
of Shemaiah the prophet" (2 Chron. 12:15); and the "events
of Uzziah's reign . . . recorded by the prophet Isaiah son of
Amoz" (2 Chron. 26:22).[10] It is generally considered to have
been written between the reforms by the prophets Haggai
and Zechariah (ca. 515 B.C.) and the Greek period (ca. 300
to 160 B.C.).[11] The last dated event in 2 Chronicles is the

[9]David Howard, Jr., *An Introduction to the Old Testament Historical Books*
(Chicago: Moody Press, 1993), 171, citing Edwin R. Thiele, *The Mysterious
Numbers of the Hebrew Kings,* rev. ed. (Grand Rapids: Wm. B. Eerdmans,
1983), 189–90.

[10]Also mentioned are the "prophecy of Ahijah the Shilonite" (2 Chron. 9:29),
the "visions of Iddo the seer" (2 Chron. 9:29), and the "annals of Jehu"
(2 Chron. 20:34).

[11]Andrew E. Hill and John H. Walton, *A Survey of the Old Testament* (Grand
Rapids: Zondervan Publishing House, 1991), 217.

record of Cyrus's decree. This decree permitted Jews to return to their homeland from the exile in Babylon (ca. 538 B.C.; cf. 2 Chron. 36:22–23). Some believe that the genealogy for Zerubbabel is arranged chronologically (1 Chron. 3:17–21). If so, this would place the final editing of Chronicles nearer 400 than 500 B.C.[12] Gleason Archer suggests a date between 450–425 B.C., following a Talmudic tradition that assigns authorship to Ezra.[13] He reasons that Ezra, "the chief architect of the spiritual and moral revival of the Second Commonwealth,"[14] would have had appropriate motivation to construct a "survey of this sort."[15]

Who Was the Audience for 1 and 2 Kings?

We now come to the issue of audience. Who were the people who originally read the books of 1 and 2 Kings? Perhaps the entire exiled Jewish community was the intended audience.

What about the emotional stability of the exiles? What were they feeling? The books of Jeremiah, Lamentations, and Ezekiel indicate that most of them experienced feelings of depression, as well as disorientation – a dark and stormy night, if you will. Their answer as to why they were in this humiliating state is not unlike our day. They said things like, ""'The way of the LORD is not just'"" (Ezek. 18:25). "God, you're not fair. We are being punished for what our ancestors

---

[12]Ibid.

[13]Gleason Archer, Jr., *A Survey of Old Testament Introduction,* updated and revised edition (Chicago: Moody Press, 1994), 450.

[14]"Second Commonwealth" refers to the restoration of Israel in Palestine after the exile.

[15]Archer, *Old Testament Introduction,* 450. Furthermore, the widely acknowledged associations between Chronicles and Ezra-Nehemiah would agree with this dating; see Hill and Walton, *Survey,* 217.

did" (see Lam. 5:7; Ezek. 18:2). Still others played the blame game, saying, "Our punishment is because of those lying prophets" (see Lam. 2:14).[16]

Psalm 137 describes a twofold picture that I believe best summarizes exilic life. In it, the exiles are tormented by the Babylonians; they vowed to never forget Jerusalem and to pray for Babylon's destruction. Those who were not taken to Babylon, however, became arrogant and unrepentant. "'[The] people living in those times in the land of Israel [Jerusalem] are saying, "Abraham was only one man, yet he possessed the land. But we are many; surely the land has been given to us as our possession"'" (Ezek. 33:24).

Finally, the author of Kings wanted his audience to be familiar with and care deeply about their nation's history, particularly the events and the covenantal laws that identified them as God's people. Furthermore, he expected them to understand why they were in captivity. If they could see their captivity as God's punishment for covenantal unfaithfulness, they would seek forgiveness and would think about returning to the land of promise.

To an audience responding to this crisis, the ultimate question was simple: Would the crisis cause them to reassert their identity or to lose their identity? The author of Kings challenged them to respond in faith. In their struggle this would keep hope alive for the future. The final four verses of the book tell of Jehoiachin's release from a prison in Babylon and of his being given a "seat of honor" in the court (2 Kings 25:27–30). Thus the future remained "open for a new work of the LORD in faithfulness to his promise to the house of David."[17]

[16]Nelson, *First and Second Kings,* 6.

[17]"1 Kings," Introduction, *NIV Study Bible,* 466.

The way the author of Kings arranged his material indicates that he was looking at Israel's history from a prophetic and covenantal perspective. His perspective is clearly summarized in 2 Kings 17:7–41. He believed, observes Bernard W. Anderson, that God would "bring blessing to those who are obedient to him and judgment upon those who flout his revealed will."[18] Each of the kings from both the Northern and Southern Kingdoms (i.e., Israel and Judah) were "strictly judged by this Deuteronomic standard of covenant obedience."[19] Israel's destruction by the Assyrians was God's punishment. They had repeatedly been unfaithful to the covenants. They had rejected the numerous prophetic warnings and calls to repentance (2 Kings 17:13). Judah followed this same path.[20]

A Pattern Is Established

First Kings 14:21 through 16:34 is called "paradigmatic history." This means these chapters establish a pattern, or example, which can either be rejected or followed. The paradigm in our story of the kings of Judah was one of sin and punishment. With only a few exceptions (which we will note) all Judah's kings followed this pattern. Richard Nelson

[18]Bernhard W. Anderson, *Understanding the Old Testament*, 3d ed. (Englewood Cliffs, N.J.: Prentice-Hall, 1975), 232.

[19]Anderson, ibid., 233, further notes that the word "Israel," which is basically a religious term referring to the tribes united by the covenant, now acquires a political meaning: the Northern Kingdom. "Judah" is the name for the Southern Kingdom, ruled by Davidic kings. Even after the division of Solomon's kingdom, however, "Israel" was often used to refer to the ideal unity of all the tribes within the covenant.

[20]Anderson, ibid., 234, notes that Judah doesn't fare much better on its report card: "Only two southern kings (Hezekiah and Josiah) come off with a clean record; six receive a grade of only 'passing,' because they failed to remove the high places; and ten 'flunk' because they 'did what was evil in the sight of Yahweh.'"

observes that, while Israel followed the common Near Eastern practices involving the king in the cult, Judah did not. He concludes, therefore, that the guilt of apostasy in Judah had to be shared by all parties involved, whether royal or lay.[21]

A "High Place" at Dan

Israel's and Judah's rebellion against God grew progressively worse.[22] God's response to their unfaithfulness is described in the language of human emotion: jealousy (1 Kings 14:22) and anger (15:30; 16:7,13).[23] The logical result was a series of disasters for Judah and Israel (15:29; 16:19). Pharaoh Shishak of Egypt attacked Jerusalem,

[21]Nelson, *First and Second Kings,* 100.

[22]Compare 1 Kings 15:30 to 21:22; 2 Kings 23:26; 1 Kings 16:7 to 2 Kings 17:17; 21:6,16; 22:17.

[23]See the *NIV Study Bible* note on Exod. 20:5 and the article "Anger" by H. C. Hahn in *The New International Dictionary of Theology,* ed. Colin Brown (Grand Rapids: Zondervan Publishing House, 1975), 1:105-13 for an excellent discussion of the concept of God's jealousy and anger.

plundering the temple and the royal palace (14:25–28). There was ongoing border war between Israel and Judah (14:30; 15:6,17,32). Brothers fought brothers and even enlisted a pagan king to help (15:16–22).

But in the midst of this pattern of sin and punishment, was there any hope of God's favor? Wasn't this also a part of the paradigm? Would only anger be experienced? For Israel there were no reforming kings who chose to lead the people in repentance and covenantal faithfulness. Consequently, this led to their inevitable destruction even though they were called God's people (16:2).

Judah, however, remained special to God and an object of his favor. Why? First Kings 15:4–5 declares that God made an eternal covenant with David. David sinned grievously before the LORD (2 Sam. 11); in his heart, however, he never served the Canaanite gods.[24] Israel's kings chose not to follow David's example. On the other hand, Judah's kings did, that is, at least some of them did. Now let's take a look at these kings.

The Parade of Judean Kings: From Abijah to Hezekiah – 1 Kings 15 Through 2 Kings 20; 2 Chron. 13 Through 32

The Pre-Assyrian Era

ABIJAH—1 KINGS 15; 2 CHRON. 13; 913–911/10 B.C.[25]

The author of Kings dismisses Abijah with a negative evaluation. First, Abijah continued the wickedness and idolatry

---

[24]See *NIV Study Bible* note on 1 Kings 15:3.

[25]Dates written with a slash (e.g., 931/930) indicate a year beginning in one year and ending in another according to our modern Gregorian calendar.

of his father, in that "his heart was not fully devoted to the LORD his God" (1 Kings 15:3). The mention of his mother, Maacah, may indicate that she also influenced him. She set up a wooden image representing the Canaanite fertility goddess, Asherah.[26] Second, he waged continual warfare against Jeroboam (1 Kings 15:6-7).

The Chroniclers' view of this warfare, on the surface, appears to be favorable. In 2 Chronicles 13, he records a great military victory achieved over Jeroboam. He also exposes Jeroboam's corrupt rule (v. 7) and his folly in establishing idolatrous worship in Israel (vv. 8-9). The author also recorded Abijah's appeal to Judah's religious tradition (2 Chron. 13:10-12). Abijah's victory over Jeroboam wasn't because of his righteousness, however. It was because of God's covenant with David (1 Kings 15:4; cf. 11:36). Abijah's life, marked by disobedience to God, exhibited only one act of faith: He appealed to Judah to remember God. Yet God may have used Abijah's victory. It prepared the people for reforms that came during the reign of his son, Asa.

ASA—1 KINGS 15; 2 CHRON. 14 THROUGH 16; 911/10–870/69 B.C.

As the saying goes, "Of a good beginning cometh a good end." Unfortunately Asa's case was one of those exceptions. Abijah and his father, Rehoboam, were "unrighteous but occasionally obedient kings." On the other hand, Asa, Abijah's son, was just the opposite:

Abijah and Abijah: Who's Who?

One of the perplexing issues in sorting out the kings is the similarity—and sometimes identical-ness—of a number of the royal names. For instance, both Jeroboam and Rehoboam had a son named "Abijah," as seen in the references below.

Son of Jeroboam (Israel)

1 Kings 14:1: "At that time Abijah son of Jeroboam became ill."

He died in his youth; 2 Chronicles contains no parallel accounts.

Son of Rehoboam (Judah)

1 Kings 14:31: "Rehoboam rested with his fathers and was buried with them in the City of David. His mother's name was Naamah; she was an Ammonite. And Abijah his son succeeded him as king."

(cont. on the next page)

---

[26]W. T. Purkiser, ed., *Exploring the Old Testament* (Kansas City, Mo.: Beacon Hill Press, 1955), 306.

"righteous but occasionally disobedient."[27] Dismayed with the rampant paganism in Judah, he began a thorough religious reformation. He destroyed idols and their altars. He commanded Judah to seek God and obey his laws (1 Kings 15:11–13; 2 Chron. 14:2–5). One of the most difficult tasks of his reformation was removing the "high places."[28] Was Asa successful in this phase of his reform? Kings seems to be at odds with Chronicles (1 Kings 15:14; 2 Chron. 14:5). (Remember, pagan worship was deeply ingrained in Judah by this time.) It would seem that Asa made an *attempt* to remove the high places. His efforts were not totally successful, since some still remained.

The author notes the result of this early reformation: peace, rest, and prosperity reigned for some ten years (2 Chron. 14:1,5–8). If the story ended here, all would be well. This decade of peace, however, came to an abrupt end with an invasion by an enormous Ethiopian army led by Zerah the Cushite.[29] The outcome of this invasion was a decisive victory for Asa's forces (2 Chron. 14:9–10).

Just at this moment of victory Asa heard from a prophet, Azariah the son of Obed. What was this prophet's message? Seek God and he'll be with you; forsake God and he'll leave you (2 Chron. 15:2–7). Hearing this prophetic word, Asa's passion for reform and covenant renewal was intensified. It drew a passionate response from the people:

---

[27]John J. Davis and John C. Whitcomb, *Israel From Conquest to Exile: A Commentary on Joshua–2 Kings* (Grand Rapids: Baker Books, 1989), 367.

[28]See the note in the *NIV Study Bible* on 1 Kings 3:2; cf. Deut. 12:2–3.

[29]Some identify Zerah with Pharaoh Osorkon I, the successor to Pharaoh Shishak, or an unknown general serving the pharaoh. See note on 2 Chron. 14:9 in the *NIV Study Bible*. Others, however, see him as a leader of an Arabian tribe. See Ernst Axel Knauf, "Zerah," in *ABD*, 6:1080-81.

"They took an oath to the LORD with loud acclamation, with shouting and with trumpets and horns. All Judah rejoiced about the oath because they had sworn it whole-heartedly" (2 Chron. 15:14–15). In accordance with basic covenant law, death was decreed for any who would not seek the LORD. So wide reaching was this reform that even the northern tribes were affected (2 Chron. 15:9).

But Asa didn't stop here. He removed his own grand-mother, Maacah, from her position as queen mother. Someone rightly called her the "Jezebel of Judah." Why? Like Ahab's Jezebel, she was instrumental in introducing pagan worship. She sponsored the worship of Asherah. Could her actions have been a deliberate attempt to counter Asa's reforms? We don't know. In any event, Asa dealt with her decisively (2 Chron. 15:16).

Despite the proverb about a good beginning presaging a good ending, it did not hold true for Asa (1 Kings 15:16–22; 2 Chron. 16). As a result of his reforms, Judah became a "magnet for revival." Large numbers from Israel flocked to Judah when they saw God was with its king. Predictably, Israel's king Baasha was alarmed by solid citizens leaving his kingdom for a neighboring kingdom, even if it was that of his kinsmen (2 Chron. 15:9).[30] So his solution was physical restraint, an outpost. For this he invaded Judah and fortified Ramah, a town about four miles north of Jerusalem. He wanted to prevent any further Israelite emigration to Judah.

Unfortunately Asa didn't trust the LORD as he had when Zerah the Cushite invaded his kingdom (2 Chron. 14:9–15). Instead, he chose to lean on his own strength and

A Cure for Self-Sufficiency and Pride

One thing seems to be missing from the Asa account. Why, in peace and prosperity, would war reemerge? The author doesn't explain why. Could it be that Judah allowed peace and prosperity to lull them into self-sufficiency and pride? Maybe they thought, "We are the chosen of God." Perhaps they took their blessings for granted. But they would once again be forced to recognize that God was their strength and source of blessing. God allowed adversity to cure them of self-sufficiency and pride. On behalf of his people, Asa prayed one of the great intercessory prayers of the Bible (2 Chron. 14:11). This prayer reminds us that our suffi-ciency, strength, and blessing are from God, not from human ingenuity.

---

[30]For a concise discussion of the chronological problem relating to Asa and Baasha, see Davis and Whitcomb, *Israel From Conquest to Exile,* 369, and the discussion note on 2 Chron. 16:1 in the *NIV Study Bible.*

Grace for Asa— and for Us

The remarkable testimony of 1 Kings 15:14 is worth noting: "Asa's heart was fully committed to the LORD all his life." On the surface this verse seems almost irreconcilable with the biblical account of the end of Asa's reign. One must realize, however, that "perfect" (KJV) or "fully committed" do not imply that Asa was faultless or sinless. The aim of Asa's heart was to do God's will. That cannot be denied. His problem was the same as yours and mine. On occasion he yielded to temptation. The Bible doesn't portray him as flawless. Rather, his reign overall promoted godliness and covenant faithfulness. The Spirit-inspired author's testimony about Asa is evidence of God's grace. This grace is also available to us.

ability (2 Chron. 16:2–6). He removed from the temple the gold and silver he had dedicated to God. Using this he bribed Ben-Hadad of Aram to break his treaty with Baasha.

Immediately Ben-Hadad invaded Israel's northern border, capturing several cities. We aren't told if Asa's conscience disturbed him, but why should it? His plan had succeeded. Didn't it prove God was the inspirer of his plan? While he was patting himself on the back, he received a visitor—the last person he expected or wanted to see—a prophet. The prophet's name was Hanani. Instead of congratulating Asa for his political savvy, he rebuked him. He told Asa that there would be war for the rest of his reign (2 Chron. 16:7–9).

Asa had a choice: repent or rebel. Unhappily, he chose to rebel. He threw Hanani into prison. And anyone else who dared to question his policies was oppressed. His unbelief and rebellion, however, did not stop there. Two years before the end of his forty-one-year reign, Asa was smitten with a disease in his feet (2 Kings 15:23).[31] But instead of seeking God for healing, he sought help from physicians. They were probably pagan foreign physicians, perhaps nothing more than witch doctors. Healing did not come and Asa died, another case in Judah's history of a sorry ending after a good beginning.

Jehoshaphat—1 Kings 22; 2 Kings 3; 2 Chron. 17 Through 21; 872/71–848 B.C.[32]

The twenty-five-year reign of Jehoshaphat,[33] son of Asa,

[31]For other examples of disease as punishment for sin see 2 Chron. 21:16–20; 26:16–23; Acts 12:23.

[32]Asa's reign ended in 870/69 B.C. The overlap with Jehoshaphat's reign indicates a coregency, wherein the heir to the throne takes over as acting king, or regent, before the death of the reigning king.

[33]The details of Jehoshaphat's reign may not be in chronological order, so this discussion will consider both its positive and negative aspects. See the Kings

is, according to some, one of the rare bright spots in Judah's up-and-down history. But a closer look at his reign will reveal a study in contrasts. The upside of his reign demonstrates a spiritual fervor. He had an earnestness to lead Judah in the suppression of idolatry. He tried to restore pure religion before God. The downside of his reign shows his repeatedly involving himself and the nation in alliances with the Northern Kingdom and wicked King Ahab. In effect, he failed to be spiritually discerning with regard to pagan, idolatrous, and God-forsaking Israel–thereby weakening the spiritual vitality of his reforms.

His reign began with great promise. The Chronicler says he "strengthened himself against Israel" (2 Chron. 17:1) and he "walked in the ways [of] his father David" (2 Chron. 17:3). Throughout Judah he sent teams to teach the people their responsibility to obey God's Word (2 Chron. 17:9). God blessed Jehoshaphat's commitment to Scripture so much that even the Philistines and Arabians brought him gifts. "The fear of the LORD fell on all the kingdoms of the lands surrounding Judah" (2 Chron. 17:10). God continued to increase his wealth and honor (2 Chron. 18:1).

Jeshoshaphat showed a great passion for teaching Judah God's Word and turning hearts to him. Yet his record contains a most serious blot. He made a decision that threatened his kingdom and the Davidic dynasty for years, nearly destroying it: "He allied himself with Ahab by marriage" (2 Chron. 18:1). That is, he allowed Jehoram, his son, to marry Athaliah, daughter of Ahab and Jezebel. This union brought with it disastrous results (1 Kings 22:1–40; 2 Chron. 18:1 through 19:3).

---

account of his reign and compare it with that in Chron.

Serving Without Compromise

Jehu's words contain a lesson for Christians today: God's work cannot be accomplished through compromise with the pagan world. We need to keep both Jehu's word to Jehoshaphat and Paul's word to the Corinthians (2 Cor. 6:14–15) ever before us.

Jehoshaphat went on a royal visit to see his son's father-in-law, Ahab. During his visit, Ahab urged him to help recapture Ramoth Gilead from the Arameans.[34] Ahab chose to listen to his own prophets instead of to Micaiah, a true prophet of the LORD. And so, to borrow the words of Tennyson, "into the valley of death . . . . into the mouth of Hell" rode Ahab. Predictably, he was killed. This fulfilled Elijah's and Micaiah's prophecy of his death (1 Kings 21:19; 22:28).

As for Jehoshaphat, after praying "one of the most famous 'foxhole prayers' in the Bible,"[35] he barely escaped with his life (2 Chron. 18:30–32). Upon returning to Jerusalem, he was severely rebuked by the prophet Jehu (2 Chron. 19:2).

Unlike his father, Asa, Jehoshaphat listened to godly counsel. He immediately instituted further reforms in Judah (2 Chron. 19:4–11). This time he personally took part in the instruction of the people. In addition, he instituted judicial reform throughout Judah. He appointed courts and judges to render verdicts in the daily lives of the people. Their judgments were always to be given with a reverent sense of God's presence. They were to avoid all partiality, injustice, and greed (2 Chron. 19:5–7).

Undoubtedly these reforms prepared Jehoshaphat for his next crisis – an invasion from Moab and Ammon to the east (2 Chron. 20). Here his spiritual leadership excelled. In one of the classic prayers of faith recorded in the Bible, he led his people in seeking God's help (2 Chron. 20:5–12). God's answer to his prayer was decisive. Jahaziel, a Levite, spoke these words by the Spirit of the LORD: "'"Do not be afraid or discouraged. . . . For the battle is not yours, but God's"'"

[34]See *NIV Study Bible* note on 1 Kings 22:1 for background information on Ahab's plan to recapture Ramoth Gilead.

[35]Davis and Whitcomb, *Israel From Conquest to Exile,* 383.

(2 Chron. 20:15). The result of the battle was never in doubt (20:16–30). Victory was total. The fear of God came upon all nations surrounding Judah and peace reigned in the land again.

The prophet Jehu's message and Jehoshaphat's zealous religious reforms were good things. But they didn't stop him from making further treaties with Israel. First, he continued his treaty with Israel through Ahab's son, Ahaziah (1 Kings 22:48–49; 2 Chron. 20:35–37). Probably tempted by the prospect of further wealth, Jehoshaphat decided to join Ahaziah. He wanted to cash in on the lucrative commercial sea trade through the Gulf of Aqaba. God then sent him another messenger, Eliezer. Eliezer criticized how Jehoshaphat had joined hands with Israel again. The result was failure; Jehoshaphat's fleet was wrecked (2 Chron. 20:36–37).

Finally, Jehoshaphat's last treaty with Israel ended in failure. Refusing to learn the lessons of his earlier disastrous alliances, he joined with King Joram of Israel to fight Moab. Thank God for sending another prophet! Elisha interceded for him and God graciously spared both him and Joram from a catastrophe (2 Kings 3).

The authors of Kings and Chronicles give positive marks to Jehoshaphat's reign. The author of Kings, however, added an appendix to his evaluation: "Jehoshaphat [made] peace with the king of Israel" (1 Kings 22:44).

Jehoram to Amaziah – 2 Kings 8; 11 Through 12; 14; 2 Chron. 21 Through 25; 853–767 B.C.[36]

Judah's dark and stormy night continues from Jehoram's reign to Amaziah's. Passages from 2 Kings and 2 Chronicles record the apostasy that resulted from

---

[36]Jehoram had a coregency with Jehoshaphat, 853–848, and reigned 848–841 B.C.

Jehoshaphat's treaties with Israel. Four kings and a wicked queen dominated the political and religious leadership of Judah for some fifty years. They were Jehoram, Joash, Ahaziah, Amaziah, and Athaliah, the daughter of Ahab and Jezebel.

Both Kings and Chronicles portray Jehoram's character as evil (2 Kings 8:18; 2 Chron. 21:6). This is clearly shown in his first official act: He murdered his six brothers, along with some of the nobility in Judah. Why? Perhaps it was to give him a free hand, unchallenged by the royal family. Part of his agenda seems to have been to introduce Baal worship into Judah. The language of the text indicates that Jehoram deliberately pressured the people to worship at idolatrous shrines (2 Chron. 21:11). God, however, was quick to respond to his deeds of murder and idolatry (2 Chron. 21:10–20). First, he permitted Edom and Libnah to revolt. Second, he prompted Elijah to send the king a letter announcing judgment on his nation, on his family, and even on his own body. Third, he moved the Philistines and Arabians to attack and plunder Jerusalem. They carried off his sons and their wives, with the exception of Ahaziah and Athaliah. Fourth, after meeting the horrible death that Elijah predicted, Jehoram was denied the customary burial of a king. The summary of his reign is recorded in 2 Chronicles 21:20: "He passed away, to no one's regret." What a sad commentary for ending one's life!

Ahaziah, his son, fared no better.[37] Named by his mother, Athaliah, after her wicked brother in Israel, Ahaziah followed her evil counsel (2 Chron. 22:3). He also followed

[37]Ahaziah's reign was short, beginning and ending in 841 B.C.

wicked counselors from the house of Ahab. The Bible says this was "to his undoing" (2 Chron. 22:4). His end came as he continued the treaty with Israel begun by his father, Jehoshaphat (2 Chron. 22:5). Shortly thereafter Ahaziah died at the hands of Jehu, who also destroyed the house of Ahab.[38] No one in his house was powerful enough to succeed Ahaziah. This opened the way for his mother, Athaliah, to ascend to the throne.

Again, this tragic period of Judah's history was the result of apostasy. This is clearly seen in the dominance of a queen, and a foreign queen at that! Having gained control over her weak-willed husband, King Jehoram, Athaliah introduced the cult of Baal Melkart into Jerusalem.[39] To accommodate this pagan worship she had a temple built for Baal. She appointed someone by the name of Mattan as the leader of the cult's priesthood.[40] She secured the throne in Judah and promoted Baal worship in Judah by killing all the male descendants of David. Perhaps some of these victims were her own grandchildren! By this time the royal family had been all but annihilated.[41]

Through God's sovereignty, Joash, the one-year old son of Ahaziah, was saved by Jehosheba, wife of the priest Jehoiada. She hid Joash in the temple for six years (2 Kings 11:2–3). The rest of the story in chapter 11 recounts

[38]Second Chron. 22:6–9; cf. 2 Kings 9:21–27; 10:12–14.

[39]John Bright, *A History of Israel,* 3d ed. (Philadelphia: Westminster Press, 1981), 252. "Melqart" (Phoenician Baal) is also spelled "Melkart."

[40]His name suggests he was a Tyrian from Phoenicia. H. H. Ben-Sasson, ed. *A History of the Jewish People* (Tel Aviv, Israel: Dvir Publishing House, 1969), trans. George Weidenfeld and Nicolson Ltd. (Cambridge, Mass.: Harvard University Press, 1976), 126.

[41]See *NIV Study Bible* note on 2 Kings 11:1. Athaliah's reign lasted from 841 to 835 B.C.

Jehoiada's plan to bring Joash to the temple and have him crowned king. Jehoiada succeeded in his goal to rid Judah of its pagan ruler. As with Elijah on Mount Carmel, the God of Israel once again defeated Baal. Mattan and Athaliah were put to death.[42]

But how would a seven-year old boy have the wisdom to reign as king over the nation?[43] The answer is simple: Joash was heavily influenced by the godly priest Jehoiada at the beginning of his reign (2 Kings 12:2). In fact, his forty-year reign may be divided into two periods: the period of Jehoiada's godly influence and the period of Joash's apostasy.

During the first period of his reign, under Jehoiada's influence, an immediate religious reformation was begun. Athaliah's detestable Baal temple was dismantled. After this, Joash sponsored the restoration of the temple (2 Kings 12:1–16; 2 Chron. 24:1–16). Had his reign ended here, Joash would have earned an honorable place among the Judean kings. It wasn't to be, however.

When Jehoiada died, Joash turned his ear to a group of princes who persuaded him to allow the return of idolatrous worship. Jehoiada's son, Zechariah, was led by the Spirit to condemn this apostasy. Joash reacted as others before him had when rebuked for rebellion against God. He ordered Zechariah to be stoned in the very precincts of the temple (2 Chron. 24:17–22). Divine judgment for this despicable act quickly followed. The Aramean army under King Hazael laid siege to Jerusalem. With only a few men, they defeated Joash's much larger army. The Arameans killed the leaders of the people and severely wounded Joash.

---

[42]Second Kings 11:15–16,18a; 2 Chron. 23:12–17.

[43]Joash reigned 835–796 B.C.

To avoid further destruction of Jerusalem, Joash gave Hazael the temple treasures as a bribe (2 Kings 12:17–18; 2 Chron. 24:23–25). His own officials, outraged at this apostasy, murdered him. He suffered one final indignity: He was "buried in the City of David, but not in the tombs of the kings." This special honor had gone to the priest of his early reign, Jehoiada (2 Chron. 24:15–16,25). So ended the career of another king who had begun with such great promise.

Similar to earlier Judean kings, Amaziah, son of Joash, began his reign well.[44] Like most ancient kings, he could have executed the entire family of his father's assassins. Instead, he followed the instructions of Scripture and spared the assassins' children.[45] However, in his planned expedition against Edom, he felt an army of 300,000 was insufficient. He hired 100,000 skilled soldiers from, of all places, Israel. Apparently he forgot the damage that earlier treaties with Israel had caused. As his reinforced army was preparing to attack Edom, God sent him a prophet, who brought this message: "'O king, these troops from Israel must not march with you, for the LORD is not with Israel – not with any of the people of Ephraim. Even if you go and fight courageously in battle, God will overthrow you before the enemy, for God has the power to help or to overthrow'" (2 Chron. 25:7–8). Regretting only the loss of his money, he sent Israel's soldiers back home. Consequently, God gave him a great victory over Edom (2 Chron. 25:9–12). He learned, at least for the time being, that he must conduct affairs of state *God's* way.

Amaziah's actions following this God-given victory are

[44]Amaziah reigned 796–767 B.C.

[45]Second Kings 14:5–6; 2 Chron. 25:3–4; cf. Deut. 24:16; Ezek. 18:2,4,20; Davis and Whitcomb, *Israel From Conquest to Exile*, 440.

hard to understand. Rather than worshiping and giving praise to God, he chose to engage in idolatry. He refused to listen when God sent a prophet to rebuke him. Amaziah's success had filled his heart with an ambitious pride and he began to prepare for war against Israel. After all, he had routed the Edomites, captured their gods, and silenced God's "meddlesome prophet."[46] King Jehoash even tried to persuade Amaziah to abandon his challenge by sending him a fable: "O Amaziah, pitiful 'thistle king' of Judah, stay in your own league and be content with the little trophies you have already won, lest you and your kingdom should come to disaster" (see 2 Chron. 25:18–19).[47]

Nevertheless, refusing to listen to God, he marched forth to do battle with Israel's army. This time God was not with him. Amaziah suffered a humiliating defeat: He saw six hundred feet of Jerusalem's wall broken down and lost both hostages and temple treasures to Israel (2 Chron. 25:21–24). This was too much for the people. Amaziah's enemies found him in Lachish several years later and killed him. So ended the career of another promising Judean king. What might have been, wasn't.

UZZIAH—2 KINGS 14:21; 15:1–7; 2 CHRON. 26:1–23; 792/91–740/39 B.C.

The story of King Uzziah,[48] or "Azariah,"[49] is similar to several of his predecessors. He began well, became enam-

---

[46]Davis and Whitcomb, *Israel From Conquest to Exile,* 441; 2 Chron. 25:15–17.

[47]Parable paraphrase by Davis and Whitcomb, *Israel From Conquest to Exile,* 442.

[48]See the *NIV Study Bible* discussion notes on 2 Kings 14 through 15; 2 Chron. 26 through 27 for discussion of the coregency of Uzziah and Jotham.

[49]Second Kings 14:21 through 15:7 uses the name Azariah; 2 Chron. 26:1–23

ored of his God-given success, then came under God's judgments. His fifty-two-year reign was the second longest of any Judean king.[50] It can be divided into two periods.

First, there was the period of prosperity. Uzziah experienced God's blessing and demonstrated exceptional leadership in economic and political matters. The brief account in 2 Kings 15:1–7 and the longer account in 2 Chronicles 26 document Judah's prosperity during his reign. Uzziah modernized the army and established control of the main commercial highways in Judah. He expanded commercial trade into Arabia. He fortified the port of Elath on the Gulf of Aqaba. This solidified and expanded trade with the south. He developed agriculture and stockbreeding. He repaired the defenses of Jerusalem that had been partially destroyed by Jehoash in the defeat of Amaziah. The Chronicler summarizes Uzziah's achievements with these words: "His fame spread as far as the border of Egypt, because he had become very powerful" (2 Chron. 26:8).

Uzziah's reign marked a rare period of prosperity during Judah's dark and stormy night. A couple of factors account for this positive assessment. First, there was the political situation of the Near East at this time. Assyria had crushed the Arameans and threatened Israel. Assyria's internal strife, however, precluded any further movement westward. Because of this, Israel and Judah enjoyed peace.[51]

---

and Isa. 1:1; 6:1, however, use the name Uzziah. One of these may have been a throne name.

[50]The regnal years for Uzziah (Azariah) consist of a coregency with Amaziah, 792/91–767, and a reign, 767–740/39 B.C.

[51]Henry Jackson Flanders, Jr., Robert Wilson Crapps, and David Anthony Smith, *People of the Covenant: An Introduction to the Hebrew Bible*, 4th ed. (New York: Oxford University Press, 1996), 318.

Through a combination of the capable leadership of Jeroboam II of Israel and Uzziah of Judah the two nations saw geographic expansion and prosperity unknown since the days of David and Solomon.

Second, and more importantly, however, are the authors' references to Uzziah's heart for God. Both Kings and Chronicles say, "He did what was right in the eyes of the LORD" (2 Kings 15:3; 2 Chron. 26:4). The Chronicler attributes Uzziah's success to his heeding the prophet Zechariah. Zechariah, it is said, "instructed him in the fear of God" (2 Chron. 26:5). Perhaps Zechariah reminded Uzziah of Moses' words about a king's responsibility, both to God and to his people (Deut. 17:18–20; 28 through 30). Uzziah's response was to seek God (2 Chron. 26:5), who then helped him greatly (2 Chron. 26:7,15).

Tragically, Uzziah's commitment to seek God didn't continue. If it had, perhaps Judah's night would not have turned out to be so dark and stormy: After Uzziah became powerful, the proud, haughty spirit that precedes a fall did its deadly work in his heart (Prov. 16:18).

The second period of Uzziah's reign is characterized by irreverence, sin, and punishment (2 Kings 15:5; 2 Chron. 26:16–23). He assumed he could participate in temple worship as though he were a priest.[52] Why he would want to do that, we cannot be sure. It seems probable, however, that his actions were prompted by a desire for more power (2 Chron. 26:16).

When Uzziah went so far as to offer incense in the temple, the priests became offended. Azariah, together with

---

[52]See Ben-Sasson, *History of the Jewish People,* 131–32, for a discussion of Uzziah's actions and the possibility of precedents. Cf. 2 Sam. 6:17–18; 1 Kings 8:62–64; also 2 Sam. 8:18 with the NIV text note.

eighty other priests, confronted Uzziah. They denounced him in the name of the LORD for his actions. Like some of his predecessors, he responded in anger. Immediately, God smote him with leprosy, a loathsome disease.[53] The disease made him ritually unclean and forced him to live apart from his people and the temple until he died (see Lev. 13:45–46).

Archaeologists, excavating at Ramat Rahel just south of Jerusalem, believe they have uncovered the dwelling of this leprous king.[54] They found striking proof of Uzziah's illness on a marble plaque, called the "Epitaph of Uzziah." This plaque bears an inscription in Aramaic, dating to about the first century A.D. It reads: "To here were brought the bones of Uzziah, King of Judah. Do not open."[55] Evidently he wasn't buried in the royal cemetery. He was found later and reburied with a new tombstone.

JOTHAM — 2 KINGS 15:32–38; 2 CHRON. 27:1–9; 750–732/31 B.C.

Succeeding Uzziah was his son Jotham[56] (2 Kings 15:32–38; 2 Chron. 27). Religiously, his reign was much like that of his father, with one exception: He carefully avoided any interference with the priestly office. He continued his father's construction and military policies. The Chronicler says that he, too, grew powerful. But unlike his father, he

> ## Twin Sins
>
> How tragic that Uzziah, having such leadership and administrative skills and so blessed by God, yielded to the twin sins of pride and self-sufficiency! He concluded his life in shame and disgrace. Uzziah's failure before God characterized the condition of the entire nation as they stood before God. This is reflected in Isaiah's confession when he saw the holiness of God the year King Uzziah died. "'Woe to me! . . . I am ruined! For I am a man of unclean lips, and I live among a people of unclean lips'" (Isa. 6:5). But let's personalize this story. We who have an ear, let us hear and learn what the Spirit would say to us through Uzziah's failure to seek the LORD all the days of his life. Remember Paul's warning to the Corinthians: "So, if you think you are standing firm, be careful that you don't fall" (1 Cor. 10:12).

[53]The Heb. word *tsara'at* can designate a wide range of disorders, ranging from acne, psoriasis, or vitiligo, to Hansen's disease (true leprosy).

[54]Francois Castel, *The History of Israel and Judah in Old Testament Times,* trans. Matthew J. O'Connell (Mahwah, N.J.: Paulist Press, 1985), 118.

[55]Ben-Sasson, *History of the Jewish People,* 132.

[56]Jotham's regnal years include a coregency with Uzziah, 750–740/39, and reign, 740/39–732/31 B.C.

realized that his success wasn't due to his own efforts; it was God's blessing. Scripture records that "he walked steadfastly before the LORD his God" (2 Chron. 27:6). Under Jotham's influence, Judah became prominent. The nation rose to a position of power and influence exceeded only by the reigns of David and Solomon. There was only one cloud on the horizon—Assyrian aggression and expansion.

Assyrian Domination

Assyrian Aggression and Expansion

Up to this point we have traced the history of two independent nations, Israel and Judah. They maintained their independence despite periodic fighting with their neighbors and with one another, suffering horrific losses and humiliation. The reason is clear: No empire existed at this time that could subject them to permanent domination. This would change, however, in the middle of the eighth century B.C. The ominous Assyrian cloud on the horizon would become a thunderstorm bringing judgment upon the nation of Israel. Isaiah says: "[God] whistles for those at the ends of the earth. Here they come, swiftly and speedily. . . . In that day. . . . if one looks at the land [Israel], he will see darkness and distress; even the light will be darkened by the clouds. . . . In that day the LORD will whistle for . . . bees from the land of Assyria. . . . the king of Assyria" (Isa. 5:26,30; 7:18,20).

The Northern Kingdom was blown away by this thunderstorm from the east. Judah would manage to survive for about another century and a half, even outlasting Assyria. But then even Judah would experience the loss of its political independence.

Isaiah and the Kings of Judah

Isaiah, like Hosea and Amos, dates his ministry to the reigns of four specific kings of Judah: Uzziah, Jotham, Ahaz, and Hezekiah. Judging from 2 Chronicles 32:32, Isaiah may have lived a few years into the reign of Hezekiah's son Manasseh. None of Israel's kings is mentioned in the superscription because Isaiah ministered primarily to Judah. Two specific events concerning Isaiah's ministry are related in this chapter. The first one is the Syro-Ephraimitic War. This war involved King Ahaz of Judah, King Rezin of Aram, and King Pekah of Israel. The second event is the invasion of Judah and Jerusalem by the Assyrian king Sennacherib during Hezekiah's reign. Through both of these crises, Isaiah's task was to discern God's will and communicate it to Ahaz and Hezekiah. With this in mind, let's look at the reigns of Ahaz and Hezekiah.

AHAZ—2 KINGS 16; 2 CHRON. 28; ISA. 7:1 THROUGH 8:22; 735–716/15 B.C.

As we have seen, Judah, as well as Israel, experienced a period of prosperity in the mid-eighth century. Two things, however, threatened to alter Judah's future. The first was the revival of Assyrian strength under Tiglath-Pileser III; the second was King Ahaz's accession to the throne.[57] Ahaz's legacy would be to change Judah's status from independence to foreign servitude. He would be known in the biblical account as one of Judah's most wicked rulers. How could he take Judah down this path of Assyrian

[57]Ahaz's regnal years include a coregency with Jotham, 735–732/31, and reign, 732/31–716/15 B.C.

servitude and leave such a legacy of wickedness? The answer may be found by examining the dilemma he faced, the counsel from Isaiah that he refused, the decisions he made, and the consequences of those decisions.

First, Ahaz faced both a political and a military dilemma in the mid-eighth century. Assyria was expanding westward under the leadership of Tiglath-Pileser III. Assyria wanted to occupy the smaller states of western Asia. It desired to incorporate them into the provincial structure of the Assyrian Empire. Assyria's objective would be accomplished in three stages. First, there would be a demonstration of Assyrian military might. Then there would be an immediate crushing of any proven anti-Assyrian conspiracy. Finally, any king or state involved in rebellion against Assyria would be made an Assyrian province ruled by a governor. Assyria hoped that these measures would make conquered territories more governable.[58]

During Ahaz's reign, a plot developed among some of the smaller states of western Asia. The key instigators of this plot were Pekah, king of Israel, and Rezin, king of Damascus. They planned to unite to stop Assyria's advance. They tried to convince Jotham and Ahaz to join this plot.[59] Ahaz refused, however. Pekah and Rezin, unwilling to have a neutral, potentially hostile power to the south, sought to force Ahaz and Judah into line. They invaded Judah and laid siege to Jerusalem (2 Kings 16:5; 2 Chron. 28:5–8). This

[58]John H. Hayes and J. Maxwell Miller, eds., *Israelite and Judean History* (Philadelphia: Westminster Press, 1977), 419.

[59]Jotham's reign was short for reasons that are unclear, falling between his coregency with his father, Uzziah (Azariah), and the coregency of Ahaz (735–732/31 B.C.). He won a victory over the Ammonites and began preparing Jerusalem to withstand the Syro-Ephraimitic menace forming in the north (2 Kings 15:32–38; 2 Chron. 27).

invasion is called the Syro-Ephraimitic War.[60]

Edom had been subject to Judah for most of the eighth century. Now it saw Ahaz's dilemma as an opportunity to revolt and to seize Elath (2 Kings 16:6b; 2 Chron. 28:17). Similarly the Philistines raided and captured towns in the Judean foothills (the Shephelah) and the Negev (2 Chron. 28:18). Ahaz's dilemma intensified; he was invaded from three sides. Ahaz's throne and nation were endangered and helpless.

You would think Ahaz would turn to God and seek his help. Instead, he chose to appeal to Tiglath-Pileser III for aid. He reinforced his appeal with gifts from the temple and the treasuries of the royal palace (2 Kings 16:7–8; 2 Chron. 28:21). He hoped Judah would be spared.

This foreign policy decision was passionately opposed by Isaiah (Isa. 7:1 through 8:18).[61] What did Isaiah say to Ahaz? Isaiah's counsel was to trust God and not to be alarmed (Isa. 7:4,9). He told Ahaz to forsake any trust in human treaties. Ahaz was to rely solely on God's sovereign will and power. Isaiah's message, although divinely inspired and politically relevant, was too hard for Ahaz.

Unwilling to give up on Ahaz, God sent Isaiah to him with another prophetic word. In the form of a question, the prophet encouraged Ahaz to ask God for a sign (Isa. 7:11); God was willing to go beyond just words to strengthen Ahaz's faith. Pretending a piety he never possessed, Ahaz declined God's invitation (7:12). Isaiah, however, told him

[60]Our knowledge of this war is based on three basic sources: (1) the accounts in 2 Kings 15 through 16 and 2 Chron. 28, (2) Isa. 7 through 12, and (3) brief reports about the end of the war and its results in the annals and inscriptions of Tiglath-Pileser III (see *ANET*, 282–84).

[61]See the excellent discussion of Isaiah's prophetic word to Ahaz in the *NIV Study Bible* notes on these chapters.

Isaiah to Ahaz to Mary

Characteristic of God is his constant presence with us. So, hundreds of years later, another child was born to a virgin girl in Bethlehem. As this child grew, the people sensed in him the presence of God. Matthew, when writing his gospel, believed this promise made by Isaiah to Ahaz was fulfilled in the life of Jesus of Nazareth. He, too, is God with us. And so this prophecy of Isaiah to Ahaz passed from the "was-ness" of eighth century fulfillment into the first century "is-ness" of fulfillment. We can be forever grateful it did!

God would give him a sign anyway (7:14): A child would be born. He would grow up among the people of Judah in the midst of the Assyrian invasion, God's judgment on both Ahaz and Judah (7:18; 8:10). But in the child's name, "Immanuel" ("God with us"), there would be the constant reminder of God's faithful promise to David. God wouldn't annihilate his people. He would preserve and refine a remnant.[62] Once the Assyrian yoke was removed, the meaning of "Immanuel" would be clearly understood.

Ahaz wasn't concerned with God's words and signs, however. Two courses of action were open to Ahaz. One, he could surrender to Damascus and Israel and join their struggle against Assyria. Or two, he could enlist Assyrian aid against the Syro-Ephraimitic coalition. He chose the latter course. Though his actions saved Judah's national life, he paid a great price for them. Judah became a vassal state to Assyria. Excessive taxes drained even the temple of its wealth. The territory lost due to the Syro-Ephraimitic War and the Edomite capture of Elath were not regained. This crippled Judah's economy throughout Ahaz's reign. Further, his reign was characterized by a period of unparalleled idolatry in Judah (2 Kings 16:10–14; 2 Chron. 28:23).

Ahaz is remembered as one of the worst kings Judah ever had. He forsook God and led Judah further into the dark night of Assyrian oppression (Isa. 8:6–8). Ahaz was not buried in the royal tombs (2 Chron. 28:27). This showed Judah's resentment of his reign.

Judah would have continued its slide except for Hezekiah, Ahaz's son. Hezekiah had faith in God and was

---

[62]See also the name of Isaiah's first son, "Shear-Jashub," which means "a remnant will return" (Isa. 7:3). The meaning of the Immanuel prophecy is discussed in chap. 16, "Hear the Word of the Lord."

willing to listen to Isaiah, God's prophet. This moved God to extend the nation's existence for another hundred years.

HEZEKIAH — 2 KINGS 18 THROUGH 20; 2 CHRON. 29 THROUGH 32; ISA. 36 THROUGH 39; 716/15–687/86 B.C.

Scholars have long struggled with biblical and extrabiblical accounts of Hezekiah's reign in Judah. There are two major difficulties, as told in 2 Kings. The first involves the chronology of Hezekiah's reign. Scholars can't agree when he came to the throne. The second concerns Sennacherib's invasion of Judah and his siege of Jerusalem. The accounts of the invasion in 2 Kings 18 and 19 seem to tell quite different stories. Further difficulty arises when attempting to reconcile the biblical account of the Assyrian invasion with Sennacherib's own account.[63] With these things in mind, let us begin our look at Hezekiah.

Since the time of the breach between Israel and Judah,[64] Hezekiah could be considered the most successful reformer to sit on the throne of Judah (2 Kings 18:5).[65] His reforms joined religious devotion and political zeal. This led to his rebellion against Assyrian domination. His efforts for political freedom have caused some to question the motivation of his religious reforms. Were they his method of expressing his resistance to Assyria?[66] Of course they were. Yet there was a more fundamental issue at stake. Hezekiah's concept of the state was not a purely political

[63]Nelson, *First and Second Kings,* 235.

[64]See chap. 13, "The Great Divorce."

[65]See the discussion in the *NIV Study Bible* on this verse.

[66]Flanders, Crapps, and Smith, *People of the Covenant,* 360.

one. In Hezekiah's mind, the separation of religious authority and state authority was a nonissue. For him and his contemporaries, the covenant was the foundation for the state. Had Israel and Judah remembered this, no storm might have ever broke over them.

The international scene during Hezekiah's reign in Judah was one of political turmoil. In Assyria, Sargon II was facing rebellion in Babylon led by Merodach-Baladan and in Asia Minor by Midas, king of Phrygia. Meanwhile, the Ethiopian king, Piankhi, having seized control of Upper (i.e., southern) Egypt, proceeded to overrun the delta area.[67] This political instability fostered a revolt of the Philistines. They refused to pay taxes to Assyria. When Ethiopian representatives sought to enlist Hezekiah's aid, Isaiah opposed it (Isa. 18 through 19). He symbolically illustrated the folly of joining such an alliance (Isa. 20) by walking around Jerusalem barefoot, wearing only a loin cloth. Hezekiah listened and a disastrous crushing was avoided. Apparently it was at this time that Hezekiah began to launch his religious reforms. It would appear, then, that those reforms *did* have anti-Assyrian implications. His primary motivation, however, was to lead Judah back to covenant observance and faithfulness (2 Kings 18:3–7a; 2 Chron. 29:2 through 31:21).

His religious reforms were both negative and positive. Hezekiah ordered his men to remove and destroy the pagan symbols of idolatry (2 Kings 18:4; 2 Chron. 31:1). Among them was the bronze serpent that Moses had made some seven centuries earlier in the wilderness as a reminder of God's salvation through obedience. Having become an idol (Num. 21:8–9; 2 Kings 18:4), it had to be destroyed.

[67]Bright, *History of Israel*, 280–81.

Hezekiah's positive reforms are noteworthy, since they concern covenantal observances and faithfulness. He opened the temple doors, which had been closed by his father, Ahaz (2 Chron. 29:3; cf. 28:24). He instructed the priests and Levites to cleanse the temple (2 Chron. 29:4–19) and offered sacrifices to God (2 Chron. 29:20–36). He planned a special Passover celebration, inviting people from both Israel and Judah (2 Chron. 30:1–12). He then made provision for contributions for worship and the support of the priests and temple. He led the way by personal example (2 Chron. 31:2–19). The Chronicler assesses Hezekiah's reforms in terms of obedience and seeking God with one's whole heart (2 Chron. 31:20–21). Is there a lesson for us today?

A number of Hezekiah's religious reforms had sent powerful political signals. He had removed pagan Assyrian elements introduced by his father (2 Kings 16:10–18). This was a clear rejection of any Assyrian authority in the land of Judah. But Hezekiah was also a realist. He knew that these reforms would be understood by Assyria as open rebellion. When Sennacherib succeeded Sargon, Hezekiah felt this was the most favorable time to throw off the Assyrian yoke. He reaffirmed his conviction that Judah was to be a nation under covenantal relationship to God (2 Kings 18:12). His hopes of success were probably encouraged by this change in Assyrian administration. It created a period of instability in the Assyrian Empire. To the southeast Merodach-Baladan saw this as an opportunity to reestablish Babylonian independence. To the west, revolt also began to spread up and down Palestine and Syria. Hezekiah ignored Isaiah's warnings. Perhaps this was due to his fervent desire to free Judah's religion from

foreign influence. On the other hand, it may reflect pressure from patriots in the nation. In any event, he joined Egypt in the rebellion against Assyria (Isa. 30:1–7; 31:1–3).

Hezekiah knew Sennacherib wouldn't tolerate this rebellion, so he took steps to strengthen Jerusalem's military position. He reinforced the walls of Jerusalem (see photo 1). He reorganized the army and fortified several Judean cities (2 Chron. 32:1–6). He walled up the Gihon spring (see photo 2), just outside Jerusalem, and brought its waters into the city (2 Kings 20:20; 2 Chron. 32:30). This was a stroke of military and engineering genius. A reliable water supply would be a key factor in resisting an Assyrian invasion. Workers with picks and axes cut from both ends through nearly a third of a mile of solid rock (see photo 3). The water channel ran from the Gihon spring, flowed beneath the city, and emptied into the Pool of Siloam (see photo 4). Then they sealed and camouflaged the spring so that it could not be discovered.

An archaic Hebrew inscription was found in the tunnel near the Siloam end. It tells how the workmen, cutting from either end, met in the middle. When they heard the voices of the other workers, they cut through the remaining rock and the water flowed.[68] Today this inscription is in the Istanbul Archaeology Museum in Turkey.[69]

[68]Bill Humble, *Archaeology and the Bible* (Nashville: Christa Communications, 1990), 33.

[69]Ibid.

As Hezekiah thought would be the case, Sennacherib didn't wait long to launch a punishing campaign. Begun in 701 B.C., it was designed to crush the rebellion centered in Tyre, Philistia, and Judah. Despite the difficulties in harmonizing the biblical texts with the Assyrian accounts, it is possible to provide a general outline of this campaign. It followed four stages: (1) crushing Tyre, (2) conquering several cities in Philistia, (3) defeating Egypt and the Philistine city of Ekron, and (4) attacking cities in Judah and laying siege to Jerusalem.[70] We will confine our attention to his campaign against Hezekiah and Jerusalem (2 Kings 18:13–37; 2 Chron. 32:1–23; Isa. 36 through 37).

Scholarly research on Sennacherib's campaign against Judah has formulated two main theories as to its program and outcome. According to the first theory, there was only one campaign with two stages taking place in 701 B.C. Both 2 Kings 18:13–16 and Sennacherib's own annals record the first stage ending with Hezekiah's surrender. In the second stage, the biblical account records Assyria's defeat. In the Assyrian account, however, no Assyrian defeat is mentioned.[71] The emphasis of the Assyrian account is on the capture of forty-six fortified Judean cities and on making Hezekiah a "prisoner in Jerusalem, his royal residence, like a bird in a cage." Sennacherib also boasts of the enormous tribute he forced Judah to pay.[72]

The second theory concludes that the biblical record combines the accounts of two chronologically separate invasions of Judah by Sennacherib. The first one was in 701

Walking the Siloam Tunnel

I will never forget the first time I walked through this tunnel. I realized I was literally walking in the steps of Hezekiah, experiencing the genius that spared both him and Jerusalem from Assyrian defeat. That feeling was overwhelming!

[70]Hayes and Miller, *Israelite and Judean History,* 448.

[71]Ibid., 450.

[72]*ANET,* 288.

B.C. (2 Kings 18:13–16). The second was ten or fifteen years later (ca. 686 B.C.). This concluded with a devastating Assyrian defeat (2 Kings 18:17 through 19:37; Isa. 36 through 37).[73] Theoretically, the editor of Kings combined the two invasions, producing the form found in the current biblical narrative.[74]

Each of these theories has evidence both for and against it. Unless some further archaeological evidence, such as other Assyrian records, is discovered, we may never know the facts. This does not negate the theological implications of this story, however, either for Hezekiah or for us. A close look at the narrative in 2 Kings 18:17 through 19:37 clearly reveals that Hezekiah was facing his own dark and stormy night, despite his godly character. Let's look at that night.

It began with Sennacherib's demand that Hezekiah surrender Jerusalem. To present his ultimatum he sent three high-ranking officials with a large army. They were met by three of Hezekiah's officials. The Assyrian army's field commander spoke for Sennacherib. Six masterful arguments were used to convince the officials of Hezekiah's court to advise him to surrender (2 Kings 18:19–35):

1. Dependence on a military alliance with Egypt is foolish and futile (18:21).

2. Reliance on your God is futile since Hezekiah has removed his holy places (18:22).

3. The Assyrian army is invincible (18:23–24).

4. Your God has commissioned us to destroy you (18:25).

5. Surrender to us and we will provide a prosperous life for you (18:31–32).

6. Other cities' gods were ineffective against the might of

[73]Hayes and Miller, *Israelite and Judean History*, 450.

[74]Ibid.

our god, Ashur, so what can your god do except surrender his city to us to prevent its destruction? (18:33–35).[75]

Each of these arguments has a certain practicality. On the
human level they were difficult to refute. So Hezekiah did
the right thing in instructing his delegation, "'Do not
answer him'" (2 Kings 18:36).

While the delegation reasoned with the Assyrians
(2 Kings 18:13–16), Hezekiah humbled himself before the
LORD (19:1). He sought counsel from Isaiah, God's prophet
(19:2). Hezekiah asked him to intercede for those in Judah
who yet survived Sennacherib's capture (19:4). The LORD's
response through Isaiah was one of assurance and promise.
He said, "Don't be afraid. I'm going to punish him for his
blasphemy" (2 Kings 19:5–7, my paraphrase).

About this time, Sennacherib heard of the encroaching
Egyptian army. Perhaps he sensed that his position was
becoming more urgent and dangerous. He sent a second
ultimatum to Hezekiah (2 Kings 19:10–13). In it the real
issue becomes clear. The rivals were now the God of Israel
and the gods of Sennacherib, the "great king of Assyria"
(see 2 Kings 18:19,28). As in the confrontation between
Pharaoh and God in Exodus or Baal and God in 1 Kings
18, the primary conflict surfaced. Was Israel's God the
only true God, or could Sennacherib reduce him to impo-
tence?

Once again Hezekiah responded by taking it to God in
prayer (2 Kings 19:14–19). In his prayer he acknowledged
God as the sovereign creator. A mere man had defied him.
He affirmed that Sennacherib's boast about destroying
other nations' gods only proved they were not real gods at

---

[75]Davis and Whitcomb, *Israel From Conquest to Exile,* 451–53.

all. Hezekiah then prayed for deliverance. He wanted God to be glorified among all nations as the one and only true God. God answered Hezekiah through Isaiah: (1) God would meet Sennacherib's arrogance and ridicule of Israel with decisive judgment (2 Kings 19:20–28); (2) the remnant of Judah would prosper again (vv. 29–31); and (3) Jerusalem would not be captured because God would defend and save it (vv. 32–35).

The final battle line was drawn. The word of the LORD could not be true (2 Kings 19:6,20,32) if the words of the king of Assyria prevailed (18:19). So that very night Sennacherib, Hezekiah, and Jerusalem learned who really was the true God. The angel of the LORD killed 185,000 Assyrian soldiers.[76] The great army was gone overnight (18:17). Returning to Nineveh, his capital, Sennacherib learned how powerless his god really was: In his own temple Sennacherib's god couldn't protect him (19:37). Sennacherib was killed by two of his sons (cf. Isa. 37:38). And so the word of the LORD prevailed over what the king of Assyria said. And it always will![77]

Two further episodes of Hezekiah's reign need some comment. They are (1) his illness (2 Kings 20:1–11; Isa. 38) and (2) his foolish response to the Babylonian representatives of King Merodach-Baladan (2 Kings 20:12–19; Isa. 39). It has become customary to accept them chronologically, as occurring after Jerusalem's deliverance from Sennacherib's siege. There are several reasons, however, for believ-

---

[76]The ancient Greek historian Herodotus suggested that the Assyrian army was overrun by a plague of mice, thus spreading bubonic plague. This is similar to the account of the plagues brought on Egypt in the exodus (cf. Exod. 12:13,29) and could explain how the LORD killed them.

[77]See Nelson, *First and Second Kings,* 242.

ing that they occurred before the siege.[78]

Why would the writers place these two stories after Jerusalem's deliverance rather than before? Could it be that they wanted to conclude by providing their audiences with two perspectives on Jerusalem's miraculous deliverance? Richard Nelson believes so. He says that the first perspective "emphasizes God's love for the Davidic dynasty," whereas the second warns us "not to take God's salvation for granted." This incident points to a "complex interplay between God's grace (Rom. 4) and human obedience (James 2:14–26)," with prayer as a crucial element. This interplay is central to biblical theology.[79]

Thus ends the story of Judah's dark and stormy night, from the division of the kingdom to Hezekiah. We can only wish it had been different. As will be seen in subsequent chapters, this period would continue with only short breaks in the clouds. In fact, it still continues today. The Old Testament prophets and the New Testament writers, however, do promise that it will end. God's kingdom will be established on earth. He will reign forever!

Conclusion

There is a guiding lesson within this period of Judah's history. Its spiritual and material welfare and its kings

[78]They are these: (1) The deliverance hadn't yet happened (2 Kings 20:6; Isa. 38:6). (2) The royal treasury was still full (2 Kings 20:13; Isa. 39:2; cf. 2 Kings 18:15–16). (3) Second Chronicles 32:25–26 indicates that after God healed Hezekiah, he became prideful. But when he saw God's wrath come upon Judah and Jerusalem, he repented. This means the payment of heavy taxes and the threat of the Assyrian siege occurred *after* he was healed of the deadly disease (Davis and Whitcomb, *Israel From Conquest to Exile,* 461). (4) The vague time references in 2 Kings 20:1,12 indicate these two stories were flashbacks to the events of the previous chapters. If 2 Kings 20:1 were expanded, these events could be placed there.

[79]Nelson, *First and Second Kings,* 246–47.

depended on their covenantal faithfulness defined in the Mosaic covenant. From this general thesis several lessons emerge for the exilic community and the restored community. First, the lives of the kings taught them that the observance of God's law and conscious dependence on him would bring God's favor. The opposite behavior would bring God's judgment. Second, God was still in control of individuals, nations, and history. He was the sovereign LORD whose will and plan would not be defeated. Third, Judah's true mission as covenant people was to live in such a way that God would be seen as the *only* God before whom people were to bow and worship. Fourth, any king who would trust in the LORD, the God of Israel, hold fast to him, and not cease to follow him would receive God's highest praise (2 Kings 18:5–6). Finally, as Paul would later say in the New Testament, "Where sin increased, grace increased all the more" (Rom. 5:20). And so, God has never forgotten, and *will never* forget, his promises. This is true no matter what the circumstances. Both Kings and Chronicles affirmed Solomon's declaration after his dedicatory prayer for the temple (1 Kings 8:59–61): "'May these words of mine, which I have prayed before the LORD, be near to the LORD our God day and night, that he may uphold the cause of his servant and the cause of his people Israel according to each day's need, so that all the peoples of the earth may know that the LORD is God and that there is no other. But your hearts must be fully committed to the LORD our God, to live by his decrees and obey his commands, as at this time.'"

God will continue to remember his "good promises" (8:56) to us as we continue to walk before him and serve him in total commitment.

Study Questions

1. Explain what the author means by the "dark and stormy night" for Judah and Israel.

2. From what perspective do we read Kings and Chronicles?

3. What problems did Judah struggle with in the time of the divided monarchy?

4. What is the general theme of the Books of Kings? How does this theme differ from the theme of Chronicles?

5. Trace the practice of reform throughout Judah's history. Who did it, when, and why?

6. How are Judah's and Israel's foreign alliances regarded by the Bible?

7. What was the single interruption in the Davidic kingship in Judah? How did it happen?

8. Trace the rise of Joash, his good intentions, and the somewhat checkered results.

9. Analyze the religious, social, and political situations that preceded and followed Joash's reign. What part does the Syro-Ephraimitic War play?

10. Analyze the principle military and political threats to Judah in the eighth century B.C.

11. The reign of Hezekiah was a very important one, both politically and religiously. Why?

For Further Reading

Ben-Sasson, H. H., ed. *A History of the Jewish People*. Tel Aviv: Dvir Publishing House, 1969. Translated by George Weidenfeld and Nicholson Ltd.; reprint, Cambridge: Harvard University Press, 1976.

Crockett, William Day. *A Harmony of the Books of Samuel, Kings, and Chronicles*. Grand Rapids: Baker Book House, 1951.

Dillard, Raymond B., and Tremper Longman III. *An Introduction to the Old Testament*. Grand Rapids: Zondervan Publishing House, 1994.

Franz, Gordon. "The Hezekiah/Sennacherib Chronology Problem Reconsidered." Master's thesis, Institute of Holy Land Studies of Jerusalem, 1987.

Thiele, Edwin R. *The Mysterious Numbers of the Hebrew Kings*. Rev. ed. Grand Rapids: Wm. B. Eerdmans, 1983.

16

Richard Israel
Steve Fettke

Hear the Word of the LORD: The Rise of the Prophetic Movement

Outline:

- What Is a Prophet?
- Prophets in Ancient Israel
- Who Were Israel's "Non-literary" Prophets?
- What Were the Prophets' Theological Themes?
- What Did the Prophets Say About Worship?
- The Book of Jonah
- The Book of Amos
- The Book of Hosea
- The Book of Micah
- The Book of Joel
- The Book of Isaiah

Terms:

interpret
prophet/prophetism
sons of the prophets

In all ages people have wondered about prophets and prophecy. Is there a way to hear from God through a divinely called person? How can we know if that person is truly from God? What does the Bible say about those things?

What about those "prophets" on television and radio who claim to speak for God—like the one who tells fortunes for callers on the air? Or the one who "reads" the stars in the sky and says your life is determined by the movement of the planets? Or the shouting preacher who predicts wealth and happiness for all who contribute to his ministry? Or what about those preachers who cry out against injustice, greed, and militarism, who do so with their voices, protests, and even their very lives? How can we make any sense of all that?

The Bible provides some answers to our questions about prophets, both the true ones and the false ones. In ancient Israel God raised up prophets to speak to his people. They declared God's word and his plans for their present and future. God provided a witness to his word and will. He sent that witness—the prophet—to people he hoped would hear and obey. Regardless of the audience's obedience or disobedience, the prophet had to obey God's call. Perhaps those ancient prophets and their obedience to God and his call can help us in some way understand the role and ministry of people today. What does it mean to be called by God to proclaim his word and will to others?

What Is a Prophet?

Perhaps the clearest passage in the Old Testament for understanding the role and work of a prophet is found in Deuteronomy 18. The one called by God is designated a *nabi'*, a prophet who would speak the word of God (Deut. 18:15). The exact meaning of *nabi'* is not clear. The word "prophet" in English comes from the Greek term *prophetes*, the word that translates the Hebrew word *nabi'* in the Septuagint.[1] But in the Hebrew Bible the words for "seer"—*ro'eh* and *chozeh*—were also used to designate a prophet.[2] In Isaiah 29:10 and 30:10, *nabi'* and *ro'eh* seem to indicate the same thing. At some point in history there appears to have been an effort to change the designation of a prophet from *ro'eh* (seer) to *nabi'* (prophet; 1 Sam. 9:9).[3]

The closest the Old Testament canon comes to explaining the use of the word *nabi'* is Exodus 7:1–2: "Then the LORD said to Moses, 'See, I have made you like God to Pharaoh, and your brother Aaron will be your prophet *[nabi']*. You are to say everything I command you, and your brother Aaron is to tell Pharaoh to let the Israelites go out of his country.'" According to one scholar, "This is one of the clearest indications in the Old Testament that the word *nabi'* can have the basic meaning of 'spokesman.'"[4] We might even say that the word indicates "one who is called (to speak for another)."[5]

In examining carefully the text of Deuteronomy 18:15,18, certain things become clear. When God raised up a

[1] J. Lindblom, *Prophecy in Ancient Israel* (Philadelphia: Fortress Press, 1962), 26.

[2] R. K. Harrison, *Introduction to the Old Testament* (Grand Rapids: Wm. B. Eerdmans, 1969), 742.

[3] See also chap. 10, "From Tribal League to Kingdom."

[4] J. P. Hyatt, *Exodus,* New Century Bible Commentary (Grand Rapids: Wm. B. Eerdmans, 1971), 101.

[5] J. Jeremias, *"nabi,"* in *Theological Lexicon of the Old Testament,* ed. Ernest Jenni and Claus Westermann, trans. Mark E. Biddle (Peabody, Mass.: Hendrickson Publishers, 1997), 2:697. (Hereafter *TLOT.*)

prophet, that prophet was to speak the words that God had commanded. In addition, the prophet had God's authority. Deuteronomy 18:19 says that those who failed to listen to the prophetic word would be judged. The prophet was "one who speaks with the authority of the one who sends him."[6] This calling was not just a one-time event. Instead, the text of Deuteronomy 18:15–22 is expressed in terms of a succession of prophets who would preach like Moses. "The sense of the passage is that a succession of prophets would arise to continue the work of Moses who surpassed them all (Deut. 34:10)."[7]

The prophet *(nabi')*, therefore, was called by God, sent by him with his word, and given his authority. Yet many claimed to have a divine message when in fact they did not. We can read in Deuteronomy 18:15 that the called prophet was to be an Israelite. This requirement helped distinguish the true prophet from a foreigner who might prophesy by some power other than God (Deut. 18:10–12).

What, then, is a prophet? A prophet is one who is called by God, given God's words, and sent with God's authority. The work of the prophet is recognized by God's authoritative word. It is not to be confused with the mystical or clairvoyant means often used by others who also claim to be prophets.

Prophets in Ancient Israel

The first time the Bible uses the word for prophet, *nabi'*, is in reference to Abraham (Gen. 20:7). There God tells a

[6]James K. West, *Introduction to the Old Testament,* 2d ed. (New York: Macmillan, 1981), 266.

[7]J. A. Thompson, *Deuteronomy,* TOTC (London: Inter-Varsity Press, 1974), 212.

foreign king in a dream that Abraham will intercede for him because "'he is a prophet.'" While it is true that prophets interceded in prayer on behalf of individuals and nations, the more typical role of prophets was bringing a message from God. The Bible holds many interesting stories of people doing that. Aaron prophesied to Pharaoh (Exod. 4:14–16). Miriam, sister to Moses and Aaron, prophesied through song (15:20–21). So did a temple singer (2 Chron. 20:14–17). Some elders of Israel who were Moses' helpers also prophesied, prompting Moses to wish that all in Israel could prophesy (Num. 11:25–29).

Balaam was known as a great prophet from Mesopotamia. He came from a culture different from that of Israel. However, he was never actually called a prophet in the Old Testament. Yet his fame and prominence in the story about him in Numbers 22 through 24 indicate his stature in the ancient world. God used him to prophesy what God wanted him to say rather than what he was paid to say. The story of Balaam thus demonstrates that prophetic figures were not unique to Israel. They also were found in other cultures of the Ancient Near East.[8]

The prophetic role of Moses overshadows all others (Num. 12:6–8). He set the standard for prophets and their prophecies. The job of the Mosaic prophet was to communicate God's word to his people. Moses demonstrated that when he mediated between God and the people at Mount Sinai.

[8]See Robert R. Wilson, "Prophecy in the Ancient Near East," in *Prophecy and Society in Ancient Israel* (Philadelphia: Fortress Press, 1980), 89–134. Even though other societies, such as Mari, Assyria, Egypt, Canaan (Palestine), and Syria involved prophets in their cultural expressions, Wilson suggests that it is *not* appropriate to conclude that Israelite prophecy was simply "borrowed from another culture."

Following the Mosaic period, the role and ministry of a prophet was shaped by the community's governance structure. For instance, in reference to the time of the tribal league (Josh. through 1 Sam.), prophets were concerned about God's will as expressed among certain tribes or in certain locales. Later, during and after the rise of the monarchy, prophets (e.g., Isaiah and Jeremiah) took on a broadened political and social awareness. They spoke to the affairs of both Israel and the Gentile nations. The prophets were concerned that the people remain faithful to the *torah*, the law of Moses. They warned that God's judgment, rather than God's blessing, would be the result of their unfaithfulness. When God's people would not turn from idolatry, oppression of the poor and weak, and immorality, God judged them through invasion of foreign armies, sending them into exile in foreign lands. However, even in exile, God had prophets like Ezekiel to tell them why they were being judged and to offer them hope for restoration. After the exile, the prophets Haggai and Zechariah were concerned about the rebuilding of the community and the temple in Jerusalem. Because the prophetic role changed as the shape of the community changed, prophets should be studied in reference to their particular historical situations.

Who Were Israel's "Non-literary" Prophets?

The terms traditionally used to describe Israel's prophets are "literary" and "non-literary." These terms can be misleading. For instance, Samuel is considered a "non-literary" prophet even though there are biblical books that bear his name. Whether or not he wrote the books is not the point. The historian who compiled them thought Samuel such a key figure that he attributed to him those books that bear his name. Likewise, prophets whose books are found in the Bible probably did not foresee their works collected in the form in which we now have them. In a sense, then, all Israel's prophets were oral prophets. It is just that major portions of some prophets' preaching and exploits were preserved and handed down to us. Others had only small parts preserved.

The Hebrew Bible calls the "historical books" of Joshua, Judges, Samuel, and Kings the "Former Prophets."[9] The Bible explains Israel's history from Joshua through 2 Kings in terms of Moses' prophetic warnings in Deuteronomy. Those warnings, sadly, proved all too necessary. As Moses had predicted in Deuteronomy, Israel came to a tragic end. The Northern Kingdom (Israel) was conquered and taken away captive by the Assyrians in 723/22 B.C. (2 Kings 17). The Southern Kingdom (Judah) met the same fate at the hands of the Babylonians in 586 B.C. (2 Kings 25). In this so-called non-literary period of prophetic history, three prophets stand out from the rest for their significance: Samuel, Elijah, and Elisha.

Samuel's prophetic role covered a wide spectrum of activity (1 Sam. 3:20). He anointed Saul and David as kings. He was instrumental in decisions to go to war. At times, he was portrayed as a leader of ecstatic prophets (1:18–24). People would also come to him to inquire of the LORD (9:9). Samuel also heard from God and proclaimed his word (3:21). All these activities in Samuel's prophetic ministry were also found in the ministries of his successors, Elijah and Elisha. Clearly, prophetic activity was a multifaceted, complex issue from its earliest appearance in ancient Israel.

Besides the prophetic activities Samuel practiced, Elijah's

[9]See chap. 1, "What Is the Old Testament?"

prophetic ministry added the work of social justice and right worship of God. During Elijah's ministry, King Ahab had married Jezebel of Sidon—who brought Baal worship with her to the northern kingdom of Israel. Elijah condemned Baal worship as incompatible with the worship of God (1 Kings 18:21). In Baal worship, the worshiper supposed he insured the changes of seasons through his worship of the gods that controlled natural forces. To combat this thinking and to show God's control of nature, Elijah prophesied a drought in Israel (1 Kings 17). After three years, he challenged the prophets of Baal to a test: The god who answered by fire would be the true God (1 Kings 18). Despite the frenzied efforts of the Baal prophets, their god gave no answer. The God of Elijah, however, answered by fire. In this dramatic story, we learn how Elijah reformed Israel's worship of God.

Elijah was also concerned with social justice, a matter prominent in later prophets (Jer. 9:23–24; Mic. 6:8). An example of this may be seen in the story of Naboth's vineyard in Jezreel (1 Kings 21). Through abuse of Israel's legal system, King Ahab took ownership of Naboth's vineyard. In doing this, the king committed murder and violated family ownership rights given by the LORD. Elijah announced a blood-for-blood death sentence on Ahab (1 Kings 21:19).

Elisha was Elijah's successor by divine commission. When Elijah called Elisha to follow him, he threw his cloak around him. On the day Elijah was taken up into heaven, the cloak fell back to earth (2 Kings 2:1–17), symbolizing a transfer of Elijah's prophetic power to Elisha. Like Samuel and Elijah, Elisha dealt with kings and political and military decisions.[10] Elisha's ministry in these areas was a reminder

[10]Second Kings 3; 6:28–33; 6:24 through 7:20; 13:10–20.

to God's people that their political fortunes were in God's hands and not their leaders' or their own. Elisha interpreted events for Israel. He helped them understand God's activity as either *judgment by* their enemies or *deliverance from* their enemies (2 Kings 8:7–14; 13:1–3). These themes—judgment, deliverance, and restoration—were utilized by later prophets.[11]

In the description of Elisha's ministry we read of an organized prophetic group called "the sons of the prophets" (2 Kings 2:15, KJV; "company of the prophets," NIV). The phrase occurs eleven times in the Hebrew text, ten times in connection with Elisha. It doesn't refer to a family relationship so much as it describes a brotherhood. Such men were dedicated to their prophetic roles and lived in communities apart from society.

We know little about their origins and what became of them. Through much of Israel's history, there must have been a tradition of prophetic activity among the people. The seventy elders prophesied in the wilderness period (Num. 11:24–29). Such activity continued, and a guild of prophets is mentioned as late as the mid-eighth century B.C. (Amos 7:14). The prophets had disciples and support groups. They were not solitary eccentrics or religious geniuses. No doubt the accounts of the non-literary prophets' exploits can be traced to such a guild of disciples.

What Were the Prophets' Theological Themes?

The prophetic books contain messages that speak to particular circumstances in the history of Israel. Nowhere did the prophets proclaim a systematic theology. Instead, their

---

[11]Examples may be found in the books of Isa., Jer., Ezek., and Amos, although other literary prophets also use these motifs.

messages were concrete expressions addressed to specific incidents. Consequently, it is difficult to extract a theology as such from the sermons of the prophets. Nevertheless, there are common theological emphases in them. In one way or another, all of them emphasized God's sovereignty, justice, righteousness, and covenant loyalty.[12]

Perhaps the passage that best illustrates and summarizes these theological themes is Jeremiah 9:23–24. Jeremiah contrasted what the world understands as qualities of success—wisdom, political and military strength, and wealth—with those qualities God wanted his people to practice: covenant loyalty *(chesed)*, justice *(mishpat)*, and righteousness *(ts^edaqah)*. As sovereign lord, God has the right to decide how people are to live. They are to imitate him, who practices these same qualities in his dealings with all humanity.

Sadly, Israel often did not practice these divine qualities in their faith history. Amos lamented the loss of justice *(mishpat)* in Israel's courts (Amos 5:12,14). Isaiah reminded those who said they were pursuing righteousness *(ts^edaqah)* that true righteousness comes from God (Isa. 51:1–8).

Covenant loyalty *(chesed)* describes the relationship between God and Israel as parties bound by a covenant. Hosea's marriage to an unfaithful wife served as a powerful indictment of Israel's unfaithfulness to God (Hos. 1 through 3). God expected Israel to be faithful and loyal to the terms of their covenant. Israel both as a people and as individuals were held accountable. Hosea accused the Israelites of being fickle. "'Your love [chesed],'" said Hosea, "'is like the morning mist, like the early dew that disappears'" (6:4). There were other ways to describe the

[12]Some passages that illustrate these themes are Isa. 1:16–17; Amos 5:24; and Mic. 6:8.

Israelites' failures in their relationship to God. They had no knowledge of God (4:6). They had forgotten him (Isa. 17:10). They had refused to obey his commandments (Amos 2:4). The point is that the prophets had a sense of how one ought to live in relationship to God.

Justice and righteousness *(mishpat, ts*e*daqah)* are terms describing appropriate social relationships. Social ethics were the focus when prophets called for justice and righteousness. The king was the person in power who was charged with maintaining justice for the community (2 Sam. 8:15; 1 Kings 10:9). The powerful, however, could easily take advantage of the poor by perverting justice and overthrowing righteousness. But such an ethic of "Might makes right" brought condemnation from the prophets. They spoke God's judgment against all who took advantage of the poor and powerless.

Justice meets a universal human need.[13] It is rooted in God as creator and sustainer of the universe. Amos accused the Israelites of turning justice into bitterness and casting righteousness to the ground (Amos 5:7). He followed this indictment with a hymnic portion describing God as creator and sustainer of the cosmos (5:8). Covenant relationship and election privileges exempted no one from the requirements of doing justice and righteousness. God's sovereignty called all creation to justice and righteousness.

The people were unfaithful in a variety of ways. In particular, they yielded to the temptation of polytheism and worshiped other gods. Similarly, they maintained a form of godliness without authentic commitment to the

---

[13]See Rolf Knierim, "Cosmos and History in Israel's Theology," in *The Task of Old Testament Theology* (Grand Rapids: Wm. B. Eerdmans, 1995), 171–224, especially 198–204 on "Yahweh and World Order."

relationship it suggested. Their religion was an empty hypocrisy. "'These people come near to me with their mouth and honor me with their lips,'" said the LORD, "'but their hearts are far from me'" (Isa. 29:13). The prophets decried Israel's disobedience to God, reporting his judgment: "'Because they have rejected the law of the LORD and have not kept his decrees . . . I will send fire upon Judah'" (Amos 2:4–5). Taking advantage of people through abuse of power was another way individuals failed to keep covenant. To worship God and trample on others was a betrayal of God's character. "'The multitude of your sacrifices—what are they to me?' says the LORD. . . . 'Your hands are full of blood; wash and make yourselves clean. Take your evil deeds out of my sight! Stop doing wrong, learn to do right! Seek justice, encourage the oppressed. Defend the cause of the fatherless, plead the case of the widow'" (Isa. 1:11,15–17).

What Did the Prophets Say About Worship?

The prophets proclaimed the importance of worshiping God. Israel had corrupted its worship with paganism and a lack of concern for the *torah* and for the poor. Many prophets were quick to respond. Isaiah complained about their offerings, observances of religious festivals, and even their prayers (Isa. 1:12–15). Instead of their worship making them good servants of God, it had become a way to salve their consciences and cover up their sins. Isaiah's advice was for them to repent, be cleansed by God, and start practicing justice. Then, and only then, would their worship be acceptable (1:13–20).

Jeremiah went to the temple where he preached against those who used the worship sanctuary as a place of safety. All along, those same people had been oppressing the helpless and worshiping Baal (Jer. 7:1–11). Jeremiah accused them of violating the Decalogue and then coming to the temple to worship. This, he said, would turn the temple into a "den of robbers." By this he meant that they made the temple a place for covenant breakers instead of a house of prayer and worship. When Jesus cleansed the temple of the moneychangers, he quoted from Jeremiah 7:11 (Matt. 21:13; cf. Isa. 56:7).

Amos was especially harsh in his denunciation of Israel's worship. They had oppressed the poor. They had focused on the style and amount of worship rather than on the changed lives worship was supposed to produce (Amos 5:12–24). For Amos, a clear sign of true worship was the practice of justice and righteousness (5:24). Micah said something very similar in regard to worship. It was not the amount of offerings or kinds of offerings or even the sincerity of one's offerings that truly mattered. What truly mattered would be the practice of justice, mercy, and humility (Mic. 6:6–8).

H. H. Rowley expressed it well when he said, "The worship of the shrine [was to] prove its reality by inspiring daily life, where the will of God had to be worked out in human relationships that reflected the character of God . . . and [had] corollaries that [touched] every aspect of life."[14]

Worship and Lifestyle

The prophets can help us take stock of our own worship practices, which in turn can help us conform our worship content and practices to our everyday life of faith.

The Book of Jonah

Who Was Jonah?

Jonah son of Amittai received a commission to go to Nineveh (Jon. 1:2). There he was to announce God's

---

[14]H. H. Rowley, *Worship in Ancient Israel: Its Forms and Meaning* (London: SPCK, 1967), 271.

judgment on the city. A prophet named Jonah son of Amittai is mentioned in 2 Kings 14:25. This would place Jonah's ministry to the Northern Kingdom during the reign of Jeroboam II (793–753 B.C.).

The Book of Jonah divides neatly into two sections, each composed of two chapters:

1:1 through 2:10	Jonah's First Commission to Nineveh
1:1–17	Jonah receives his commission, flees
2:1–10	Jonah's prayer and deliverance
3:1 through 4:11	Jonah's Second Commission to Nineveh
3:1–10	Jonah preaches to Nineveh, the city repents
4:1–11	Jonah sulks, God reasons with him

What Was Jonah's World Like?

Jeroboam II reigned during a period when Assyria was relatively weak. A coalition of Aramean and Israelite armies had stopped the Assyrians in 853 B.C.[15] Since that time, the Assyrians had not been able to expand their empire. Assyrian weakness allowed Jeroboam II of Israel to expand Israel's borders. Jonah himself had prophesied Jeroboam's success (2 Kings 14:25).

Assyria, after Tiglath-Pileser's accession to the throne in 745, renewed their bid for world domination. The Assyrian campaign targeted civilian populations for ruthless atrocities. Israel would experience those atrocities in 723/22 B.C., when the Assyrians conquered the Northern Kingdom.[16]

[15]See chap. 14 of this book, "Long Day's Journey Into Night," and *ANET,* 276.

[16]Edwin R. Thiele, *A Chronology of the Hebrew Kings* (Grand Rapids: Zondervan Publishing House, 1977), 51. Thiele's chronology, followed in

It is important to distinguish between the time of the event and the time of the book's writing. Apparently, the narrator looks back on the period of Jonah.[17] The wickedness of Nineveh was bad in Jonah's time. Later on, however, the Israelites would be victimized even more. At that time the teaching of the Book of Jonah concerning God's forgiveness and compassion would sound still more radical.

What Does Jonah Teach Us?

There is a wide diversity of opinion about how to understand the Book of Jonah. The key issue is whether Jonah is a work of fiction or of nonfiction. On the fiction side, people understand the book as a parable,[18] a midrash,[19] an allegory,[20]

---

this textbook for the most part in the reigns of the kings, is probably a year too early for the fall of the Northern Kingdom. He dates the fall of Samaria as 723 B.C. It now appears that Samaria fell in 722/21 B.C.

[17]William C. Williams, "Jonah," in *ISBE*, 2:1112–16. Williams notes that the verb (*waw* disjunctive followed by a perfect tense) probably indicates that the author of 3:3b was looking back on Jonah's time from some time after the fall of Nineveh in 612 B.C. However, because it interrupts an obvious parallelism with the opening verses of chap. 1, he considers 3:3b to be a gloss that was added later, and thus need not reflect the date when the book was written.

[18]The historical references to actual people, places, and events argue against this view. The parable of Nathan to David in 2 Sam. 12, for instance, makes a point of using nameless characters, as do the parables of Jesus.

[19]When we call it a midrash, we are assuming that it is a story told to explain what a certain text means. In this case the text would be Jon. 4:2: "'You are a gracious and compassionate God, slow to anger and abounding in love, a God who relents from sending calamity.'" Similar descriptions of God's character occur frequently in the OT as at Exod. 34:6, Ps. 86:15, and elsewhere. The text, though, seems to support the story, rather than the story support the text. A midrashic method may have been at work here, but a haggadic (narrative style) commentary on a verse does not seem to take in the whole story.

[20]This view "purports to see in Jonah a complete allegory in which each feature represents an element in the historical and religious experience of the

or a theological lesson in narrative form. On the nonfiction side, people interpret it either as history or as a theological lesson in narrative form based on Jonah's mission to Assyria.

Two problems complicate the question. The first asks, "Is it possible for a person to survive three days inside a great fish?" Accounts of sailors who underwent an ordeal similar to Jonah litter the commentaries. But that misses the point. The God who parted the Red Sea to save Moses and the Israelites could employ a fish to save this prophet even if it never happened to anyone else. The real issue under discussion by interpreters is whether God works miracles or not. That is not an issue in Jonah (or the rest of the Bible for that matter). That is an issue raised by the philosophy of the interpreter.

The second problem poses the question, "Why are there no Assyrian records of the conversion of Nineveh?" Two logical explanations have been proposed to explain the silence of the Assyrian chronicles regarding Jonah's ministry. Either the Assyrian historians did not deem it a noteworthy event, or the records have disappeared.

While interpreters may differ on the matter of historicity, they concur that the Book of Jonah is a theological lesson in narrative form. Jonah differs from other books named after prophets because it is a story about a prophet, not a collection of the prophet's messages. The story divides itself into two parallel movements. These movements are introduced by the statements "the word of the LORD came

---

Israelites." Harrison, *Introduction to the Old Testament,* 911. See his fuller description of the allegory's component elements. He rightly rejects this interpretation because the story has neither "implicit nor explicit" indicators that it stands for another "series of happenings" beyond the events involving Jonah himself (912).

to Jonah" (1:1 through 2:10) and "the word of the LORD came to Jonah a second time" (3:1 through 4:11).

In the first movement, Jonah received a commission to go preach judgment on Nineveh. Instead, Jonah boarded a ship and sailed in the opposite direction. The LORD's response to Jonah's disobedience was to send a life-threatening storm. This terrified the ship's crew. At Jonah's advice, the sailors reluctantly threw him overboard to quiet the storm and save the ship. God prepared a great fish to swallow Jonah and the storm subsided. The thankful sailors converted to Yahwism. While he was still in the belly of the fish, Jonah offered a psalm of thanksgiving to Yahweh for deliverance. The fish then took him back to land and the second movement begins.

This time Jonah obeyed the word of the LORD and went to Nineveh to preach the message of judgment. The city sought forgiveness and God responded accordingly, but Jonah took exception to God's show of mercy. God's reluctant prophet, it seems, knew God's character. He confessed that God was "a gracious and compassionate God, slow to anger and abounding in love, a God who relents from sending calamity" (Jon. 4:2). Yet Jonah would rather die than live in a world with a God like that (4:3). Jonah, in a bizarre outpouring of compassion about a shade plant, got a lesson about God's perspective on his creatures.

Important Theological Issues in the Book of Jonah

The Book of Jonah addresses some issues of theology. First, Jonah's disobedience to God's commission to go preach to Nineveh highlights a real problem for those God calls. Sometimes interpreters assume that Jonah's reason

Blessing Your Enemies

All who prophesy must struggle with a basic question. They must ask themselves if they will obey God's command even when it does not lead to their preferred outcome. Presumably it was easy for Jonah to assure Jeroboam II of God's promised success (2 Kings 14:25). His own king, his own country, his own people, received the benefit. In contrast, Jonah resisted sharing the good news with the enemy Assyrians. The question in the Book of Jonah remains open to all readers: whether they will minister in conformity with God's own character.

for running was embarrassment. He knew that if God did not destroy Nineveh it would leave him looking like a fool, or worse, a false prophet. Jonah's anger toward God stemmed from his feeling betrayed. The story, though, gives a more immediate reason for his disobedience: Jonah knew God's merciful character. He did not wish the hated Ninevites to have an opportunity to repent and experience God's mercy (Jon. 4:2).

Second, the story also raises the issue of God's changing his decision, or "relenting" (*nacham;* Jon. 4:2). Sometimes readers ask how an unchangeable God, who knows the end from the beginning, can "change his mind." After all, Numbers 23:19 claims that such change is a characteristic of humans, not of God. Yet, Jonah described God as one who "relents from evil." How may one hold those two views together theologically?

The sense of the Hebrew verb *nacham* is "to be sorry."[21] God was sorry for the evil that he had decreed against the inhabitants of Nineveh. One should not infer, though, that God's mind changed. Jonah knew what God had in mind from the beginning. He knew that God wanted to spare those wicked sinners, so he fled to avoid preaching to them. God's character, however, requires him to relent from sending calamity any time humans repent from evil (Jon. 4:2). What he actually "has in mind," therefore, is to be gracious, compassionate, slow to anger, abounding in love, and relenting from evil. It was God's grace that motivated him to send prophets like Jonah to preach to their enemies. God's mind does not change. He turns (3:9) from judgment when humans turn (3:10) from evil. Jonah is to the Old Testament what

---

[21]H. J. Stoebe, "NHM," in *TLOT,* 734–39.

John 3:16 is to the New Testament.

Third, the Book of Jonah engages another important question. How does justice relate to mercy in God's actions? The prophet Jonah may seem like a petty person who cannot get past his antipathy for Assyrians. He appears uncompassionate, ethnocentric, and prejudiced. He deserves a more sympathetic reading than that.

At a later time, the prophet Nahum reflected Israelite sentiment against Assyrian brutality. When Nineveh fell, he cried, "Who has not felt your endless cruelty?" (Nah. 3:19). At stake for Jonah, however, was the morality of God. How could God, the judge of all the earth, not do justice?

Jonah learned the answer in the incident of the shade plant. God had "provided" the great fish to save Jonah. In the same way, God "provided" the shade plant and "provided" the worm that killed it. Finally, he "provided" a scorching wind to make Jonah faint. Jonah became angry, motivated by his "concern" (chus) for the plant. This forms the link for God's argument. If Jonah was concerned (chus) about the vine, couldn't God be concerned (chus) about Nineveh? There were 120,000 innocent people and many cattle in the city. It was not a choice between justice or mercy. God is committed to being merciful (Jon. 4:2). To be just, therefore, God must be merciful. God revealed to Jonah his justice *through* his mercy.

However, the story ends with a question that goes unanswered. In posing it, the narrator puts us all in the hot seat. Do we feel compassion only for our own comfort? Can we get beyond that to share in God's compassion for the world, including our enemies?

The Book of Amos

Who Was Amos?

Amos was a shepherd from Tekoa in Judah (Amos 1:1) who "took care of sycamore-fig trees" (7:14). He was not a prophet by heritage or profession. He prophesied because he had received a commission from the LORD.

Since Amos was from Judah but prophesied in the Northern Kingdom, the Israelites probably resented him as an outsider (7:12–13). Perhaps 3:3–8 is Amos' defense of his call. Some scholars think the whole book is the remains of a single sermon. Others detect several stages of ministry in his words spanning several years.

Amos was a person with great communication skills. He used literary devices to influence his audience. These included a funeral lament about his listeners (Amos 5:2), a parody of a priest's instructions to pilgrims (4:4), biting sarcasm (6:1–7), verses from hymns (4:13; 5:8–9; 9:5–6), and other rhetorical strategies. We get the impression of a courageous person wading into controversy. He was compelled by the roar of the Lion to prophesy God's word to a hostile audience (3:8).

What Was Amos's World Like?

Amos prophesied during the reigns of Jeroboam II (793– 753 B.C.) in Israel, and Uzziah in Judah (792–740; Amos 1:1). The reign of Jeroboam II is described in 2 Kings 14:23–29. The reign of Uzziah/Azariah is described in 2 Kings 15:1–7; 2 Chronicles 26.

Israel and Judah had recaptured some of the territory that they had lost since the time of David (2 Kings 14:25,28; 2 Chron. 26:6–8). A big reason for this military success was

What Happened to Amos?

How Amos's ministry ended is as mysterious as how it began. Amaziah, priest at Bethel, accused Amos of inciting a revolution (Amos 7:10–17, esp. v. 10). We do not know if he was allowed to go free after that. He may have been executed. What is clear is that Amos put his life on the line to proclaim his message. Obedience to his calling became the sole purpose of his existence. He was willing to pay whatever this cost him: his profession, his reputation, perhaps even his life.

a power vacuum in the Near East. Neither Assyria nor Egypt was expanding its empire in those decades. Moreover, the kingdoms of Israel and Judah enjoyed friendly relations at this time. Thus they took advantage of an opportunity to expand their borders. Control over other territories brought a peace dividend that was good for the economy. Consequently, those decades became a period of prosperity, at least for some Israelites.

Amos, however, denounced the merchant class that disregarded the covenant regulations of the *torah*. A corrupted system of religion and politics supported their greed. It left two classes of Israelites, the rich and the poor. The poor were oppressed and exploited by the powerful rich. This perversion of justice was the central issue of Amos's preaching. He saw it as the reason for Yahweh declaring an end to his people.

What Does Amos Teach Us?

The Book of Amos falls into four distinct sections. The speeches that introduce each of the sections indicate the divisions. Chapters 1 through 2 are a series of oracles against certain nations. Chapters 3 through 6 are speeches of varying types. Chapters 7 through 9 record five visions. Words of hope for the future conclude the book (9:11–15).

1:1 through 2:16	Judgment on the Nations
3:1 through 6:14	Warnings of Judgment on Israel and Judah
7:1 through 9:10	Visions of Judgment
9:11–15	Hope Beyond Judgment

JUDGMENT ON THE NATIONS — AMOS 1 THROUGH 2

Amos used the same forms of prophetic speech that other prophets used.[22] His style, though, was distinctive. The following pattern recurs in Amos 1 through 2: "For three sins . . . for four, I will not turn back my wrath." That is, three sins could have been overlooked; the "fourth" was the one that tipped the scales. This formula suggests completeness, that is, the nations were completely sinful. God would judge them.

Amos set a rhetorical trap to indict his Israelite audience. He first got their attention by announcing judgment on the breakaway nations of the former Davidic empire.[23] The climax to his sermon came when he pronounced a more severe judgment on his Israelite listeners (Amos 2:6–16). For them, that was probably an unpleasant and unexpected turn of events. In their desire for judgment on their enemies, they had set themselves up for the same.

God's accusations against the nations other than Judah and Israel stemmed from crimes against humanity. Excessive cruelties in warfare were typical reasons for judgment. Some of those practices included deporting whole populations, ripping open "pregnant women" (Amos 1:13), and treaty violations. They were actions that every moral person would condemn as extreme. They were the reasons for God's judgment on those nations. Yahweh was the judge of all nations. He would judge and punish all injustices.

[22]Modern interpreters might term Amos's speech "oracles against foreign nations" or something similar; see Isa. 13 through 23 or Jer. 46 through 50.

[23]Francis I. Andersen and David N. Freedman, *Amos: A New Translation With Notes and Commentary,* AB (New York: Doubleday, 1989), 27.

By contrast, Israel's and Judah's covenant with the LORD was the foundation for their indictment. Those who knew Yahweh as their savior received judgment in light of that knowledge (Amos 2:4). Amos accused the nations of rebellion *(pesha')*. He indicted them for failure to live by the rules of decency. He charged Israel and Judah with violating God's direct commands. Israel's special knowledge of God did not exempt them from the punishment announced against other nations. Rather, it shifted the terms of judgment onto more dangerous ground. Their judgment as a nation flowed from their special relationship with God (2:4,11–12).

WARNINGS OF JUDGMENT ON ISRAEL AND JUDAH — AMOS 3:1 THROUGH 6:14

The markers for this section of judgment are three prophetic "words" that Israel was to "hear." The first of them based God's punishment of Israel on their special election (Amos 3:1–2). The second promised judgment for the rich women of Samaria who oppressed the poor (4:1–3). The third was a funeral song for fallen Israel (5:1–2).

Apparently Israel had an attitude of superiority growing out of their special relationship with God. In fact, the privilege of Israel's election was at the root of their problem. They assumed that their standing with God excused them from his judgment. How could God's "most favored nation" lose its status? Was God not prospering their economy and politics? Amos argued that God's special election was the basis for his judgment (Amos 3:1–2). Then he rhetorically summoned the Philistines and Egyptians to witness Israel's sins (3:9–12). Since Samaria was Israel's capital city, its sins would testify against the whole nation in the time of God's judgment (3:13–15).

Amos's message of judgment must have brought questions about his legitimacy as a prophet. In any case, he made a passionate defense of his ministry (Amos 3:3–8). His claim to have received his message from God was its sole basis. He needed no other authorization.

Chapter 4 contains a series of warnings based on judgments sent on the unrepentant Israelites. "'Yet you have not returned to me'" is the refrain (Amos 4:6–13). Because of this, they were summoned: "'Prepare to meet your God, O Israel'" (4:12).

Chapter 5 opens with a lament (Amos 5:1–2) over Israel's death. The funeral motif continues through 5:17. Appeals to seek God and live (5:4–6,14–15) contrast with the funeral songs of the surrounding verses. These appeals highlight God's willingness to relent even at the last moment.

Amos challenged the Israelites' perception of the "day of the LORD" (Amos 5:18–20). They perceived it as the dawn of a day of salvation. Amos, however, warned that it would bring darkness, not light. There was a lot of religious activity in Israel, but there was no justice (5:21–27). As a result, God despised their religion. "'Let justice roll on like a river, righteousness like a never-failing stream'" (5:24).

Judgment through exile, already sounded in 5:27, becomes the dominant note in chapter 6. Other nations had suffered God's punishment. Judah and Israel would not be exempt (6:1–7). Israel's pride in their conquest of other nations motivated God to raise up a nation to oppress them (6:8–14).

VISIONS OF JUDGMENT—AMOS 7:1 THROUGH 9:10

Five visions form the core of the final major section of Amos. Visions one (Amos 7:1–3) and two (7:4–6) show

Amos's role as a prophetic intercessor. In response to his intercession, God twice relented from his judgment. These texts show that Amos's compassion for God's people paralleled his passion for God's word. He dared to speak back to God. His courageous proclamation *to* the people matched his courageous intercession *for* the people.

Visions three (7:7–9) and four (8:1–2) announce God's verdict: "'I will spare them no longer.'" The time for intercession and relenting from judgment was past. The end had come for God's people. Amos was apparently the first prophet to proclaim this. His radical message must have struck the listeners as inconceivable. They may have known of Moses' warnings (Deut. 28:15–68), but to have "the end" come in their generation must have been hard.

Sandwiched between these visions is the report of the impact of Amos's message. In the third vision, Amos threatened that God would raise a sword against Jeroboam II (Amos 7:9). This made Amaziah, the priest who officiated at the Bethel shrine, suspicious. He reported to the king that Amos was forming a conspiracy against him (7:10–11).[24] A confrontation followed between Amos and Amaziah, set against the Bethel shrine (1 Kings 12:29). Amaziah called the shrine at Bethel "the temple of the kingdom" *(beyth mamlakah)*. The term contrasts ironically with the meaning of Bethel as "the house of God" *(beyth 'el)*. The (northern) kingdom had assimilated the temple: Politics now dominated religion!

The fifth vision follows a series of judgments introduced by the formula "In that day . . ." or "The days are coming . . ." (Amos 8:3,9,11,13). Amos ended this series of

---

[24]See 2 Kings 9 for the story of just such a "conspiracy" by Elisha. Jeroboam would take Amos's words as treasonous.

visions by citing a doxology that must have been known at the Bethel shrine (9:5–6).

Amos 9:7 reintroduces the theme of Israel among the nations. Those nations would play a role in God's judgment of his people. They would be his "sieve," (v. 9) his tool, to destroy the sinners in Israel. The verses also introduce hope in a remnant who would be saved through judgment.

HOPE BEYOND JUDGMENT—AMOS 9:11–15

Amos gives two descriptions of hope beyond judgment. The first (Amos 9:11–12) recalls God's promise to David (2 Sam. 7:12–16). The tradition of the promise speaks of God's faithfulness to his own purposes for Israel. David's lineage would be reborn! Human unfaithfulness would not deter the purposes of the Sovereign LORD. The promise to David reflected God's continuous commitment to his people.

The second description envisions a future agricultural bounty (9:13–15). God would plant Israel and they would never again be uprooted. Exiles would return and they would live in the land promised so long ago to Abraham's descendants.

The Book of Hosea

Who Was Hosea?

The Bible does not tell us anything of Hosea's life except what is mentioned in the book that bears his name. His own life became a dramatic portrayal of the relationship between Yahweh and Israel (see chart "Symbolic Representation in Hosea's Marriage" later in this chap.). Marriage became the metaphor. Israel was like a wife who forsook her husband and turned to other lovers. To depict that reality, the LORD commanded Hosea to marry a woman of questionable morals. The children she would bear would be illegitimate (Hos. 1:2).

What Was Hosea's World Like?

Hosea prophesied "during the reigns of Uzziah, Jotham, Ahaz and Hezekiah, kings of Judah and during the reign of Jeroboam . . . king of Israel" (Hos. 1:1). Apparently, at some point, the ministries of Hosea and Amos overlapped. Hosea's ministry, though, seems to have extended to the termination of the Northern Kingdom in 722 B.C. Hosea witnessed Israel's prosperity under Jeroboam II and Israel's demise at the hands of the Assyrian Empire. In a sense, he witnessed the fulfillment of Amos's prophecies against Israel. Perhaps he made his way south to Judah after Israel's destruction.

These were times of tumult for the Northern Kingdom. (Because Ephraim was the most powerful of the northern tribes and contained the shrine at Bethel, Hosea often referred to the Northern Kingdom as Ephraim.) Jeroboam II passed from the scene in 753 B.C. With him went the tranquility of his era. An ominous shadow fell over Israel when Tiglath-Pileser III seized the throne of Assyria in 745. This powerful king developed an aggressive foreign policy toward western Asia. He launched a series of campaigns to bring those territories under Assyrian control. Israel's attempts to form defensive coalitions with neighboring countries proved futile, including its efforts to coerce Judah to join the fight against Assyria (2 Kings 16:5–9). By 732 Assyria had conquered Damascus, Israel's neighbor to the north. It gained control of Israel as well–except for

Samaria, the capital city. But in 722 B.C., even it fell to the Assyrians.

The Assyrian threat, coupled with Israel's lack of faith, generated unrest throughout most of Hosea's ministry. At least two political parties in Israel struggled for power. One party advocated compromise with and capitulation to the Assyrians for the sake of survival. The other party wanted to resist Assyria and form an alliance with Egypt. They hoped that they could play off one superpower against the other. Consequently Hosea called Israel a "'dove, easily deceived and senseless – now calling to Egypt, now turning to Assyria'" (7:11). This had drastic implications for the kings. Assassinations and revolutions followed the changing tide of political strategies. After Jeroboam II, six kings came to power in a span of fifteen years. Only one of them, Menahem, died peacefully (2 Kings 15:17–22).

In addition to political topics, Hosea also addressed theological issues. Israel was guilty of spiritual adultery, forsaking Yahweh and turning to the Baals. The Israelites hoped that the local fertility deities would bring them prosperity. This led them into cultic prostitution (Hos. 4:10–14). Baal worship often involved sacrifices to fertility gods and sexual intercourse with shrine prostitutes. Some Israelites hoped this would assure the prosperity of their agriculture. Hosea, in his own marriage to an unfaithful spouse, dramatized Israel's apostasy. They had left the LORD, their sustainer and savior.

Despite the scandal Hosea's marriage implies, it seems best to assume that it was literal:[25] a symbolic but real relationship lived out among his neighbors to dramatize Israel's

[25]For a detailed treatment of the various views concerning Hosea and Gomer's marriage, see Harrison, *Introduction to the Old Testament*, 861–68.

unfaithfulness. Through his failed marriage, Hosea suffered the divine pathos. He felt the pain of a husband deserted by his unfaithful wife. Like God, he endured his people's hostile rejection of his message.

What Does Hosea Teach Us?

All interpreters agree that Hosea 1 through 3 form a unit. Their theme is Hosea and his family. Chapters 4 through 14 are not so easily subdivided. For convenience we will consider chapters 4:1 through 11:11 as a section and 11:12 through 14:9 as another. A distinctive pattern makes up each section: First come words of judgment, followed by words of promise. The book concludes with promises made by God to his people (11:8–11; 14:4–8). They are the final word: Hope lies beyond judgment.[26]

1:1 through 3:5	Hosea's Broken Marriage, Israel's Broken Covenant
4:1 through 11:11	Judgment on Israel and Judah
11:12 through 14:9	Israel's Past Defines Who They Are

HOSEA'S BROKEN MARRIAGE, ISRAEL'S BROKEN COVENANT—HOS. 1 THROUGH 3

The theme of the first two chapters of Hosea moves from judgment to hope. Hosea's wife, Gomer, bore three children who received symbolic names. The eldest was Jezreel *(yizrᵉ'e'l)*, "God Sows." His name symbolized judgment on Israel's kingship by blaming Jehu, Jeroboam II's

[26]H. W. Wolff, *Hosea*, Hermeneia (Philadelphia: Fortress Press, 1974), divides the book into the same three sections, identifying each as a separate "tradition complex." This implies a model of the book's formation which has not won universal agreement from interpreters; nevertheless, the insight concerning the thematic movement from judgment to hope remains valid.

great-grandfather, for a "massacre at Jezreel" (Hos. 1:4).[27]
Jezreel as a symbol of punishment was also to become a symbol of hope. God promised to sow *(zara')* Israel in the land
(2:23). The "day of Jezreel" was to signify that what the LORD
sowed would sprout anew (1:11). The judgment would then
be reversed and hope renewed for God's people.

Hosea's other two children also received symbolic
names. He called them *Lo-Ruhamah,* "Not Loved," and *Lo-
Ammi,* "Not My People," perhaps implying that their
paternity was in doubt.[28] As such they mirrored God's relationship with Israel. God, like Hosea, had been forsaken by
his lover, Israel. Israel, like Gomer, had played with other
"lovers," the surrounding nations. Born of these unwhole-
some dalliances were pagan influences ("children") among
the people. God would then "divorce" Israel and leave her
to her "lovers." After a period of judgment had passed, *Lo-
Ruhamah* and *Lo-Ammi* would become *Ruhamah,*
"Loved," and *Ammi,* "My People" (2:1,23).

Symbolic Representation in Hosea's Marriage	
Character	**Person or Idea Represented**
Hosea	God
Gomer	Israel
Lovers	Foreign Nations
Children	1. Foreign influences that are religious and/or moral. 2. Symbols of God's impending judgment on Israel (see 1:4,6,8)

[27]Second Kings 9 through 10 narrates the incident from a more positive perspective.

[28]It is noteworthy that only Jezreel's name takes the form of a finite verb compounded with the word for "God" *('el),* and only he is said to be born to
Hosea (Hos. 1:3–4). The later children, both of whom have names beginning
with *Lo-,* are not said to be Hosea's, but are born of Gomer's promiscuous
sexuality (2:4).

In a bold metaphor of a legal divorce proceeding, Hosea describes the end of his failed marriage (Hos. 2:2–13). In it, the children received a summons to contend against their mother (2:2a). Gomer was to be punished (2:5–13). The threat of punishment would also include the children (2:4). At first, the "therefore" in 2:14 would seem to signal a continuation of the preceding announcements of judgment (2:6,9). But the surprise of grace is that Hosea's message is one of renewal (2:14–23). The reason for the two preceding judgments was the unfaithfulness of the Israelites. But this third speech offers no reason for its blessing. The action describes a gift founded in God's own choice. He wanted to start over and make the relationship work. He would show love to Israel, the unloved one, and reunite with them (2:23). Chapter 3 describes how Hosea's renewed marriage to Gomer signified the renewed relationship between God and Israel.

JUDGMENT ON ISRAEL AND JUDAH — HOS. 4:1 THROUGH 11:11

Israel's moral corruption had polluted the land. All that lived in it suffered, whether people, fish, animals, or birds (Hos. 4:1–3). Hosea held the religious leaders responsible for this catastrophe. They had failed their responsibility to teach God's *torah* (4:4–9). A spirit (desire) of apostasy had led them astray. They found themselves reaping the harvest of what they had sown (4:10 through 5:7). Judah was in danger of succumbing to the same temptations; they stumbled in the same sins (5:5).

Hosea 5:8 through 6:11 probably refers to a civil war between Israel and Judah. Assyria's invasion of western Asia seemed imminent. To resist the encroaching

Assyrians, Israel formed an alliance with Damascus. Judah refused them all military assistance. Accordingly, the armies of Damascus and Israel marched against Jerusalem. They hoped to force Judah to provide them with military support. Instead, Ahaz, acting king (regent) of Judah, paid tribute to the Assyrians. He hoped that they would rescue Judah from the "Syro-Ephraimitic coalition."[29] Apparently Judah took advantage of Israel's preoccupation with Assyria to annex some of Israel's territory. Therefore, Hosea accused Judah of being like one who moves boundary stones (5:10; see Deut. 19:14). Hosea prophesied that Ephraim would indeed receive punishment, but Judah would reap the harvest of their actions as well (Hos. 6:11).

There was political chaos within Israel (Hos. 7:1–7) and in their foreign policy (7:8–16). Samaria, the capital city, had "sowed the wind" with its illegitimate kings and calf idol (8:1–14). They would "reap the whirlwind"—exile to Assyria (8:7a), and death in Egypt awaited those who would flee there to escape (9:1–9).

The prophet skillfully contrasted Israel's apostasy with its former devotion to God (Hos. 9:10 through 11:7). God's delight in Israel was like finding "grapes in the desert" (9:10). But Israel had become corrupt, a dying plant bearing no fruit (9:16). They were a "spreading vine" whose apostasy fed prosperity (10:1–2). Now they would reap the harvest of what they had sown (10:13). Israel was a child cared for in its youth by God, but who turned from God in later years (11:1–7). The motif of a delightful beginning and a tragic ending unites these verses. They tell a story of wasted

[29]The "Syro-Ephraimitic War" occurred about 735/34 B.C. Apparently Jotham, king at the time, had turned over the government to his son Ahaz. See 2 Kings 16:1–9; 2 Chron. 28; Isa. 7:1–9.

opportunities and squandered potential.

The second main section (4:1 through 11:11) ends in the triumph of love through God's pain and struggle. In a deeply moving passage, the rejected parent would bring the wayward children home. The initiative would come solely from God's divine character. God would not abandon his promise to settle his people in the land (11:8–11).

Israel's Past Defines Who They Are —Hos. 11:12 Through 14:9

The third unit of the book uses the stories and traditions of Israel's own history for illustrations. The narrative recounts the story of Jacob's birth. It tells how he wrestled with God (Hos. 12:3) and worked for his uncle to get his wife (12:12). It recalls how a prophet, Moses, led Israel from Egypt and how God cared for them in the desert (12:9–10,13; 13:4–6). Human rebellion, in the face of divine faithfulness, drew the judgment of God (13:16).

The concluding chapter of Hosea's book was probably written on the eve of Samaria's fall. Hosea called the Israelites to repent. He even provided a prayer for them to recite (14:1–3). A favorable response by Israel would bring about God's favorable reply (14:4–8). Once again God's grace and love would emerge in promises of healing and blessing.

The triumph of God's love over all obstacles shines through in Hosea. Human rebellion receives divine judgment. But beyond that, God remains committed to his people in unrelenting love. Hosea dramatically pictured God's love as devotion that does not falter under the gravest circumstances. He responded graciously as the husband of an adulterous wife (3:1–5) and as the parent of a wayward child (11:8–11). He lived out God's love for his rebellious people (14:1–8).

The Book of Micah

Who Was Micah?

As with many of the "literary" prophets, we know little about Micah's personal history. We know he came from Moresheth (Jer. 26:18; also called Moresheth Gath, Mic. 1:14). Moresheth was a small town that lay about twenty miles southwest of Jerusalem. Micah spoke as one of the "people of the land" (Ezek. 39:13) who preached against Jerusalem and its inhabitants. He spoke as an outsider more than an insider. He described the good life in farming images. In the coming age, for example, each Israelite would sit under his own vine and fig tree (Mic. 4:4). Israel would be God's flock ruled by a shepherd, peacefully grazing in the land (2:12; 5:4; 7:14). The city of Jerusalem was the problem. It had to be cleansed of its evil ways (2:9–12). Micah, then, appears to be a prophet from the periphery of Judah's society. He protested against powerful landowners who displaced farmers from their tribal inheritances to increase their own holdings (2:2).[30]

Micah's ministry is set in the reigns of Jotham, Ahaz, and Hezekiah (750–686 B.C.). The first chapter seems to refer to the Assyrian encroachment on Judah in 701 B.C. His ministry, then, could be dated conservatively as being from the last year of Jotham (735) to shortly after 701 B.C. Thus Micah would have been a contemporary of Hosea and Amos in Israel and of Isaiah in Judah.

[30]Wilson, "Prophecy," 276; see also Joseph Blenkinsopp, *A History of Prophecy in Israel* (Philadelphia: Westminster, 1983), 121–22.

What Was Micah's World Like?

The locales for Micah's prophecies alternate from the northern kingdom of Israel to the southern kingdom of Judah (Mic. 1:1,5). Several issues distinguished the theology of the South from that of the North. Judah found itself preoccupied with Jerusalem, the temple, and the Messiah. These issues stemmed from the time of David. When David conquered Jerusalem, he made it the capital of the United Monarchy (2 Sam. 5). He wanted to build a house for God there but was prohibited from doing so (2 Sam. 7). Instead, his son Solomon built the temple (1 Kings 7). But God promised to build David's house so that he would have a descendant—an "anointed one," a Messiah (*mashiªch)—*to sit on the throne forever (2 Sam. 22:51).

Jerusalem was heralded as the city of God. It was the place where God had promised to put his name (Deut. 12:5). From there, God would rule through his Anointed One. Some even thought Jerusalem could not be conquered (Ps. 46:6; Jer. 7:4): The temple was the focal point for God's presence on earth. His Anointed was God's agent of justice for his people. By the time of Micah these issues had even displaced the law of Moses in the minds of some Judeans. The *torah* had fallen out of common usage. Decades after Micah, it would be rediscovered in the temple during Josiah's reign (2 Kings 22).

These popular notions about Jerusalem, the temple, and the king as God's Messiah proved a disappointment in real life. God had set up Jerusalem as the throne of justice and the city of God. Its institutions, however, were corrupted by humans. They had become instruments of oppression for greedy kings and powerful citizens. The eighth-century prophets Isaiah and Micah cried out against the oppressors. They saw a vision of a future Messiah and a renewed Jerusalem from which God would reign to the ends of the earth.

The Assyrian conquest of the Northern Kingdom in 722 B.C. resulted in a large number of refugees going to Jerusalem. Within a few decades its population increased three or four times.[31] No doubt these refugees brought their social turmoil with them. This must have taxed the resources of Judah. An upheaval in society followed. The need to cope with new realities brought occasions for injustice and abuse of power. Micah speaks for a rural population that was being disenfranchised by a new order. They felt betrayed by the authorities. Government officials were supposed to have been divinely appointed to safeguard justice. Instead, the people found their leaders to be in league with their oppressors. Hoping for a new age, Micah saw their present sufferings as preparation for the coming of a new David. He would be a Shepherd-Messiah from Bethlehem who would usher in an era of peace and prosperity (5:2,4; 7:14).

What Does Micah Teach Us?

After the superscription (Mic. 1:1) the book falls into three sections (chaps. 1 through 2; 3 through 5; and 6 through 7). Much like the Book of Hosea, the pattern moves from judgment to promise. Each section begins with the command "Hear!"[32]

---

[31]Delbert Hillers, *Micah,* Hermeneia (Philadelphia: Fortress Press, 1984), 5.

[32]See Hillers, *Micah,* 8. It should be noted that the command "Hear!" also occurs at 3:9 and lessens the force of this argument. The Heb. term is translated in 3:1 as "Listen" in NIV.

1 through 2	Judgment and Deliverance
3 through 5	False Leaders and a True King
6 through 7	Hope in the Face of Despair

JUDGMENT AND DELIVERANCE — MIC. 1 THROUGH 2

The first section opens with a proclamation: The LORD was a witness against all the nations of the earth (Mic. 1:2). What follows is a theophany (1:3–4):[33] God had come to judge Israel for its sins (1:5–7). Israel's "incurable wound" had spread to Judah (1:9). Micah would "howl like a jackal" in lamentation for his people (1:8–15). In the Hebrew text, a series of alliterations and puns on place names draws the listener into the message (for example, see NIV text notes at verses 10–11), adding to the rhetorical force of Micah's words.

Chapter 2 announces judgment on those who dispossess the people of the land (2:1–5). Micah denounced false prophets. They had proclaimed that the Spirit of the LORD was not angry with his people and that disgrace would not overtake them. These false prophets had in effect endorsed oppression by the powerful. But Micah saw it differently. The oppressors had defiled the land; it would be ruined (2:6–11). But a message of comfort immediately follows: Micah promised that a "remnant of Israel" would return as the flock of God. They would be shepherded by their king; the LORD would lead them (2:12–13).

[33]A theophany is a poetic description of the impact on creation of God's coming to earth occurring occasionally in the OT (see Pss. 18:7–15 and 97:4–5 for examples).

FALSE LEADERS AND A TRUE KING
—MIC. 3 THROUGH 5

The second section proclaims judgment on Israel's (that is, Judah's) leaders (Mic. 3). After the fall of the Northern Kingdom (Israel) to the Assyrians (e.g., 2 Chron. 30:18), a remnant had fled south. Accordingly, since the Southern Kingdom (Judah) embodied what was left of the North, the Judean prophets often considered Judah to be Israel (cf. Isa. 1:2–3). In grisly language, Micah describes Judah's rulers as butchers, as cannibals who ate their own people (Mic. 3:1–4). Micah contrasted their motives to his. He was compelled by the Spirit to preach justice in the face of opposition (3:5–8). Because of these false rulers and prophets, Jerusalem (Zion) would become desolate.

Once again harsh words of judgment are followed by promises of restoration (Mic. 4 through 5). Much of 4:1–5 parallels Isaiah 2:1–5. Jerusalem's temple would become the center of *torah* instruction for all nations. The restoration would usher in an era of peace and security (4:1–8). At this point, the text abruptly turns to the political crisis that faced Judah (4:9–13). Jerusalem would be besieged by the Babylonians, in 598–597 B.C. and again in 587–586. The first siege resulted in surrender to the Babylonians. The second was followed by the total destruction of Jerusalem and the temple by the Babylonians. Micah compared Jerusalem's impending agony to the pain of a woman in labor, about to give birth. The nations would misunderstand the labor pains as pangs of death. God, however, would be birthing a new era. At that time, he would punish the nations and restore Israel.

What kind of city should be the center for God's restored kingdom? It would have a shepherd as its king. He would,

---

When Leadership Had a Price

Micah exposed the merchandising going on among God's leaders. "Her leaders judge for a bribe, her priests teach for a price, and her prophets tell fortunes for money. Yet they lean upon the LORD and say, 'Is not the LORD among us? No disaster will come upon us'" (Mic. 3:11).

like David, come from Bethlehem (5:2–4). God would raise up a community of shepherds to defeat Judah's enemies. They would restore Judah, "the remnant of Jacob" (5:5–9). But first, Judah must suffer captivity (5:1,3); exile would purge its corrupt government and religion (5:10–14).

HOPE IN THE FACE OF DESPAIR
— MIC. 6 THROUGH 7

The final section of Micah's prophecy repeats the cycle of judgment (Mic. 6:1 through 7:7) and restoration (7:8–20). It opens with a lawsuit metaphor. God was holding court as prosecutor and judge (6:1–5).[34] In brilliant prophetic rhetoric, Micah showed how Judah had to mend their broken relationship with God. It could not be done by sacrifice alone. God required justice, mercy, and humility (6:6–8). The chapter ends with judgment speeches. They proclaim doom to those who walk in the ways of Ahab.[35]

Judah's corrupt leaders would bring great suffering on the people (7:1–7). Micah's only hope was the LORD (7:7). The book closes with a text that expresses the community's repentance and hope.[36]

A Crib From Micah

The New Testament applies Micah 5:2 to Jesus. "'But you, Bethlehem, in the land of Judah, are by no means least among the rulers of Judah; for out of you will come a ruler who will be the shepherd of my people Israel'" (Matt. 2:6).

[34]Kirsten Nielsen, *Yahweh as Prosecutor and Judge,* Journal for the Study of the Old Testament, Supplement 9 (Sheffield, England: JSOT Press, 1978), 5, 9.

[35]Omri was a king of Israel who promoted false worship in Israel (1 Kings 16:25–26). The Bible calls Ahab, Omri's son, the most wicked of all of Israel's kings (1 Kings 16:30,33).

[36]It is possible that the words of this passage stem from a communal liturgy that was used from time to time in ancient Israel. Hermann Gunkel noted this first and his view remains dominant. Such a liturgy may lie behind the Psalms of communal complaint such as Pss. 74 and 79. Prophets were probably key figures, giving divine oracles of response at key points in the liturgy. Following Hillers (*Micah,* 88), we may analyze the passage thus: 7:8-10 is spoken by the people; 7:11-13 is spoken by a prophet; 7:14-17 is a prayer of the people; and 7:18-20 is a hymn.

The Book of Joel

What Was Joel's World Like?

Unfortunately, we know little about the prophet Joel or the time of his prophecy. The book itself contains little specific information to help us know him. One theme treated in the book is based on the agricultural dilemmas of drought and locusts. Since disasters like these happened from time to time, they do not help us identify a particular time in history. The other theme in the book is the "day of the LORD." Joel conceived this to be a time of judgment (Joel 2:1-11) or vindication (3:9-16). But neither do these prophecies help us locate Joel historically.

The people of Tyre, Sidon, and Philistia, as well as the Greeks and the Sabeans (3:4-8), had interacted with Israel and/or Judah over long periods of time. The looting of Jerusalem and the captivity of its inhabitants (3:2b-3,5-6) may refer to the destruction of 586 B.C. But Jerusalem was conquered and plundered before that time.[37] Suggested dates for Joel range from the time of Joash (about 835 B.C.) to the capture of Jerusalem by Ptolemy I Soter in 312 B.C.[38] Most evangelicals prefer a preexilic dating.

Regardless of when the events of the book took place, they show us glimpses of religious life in those times. The community of faith was organized around the temple. In addition to Israel's regular schedule of fasts and festivals, there were special occasions that required sacred assemblies. In times of crisis, the total community of faith was called together to lament.

[37]See 1 Kings 14:25–28 and perhaps 2 Chron. 20:10–11.

[38]H. G. M. Williamson, "Joel," in *ISBE,* 2:1077.

Joel seems to have been a participant in the temple system. He called the people to assemble and the priests to lament. He exhorted the people to return to God. Scholars often call such a person a "cult prophet,"[39] a term meaning a prophet who ministered as part of the religious system.

What Does Joel Teach Us?

Most commentators divide the Book of Joel into two sections. The first section, Joel 1:2 through 2:27, speaks about a present crisis. The land was about to be overrun by locusts. The second section, 2:28 through 3:21, speaks about the more distant future.

1:1 through 2:17	The Present Crisis: A Locust Plague, Prayers, and Repentance Predict the Day of the LORD
2:18 through 3:21	The LORD Answers the Prayers of His People: Judah Will Be Spared in the Day of the LORD

H. W. Wolff differs. He believes that 2:1–11 already departs from the locust plague. These verses speak of a more ominous time of judgment foreshadowed by the locusts.[40] The near future (1:2 through 2:27) cannot be sharply distinguished from the distant future (2:28 through 3:21). Instead, the dividing point is the simple statement in 2:18: "Then the LORD will be jealous for his land and take

[39]See for instance, G. W. Ahlstrom, *Joel and the Temple Cult of Jerusalem* (Leiden, Netherlands: E. J. Brill, 1971). Wilson notes, however, that the "apocalyptic" materials in Joel may imply a peripheral rather than a central sociological location for Joel. "Prophecy," 290. The term "cult" in this usage is not related to the term "occult" but is derived from the Lat. *cultus,* and simply denotes a religion in terms of its liturgy.

[40]H. W. Wolff, *Joel and Amos,* Hermeneia (Philadelphia: Fortress Press, 1977), 7.

pity on his people."[41] In this verse, Yahweh has answered his people's prayer regarding the locust plague (2:12–17). The first section consists of calls to repent and prayers from the people (1:2 through 2:17). In the second section, the LORD responds (2:18 through 3:21). Each of the major sections is introduced by a narrative sentence (1:2–4; 2:18).[42]

THE PRESENT CRISIS: A LOCUST PLAGUE, PRAYERS, AND REPENTANCE—JOEL 1:1 THROUGH 2:17

A locust plague, worse than any in memory, is described in Joel 1:2–4. A call to lamentation follows: Joel summoned people and priests to wail, mourn, despair, and grieve. Their crops would be lost. Economic devastation would follow. In language that echoed the communal complaints in the Psalms, Joel called for a sacred assembly. It was God who had brought this calamity against his people. He called for a "return" to him (2:12–17). The rituals of lament were to flow from sincere hearts.

The crises of drought (1:19–20) and locust plague foreshadowed a more ominous time. The prophet turns to the "day of the LORD," introduced in 1:15 and developed in 2:1–11. The LORD calls the swarm of locusts "my great army" (2:25). If the people did not return to the LORD, his army would attack Jerusalem (2:12–17). The people had to repent or face the Day of the LORD.

THE LORD ANSWERS—JOEL 2:18 THROUGH 3:21

The second major section informs us that the people really did return to the LORD (Joel 2:18 through 3:21).

A Day to Come

Though the crisis in Joel's time was not the final day of God's judgment, the events of that time pointed to that day (1 Cor. 5:5; 2 Pet. 3:10). As it was in Joel's time, a community's life today also has implications for "that day" (Joel 1:15) when God will judge the world (Obad. 15).

---

[41]NIV translates this as a future tense statement. The verbs, however, are typical Heb. grammar for narrating a past event (*waw* consecutive imperfects). Wolff, therefore, argues that poetry is abandoned for this verse and prose narrative is the signal for the turning point of the book (*Joel and Amos*, 9).

[42]Ibid., 7–8.

Consequently, the LORD would bless them. Their losses from devastation would be restored (2:21–27). In the more distant future an age of the Spirit's outpouring would precede the Day of the LORD. All who would call on the name of the LORD would be delivered from the anguish of that day (2:32). God would pour out his Spirit on all people. Moses had wished that all the LORD'S people could prophesy (Num. 11:29). Joel proclaimed that they would, when God's Spirit is outpoured (Joel 2:28–29). Joel's final chapter depicts the fate of the nations God would act against. The nations would be judged; Israel would rest secure in God's protection.

The Book of Isaiah

Who Was Isaiah?

Isaiah was a man who saw God enthroned in the temple (Isa. 6:1–13). In his vision, he witnessed a stunning manifestation of God's presence: singing angels, a live coal from the altar, a heavenly council. Who was this man so blessed as to have been ushered into God's very presence, a participant in the divine council? Of the prophets experiencing the LORD'S call, only Ezekiel's experience (see Ezek. 1 through 3) rivals that of Isaiah—indeed, he is a man who commands our attention!

The public ministry of Isaiah, son of Amoz, began with his call in the last year of Uzziah's reign (740 B.C.). Nothing is known of Isaiah's life prior to that time. Glimpses of his life are given in his book: He was married—he gave his children names that had prophetic symbolism. Isaiah 7 tells of one son named *Shear-Jashub,* "a remnant will return." Isaiah 8 tells of another named *Maher-Shalal-Hash-Baz,*

Citing Joel

The Day of Pentecost is claimed by the New Testament as the fulfillment of Joel's promised outpouring and the inauguration of the age of the Spirit. Peter cited Joel to explain the phenomena that the people observed (Acts 2:16–21).

"quick to the plunder, swift to the spoil." Like Hosea's children, they were a part of the prophet's ministry. Every time a friend or neighbor spoke or heard those names, they were reminded of a prophetic message. One name recalled doom, the other, hope.

Isaiah's wife is called a prophetess in 8:3. She may have had her own ministry independent of Isaiah. Or perhaps she was considered a prophetess because she conceived children of prophetic significance. In any case, the family served as "signs and symbols in Israel" (8:18).

The prophet also used symbolic actions. For example, he went around "stripped and barefoot" (Isa. 20:2) for three years. In doing this, he illustrated the plight of Egyptians whom the king of Assyria would take captive. This action was to discourage Judah from relying on Egypt for deliverance from Assyria (Isa. 20).

Apparently Isaiah had disciples. Mention of them in Isaiah 8:16 gives us a glimpse into the prophet's ministry as well as suggests how his message was preserved and passed on.[43]

Isaiah had access to royalty. Without appointment, he would take God's message into Ahaz's presence (Isa. 7). King Hezekiah consulted with him (2 Kings 20:8). A royal administrator named Eliakim was one of the messengers whom Hezekiah sent to Isaiah during the Assyrian siege. Perhaps Eliakim was Isaiah's means of access to Hezekiah.[44]

We know few other specifics about Isaiah's life. His prophecies show a strong faith in the temple and the

[43]Isa. 8:16 says, "Bind up the testimony and seal up the law [i.e., *torah*] among my disciples." The "law" here refers to the prophet's teachings.

[44]Isaiah prophesied about him (Isa. 22:20–25). Apparently he would have some success as palace administrator, but that success would be short-lived.

monarchy because of God's promise to David. Even when kings and leaders failed miserably to rise to the calling of their office, Isaiah's hope remained unshaken. God would send an anointed king—"a shoot" from the "stump of Jesse"—who would fulfill the hopes and expectations of God's promise (Isa. 11:1–5).

What Was Isaiah's World Like?

Isaiah ministered over the course of decades, from 740 until 701 B.C. or later. He prophesied during the reigns of Uzziah, Jotham, Ahaz, and Hezekiah. Uzziah (also called Azariah) reigned in an era of peace and prosperity; he died, however, from leprosy (2 Chron. 26:21). Isaiah's call to prophetic ministry happened in the year of Uzziah's death (Isa. 6:1–10).

When Uzziah became ill, his son Jotham served him as regent (2 Kings 15:5)[45] and continued his policies. The Bible gives Jotham high marks, even while acknowledging his shortcomings. During his reign, the northern kingdom of Israel began to conspire with Damascus. They intended to take over Judah. This threat grew into a crisis at the time of Jotham's successor, Ahaz.

Ahaz faced the threat of the "Syro-Ephraimitic coalition" in 735/34 B.C. Damascus and Israel (Ephraim) attempted to capture Jerusalem. They wanted to depose Ahaz and put their own man on the throne. It seems that Ahaz had refused to join their anti-Assyrian coalition. They hoped his replacement would be more cooperative. Their armies

[45]A regent was an acting king. His term of office is called a "coregency" because he reigned with the king until the kingdom was turned over to him, often at the death of the reigning king. A coregency was a common arrangement during the monarchy to facilitate a smooth transfer of the throne to the king's successor.

were fairly effective in subduing the countryside of Judah. But when they threatened Jerusalem, Isaiah went to Ahaz with a message of deliverance (Isa. 7:3–9). He challenged Ahaz to trust the LORD. Instead, Ahaz paid Tiglath-Pileser III, the Assyrian king, to attack Damascus and Samaria, Israel's capital. This forced the coalition to abandon its siege of Jerusalem. But by this action, Judah was made a vassal state of Assyria. Vassalage to Assyria brought with it pressures to conform to pagan religion. This would cause Judah much distress in the future (2 Kings 16:10–18).

Ahaz had trusted diplomatic strategy instead of the LORD; he had departed from the faith of his ancestors. Both Kings and Chronicles record scathing critiques of this king (2 Kings 16:2–4; 2 Chron. 28:1–5). Isaiah found a better reception with Ahaz's successor, Hezekiah.

Three episodes from Hezekiah's reign are important for understanding Isaiah. The first was the Assyrian siege of Jerusalem. Unlike Ahaz, Hezekiah listened to Isaiah and believed his message of deliverance. As a result, he saw the Assyrian army destroyed by a plague from God (Isa. 36 through 37). The second episode was an illness that threatened Hezekiah's life. When Isaiah told him that he would die, he cried out to the LORD. So God extended his life by fifteen years (Isa. 38). The third episode was brought about by Hezekiah's healing: Royalty from Babylon sent messengers to Hezekiah, supposedly to congratulate him on his healing. Hezekiah gave them a thorough tour of his palaces. As a result, Isaiah prophesied that all Hezekiah's wealth and some of his descendants would be carried off to Babylonia (Isa. 39).[46]

[46]The biblical text records that the reason for the visit was to congratulate Hezekiah on his healing. It seems probable, however, that the Babylonian motive was more sinister. Merodach-Baladan was a Chaldean who had

Chapters 40–66 look forward to Judah's return from such captivity. Cyrus, king of Persia, defeated the Babylonians in 539 B.C. Isaiah called him God's "shepherd" and "anointed" (Isa. 44:28; 45:1). God would raise him up to play a special role in Judah's future. In 539, Cyrus issued a decree. Any of the captives from Judah who wished to could return and build a temple to the LORD (2 Chron. 36:23; Ezra 1:2–4).

The historical setting for Isaiah 56 through 66 seems to reflect the situation in Judah after the return from Babylonia.[47] The chapters depict a situation of conflict: Some powerful people in Jerusalem were threatened with destruction. They had disobeyed God's laws and persecuted other people. Those who controlled the temple abused those who suffered for God's name (66:5). The return from exile and restoration of the temple did not mean that the kingdom of God had come. Hope for the complete fulfillment of that vision still lay in the future.

What Does Isaiah Teach Us?

The Book of Isaiah contains sixty-six chapters. Many scholars divide the book into three sections: 1 through 39; 40 through 55; and 56 through 66. Others, however, note what they consider a significant mood change at Isaiah

---

seized the throne of Babylon and held it for a short while (721–710 B.C.). He probably wanted to enlist Hezekiah's support against Assyria. But the Bible suggests that the Babylonian envoy was also noting the royal inventory. It was a Chaldean king, Nebuchadnezzar, who carried captives and loot from Jerusalem to Babylonia in 586 B.C.

[47]Stanley M. Horton prefers to see all of 40 through 66 as referring to Judah in Isaiah's lifetime. See Horton's *Isaiah* (Springfield, Mo.: Logion Press, 2000), 298, citing Joseph A. Alexander, *Commentary on the Prophecies of Isaiah,* 2 vols. in 1 (1875; reprint, Grand Rapids: Zondervan Publishing House, 1975), 2:93.

40:1: "Comfort, comfort my people, says your God." As a result, they divide the book into two sections: words of doom, 1 through 39, and words of comfort, 40 through 66. Prophecies of judgment dominate the first section. Prophecies of hope beyond judgment characterize the second. Between 1 through 39 and 40 through 66 lies God's judgment. After judgment comes God's comfort. On the one hand, the two sections together show God's justice in judgment; on the other, they show God's faithfulness to his promises.

For other interpreters, that arrangement seems inadequate. They see hopeful oracles in chapters 1 through 39 and judgment oracles in 40 through 66. Accordingly, they divide the book into 1 through 33 and 34 through 66.[48] According to one such interpretation, both sections deal with the theme of the LORD's worldwide sovereignty at Zion: Chapters 1 through 33 announce God's plans; chapters 34 through 66 declare that the fulfillment of Yahweh's plans for worldwide sovereignty has begun.[49] The LORD's judgment on Edom and the return of Judah's captives from Babylonia testified to the nations and God's people. They declared that God was beginning a new thing in their time. The "former things" include God's judgment of his people to purify Zion; the "new things" represent a new start that

[48]See Harrison, *Introduction to the Old Testament,* 764, 787–89. W. Brownlee notes the significance of the great Isaiah scroll from Qumran that skips several lines to begin at the top of a new column with chap. 34, perhaps indicating the start of a new section. Brownlee, *The Meaning of the Qumran Scrolls for the Bible* (New York: Oxford, 1964), 247–59.

[49]Marvin A. Sweeney, *Isaiah 1–39, With an Introduction to Prophetic Literature* (Grand Rapids: Wm B. Eerdmans, 1996), 39–41. He titles chapters 1 through 33 "Concerning YHWH's plans for worldwide sovereignty at Zion" and chapters 34 through 66 "Concerning realization of YHWH's plans for worldwide sovereignty at Zion."

would lead to the LORD'S worldwide sovereignty in Zion.[50]

JUDGMENT AGAINST JUDAH, ISRAEL, AND THE NATIONS—ISA. 1 THROUGH 33

The first half of the Book of Isaiah contains three subsections. Chapters 1 through 12 deal with the purification of Jerusalem through judgment. Chapters 13 through 27 describe the coming judgment of God against other nations. Chapters 28 through 33 unmask Jerusalem's false hope in Egypt as the power that will deliver them from the Assyrians, at the same time pointing to the coming reign

1 through 33	Judgment Against Judah, Israel, and the Nations
1 through 12	Purification of Jerusalem Through Judgment
13 through 27	Judgment of God Against the Nations
28 through 33	Woes Against Israel's Alliance With Egypt
34 through 66	Promise and Fulfillment
34 through 35	Edom's Ruin, Judah's Salvation
36 through 39	Assyria's Siege of Jerusalem, Hezekiah's Illness, and Merodach-Baladan
40 through 55	Words of Comfort to Those Returning to Jerusalem
56 through 58	False Religion and True
59 through 66	Zion's Repentance, Restoration, and Future

[50]"Former things" and "new things" are contrasted at Isa. 42:9 and 48:3 as well as at other places. Brevard S. Childs argues that "former things" pertain to prophecies of judgment from the eighth century and their fulfillment. "Latter thing" applies to the new work that begins with the return from captivity in the sixth century. See his *Introduction to the Old Testament as Scripture* (Philadelphia: Fortress Press, 1979), 328–30. Although Childs sees the canonical shape of Isa. in two sections comprising chapters 1 through 39 and 40 through 66, his arguments are pertinent to Sweeney's view as well.

of God as the genuine depository of hope.

Chapters 1 through 4 describe Jerusalem's sorry spiritual and moral condition. "See how the faithful city has become a harlot! She once was full of justice; righteousness used to dwell in her — but now murderers!" (Isa. 1:21). The day of God's judgment would come on Jerusalem and purge the evildoers from it. Then God would restore the city and it would become the center of the nations in a time of peace (2:1–4), enjoying God's canopy of protection (4:2–6). These chapters lay out the basic themes of the entire book: There would be a day of judgment to punish and purify, followed by a day of restoration.

Chapters 5 through 12 focus on the period of Assyrian threat to Israel and Judah. Chapter 5 is an allegory of God's people. They were a vineyard that had failed to produce fruit. As a result, they would be laid waste. God would summon "distant nations" to act as his agents of judgment (5:26). Isaiah 6 narrates the call of Isaiah to prophetic ministry. God commissioned him to an unpleasant task. God would use him to blind the eyes and make deaf the ears of the people. His ministry would bring his people punishment rather than repentance (6:9–13a). Chapters 7 through 8 identify the king of Assyria as this agent of punishment. Afterward, he, too, would be judged by God for his pride (10:5–34).

Words of hope intermingle with words of judgment. The prophet promised that a holy seed would remain in the land as "a stump" (Isa. 6:13b). The sign of Immanuel assured the people that God was with them (7:13–16).[51] An

[51] For a discussion of the meaning of the Immanuel prophecy and how it relates to Matt. 1:23, see J. Alec Motyer, *The Prophecy of Isaiah: An Introduction and Commentary* (Downers Grove, Ill.: InterVarsity Press, 1993), 84–86, as well as Horton, *Isaiah*, 100–102.

anointed ruler would descend from David (9:2–7; 11:1–5). He would bring about a future age of peace and prosperity (11:6–9, 12:1–6).

A series of oracles against foreign nations occurs in chapters 13 through 23. A superscription introduces each section: "An oracle *[massa']* concerning . . ." This shows "how YHWH's actions are manifested in the realm of human affairs."[52] The prophet saw the LORD's intention revealed in the events of human history. He spoke to show his hearers how political and military events correspond to God's work.

Chapters 24 through 27 shift from a localized judgment to the LORD's great Day of Judgment. In it, God would judge his enemies. He would restore and exalt Jerusalem. These chapters are frequently called "the Isaianic apocalypse." They form the climax to the preceding chapters, God's work in the history of nations (13 through 23). God's rule and reign from Jerusalem would appear before the entire world.

A common historical background stands behind chapters 28 through 33. Assyria posed a threat to western Asia following the death of Sargon II, particularly with the accession of Sennacherib to the throne in 704 B.C.[53] Egypt promised support for Hezekiah if he revolted against Assyria. Isaiah called the Egyptian alliance a covenant with death and the grave, and warned against it (Isa. 28:15,18); it would fail. Disregarding the prophet's counsel, Hezekiah

---

[52]Sweeney, *Isaiah 1–39*, 534–35, following R. D. Weis, "A Definition of the Genre Massa' in the Hebrew Bible" (Ph.D. diss., Claremont Graduate School, 1986).

[53]Following Motyer's reconstruction of the text's background in *Prophecy of Isaiah*, 20–21.

entered an alliance with Egypt against Assyria. As a result, Sennacherib invaded Judah. The promised Egyptian aid never materialized. In these chapters Isaiah describes the role of Assyria as the LORD's instrument of punishment on Jerusalem. A promise of hope emerges in chapters 32 through 33: A king would rule in righteousness, bringing a new era of deliverance for Jerusalem.

A series of "woe" *(hoy)* speeches (or cries of anguish) sets off chapters 28 through 33.[54] The first woe is directed against Samaria, the "pride of Ephraim's drunkards" (and capital of the Northern Kingdom; 28:1–3). It would fall to Assyria. The second woe predicts Assyria's siege of Jerusalem (Ariel), in 701 B.C. (29:1).[55] Three more woes follow, proclaiming the failure of Judah's alliance with Egypt (29:15; 30:1; 31:1). Assyria would be punished, but not by Egypt (31:8–9). Deliverance for Judah would come in "repentance and rest"; strength would come from "quietness and trust" (30:15). God, not Egypt, was the one who would fight to deliver Jerusalem (31:4–9). The final woe targets Assyria, the destroyer of Jerusalem (33:1). Beyond this lies the hope of a king whose kingdom would destroy the destroyer. Jerusalem would one day become what God had intended (32 through 33).

PROMISE AND FULFILLMENT—ISA. 34 THROUGH 66

The second half of the book continues the themes begun in Isaiah 1 through 33. The perspective, however, shifts from promise to the beginning of fulfillment. The judgment of the LORD against Jerusalem was coming to an end. The

[54]Sweeney, *Isaiah 1–39*, 353–54.

[55]Jerusalem is called "Ariel." This may mean "God's lion" or perhaps "altar hearth."

former things would be replaced by a new thing (see 43:18–19). It would begin when the LORD returned the captives to Zion (40:2,11) and restored Jerusalem (52:1–2; 62:7). These chapters describe what is "already but not yet." This phrase means that God's plan for the future was expressed in ways that gave the impression that it was already happening in the end of the old, failed monarchy and would also happen in the restoration of the people to Israel in the future. The return from captivity would be the beginning of the plan. Its culmination would remain a future hope. The wicked would be purged from the community of the redeemed (65 through 66).

Chapters 34 and 35 correspond to one another by way of contrast. The nations would be summoned to slaughter (34:1–4). Edom's defeat would serve as an example to all the nations that opposed God (34:5–17). It would be made a desert, uninhabitable except for wild creatures. The opposite would be true for Israel (35). The desert would become a garden. Dangerous animals would not threaten the redeemed who return to Zion (35:8–10).

Chapters 36 through 39 parallel in part 2 Kings 18 through 20 and 2 Chronicles 32. They play a significant role in the Book of Isaiah. Chapters 36 through 37 narrate Assyria's ensuing attack on Jerusalem in 701 B.C. Hezekiah trusted God to deliver him. Miraculously, Jerusalem was saved (37:36).

Before Assyria's siege of Jerusalem, Hezekiah became sick. When God healed him, Merodach-Baladan, the son of the king of Babylon, sent a delegation to congratulate Hezekiah on his recovery (Isa. 39:1). Hezekiah opened his palace to the Babylonian envoy (see the section "What Was Isaiah's World Like?"). Because of this, Isaiah prophesied

Like Father, Like Son—Not!

The portrait of Hezekiah, the son, as a believing king contrasts with the portrait of Ahaz, the father (under threat similar to that of his son), as an unbelieving king (Isaiah 7 through 9). Ahaz functions as the epitome of disbelief in the period of Judah's judgment prophesied in Isaiah 1 through 33; Hezekiah functions as a model of faith for the period of its restoration envisioned in Isaiah 34 through 66.

that Judah would be deported to Babylonia (39). Isaiah's prophecy prepares the reader for the message of hope found in chapters 40 through 66. These chapters serve as a transition from the Assyrian era to the Babylonian era in the Book of Isaiah.[56]

Words of comfort open the next subsection (40 through 55). The LORD would return to Jerusalem in glory. He would gently tend his flock as they returned from captivity (40:1–11). The LORD made his case to the survivors from Jerusalem and to their descendants. He is God and there is no other. "'You are my witnesses,' declares the LORD, 'and my servant whom I have chosen, so that you may know and believe me and understand that I am he. Before me no god was formed, nor will there be one after me'" (43:10).

In these chapters the people are called to trust the word of God. It would stand forever (Isa. 40:8) and would accomplish its purpose (55:10–11). God spoke the former things, the prophecies of judgment against Jerusalem, and they had come to pass. God now spoke a new thing, a return from captivity. He called on the people to trust him to do this.

Apparently some of the people were in danger of apostasy. Babylonia was full of idols. Isaiah described idolatry as something ridiculous (46:5–7): In one example the prophet ridiculed the idol maker for using half a tree as firewood to cook his lunch and then turning around and using the other half to make an idol—which he would then bow down to and worship (44:9–20). The LORD's case against

No Other Gods!

Isaiah 40 through 55 reaches a high-water mark for the Bible in its monotheistic theology. There are no other gods, only powerless idols who are deaf and dumb, unable to help and who know nothing. Other passages in the Old Testament forbid the worship of other gods, but these chapters go beyond that to deny the existence of any god except the One who created everything!

---

[56]Isa. 40 through 66, then, do not constitute a separate "book." Instead, these chapters depend on chapters 36 through 39 for their literary context. See R. Melugin, *The Formation of Isaiah 40–55*, BZAW 141 (Berlin and New York: deGruyter, 1976), 82–84.

idols was that he as Creator had made everything. He knew the end from the beginning (46:10). When the LORD announced a new thing, it was as trustworthy as the former things he had announced. The idols never knew anything (41:22–24). God, on the other hand, ordered the nations to do his bidding. He had sent Babylonia to punish God's people. He would raise up Cyrus the Persian to punish Babylonia. He would return his people to their land (43:24 through 45:13).

A distinctive use of the title "The Servant of the LORD" occurs in these chapters. Four songs (called Servant Songs) in Isaiah 40 through 55 describe "The Servant": 42:1–4; 49:1–6; 50:4–9; and 52:13 through 53:12. These four texts relate to one another, independent of the rest of the material in the chapters. In the first song, God calls the Servant to establish justice on the earth. In song two, the Servant discovers that his mission, to "restore the tribes of Jacob," has been expanded to bring "salvation to the ends of the earth" (49:6). In the third song the Servant speaks, though the term "servant" does not occur in the verses. The Servant would experience violent opposition, yet God would continue to instruct him morning by morning. In spite of suffering, the Servant remains persuaded that God would vindicate him. In song four, the Servant has suffered a violent death that serves to bring healing and forgiveness for others (53:4–5). Through the words of the prophet, God promised vindication for the Servant's ministry and resurrection for the Servant himself (53:11-12).[57]

Isaiah's Songs About Jesus

The Servant Songs in Isaiah correspond so closely to the life and ministry of Jesus that from the early days of the Church, Isaiah 53 was interpreted as fulfilled in Jesus (see Acts 8:26–40). Later interpreters argued that the Servant was Israel, or a faithful group within Israel, or the prophet who himself spoke the songs. The complexity of the issue prevents detailed discussion of the arguments here. The ambiguity of the allusions to the Servant make it susceptible to different interpretations so that no interpretation satisfies everyone. But the New Testament applies the prophecies to Jesus, using them to illumine important truths about his life and ministry. The prophecies in the Servant Songs clarified the nature and des-

(cont. on the next page)

[57]This summary follows C. R. North, *The Suffering Servant in Deutero-Isaiah* (London: Oxford University Press, 1948), 139–55. North also discusses the identity of the Servant (6–103); see also Raymond B. Dillard and Tremper Longman, *An Introduction to the Old Testament* (Grand Rapids: Zondervan Publishing House, 1994), 278–79.

*Isaiah's Songs About
Jesus (cont.)*

tiny of Jesus' messianic
mission. God called Jesus
the Messiah to a suffer-
ing, atoning death. That
much is revealed by the
Servant Songs regardless
of whether they are iden-
tified as direct prophecy,
prophetic double refer-
ence, or typological
interpretation.

The fourth Servant Song has held the fascination of people of faith for centuries. Even its literary construction is
interesting: five stanzas of three verses each (52:13 through
53:12). This song emphasizes the Servant's suffering.
Another servant of God, Moses, was said to have suffered
God's anger because of Israel's sin (Deut. 4:21). Likewise,
Ezekiel was told to bear the sin of the nation (Ezek. 4:4).
Many other prophets suffered for their messages, but none
suffered in the way described in this song. "The prophet's
utterances are concerned with a saving act that lies in the
future. . . . The atonement of the Servant is a part of the
future saving act."[58]

In the first stanza of the fourth Servant Song (Isa.
52:13–15), God introduces the divine Servant whom God
will "exalt," even though he will be "marred," "disfigured."
As a result, the Servant will have a worldwide influence.
Nations and leaders will be "startle[d]" (52:15, RSV) into
silence because of the Servant's work. "The character of the
saving act is such that it should astonish nations and close
the mouth of kings."[59]

In the second stanza (Isa. 53:1–3), the prophet reveals the
Servant's humble origins. He was born a "tender shoot" of
Jesse (see 11:1), the lineage of David. Micah prophesied this
One would be born in Bethlehem (Mic. 5:2–5a). The
Servant would also be rejected by people. They would view
his suffering as God's curse (Isa. 53:3). They would think it
dangerous to look at one who had been cursed, fearing the
curse would come upon them as well. However, the
prophet reveals a secret. As John L. McKenzie says, "The

[58]John L. McKenzie, *Second Isaiah*, AB (Garden City, N.Y.: Doubleday & Co.,
1968), 136.

[59]Ibid., 133.

curse may not lie upon the person who suffers; it may be the curse . . . lies upon another and has been transferred to the person who suffers."[60]

The third stanza (Isa. 53:4–6) reveals an exchange of roles. People have exchanged their sins, iniquities, and sorrows for the Servant's peace and healing! The pronouns move from "we" and "our" to "he" and "his." It was his vicarious suffering that brought peace; he suffered the judgment that would have been rightly applied to others, not to him.

The fourth stanza (Isa. 53:7–9) indicates that the Servant died by judicial process, the victim of an unjust judgment. Although the Servant's enemies hoped to give him a disgraceful burial with the wicked, he wound up honored in burial with the rich.

In the fifth stanza (Isa. 53:10–12), we learn of the purpose of the Servant's suffering: God's will! It was the divine plan that called for this suffering on behalf of "many." The Servant became a "guilt offering" (see Lev. 5:15 through 6:7). The results of the Servant's suffering would be justification for "many." Perhaps there is yet another exchange in 53:11: The Servant possesses righteousness; the "many" possess iniquities. In the work of the Servant, the iniquities of the "many" are exchanged for the Servant's righteousness. In the last verse (53:12), the work of the Servant continues after he has won the victory for sinners. His work goes on in his intercession. "Here the Servant comes voluntarily to stand with us . . . so that he might bring us to God."[61]

[60]Ibid.

[61]Motyer, *Prophecy of Isaiah*, 443.

Luke Proclaims Isaiah Fulfilled

Foreigners and eunuchs were barred from the assembly under Moses (Deut. 23:1–8), but with the coming of God's kingdom, they would be included. Luke's recording of the Ethiopian eunuch as a convert proclaims the fulfillment of Isaiah's prophecy and the inauguration of a new order, the Kingdom of God, in which all who confess faith in Christ are accepted. (See Isa. 56:3–7; Acts 8:27–39.)

The final section of the Book of Isaiah, chapters 56 through 66, moves from the inauguration of God's plan to its culmination. These chapters define the character of the covenant community that God had already promised to David (55:3). Those who wished to participate in that community were to keep their covenant commitment.

Chapters 56 through 59 tell us that not all was well in the community. On the one hand, all who kept covenant were to be welcomed (56:1–8). On the other hand, those who were wicked were to be punished. Sadly, however, the wicked controlled Jerusalem. They were the "watchmen" and "shepherds" greedy for selfish gain (56:9–12). They had been false to God. They would be carried off in a wind of judgment (57:1–13). The LORD did not acknowledge their days of fasting. They were occasions for quarreling. The LORD'S chosen fast was "to loose the chains of injustice." They were to share their "food with the hungry and to provide the poor wanderer with shelter," and to clothe the naked (58:6–7). Chapter 59 summons all to repent. To those who do, God will come as Redeemer and enter into covenant with them (59:20–21).

Chapters 60 through 62 express visions of a renewed Zion that would fulfill God's plan. Zion would be the light for the nations. Their wealth would flow to it. The LORD would be its light. The righteous would inherit the land forever (60). Zion's shame would be replaced with glory. God would change its reputation. It would receive a new name from the LORD: *Hephzibah*, meaning "My delight is in her" (62:4 with NIV footnote). The city would be called "Sought After" and "the City No Longer Deserted" (62:12).

In chapters 63 through 66 the covenant community is called God's "servants." The prophet warned that they would experience abandonment and mistreatment. Some passages indicate that opposition might even come from God's own people. He cautioned them: "'Your brothers who hate you'" will "'exclude you because of my name'" (66:5).[62] The LORD would repay those enemies. He would reverse the distress of the LORD'S servants (65:13–16). God would create a new heaven and a new earth (65:17). They would endure before him, as would the name of his servants and their descendants (66:22). Their enemies would receive a final and permanent punishment (66:24).

Isaiah had called the covenant community to faithfulness. They were to live in covenant observance, justice, and mercy. What the LORD had begun, he would finish gloriously. Present sufferings would be forgotten when the LORD'S plans for his people were culminated.

Isaiah and Critical Studies

Controversy surrounds the Book of Isaiah like no other book among the prophets.[63] The debate comes from questions about the book's authorship. Historically, interpreters assigned the authorship to Isaiah ben Amoz who prophesied from about 740 B.C. (Isa. 1:1; 6:1). In the last two centuries some interpreters have questioned the accuracy of that view. Both groups of interpreters agree that

[62]Paul Hanson, *The Dawn of Apocalyptic* (Philadelphia: Fortress Press, 1979), considers the "servants" to have been a prophetic "visionary community" marginalized from the power structures by the hierocrats of the temple. This group of servants received an apocalyptic vision of the new heavens and new earth and a purified Zion that they were called to wait for patiently (69–75).

[63]For more detailed discussions of authorship, see John N. Oswalt, *The Book of Isaiah: Chapters 1–39,* NICOT (Grand Rapids: Wm. B. Eerdmans, 1986), 17–28; Horton, *Isaiah,* 22–28. Both Oswalt and Horton advocate a single authorship for Isaiah, as do most evangelicals.

Isaiah 40 through 66 deals with a time period well after the eighth century. In Isaiah's time the Assyrian empire threatened Jerusalem (701 B.C.). Chapters 40 through 66 deal with the Babylonian empire's exile of Israel (586 B.C.) and the Persian empire's overthrow of the Babylonians (539 B.C.).

Some interpreters, therefore, have suggested that chapters 40 through 66 do not look forward to that period from an eighth-century perspective. According to their view, those chapters look back on the exile and forward to the return. Some conclude from this that chapters 40 through 66 must have originated between the exile and the return. Therefore they hypothesize a Second Isaiah ("Deutero-Isaiah"). This "anonymous" prophet, presumably a member of a group who treasured and preserved Isaiah's prophecies, lived in the Babylonian exile. The Spirit anointed this prophet afresh to prophesy the end of God's judgment and a new beginning for God's flock (Isa. 40:1–11). We now read this prophet's words in chapters 40 through 66.

Others divide the material even further, calling 40 through 55 "Deutero-Isaiah" and 56 through 66 "Trito-Isaiah" (that is, Third Isaiah). They say a prominent figure arose in the postexilic period who spoke forcefully against the complacency of God's people. As a "disciple" of the historical Isaiah, he spoke in the "spirit" of Isaiah when the second temple was being built (520–515 B.C.).[64]

These views evoke strong reactions from conservative interpreters who favor the view that Isaiah predicted these events in the eighth century. They argue that divided authorship undermines both the supernatural character of

[64]Bernhard W. Anderson, *Understanding the Old Testament* (Englewood Cliffs, N.J.: Prentice-Hall, 1986), 502–3.

prophecy and the authority of Scripture.[65] Prediction has a place in the message of the prophets, and references to events and persons yet future may find a place in their words. "If specific prediction is denied to the prophet (or prophets)," says one who argues for Isaiah's authorship of the whole book, "then their theology is groundless."[66]

Other more detailed arguments fly back and forth between the two camps, but these are the biggest issues in the discussion. The data, it seems, can be interpreted in different ways. Neither view has compelled the other to abandon its position. The discussion is stalemated, with most evangelicals advocating a unity of authorship and nonevangelicals holding to two or three authors.[67] For the purposes of this study, however, the position advocated in the New Testament attributing quotations from all parts of Isaiah to the historical Isaiah will be affirmed. If, as the saying goes, scripture interprets scripture, then surely the noncritical acceptance of Isaiah's writings from all its sections by Jesus and the apostles should be given great weight and lasting authority.

A particularly helpful position is to view the biblical material from its canonical form. That means we read the

Learning to Think for Yourself

Some people think that those who disagree with them don't believe the Bible or are unwilling to accept the scholarly evidence. Interpretation is not a simple "yes" or "no" matter. Interpreting Isaiah (and many other biblical books) calls for critical thinking. You must not simply accept everything you read about the Bible as true and/or authoritative. You must not only interpret the text; you must also interpret the interpreters. You need to learn to assess each interpreter. Theological and philosophical convictions influence every exegesis. Part of interpretation is learning to observe how an interpreter's position influences his or her conclusions. Then you must adopt your own hermeneutical position, interpret the text, and evaluate the conclusions of others in light of that. Finally, discerning what is good and profitable, you may use that in pursuit of truth and godliness.

[65]Multiple authorship seems to diminish the supernatural character of prophecy by limiting predictions to the particular generation the prophecy was given in. God, however, frequently revealed distant events to prophets. For example, Jesus and the writers of the NT quoted from chapters 40 through 66, attributing them to the prophet Isaiah.

[66]Oswalt, *Book of Isaiah,* 49; see also Herbert M. Wolf, *Interpreting Isaiah: The Suffering and Glory of the Messiah* (Grand Rapids: Zondervan Publishing House, Academie Books, 1985), 31–36.

[67]The multiple-authorship advocates dismiss the single-author advocates in a footnote without serious engagement. The single-author advocates dismiss the multiple-author advocates with doctrinaire caricatures that cast aspersions on their faith or spirituality.

biblical text as it has been preserved in the canon. The canon presents the Book of Isaiah as the product of the eighth-century B.C. prophet Isaiah. As Brevard S. Childs suggests, Isaiah's message of promise, therefore, relates not only to Isaiah's time, but also "to the redemptive plan of God for all of history."[68] The seriousness with which Isaiah's words were taken by Jesus and the apostles indicates also the seriousness with which we should take Isaiah's words.

Study Questions

1. What are the key Hebrew terms and phrases presented from the biblical text on the prophets?

2. Know the background material for each prophet: Where did he come from? Who was his audience? When did he preach?

3. What controversial issues related to the prophets' works have been raised by contemporary scholarship?

4. What section or division of the Hebrew Bible do these prophets belong to? What does that section consist of?

5. What literary devices (e.g., metaphor) as well as what typical patterns of prophetic speech were discussed in this chapter?

6. What is the definition of a prophet? A cult prophet?

7. Make certain you know these things about each prophet:

   a. Who was he?

   b. Where did he minister?

   c. What was the setting for his book?

   d. What does his book teach us (i.e., identify the over-riding themes of the major sections)?

[68]Brevard S. Childs, *Introduction to the Old Testament*, 326.

For Further Reading

Brueggemann, Walter. *The Prophetic Imagination*. Philadelphia: Fortress Press, 1978.

Bullock, C. Hassell. *An Introduction to the Old Testament Prophetic Books*. Chicago: Moody Press, 1986.

Huey, F. B. *Yesterday's Prophets for Today's World*. Nashville: Broadman, 1980.

Lindblom, Johannes. *Prophecy in Ancient Israel*. Philadelphia: Fortress Press, 1962.

Young, E. J. *My Servants the Prophets*. Grand Rapids: Wm. B. Eerdmans, 1952.

For commentaries on the individual prophets, the Tyndale Old Testament Commentaries, published by InterVarsity Press (Downers Grove, Ill.), are written in nontechnical language and are quite helpful.

17

Malcolm Brubaker

On the Edge of Night: Judah From Manasseh to the Exile

Outline:

- Who Were the Last Kings of Judah?
- What Do We Learn From This?
- The Late Judean Prophets
- Prophets of the Exile
- Wrapping It All Up

Terms:

Septuagint (LXX)
Masoretic Text (MT)

After Hezekiah died, Judah faced serious challenges in the years ahead. Hezekiah had followed a foreign policy of independence from such countries as Egypt and Assyria. Could Judah remain free of foreign domination? Then there was the question of religion. Could Judah continue the monotheistic worship of Yahweh that Hezekiah promoted? Or would it be compromised by external pressure from pagan cultures? Would it become syncretistic—mixing the worship of Yahweh with that of pagan gods and goddesses?

In this chapter we will look at the kings who faced these political and spiritual challenges. We will also survey the preexilic and exilic prophets God raised up to guide Judah. These prophets were called to keep the nation and its kings on the right track. This chapter will document the unfortunate end of the kingdom of Judah, which came because it ignored God's revealed will.

Who Were the Last Kings of Judah?

With only a few exceptions, the last kings of Judah were a sorry lot, bearing the fruits of an evil life. One king, Amon, was even assassinated by his own people. Let's look at them one at a time.

Manasseh: A Wickedly Long Reign
—697/87–643 B.C.

Ten years before his death, Hezekiah appointed his son Manasseh to be his coregent. Adding those years to Manasseh's rule as king produced the longest reign of any Israelite or Judean king. Unfortunately, Manasseh is also known as the most evil of any Judean king. Years later the prophet Jeremiah would announce that God was bringing judgment upon Judah "because of what Manasseh son of

Hezekiah king of Judah did in Jerusalem" (Jer. 15:4). What Jeroboam was to the Northern Kingdom, Manasseh became to the Southern Kingdom (see chap. 14 of this book). The kings of Judah after Manasseh would be compared to him.

The historical accounts in 2 Kings 21 and 2 Chronicles 33 describe his violations of the covenant. He built high places outside Jerusalem, altars to Baal, and Asherah poles. He consulted astrologers, spiritists, and diviners. He practiced child sacrifice. His reign was full of violence (2 Kings 21:16). The writer of 2 Kings noted, "Manasseh led them [the people of Judah] astray, so that they did more evil than the nations the LORD had destroyed before the Israelites" (21:9). The analogy is obvious: Just as God had rid the land of the wicked Canaanites, so he would rid the land of his own sinful people (Deut. 30:15–20).

DOES A LONG REIGN MEAN GOD'S APPROVAL?

Manasseh's long reign was not necessarily a mark of God's approval.[1] The Chronicler may give us the theological reason. He recounts the repentance of Manasseh after he was captured by the Assyrians and taken to Babylon. Historians suggest that Manasseh may have supported a revolt against Assyria (652–648 B.C.). The revolt led by Shamash-shuma-ukin, viceroy of Babylon, failed; Manasseh, who had joined in the revolt, was punished.[2]

[1]In 1 and 2 Chron. the usual indicators are peace and prosperity, building projects, success in warfare, and large families; see note on 2 Chron. 33:1–20 in *The NIV Study Bible* (Grand Rapids: Zondervan Publishing House, 1985).

[2]Manasseh's name appears as one of twenty-two tributaries on Assyrian monuments, the Prism of Esarhaddon and the Prism of Ashurbanipal. See *ANET,* 291, 294.

He sought God's mercy. God heard this wicked king's prayer of confession and restored him to his kingdom (2 Chron. 33:10–13). Can you believe the quick turn of spiritual direction? It highlights the long-suffering grace of God to an aging but repentant king.

Unfortunately, the evil he had done through most of his reign could not be undone. Pagan idolatry would never be eradicated from the hearts of Judah's people. The efforts made by a later king, Josiah, and righteous prophets, such as Jeremiah, would be unsuccessful. Hezekiah had sought the LORD and divine blessing had followed. His son Manasseh rejected God and turned the nation towards doomsday. Even the king's conversion at the end of his life could not reverse the consequences for the nation.

Amon: A Short, Evil Rule – 643–641 B.C.

The sins of the father, Manasseh, bore immediate fruit in the short and tragic reign of his son, Amon. The biblical record simply mentions that the sins of Manasseh were repeated by Amon. His life and reign were ended by assassination. It happened in a palace intrigue by courtiers whose reasons and motives are not mentioned. Their actions, however, were not publicly supported and they were punished for their deed.

Josiah: Judah's Last Godly King – 641–609 B.C.

The aborted reign of Amon resulted in his son, Josiah, coming to the throne at the age of eight. During Josiah's early reign the godly influences of Hilkiah the high priest and Huldah the prophetess produced positive results. Josiah became the last Judean monarch who sought to restore the worship of God. He worked hard to remove the pagan religious influences of his sinful predecessors.

WHAT TRIGGERED JOSIAH'S GODLY REFORMS?

During Josiah's reign, a revival of righteousness was sparked in two ways by the Word of God. During Manasseh's reign, the temple had been defiled. Josiah decided to repair it. While the temple was being renovated, the *written* form of the law of Moses, forgotten in the wicked reign of his grandfather, Manasseh, was found and read. At the same time, the *living* word of God was being spoken through prophets, such as Jeremiah. The effect of God's Word on Josiah was twofold: It convicted him of sin, and it motivated him to rule righteously. Josiah initiated a purge of idolatry in the land.

The reformation began in the temple and radiated to the king's palace. Jerusalem and the rest of Judah were affected. Even the northern religious cult-site of Bethel and the region of Samaria were influenced. Huldah the prophetess and Jeremiah the prophet supported the king's reforms. Both, however, spoke of an inevitable judgment upon the Southern Kingdom's wickedness, which Josiah's reign only delayed (2 Kings 23:1–25).

GOODBYE ASSYRIA, HELLO NEO-BABYLONIA

Fortunately for Judah, pressure from Assyria decreased throughout Josiah's reign. Revolts by Babylon, Media, and Egypt reduced the influence the Assyrians once had on Judah. In Egypt the reign of Psammetichus (664–610) reunited Lower and Upper Egypt into a powerful nation; he stopped sending tribute money to Assyria by 656 B.C. Assyrian dominance in the Ancient Near East further

Josiah's Reforms and the Heart of the Matter

At first glance the historical record of Josiah's reign emphasizes his successful eradication of idolatry in Judah: Idols are smashed; pagan worship sites purged. Furthermore, the temple was renovated. In the process a scroll of God's law was found. Moses' warnings about violating the covenant drove Josiah to repentance. There seemed to be hope for Judah after all. But a prophetic word from a woman, Huldah, set the matter straight (2 Kings 22:14–20; 2 Chron. 34:22–28): God would only delay his judgment of the nation during the reign of Josiah; the previous reign had gone too far (see also 2 Kings 21:14–15; 23:26–27).

The question still remains, Was Josiah able to effect a deep change in the people's hearts? Jeremiah's ministry revealed that Josiah's

(cont. on the next page)

Josiah's Reforms and the Heart of the Matter (cont.)

reforms were superficial. The land only appeared to be rid of idolatry; soon after Josiah's death the people returned to publicly worshiping pagan gods and goddesses (Jer. 11:9–13). Idolatry was still in the people's hearts (Ezek. 14:1–6). The human heart cannot be changed by outward laws but only by a radical transformation (Jer. 17:1,9). The promise of the new covenant centered on an internal conformity to the law of God (Jer. 31:33; cf. Ezek. 36:26).

eroded after the death of Ashurbanipal (668–627). In 626 B.C. the Chaldean prince Nabopolassar captured Babylon. His reign (626–605) produced separation from Assyria and yielded the next superpower, Neo-Babylonia.

Josiah ruled in that brief window made possible by the decline of Assyria and the rise of Neo-Babylonia. This allowed Josiah freedom to do as he wished in the local religious arena.

A SUDDEN END TO A LONG REIGN

In an attempt to thwart the military movements of the Egyptian pharaoh Neco, Josiah ended his reign and life. In 612 B.C. Assyria's capital, Nineveh, fell to a coalition of Chaldeans, Medes, and Scythians. Assyria's armies were driven back to Haran. In 609 B.C., Egyptian forces under Neco traveled north. They were trying to reach the fragments of the Assyrian forces in time to help them stop the Babylonian (Chaldean) advances. Josiah attempted to prevent Assyria from ever again becoming a threat. He and the Judean forces met the Egyptian army in battle on the plain of Megiddo. In this futile effort, Josiah was mortally wounded (2 Kings 23:29). The Bible does not say whether he had consulted the LORD before this battle. Apparently he simply made a military decision that proved unsuccessful.

Jehoahaz: A Victim of Egyptian Interests – 609 B.C.

Following the death of Josiah, Jehoahaz, supported by the people, became king. His brief reign of three months ended when Neco, king of Egypt, deposed him. Neco, on his return from Haran, appointed Jehoahaz's brother, Eliakim, in his place. He took Jehoahaz to Egypt, where he died in oblivion. The writer/editor of Kings added his characteristic commentary that Jehoahaz had continued in the evil ways of most Judean kings (2 Kings 23:32).

Jehoiakim: Coping With Babylonian Dominance —609–597 B.C.

Judah had become a vassal state to Egypt. Egypt's power over Judah's internal affairs can be seen when Pharaoh Neco changed Eliakim's name to Jehoiakim (2 Kings 23:34). This power ended in 605 B.C. following the battle at Carchemish, a ford on the upper Euphrates River. There Neco's army fought against the army of Nebuchadnezzar, son of King Nabopolassar of Babylon. Nebuchadnezzar led the Babylonians to victory over the Egyptians and the remnant of the Assyrian army (see Jer. 46). As a result of Egyptian flight and Babylonian advance south, Judah's vassalage shifted to Babylon (2 Kings 24:1). At this time Daniel and other young Judean noblemen were taken to Babylon to be trained for the king's service (Dan. 1:1–6).

LIVING LIKE A KING, DYING LIKE A DONKEY

Despite the chastening effects of the Babylonian takeover, Jehoiakim ruled poorly. The Book of Jeremiah records several examples of this. Using forced labor, he built a palace extravagantly furnished with cedar. When a scroll of Jeremiah's prophecies was read to him, Jehoiakim burned it (Jer. 36:22–23). Little wonder that Jeremiah prophesied that Jehoiakim would receive a donkey's burial (22:13–19).

Following a Babylonian defeat in Egypt in 601 B.C., Jehoiakim revolted against his vassalage to Babylon. Nebuchadnezzar responded by sending Arameans, Moabites, and Ammonites to raid Judah. In 598 B.C. he sent another army to Jerusalem to squelch its rebellion. As the siege began, Jehoiakim died, possibly in battle or assassinated by political enemies.

Jehoiachin: Brief Rule, Long Captivity
− 597 B.C.

Jehoiakim's death brought his eighteen-year-old son, Jehoiachin, to the throne. Though his reign was brief, it is labeled an "evil" one by the writer of Kings. Jehoiachin had continued the covenant-violating practices of his predecessors. He surrendered to the Babylonian forces after a three-month siege and was taken captive to Babylon. Along with Jehoiachin, the Babylonians took about ten thousand Judeans into captivity. This event is often referred to as the first deportation of Jerusalem to Babylon. The people taken were largely the educated classes, skilled laborers, and military leaders. The young man Ezekiel was part of this group of exiles (Ezek. 1:1–3).

Thirty-seven years into captivity, Jehoiachin was removed from prison and given a measure of respect at the Babylonian court (2 Kings 25:27–30).[3] This was viewed as a sign indicating that God's favor was returning to his people.

Zedekiah: Split Allegiances and Weak Character
−597–586 B.C.

Nebuchadnezzar believed a vassal king would best govern a subject people. The godly Josiah had died years previous, in 609 B.C. His first son and successor, Jehoahaz, died in Egypt. A second son, Jehoiakim, died in 597 B.C. His successor, the youth Jehoiachin, was now in Babylonian exile.

---

[3]This is attested in Babylonian royal ration records. See D. Winton Thomas, *Documents from Old Testament Times* (New York: Thomas Nelson, 1958), 84–86.

The Fall of Jerusalem

Television brought the Vietnam war into America's living rooms. Saigon, capital of South Vietnam, fell to the Vietnamese communist forces on April 30, 1975. Although I was not there, I witnessed it via television. It is a fixed moment, a part of my baby boom generation's psyche. The final television news images relayed a city in panic. The sound of heavy artillery echoed through the streets. Communist tanks rumbled toward the governmental palace. Desperate people tried in vain to scale the fence around the American embassy and board the last helicopters from the compound. The atmosphere was one of chaos and dismay.

Such emotions are what I picture taking place as the Babylonian army forced its way into the city of Jerusalem on July 18, 586 B.C.

The unthinkable had happened! The City of David and the earthly residence of Yahweh were destroyed. Corpses littered the streets. The survivors' faces were drawn tight with hunger and fear. A march of seven hundred miles to Babylon awaited them.

The Book of Lamentations catches the spirit of this event. Its five poetic chapters record a sense of loss and hopelessness. Humanly speaking there would be no future for Judah. But there was still God. And Jeremiah recognized that his mercies are "new every morning" (Lam. 3:22–24), that with him all things are possible (Jer. 32:26). The LORD is able to bring a remnant back to the land and start afresh (Zeph. 3:12). "'The LORD your God is with you, he is mighty to save'" (3:17). It was a word the faithful would take to heart.

Nebuchadnezzar decided to put Jehoiachin's uncle, Mattaniah, on the Judean throne. To show his authority over him, Nebuchadnezzar changed his name from Mattaniah to Zedekiah. He would be the last king of Judah. Because he was not in the direct line of succession, Zedekiah may have felt unsure of himself. He was a mixture of good intentions and weak character. This is supported by the accounts of Jeremiah's relationship with him. Jeremiah saw a man torn between the desire to do right and the temptation to do the expedient (Jer. 37 through 39). Zedekiah vacillated in his sworn allegiance to Babylon. He hoped Egypt would come to help Judah throw off the Babylonian yoke (Jer. 28; Ezek. 19). Ultimately Zedekiah listened to his pro-Egyptian advisers and sought independence from Nebuchadnezzar. The result was catastrophic, both for him *and* the nation. The armies of Babylon returned to lay siege against the cities of the land. One by one they were taken, till only Jerusalem remained. It fell on July 19, 586 B.C., in the eleventh year of Zedekiah's reign.

What Do We Learn From This?

After the death of the godly king Hezekiah, the southern kindgom of Judah had entered a religious and political decline. A hundred years after Hezekiah, the worship of pagan gods still rivaled the worship of Yahweh, so mighty Babylon defeated Judah. God had forewarned Israel through Moses of this link between sin and its consequences. He had said: "See, I set before you today life and prosperity, death and destruction. . . . But if your heart turns away and you are not obedient, and if you are drawn away to bow down to other gods and worship them, I declare to you this day that you will certainly be destroyed. You will not live long in the land you are crossing the Jordan to enter and possess" (Deut. 30:15,17–18).

Despite the preaching of faithful prophets and the rule of one godly king, in the seventh century B.C. Judah chose in effect "death and destruction." The end came in the second decade of the sixth century B.C. In 586–582 B.C., Babylon destroyed Judah and took the survivors into exile.

Thus, the night of exile settled over the Southern Kingdom. God's judgment on his people was complete. Both the histories of Kings and of Chronicles reveal sad stories of what happened to a people and their kings when they were consistently disobedient to God's covenant. The words of God to Moses came true. Violation of the commands of God brought death and a seventy-year "night" of exile.

The Late Judean Prophets

From the death of Hezekiah to Zedekiah's exile in Babylon, God called five prophets. They were to reveal his will to Judah. He raised up Nahum, Jeremiah, Zephaniah, and Habakkuk to be his spokesmen. Obadiah, if dated about the time of Jerusalem's fall, interpreted God's involvement with the nation of Edom. We will take a look at each of these five prophets of God.

Nahum: Prophet of Assyria's Demise
–Late 600s B.C.

1:1	Superscription
1:2 through 2:2	God's character revealed in his promises to Judah and warnings to Nineveh
2:3–13	Verbal pictures and taunts about Nineveh's destruction
3:1–18	Woes, more taunts, and a funeral dirge about Nineveh's fall

WHAT DO WE KNOW ABOUT NAHUM?

Of the prophet Nahum, little is known, not even his father's name. His hometown is given as Elkosh (Nah. 1:1). Its location, however, is disputed. Some suggest it was in Assyria (which would make Nahum a northern Israelite in exile); others think it was in Galilee or Judah.[4] Fortunately, the historical setting of the book is identifiable. It can be dated no earlier than 663 B.C., when the Egyptian city of Thebes fell to the Assyrians. The latest possible date would be about 612 B.C., when Nineveh, capital city of Assyria, fell to the Medes and Babylonians. Nahum cites the fall of Thebes (Heb. *No-Amon*) to the Assyrians (3:8–11), using it as a model for Nineveh's own fall.

WHAT DO WE KNOW ABOUT NINEVEH?

Archaeologists have uncovered the ruins of Nineveh. It was a city that boasted a large wall eight miles in circumference. It utilized a water system employing an aqueduct. Archaeologists have unearthed a royal library containing twenty thousand clay tablets. The seventh century B.C. witnessed the peak of Assyrian power when Thebes was captured. During this same century Assyria also faced its demise. Internal strife among the sons of King Esarhaddon (ca. 681–669 B.C.) weakened the empire. Though Ashurbanipal (668–627) defeated his brother, Shamash-shuma-ukin, in 652 B.C. and kept the empire together, his successors could not.[5] The Chaldeans (Neo-Babylonians),

[4]R. K. Harrison, *Old Testament Introduction* (Grand Rapids: Wm. B. Eerdmans, 1969), 926.

[5]Raymond B. Dillard and Tremper Longman III, *An Introduction to the Old Testament* (Grand Rapids: Zondervan Publishing House, 1994), 405.

under Nabopolassar, eventually broke away from Assyria and became the dominant power in that region.

WHAT'S IN A NAME?

Two ironies confront the reader of Nahum. First, although the prophet's name means "comfort," he left a prophecy for Assyria that was anything but comforting. The comfort he offered was for the people of God. They had suffered long under the harsh rule of Assyria, whose end he foretold. Second, for a book whose main theme is death and destruction, scholars judge Nahum as one of the most skilled Judean poets: "As a literary craftsman Nahum has no superior and few peers among the Old Testament poets."[6]

Nahum opens his book with a portrait of God: He is coming to take vengeance on his foes and provide refuge for his people (a picture that matches the cosmic grandeur of Ps. 18:7–15). The prophet writes like a battle general. Nahum prophetically barks out commands to the Assyrian army as they prepare for an invasion (Nah. 2:1; 3:14). His metaphors and similes vividly capture the agony of defeat: "[Nineveh's] slave girls moan like doves" (2:7). He adds: "All your fortresses are like fig trees with their first ripe fruit; when they are shaken, the figs fall into the mouth of the eater" (3:12). Other figures of speech picture Assyria like a lion that is no longer a threat (2:11–12). It is also likened to a harlot exposed to ridicule and filth (3:4–7). The book is a collection of hymns (1:2–8), battle reports (2:3–10), taunts (3:15–17), woe-speeches (3:1–3), and even insults (3:11–15).

[6]William S. LaSor, David A. Hubbard, and Frederic W. Bush, *Old Testament Survey: The Message, Form, and Background of the Old Testament,* 2d ed. (Grand Rapids: Wm. B. Eerdmans, 1997), 319.

CAN ANY GOOD COME OUT OF NAHUM?

In a day when the *grace* rather than the *wrath* of God is more palatable to our moral tastes, Nahum comes as a tart reminder: God never overlooks wickedness. Nahum, along with John in the Book of Revelation, presents a frightful picture of God's coming judgment. For both Old and New Testament believers, this provides hope in the midst of a "crooked and depraved generation" (Phil. 2:15): Evil will be punished; righteousness will be rewarded.

Zephaniah: Prophet of Doom
— Middle to Late 600s B.C.

1:1	Title
1:2 through 2:3	God's global judgment will include Judah
2:4 through 3:8	God's judgment on Judah's neighbors
3:9–20	God's restoration of Judah

Little is known about Zephaniah (see Zeph. 1:1). He lived in Jerusalem and prophesied in the reign of Josiah (641–609 B.C.). His unusual genealogy mentions four ancestors. Perhaps this was to connect him with the righteous reign of Hezekiah. Most scholars suggest that his prophecies came after the religious reforms of Josiah, begun in 621 B.C., and that his words supported the king's attempt to eradicate idolatry. Other scholars argue that the book comes from a time *before* 621 B.C., that Zephaniah was a catalyst for Josiah's religious purge. Part of this debate hinges on which imminent invasion of Judah was at hand. Was it the Scythian incursions (bands of marauding nomadic peoples from the Black Sea region) in the seventh century? Was it the Assyrians who had dominated the Ancient Near East for the past hundred years? Or more likely, was Zephaniah's vision of coming destruction that of the Babylonians? After the Battle of Carchemish in 605 B.C., they swept through Judah repeatedly (605, 597, and 587; perhaps also in 582. See Jer. 41:17–18).

WHAT KIND OF MINISTRY DOES A VOICE OF ALARM HAVE?

Though little is known of Zephaniah, God raised him up as a voice of alarm. The long and wicked reign of Manasseh had left a legacy of syncretism in Judah. Its people had worshiped Baal, astral deities, Molech, *and* Yahweh. Manasseh's political ties to Assyria likely had encouraged the recognition of Assyrian gods and goddesses. Judah's compromising attitude toward religion was permanently written on the hearts of the people. The voice of Zephaniah joined Jeremiah and Habakkuk in condemning this violation of the Mosaic covenant. Their messages, however, fell on deaf ears. The result was catastrophic. God rejected his own people and orchestrated their destruction via the hand of the Babylonians.

WHAT DOES ZEPHANIAH SAY ABOUT WICKEDNESS?

The opening lines of the Book of Zephaniah set the mood: "'I will sweep away everything from the face of the earth,' declares the LORD. 'I will sweep away both men and animals; I will sweep away the birds of the air and the fish of the sea. The wicked will have only heaps of rubble when I cut off man from the face of the earth,' declares the LORD" (Zeph. 1:2–3). This declaration of universal annihilation echoed the worldwide Noachian flood. It is repeated in

Oracles Against
the Nations

Oracles Against the Nations (OAN) are a common feature of prophetic books. They are found in Isaiah 13 through 23, Jeremiah 46 through 51, Ezekiel 25 through 32, Amos 1 through 2, and Zephaniah 2. Nahum and Obadiah are primarily directed to Assyria and Edom, respectively. God had a prophetic word about their future. He expected them to live up to the universal norms of justice in their dealings with other peoples.

These OAN addressed nations such as Egypt, Babylon, Philistia, and Moab. The real audience, however, was the people of God. They needed to know that their God was active on the stage of world events. Their God held all nations to account before heaven's court of law. Israel was a small nation, but it had a big God. He was sovereign over *all* the earth.

Zephaniah's "great day of the LORD" announcement in 1:14–18. It appears again in the global fire of God's anger described in 3:6–8.

Who are these wicked people of the world who await the fulfillment of Zephaniah's apocalyptic vision? They are the nations that surrounded Judah. Zephaniah 2:4–15 is a miniature collection of oracles against these nations (see sidebar). All the lands to the north (Assyria), south (Cush), east (Moab and Ammon), and west (Philistia) would come under God's wrath. God's wrath would also come upon his own people. Zephaniah describes a Judah rife with idolatrous practices. Jerusalem was filled with worship of Baal, astral deities, Ammon's god Molech, and superstitious ways (1:4–5,8–9). Yet they professed to worship Yahweh (v. 5). Zephaniah also accused the people of flagrant disobedience to God. They rebelled at every level of society: the merchants and the rich (1:10–13), the officials, the prophets, and the priests (3:1–5).

IS THIS PROPHET ALL BAD NEWS?

There is more to Zephaniah than predictions of doomsday. Like Hosea and Amos before him, he ended his book with hope. Though he had briefly spoken of sparing a humble remnant (Zeph. 2:1–3), still he declared God's favor to his people (1:9–18). But how could God restore such a wicked group of people? By his corrective judgment a people would be purified by the fire of national doom. They would be saved and returned to the land rejoicing. Such is the grace of God!

The Book of Zephaniah exerted some influence on the thought of the New Testament. Paul's teaching on the "day of the Lord" (2 Thess. 2:2) is parallel to Zephaniah's "day of the LORD." Also, the Battle of Armageddon, called by John "the

great day of God Almighty" (Rev. 16:14), has the same apocalyptic tone as Zephaniah's prophecy. Just as the hand of God
fell upon an unrighteous Judah after Zephaniah's day, so in
the last days it will fall on all nations who oppose God.

Jeremiah: Prophet of the New Covenant — 626–586 B.C.

1	Introduction and call
2 through 25	Collection of prophetic warnings (e.g., 2:1 through 3:5), symbolic actions (e.g., 13:1–11), and honest complaints to God (e.g., 15:10–21)
26 through 45	Stories about Jeremiah (e.g., 28) and the book of consolation (30 through 33)
46 through 51	Oracles against the nations
52	Historical appendix

WHY IS JEREMIAH SO AUTOBIOGRAPHICAL?

Jeremiah is a unique prophetic book. More is known
about this ancient preacher than any other prophet of God:
his birthplace, call, time references, friends, enemies.
Specific settings for some messages are clearly understood.
His personal walk with God and his experiences at the end
of his life are detailed. Jeremiah was born into a family
from Anathoth, a town given to priests. Anathoth was a
few miles northeast of Jerusalem (Jer. 1:1; Josh. 21:13–18;
1 Kings 2:26–27). Jeremiah's public ministry would be
mainly spent in Jerusalem.

While yet a youth, Jeremiah received his call to prophet-
hood in King Josiah's thirteenth year (Jer. 1:6). God
warned him that his ministry would be difficult. People
would oppose him but God would give him strength.

Jeremiah was to fear God and not people (1:17–19). Jeremiah's life became a model of courage.

Because the historical and political times were uncertain, God prohibited Jeremiah from marrying (in contrast to other OT prophets such as Isaiah, Ezekiel, and Hosea). Also, he was not allowed even to participate in social functions like weddings and funerals (16:1–9).

In his early ministry Jeremiah supported the religious reforms of King Josiah, and the king supported him. Their common goal was to rid the land of idolatry and return the people to the true worship of God at Jerusalem. They were only partially successful (see discussion above on the reign of Josiah). When later kings proved spiritually deficient, Jeremiah delivered outspoken messages against them. His actions created enemies in the royal court and the Jerusalem temple establishment. He was put in stocks by temple officials (Jer. 20:1–2) and was mobbed by angry crowds (26:7–9). Later Jeremiah was sent into hiding when King Jehoiakim burned a scroll of his prophecies (36:1–27). He was mistaken for a defector and imprisoned (37:11–15). And he was nearly hauled off to Babylon (40:1–6). Finally, he was carried to Egypt by fearful survivors of the 586 B.C. holocaust.

But God did send him people throughout his life to befriend and support him. For example, during the final siege of Jerusalem, King Zedekiah permitted Jeremiah to be put into a cistern or well. He would have died there, but Ebed-Melech, a man from Cush in North Africa, pulled him out (38:1–13). Baruch, Jeremiah's scribe, proved to be a loyal colleague and friend (36:8).

Despite the hard knocks people gave him, Jeremiah had a soft heart. His compassionate cry for them can be heard,

"Is there no balm in Gilead? Is there no physician there? Why then is there no healing for the wound of my people? Oh, that my head were a spring of water and my eyes a fountain of tears! I would weep day and night for the slain of my people" (Jer. 8:22 through 9:1).

Jeremiah is unique among the Old Testament writing prophets for the number of his written complaints, or "confessions," against God (11:18–23; 12:1–4; 15:10–21; 17:12–18; 18:18–23; 20:7–18). He cried out to God in the depths of despair for the trials God permitted. Like the psalmist (e.g., Ps. 6), Jeremiah was honest with the Lord. He felt lonely, afraid, confused, and angry. This venting revealed a genuine human being expressing universal human emotions.

Jeremiah is autobiographical because the life of Jeremiah is a major lesson of the book. This book models the character of a godly person in the face of trials. Like Jeremiah, believers have their doubts and trials but their faith sustains them.

WHAT DO WE KNOW ABOUT THE STRUCTURE OF JEREMIAH'S BOOK?

Jeremiah is the longest book in the Bible. It represents the literary distillation of a prophet's ministry covering over forty years. Most of Jeremiah's messages seem to follow Judah's difficult years after Josiah's death (609 B.C.). After the king's demise, the religious reforms supporting the sole worship of God in Jerusalem were discontinued.

The chapters are not arranged chronologically. King Jehoiakim had burned a scroll of Jeremiah's prophecies but God told the prophet to write them down again (see Jer. 36:28–32). This may account for an overlap of content found in the book (e.g., the "righteous Branch" prophecy is found in Jer. 23 and 33). The first chapter is a classic account of a prophetic call. Like Moses before him, Jeremiah offers reasons why he was not a good candidate, and God gave a firm answer that he knew his man. Jeremiah learned that it is hard to argue with the Lord.

Jeremiah 2 through 25 presents some of the prophet's fervent sermons against sin. At times God instructed him to include object lessons in his preaching: An expensive belt is ruined to teach what will happen to Judah (chap. 13). The craft of a potter taught God's sovereignty over his people (chap. 18). The smashing of a clay jar illustrated the destruction of Jerusalem (chap. 19).

Jeremiah 26 through 45 is biographical. The prophet is befriended by some people and hated by others. He survives the fall of Jerusalem only to be forced into Egyptian exile by unbelieving remnants of Judah. Through it all, Jeremiah remained faithful to his call to be God's spokesman.

Jeremiah 46 through 51, like Isaiah and Ezekiel, includes messages against some of Judah's neighbors and enemies. Egypt, Moab, Philistia, and Babylon received particular attention. Jeremiah 52 is a near repeat of 2 Kings 24:18 through 25:30. Both give the tragic details of Jerusalem's fall.

WHAT KIND OF WRITER WAS JEREMIAH?

The length of Jeremiah's book is matched by the variety of its literary forms. For example, it includes narratives of Jeremiah's ministry (28:1–17). Also, Jeremiah constructed oracles (46:1–12), complaints (12:1–13), symbolic actions (13:1–11), salvation speeches (30:12–17), hymns (31:7), letter writing (29:4–23), and prose sermons (7:1–15). Within these literary types, Jeremiah used skillful writing techniques. Using chapter 2 as an example, we can find a rapid change of tone (compare vv. 2–4 with v. 5), memorable phrases (2:13), rhetorical questions (2:11,14,31–32), graphic imagery (2:23–24), satire (2:28c), as well as historical reminders (2:2–3,6,16).

WHAT IS THIS BUSINESS ABOUT LXX AND MT?

Another unique feature of the Book of Jeremiah is its relationship to its Greek counterpart in the Septuagint (LXX; see glossary). The Greek version of Jeremiah is about 2,700 words shorter than its Hebrew version (in the Masoretic Text, or "MT" for short).[7] The LXX is also arranged differently. It puts the oracles against the nations (Jer. 46 through 51) in the middle of the book, at 25:13.[8]

Evidence for a complex textual history comes from the book itself. After Jehoiakim burned Jeremiah's scroll, God instructed Jeremiah to dictate it again it to his scribe, Baruch (Jer. 36:32). The text notes, "And many similar words were added to them." However, the differences are not substantive. The MT contains passages that are expansions of the LXX. Conversely, one could say that the LXX is a condensed version of the MT. God's preservation of his Word ensures us that we do have an inspired text. When God told Jeremiah, "'Now, I have put my words in

[7] J. G. S. S. Thompson, "Jeremiah," in *New Bible Dictionary,* 2d ed. (Wheaton, Ill.: Tyndale, 1982), 562.

[8] Heb. fragments of Jer. have been found in Cave 4 near Qumran. They support a Heb. text like that from which the LXX could have been translated. Some scholars, therefore, argue that the LXX reflects a form nearer the original. Perhaps it was the LXX version that was later expanded and rearranged to be the MT we know today. More scholars presently accept the likelihood of two early versions of Jer. They do not argue for the superiority of one over the other.

Second Verse, Same as the First

Jeremiah 44 is one of those unbelievable chapters in the Bible. It takes place after the fall of Jerusalem. Judean survivors had forced Jeremiah to go with them to Tahpanhes in Egypt. There, among the Jewish exiles, he continued his prophetic ministry. He told them to leave their idolatries. Going after pagan gods was a major reason for the judgment of God they were experiencing as exiles. They still didn't get it. He received the same response from them as before—denial. They thought it was because they had quit worshiping "the Queen of Heaven" under the reform of Josiah that things had gotten worse (44:18).

The irony was they had brought the exile on themselves. It was Yahweh who had caused their nation's destruction, not some pagan goddess.

Chapter 44 portrays the amazing rationaliza-

your mouth,'" (1:9) we know he has kept watch over those words.

WHAT LESSONS CAN WE LEARN FROM JEREMIAH?

Let me suggest four lessons from Jeremiah. First, we learn that Jeremiah's God is *the* big God who created the universe (e.g., Jer. 10:1–16). His dealings with us are sometimes beyond our comprehension (see 12:5–13). Yet this same God knows every atomic particle of our being (1:5). He promises to care for us as he cared for Jeremiah (1:19).

Second, human nature is sinful and rebellious. Jeremiah wrote, "The heart is deceitful above all things and beyond cure. Who can understand it?" (17:9). He echoed this theme in sermon after sermon (e.g., 2:1–19). Judah's people had rejected God's instructions on how to live righteously (7:9–11), and Judah's kings had been in the lead (22:1–30).

Third, sin must be judged. By the close of Jeremiah's life the armies of Babylon had come and completely destroyed the country of Judah: its people, kings, capital city, and temple. Jeremiah's long years of warning proved right (Jer. 25:3). God judged his own people for their rebellion.

Fourth, God's love and mercy would not allow him to abandon his people. Jeremiah 30 through 33 is a collection of Jeremiah's promises of restoration. The LORD promised to bring Israel back from their Babylonian exile (32:36–44); Israel would be his people again (30:22).

WHY IS JEREMIAH MENTIONED IN THE NEW TESTAMENT?

The Gospels reflect a popular view of Jesus as a contemporary Jeremiah. Jesus' teaching and life often reflected Jeremiah. Both knew that the human heart needed a radical change (Jer. 17:9; John 3:3–5). Both knew the disappointment of people listening but not obeying (Jer. 25:3; Matt. 19:22). Near the end of his life, Jeremiah, exiled to Egypt, heard the people complain. They said that their troubles had begun when they stopped worshiping the goddess called "Queen of Heaven" (Jer. 44:18). Earlier he had seen the unalterable drift of the people's heart toward sin and observed, "Can the Ethiopian change his skin or the leopard its spots? Neither can you do good who are accustomed to doing evil" (13:23). Little wonder that chapters 30 through 33 are called Jeremiah's "book of consolation" and include the expectation of a righteous king. He would bring victory over enemies and over sin (33:14–16). It also speaks of a new covenant that will be superior to the Mosaic law in dealing with sin and achieving righteousness (31:31–34; quoted in Heb. 8:8–12). Jesus is that promised "righteous Branch" whose eternal reign will bring salvation to the world (33:14–18).

tion process of human nature. The human heart is capable of explaining away anything to avoid the truth of God's Word. My own frequent prayer is that God will show me *my* faults. The Bible is that lamp which exposes our faults and lights our way (Ps. 119:105).

Lamentations: The Cry of Jerusalem's Heart — About 580 B.C.

1	Jerusalem (Zion) sits alone, conquered, desolate, and miserable
2	The LORD has punished Jerusalem and its people
3	The lament of the people, and God's great love
4	Jerusalem's past wealth and present wretchedness
5	The poet's appeal to God to forgive his people

WHAT IS THE BOOK OF LAMENTATIONS?

Lamentations is not, strictly speaking, a prophetic book. Instead, it is a poem written to describe the misery of the people following the conquest of Jerusalem by the Neo-Babylonians.

WHO WROTE LAMENTATIONS?

The author of Lamentations is unknown. Because of its doleful tone, traditionally it has been ascribed to Jeremiah, the "weeping prophet" (see Jer. 4:19; 9:1; 10:19–20; 23:9). Whoever the author may have been, it is clear that, like Jeremiah, he was a witness to and survivor of Jerusalem's capture. He had witnessed the brutality of the invaders.

WHAT IS ITS LITERARY STRUCTURE?

Prophetic speech often uses poetry (for example, Isaiah's "Song of the Vineyard" in Isa. 5:1–7). Or prophetic books may contain poetic portions (as Hab. 3). But Lamentations is entirely poetic. It consists of five lament songs, written largely in a *qinah* rhythm. This particular poetic meter was used by the Israelites and Judeans for funeral songs (for example, Amos 5:1b–2). The first four laments are alphabetical acrostics. The first two laments are 22 verses long; so are the fourth and fifth. The third is 66 verses (22 times 3). An acrostic means that each verse begins with a different Hebrew letter in alphabetic sequence. Since there are 22 Hebrew letters (counting *shin* and *sin* as variant forms of the same letter), this yields 22 verses per chapter. The last chapter keeps the form of 22 verses but drops the alphabetic form.

WHAT IS ITS MESSAGE?

The book's formal structure as a funeral dirge makes clear its purpose: The poet describes the grief of the survivors over the death of their city. He likens the city to a widow whose children have been taken from her. The poet uses this metaphor to describe in vivid detail how Jerusalem was once full of people but was now empty (Lam. 1:1). Her women have been ravished (5:11), her young men and maidens, slain (2:21) or driven into exile (1:3), and her foes have become her masters (1:5). For this she weeps at night (1:2). The survivors have no food or water so they barter their treasures for a morsel or a drink (1:11; 5:4,9). Those who can get no other food eat their own children (2:20). The enemy's brutality is described in terms of the LORD's wrath, tearing the city apart (2:4–9). The poet's own anguish over the great catastrophe is described in 3:1–20. Yet amid all the agony of poet and people, there is hope: "Yet this I call to mind," he says, "and therefore I have hope: Because of the LORD's great love we are not consumed, for his compassions never fail. They are new every morning; great is your faithfulness" (3:21–23).

WHAT CAN WE LEARN FROM LAMENTATIONS?

There is a pop theology circulating today that says if believers have faith, they will not suffer. However, Lamentations suggests life's most intense cruelties can prove our faith. Out of the black abyss of chaos, out of the fires of torment, out of the depths of agony, rises that majestic hymn of the church, its words taken from Lamentations 3:22–23:

"Great is Thy faithfulness, Oh God my Father
There is no shadow of turning with Thee

Thou changest not, Thy compassions they fail not
As Thou hast been, Thou forever wilt be."[9]

[9]Words by Thomas Chisholm; music by William Runyan (1923).

Habakkuk: The Prophet of Questioning Faith
– About 605 B.C.

1:1	Title
1:2 through 2:20	Dialogue between Habakkuk and God
1:2–4	Habakkuk: "God, do you see this wicked society?"
1:5–11	God: "Prophet, Babylon will destroy this wickedness."
1:12 through 2:1	Habakkuk: "God, how can you use pagan people to judge us?"
2:2–20	God: "Prophet, woe will come to them. You, have faith in me."
3:1–19	A psalm of difficult times

HABAKKUK WHO?

As with Nahum, biographical information on Habakkuk is scarce. The book simply opens, "The oracle that Habakkuk the prophet received" (Hab. 1:1). What follows is the record of his struggle to understand his times and the God he served. Some scholars argue that he was one of the temple prophets, individuals the temple authorities hired to answer worshipers' requests to God (a kind of prophecy-on-demand). The psalmlike style of the third chapter, complete with instructions to the Levitical musicians, points to this possibility (3:19b). Yet temple prophets were viewed negatively by biblical prophets like Micah (Mic. 2:6–11) and Jeremiah (see Jer. 23:14). So Habakkuk probably was not a professional prophet. Instead he seems to have been called by God from ordinary life to deliver his message.

Several details in the book help us to date the prophecy in the closing decade of the seventh century B.C. (ca. 612–605). First, the approaching storm of Babylonian conquests in Habakkuk 1:5–11 fits the activity of Nebuchadnezzar's armies in 605 B.C. Second, the violence, injustice, and disregard for the *torah* fit the times of the Judean kings following Josiah's death. Perhaps Habakkuk prophesied during the reign of Jehoiakim (608–597 B.C.), whom Jeremiah described as an unrighteous king who used force to oppress the people (Jer. 22:13–17).

WHAT IS THIS BOOK ABOUT?

The structure of the book is twofold: Habakkuk 1:2 through 2:20 is the dialogue between the prophet and God; 3:1–19 is the psalm of Habakkuk. In the first section, Habakkuk complains to the LORD about his delay in sending judgment on Judah (1:2–4). God answers that he is raising up the Babylonians to judge Judah (1:5–11). Habakkuk then expresses bewilderment that God would judge his people by the Babylonians. Habakkuk asks, How could that be? How could God use a people more wicked than the Judeans to judge them? (1:12 through 2:1, esp. 1:13). God, however, reminds Habakkuk that he is sovereign (2:14,20). In a series of five woes, he says that he will also judge the Babylonians (2:2–20). Habakkuk's relationship to God would have to be one of faithfulness (2:4).

In the second section, the psalm of Habakkuk, the prophet puts his faith to work. He calls on God (3:1–2) to perform miraculous deeds, like those in Israel's past under Moses and Joshua (3:3–15). The book closes with one of Scripture's great statements of faith. Despite evidence to the contrary, Habakkuk affirms his trust in God:

> Though the fig tree does not bud
> and there are no grapes on the vines,
> though the olive crop fails

Corrie ten Boom— Habakkuk's Companion in Doubt

The ten Boom family of father and two adult daughters hid Jews from the Nazis in World War II Netherlands. Betrayed, arrested, and sent to concentration camps, they suffered greatly. Corrie's father and her sister, Betsy, died while imprisoned. Corrie survived and went on to become an international speaker about the love of God. The ten Boom story was published and made into a film, *The Hiding Place*.

Corrie was not always a rock of faith and trust in God. It was Betsy. The telling moment in the story occurred when their prison barracks was overrun with fleas. Corrie reached her limit: "Why did God allow all these horrible things to happen? And now fleas! Why God? Why?" It was Betsy

and the fields produce no food,
though there are no sheep in the pen
and no cattle in the stalls,
yet I will rejoice in the LORD (3:17–18).

WHAT DOES HABAKKUK TEACH US?

We can learn at least three lessons from Habakkuk. First, believers do experience doubt. Evil in the world troubles our belief in God's rule. If he is all-powerful, why doesn't he do something about evil? We too will have questions and concerns about why God allows evil to run its course. We too join with Habakkuk in crying, "How long, O LORD, must I call for help, but you do not listen?" (Hab. 1:2). Throughout biblical and church history the most deeply spiritual believers have sometimes had the most troubling questions (e.g., Martin Luther). It's not wrong to ask God, "Why?"[10]

Second, God tells us to have faith in his providence. He alone governs the world. We may not see or understand his work in our lives or in history but he is still on his throne. The life of the believer will be securely grounded in God by faith. Paul used the final phrase of Habakkuk 2:4 as his cornerstone of salvation: "the righteous will live by his faith" (see Rom. 1:17; Gal. 3:11; Eph. 2:8). Despite doubts and trials, the believer's walk will be marked by trust in a good and great God. It was so with Abraham (Gen. 15:6). It was so with Habakkuk. It will be so with us.

---

[10]Sometimes Christians mistakenly think that questioning God is sinful and shows a lack of faith. But asking God "why" really shows where our faith is directed—to God. Job, Eccles., and several of the Pss. also ask the same question.

Third, despite our questions and doubts, we are to worship God (Hab. 3). Habakkuk reviewed the saving acts of God. That led him to write a psalm of praise. How much more do we have reason to praise God than did Habakkuk! We know of God's greatest saving act—Jesus' coming as Messiah.

Obadiah: The Prophet of Edom's Doom — About 580 B.C.

Verse 1a	Superscription
Verses 1b–14	God will judge Edom for pride and its treatment of Judah
Verses 15–21	The Day of the LORD will bring judgment to the nations but restoration to Israel

WHEN DID OBADIAH WRITE HIS BOOK?

Other than his being a prophet, nothing is known about Obadiah. Like the prophecies of Nahum and Habakkuk, the Book of Obadiah does not explicitly state its historical setting. Scholars hold two primary views. A minority position sees this book as a response to Edom's ninth century B.C. attack upon Jerusalem (2 Kings 8:20–22; 2 Chron. 21:8–20). The majority view, however, considers the book to be a response to the 587–586 B.C. attack by Babylon and its allies, such as Edom. If the majority view is correct, Obadiah's prophecy was a divine word of retribution for Edom. This nation took particular delight in Judah's humiliation. Following the fall of Jerusalem, it made raids on the Judean people, kicking them when they were down, so to speak.

who answered Corrie's bitter questions with the call to thank God even for fleas. As it turned out, because of their flea-infested barracks, the night prison guards left its women alone and did not molest them. Corrie learned a lesson like Habakkuk had—God is worthy of our trust and praise even when circumstances seem to dictate otherwise (see Hab. 3:16-19).

WHAT AND WHERE WAS EDOM?

The country of Edom, also known as the land of Seir (Gen. 36:9), lay south and east of the Dead Sea. Its rugged mountains permitted its people to build highly defensible fortresses (Obad. 3–4). Jacob was a patriarch of the Israelite people. His brother, Esau, was the patriarch of Edom. In spite of this familial tie, biblical history is stained with the blood shed between Israel and Edom (Num. 20:14–21; 1 Sam. 14:47; 2 Sam. 8:13–14; 1 Kings 9:26–28; 11:14–22; Lam. 4:21–22). Renowned for its wisdom (Obad. 8), Edom was the home of at least one of Job's friends, Eliphaz. Two north-south trade routes passed through the country. This provided the nation with a primary source of revenue: Edom taxed the caravans passing to and from Africa, Europe, and Asia.

By the close of the Old Testament period, the Edomites had been displaced by Arabian tribes. They had resettled in the Negev region and, as a country, were renamed Idumea. Herod the Great was an Idumean, an Edomite! His rule over the Jews in the New Testament period was endured with bitterness by the Jews.

In light of this history, Edom became the object of more frequent prophetic attention than any other Gentile nation (Isa. 34; Jer. 49; Ezek. 25; 35; Amos 1). Obadiah, the shortest book of the Old Testament, is devoted to God's dealing with Edom.

WHAT IS OBADIAH'S STRUCTURE?

Obadiah consists of two parts. Part one, verses 1–14, is the direct prophecy about Edom. Part two, verses 15–21, is a wider prophecy involving all nations and Israel. Like Joel,

Obadiah begins with an immediate historical situation. It also ends with God's triumph over Israel's enemies. Obadiah's final words were "And the kingdom will be the LORD's" (v. 21).

Obadiah 1–9 parallels material found in Jeremiah 49:7–16. It is clear that either one is citing the other or both are citing a common source.[11]

LESSONS FROM OBADIAH—SMALL BOOK, BIG LESSONS

Despite its brevity and sharp tone, Obadiah offers us some important themes.[12] There is the theme of God's reciprocal relationship to his people: "'I will bless those who bless you, and whoever curses you I will curse'" (Gen. 12:3). Edom's hostile actions against its cousin Judah brought the curse of God back upon them. The theme of *lex talionis,* the law of appropriate judgment, is witnessed in God's judgment against Edom. In the manner it treated Judah, God would treat Edom. The theme of the universal rule of Yahweh has been noted. Obadiah's small voice joins a whole chorus of voices in the Bible. They all declare the ultimate triumph of the LORD over his enemies.

Prophets of the Exile

The promised dark night of defeat and exile became a reality for both the kingdoms of Israel and of Judah. The Babylonians gained victory over Judah and Jerusalem in the summer of 586 B.C. Thousands of surviving Judeans joined

---

[11]For more on this subject, see Dillard and Longman, *Introduction to the Old Testament,* 388; Harrison, *Old Testament Introduction,* 899–903.

[12]The following summary of the themes of Obad. is borrowed from Dillard and Longman, *Introduction to the Old Testament,* 389–90.

earlier waves of forced expatriates living in Mesopotamia. The preexilic prophetic warnings of judgment to both Israel and Judah had come true. The fall of Israel in 722 B.C. and now Judah in 586 B.C. raised serious theological questions for the Jews. Would the preexilic pictures of restoration and forgiveness also be fulfilled? Would God abandon his people forever? Would there be a word of hope to them in exile?

How Did God Answer His People's Crisis of Faith?

During this time of national despair, God raised up two prophetic voices. They gave the Judean exiles hope for their present and for their future. These two men had themselves experienced the disorientation and alienation of exile in Babylon. In 605 B.C., the young man Daniel was taken in the first group of select captives to Babylon. Like Joseph in Egypt centuries before him, Daniel's role was political. He became an insider for the Judean people. God placed him in the upper echelons of Nebuchadnezzar's government. Daniel lived until the very end of the Babylonian captivity in 538 B.C. He secured religious freedom for his people and presented them with prophetic visions of God's kingdom.

In 597 B.C., the young priest Ezekiel was taken to Babylon with the second wave of Judean captives. Four years later God called him into a two-phase prophetic ministry. The first phase occurred before the fall of Jerusalem. Ezekiel's main mission was to purge the people of their false hopes of a quick release and return to Judah. But the people of Judah did not repent. They continued their wicked ways despite warnings from Zephaniah, Habakkuk, and Jeremiah. After the fall of Jerusalem in 586 B.C., God gave

Ezekiel a second phase of ministry. He revealed words of hope and visions of restoration.

God used Daniel and Ezekiel to preserve his people during their long night of captivity. When circumstances were darkest, Daniel's and Ezekiel's ministries were beacons of hope. I present them here in canonical order.

Ezekiel: The Prophet of God's Presence —593–571 B.C.

1 through 3	The call of Ezekiel
4 through 24	Messages, visions, and symbolic actions warning of judgment against Judah
25 through 32	Messages warning of judgment against other nations
33 through 48	Messages of restoration of Judah and Israel

HOW DID EZEKIEL FIND HIMSELF A DISPLACED PERSON?

Ezekiel was born to a prominent priestly family (Ezek. 1:1–2). The reference to the "thirtieth year" in 1:1 probably refers to his age. Ezekiel's birth, therefore, would have been during the godly reign of Josiah (ca. 623 B.C.). Ezekiel was taken into exile when the Babylonians deported King Jehoiachin and ten thousand other Judeans (see the history of this period above). Ezekiel's life was altered forever. He could no longer serve God in the sacred temple of Jerusalem. Instead, he was settled in the rural Babylonian village of Tel Abib to serve his pagan captors. Perhaps he and his compatriots worked farms or maintained the canals necessary for irrigation. One such canal was the "Kebar River" (1:1,3; 3:15). It lay on the plain of lower

Mesopotamia between the Euphrates and Tigris Rivers.

While Ezekiel was standing beside the Kebar River in his fifth year of exile, God called him to be a prophetic "watchman" (1:2; 3:17). Like Isaiah's and Jeremiah's experiences, the call was dramatic and personal. Ezekiel's call was unique, however, because of its pagan setting hundreds of miles from Israel. Ezekiel and his countrymen felt cut off from fellowship with the LORD. Yet the thrust of the opening vision and call of Ezekiel proved otherwise. The opening theophany revealed to Ezekiel that God was with his people even in a pagan land (Ezek. 1 through 3). God later told the people that he was a "sanctuary" for them during their time of banishment (11:16).

WHAT'S THE BIG IDEA IN EZEKIEL?

This is the central theme of the Book of Ezekiel: God's presence among his people brings his blessings and ultimate triumph over their enemies. The book opens with the arrival of God. The book ends with the end-time name of Jerusalem, "THE LORD IS THERE" (Ezek 48:35). Ezekiel's prophetic ministry lay between those two points. He witnessed the glory of God leaving the temple (chaps. 8 through 11). He warned about God's final judgments on Judah (chaps. 6 through 7 and 12 through 24). He pronounced the control of God's power over foreign nations (chaps. 25 through 32). He prophesied the promised restoration of God's fellowship with his people after their cleansing and return to the land (chaps. 33 through 37). He predicted future protection for Israel from its enemies (chaps. 38 through 39). He envisioned the bright future of a renovated land, purified people, and glorious return of God to the new temple (chaps. 40 through 48). Ezekiel's main task was to build confidence in the faith of the exiles. They were to become the remnant of righteousness and future hope of God's plans for the world. God was with them!

WHY THE PRECISE DATING IN EZEKIEL?

Ezekiel's dating method is a unique feature of the book. More than any other prophet, he gives the day, month, and year for many of his prophecies and visions. The fourteen dates he gives generally follow a chronological order from 593 to 573 B.C. The seven dates in the oracles against the nations (Ezek. 25 through 32) are arranged topically. This overrides any chronological order. Haggai and Zechariah also date their prophecies. There is significance to such precise dating. It fixes the acts of God in human history. It reminds us that God is not a distant deity. He is an active God, one who brings judgment and salvation to the world.

WOULD EZEKIEL HAVE PASSED ENGLISH 101?

The Book of Ezekiel displays a wide variety of literary features and forms. Though largely written in prose, there are rich poetic passages employing metaphors. For example, the metaphor of God's judgment as a sword is skillfully used in Ezekiel 21. The lion as a symbol for a king's rule is put to cunning use in Ezekiel 19. Poetic form is predominant in the OAN sections. Tyre, pictured as a majestic merchant vessel, sinks. All hands and cargo are lost on the high seas (chap. 27). The king of Tyre is portrayed as a majestic figure in the garden of God. His pride leads to his fall (chap. 28). Egypt, symbolized as a ferocious crocodile, is snared. Its carcass is thrown onto the land, to bloat and explode (chap. 32).

Ezekiel's prose speeches also represent a variety of forms. Dire and apocalyptic warnings are given: "'The end has come! The end has come!'" (Ezek. 7:6). Straight historical reviews of Israel's record of moral and spiritual failures are recounted (e.g., chap. 20). Lengthy allegories describe the nature of the people's sins (chaps. 16 and 23). Whole sermons are built upon a single proverb (chap. 18). Major sections of the book are recollections of visions (1 through 3; 8 through 11; 40 through 48).

Ezekiel also employed nonverbal forms of communication. He used drama and symbolic actions. These acted-out sermons may have resulted from the restriction set upon him by God. He could speak only when God told him to speak (see 3:24–27; 33:22). In Ezekiel 4 through 5 he builds models of Jerusalem in sand. He eats siege rations cooked over the fuel of dried cow manure. For days on end, he lies on his right side, then on his left. The prophet then cuts off his hair.

Why did Ezekiel employ such a variety of poetic and prose styles? He used every technique of verbal and nonverbal communication available to him to convey God's message. He was *compelled* to get through to his listeners. Apparently Ezekiel got quite a following. People were intrigued. What would he do or say next? God told him that people were listening to him. However, God also warned him that there can be a gap between listening and obeying (see 33:30–33).

Ezekiel's writing is marked by a repetition of phrases.[13] Several deserve attention. The vocative phrase "son of man" occurs over ninety times when God addresses Ezekiel. This usage highlights the humanity of the prophet. The NRSV uses the word "mortal" to bring out that sense. That the great

---

[13]H. G. May provides a list of forty-seven such repeated phrases; see "Ezekiel" in *The Interpreter's Bible* (Nashville: Abingdon, 1956), 6:50f.

sovereign God would speak with humanity is remarkable. This emphasizes his desire to reveal his will and character.[14]

The phrase "then they/you will know that I am the LORD" is found over fifty times. Found in judgment speeches (e.g., Ezek. 6:10) as well as restoration prophecies (e.g., 33:29), it is called the "recognition formula." Ezekiel's God is a revealing God: He wants to make himself known. His mercy and righteousness are taught by his deeds.

WHAT IS EZEKIEL'S THEOLOGICAL LEGACY?

Finally, using three critical movements of God's presence narrated in the book, some theological observations about Ezekiel can be made. The first is the awesome display of God's glory in chapter one. The storm cloud, four creatures, eye-covered wheels, and the humanlike form command attention. This chariot-throne was illuminated with "brilliant light" and rainbow colors (Ezek. 1:27–28). The visual effects were accompanied with a rush of sound like a mighty waterfall. In coming to the exiles, God signified that he had not abandoned them. Later messages (e.g., 5:3; 6:8–11) underscored this fact. God's future dealings with Israel, however, would be with the exiles in Babylon. They would not be with the people left in Judah (22:18 calls them "dross," worthless). Where the presence of God is, there is hope. He is too great to fail. When God's glory comes, it is understandable that Ezekiel falls down before him in worship (1:28).

Ezekiel's opening vision of God also teaches God's mobility and freedom. He is no mere local deity, bound to a city or region. He is Lord of all the earth. He is free to

[14]Jesus' use of the phrase seems to be drawn from the heavenly "son of man" who approaches the "Ancient of Days" in Dan. 7:13. See discussion later in this chapter.

A Sexist Prophet?

In chapters 16 and 23, Ezekiel used the imagery of immoral women to teach his listeners how God regarded their apostasy. They had turned away from their covenant with God like a wayward wife turns away from her marital pledge to her husband. Ezekiel employed explicit language in his portrayal of unfaithful Israel.[15] Some readers may find it offensive.

The most intimate human relationship is marriage. Marriage provides the closest analogy to the way God feels toward his people. Just as believers regard the behavior of a wayward spouse as abhorrent, so God regarded Israel's spiritual waywardness abhorrent.

Why did Ezekiel use such offensive language? Because the people's hearts were deadened to God's Word. They did not grasp the seriousness of their rebellion against him. Ezekiel had to use extreme measures to

roam as he wishes. The speed of the chariot-throne and the eyes on the wheels teach that God is all-present and all-knowing. The faces of the eagle, ox, human, and lion represent all creation over which the LORD rules and reigns.

The second critical movement of God's presence is the vision of Ezekiel 8 through 11. Tragically, these chapters detail his abandonment of the temple and Jerusalem. The four scenes of wickedness in the temple in Ezekiel 8 reveal that Israel had abandoned him first. God is a holy God and they who worship him must do so "in spirit and in truth" (John 4:23–24). He is a jealous God who covets our sole worship. He is the true Deity. As in the days of Eli, "Ichabod" could apply to God's people here too (see 1 Sam. 4:21–22). Holiness is not optional for the people of God. Unless we are obedient to his will, we cannot assume that he is with us.

God holds people accountable (see esp. Ezek. 18). There is a limit to his mercy: Rebellion can result in a hardened heart (see 20:1–29). God sees our hidden sins as well as our flagrant ones. Ezekiel saw judgment come upon Jerusalem (chap. 9). Likewise the New Testament reveals a coming day of judgment upon all humanity (Heb. 9:27; Rev. 20:11–15).

The third critical movement of God's presence is Ezekiel's vision of his glory returning to his new temple (Ezek. 40 through 48). Despite the many interpretive problems these chapters pose, the message is clear: God would be true to his covenants with Abraham, David, and Israel. After purifying the people from their sins (e.g., 36:25–26)

[15]Here are two recent works on this theme: Phyllis A. Bird, *Missing Persons and Mistaken Identities: Women and Gender in Ancient Israel,* Overtures to Biblical Theology, ed. Walter Brueggemann (Minneapolis: Fortress, 1997); Raymond C. Ortlund, *Whoredom: God's Unfaithful Wife in Biblical Theology*, New Studies in Biblical Theology, ed. Donald Carson (Grand Rapids: Wm. B. Eerdmans, 1996).

God would renew fellowship with them. He would receive their worship in the new sanctuary.

But in this last vision, even the city and the land beyond the temple had changed. From the temple came an ever-growing volume of water. It would change the desert into a fruit-growing garden. The Dead Sea would be transformed into a fishing paradise (Ezek. 47:1–12). The land would be divided into tribal allotments with every tribe represented (47:13 through 48:29). The city would no longer be called Jerusalem. It would be spiritually refurbished and bear God's name: "THE LORD IS THERE" (48:35). Centuries later, John saw the New Jerusalem without a temple—"because the Lord God Almighty and the Lamb are its temple" (Rev. 21:22). In the interim, believers have God's presence by his Spirit. His Spirit lives in us (1 Cor. 3:17; 1 Pet. 2:4–5).

communicate effectively.

The analogy of marriage to our relationship with God is found in the New Testament as well. Jesus told the parable of the ten virgins who had been invited to a wedding feast (Matt. 25:1–13). In the parable he is the bridegroom. Paul parallels Christ's love for the Church with the love of a husband for his wife (Eph. 5:22–33). The Book of Revelation speaks of a coming bridal feast when Christ and his Church will celebrate their union in heaven (19:9; 21:9).

Daniel: Long-Lived Prophet of God's Enduring Kingdom – 605–535 B.C.

1 through 6	Stories about the life and ministry of Daniel
1	Daniel and friends put God first
2	Nebuchadnezzar's dream of a metallic statue
3	Daniel's three friends take a stand for God
4	Nebuchadnezzar's dream of a great tree
5	Belshazzar's banquet and judgment
6	Daniel in the lion's den
7 through 12	The visions of Daniel
7	Four animals represent four kingdoms
8	Two more animals and a little horn
9	Jeremiah's 70 years, Daniel's prayer, and Gabriel's 70 "sevens" answer
10 through 12	Spiritual warfare, rival kingdoms, and the resurrection

How About a George Lucas Trilogy of Daniel?

There are some literary connections between the *Star Wars* film series and Daniel's stories and visions. Both involve the struggle between good and evil (see Dan. 9). Both portray strange creatures (see Dan. 7 through 8). Both have action scenes of a cosmic scope (see Dan. 12). Both involve defeat and victory (see Dan. 6). Writings with such themes are called "apocalyptic literature." The Book of Daniel, Isaiah 24 through 27, and Ezekiel 38 through 39 are biblical examples of this style of writing that became popular in the intertestamental and early Christian periods. They provided God's people with hope. The forces of evil in this world will ultimately be defeated. God will rule supreme. God's people will prosper. Meanwhile, patience and faithfulness are the virtues to live by (see Dan. 12:1–4).

Why Was Daniel a Babylonian Bureaucrat?

Daniel was exiled by the Babylonians in 605 B.C. for governmental service. He, along with other young men from various conquered lands, was taken to the great city of Babylon. There they received an education in Babylonian language and literature. Daniel's divinely anointed and natural abilities propelled him into a position as a counselor for King Nebuchadnezzar. Daniel faithfully and competently served his foreign masters for many decades. In 539 B.C. the Persians, under Cyrus the Great, took control of Babylon. Thus Daniel's last years were lived as an official in the Persian government.

Daniel's ministry benefited his exiled fellow Judeans in at least two ways. First, through Daniel's influence and accomplishments, they were permitted to worship God without hindrance; the Jews could practice their religion and culture. Second, through Daniel's prophetic visions, the Jewish people received powerful predictions. Daniel's visions foretold both coming trials and glorious triumphs. They would suffer persecution by future kings who hated them and their Lord. God promised, however, to intercede in history and usher in his eternal kingdom.

A Book About Lions and Leopards and Bears . . .

The structure of the book is built on stories and visions. Daniel 1 through 6 contains court narratives. These stories are accounts of Daniel and his friends. They detail their education and work as administrators and wise men. These narratives resemble the centuries-old hero stories and court tales of Joseph and Moses in the land of Egypt. In form, the Book of Esther mirrors these stories decades later. Like Joseph and Moses, Daniel the outsider influenced the government of a pagan land. He offered supernatural demonstration of the power of God. Like Esther, Daniel risked offending the monarch for the sake of principle and people. These stories of Daniel offer inspiring lessons of how obedience to God will be vindicated.

Four dreams, narrated in the first person, make up Daniel 7 through 12. They deal with apocalyptic scenes of coming empires and events. Beginning with biblical passages like Isaiah 24 through 27 and Zechariah 9 through 14, apocalyptic literature after Daniel took on a life of its own in the intertestamental period. At that time Jewish works like 1 Enoch were composed. Common features of apocalyptic writings are end-times events, use of angels as mediators or guides of divine revelation, unusual imagery, the author living in a time of oppression, and certainty of judgment and of hope. This type of literature was intended to encourage the people's moral resolve and spiritual hope.

DANIEL—A BILINGUAL BOOK?

In Daniel the Hebrew language is used in 1:1 through 2:4a, Aramaic in 2:4b through 7:28, and Hebrew again in 8:1 through 12:13. Much like English today, Aramaic was the international language of this period. Using Aramaic in Daniel 2 through 7 emphasized the sovereign control of God over the Gentile kingdoms of the world, which he was addressing at this point. Human kingdoms rise and fall, but the reign of God endures.

WHY IS DANIEL SO DEBATED?

Daniel is a controversial book. There are questions of interpretation. What nations are represented by the different metals in Nebuchadnezzar's dream (Dan. 2:31–45)? Who is the "little" horn with the boastful mouth (7:8)? What do the "seventy 'sevens'" mean (9:24–27)? Who is the king of the North that will threaten Israel (11:41)? Does Daniel teach the resurrection of the dead (12:2–3)?

There are also questions about its authorship and dating. The traditional view is that the book was written by the prophet Daniel. He was living as a Judean exile in the sixth century B.C. in Babylon. The book is a unified work of stories and dreams from his life. God gave supernatural revelation of the future to Daniel. Subsequent history has verified the accuracy of these revelations. A common view of Daniel 2 is that the four metals in the statue predicted the four major empires of Babylon, Medo-Persia, Greece, and Rome.

Questions have long been raised about the book, as early as the Greek scholar and Neoplatonic philosopher Porphyry (A.D. 233–304). Only in the last few hundred years, however, has a significant challenge to the traditional view been raised. Today, the majority of critical scholarship argues that Daniel was written in the second century B.C. by an unknown author. This writer supposedly lived in Palestine during the intense persecution of the Seleucid king Antiochus IV (ca. 165 B.C.) and wrote the book in a pious attempt to encourage the Jewish people. They were resisting pagan pressures to Hellenize their religion and culture. This unknown writer is said to have utilized the apocalyptic style and content of such noncanonical works such as 2 Esdras, 1 Enoch, and 2 Baruch.

In response, consider two comments about the questions of authorship and dating of Daniel. First, fragments of the Book of Daniel were found among the Dead Sea Scrolls (DSS). The Qumran community hid these scrolls during the Jewish Revolt against Rome around A.D. 66–70. This meant that Daniel had been written, copied, and recognized as canonical by that time. Such a process favors an earlier date of authorship than the second century B.C. Second, Jesus referred to the Book of Daniel in Matthew 24:15, warning of "'"the abomination that causes desolation," spoken of through the prophet Daniel.'" The reference is to Daniel 9:27; 11:31; and 12:11. In other words, Daniel's book was a part of Jesus' Scriptures, and Jesus assumed a traditional understanding of authorship.

WHAT DOES DANIEL TEACH ABOUT THE MESSIAH?

Traditional Christian interpretation of the Old Testament saw messianic teachings in Daniel. There are theological

Daniel's "Seventy 'Sevens'"

One of the most debated parts of the Book of Daniel is chapter 9. Daniel had read Jeremiah's prophecy of the length of the exile—seventy years (9:2; see Jer. 29:10). (This shows that the Book of Jeremiah had attained status as Scripture by the end of Daniel's long life.) The number "seventy" is related to the Mosaic concept of the sabbatical rest of the land every seven years. God considered the seventy years of exile an extended sabbatical rest. This would ensure the cleansing of the land stained by Israel's sins.

Believing the exile's end was near, Daniel prayed to God. The angel Gabriel brought him an answer: God's program of redemption would now take "seventy 'sevens'" (Dan. 9:24). This

and thematic arguments for supporting a Christocentric understanding.[16] Four texts in particular reveal information about the person and program of the Messiah.

In Daniel 2 the rock uncut by human hands destroys a statue that represents the kingdoms of this world. This rock grows into a mighty mountain. Daniel interprets the rock as an eternal kingdom (v. 44). Other OT texts utilize rock and mountain motifs in describing God himself (e.g., Deut. 32:4) and his kingdom (Isa. 2:2–3). Biblical teaching is that this kingdom is Christ's kingdom (Rev. 11:15).

In Daniel 3 the identity of the fourth man in the furnace is of particular interest. The pagan king Nebuchadnezzar says the man resembles "a son of the gods" (3:25). Because of the ambiguity of the Aramaic word "gods," the phrase could be understood by a believer as "the Son of God." The appearance of God in human form has biblical precedence. For example, God appeared to Abraham as a human visitor (Gen. 18:2,13). Also, "angel of the LORD" passages provide possible support of Old Testament appearances of the second member of the Trinity (e.g., Judg. 13:3,19–22). In the case of the young Judeans, this "Son of God" provided deliverance, an activity that is directly related to divine acts of salvation.

The third messianic text is the most important one. Chapter 7 communicates Daniel's vision of a heavenly court scene. The wicked fourth beast is judged before God, and the kingdoms of the world are given to "one like a son of man, coming with the clouds of heaven" (v. 13). This is the language Jesus used to describe himself (e.g., Matt. 24:30).

[16]For a thorough discussion see Gerard Van Groningen, *Messianic Revelation in the Old Testament* (Grand Rapids: Baker Book House, 1990), 788–846.

The last text, Dan. 9:25, speaks of "the Anointed One, the ruler" who will come in during Daniel's "seventy 'sevens' [traditionally interpreted as "weeks"]." Apart from the discussion concerning the nature and length of these "sevens," traditional Christian interpretation has taught that this "Anointed One" refers to the coming of the Messiah.

What Is Daniel's Message for Us?

Despite many critical questions, the message of the Book of Daniel is clear enough. First, God's sovereign power ensures the endurance of his eternal kingdom. The passing, and sometimes antagonistic, kingdoms of this world will not prevail. Daniel knew he was a citizen of a superior kingdom. Even Nebuchadnezzar came to that conclusion, confessing, "'His dominion is an eternal dominion; his kingdom endures from generation to generation'" (Dan. 4:34). This is a central message in the New Testament as well: It is Jesus' teachings about the "kingdom of God," Paul's Christological center of salvation, the Book of Hebrews' unshakable kingdom, and John the Revelator's heavenly visions.

Second, human pride is self-destructive.[17] Nebuchadnezzar lived like an animal for seven years until he surrendered to God (Dan. 4). Belshazzar is criticized for his pride (5:22–23). Darius's pride clouded his common sense (6:6–9). The "little horn" is destroyed because of its boasting (7:11). The "stern-faced king" believed himself superior to others (8:23–25). The final "king of the North" also is described as exalting himself (11:28,36).

revelation must have been a shock to Daniel. He had lived through the Babylonian exile. He then hoped to see God's final breaking into human history and the coming of the Messiah. But no, he and the rest of humanity would have to wait.

Scholars continue to debate the meaning of Daniel's "seventy 'sevens.'" Does this phrase refer to weeks or to years? Can we use this time period as Daniel's forecast of the time between him and the Messiah? What about that *seventieth* "seven"? Is it referring to John the Revelator's "great tribulation"? (Rev. 7:14). Despite all these questions (and more), believers can be sure that God's program of redemption is on track. Let us anticipate with confidence the day when wickedness will be gone and righteousness will rule.

[17]William T. Arnold, "Daniel," in *Evangelical Dictionary of Biblical Theology*, ed. Walter A. Elwell (Grand Rapids: Baker Book House, 1997), 140–42.

Third, God blesses his faithful followers. He rewarded Daniel and his friends with wisdom and honor (Dan. 1). He delivered Shadrach, Meshach, and Abednego because of their testimony of trust in him (3:16–18). And he saved Daniel from the lions because of his faithful piety (6:21–22). Deliverance in the end will come to those whose names are found in God's Book of Life. Whether we live to see that final day, or like Daniel, go to our rest to await the final consummation of the ages (see 12:13), we can find hope and strength in the "Ancient of Days" (7:9).

Eugene H. Merrill summarized the Book of Daniel this way: "The central theme of Daniel—that the arrogant, God-denying sovereignty of man will be overturned so that God might reign—finds unequivocal fulfillment in the eternal dominion of His saints who, despite all apparent evidence to the contrary, will eventually prevail."[18]

Wrapping It All Up

We have reviewed the closing days of the kingdom of Judah and her last kings. Although God sent his prophets to warn them, their disobedience brought them down. Or so it would seem. The preexilic visions of restoration were supplemented by the exilic visions of Ezekiel and Daniel. These prophets provided the Babylonian exiles with hope and light, which sustained them till the dawn of a better day.

---

[18]Eugene H. Merrill, *A Biblical Theology of the Old Testament,* ed. Roy B. Zuck, consulting eds. Eugene H. Merrill and Darrell L. Bock (Chicago: Moody Press, 1991), 395.

Study Questions

1. What was the dominant characteristic of Manasseh's reign? How long was it? What was his end?

2. What important events marked the reign of Josiah? What was the prophetic response to these happenings?

3. What events precipitated the invasion that caused Josiah's death? Describe the international scene and how and when it was being transformed.

4. How did these events lead to the fall of Jerusalem? Who captured it? When? Who were the Judean kings involved?

5. Who was Nahum? Whom did he prophesy against? Was it fulfilled? When? By whom?

6. Who was Zephaniah? What did he prophesy about?

7. Who was Jeremiah? What family did he come from? What was the burden of his message? What is the problem posed by the LXX text of the Book of Jeremiah? What distinctive prophecy is cited by the author of the Book of Hebrews?

8. What is the message of Habakkuk? When did he prophesy?

9. What is the message of Obadiah? When did he prophesy?

10. Who was Ezekiel? Where did he prophesy? What unique features does his book contain? How did he illustrate his sermons? How does his book close?

11. Who was Daniel? Where did he prophesy? When? What unique features are found in his book? What languages were used? Why? What parallels to the New Testament do you find?

For Further Reading

See also suggested reading for chap. 18.

Dillard, Raymond B., and Tremper Longman III. *An Introduction to the Old Testament*. Grand Rapids: Zondervan Publishing House, 1994.

Harrison, R. K. *Old Testament Introduction*. Grand Rapids: Wm. B. Eerdmans, 1969.

18

Malcolm Brubaker

The LORD Brought Back the Captives to Zion

Outline:

- How Did the Jews Get Home?
- What Did They Do After They Got There?
- What Other Opposition Did the Jews Face?
- What Spark Reignited the Jews to Complete the Temple?
- Haggai
- Zechariah
- Where Does Ezra the Priest Fit in His Own Book, and What Makes Him So Special?
- The Book of Nehemiah: How Do Politics and Religion Mix?
- Esther: What's a Classic Story of Humor, Heroism, and Haman Doing in the Bible, Without

"God" Being Mentioned!
- The Book of Malachi: What Happens in a Spiritual Cooldown?
- What Next? The Old Testament as an Unfinished Drama

Terms:

Jew
laws of the Medes and the Persians

It must have been electrifying news to the Jewish captives throughout the Babylonian Empire in 538 B.C. Their new political overlord, King Cyrus of Persia, had published a proclamation of freedom. It said they could return home! The long night of national and religious humiliation was ending. The coming day was rosy with anticipation.

But rose-colored glasses were soon pulled off by stark reality. This postexilic period would produce several challenges for the Jews.[1] First, there was the cultural challenge. The Jews were a minority in the world of nations that made up the Persian Empire. They were just one ethnic group in a multicultural kingdom that stretched from India to Egypt and from the Black and Caspian Seas to the Red and Arabian Seas. The pressure to merge with the cultural ways of pagan neighbors was strong. Why not just blend in?

Second, there was the political challenge. The Persian government granted only a dependent status to the community of Jews who would return to their homeland. Judah would become a minor province in the Persian sphere of governance. No Davidic king sat upon the throne in Jerusalem, just Persia-approved governors who answered to a satrap[2] in Samaria. Various ethnic groups would threaten even this limited political freedom. The threat of attack and legal action by hostile neighbors faced the Jews. Why not just give up?

---

[1] From the time of the Babylonian exile and their separation from the temple, the term "Jew" becomes appropriate for the Judeans who survived the hardships of that time. The term denotes a new historical phase for the descendants of Abraham. In exile they started what would later become the Talmudic academies in Babylonia and, eventually, the rise of the synagogue. Ezra would be an example of this new religious orientation and training.

[2] A satrap governed a province in the Persian Empire. Under the satrap were often several regional governors; cf. Ezra 1:8; 5:14.

Third, there was the spiritual challenge. The preexilic prophets had cast a vision of messianic grandeur that had sustained the exiles in their captivity. Faith in God and in his program of prophetic restoration had given them hope. But when the Jews returned to Judah they found adversity and hard work. Isaiah, Jeremiah, Ezekiel, and Micah had spoken of a prosperous land, a restored throne, and a purified people.[3] Why not just discard these pie-in-the-sky visions and the God who had promised them?

In this chapter we will look at six biblical writings that came out of this postexilic aftermath of Cyrus's decree. A likely chronological order of composition would be Haggai and Zechariah; Esther, Ezra, and Nehemiah; and Malachi. The Old Testament historical books of Ezra and Nehemiah record the story of the Jewish people who returned to rebuild their land, religion, and nation. The story of Esther records the saving role of a Jewish queen of Persia. The prophetic books of Haggai, Zechariah, and Malachi preserve the spiritual voices that guided the Jews' life with God. Collectively, these books reveal that God was faithfully working in history on behalf of his people. With God's help they would be up to the challenges facing them.

How Did the Jews Get Home? – Ezra 1 Through 2

Cyrus's decree of 538 B.C. ends 2 Chronicles and begins the Book of Ezra. The first six chapters of Ezra deal with the early Jewish returns to Judah: Ezra 1 through 2, the return under Sheshbazzar and Zerubbabel; Ezra 3 through 4, the altar rebuilt, the temple begun, and the Jews opposed; Ezra 5 through 6, the temple work completed. The Persian

A Time Line of Main Events

586 B.C. The Babylonian forces besiege Jerusalem, destroying the city and taking thousands of Hebrew people into captivity in Babylon.

538 B.C. The Medo-Persian forces under Cyrus the Great conquer Babylon, setting free captive peoples such as the Jews. They are allowed to either remain in Babylon or return to their homeland.

520 B.C. After a sixteen-year delay, the Jews begin again to rebuild their temple in Jerusalem. Four years later it is completed.

458 B.C. Ezra the scribe comes to Jerusalem with a royal order from King Artaxerxes to take charge of the religious life of Judea.

445 B.C. Nehemiah is appointed governor over Judea by King Artaxerxes.

[3]See Isa. 2:1–4; 9:1–7; 35:1–10; Jer. 31:31–37; 33:14–18; Ezek. 34:25–31; 36:24–38; 37:1–14; Mic. 4:1–5; 5:2–5.

Those Lists of "Begats"— The Bible's Family Tree

Have you ever wondered why biblical authors such as Ezra were so interested in genealogies? Those lists of names can be so boring! Despite teaching Old Testament survey classes for years, I dreaded those endless lists of "begats." But one day a thought hit me: *The reason why these lists bore me is that I have no ancestors in them!*

In fact, I am very interested in genealogy— mine! An hour away from where I live is the Mennonite Historical Society. It houses thousands of genealogies of people descended from Pennsylvania Germans— including the Brubakers. I have gone there, have spent time looking up

king's approach to conquest was to work with the grain of ethnicity rather than against it. The Assyrians had moved whole groups around. They deported huge numbers of Israelites from the Northern Kingdom and moved other peoples in (see 2 Kings 17:22–24). Babylon had followed suit. They took the survivors of the 586 B.C. Jerusalem holocaust to Babylon. By contrast, Cyrus, king of Persia, chose to allow displaced populations to return to their native lands. His decree authorized the Jews to rebuild their central temple at Jerusalem and live in Judah under Persian rule.

But would anyone want to leave the growing comfort of prosperous Babylon, risk the journey, and endure pioneer life? Ezra 1 and 2 record that over forty thousand Jews answered yes. Exile in a pagan land had not extinguished their hopes and dreams. They were still God's people. This hope was built upon the preexilic prophets and historians. Historians had recorded the causes for that judgment (2 Kings 17:7–20; 24:20). Preexilic prophets like Isaiah and Hosea had predicted that God would restore Israel after such a time (Isa. 40:1–2; Hos. 14:4–8). The exilic prophets Ezekiel and Daniel had sustained this hope.

Cyrus showed wisdom in allowing the Jewish people to reclaim the gold and silver temple utensils taken by the Babylonians (Ezra 1:7–11; see also Dan. 5:2–3). These were sacred objects, reminders of God's fulfilled promises of restoration. Sheshbazzar,[4] the appointed Jewish governor, oversaw the return of these temple objects.

[4]Sheshbazzar is probably a variant spelling for Shenazzar (1 Chron. 3:18), the fourth son of King Jehoiachin. Zerubbabel would then have been Sheshbazzar's nephew (cf. 1 Chron. 3:18; Ezra 3:2). Sheshbazzar may have been the leader of the returning exiles but may have died shortly after work on the temple was begun. It seems a lapse then set in, causing great distress to the prophets Haggai and Zechariah, who wanted the temple finished. As

What Did They Do After They Got There? – Ezra 3

The first community action taken by the repatriated Jews was to rebuild the altar of burnt offerings (Ezra 3). This action showed that they were returning not just to the land but also to their religious values. God had cast their ancestors out of the land because of disobedience. This first postexilic generation desired to please God. Pleasing God meant offering to him the appropriate sacrifices. They were able to celebrate the Feast of Tabernacles in their first year back home (Ezra 3:4). This feast reminded them of their people's time in the wilderness under Moses. As God had taken care of Israel then, so he would take care of them now.

After work on the altar, the people began work on the temple itself in the spring of 536 B.C. The ceremony marking the early foundational work produced different responses (Ezra 3:12–13). The survivors of the exile, now advanced in years, remembered the glory of Solomon's temple. Looking on the smaller size of, and inferior materials in, the reconstruction, they wept in sorrow. The younger generation, however, saw the beginning of God's new temple and wept in joy.

What Other Opposition Did the Jews Face? – Ezra 4

Progress in God's kingdom faced opposition in the postexilic community of faith. Many of the people living near Jerusalem had moved in after the Babylonians destroyed the temple. At first they offered to help, but when the Jews

names, and have even bought a book on the genealogy of the Brubakers.

My lack of interest in biblical genealogies stemmed from their listing no Brubakers! That realization made the difference for me. Lists of biblical names are now meaningful because they represent somebody's family tree. Furthermore, the point of a biblical genealogy is God's faithfulness to the families of Abraham in ancient Israel. I can now relate their interest in their past to my interest in my past. Just as God had been faithful to the families of Abraham in Israel, he has been faithful to the Brubaker families in America. And that's the significance of those "begats"!

a result, Zerubbabel, together with Joshua (Jeshua), the high priest, saw the foundation completed about sixteen years later (Hag. 1:14–15; Zech. 4:6–10).

It's Aramaic to Me!

Why did Ezra write 4:8 through 6:18 and 7:12–26 in the Aramaic language? This is a question asked at times by students of the Old Testament.

A short linguistic history lesson may answer that. Aramaic is a close relative of biblical Hebrew. Both languages stem from the descendants of Shem. So they are part of the Semitic family of languages. By the late Old Testament period, Aramaic had become the dominant language of government, trade, and learning in Assyria, Babylon, and Persia. The Jews taken into exile in Babylon and later released by Persia would have learned Aramaic.

Back to our original

declined, they then opposed the Jewish efforts at rebuilding (Ezra 4:1–5). The Jews regarded Yahweh's temple as particularly holy and they were Yahweh's people. Cyrus had given them permission to rebuild it. But through a combination of continual opposition, physical intimidation, and legal processes, these "enemies of Judah and Benjamin" had halted the temple project (4:1,24). It looked like the Jews' dreams of rebuilding their country were disappearing before the ugly reality of hate.

Ezra 4:6–23 is a parenthetical note about a time of later opposition.[5] The Gentile opposition continued after Haggai and Zechariah's era. Antagonistic letters were sent to Xerxes (486–465 B.C.) and Artaxerxes (464–423) requesting that the Persian government stop the Jewish reconstruction of the city. These written interventions may have had some success.[6] But the Book of Nehemiah documents their ultimate failure. God's kingdom would not be stopped by external threat.

What Spark Reignited the Jews to Complete the Temple? – Ezra 5 Through 6

After sixteen years of work stoppage on the temple, God raised up two prophets to get the work restarted in 520 B.C. (Ezra 5 through 6). Haggai and Zechariah's divinely inspired messages renewed the people's vision. The response

[5]Derek Kidner sees evidence of three letters of opposition in Ezra 4:6,7,8–23. See *Ezra and Nehemiah: An Introduction and Commentary,* TOTC (Downers Grove, Ill.: InterVarsity Press, 1974), 51. Artaxerxes' note in v. 21 that the work would stop only until he made further inquiry opened the door for Nehemiah's return with official approval to rebuild.

[6]Some argue that Neh. 1:2 refers to an attack upon Jerusalem in this postexilic time. Others argue that this reference is to the Babylonian attack in 586 B.C.

was another legal challenge from their enemies and the Persian bureaucracy. But the Persian king, Darius I, commanded his provincial administrators not only to allow the work to continue but also to provide assistance. And this time the people completed the task. The Jews dedicated the temple four years later, in 516 B.C. They marked this milestone with a joyous celebration of Passover and the Feast of Unleavened Bread (6:13–22).

The writings of Haggai and Zechariah further highlight the spiritual and religious aspects of the early postexilic period. Haggai's simple messages and Zechariah's complex visions renewed and sustained the temple project. Let's take a look at each of these two books in turn.

Haggai

Who Was Haggai?

We have minimal information about Haggai. He was one of the Babylonian exiles who took up Cyrus's offer to return. Jewish traditional teachings argue that he was an old man who had seen the former temple before its destruction (Hag. 2:3).

What Does Haggai Tell Us?

Four brief messages compose Haggai's prophecy. It is the second shortest book in the Old Testament (only Obadiah is shorter). In 520 B.C., over a period of four months, these four "words" were given: (1) Finish the temple, Haggai 1:1–15. (2) Be encouraged that God will help you, 2:1–9. (3) God will bless you, 2:10–19. (4) Zerubbabel–you are God's chosen governor, 2:20–23. We will briefly look at each message.

question. A quick look at the Aramaic section in Ezra 4:8 through 6:18 reveals that it contains copies of official correspondence between Persian provincial officials and Persian monarchs. The topic was the Jewish rebuilding of the Jerusalem temple. Ezra 7:12–26 is a copy of the decree from King Artaxerxes commissioning Ezra to go to Judea as head of religious affairs.

Thus the answer to the question. Ezra desired to accurately inform the reader of the relationship between the Jews and the Persian government. The Aramaic sections of the Book of Ezra reflect original documents, or excerpts from them, used in these transactions. It wasn't simply an arbitrary shift; it was a wish to accurately and emphatically reflect the official source.

First, on August 29, 520 B.C., God's message to the Jewish community was simple: Get to work! Haggai charged the people with wrong priorities. They were consumed with their own houses and lands while neglecting God's house. No wonder that they hadn't received divine blessings (1:9–11). Zerubbabel the governor and Joshua the high priest led the people in fearful obedience to God's word. God had stirred their hearts to respond to the prophetic message. They started the work.

Second, on October 17, God's word in Haggai 2:1–9 to the Jewish community was encouragement. The postexilic community was poor in comparison to the wealth of Solomon's era. He had lavished the first temple with the best materials crafted by the best skilled workers, brought in for the task from Phoenicia. Any survivor of the 586 B.C. defeat realized that the second temple could be built only with limited materials and craftsmanship. Apparently some of these "senior saints" made their observations in a critical spirit. Haggai reminded them that God's Spirit was with them (2:5). He prophesied that God would bring greater glory to this second temple than to the first. Scholars debate how this prophecy was fulfilled. It is possible that the resources promised by Darius's decree arrived at this time.[7] Also, some argue that the words have relevance to the coming of the Messiah. In any case, it is clear that Haggai's words motivated the people to continue the work. God was pleased with their labor.

Third, on December 18, God's word in Haggai 2:10–19 to the Jewish community was blessing. The Jewish people's

---

[7]Joyce Baldwin, *Haggai, Zechariah, Malachi: An Introduction and Commentary*, TOTC (Downers Grove, Ill.: InterVarsity Press, 1972), 48.

disobedience had resulted in God's disfavor upon all the work. It had defiled everything they touched. But now God announced that blessings would come to them because of their positive response in completing the temple.

Fourth, on December 20, God's word in 2:20–23 to the Jewish community was messianic. The message was directed to Zerubbabel, the Jewish governor appointed by the Persians. A Davidic descendant, Zerubbabel was called God's "signet ring" (v. 23). This piece of jewelry would be used for sealing official documents. It was a sign of authority. That the message had a messianic aspect is confirmed by Matthew's genealogy of Jesus. Zerubbabel is listed in the line of Christ (Matt. 1:12). His "royal" personage was an installment of Old Testament messianic hope. Some day God would send his Messiah.

Zechariah

Who Was Zechariah?

Haggai's contemporary and coworker Zechariah came from a priestly family. His grandfather Iddo is listed as one of the priests who had returned to Judah with Zerubbabel (Neh. 12:4). It is likely, therefore, that Zechariah was still a young man at the beginning of his ministry.

Who Wrote the Book?

The prophetic book that bears Zechariah's name is the longest of the Minor Prophets. Its visionary character, added to its length, makes it a challenging book to read and understand. Furthermore, scholarly debate on the unity of the book adds to the confusion. Some say that Zechariah 1 through 8 comes from about 520 B.C. but that chapters 9 through 14 come from someone writing at a later time.[8] Others say that any apparent differences in style or content between the two halves of the book overlook the many similarities.[9] My presentation assumes a traditional unity of the book while acknowledging that others may disagree.

What Sort of Literature Is It?

Zechariah 1 through 8 can be called "historical eschatology." In these chapters Zechariah expresses God's concern for the sixth century B.C. postexilic community. The theme is the same as Haggai's: The temple should be rebuilt. The remaining chapters (9 through 14) share an apocalyptic style with Daniel and parts of Isaiah, Ezekiel, and Zephaniah. These prophecies describe what we commonly call "the last days," when God will break into history for the last time. He will bring history to a climactic moment of military victory and the establishment of his kingdom.[10] These writings are rich with animal and numeric symbolism conveyed by visions and dreams. Accordingly, Zechariah 9 through 14 can be called "apocalyptic eschatology." The message of these chapters is the radical new world that God's intervention will bring.[11]

What Does Zechariah Tell Us?

The following outline shows how the two sections of Zechariah may be broken down:

[8]William LaSor, David Hubbard, and Frederic Bush, *Old Testament Survey: The Message, Form, and Background of the Old Testament,* 2d ed. (Grand Rapids: Wm. B. Eerdmans, 1996), 401–2.

[9]Baldwin, *Haggai,* 68–70.

[10]See, for example, Isa. 24 through 27; Ezek. 38 through 39; Dan. 7.

[11]LaSor, Hubbard, and Bush, *Old Testament Survey,* 411.

Chapters 1 Through 8: Night Visions and Messages
to Encourage the People

Ref.	Vision	Meaning
1:1–6	Introduction	
1:7–17	First Vision: God's Commander and His Scouts	The world is at peace.
1:18–21	Second Vision: Four Horns and Four Craftsmen	God will punish Judah's tormentors.
2:1–13	Third Vision: A Man With a Measuring Line	Jerusalem would be repopulated.
3:1–10	Fourth Vision: Clean Garments for the High Priest	The priesthood would be restored.
4:1–14	Fifth Vision: A Menorah With Two Olive Trees	The restoration of civil and religious authority.
5:1–4	Sixth Vision: A Flying Scroll	A curse on thieves.
5:5–11	Seventh Vision: A Woman in a Basket	Wickedness banished from the land.
6:1–8	Eighth Vision: Four Chariots	God controls the earth.
6:9–15	Crown for the High Priest	
7:1 through 8:23	A Question About Fasting and Four Sermons	

Chapters 9 Through 14: Prophetic Oracles

9:1–17	Coming of the Messianic King
10:1–12	The Lord's Care of His People
11:1–17	Two Shepherds: One Foolish and One Good
12:1 through 14:21	The Future of Jerusalem and God's People

The opening paragraph (Zech. 1:1–6) notes the date (October–November 520 B.C.) and reviews Israel's past disobedience that resulted in God's judgment. Verse 6 mentions that the people had accepted their judgment and had repented.

Eight night visions follow (1:7 through 6:8). They are

dated February 15, 519 B.C. (1:7).[12] There is a pattern repeated through much of these visions: Zechariah records the vision, he asks his angelic guide the meaning, and the guide gives the interpretation.[13] While the imagery is difficult at times, the overall teaching is clear: God is with his people, their leadership, and their rebuilding the land. One of the better-known verses makes this point well, "So he said to me, 'This is the word of the LORD to Zerubbabel: "Not by might nor by power, but by my Spirit," says the LORD Almighty'" (4:6).

Two additional messages end the first part of the book. First, Zechariah 6:9–15 is a message of encouragement for the high priest. God told the prophet to make a crown and place it on the head of Joshua the high priest. This was to indicate that God had chosen him to lead the temple rebuilding effort. Second, Zechariah 7 through 8 contains messages about past problems of disobedience contrasted with God's promised blessing. Zechariah 7:1 dates the first message December 7, 518 B.C. Zechariah 8 contains ten blessings God will bestow on his people. They include promises of safety, longevity, and rich crops for the people. They would be a people marked by truth and righteousness. They would all seek the LORD.

The title "An Oracle" divides the second half of Zechariah (9 through 14) into two sections: chapters 9 through 11 and chapters 12 through 14. These chapters contain a series of prophecies about God's ultimate victory in history. Jerusalem will be invincible against its enemies (9:13; 12:2–3). The messianic king will enter the city to bring peace

[12]Apparently Zechariah had all eight visions in one night (Zech. 1:8).

[13]Bill T. Arnold and Bryan E. Beyer, *Encountering the Old Testament: A Christian Survey* (Grand Rapids: Baker Book House, 1998), 466.

(9:9–17). In the final days God himself will return to the city: "On that day his feet will stand on the Mount of Olives, east of Jerusalem" (14:4).

The Book of Zechariah was a powerful word of encouragement to postexilic Jews. The colorful imagery of the night visions gave the people incentive to rebuild their temple. God was still very much involved in present history. The prophetic promises of the later oracles reminded them that they were God's people; he had not forgotten them. Though future trials would come, God would be with them. They would experience his forgiveness, spiritual cleansing, and holiness. God would be with them till the end of time.

Where Does Ezra the Priest Fit in His Own Book, and What Makes Him So Special?

Seven chapters into the Book of Ezra, Ezra himself makes his debut. The first six chapters have brought the reader up to date on the early days of the Jewish return to Judah, and the writer emphasizes the physical reconstruction of the temple. The last four chapters emphasize the spiritual rebuilding of the people themselves. In particular, the focus is on the need for God's people to keep their distinctive culture rooted in the covenant. Ezra played a key role in preserving the Jewish people from being corrupted by a pagan environment. He was commissioned by the Persian king Artaxerxes to leave Babylon and take charge of the religious affairs of the Jews in Judah.

Here is an outline of the final chapters of Ezra:

7:1–10	Summary of Ezra's Return
7:11–28	Ezra's Royal Authorization to Go to Jerusalem
8:1–14	List of Jews Who Came With Ezra
8:15–36	Preparations for the Trip and Safe Arrival
9:1–15	Ezra's Reactions and Prayer Concerning the Jews' Intermarriage With Pagans
10:1–17	Community Repentance and Council Concerning Intermarriage With Pagans
10:18–44	List of People Who Had Married Pagans

Who Was Ezra? – Ezra 7

Ezra is a perfect example of God's preparing a person to carry out a task. Ezra's task was to preserve Jewish faith and practice. Chapter 7 suggests four qualifications Ezra had for the job: The first was his pedigree. He was a priest descended from Aaron, Israel's first high priest (7:1–5). Ezra's link to Aaron would give him credibility among the Jews. The second was Ezra's training. He was a scribe learned in the Torah of Moses, which governed the Jewish people (7:6,11).[14] Failure to keep the Torah had resulted in the exile to Babylon. Postexilic obedience to the Torah would bring God's blessing. Ezra's third qualification was divine empowerment, expressed in the phrase "the hand of the LORD his God was on him" (7:6; cf. vv. 9,28). The Holy Spirit blessed Ezra with success. Ezra 7:11–26 records the letter from King Artaxerxes authorizing Ezra to go to Jerusalem from Babylon. The king gave him permission to raise funds and even tap into Persian

---

[14]In biblical times the ability to read and write was not something taken for granted. A scribe *(sopher)* was one who had those skills and who, therefore, could keep records (as Shaphan, 2 Kings 22:3) or could write down what was orally given to him (as Baruch, Jer. 36:32). In Ezra 7:6,11,12,21 and Neh. 12:26 the term is used as a title of respect for Ezra, meaning one who is learned (Ezra 7:10) and who therefore could teach others (Neh. 8:1–5,6,9,13), as one would use the term "scholar" or "professor" today.

treasuries for the trip's expenses. Ezra's fourth qualification was his mission. The text stresses that the purpose for his trip was to teach the Torah to the people (7:10,25). Artaxerxes' letter also commissioned Ezra to go to Jerusalem as a teacher of God's law with the power to regulate religious matters (7:14,25–26). All these qualifications made Ezra a model of both preparation and piety.

Ezra's Travel to Jerusalem – Ezra 7 Through 8

Ezra 8 summarizes the preparations, personnel, and perils faced by the Jewish repatriates in 458 B.C. Over 1,500 men, plus women and children, joined Ezra in the journey back to Judah (listed in 8:1–14). Many of the family names are the same as those of the Jews who had returned under Sheshbazzar and Zerubbabel.[15] Ezra recruited Levites and descendants of temple servants to join his group (Ezra 8:15–20). He divided the gold and silver intended for the temple. He gave a portion of the money to different families to keep safe while traveling. After prayer and fasting the people set out on their long journey. They trusted in God's protection from the dangers of armed attack.

Four months later Ezra and his party arrived in Jerusalem safely (7:8–9). God had protected them without incident. They celebrated their arrival with a series of burnt offerings to the Lord (8:35).

What Cultural Challenges Did Ezra Face?
– Ezra 9

Within a few months after arrival in Jerusalem, Ezra faced a major problem (Ezra 9:1–2). He was told that many

---

[15]Kidner, *Ezra and Nehemiah*, 65.

were taking as wives women from among the Gentiles living nearby. Ezra's list of nations sounds like a list of those
people who occupied the land of Israel in the days of Moses
and Joshua (Exod. 34:11–16; Deut. 7:1–4). The parallel is
intentional.[16] The Jewish people were in jeopardy. Their
danger lay not in military defeat but in cultural compromise. Levites, priests, and community leaders had married
Gentiles. The language of the report to Ezra is strongly
worded. It says, "'They . . . have mingled the holy race with
the peoples around them'" (Ezra 9:2).

"So what!" you might say. "There is no sin in marrying
people of another race." This statement, however, was not
true for the returning exiles. The real issue was not one of
race but one of religion and ethics. Just as with Solomon,
these marriages to non-Jewish people had resulted in the
decline of the Jews' spiritual and religious fervor. The Jews'
social, religious, and ethical teachings had given them a distinctive faith and way of life. The recent Babylonian exile
had been the result of Judah's violations of those very pre-
cepts. The Gentile partners in these marriages had little
interest in keeping the terms of the Mosaic covenant.
Would the Jewish people again slip into pagan ways of living and believing that contradicted their relationship with
God? That is the crisis represented by their intermarriage,
which Ezra faced when he came to Jerusalem.

Ezra's reaction to the problem was dramatic: He tore his
clothes, pulled hair from his head, and sat down. These
were customary reactions to bad news, such as the death of
a loved one. He remained in this dejected state all day.
Others who were also appalled by these "mixed marriages"
joined him.

16Ibid., 68.

Ezra's reaction to the problem was also verbal. At the close of the day he prayed (Ezra 9:6–15). His prayer was a corporate one: He uses "we" and "our." His prayer had a historical tone: It reviewed the disobedient history of Israel. His prayer was also hopeful: Perhaps God's mercy would yet be sufficient to forgive.

What Impact Did Ezra Have on the People? –Ezra 10

Ezra's lament and prayer moved the Jewish community to repent of their sinful marriages (Ezra 10). The religious and civic leaders themselves took an oath to sever any such marriages. They also called a special convocation to deal with the matter. The winter rain that fell upon the people who had gathered before the temple added to their distress. The assembled people established an investigative commission to review every mixed marriage. Ezra appointed men to the commission. In the following three months each case was reviewed. The Book of Ezra closes with the list of men who had married foreign women. These women and any children born to these marriages were sent back to their own people to care for them.

Ezra had succeeded in his mission to teach and uphold the laws of God. His personal example and righteous leadership ensured the preservation of God's people. We will later see a more joyful side of Ezra's religious influence in the Book of Nehemiah.

The Book of Nehemiah: How Do Politics and Religion Mix?

Nehemiah's book continues the story of the struggles of the small Persian province of Judah in the postexilic period.

While Ezra was a religious figure, Nehemiah was a political one. Yet we will find that Nehemiah was no less an exemplary spiritual person. His book outlines a story of personal piety joined with official duties:

1:1–4	News of Jerusalem's Plight
1:5–11	Nehemiah's Prayer
2:1–10	Artaxerxes Sends Nehemiah to Jerusalem
2:11–20	Nehemiah's Inspection of the City, and Local Gentile Opposition
3:1–32	Organization of Laborers for Rebuilding the Wall
4:1–23	Progress of Work on the Wall Despite Threats
5:1–19	Nehemiah's Social Reforms and Personal Example
6:1 through 7:3	More Opposition but the Wall and Gates Are Completed
7:4–73	List of Families Who Had First Returned from Babylon
8:1–18	Public Reading of the Torah and Celebration of Feast of Tabernacles
9:1–37	Public Repentance and Corporate Prayer of Confession
9:38 through 10:39	Public Agreement to Keep the Torah
11:1–36	Forced Repopulation of Jerusalem
12:1–26	List of Priests and Levites
12:27–47	Wall Dedication
13:1–31	Issues During Nehemiah's Second Term as Governor

How Is Judah Faring?

Our last look at the people of Judah was promising: By 458 B.C. they had rebuilt the temple. They had begun to rebuild the city. They had constructed homes. They had pledged to follow the Torah of God. But as we turn the biblical page from the Book of Ezra to that of Nehemiah, we advance thirteen years to 445 B.C. to discover difficulties. Their Gentile neighbors continued to be antagonistic. These enemies actually attacked Jerusalem (Neh. 1:2–3). Its walls had been made rubble, and its gates, ashes. A walled city was a symbol of status as well as security. The Jews felt humiliated and vulnerable.

How Did Nehemiah Respond to the Crisis? – Neh. 1

At the time, Nehemiah was employed as a cupbearer[17] to King Artaxerxes of Persia. When he heard the news of the attack upon Jerusalem from his brother, Hanani, his piety is immediately evident. This Persian-employed politician mourned, fasted, and prayed (Neh. 1:4–11). Throughout his memoirs we see a person fully relying upon God. He prays to the Lord both formally (as here) and informally (2:4). His opening prayer is a model of biblical faith and intercessory prayer. In it Nehemiah recognized God's might and faithfulness (1:5). He used the pronoun "we" to confess the sinfulness of his people, even though he himself had not been a part of that sin (1:6–7). He based his prayer on God's past promises (1:8–9). He concluded with a request for his success in pleading for Jerusalem with the king (1:10–11).

What Obstacles Did Nehemiah Face in Completing His Goals? – Neh. 2

Nehemiah 2 records God's answer to Nehemiah's prayer. King Artaxerxes granted Nehemiah permission to go to Judah to rebuild Jerusalem's gates and walls. This was

The Praying Governor

Nehemiah is remembered as the skilled administrator appointed by Artaxerxes to rebuild the broken-down walls and gates of Jerusalem in 445 B.C. But his venture was blessed by God because he was a person of prayer. He responded to the original report about the city with prayer (Neh. 1:4,6,11). He prayed while he worked on the walls (6:9). He interjected brief prayers in his book for God to remember him (e.g., 5:19; 13:22,31).

My favorite prayer of Nehemiah is also his shortest—as well as being unrecorded! Chapter 2 recounts his talk with King Artaxerxes. The king had noticed Nehemiah's sadness. Nehemiah related the report of Jerusalem's destroyed walls and gates. Then the king

(cont. on the next page)

---

[17]A cupbearer in the Persian Empire tasted the wine to see if it was poisoned, before passing it to the king. He was someone who had immediate access to the king. The position thus speaks of someone who enjoyed the complete confidence of the king and sometimes became the royal confidant.

The Praying Governor (cont.)

asked him, "'What is it you want?'" The text (2:4–5) notes his silent response: "Then I prayed to the God of heaven, and I answered the king."

Nehemiah is a good role model for us. We too can be assured that God hears our prayers whether they be short or long, formal or informal—including abrupt cries for help.

to be done at the Persian government's expense. Nehemiah would assume the role of governor. His arrival in Judah marked the beginning of a twelve-year term of office (5:14).

Nehemiah encountered several obstacles. First, he needed information about the size of the task. He gained it by a secretive inspection of the city by night (2:11–15). He followed this with his first appeal to the leaders to rebuild the walls and gates. This met with a good response (2:16–18). The Jews seemed eager to begin the work.

But there were those threatening Gentile neighbors! Scripture names three of them as Nehemiah's key opponents (2:19). They were Sanballat the Horonite, Tobiah the Ammonite, and Geshem the Arab.[18] They were regional leaders of different ethnic groups who had a vested interest in keeping the Jews from prospering (2:10). Possibly they had been responsible for the work stoppage mentioned in Ezra 4:6–23 and the destruction cited in Nehemiah 1:3. They had sufficient military capability to be a genuine threat. They seemed even more confident in their ability to use military threats as a propaganda tool to stop the work (2:19; 4:1–3,7–8,11). These enemies even hired false prophets to frighten Nehemiah into a fearful retreat to the temple sanctuary (6:10–14). There were enemies outside the city in the countryside and there were informants inside. Nehemiah had to be careful. For example, his initial survey of the city's fallen walls had been at night to avoid the hostile scrutiny of his enemies.

[18]Sanballat's town was probably Upper or Lower Beth Horon, towns northwest of Jerusalem. Tobiah was probably governor of the Transjordan. Geshem was probably a leader of people from Arabia who had moved into the Transjordan after Assyria invaded it in the late eighth century B.C.

How Did Nehemiah Win the Hearts of His Countrymen? – Neh. 3 Through 5

Despite threats from the enemy, Nehemiah's encouraging words to the people and clever tactics kept the project going. Dividing the task into family-assigned sections made the total project feasible for the workers (Neh. 3:1–32). Keeping the workers armed with weapons as well as tools inspired a spirit of patriotic courage (4:13–23). The blast of a trumpet (ram's horn) served as the mode of communicating any place of attack. But ultimately it was Nehemiah's trust in God that won the day. He told the people, "'Our God will fight for us!'" (4:20).

Nehemiah's courage and detailed planning brought him success in his mission. But it was his administrative style that brought him respect (5:14–18). In contrast to recent governors, Nehemiah refused to burden the people by making them support him.[19] Further, he provided a daily meal to 150 people and paid for it out of his own resources. Neither he nor his subordinates used their influence to gain land.

Nehemiah also reformed Judah economically. Times were hard.[20] The landless had no money for food. The landowners didn't have enough money to pay the king's tribute. They borrowed money. In violation of the Mosaic laws, the rich began charging interest for loans (Neh. 5:7;

[19]Other governors had taxed the people for both food and money. Nehemiah's indictment probably does not refer to Sheshbazzar and Zerubbabel. Although translated "governor," the Heb. word is used for various Persian officials (Ezra 5:3,6; 6:6–7,13; 8:36; Neh. 2:7,9; 3:7) and probably speaks of those after Zerubbabel but before Nehemiah.

[20]See note on Neh. 5:1–19 in The NIV Study Bible (Grand Rapids: Zondervan Publishing House, 1995).

cf. Exod. 22:25–27).[21] Some even had to sell family members into slavery to other Jews to gain enough money to live on.

How were these matters to be handled? The construction project would be threatened by lack of support if every social class were not treated justly. Nehemiah's reaction was immediate—anger! Then after reflecting upon the problem he called the nobles and officials. He confronted them with the social discontent that was brewing (Neh. 5:1–13). The wealthy class responded positively to his rebuke. They agreed to return money exacted in interest. They took an oath before God not to charge interest again.

Is it any wonder that God's people treasured the memoirs of Nehemiah? Here was a people's politician who administered fairness out of the fear of God (5:15).

So What Happened?–Neh. 6 Through 7

Nehemiah achieved his primary goal. The walls and gates were rebuilt despite the obstacles (6:15 through 7:3). The total time for this construction was fifty-two days! The gates were set in place. Guards were assigned their posts. The city was secure. When God's people are in unity and have a mind to work, who knows what they can do?

Where Did the Word of God Fit Into Human Effort and Ability?–Neh. 8 Through 10

At this point, the narrative in the book shifts from Nehemiah the governor to Ezra the learned scribe. Ezra released the power of God's Word in a series of events that

---

[21]The biblical principle is that you loan to a brother or sister to help, not to victimize. "Interest" in biblical terminology does not mean the modest amounts paid *by* banks on deposits or *to* banks for loans in modern society. Rather, it means charging exorbitant rates, rates more in keeping with loan-sharking today.

began with a public reading of the Torah. On the Feast of Trumpets,[22] the people gathered in the Water Gate square. Ezra, standing on a high platform, read from the Torah of Moses. From time to time he would stop to let the Levites explain or interpret what had been read.[23] The people stood to listen. They raised their hands and shouted, "Amen! Amen!" They bowed in worship. The Word convicted their hearts and they wept. Ezra, Nehemiah, and the leaders recognized the hand of God upon this event. They called for a season of celebration because the people had heard and understood the Scripture.

A second event was the eight days the people celebrated the Feast of Tabernacles (Neh. 8:14–18). The feast recalled Israel's forty years of desert wanderings (Exod. 23:14–17; Lev. 23:34,42). The Jews showed their obedience to the LORD by observing it.

On a third occasion when the Word of God was read, the Levites led a public prayer of confession (Neh. 9:5–38). It summarized Israel's years of rebellion against God and closed with an appeal to God's mercy for continued help.

And lastly, the people signed a covenant to God (Neh. 10). They pledged to remain separate from their pagan neighbors, keep the Sabbath, and support the temple financially. All these events took place because Scripture was given its proper place in the people's lives and beliefs.

---

[22]The first day of the civil new year, October 8, 444 B.C.

[23]After more than a century of Babylonian and Persian rule, Aramaic had become the language of the common people. It is thought that Ezra read the Torah in Hebrew and another Levite gave the sense of the passage in Aramaic. Later on, these Aramaic paraphrases would become more or less fixed. They eventually were written down and became known as "the translations," that is, the Targums.

What's a Wall Without People?
—Neh. 11 Through 12

Nehemiah ordered a census of the province to determine the Jewish population in the ninety-some years since the first Babylonian exiles had returned in 538 B.C.[24] The census found that most of the people were living in the surrounding towns and villages. The city of Jerusalem was sparsely populated. The people agreed to increase Jerusalem's numbers by voluntary and forced relocation (Neh. 11:1–2). One tenth of the total population would live in the holy city. The lists reflect the importance of the tribes of Judah, Benjamin, and Levi.[25] They were the ones who stayed true to the Davidic kings in preexilic times, and they were the ones who formed the core of postexilic Judah.[26]

Nehemiah 12 records the great day of celebration and dedication of Jerusalem's wall. The first generation of returnees had rejoiced in completing the second temple (Ezra 6:13–18). Nehemiah's generation rejoiced in rebuilding Jerusalem's walls and gates. Two great columns of Levitical singers and musicians formed at one location. Ezra led one group around in a counterclockwise direction. Nehemiah led the second group in a clockwise direction. What a meeting they must have had as they reunited on the other side of the city! The circle of Jerusalem's defenses was complete.

Whatever Happened to Nehemiah?—Neh. 13

Nehemiah's later years are obscure (Neh. 13). Apparently his term as governor lasted twelve years (445 to

[24]Neh. 7:4–73 duplicates Ezra 2:1–70. The list in Neh. 11:3–19 duplicates one in 1 Chron. 9:1–17.

[25]See Neh. 12:1–26 for another list of the postexilic priests and Levites.

[26]Kidner, *Ezra and Nehemiah,* 117.

433 B.C.). Afterward, he returned to serve Artaxerxes again. Some time later he was reappointed governor of Judah. He again was faced with apostasy among the Jews. He again dealt with marriages to foreigners, neglect of the temple area, and the lack of financial support for the temple. His tactics were tough but the issues were critical.[27] The closing verse could be a prayer for all believers: "Remember me with favor, O my God" (13:31).

What Lessons Can We Learn From Ezra-Nehemiah?

Ezra-Nehemiah suggests four lessons.[28] First, we must value historical continuity. The postexilic community saw itself as part of God's ongoing kingdom. Thus they valued genealogies because these lists linked them to preexilic Israel. They felt connected to their physical and spiritual ancestors. Similarly, we the New Testament church are a part of God's kingdom. We too should prize our spiritual predecessors. Second, we should value the role of worship and the Word of God. The temple represented the presence of God to postexilic people; it was where they expressed their public worship of God. The value of God's Word caused Ezra to study it, learn it, and teach it.

---

[27]Contrast the actions of Ezra with those of Nehemiah. When Ezra first heard about the mixed marriages, he tore his clothes, pulled his hair, sat down appalled, and prayed (Ezra 9:2–6). Nehemiah rebuked some men involved in such a marriage, beat *them,* pulled some of *their* hair, and made *them* take an oath to abstain from marrying Gentiles (Neh. 13:25). The difference may be in the differing circumstances: Ezra's authority was primarily a spiritual one; moreover, he had just arrived in Jerusalem. The reference to Nehemiah describes his actions in his second term as governor, years after Ezra had dealt with the problem. Nehemiah knew that these men knew better and could be held to greater accountability.

[28]LaSor, Hubbard, and Bush, *Old Testament Survey,* 563–65.

Scripture had an important place in their religious lives. It revealed their sins and encouraged their repentance. It gave them their identity as a people holy to the LORD. Third, we should value the importance of writing. The books of Ezra and Nehemiah begin with a king's decree. Both include correspondence between provincial officials and the royal government. Both stress the value of God's written Word. In the postexilic world, Judaism became centered on preserving and interpreting divine revelation. The early Christians adopted the same focus, passing along the legacy of being people of the Book. Fourth, we should value God's future work. In Ezra-Nehemiah there is an expectation that God was not done with Israel. He had a purpose and plan for the postexilic community of faith. This gave them a hope for what God would do in the future.

Esther: What's a Classic Story of Humor, Heroism, and Haman Doing in the Bible, Without "God" Being Mentioned!

Esther is a book of Jewish humor. It describes the heroism of a beautiful queen. It has a villain, Haman. It contains elements of supreme irony and poetic justice. But the unique thing about the Book of Esther is the conspicuous absence of any mention of God. So we are back to the original question: How did a book without God's name get into God's Book? We will come back to this matter later. But first we'll look at some other matters.

What Is the Setting of the Story of Esther?

The story takes place in Susa, one of three Persian royal cities. It had been the capital of Elam until taken over by the Persians (see Dan. 8:2). Darius rebuilt it and Xerxes reno-

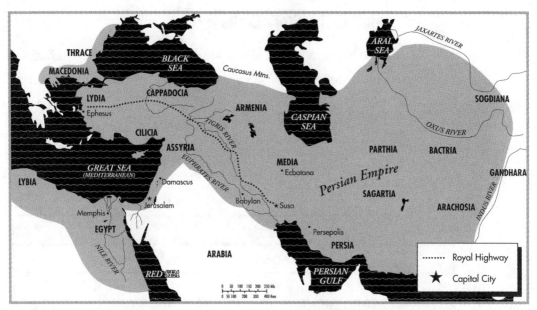

World of Nations Making Up the Persian Empire

vated it. Nehemiah would later be the cupbearer to King Artaxerxes in this same city. The time is the reign of Xerxes (486–465 B.C.). He was the fourth Persian monarch, following Cyrus, Cambyses II, and Darius.

What Is This Book About?

The Book of Esther narrates the tale of a young Jewish girl who became a queen. The villain Haman, an honoree of the king, wanted to kill all Jews. He tricked the king into decreeing a special day so he and his coconspirators could attack them, being without defense. At the urging of Mordecai, an elder cousin, Esther crafted a plan to expose Haman's plot. It worked: Haman was executed; Xerxes, unable to rescind the law (because a law of the Medes and the Persians was immutable; cf. Dan. 6:15), allowed the Jews to defend themselves on the designated day, and they defeated all their foes.

How Is This Story Crafted?

This is a well-crafted story: Its setting, key characters, plot, action, and resolution are a seamless production. Some see a chiastic[29] structure (see chap. 12). Others suggest a "problem-solution" format.[30] An easy-to-remember approach organizes the story around three series of feasts.[31] Here is an outline based on that approach:

1:1 through 2:18	The Feasts of Xerxes
1:1–22	Vashti Deposed
2:1–18	Esther Made Queen
2:19 through 7:10	The Feasts of Esther
2:19–23	Mordecai Uncovers a Plot
3:1–15	Haman's Plot
4:1–17	Mordecai Persuades Esther to Help
5:1–8	Esther's First Banquet
5:9 through 6:14	A Sleepless Night
7:1–10	Esther's Second Banquet
8 through 10	The Feasts of Purim
8:1–17	The King's Edict on Behalf of the Jews
9:1–32	The Institution of Purim
10:1–3	The Promotion of Mordecai

[29]See Joyce Baldwin, *Esther: An Introduction and Commentary*, TOTC (Downers Grove, Ill.: InterVarsity Press, 1984), 30.

[30]Arnold and Beyer, *Encountering the Old Testament*, 272.

[31]Raymond B. Dillard and Tremper Longman, *An Introduction to the Old Testament* (Grand Rapids: Zondervan Publishing House, 1994), 190.

How Did Esther Become Queen of Persia?
—Esther 1 Through 2

The story begins with Xerxes and Vashti, king and queen of Persia, hosting two feasts. One was for men and the other for women (Esther 1:1–9). These feasts were sumptuous affairs, with plenty of food and drink served on the palace grounds. Vashti, however, declined Xerxes' invitation to show off her beauty before the men at their feast. Xerxes felt pressure to publicly respond with a royal edict that wives should obey their husbands (1:10–22). He also demoted Vashti and looked for another woman to be his queen (2:1–4).

In the search for a new queen, Esther, a beautiful Jewish girl, was added to the king's harem. She so pleased the king that Xerxes declared her the new queen (2:5–18). The king, however, did not know she was Jewish. Mordecai, a close relative, had raised her as his daughter. While sitting at the city gate, Mordecai overheard a plot to assassinate the king. Mordecai sent word to Esther, who informed the king. The plot failed and the men were executed (2:19–23).

Why Was Haman the Villain?
—Esther 3 Through 7

Haman, a close adviser to Xerxes, hated the Jews and received permission to attack them (Esther 3:1–15). Mordecai informed Esther of Haman's plot and pressed her to act on behalf of her own people. She agreed to approach the king (4:1–17). Esther arranged two private dinners with Xerxes and Haman to disclose Haman's plot. Just before the second dinner, the king's insomnia resulted in his finding out that Mordecai had not been rewarded for discovering the assassination plot. For his reward, Xerxes commanded Haman to honor Mordecai by taking him around town on the king's horse. At the second dinner Esther told Xerxes that she was Jewish and that Haman desired to kill the Jews. The king commanded Haman's death.

What Became of Haman's Plot? – Esther 8 Through 10

Xerxes could not change the original edict allowing for the attack on the Jews. He did issue a new edict allowing the Jews to prepare and arm themselves for the day of the attack (Esther 8:1–17). The Jews successfully defended themselves when the day came (9:1–17). To commemorate their victory they established a series of feasts (9:18–32). These feast days were called "Purim." They were named after the casting of a lot (*pur*) that was used by Haman to choose the day of attack (see vv. 24,26). The story concludes with a note about Mordecai's later successful career.

Why Did Haman Hate the Jews?

Look at Haman's initial entry into the story. Esther 3:1 notes, "After these events, King Xerxes honored Haman son of Hammedatha, the Agagite." It is Haman's ethnic identity that unlocks the reason for his hatred. Look back five hundred years to 1 Samuel 15. There we find the clue. King Saul's campaign against the Amalekites resulted in their decimation and the death of their king, Agag. Haman's ancestors had recounted this ancient feud and passed its hatred down to him. He hated the Jewish people for nearly destroying his own people five hundred years earlier! Mordecai had refused to bow to Haman in the streets of Susa. This further angered

Haman. Mordecai was from the tribe of Benjamin and the family of King Saul (Esther 2:5). So Haman and Mordecai were descended from ancient foes!

Why Didn't the Jews Plunder Their Defeated Foes?

Three times in Esther 9 the writer notes that the Jews "did not lay their hands on the plunder." The Jews had permission to defend themselves and take anything they wanted from their defeated foes, yet they did not (9:10,15,16). Again, the key is found in 1 Samuel 15. God's instructions had been not to plunder the Amalekites but to destroy them. That is what God had instructed Joshua to do at Jericho (Josh. 6:18–19,24). Saul had failed to follow such instructions. Instead, he kept the best of the spoils. God, however, exposed his disobedience and deposed him from being king. In Esther's day, the Jews did not want to commit the sin of Saul.

Okay . . . But Why Is Esther in the Bible?

By now you may have a sense of how this question may be answered. The Book of Esther is a story of deliverance from cruel and powerful forces. The deliverance did not come about through Queen Esther's cleverness. Nor did it happen because of just plain chance, a roll of the dice. Neither was it the result of Xerxes' insomnia. Rather, deliverance for God's people came about because of God's sovereign intervention. Though the narrative or the characters never mention his name, his influence is on every page. It may be seen in Vashti's demotion, Esther's selection, Mordecai's discovery of a plot, his counsel of Esther, Esther's warm reception by the king in his court, her

"Booing" the Villain

The Jewish tradition for reading the Book of Esther at the feast of Purim is fascinating. Each Jewish child is given a noisemaker (whistle, sticks to strike together, small drum or percussion toy, etc.). The synagogue reader instructs the children to listen carefully as the story is read. Whenever they hear the name "Haman," they are to make a noise! That way the very sound of this ancient evil foe can be drowned out with their racket.

So the next time you read aloud the story of Esther (or even just a passage having Haman's name), instruct your audience to get anything out of their pockets or purses that makes a noise (tip: a ring of keys works well). Have them join in the tradition of drowning out the evil name of "Haman."

skillful plan, Xerxes' insomnia, and Haman's blind hatred. These all point to divine involvement. As one source observes, "Coincidences in Esther are the fingerprints of God's hand at work."[32]

The book's central verse points to God's unseen role. Mordecai said to Esther, "'If you remain silent at this time, relief and deliverance for the Jews will arise from another place, but you and your father's family will perish. And who knows but that you have come to royal position for such a time as this?'" (4:14). Esther's story is about the God who saves his people and delivers them from their enemies.

Who Wrote the Book of Esther, and When?

There is no information on the author. Presumably a Jew in the Persian diaspora wrote it shortly after the events recorded in it. What is obvious is that this person was skilled in storytelling. We can be grateful to God for such a brilliant story of his providence and preservation.

The Book of Malachi: What Happens in a Spiritual Cooldown?

Our last book in this chapter—and in the Old Testament—tells how the prophet Malachi confronted indifference in the people of Judah. Indifference had stunted their spiritual growth. Mediocrity, worldliness, and even cynicism had resulted. Malachi saw that marital bonds had weakened, support for the rebuilt temple had declined, and the people had lost their messianic fervor. We will examine these issues as well as others in our study of the "last prophetic voice" of the Old Testament.

[32]LaSor, Hubbard, and Bush, *Old Testament Survey,* 538.

What Do We Know About Malachi Himself?

As with the prophets Joel and Obadiah, we know very little about Malachi except that he lived in Jerusalem. Even his name is questioned (Mal. 1:1). It literally means "my messenger." Some argue that the book is anonymous. They interpret the opening verse to say, "An oracle: the word of the LORD to Israel by my messenger."[33] The Septuagint supports that view by translating the last phrase "by the hand of his messenger." Moreover, "Malachi" is not found as a name elsewhere in the Old Testament. Others argue that the verse reads naturally as an opening ascription of authorship and that "Malachi" should be retained as a name.[34]

The book contains no dates or historical references. The internal evidence, however, requires a postexilic dating. A governor and a temple are mentioned (1:8,10). Social conditions appear to be similar to the days of Ezra and Nehemiah.[35] Since they are not mentioned by name in the book, Malachi may have prophesied before their arrival in Judah (Ezra, 458 B.C.; Nehemiah, 445).

What Unique Literary Traits Characterize Malachi?

There is one dominant literary feature in the book: disputation. The Book of Malachi relays to the reader what the people thought as they listened to the prophet's messages. They frequently objected to what they heard, whether negative or positive. The prophet would then

[33]See ibid., 415.

[34]Baldwin, *Haggai,* 212.

[35]Dillard and Longman, *Introduction to the Old Testament,* 439.

respond with God's rebuttal. Malachi used this technique six times. This produces a six-part outline for the book:

1:1–5	Dispute About the Love of God
1:6 through 2:9	Dispute With Priests Who Despised God
2:10–16	Dispute With Judah About Broken Faith With God
2:17 through 3:5	Dispute With the People Who Had Wearied God
3:6–12	Dispute About Repentance and Tithing
3:13 through 4:3	Dispute About the People's Harsh Words Toward God
4:4–6	Final Encouragement to Remember the Torah and Look Forward to "Elijah"

What Does Malachi Teach Us About God?

The six disputations center on God's nature.[36] First, the prophet proclaims that God loves his people (Mal. 1:2; 1 John 4:8). The hard conditions faced in rebuilding their capital and temple had led some to question the LORD's benevolent care for them. He cares for his people despite what negative circumstances might suggest. Second, the prophet declares that God is the Father and Master of his people (Mal. 1:6). He deserves proper respect and reverence. Our worship of the LORD should attribute to him praise and honor. Third, since God is Father and Creator of his people, the people should uphold their covenant with him (2:10). God's people should live holy lives free of worldliness. Fourth, God is just (2:17). When evil seems to triumph, we, like Judah, tend to forget that God still rules. But right will win out. God will see to it. Fifth, God is changeless (3:6). Our modern society may need this truth

[36]Ibid., 441–42.

even more than fifth century B.C. Judah. We need to know that his character is constant. His ways with us are the same as with Old Testament Israel. Sixth, serving God is not pointless but will result in his blessings (3:14–18). His word is true. We should not doubt either his resolve to save repentant hearts or his punishment of the wicked.

What Significant Legacy Does Malachi Leave Us?

The book closes on a command and a promise.[37] The command is to remember the Torah of Moses (Mal. 4:4). God had given Israel his words of guidance for a blessed life (Ps. 119). We, too, should heed God's commands.

The Jews were to wait for the promised "Elijah" (4:5–6).[38] This "Elijah" would be the forerunner of the great day of the LORD. God had future plans for his people. Thus the Old Testament ends on a note of expectancy for the Lord's coming. We leave its pages looking for the ultimate wrapping up of divine history.

So, Is Postexilic Judah the Zenith of Old Testament Spirituality?

We have seen some great people. There are the prophets, Haggai, Zechariah, and Malachi. By their preaching and visions they encouraged the Jews who had returned to Judah. There are the governors, Zerubbabel and Nehemiah. They guided the rebuilding of Jerusalem. There is the priestly scribe Ezra. He centered the Jewish community

Malachi's "Adolescent" Audience

Is there anything as annoying as someone who talks back using your own words? Parents tell their young teen, "Take out the trash." The teen retorts, "Who me? Take out the trash?" Or, "Set the table for dinner." "Who me? Set the table?"

I find the Israelites' retorts to Malachi's preaching similar. God revealed to the prophet certain truths or judgments about Israel. But they wouldn't listen. They talked back to Malachi ("disputation"). Six times the people attempt to deflect God's word to them. Each time God responds to their "adolescent" talk with an explanation.

A proof of spiritual adulthood is receiving God's criticism as well as his encouragement (Heb. 12:5–11). In that case, Malachi dealt with spiritual adolescents!

[37]Arnold and Beyer, *Encountering the Old Testament,* 473.

[38]Matt. 11:14; 17:12; Mark 9:11–13; and Luke 1:17 interpret "Elijah" as John the Baptist.

on holiness and Scripture. There are Esther and Mordecai. God helped them to thwart a vicious attack against their people, the Jews.

But we have also seen that there were spiritual problems to be faced. Haggai and Zechariah fought discouragement and disappointment. Ezra and Nehemiah fought worldly compromise. They along with Esther had to overcome opposition from other ethnic groups who opposed the success of the Jews. Malachi contended with an indifferent Jewish community in need of a message of hope for the future.

What Next? The Old Testament as an Unfinished Drama

One distinguished twentieth-century biblical scholar spoke of a sense of incompleteness to the Old Testament.[39] Perhaps we could describe the canon of Scripture at the end of the Old Testament period as the end of "act one" of a two-act play. Let me work with that imagery a bit more. The plot has been established: A fallen human race needs redemption and reconciliation. The key players have been introduced: a holy God and his chosen people. That last component has included kings and queens, prophets and prophetesses, priests, wise men and women, good and bad, and many more. Even a few animals have had cameo roles (e.g., a talking donkey, a great fish). But the tension of the story remains unresolved. God's people are back in their own land, but they are a subject nation. What happened to the visions of national grandeur? There is a sense of unfulfilled expectations: Where is that final messianic figure who

[39]See John Bright, *The Authority of the Old Testament* (Nashville: Abingdon Press, 1967; reprint, Grand Rapids: Baker Book House, 1975), 136–40.

will both break the chains of sin and usher in a new age of peace?

That is the message of the New Testament. The first word of its canon ties the past period of divine revelation to "act two" of God's plan of redemption. Matthew 1:1: "A record of the genealogy of Jesus Christ the son of David, the son of Abraham." It is this Jesus who is presented as the fulfiller of the Law (Matt. 5:17), the Beginning and End of History (Rev. 21:6; 22:13), the Wisdom of God (1 Cor. 1:24), and God's ultimate Prophet. Hebrews 1:1–2 also takes up this theme: "In the past God spoke to our forefathers through the prophets at many times and in various ways, but in these last days he has spoken to us by his Son."

It would be four hundred years between Malachi and Matthew. History didn't stop. Kings and kingdoms came and went. But God's redemptive plan stayed on schedule. When the time was right, Jesus would bring salvation to both Jews and Gentiles (Gal. 4:4). God's kingdom arrived in the person of his Son.

Study Questions

1. What is the political and historical background for these books?
2. Who led the first wave of returning Jews and when?
3. Trace the cycles of opposition to the returned Jews and the letters their enemies sent to the Persian king.
4. Trace the cycles of work stoppage on the temple and the walls of Jerusalem.
5. Describe Ezra and Nehemiah. Who were they? What sort of people were they?
6. Analyze the intermarriage problem that faced Ezra.

7. Summarize the Book of Esther: its problems, setting, plot, and main characters.

8. For the books of Haggai, Zechariah, and Malachi, give the setting, structure, and message of each.

For Further Reading

House, Paul R. *Old Testament Theology.* Downers Grove, Ill.: InterVarsity Press, 1998.

Merrill, Eugene H. *Kingdom of Priests: A History of Old Testament Israel.* Grand Rapids: Baker Book House, 1987.

Walton, John H., Victor H. Matthews, and Mark W. Chavalas. *IVP Bible Background Commentary: Old Testament.* Downers Grove, Ill.: InterVarsity Press, 2000.

Glossary and Indexes

Glossary of Terms

Within the definitions an asterisk (*) next to a term indicates a glossary entry.

acrostic. A poem that begins consecutive lines or stanzas with letters in the alphabet that form a pattern, most often the sequence of the letters in the alphabet.

Aegean. An inclusive term denoting the lands bordered by the Aegean Sea, including mainland Greece, the coast of western Turkey, and the Greek Islands.

Akkadian language. The Semitic language spoken in Mesopotamia from the third through the first millenniums B.C. The principal known dialects are Assyrian and Babylonian.

allegory. Abstract ideas or principles represented by characters, figures, or events in narrative, dramatic, or pictorial form. Assigning allegorical meanings to the plain sense of a text, in effect producing a hidden meaning, is called "allegorization."

amphictyony. A league of states or tribes that took part in the cult of a common deity. The Delphic league was an amphictyony.

Anatolia. The area often called Asia Minor, now occupied by the Asian portion of Turkey.

annals of the kings. A record of the reigns of the kings of Israel (1 Kings 14:19) and Judah (14:29) used as a source by the authors of 1 and 2 Kings.

apocalyptic literature. A style of Jewish writing that focused on God's breaking into human history in the end times, commonly related as a dream or vision. Examples are Isaiah 24 through 27, Ezekiel 40 through 48, and the visions of Daniel.

apocalyptic style. Portions of Isaiah, Ezekiel, Daniel, and Zechariah were written in a prophetic style that included visions and dreams, angelic guides, end-of-the-world scenarios, and the triumph of God's people against the forces of evil. Between the end of the Old Testament and the beginning of the New Testament, it developed as an entire genre of literature.

Apocrypha. A collection of books that were included in the Septuagint but which were not accepted into the Jewish or Protestant canons.

apostasy. Renunciation of one's religion or belief. In the case of Israel, it denoted the actions of anyone who ceased to worship Yahweh or decided that Yahweh was not the one true God.

Aram. The territory lying northeast of Canaan, stretching to the Euphrates River. The people were the Arameans, who spoke Aramaic. Damascus was a city-kingdom in Aram.

ark of the covenant. A rectangular wooden chest the LORD had Israel construct to represent his throne in the sanctuary. Above it he showed his presence (his "glory") between two statues of a winged heavenly creature called a cherub (pl. "cherubs" or "cherubim"). The ark contained the two stone tablets on which were inscribed the Ten

Commandments, representing the covenant relationship between the LORD and Israel. It also contained Aaron's staff that sprouted and a jar of manna (Heb. 9:4). The lid was the place of atonement, traditionally called the "mercy seat," where the high priest offered blood once a year for atonement of all their sins not already covered.

Asherah. A Canaanite goddess who appears in the Old Testament as a wife of Baal. Most biblical references to this name point to some cult object of wood bearing her image. See 1 Kings 14:15.

Assyria. The northern part of Mesopotamia that is today the Kurdish part of Iraq.

atonement. The restoration of a relationship through an act of substitution.

attributes. The characteristics of a person or thing. Among God's attributes are holiness, righteousness, love, omnipotence, and omniscience.

authority. Authority generally means legal power or right. Innate authority refers to an inherent right, or power, in virtue of the person or position the person holds. Derived authority is a delegated legal power or right.

autograph(on, a). An original writing(s). Used of Scripture, it refers to the original manuscript of a given book(s).

Baalism. A general term referring to the worship of a number of deities addressed as Baal. At Ugarit, for example, Baal was Hadad, god of thunder, rain, and fertility. At Tyre, Baal was Melqart (the variant worshipped by Jezebel).

Babylonia. An area of southern Mesopotamia, often called Shinar, taken over by the city of Babylon.

bless/blessing. In Israelite culture, to bless someone was to ask God to bring the person success. The blessing, then, was a request that God would fulfill the person's destiny. Inanimate objects could also be blessed in this manner.

canon. Derived from the Hebrew term *qaneh*, meaning a "reed" or "rod" used for measuring, the term has come to mean "a standard." The canon of Scripture refers to the books of the Bible that have been accepted as inspired by God, and therefore authoritative.

canonicity. That quality, intrinsic to a book because it is divinely inspired, that gives it the right to inclusion in the Bible.

case law. A legal interpretation of a law, normally by a court hearing, that furnishes a precedent for such cases in the future. The Hebrew term for case laws is *mishpatim* (plural).

Chaldeans. Inhabitants of southeastern Mesopotamia, who, under a succession of kings, developed from tribe to nation and later founded the Neo-Babylonian Empire. The best known of their kings was Nebuchadnezzar.

cherem. (KHER-em) Devoted to the LORD, usually to be destroyed.

chesed. (KHES-ed) Duty, loyalty, obligation.

chiasm. Reversed parallels. In its simplest form A–B is paralleled by B'–A' (instead of A'–B'). This can be expanded to form lengthy chiasms (e.g., A–B/C/B'–A', or A–B–C–D /E/D'–C'–B'–A').

Christ. From the Septuagint* *christos,* which translated the Hebrew term *meshiªch* (see Messiah).

Chronicler. The author, compiler, or editor of 1 and 2 Chronicles.

clean and unclean. Qualification (clean) for or disqualification (unclean) from the worship and presence of God. It refers to spiritual purity versus contamination.

Unclean things were not allowed to come before the LORD.

Code of Hammurabi. A collection of laws compiled shortly before 1750 B.C. and inscribed on an eight-foot pillar of black diorite. Hammurabi was the sixth ruler of the First Dynasty of Babylon. This is the longest and best organized of the ancient Mesopotamian law collections or "codes" (they are not codes in the modern sense). Many of the laws are found in earlier ANE collections. It contains a lengthy prologue, 275–300 laws, and an epilogue including blessings and curses. One of its main purposes was to show what a just king Hammurabi was.

command, commandment. Though often confused with "law," commands are not law, although laws may be compiled to enforce them. An example of a command would be a stop sign at a traffic intersection. The actual law, describing the penalty, would not be written on the sign.

consort. A husband or wife, particularly of a ruling official.

coregent/coregency. In old age, or in times of war or sickness, a ruling monarch would make certain his dynasty would continue by making one of his sons a coruler. This political relationship insured a smooth transition of power when the monarch died.

covenant. A formal agreement between two or more parties. A covenant often included specific responsibilities for each participant and was often considered legally binding.

creationists. Persons who advocate a theology that explains existence in terms of a creation by God, rather than by a theory of spontaneous generation.

cult. This term, derived from the Latin *cultus,* refers to a religion as it is described in terms of its liturgy, or speaks of a rite within that religion. In such scholarly usage, it has no relationship to the word "occult."

cuneiform. A form of writing for use on clay tablets. Wedge-shaped characters were made by pressing a sharpened stylus, often a reed, into wet clay. It was used in Mesopotamia and neighboring regions.

curse. In Israelite culture, to curse someone was to wish that God would bring misfortune on him or her.

cycle. In literature, cycle is a term for describing a recurrence of a sequence of events, such as the speeches in Job, to advance the plot.

Damascus. An Aramean city lying northeast of Israel. Damascus was Israel's principal rival for power in the area.

Davidic covenant. An expansion of the Abrahamic covenant. Mainly it identified more precisely the descendants through whom the blessing promised to Abraham was to find fulfillment: the house of David, and later, Christ.

Day of the LORD. Denotes a time when God would come in righteous anger to punish those who oppose him. Sometimes, as in Amos 5:18–20, the reference applies to a national calamity, such as the Assyrian destruction of Israel in 722 B.C. In Joel 2:31 and 3:14 it seems to refer to an event still future.

Decalogue. Literally "ten words," specifically the Ten Commandments.

Diaspora. The dispersion of the Jews following the destruction of Judah by the Babylonians (sixth century B.C.), followed by a second dispersion by the Romans after the destruction of the temple in A.D. 70.

disputation. A prophetic literary technique that

revealed the unrighteous thinking of the people. This technique allowed the prophet to give God's response to the public mindset. It is found six times in the Book of Malachi.

dynasty. A succession of rulers that are in some way related or similar.

ecclesiastical. From a Greek word meaning "to call out"; the word pertains to the congregation, or assembly.

election. God's choice of Abraham and his descendants, Israel, as the means of his revelation of himself to the world.

'eleph **(EL-eff).** One thousand, subtribe, military unit.

Elohim. The most common Hebrew word for god. It is not a name but a title and is used for all manner of gods. Technically, the word is plural. When it refers to Israel's God, the plural denotes the supreme God and is constructed with singular verbs and adjectives.

ephod. A jacket or vest worn by priests. Israel's high priest had a special one. From it hung a breastpiece that carried the Urim and Thummim*, with twelve gemstones on its front that represented the twelve tribes of Israel before the LORD.

eschatology. The study of "last things," or end-time prophecies. Zechariah 1 through 8 has been described as "historical eschatology" because it emphasizes a historical continuity with current events; Zechariah 9 through 14 has been described as "apocalyptic eschatology" because it emphasizes a radical break with history by God's intervention in time and space.

etiology. A story that explains the origin of a name, custom, or place (e.g., Judg. 2:4,5).

evangelical. For the purposes of this textbook, those Christian scholars who accept the doctrine of a verbal plenary inspiration of Scripture.

exile. The period of time in the sixth and fifth centuries B.C. when many of the people of Judah* were deported to Babylon by Nebuchadnezzar, its king. This was prophesied particularly by Jeremiah as God's judgment on Judah for its unfaithfulness.

Exodus/exodus. Begun with a capital letter, the word indicates the biblical Book of Exodus. Begun with a lower-case letter, it refers to Israel's departure from Egypt.

fertility gods. Certain Canaanite religions were designed to control the forces of nature and, through them, bring fertility to agricultural crops and livestock. Religiously sanctioned sexual activity would cause the gods to produce rain for crops or offspring in livestock.

firstborn. The first offspring of animals or humans. Firstborn males were claimed by God. They were either to be sacrificed or redeemed. The firstborn represented the future of the parents since children assured the perpetuation of the family name.

genre. The "kind" or "sort" of something. In biblical hermeneutics, "genre" refers to the type of literature one is interpreting. Some examples of genre are poetry, prose, law, and wisdom.

Gilgamesh. A quasi-legendary Mesopotamian king of Uruk (biblical Erech, Gen. 10:10) whose quest for immortality is told in the *Epic of Gilgamesh,* a story that also refers to a great world flood.

glory. Derived from a Hebrew word that means "heavy" *(kabed),* "glory" *(kabod)* came to mean honor or splendor. When used of God, it refers to a special, tangible presence. In the Bible his glory was experienced as the awesome weightiness of his person, the holy, all-powerful, all-wise, infinite king of all creation.

go'el. Derived from the root *ga'al*, to reclaim as one's own, restore, redeem. The word designates the near kinsman who was responsible for looking after the welfare of his relative. His most common duties included marrying the widow of his relative to produce an heir to the dead man's estate, buying his relative out of debt, and tracking down the person who killed his relative.

Habiru. Displaced immigrants viewed as an inferior social class. The *Habiru* could be found throughout the Ancient Near East (ANE) and were made up of many ethnic groups, including several Semitic* peoples.

heart. In Scripture, "heart" refers primarily to a person's will or disposition.

Hebrew. Denotes the language spoken by the Israelites in Old Testament times. When designating ethnicity, the term most properly refers to Abraham (e.g., Gen. 14:13), perhaps denoting either his descent from Eber (Gen. 10:24; 11:14) or designating a class of people that adopted a semi-nomadic lifestyle. By contrast, "Israelite" designates a person from one of the twelve tribes descended from Israel, i.e., Jacob, or one adopted into one of those tribes. After the split of the kingdom in 931 B.C., the name "Israel" designated the confederation of northern tribes, while the southern tribes were called "Judah." "Jew" is derived from "Judah" and designates a person with ancestral ties to the kingdom of Judah, whose lineage had survived the Babylonian exile in the sixth century.

hermeneutics. The science and art of interpretation. Biblical hermeneutics seeks to answer three basic questions in order to understand and communicate the message of the text: (1) What does the text say? (2) What did it mean to those who first received it, and what does it mean to me now? (3) What am I going to do about it?

hieroglyphics. A writing system developed in Egypt in which the characters for words or syllables are mostly identifiable pictures.

high places. Worship centers for gods and/or goddesses. Originally these were Canaanite ritual altars located on a mountain or a hill and were associated with a shrine to their gods. An elevation was preferred for such shrines because worshipers believed it brought them physically nearer to their gods, who were thought to dwell there. The Israelites were forbidden to use these sites for the worship of the Lord. See the *NIV Study Bible* note on 1 Kings 3:2.

historiography. The theory, method, and resources for constructing a history.

holiness. The only appropriate term for describing the person and nature of God, distinguishing him in his transcendence (see transcendent) from the human realm of time and space. People and things become holy only when they are set apart for God's purposes. Their holiness is based entirely upon their association with God.

holocaust. The word is derived from "whole-burning." It was first used of a sacrifice completely consumed by fire, such as the "burnt offering" of Leviticus 1. In modern usage, the word is applied to the destruction of Jerusalem in 586 B.C. and to subsequent Jewish tragedies (e.g., the Roman conquest in A.D. 70 and the Nazi extermination of Jews during World War II).

holy war. A term often applied to the wars waged under Joshua for the conquest of Canaan, in which

Canaanite cities were declared *cherem**, i.e., devoted to the LORD to be destroyed.

honor. In Ancient Near Eastern culture, one's honor was the substance of one's being—his or her personal value. One's honor was seen in the ability to give, the ability to win, and the ability to sustain a large family.

hospitality. Life is hard on the edge of the desert. In such conditions, generosity and hospitality become moral values. Examples may be seen in Abraham's eager reception of the three strangers (Gen. 18:2–8) and Job's protests (Job 29; 31). Lot's feeble attempts to shelter his guests (Gen. 19:6–9) are mirrored in the Gibeah tragedy (Judg. 19:14–26), and the host's failure in both cases adds to the horror of the situation.

Hyksos. A mixed group of Asian invaders who dominated Egypt from about 1786 to 1567 B.C. during the Fifteenth through the Seventeenth Dynasties.

hyperbole. An overstatement, an exaggeration, made for emphasis.

imminent. When used of God, this term means that God is near at hand and can be reached by human beings and their needs. See also transcendent.

imprecation. Language calling for a judgment, calamity, or curse upon one's enemies.

inspiration. Describes that supernatural operation of the Spirit of God on the human writers of the Bible through which they were enabled to communicate the Word of God without error, omission, or misrepresentation.

interpret. To explain the meaning of a thing, such as a passage of Scripture.

Israel. A title given Jacob when he wrestled with the

man at the Jabbok ford (Gen. 32:22–30) and later applied to his descendants, the nation of Israel. Still later the term designated the United Kingdom under Saul, David, and Solomon. Following the schism at Shechem, "Israel" designated the confederation of northern tribes that split from the south (Judah).

Jehovah. The name of God given to Moses in Exodus 3:15 is represented by four Hebrew consonants: YHWH, often referred to as the Tetragrammaton*. After the Babylonian exile, Jews became increasingly reluctant to pronounce the name, lest they be held guilty of misusing it (Exod. 20:7). As a result, the exact pronunciation of the Tetragrammaton was lost and a substitution was made. "Jehovah" represents the English equivalent of the four consonants using the vowels of *'adonay,* "my Lord," indicating that the reader was to pronounce *'adonay* and not attempt the Tetragrammaton itself. The rendition "LORD" reflects this circumlocution. A better effort at rendering the divine name is "Yahweh"*.

Jew. Derived from Judean*, those exiled to Babylon (following the destruction of Jerusalem) and their descendants.

Jubilee. A holiday celebrated every fiftieth year. All land reverted to the Israelite families the LORD had originally given it to. This custom gave a fresh start to the poor who had lost their land. It also prevented the rich landowners from amassing unlimited wealth.

Judah. Land occupied by the tribe of Judah, later becoming a part of the United Kingdom, and after the division in 931 B.C. becoming a separate state.

Judea. Geopolitical term to describe the Jewish land after the decree of Cyrus allowed them to return. It was centered around the city of Jerusalem. During the period between the end of the Old Testament and the beginning of the New it was expanded to include Samaria and Galilee.

Judean. As a noun, "Judean" means an inhabitant of Judah* or Judea*. As an adjective, it means coming from, or of, Judah or Judea, e.g., Judean hills.

kinsman-redeemer. In ancient Israel, a man's nearest male relative had such duties as avenging his murder, redeeming the estate that he may have sold in an attempt to escape poverty, and marrying his widow to provide him an heir.

lament. A prayerful expression of sorrow, generally coupled with a petition for God's deliverance.

law. Coercive force applied on a community by a governing person or body to ensure conformity to a norm. The force may be applied through political or religious bodies. Many modern translations have translated *torah** as "law," but this is misleading. See *torah* below.

law of the Medes and the Persians. These laws were considered immutable and unalterable.

Levant. The lands bordering the Eastern Mediterranean, e.g., Syria, Lebanon, Israel, Jordan.

Levites. The qualified men of the tribe of Levi who assisted the priests in the ministries of the tabernacle*.

***lex talionis* or talion.** The law commonly known as "an eye for an eye and a tooth for a tooth," requiring that the punishment fit the crime. Repeated in each of the three Old Testament law collections and throughout the ANE, it stresses fairness in public justice (Exod. 21:23–25; Lev. 24:20; Deut. 19:21). It was intended to curb abuses from favoritism or vengeance. It does not refer to personal, private retaliation in relationships.

LXX. See Septuagint.

ma'at. The Egyptian wisdom term for something similar to "justice," which has close parallels with the use of *chokhmah* in Hebrew wisdom literature.

mashal (ma-SHAL). The Hebrew term for proverb, but can include an extended comparison such as a parable.

Masoretic Text (MT). The traditional Hebrew text of the Old Testament. It is named after the Masoretes, the group of rabbis who, from the eighth to the eleventh centuries A.D., brought it into its present form. Although the MT is comparatively late, recent discoveries of biblical texts a thousand years older found among the Dead Sea Scrolls have confirmed it as a very accurate textual tradition.

Messiah. The Hebrew word for an anointed one, such as a prophet, priest, or king. It especially indicates the anointed kings of David's line who typified the Messiah. The Greek term in the LXX* and New Testament was *christos*.

metaphor. A figure of speech that names one thing and applies it to another, implying a comparison between the two (e.g., the "I ams . . ." of Jesus—John 6:48 et al.).

Midian. The location of this ancient land seems to have changed over time. In the Old Testament, it appears to have been located in southeastern Sinai but later moved to west central Arabia. Moses sought refuge there from Egypt's wrath.

monotheism. The belief that there is only one God ("monotheistic," adj.). It developed in Israel and stood in opposition to the popular belief in many gods and goddesses.

Mosaic covenant. The agreement the Israelites made with God at Sinai to accept and be faithful to the words of the covenant as found in the Ten Commandments (Exod. 24:7–8). Their obedience to the covenant would be rewarded by God's blessings; their disobedience would bring God's judgment.

myth/mythology. An essentially polytheistic practice of personifying the forces of nature as various divinities and writing a pseudohistory that tells their tales.

name. In Near Eastern culture, people's names expressed the essence of their being. To know a person's name was to know the person. One's name also became associated with one's honor. Family members usually bore the name of their father, showing their mutual relationship. As family members preserved the father's name from generation to generation, he continued to live through them, his descendants.

Neo-Babylonian/Chaldean Empire. In 626 B.C., the nationalism that had festered for some time caused the Chaldeans* to seize Babylon and, together with the Medes and Scythians*, begin attacking city after city held by Assyria. The fall of Nineveh is the setting for the Book of Nahum, and the Battle of Carchemish is the subject of Jeremiah 46. The best known of the Neo-Babylonian kings is Nebuchadnezzar, the king who conquered Jerusalem in 597 B.C. and again in 586 and led its inhabitants into exile in Babylonia. The empire ended when Cyrus the Great of Persia conquered Babylon in 539 B.C.

offerings. See Old Testament Offerings chart in chapter 7.

oracles against the nations. Often abbreviated OAN, these are prophetic messages from God, directed through his prophets, to the foreign nations surrounding Israel.

parallelism. The state, or condition, of balanced

grammatical construction for rhetorical effect..

Passover. An annual Jewish feast in which the participants reenact the events of the Israelites' last night in Egypt. It is so named because the LORD "passed over" the houses marked by blood (see Exod. 12:12,13).

patriarch. A head of a family or a people. While some authors may refer to the descendants of Noah as patriarchs, the most common use of the term denotes Abraham (Heb. 7:4), Isaac, and Jacob, although Acts 2:29 uses the term to describe David.

Pharaoh. A title used in the Old Testament for the reigning kings of Egypt.

prophet / prophetism. One who speaks or acts or predicts for God, as by divine guidance. The practice of such conduct.

Psalter. Another title for the Book of Psalms.

Purim. The Jewish feast days commemorating the Jews' victory in Persia over Haman and his family and associates. The word is a plural of the Persian term for "lot," which was used to originally decide on which day Haman would be permitted to attack the Jews (Esther 3:7).

Qarqar. Site in northwestern Aram of an important battle between Shalmaneser III of Assyria and an alliance of West Asian kings, among whom were Ahab of Israel and Ben-Hadad of Damascus. It forms the background for the events of 1 Kings 22.

Qoheleth. The Hebrew title for the Book of Ecclesiastes, meaning Preacher or Teacher, leading an assembly of people.

recombinant DNA. DNA in which one or more segments or genes have been inserted, either naturally or by laboratory manipulation, from a different molecule or from another part of the same molecule, resulting in a new genetic combination.

redemption. The retrieval of something one owns, through payment. In the Bible, this refers to God's restoration of human beings to himself through some sort of vicarious sacrifice.

reform/reformation. A legislated, national return to *torah*.

remnant. Those Israelites who would survive God's judgment on the nation of Judah and return from exile to Israel to take possession of the land.

retribution theology. The theology that assumes, on the basis of faith in a just God, that justice will prevail: The righteous will be rewarded and the wicked will be punished. In the Old Testament, the administration of justice was handed to human agency in the Noahic covenant (Gen. 9:1–7). This first took the form of charging the *go'el**, the near kinsman to one wronged or injured, to track down the guilty party and administer justice. This often led to tribal feuds, such as the one recorded in Judges 20:8–48. The *lex talionis** was instituted by Moses to curb such abuses (Exod. 21:23–25; Lev. 24:20; Deut. 19:21).

revelation. God's making known to humanity what he chooses to disclose. "General" revelation deals with God's disclosure in creation, and is sometimes called "natural" revelation. It still operates, but within the limitations of human fallenness. "Special" revelation addresses the remedy for this fallenness through the Word of God.

ruach (RU-ach). Wind, breath, spirit.

Sabbath. The seventh day of the week (Saturday, from sunset on Friday to sunset on Saturday; cf. Gen. 1:5b). It was instituted by God as a day wherein all labor ceased. People were to "keep it holy," i.e., devote it to the LORD and to spend time with family, workers, and the community of faith. God declared it to be a sign for Israel of their covenant relationship with the LORD. The New Testament indicates that one certain day is no longer a sign of the covenant. Taking one day a week, however, to rest and to gather with God's people in worship and to hear the Word is important (Rom. 14:5–8; Col. 2:16–17; Heb. 10:25).

Sabbath Year. Every seventh year the land was to be given a rest and allowed to lie uncultivated. The poor were allowed to eat what grew by itself.

schism. When Solomon died about 930 B.C. the United Kingdom was divided into two rival nations—Israel* in the north and Judah* in the south. Its cause was Jeroboam's request to Rehoboam that he address the people's grievances (1 Kings 12:1–17). Rehoboam's harsh answer made this schism inevitable. Thus Rehoboam remained king of Judah; Jeroboam became king of Israel.

Scythia, Scythian. Scythia extended from the mouth of the Danube River on the Black Sea to the territory east of the Aral Sea. The Scythians were a nomadic people that flourished in the region from the eighth to fourth centuries B.C.

seer. An early term for a prophet (1 Sam. 9:9; Amos. 7:12). Later, it referred to one who predicted the future by various means.

Semite/Semitic. A group of languages and the people who speak them, so named because of their association with Shem in the Table of Nations (Gen. 10:21–31). The languages include Akkadian*, Eblaite, Canaanite, Amorite, Ugaritic, Phoenician, Aramaic, Hebrew, and Arabic.

Septuagint (LXX). The ancient Greek translation of the Hebrew Old Testament begun about 250 B.C. in

Alexandria, North Egypt, probably as a Greek Targum* to the Jewish community there. Later it became the Bible of the Early Church. It preserves some interesting and useful textual variants, and also includes additional books that are not in the Hebrew canon* of Scripture (Protestants call these "the Apocrypha*," from the Gk. term for "obscure," "hidden").

shekel. Two-fifths of an ounce.

Shephelah. Foothills.

simile. A figure of speech that makes an explicit comparison between two essentially unlike things, using the word "like" or "as" (e.g., Matt. 3:16, 1 Pet. 5:8).

sins of Jeroboam. When Jeroboam erected two golden calves at Bethel and Dan and told Israel these were their gods who had brought them out of Egypt (1 Kings 12:25–33), he violated the second commandment (Exod. 20:4–6). This opened the door for the entrance of pagan practices in Israel's religious observances and eventually led to God's judgment on them as a nation.

Sitz im Leben. "Life-setting." Form critical studies try to locate each type of literature in its social and religious setting. For example, law would be located in the courts, prophetic speech in the prophetic "schools," etc.

sons of the prophets. The use of the term by the NIV in 1 Kings 20:35 represents the same Hebrew construction rendered "company of the prophets" in 2 Kings (e.g., 6:1; 9:1 and elsewhere). It is thought that these people were disciples of Elijah and Elisha, a later development of the "group of prophets" who had followed Samuel (1 Sam. 19:20), and who also are simply designated "the prophets" (1 Kings 19:1).

stanza. A division of a poem of at least two lines constituting a pattern of rhythm, length, etc., comparable, for example, to what we would call a "verse" in a hymn.

statute, statutory law. A statute is a law coming directly from a lawgiver or lawgiving body, as contrasted with case law*. The Hebrew word for "statute" is *choq, chuqqim*.

stele. A stone monument, often set up by a ruler. Stelae (plural) were often inscribed and had sculptured images carved on them.

suzerain. The dominant nation or ruler who controlled one or more subordinate (vassal*) states.

suzerain-vassal treaty. An agreement between a great king and a lesser king that the lesser would serve the greater, giving him what he requires, and fighting for him when called upon. The great king will come to the lesser's defense. Both are to be loyal (perform *chesed**) to each other.

syncretism. Sometimes called "supermarket" or "shopping basket" religion, this approach to religious belief is selective: A person picks out attractive elements of many different faiths and works them into an original religion. This is usually done with the presumption that all ways to God are equal. It results in a gross distortion of each religion it incorporates. This was a live issue for ancient Israel. The people of Israel and Judah often merged their worship of Yahweh* with the religious beliefs and practices of their ANE neighbors. The Old Testament states clearly that no other god(s) could be given any sort of acknowledgment if Yahweh was to be worshiped (Exod. 20:3). The best known examples are Aaron's and Jeroboam's golden calves, pagan symbols that were used to represent Yahweh (Exod. 32:1–35; 1 Kings 12:25–30).

Syro-Ephraimitic War. A war against Judah* that

involved Damascus, principal city of Aram, and Israel, called Ephraim (the most powerful of its territories). Probably initiated to form a defensive league against the aggression of Tiglath-Pileser III in western Asia.

tabernacle. Also called the Tent of Meeting, it was the portable structure the LORD directed Israel to build during their desert wanderings. Likely, it was looked upon as the palace of God as king, with the cherubs-adorned ark as his throne in the Holy Place. God made this his headquarters where he would dwell among his people.

Targum. A translation of the Hebrew Bible into Aramaic for the benefit of Jews after the Babylonian exile who did not understand Hebrew.

taunt. A direct, sarcastic statement addressing folly, presumption, and the like (e.g., Ps. 2:4; Prov. 1:26–27).

tell. A mound containing the layers of debris from ancient settlements having built one on top of the other.

testament. In the Old Testament, the word rendered "testament" *(berith)* is better translated "covenant"*.

Tetragrammaton. The four-letter rendering of the divine name revealed to Moses (YHWH). It is related to the verb "to be" and probably means "he is." See Yahweh below.

theocracy. A type of government whose agencies exist only to announce and execute the will of God as declared by priest and prophets or by the Scriptures. Everything, even civil and criminal law, is looked at from the religious standpoint.

theophany. Literally, "God-appearance." An appearance of God in some visible form. The term applies to divine self-manifestations such as occurred at Mount Sinai in the thunder, fire, smoke, and voice. God chose to appear to various people in the Old Testament (e.g., Abraham, Gen. 15:17; Moses, Exod. 3:2–6; and Ezekiel, Ezek. 1 through 3).

tithe. Literally, a tenth part of something. In the Old Testament, it was to be paid on everything one owned (Lev. 27:30–32). The recipients were the Levites*, who were, in turn, expected to tithe to the priests (Num. 18:26–28).

***torah*/Torah.** A Hebrew word meaning "a teaching," it denotes the revelation of God, especially that given through Moses, to Israel in the Bible. In Hosea it is used to denote "Scripture." As a proper noun within Judaism, Torah is another title for the Pentateuch, the first five books of the Old Testament. Many modern translations have followed the Septuagint* in rendering it as "law," but this is misleading. Torah contains law but also much else.

transcendent. When used of God, this term means he is above and beyond nature, history, and humanity, that is, the limits of time and space, the domain of human beings. See holiness and imminent.

Transjordan. Literally, "beyond (the) Jordan." Denotes plateau east of the Jordan River. In biblical times this included the biblical land of Bashan, the Hill Country of Gilead, and the territories of Ammon, Moab, and Edom. The Bashan is in the Golan Heights today. The other four zones of this plateau are in the kingdom of Jordan.

tribal standard. A battle standard on a pole, often of a particular color and design that identified the tribe.

typology. Interpretive approach to Scripture that recognizes that persons, events, and institutions in the Old Testament often find their counterparts in the New. Thus they assume a wider spiritual significance with a climactic fulfillment in the New Testament work of Jesus Christ. To be distinguished from "allegory"*.

Urim and Thummim. Two lots, probably stones, carried in the breastpiece of the high priest's uniform, used for determining the will of God in the absence of direct revelation.

vassal. The subordinate nation or ruler in a suzerain-vassal relationship. See suzerain.

vassal state. A territory or nation controlled by, and subservient to, a more powerful nation, e.g., Israel to Assyria.

vassalage. The relationship between conquered territories and a dominant nation. The dominant nation (suzerain*) determined who would be king in each vassal state*. The suzerain also set the amount of tribute money that the inhabitants of the vassal state would pay and often imposed his gods on the vassal.

wadi (WAH-dee). Ravine, gorge.

Yahweh. The personal name by which God revealed himself to the Israelites, initially through Moses (Exod. 3:15). The name probably means "He is," alluding to the "I AM" of Exod. 3:14. The name suggests God's infinite existence and self-determining nature.

Yahwism. The worship of Yahweh*.

Scripture Index

OLD TESTAMENT

NEW TESTAMENT

Name Index

Aaron
  criticism of Moses by, 324
  priesthood of, 289, 327
  prophesying of, 693
  sin of, 257
  sons of, 292
Abednego, 798
Abel, 110
Abiathar, 440, 465, 471, 488, 490
Abigail, 442, 443, 464
Abijah (king of Judah), 588
  fights Jeroboam, 657
  following ways of parents, 592
Abijah (son of Jeroboam), 657
Abimelech (king of Gerar), 187, 200
Abimelech (son of Gideon)
  death of, 394
  as usurper, 382, 383n, 393
Abinadab, 446n
Abishag, 490
Abishai, 443, 480
Abner, 443, 466–67, 468
Abraham
  call of, 22, 180, 183
  change of name of, 22, 192n, 198
  as channel of redemption and blessing, 60, 116, 135, 192

Abraham *(cont.)*
  as citizen of Mesopotamia, 179
  descendants of, 802
  God's choice of, 187–88, 189, 192
  God's covenant with, 192, 196–97
  lifestyle of, 157, 184
  as a prophet, 692–93
  travels of, 140
Abram. *See* Abraham
Absalom
  death of, 476, 479
  kills Amnon, 476, 477
  plots against David, 477
  takes the throne, 478
Achan, 353, 368
Achilles and Hector, 434n
Achish, 439n, 444, 445
Acsah, 374
Adad-nirari III, 634
Adam, 91n, 92n, 107
Adam and Eve, 22, 102, 108, 110, 111
Adoni-Bezek, 387
Adonijah, 476, 488, 489, 490
Adoniram, 578
Agag, 623n, 830
Agur, 534
Ahab, 559, 616
  and Ben-Hadad, 622–23
  death of, 627
  and Naboth's vineyard, 696

Ahab *(cont.)*
  sins of, 621–22
Ahaz
  appeals to Tiglath-Pileser III, 675
  and Isaiah, 675, 732, 734
Ahaziah (king of Israel), 627
Ahaziah (king of Judah)
  death of, 665
  sin of, 664–65
Ahijah (priest), 429
Ahijah (prophet), 493, 570, 588n
Ahimelech (priest), 439
Ahinoam, 443
Ahithophel, 478, 479
Ahmose I, 221
Akhenaten, 150n
Albright, William Foxwell, 172
Amasa, 478, 480
Amaziah (king of Judah)
  defeated by Israel, 668
  hires soldiers from Israel, 667
  idolatry of, 668
  warned by Jehoash, 668
Amaziah (priest), 713
Ambrose, 544
Amen-em-Opet, 531, 534
Amnon, 476, 477n
Amon, 756
Amos, 699, 701, 708
Amunhotep II, 260

Subject Index

tabernacle
  functional significance of, 285–86
  furnishing of, 288–89
  instructions for, 282–83
  layout of, 284, 286–87
  overview of, 283–85
  theological message of, 284
Table of Nations, 132
Tel Abib, 785
tells, 171
temple, 679, 701, 726
  construction of, 496
  preparations for, 484
  as presence of God, 825
  reconstruction of, 805, 806–7, 808, 813
  as residence of God, 581, 723
temptation, 343
Ten Commandments
  context of, 266–67
  giving of, 254–56
  as stipulations of God's covenant with Israel, 268, 272, 339–41
  See also Mosaic covenant
Tent of Meeting, 286. *See also* Tabernacle
Tetragrammaton, 236
theft, 277–78
theocracy, 506
theophany, 254, 258, 725, 786

Tirzah, 581, 612
tithes, 300
torah, 267–68, 290, 723. *See also* Law, biblical
Torah, 814, 815, 823. *See also* Pentateuch
tower of Babel, 134–35
trade, foreign, 494–96
Transjordan, 169–71
typology, 285–86
Tyre, 473–74, 492, 494, 617

Urim and Thummim, 290, 291

virginity, 349–50, 544
Vulgate, 48

war
  cruelties in, 710
  rules of, 348–49
Waters of Merom, 371
western Asia
  at the time of the patriarchs, 180–81
wisdom
  as applied knowledge, 517
  divine, 521–22
  expression of, 516
  human, 520–21
  in the New Testament, 517
wisdom literature
  overview of, 512, 515–17
witch of Endor, 444–45

woman, as help for man, 96–98. *See also* Creation, of woman
women in the Bible, 333–34, 379, 392
worship, Israelite, 248, 283, 294, 344–45, 700–701. *See also* Priesthood; Sacrifices; Tabernacle
Writings, 47–48

Yahweh, 235–36, 238

Zechariah, Book of, 809–13
  as apocalyptic eschatology, 810
  authorship and dating of, 809–10
  as historical eschatology, 810
  night visions of, 811–12
  outline of, 811
Zephaniah, Book of, 766–69
  hope in, 768
  outline of, 766
ziggurats, 134
Ziklag, 444, 445
Zion. *See* Jerusalem
Ziphites, 441